ICND
INTERCONNECTING CISCO®
NETWORK DEVICES

ICND
Interconnecting Cisco® Network Devices

Thomas M. Thomas II,
Michael Coker, Daniel Golding,
Andrew Mason, Mark Newcomb,
Adam Quiggle, Peter Van Oene

McGraw-Hill
New York   San Francisco   Washington, D.C.
Auckland   Bogotá   Caracas   Lisbon   London
Madrid   Mexico City   Milan   Montreal   New Delhi
San Juan   Singapore   Sydney   Tokyo   Toronto

McGraw-Hill

A Division of The McGraw·Hill Companies

1 2 3 4 5 6 7 8 9 0   PBT/PBT   0 5 4 3 2 1 0 9 0

P/N 0-07-212520-9
PART OF ISBN 0-07-212522-5

The sponsoring editor for this book was Steven Elliot, the associate development
editor was Franny Kelly, and the production supervisor was Clare Stanley. It was
set in Century Schoolbook by D&G Limited, LLC.

Printed and bound by Phoenix Book Technology.

I would like to dedicate this book to my brother Ken. He not only is my brother but also a true friend that I have shared many good times and bad. No matter what the experience or situation we have faced in our lives he has always stood with me and through it all. Ken thank you for being more than a brother, I know you will achieve all your goals in life and thanks for supporting me in mine. I can only hope that I have been as good of a brother to you as you have been to me.

THOMAS M. THOMAS II

I'd like to dedicate this to my wife. Without her love and understanding this would not have been possible.

MICHAEL COKER

To my daughter, Rachel

DAN L. GOLDING

I would like to dedicate this book to my parents, Michael and Ann Mason. They brought me up with what I believe to be good moral values and always showed an interest and gave support to my many hobbies. My upbringing is even more apparent after the birth of my Daughter, Rosie. My father and I, spent countless hours on our first computer back in the 1980s, and it all started there...

ANDREW G. MASON

This book is dedicated to my lovely wife Jacqueline, without whose help I could never have accomplished this work.

MARK J. NEWCOMB

To my wife and best friend, Meg who is the source of my joy.

ADAM QUIGGLE

To Merideth, Catherine, Alan and Jonathan, whose consistent support has made this work possible

PETER A. VAN OENE

CONTENTS

Acknowledgements   xix
About the Authors   xxi
About the Reviewers   xxiii

Chapter 1   Network Concepts Review   1

Objectives   2
Network Organization: Size and Geography   2
   The Main Office   4
   The Branch Offices   5
   Home Offices   5
   Remote Users   5
Network Organization: Hierarchical Design Model   6
   The Access Layer   6
   The Distribution Layer   8
   The Core Layer   9
The OSI Model   10
   Why Have an OSI Model?   11
   Application Layers   12
   Lower or Data Flow Layers   12
   The Transport Layer (L4)   14
   The Network Layer (L3)   16
   The Data Link Layer (L2)   19
   The Physical Layer (L1)   25
Cisco Network Devices   29
   Cisco Hubs   30
   Cisco Switches   30
   Cisco Routers   31
Chapter Summary   32
From the Real World   33
Frequently Asked Questions (FAQ)   34
Questions   35
Answers   39

Chapter 2   Identifying, Cabling, and Attaching to Cisco Devices   43

Objectives   44
LAN Physical Layer Implementations   45
   Ethernet   45

Identifying Ethernet Connectors on Cisco Routers 53
    RJ-45 54
    AUI 54
    Fiber Connector 55
    Full Duplex/Half Duplex 55
Cabling Ethernet 57
    Cat 3, 4, 5 58
    Crossover Cables 59
    Fiber, SC/ST 60
WAN Physical Layer Implementations 61
    Cisco Serial ports 61
    ISDN Connections 65
DTE/DCE 67
Cisco Routers with Fixed Ports 68
Cisco Routers with Modular Ports 69
Connecting to Cisco Devices via the Console Port 70
Chapter Summary 72
From the Real World 74
Frequently Asked Questions (FAQ) 75
Questions 77
Answers 81

Chapter 3   The Basics of Cisco Configuration and Operations 83

Objectives 84
An Introduction to the Cisco Internetwork Operating
    Systems (IOS) 84
    The Cisco Boot Process 86
Cisco Device Startup 87
    Catalyst 1900 Series Switches: POST 87
    The Front Panel LEDs 88
    Cisco Routers 90
Methods of Interacting with Cisco Devices 93
Catalyst 1900 Switch: Basic IOS Commands 96
    Show Version 97
    Show Running-Configuration 98
    Show Interfaces 99
    Show IP Command 102
    Configure Terminal 103
    Hostname 104
    IP Address 105

Contents

Cisco Routers: The Initial Configuration Dialog   105
  Basic Management Setup   106
  Protocols   108
  Interfaces   108
  Script Review   109
Cisco Routers: Basic IOS Commands   110
  Keyboard Help and Command Completion   111
  Command History   113
  Show Version   115
  Methods of Viewing the Configuration   116
Cisco Routers: Configuration Mode   119
  Hostname   119
  Changing the Login Password   120
  Changing the Enable Secret and Enable Password   121
  Console and VTY Settings   121
  Interface Configuration   122
Cisco Routers: Show Interfaces Commands   124
Chapter Summary   126
From the Real World   127
Frequently Asked Questions (FAQ)   128
Case Study   129
  Switch Configuration   130
Questions   131
Answers   135

Chapter 4   Network Management   139

Objectives   140
Cisco Discovery Protocol   140
Network Troubleshooting Commands   144
  Telnet Protocol   144
  Ping Commands   150
  Traceroute Commands   158
Router Management   161
  Startup Sequence   162
  Boot Command   164
  Running and Startup Configurations   165
Chapter Summary   168
From the Real World   169
Frequently Asked Questions (FAQ)   170
Case Study # 1   171

Case Study # 2   173
Questions   175
Answers   178

Chapter 5   Catalyst 1900 Switch Operation   181

Objectives   182
Introduction   183
Understanding Layer-Two Switching Fundamentals   183
    Bridging versus Switching   184
    How Layer-Two Switches Learn MAC Addresses   185
    The Switching Process within the Switch   189
    How Switches Filter Frames   192
    Broadcast and Multicast Frames   193
How Switches Complicate LANs   196
    Broadcast Storms   196
    Multiple Frame Copies   198
    MAC Database Instability   201
    Multiple Loop Problems   201
Spanning Tree   202
    How Spanning Tree Works   203
    Topology Changes   209
Configuring the 1900 Switch   210
    User Interfaces   210
    Default Configuration   212
    Ports on the 1912/1924   214
Configuring the Switch   215
    Enable Password   218
    Setting Duplex   220
Maintaining the Switch   222
    Using the Show Commands   222
    Managing the MAT   227
    The MAC Address Table   228
    Managing the Configuration File   231
Chapter Summary   234
From the Real World   235
Frequently Asked Questions (FAQ)   236
Case Study: Configuring a New Switch   237
Questions   238
Answers   242

Chapter 6   Extending Switched Networks with VLANs   245

Objectives   246
The Domains of a LAN   246
   The Collision Domain   247
   The Broadcast Domain   248
Virtual Local Area Networks   250
   VLAN Defined   251
   VLAN Transparency   253
   VLAN Membership Techniques   253
   VLAN Technology Drivers   254
VLAN Configuration   256
   VLANs and Switch Support   257
   VLAN Trunking Protocol   257
   How VTP Works   259
   The Significance of VLAN1   262
   Managing VLANs   263
   Defining Trunks   265
   VLANs and Spanning Tree   271
Chapter Summary   273
From the Real World   275
Frequently Asked Questions (FAQ)   276
Case Study: Creating VLANs to Departmentalize Your LAN   277
Questions   278
Answers   281

Chapter 7   Interconnecting Networks with TCP/IP   283

Objectives   284
Introduction to TCP/IP   284
   IP as a Universal Protocol   285
   How the TCP/IP Protocol Suite Fits into the OSI Model   285
   TCP Segment Format   288
   Port Numbers and How TCP/IP Handles Multiple
      Applications Simultaneously   290
   Well-Known Ports   290
TCP, a Connection-Oriented Protocol   291
   The Three-Way Handshake/Open Connection   292
   SYN/ACK DoS Attacks   292
   TCP Windows and ACKs   293
   Sequence Numbers   294

UDP, a Connectionless Protocol   294
Internet Layer   295
    IP   296
    IP Datagram Format   296
    Protocol Field   298
    ARP   299
    RARP   300
    ICMP   301
IP Addresses   303
    Classes of Addresses   304
    Subnetting   309
Router Concepts   324
    Physical Interfaces   324
    Subinterfaces   324
    Encapsulation Types   325
Router Configurations   326
    Setting up the IP Address of an Interface   327
    IP Host Names   327
    Routing from One VLAN to Another   329
    Routing between WANs   331
Chapter Summary   332
From the Real World   334
Frequently Asked Questions (FAQ)   336
Case Study: Building a LAN with WAN connections   337
    Configure Router B   338
    Configure Router C   338
Questions   341
Answers   345

Chapter 8   IP Routing Fundamentals   349

Objectives   350
Routing Overview   350
Static versus Dynamic Routing   353
    Static Routes   353
    Dynamic Routing   357
Overview: Routing Protocols versus Routed Protocols   358
Interior and Exterior Gateway Protocols   358
Dynamic Routing Protocols   359
    Distance Vector   360
    Link State and Hybrid   363

Contents

Routing Information Protocol (RIP)   364
Interior Gateway Routing Protocol (IGRP)   372
IP Classless   384
Chapter Summary   385
Frequently Asked Questions (FAQ)   387
Questions   388
Answers   392

Chapter 9   Access Lists and Traffic Management   395

Objectives   396
Access List Overview   396
Access List Implementation   397
Inbound versus Outbound Access Lists   397
Access List Commands   398
IP Access Lists   399
IPX Access Lists   410
Telnet VTY Access Restriction   415
Named Access Lists   416
Breakout Box: Access List Tips and Tricks   417
Applying Access Lists: Cut and Paste   417
Access List Order   418
Monitoring and Verifying Access Lists   418
Show running-configuration   419
show ip interface   419
show ip access-list   420
show access-lists   421
Chapter Summary   421
Frequently Asked Questions (FAQ)   423
Questions   424
Answers   427

Chapter 10   Internetwork Packet Exchange (IPX)   429

Objectives   430
Introduction to IPX Protocols   430
IPX, SPX, SAP, NCP, and NetBIOS   430
Routing IPX with RIP, NLSP, and EIGRP   442
SAP Updates   449
Where IPX Protocols Fit into the OSI Model   450
NetWare Addresses   451

Basic NetWare Operation	452
GNS	452
RIP	453
SAP	453
Encapsulations of IPX	456
Configuring IPX on Cisco Routers	458
IPX Routing	459
IPX Addresses on Interfaces	459
Verifying and Monitoring IPX Routing	461
Show Commands	462
Debug Commands	462
IPX Ping	468
IPX Routing Tables	473
IPX Server Table	474
IPX Access Lists	476
Controlling Overhead on IPX Networks	480
SAP Filters	484
Chapter Summary	486
From the Real World	487
Case Study: Building an IPX LAN	488
Configure Router A	488
Configure Router B	488
Configure Router C	489
Questions	493
Answers	497
Chapter 11 Point-to-Point Serial Connections	501
Objectives	502
WAN Overview	502
LAN versus WAN	502
WAN Services	503
Working with Service Providers	506
Serial Connections	507
WAN Encapsulation	508
HDLC	509
PPP	509
SLIP	510
X.25/LAPB	510
Frame Relay	511
ATM	511

Configuring HDLC   511
Configuring PPP   512
  Link Control Protocol (LCP)   513
  Network Control Protocol (NCP)   520
Monitoring and Verifying WAN Connections   521
  Show Interface   521
  Debug PPP Authentication   521
Chapter Summary   523
From the Real World   524
Frequently Asked Questions (FAQ)   525
Case Study: Connecting to an Internet Service Provider   526
  Task 1: Configure Central Site   527
  Task 2: Configure Remote Site A   528
Questions   531
Answers   535

Chapter 12 Integrated Services Digital Network (ISDN)   539

Objectives   540
ISDN Overview   540
  Analog versus ISDN   540
  B Channel versus D Channel   541
  ISDN Reference Points   542
  ISDN BRI   545
  ISDN PRI (T1/E1)   545
  ISDN Protocols   546
Configuring ISDN BRI   548
  Switch Type   548
  Service Profiler Identifier (SPID)   549
Overview of Dial on Demand Routing (DDR)   549
Configuring Dial on Demand Routing (DDR)   550
  Dialer-list   550
  Dialer-group   553
  Dialer-map   554
  DDR Summary   555
  Default Route   555
Optional Configuration Issues with DDR   555
  Authentication   557
  Dialer idle-timeout   557
  Multilink PPP   559
  Dialer load-threshold   560

Monitoring and Verifying ISDN Connections 561
   Show Commands 561
   Debug Commands 562
Chapter Summary 566
From the Real World 567
Frequently Asked Questions (FAQ) 568
Case Study: Remote Office Connectivity with ISDN 569
   Task 1: Configure the Central Site 570
   Task 2: Configure the Remote Site 572
   Case Study Summary 573
Questions 576
Answers 580

Chapter 13 Frame Relay 583

Objectives 584
Frame Relay Overview 584
   How Frame Relay Saves Money 585
   Virtual Circuits within the Cloud 586
Frame Relay in the OSI Model 588
Frame Relay Terminology 590
   PVC 592
   SVC 592
   CIR 593
   DLCI 594
   Locally Significant 595
   Local Loop 595
   LMI 596
   FECN 598
   BECN 599
   DE 600
Frame Relay Address Mapping 602
Frame Relay Signaling 602
Frame Relay Inverse ARP 604
Configuring Frame Relay 605
   Interface Settings 605
   Encapsulation 605
   LMI Type 605
   Static Mappings 606
Verifying Frame Relay 608
   Show Commands 608
   Debug Commands 611

Contents

Designing Frame Relay 613
   Full-Mesh 613
   Star 614
   Partial Mesh 616
Frame Relay as a NBMA Network 617
   How Frame Relay Complicates the Routing Update Process 617
   Subinterfaces 619
Chapter Summary 622
From the Real World 624
Frequently Asked Questions (FAQ) 625
Case Study: Building a Frame Relay Network 626
   Configure Router A 626
   Configure Router B 626
   Configure the Frame Relay Switch 627
Questions 630
Answers 633

Appendix A OSI Model 637

Layer 1: The Physical Layer 637
   Cables and Wires 637
   Physical Terminations and Connectors 640
   Physical Encoding Methods 644
   Conclusion 647
Layer 2: The Data Link Layer 647
   Data Link Layer Example 649
   Conclusion 652
Layer 3: Network Layer 652
   The Internet Protocol (IP) 655
   IP Node Operation 655
   Internetwork Packet Exchange (IPX) Operation 658
Layer 4: Transport Layer 658
   Transport Layer Protocol Examples 660
   Conclusion 662
Layer 5: Session Layer 662
Layer 6: Presentation Layer 664
Layer 7: Application Layer 665
   Conclusion 666

Index 667

ACKNOWLEDGMENTS

I would like to acknowledge Dan Golding for his initial vision and assistance in getting this book going. Dan I hope everything turned out like you wanted! I would also like to acknowledge the assistance of Franny Kelly in juggling all the parts of this book. The publishing part of this book was anything but simple - thanks Franny! The folks that deserve to be mentioned the most are of course the authors. You may have noticed that this book is the work of many people that came together seamlessly and at a moments notice. Thank you all!

Thomas M. Thomas II

There are a few people that I would like to acknowledge for their assistance. Firstly I'd like to thank Tom Thomas, co-author and series editor for putting together such a great book. Thanks to John Akers, friend and colleague, for his assistance. Thanks to Earl Elliot and the rest of the FHS team for the knowledge and experience gained. Thanks to my current team in Sacramento at Netigy Corporation for the giant brain trust, and the opportunity to work at such a great company. Lastly, I'd like to extend the biggest thanks to my wife for putting up with the long hours over the last few months.

Michael Coker

Writing is a time consuming activity that eats into your social life. I do my writing after my day job and at weekends. I would like to thank my wife, Helen, again for her understanding and never ending support. I would like to acknowledge the co-authors of this book, Tom Thomas, Francis Kelly, and all at D&G for bringing it together.

Andrew G. Mason

I would like to acknowledge all of the authors on this work, especially Tom Thomas who coordinated getting us all together and made sure this was the quality of work we all wanted. I also want to thank the technical reviewers Neal Allen and John Vacca who made sure that our work was accurate and timely. Finally, I want to thank the crew at both McGraw-Hill and D&G Limited who made sure that the book looks as good as the content within.

Mark J. Newcomb

Many thanks, also, to my co-authors, Beth Brown at D & G, Ltd., Franny Kelly and the McGraw-Hill staff and all others involved in the creation of this book.

Adam Quiggle

I never imagined putting knowledge and reseach to paper would represent such a daunting challenge. The following people made this possible. Merideth Ritchie, my best friend and companion for her most valuable technical and literary input, guidance and motivation. The UNIS LUMIN technical team and its leader, Mauro Lollo, for their professional guidance, friendship and support, as well as numerous editorial contributions. The series Editor Tom Thomas II **Please ensure i reference his name correctly** for offering me the opportunity to participate in this work and his constant literary guidance. Finally our esteemed technical editors Neal Allen and John Vacca for exceptional insight and attention to detail.

Peter A. Van Oene

ABOUT THE AUTHORS

Thomas M. Thomas, II is a Certified Cisco Systems Instructor (CCSI), CCNA, CCNP & CCDA as well as the founder of NetCerts.com (www.netcerts.com), and the Cisco Professional Association - Worldwide or CPAW for short (www.ciscopaw.org), a not for profit organization bringing together users of Cisco equipment to learn and network. He was previously a Course Developer for Cisco Systems and was a Group Leader of the Advanced Systems Solutions Engineering Team for MCI's Managed Network Services. In his spare time, he has also authored OSPF Network Design Solution & Thomas' Concise Telecom & Networking Dictionary. Tom is currently working as an Instructor/Consultant for Mentor Technologies (www.mentortech.com).

Michael Coker, CCNA, MCSE, MCP+I, CNA, is a consultant at Netigy Corporation (Sacramento, CA), a Strategic Alliance Partner with Cisco, where he provides e-business infrastructure planning, design and implementation. Michael is a member of Netigy's Global Security Practice, focusing on VPN design solutions as well as vulnerability assessments and facilitated risk analysis of customers' e-business architectures. Michael is also a list moderator and an active member in many Cisco study groups assisting newcomers to the field of networking.

Andrew G. Mason, A+, Network+, CNA, Cisco Sales Expert, MCSE+Internet, CCNP, CCDP, is the CEO of Mason Technologies Limited (www.masontech.com), a UK-based Cisco Premier Partner involved in Cisco consulting for numerous UK-based companies. He has over 8 years experience in the computer industry.

Mark J. Newcomb, CCNP (Security), CCDP, MCSE is a consulting network engineer working for Aurora Consulting Group (www.auroracg.com), where he provides network design, security, and implementation services for clients throughout the Pacific Northwest. He has more than 20 years' experience in the Microcomputer industry. His other publication credits include co-authorship of McGraw-Hill's Cisco Internetwork Troubleshooting.

Adam Quiggle is a Senior Network Engineer at an MCI Worldcom Network Operations Center supporting a Fortune 50 company's international network. He has worked in numerous enterprise environments designing, implementing, and supporting complex environments. He holds a Bachelor of Science in electrical engineering, a CCNA, Master CNE, and MCSE. In addition, he has written *Building Cisco Remote Access Networks*, published by McGraw Hill and *Windows 2000 Server Administration Handbook*, published by Syngress.

Peter A. Van Oene, CCIE #5177, is a Technical Marketing Specialist at UNIS LUMIN Inc, a Toronto based technology consulting firm. He has numerous years designing, integrating and supporting large scale enterprise networks.

ABOUT THE REVIEWERS

Neal Allen was the Product Manager for the LANMeter Series hand-held network analyzers for Fluke Corporation in Everett, Washington for seven years. He presently supports all of the Fluke Networks products for training development and continues to assist with new products in the Alpha and Beta stages of development. Allen contributes to and is closely involved with all aspects of Fluke Networks' growing participation in the Cisco Networking Academy's CCNA and CCNP programs.

Allen has been involved in the design, installation, and troubleshooting of networks since 1987. Although his focus has been primarily OSI layer three and below, he has designed and taught a number of short seminars and three-quarter introductory networking courses at local community colleges. Allen has been a member of the NetWorld+Interop trade show *Network Operations Center* (NOC) Team since 1993 and, in addition to other responsibilities, is responsible for troubleshooting show floor problems at the Las Vegas and Atlanta Interop trade shows.

Allen was also chosen to help support and troubleshoot the network for the 1996 Atlanta Olympic Games. He participates in the local community college system as a member of program advisory boards in electronics, computer service, and networking technologies.

John Vacca is an information technology consultant and internationally know author based in Pomeroy, Ohio. Since 1982, John has been the author of 26 books and more than 350 articles in the areas of Internet and Intranet security, programming, systems development, rapid application development, multimedia and the Internet. John was also a configuration management specialist, computer specialist, and the computer security official for NASA's space station program (Freedom) and the International Space Station Program, from 1988 until his early retirement from NASA in 1995. John can be reached on the internet at jvacca@hti.net.

Network
Concepts
Review

Objectives

On completion of this chapter, you will be able to do the following:

- Identify different methods of network organization and apply them to a network design.

- Identify and describe the differences between main office, branch office, *small office/home office* (SOHO), and remote users as they apply to Cisco internetworks.

- Be able to understand the hierarchical model of network organization: access, distribution, and core layers.

- Have a thorough understanding of the OSI model as well as its correspondence to actual network devices, such as hubs, routers, and switches.

- Understand the various families of Cisco routers, hubs, and switches as well as their function in a small network.

This chapter can also help you fulfill the following CCNA Exam objectives:

- Identify and describe the functions of each of the seven layers of the OSI reference model.

- Describe connection-oriented network services and connectionless network services, and identify the key differences between them.

- Describe data link addresses and network addresses, and identify the key differences between them.

- Identify at least three reasons why the industry uses a layered model.

- Define and explain the five conversion steps of data encapsulation.

- Define flow control and describe the three basic methods used in networking.

- List the key internetworking functions of the OSI network layer and how they are performed in a router.

Network Organization: Size and Geography

Networks can be designed and examined in a variety of ways. These include functional definitions, geographic definitions (locations), and definitions based on upon placement in a network hierarchy (see Figure 1-1).

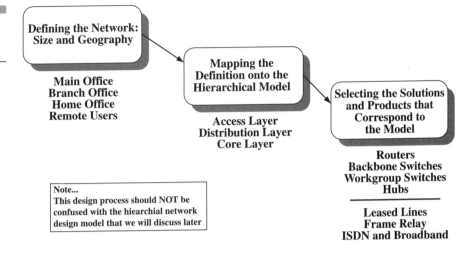

Figure 1-1
The network design process

The first method of organization we will examine is one based on size and geography. In almost all enterprise networks, four types of network users/sites exist:

- The main office
- Branch offices
- SOHOs
- Remote users

In order to compare these differing components, we will examine a fictional company, the *West Coast Router Works* (WCRW), shown in Figure 1-2. WCRW has a main office located in San Diego and several large branch offices located in Dallas, New York, and Boston. These branch offices are, respectively, the main sales, engineering, and accounting departments. WCRW also has a number of employees who work from home in and around San Diego; thus, each will be maintaining a home office. Finally, travel is a never-ending task for the hard-working sales force at WCRW.

Figure 1-2
West coast router
works

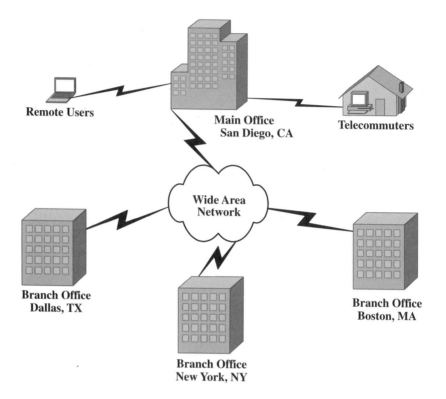

Thus, the remote sales people need a way to access network resources wherever they may be.

When designing a network, it is valuable to divide and subdivide the network in the same manner in which the company itself is organized. The needs and requirements of each branch office may be different, but they have far more in common with the other branch offices than the typical home office user or salesman on the road. In light of this, let's examine each of the distinctive units that make up WCRW.

The Main Office

This corporate office has about 300 workers spread throughout four floors at the WCRW building in San Diego. The computing resources are diverse and include a large AS/400 computer used by accounting, numerous file and print servers, and a large e-mail server. Additionally, the main office contains WCRW's link to the Internet, a high-speed leased line. A high-speed,

Fast Ethernet *Local Area Network* (LAN) runs throughout the headquarters, connecting users to these resources.

The Branch Offices

Each branch office has its own local file server and a LAN-running Ethernet. Each user has his or her own workstation, and numerous workgroup printers are available. Although these resources are enough for most tasks, access to the main office's systems are required for many business critical tasks. Thus, a *Wide Area Network* (WAN) link is required from each branch office back to the main office. As the main office is located in a different state from the branches, leased-line connectivity, probably Frame Relay, is used for the WAN. If the branch offices make a local call to the main office, an *Integrated Services Digital Network* (ISDN) or other dialup technology may be used.

Home Offices

Telecommuting is becoming more and more common for businesses. Typically, a home user will have a PC and possibly a printer. Access to file servers, e-mail systems, and the Internet are usually accomplished through a larger office. Due to the cost of leased lines, a dialup or residential broadband access is normally used for home offices. At this time, the most popular technology for home office connectivity is ISDN. A SOHO router can be configured to dial up as necessary and then disconnect when not in use in order to lessen costs.

NOTE: *ISDN is currently widely deployed as a solution for companies, but the future remains a bit unclear as the continuing deployment and growth of Digital Subscriber Lines (DSLs) and cable devices. They are cheaper and faster than ISDN, thus filling the need for increased bandwidth and at a lower cost.*

Remote Users

Typically, remote users need to be able to connect from any number of locations. This may include their home, hotel room, or the offices of business partners. For this reason, standard analog modems are typically used for these individuals. They may dial into the main office, a branch office, or perhaps one of the *Points of Presence* (POPs) that belong to WCRW's *Internet Service Provider* (ISP).

Network Organization: Hierarchical Design Model

After mapping WCRW's network into its business organization, the next step in the network design process is to identify the three main hierarchical model layers of the WCRW network. These layers are generally defined as

- The core layer
- The distribution layer
- The access layer

Although previously used only to define layers of a campus network environment, these layers have been extended to encompass an entire decentralized enterprise network.

The evolution of the hierarchical model parallels the evolution of networking. In the past, the core layer was composed of routers and had much of the network resources, including file and printer servers, mainframe and minicomputers, and other shared resources. The distribution layer may have been composed of bridges or other routers with hubs or repeaters occupying the access layer. However, the availability of inexpensive workgroup switches and the increased speed of enterprise backbones has resulted in a reorientation in this model.

Bridges, in the form of switches, have moved down to the access layer. This suggests a change in where the OSI layer 2 device has moved to and also introduces switches as a multi-port bridge, instead of a new thing entirely. On the other hand, routers now mostly reside in the distribution layer, with high-speed backbones dominating the network core. The core has evolved to include highly efficient switching devices that perform functions such as multi-layer switching.

The Access Layer

This is the layer that most users will interact with. The access layer is composed of switches, all user workstations, department servers, network printers, and other user peripherals such as network scanners (see Figure 1-3). It is easiest to envision the access layer as a series of discrete units, each

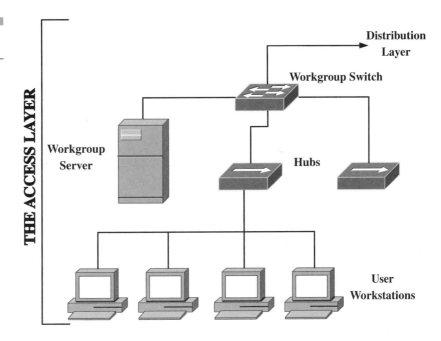

Figure 1-3
The access layer

corresponding to a workgroup. Each workgroup could correspond to a department at the main office, such as the payroll department, one of several divisions at a branch office or home office.

As a general rule, the following characteristics are shared by each unit at the access layer:

- The same network media, such as Ethernet, Fast Ethernet, Token Ring (like Cisco Catalyst 1912 Switch)
- Similar network bandwidth requirements, that is, a discrete unit of users (such as Payroll) having similar network bandwidth requirements as another unit. One group may require a huge database on a mainframe but won't push the database around the network, another may be moving large graphic files over the network frequently, while still a third may simply type a lot and move moderately small files periodically. Within the group of users, the discrete unit of users will have very similar network bandwidth requirements.
- Similar needs for data resources, that is, sharing a group of servers
- Similar needs for network resources, that is, sharing a large-format printer or network scanner

In order to have the most efficient network possible, it is desirable to place network resources as close to their consumers as possible. Thus, if a majority of users for a particular server are in the same unit at the access layer, the server should be in the same unit. Generally, an access-layer unit is connected to the distribution layer via a workgroup switch. Individual users and workstations may be attached directly to the switch or may be attached to it through hubs or repeaters. Servers or other shared resources are generally connected directly to the switch.

The Distribution Layer

The distribution layer is generally the area where interconnections between disparate media types occur. Each of the access-layer workgroups is carried back to the core on its own media type, such as Fast Ethernet, Ethernet, *Fiber Distributed Data Interface* (FDDI), or Token Ring, and is translated into the media used at the network core. Additionally, other types of translations occur (see Figure 1-4):

- The distribution layer is where remote access servers enable remote users to dial into your network.

- Internet connections are typically accomplished at the distribution layer and involve a router that connects your network to your ISP's network and the Internet.

Figure 1-4
The distribution layer

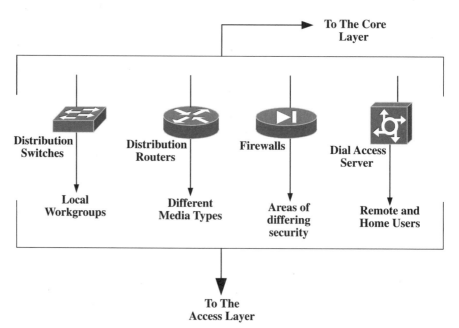

■ Security policies may vary inside an organization in response to the needs of the organization. These policies come together in the distribution layer, sometimes through the use of firewalls, *access control lists* (ACLs), or other filtering mechanisms. In this book, we will be discussing ACLs.

The primary purpose of the distribution layer is to perform "whole network" functions that involve significant resources. These include routing, filtering, routing summarization, security, packet filtering, and IP address or area aggregation. It is desirable to perform these functions at this layer that is outside of the network core in order to achieve the fastest possible performance in the core.

The Core Layer

The core layer exists to move data as quickly as possible from one section of the enterprise network to the next without sacrificing redundancy (see Figure 1-5). Thus, in many cases, you will hear the core layer referred to as a *transit area*. Although it is desirable to keep the majority of traffic inside each access-layer unit, it becomes necessary to communicate between these

Figure 1-5
The core layer

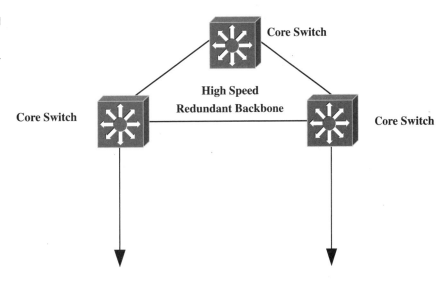

units and to access enterprise-level resources. These resources could include Internet access, groupware services, or a company intranet.

When a request for that type of data is received at the access layer, it is forwarded to the distribution layer. In this layer, the data stream is "normalized" with the rest of the network, allowing for differences in the media type, bandwidth, and security policy adjustments. From there, the data stream flows into the core layer where it is quickly redirected back down into the appropriate distribution layer device, so that it may reach its final destination.

Most core layers are composed of high-speed core switches with redundant connections between them. It is extremely rare for any actual network resources to be located at the core. It would only slow down the network, thus degrading the purpose of the network core. In recent years, advances in technology have lead to this exodus of resources from the network core, starting with the development of FDDI, then Fast Ethernet, and finally Gigabit Ethernet.

With the network defined and modeled, the next step is to build the network using the various network building blocks, such as switches, hubs, and routers. However, it becomes necessary to understand the purpose of these devices before they can be selected. The commonly used model to understand how networks are constructed is the OSI model.

NOTE: *Keep in mind the hierarchial design model and OSI model serve different purposes and should not be confused.*

The OSI Model

The *Open Systems Interconnect* (OSI) model is used to help us differentiate network functions (and the devices that perform them) from each other. The OSI model is your key to understanding how internetworks function. Although it is possible to work as a low-level network administrator without a full understanding of OSI, large-scale network design and engineering will not be possible. In order to implement Cisco networks, it is necessary to truly understand OSI, rather than simply memorize the names of each layer, as most industry certification programs would require.

This understanding will help you select the correct network device for each requirement and will promote the ease of troubleshooting once the network is constructed.

Why Have an OSI Model?

Why have an OSI model? It provides a clear delineation between networking functions. Thus, a router manufacturer knows which functions a router would be expected to perform, as opposed to a switch. The consumer would also know this, allowing an "apples to apples" comparison of various routers. Similarly, an application developer would know that his application could count on the presence of drivers for whatever type of network card happens to be in the user's workstation, rather than having to build in support for every type of hardware into every application.

For the purposes of this discussion, we will divide the OSI model into two areas (see Figure 1-6). The top layers, known as the *upper layers* or *application layers*, are used by software developers to create software that utilizes network resources. We will touch on these upper layers but will spend more time concentrating on the lower layers of the OSI model, known as the *data flow layers*, or the networking layers. These lower layers are utilized by the network devices that we use each day, such as hubs, routers, switches, network cards, and others.

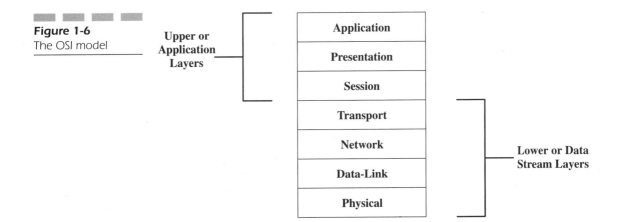

Figure 1-6
The OSI model

Upper or Application Layers

Application

Presentation

Session

Transport

Network

Data-Link

Physical

Lower or Data Stream Layers

Application Layers

The upper or application layers are used by software or application developers to create network-enabled applications, such as Web browsers, Telnet clients, *Network Interface Card* (NIC) drivers, as well as operating systems.

The application layer (layer 7) proper is perhaps the most familiar layer to many of us. It's the layer that end users interact with when using any computer or computer application. It's easy to think of software that operates at the application layer. Examples can include Web browsers, operating system *Graphical User Interfaces* (GUIs), Telnet clients, and FTP clients. Although many of these applications do much of their work on lower layers (for example, FTP does most of its "heavy lifting" at the transport layer), the aspect of these applications that you and I work with exists at the application layer.

The presentation layer (layer 6) deals with the way we see and perceive data. The old cliché that computers store data as "ones and zeros" is certainly correct. The presentation layer is essentially a translator for deciphering that data (ones and zeros) and presenting it to us in a human-readable format, as opposed to its true, machine-readable format. Examples of the presentation layer in action are abundant. The two best examples are file formats and cryptographic software. File formats such as ASCII, JPEG, MPEG, AVI, and others are familiar to us. They are simply rules for the computer to present information in a format that we understand. Cryptographic programs such as the *Data Encryption Standard* (DES) and *Pretty Good Privacy* (PGP) also function as rule engines. Their function as data decryption engines is more deliberately designed than standard file formats, but it is still functionally equivalent.

The session layer (layer 5) is the primary layer at which operating system kernels exist. The session layer enables multiple instances of network access to exist and co-exist. This layer enables your Web browser to function. Almost all Web browsers work by opening simultaneous sessions to Web servers. Multiple threads work in parallel to download content; this is the primary function of the session layer. Table 1-1 summarizes the functions and gives examples of upper-layer functionality.

Lower or Data Flow Layers

The lower layers of the OSI model perform the remainder of networking functions. These run the gamut from specifying the types of wiring the network is running through to the proper format for the data running through

	Layer	Function	Examples
Table 1-1	**Application**	Provides an interface between the user and the network.	Web browsers, Telnet clients, FTP programs, GUIs
The OSI model's upper-layer functionality summary	**Presentation**	Directs the encoding and decoding of data for network applications.	MPEG, JPEG, ASCII, PGP
	Session	Enables multiple instances of specific network applications to co-exist.	Operating system kernels and network drivers

that cable. We will examine each of these layers individually as well as the specific network devices that are associated with each layer. However, before we can do that, we need to examine the way our data will interact with each layer: through encapsulation.

When we transmit data through a network cable, it travels as a series of voltages and currents. But how does it make the leap from the data at the session layer, supplied by the operating system, to those electrical signals? And more importantly, how does the receiving computer know what to make of those signals? Significant information must be attached (in a process known as *encapsulation*) as the data moves down the OSI model so that the receiver can remove that information to determine what to do with the data. One might ask why all of this discrete information is necessary; some of it even appears repetitive. This is because the OSI model lets you "mix and match" technologies, so that you might have IPX/SPX running over Ethernet, or TCP/IP running over Token Ring. In both of these cases, each layer requires specific information to ensure correct delivery. Figure 1-7 illustrates the encapsulation process, as each additional item is known as a header. When combined with the existing information, these pieces are collectively known as *Protocol Data Units* (PDUs). However, each lower layer has a more specific name that we will discuss at each layer.

A header is added as data moves down the OSI model on the transmitting computer. At the receiving end, the headers are stripped off in reverse order, giving the upper layers useful data. This process explains how computers can communicate and how they can't. Let's say we have two PCs, one running TCP/IP, the other running IPX/SPX, both over an Ethernet network. The first computer transmits some information to the second. The second computer receives data that looks good, at first. The second computer has no problem stripping off the data link header; after all, the computers are both running on an Ethernet network. However, when the data

Figure 1-7
Data encapsulation

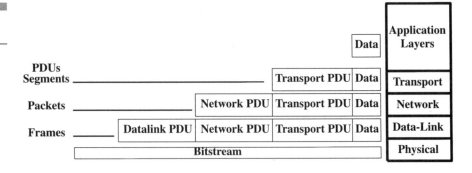

Layer	PDU Name	TCP/IP	IPX/SPX	Match?
Transport	Segments	TCP Header	SPX Header	No
Network	Packets	IP Header	IPX Header	No
Data Link	Frames	LLC+MAC Header	LLC+MAC Header	Yes
Physical	Raw Bits	Bitstream	Bitstream	Yes

Table 1-2

Protocol data units—TCP/IP vs. IPX/SPX over Ethernet

is passed to the receiving computer's network layer, it runs into trouble. The second computer can't understand the network layer header at that level and rejects it. We can see how a success or failure can occur in Table 1-2.

Now that we have briefly discussed the lower layers and a bit about the operations that go on at this layer, let's look at each layer individually.

The Transport Layer (L4)

The transport layer (layer 4) is used to differentiate between applications running over network protocols as well as to determine how connectivity between devices is established. Most network protocols are defined in terms of a pair or suite, such as IPX/SPX and TCP/IP, for example. This pairing corresponds to the network layer and the transport layer. Although IP and IPX each define information such as network addressing, SPX and TCP define how to establish a reliable connection between two end stations, complete with error checking and congestion control. This combined package of addressing between workstations, along with reliable end-to-end messaging is the defining paradigm of a network protocol. These functions are interdependent on each other; the post office needs

Table 1-3

		Examples
Application	User Interface	Telnet FTP
Presentation	• How data is presented • Special Processing such as encryption	ASCII EBCDIC JPEG
Session	Keeping different applications' data separate	Operating System/ Application Access Scheduling
Transport	• Reliable or unreliable delivery • Error correction before transmit	TCP UDP SPX
Network	Provide logical addressing which routers use for path determination	IP IPX
Data Link	• Combines bits into bytes and bytes into frames • Access to media using MAC address • Error detection not correction	802.3/802.2 HDLC
Physical	• Move bits between devices • Specifies voltage, wire speed and pin-out cables	EIA/TIA-232 V.35

both a house address (IP and IPX) and the mail carriers (SPX and TCP) to get a letter from your house to a friend's. Without both elements, reliable delivery is not possible. Network protocols are similar; they need an element that handles addressing such as IP, and an element that handles reliable delivery such as TCP. That's why we have whole suites of protocols such as TCP/IP and IPX/SPX. They combine both elements into a smoothly functioning whole.

The transport layer protocol, TCP, also defines a specific form of addressing: ports. A unique port number that enables the TCP/IP protocol stack to correctly pass data to the upper layers of the OSI model identifies each application under TCP. Therefore, when information is received at the transport layer, the port number is checked. If the port number is 25, for example, the data is passed to the application running on that port, usually a mail server. If the port ID is 23, the information is passed to the running Telnet program. We will use this port information later on to define methods of blocking and filtering certain transmissions in router configurations.

Equally important with port addressing is the establishment of connections between machines. These connections usually have error checking and congestion control if established by TCP. *Error checking* evaluates the segments that are received for errors and signals for a retransmission as necessary. *Congestion control* ensures that the receiving station isn't overwhelmed with too much traffic and provides communications between both stations to ensure that.

Finally, the transport layer regulates the reordering of segments as they are received. Because segments may need to be retransmitted due to errors or congestion, or because they may have taken different routes to reach their destinations, they may arrive in the wrong order. The transport layer puts them back into the correct order before handing them off to their respective applications.

In addition to the familiar TCP, there is also a protocol known as the *User Datagram Protocol* (UDP). The key difference is that UDP is connectionless and does away with error checking and congestion control. It just trusts that the data will be received. Although much less reliable, it is much faster and is used in numerous streaming media applications for this reason.

TIP: *How does the transport layer at the receiving end know how to put the segments back together in the correct order? TCP places sequence numbers on all of the segments as they go out the sender's transport layer. The receiving transport layer uses these sequence numbers to correctly order the data.*

The Network Layer (L3)

The third layer of the OSI model is known as the network layer (layer 3) and many of us are familiar with IP and IPX. These are standard network layer protocols that transmit user data. Additionally, another class of network layer protocols is used here, routing protocols. We will examine two of these in this text: *Routing Information Protocol* (RIP) and *Interior Gateway Routing Protocol* (IGRP). These routing protocols are methods for network layer devices to communicate with each other and spread routing information, that is, information on how to get from one physical network to another. Therefore, we call protocols like IP and IPX *routed protocols*, while RIP and IGRP are known as *routing protocols*. But more on those differences later.

The network layer also gives us hierarchical *logical* addressing. One part of these addresses is the host address, which is user-definable. It's the other address that makes all the difference, the network address. The network address enables us to define multiple physical networks and route between them. Thus, the network layer is chiefly concerned with addressing and routing.

Network Layer Addressing   Unlike the data link layer with its static MAC addresses, network-layer addresses are much more dynamic. They can be changed by the user and differ from protocol to protocol. Regardless of which protocol is being used, though, there is always one significant feature of network layer addresses that is the same. Each IP address always has separate network and host sections. Let's examine how an IP address is formed:

```
192.168.10.10 (decimal)
11000000.10101000.00001010.00001010 (binary)
```

is a standard TCP/IP address. Such addresses are composed of four equal parts, and each part is eight bits in length, for a total of 32 bits. The *period* between the groups of eight binary bits (shown in the preceding example) is known as a *dotted decimal* notation, a syntactic representation for a 32-bit integer that consists of four eight-bit numbers written in base 10 with periods (dots) separating them. It is used to represent IP addresses in the Internet, as in 192.168.10.10. Included within this single address are both network and host address portions.

The method of determining which portion of the address is for the network and which portion is for the node is determined by using a subnet mask. This mask is a series of 32 bits that is compared with the IP address. For address 192.168.10.10 with subnet mask 255.255.255.0, the comparison works like this:

```
Address: 11000000.10101000.00001010.00001010 (binary)
Mask:    11111111.11111111.11111111.00000000 (binary)
```

The ones of the subnet mask define that part of the IP address that is the network address. The zeroes mark off that part of the IP address that represents the node address. For the previous example, the first three octets (or eight-bit sections) are the network address, because they are delineated by ones in the subnet mask. This makes the network address 192.168.10.0. The node address is therefore 0.0.0.10. Other machines on the same local network would have IP addresses from 192.168.10.1 to 192.168.10.254. In order to reach other networks, such as 192.168.50.0, a network-level device, such as a router, must be used. This is but a brief introduction to IP addressing; we will explore IP addresses in more detail in later chapters.

Routers   Routers are network devices, much as switches and hubs are. Unlike switches or hubs, their function is to move data between networks, rather than within networks. Routers take packets that come to their interfaces and examine the network addresses. If the network address matches the address of the router's interface, the router does nothing. However, if the network address is different, the router will endeavor to transmit the packet to its destination. Routers know how to get packets to their destination by looking in their routing table. This table has a list of all the networks known to the router and how to get there, as well as the "cost" or metric for that path. This metric is used if several paths are available and it is necessary to determine which path is utilized (that is, the lowest cost path is used.). Routers learn how to get to networks in a number of ways:

- *Directly connected*   Routers put all directly connected networks into their routing tables. A directly connected route is a network that is physically connected to the router.
- *Static routes*   Routers can be issued a command to tell them how to reach a network. For example, Network 10.10.0.0 can be reached through interface Ethernet 3.
- *Routing protocols*   RIP, IGRP, and other protocols enable routers to send each other lists of reachable networks that can be incorporated into routing tables.

Routers are similar to switches, in that they segment networks. Unlike switches, routers do not propagate broadcasts, as broadcasts are normally only used for communications inside a local network. Thus, each network is its own broadcast domain and its own collision domain. In very large local networks, it is sometimes necessary to split the network using routers, because the large number of broadcasts uses too much capacity.

NOTE: Because most routers are slower than switches and can't operate at the full speed of many LANs, special routers called layer 3 switches are available, such as the Cisco 12000 GSR or Catalyst 8500. These are essentially very fast (or wire-speed) routers. The key difference is that normal routers operate by using routing software; that is, the routing decisions are made in a software program, whereas in a layer 3 Switch, routing decisions are made using special Application-Specific Integrated Circuits *(ASICs). Layer 3 switches are still more expensive than routers, but routers are getting faster and less expensive. Eventually, all routers will be able to operate at switching speeds.*

Typically, routers are used to connect LANs together. Usually, these LANs are at some distance, be it a campus network over a few miles, or a WAN over thousands of miles. For this reason, most routers have both WAN interfaces, such as ISDN connections, and LAN interfaces, such as Ethernet and Token Ring connections. Typical applications for such routers would include the connectivity between main offices, branch offices, home offices, and remote users.

The Data Link Layer (L2)

The data link layer (layer 2) describes the methods and practices used to take data supplied by network protocols like TCP/IP or IPX/SPX and transform it into a form that can be transmitted over a network. It is the lowest layer where this data is formed into discrete units. These units are known as *frames*, and their length and form is highly dependent on the physical media being used. Thus, Ethernet frames are much different than Token Ring frames, since each is a different physical media.

The two main functions of the data link layer are to communicate with the physical layer, such as 10Base-T Ethernet, and with the network layer, such as IP or IPX. Thus, the Ethernet data link layer itself is broken up into two sublayers: the *Media Access Control* (MAC) layer and the *Logical Link Control* (LLC) layer.

The MAC layer is defined by IEEE standard 802.3 and is closely associated with the physical layer. It governs the physical addressing of network devices, known as the MAC address. The MAC address is represented by a series of 48 bits that uniquely identifies every network device not just on your network, but also anywhere in the world. The first 24 bits are a manufacturer code prefix, while the last 24 bits are a unique device code. The prefixes are issued as address blocks, and some manufacturers, like Cisco, obtain additional new blocks of addresses regularly. In most circumstances, the MAC address is assigned at the factory and *burned* into the device's firmware, rendering it unchangeable. Routers, switches, NICs, and all other network devices contain MAC addresses.

The LLC takes care of encapsulating various network protocols for transmission on physical media. The LLC of the transmitting machine signals

Figure 1-8
The Ethernet frame

0	7 8	13 14	19 20	22 23		23+n 24+n	28+n
Preamble	Destination	Source	Length(=n)	Data		FCS	

the receiving machine's LLC by using the *Service Access Point* (SAP) identifier, which breaks out various LLC frames by the network protocol. If a workstation running both TCP/IP and IPX/SPX were to transmit a frame to another workstation, the receiver would know which network-layer protocol to pass the frame to, based on the SAP identifier. The LLC has several other functions, including some flow control, support of LAN-based applications, and sequence control bits.

The Cisco Discovery protocol runs at the data link layer only. This is a highly useful protocol that identifies Cisco devices to each other. It will be discussed at a later point in the text.

In this section, we are only talking about the data link layer for Ethernet. Although it's a good place to start, we should always remember that other data link layers are used for other types of communications. The *High-Level Data Link Control* (HDLC), Frame Relay, and the *Point-to-Point Protocol* (PPP) are all data link protocols used for various types of links, usually modem or WAN connections. Many of the principles discussed here will also apply to them and we be discussed in other chapters.

Ethernet Frame Anatomy   It is important to understand the basic organization of an Ethernet frame (see Figure 1-8).

The MAC Frame   Ethernet frames begin with a preamble, a series of 64 bits alternating in value between one and zero. The preamble acts as an attention sequence, signaling the listening devices that data will soon be coming in. You can think of a preamble like an announcer because there is really nothing of interest happening, but they are telling you the good stuff is coming!

After the preamble are the *destination and source MAC addresses*. In all cases, the source address will be the actual MAC address of the sending station. Usually, the destination address matches a specific destination station's MAC address. However, sometimes the destination MAC will signify a broadcast, or a message going to all local stations by being all ones in binary or all F's in hexadecimal. The destination MAC address can also signify a multicast, or a message going to a specific group of stations.

After the destination and source MAC addresses, a two-byte *length* field indicates the size of the frame's data payload, rather than the entire length of the frame. Immediately after the length field comes the *data*. This is the encapsulated information being sent from the upper layers of the OSI model, destined to be de-encapsulated by the receiving station. The data field is of varying lengths and is dependent on the type of physical media used in your network.

Figure 1-9
The Ethernet
LLC frame

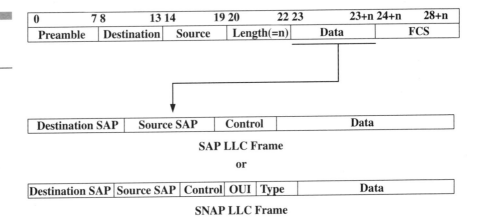

Finally, a four-byte *Frame Check Sequence* (FCS) contains error-checking information. This field holds a *Cyclic Redundancy Check* (CRC) value, which is calculated by performing numeric operations on the contents of the frame. The receiving station checks the CRC value in this field and then calculates a CRC value on its own. If these don't match, it indicates potential damage to the frame during transmission.

NOTE: *The MAC address is also sometimes called the* Burned-In Address *(BIA).*

The LLC Frame The LLC information we discussed earlier is tucked away inside the data area of the MAC frame. Two types of LLC frames exist: a *Service Access Point* (SAP) and a *Subnetwork Access Protocol* (SNAP). These type frame types are extremely similar. SNAP is simply an extension of SAP (see Figure 1-9).

The LLC SAP frame is composed of destination and source SAP values followed by a one- or two-byte control field and then the frame data. The SAP values correspond to specific protocols in higher levels of the OSI model, such as E0 for TCP/IP. In almost all cases, the source and destination SAP values will be the same. Each SAP value is one byte in length, and the definitions for the SAP values are controlled by independent standards bodies.

On the other hand, the LLC SNAP frame is a subtype of the SAP structure. This is accomplished by setting the SAP types to AA for both the source and destination as well as by placing a value of 3 in the control field. This is a signal to use the two-byte type field to specify the upper level protocol. The SNAP frame is necessary to enable many upper-level protocols, such as TCP/IP, to differentiate between different frame types. For example, ARP and IP packets are both part of the TCP/IP protocol suite. However, the SNAP type field is required for TCP/IP stacks to differentiate between the two. The SNAP frame also contains a three-byte vendor code or *Organizationally Unique Identifier* (OUI).

Ethernet Switching Methods   Ethernet switches are devices used to connect Ethernet stations in a manner similar to that of Ethernet hubs. The primary difference between switches and hubs lies in the OSI model. While hubs operate at the physical layer, switches operate at the data link layer. This provides a huge advantage to switches in terms of performance. Because a switch has access to the MAC address information in Ethernet frames, it can make *intelligent* decisions.

A switch's intelligence is basic in its ASICs, which are chips that make forwarding decisions. They can perform these decisions at a high rate of speed because they are hardware-based.

Furthermore, Cisco has recently made the default switching method for frames using anything but store-and-forward. In addition, two other fairly common forwarding techniques are being used as well as one that changes between forwarding techniques depending upon the detected error levels. The four techniques are listed below:

- *Store and forward*   This switching technique requires the switch to read in the *entire* frame before acting upon it. This is results in higher latency through your switch but reduces possible errors since the entire frame is checked for errors. If an error is found, the entire frame is discarded.

- *Cut-through*   This switching method forwards the frame *as soon as it receives* the destination address, which is in the first six bytes of the frame. The drawback is that a cut-through switch will forward errors across the network, since it does not check the CRC before forwarding the frame.

TIP: *Since a cut-through device forwards frames long before they can be error-checked, they are really just fancy repeaters. Furthermore, a cut-through switch must be counted as a repeater hop when calculating the 5-4-3 rule. Many companies have designed errors into their network by not including the switch as a repeated connection and have gone on to have*

substantially more than four repeated connections between distant stations.

■ *Fragment-free*   This switching method requires that the switch read the first 64 bytes of the frame before acting upon it. This is the minimum size frame allowed on Ethernet so that collisions can be detected. Normal collisions always occur before the first 64 bytes of a frame are transmitted.

TIP: *Fragment-free switching is a type of low-latency forwarding technique determined by the 802.3 parameter slot time. The switch does not forward the frame until slot time is over, and according to the 802.3, that means that the transmitting device has acquired the medium. Since all collisions are supposed to be over by the time 64 bytes has been transmitted, then only failures and design faults could possibly cause an error after 64 bytes. Thus, by waiting this long, the likelihood of forwarding an error is greatly diminished. It is not eliminated though!*

■ *Adaptive (also known as error sensing)*   This switching technique uses one of the low-latency forwarding techniques until the detected error level exceeds a threshold level. Then it switches to store and forward. An adaptive switch uses either cut-through or fragment-free operation, but monitors the network for error levels. At a pre-established error threshold, the switch changes methods to store and forward in order to reduce error levels on the network.

TIP: *Cisco frequently refers to switches as bridges or transparent bridges. Bridges are two-port switches, typically used to connect different networks. With the proliferation of inexpensive multi-port switches, the term "bridge" has become obsolete.*

As you can see in Figure 1-10, each type of switching causes the switch to act at different points within a frame, each with its own benefits and drawbacks.

All devices connected to an Ethernet hub are considered to be on the same segment or Ethernet collision domain. Switches act to segment networks; every port is a separate segment. Therefore, if you plug two 10-port hubs into a switch, you would get two segments of up to 10 stations each. If you plug all 20 stations into the switch, you would have 20 different segments. When

Figure 1-10

Switching decision point by the method used

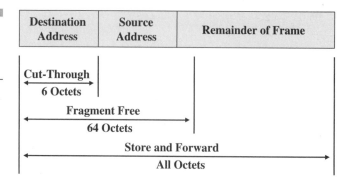

a frame from an attached segment reaches a switch port, the switch reads the destination MAC address of the frame. It compares the address to its MAC table (also called a CAM table on some Cisco switches).

This table contains a list of MAC addresses and the switch port on which they reside. A single port could have thousands of MAC addresses listed. This table is important, because it enables the ASIC to make its forwarding decision. If the destination address is local to the port that the frame is being received on, the frame won't be forwarded to any other ports. If the MAC table contains the port that the destination address is on, the frame is forwarded to that port only. This process means that collisions can't occur between these segments. Thus, each port of the switch has its own collision domain. A hub connected to a switch could still have collisions among its own devices, but it would not be possible for two devices on two different switch ports to cause a collision.

This process raises certain questions regarding how a Cisco switch handles the frames it receives. First, how is the MAC table built? The switch also looks at the source MAC address of *each* frame it receives and records the source MAC Address, along with its port of origin, in the MAC table, thus in effect *learning* its location.

Second, what happens when the destination MAC address indicates that the frame should be broadcast to all stations? The switch complies and forwards the frame to all segments. For this reason, we say that though a switch can have many collision domains, it still has only one broadcast domain. The final question that is posed, is what happens if a destination address is not in the MAC table? The frame is forwarded to all ports, and the return traffic from the destination back to the source normally gives the switch enough data to incorporate the missing address into the MAC table.

The Physical Layer (L1)

When working with the data stream elements of the OSI layer, it usually works better to start off on the most basic level, the physical layer (layer 1). When we see a Web page transmitted to us, it looks a lot different than what we see on the physical layer. In fact, the only way to really *truly* see the physical layer is on an oscilloscope or multi-meter because the ones and zeroes that represent data at this layer are in fact just electrical impulses. These are important tools for the network engineer and you are encouraged to become familiar with them, although their use is outside the scope of this text.

The physical layer is the nuts and bolts of networking. It defines the type of cable your network will be run on, the voltages and currents that will travel across the cable, and exactly what those electrical signals will represent. Other areas within your network where the physical layer rules supreme include defining the types of physical connectors that are used on your network cables, the bandwidth of your network, and the maximum distance that your network cabling can be.

TIP: Keep in mind that Ethernet will operate over other types of cables besides thick coax, thin coax, and twisted pair, for example. For instance, most of the high-speed Ethernet is commonly being installed on fiber in enterprise networks.

As this book concentrates on Ethernet, we will examine different physical-layer implementations of that popular networking method. Ethernet is defined by the *Institute of Electrical and Electronic Engineers* (IEEE) in a standard known as IEEE 802.3.

NOTE: The current IEEE 802.3 standard (1998 edition) incorporates all working group changes up through 802.3aa and is about three inches thick. The latest information, relating to Gigabit over 100-meter twisted pair copper, did not make the 1998 printing of this standard and is found in working group document 802.3ab.

This standard defines Ethernet as a networking standard operating at least at 10 megabits per second. It is also defined as operating over one or more of a number of different cabling standards and popularly installed Ethernet technologies as follows:

- *10Base-T*   Also known as twisted pair, this is the most common implementation of Ethernet and is run on standard twisted pair copper wiring, Category 3 (CAT3) or higher. 10Base-T utilizes devices known as *repeaters* or *hubs* to provide termination and signal boost. A maximum network diameter of five 100-meter segments and four repeated connections is allowed between any two distant stations.

- *10Base2*   Also known as coax or Thinnet, this is a slightly older version of Ethernet, popular in the early 1990s. It runs on coaxial cable and requires termination on either end of each coaxial segment in the form of a 50-ohm resister. In other words, coax Ethernet uses 50-ohm termination resistors at each end of each cable run, not 25 ohms. Taken in parallel, they measure 25 ohms and appear that way to the station, but they are 50 ohms each. A maximum of five 185-meter segments and four repeated connections is allowed between any two distant stations. Only three of the segments may have station connections, with the other two intermediate segments being used as inter-repeater link segments to extend the distance between stations.

- *10Base5*   Commonly known as Thicknet, this is an older cabling standard utilizing large coaxial cables. This standard requires termination devices on either end of each coaxial segment in the form of 50-ohm resistors. A maximum of five 500-meter segments and four repeated connections is allowed between any two distant stations. Only three of the segments may have station connections, with the other two intermediate segments being used as inter-repeater link segments to extend the distance between stations. Each 10Base5 device transmits through a transceiver attached to the coaxial cable and connects to the transceiver through an AUI cable that may be up to 50 meters long.

- *100Base-TX*   Commonly referred to as Fast Ethernet, even though the term applies to all of the 100-Mbps forms of Ethernet. It runs on the same pairs as 10Base-T but requires Category 5 (CAT5) or higher cable. For timing reasons, the maximum diameter of the Ethernet is restricted to two 100-meter segments with one Class I hub between them, or two 100-meter segments with two Class II hubs and a maximum five-meter cable between the hubs. Many Fast Ethernet interconnection devices are actually switches that perform OSI layer 2 bridging, and thus in those instances the segment count limits do not apply because each segment connects directly to a bridge.

- *100Base-FX*   Also referred to as Fast Ethernet, this implementation runs over fiber optic cable. The maximum segment lengths vary considerably (between 228 meters and 2000 meters), depending on half- or full-duplex operations, whether Class I or Class II hubs are present, or whether mixed media is used on those hubs. The most commonly referenced maximum segment length is 412 meters (see Clause 29 of IEEE 802.3 for details), which would be suitable between two bridged connections, such as the uplink between two switches, for instance.

- *1000Base-SX and 1000Base-LX*   These two fiber optic specifications for Gigabit Ethernet enable configurations that are similar to those found in half- and full-duplex 100Base-T. The SX implementation is used for shorter runs and the LX implementation for longer runs. The minimum segment length is two meters. The maximum segment length varies from 220 meters to 5000 meters, depending on half- or full-duplex operations and the type and size of fiber optic cable (see Clause 38 of IEEE 802.3 for details).

IEEE 802.3 also covers the MAC layer. The MAC layer covers network topology, frame delivery, optional flow control, and basic error-checking. In other words, the topology is greatly influenced by the limitations of the implementation you chose (10Base5, 100Base-TX, and so on). The controlling factor is end-to-end round-trip travel time (slot time), but that is defined frequently in each of the physical layer implementations as distance limits and such.

The flow control is largely determined by how an error is detected and handled, such as a collision that is detected by the physical layer in some instances and the MAC layer in others. The overvoltage state on a coax cable causes the chipset to realize that a collision has taken place, even if the *Frame Check Sequence* (FCS) checksum worked! On half-duplex twisted-pair Ethernet the mere presence of data on the RX pair while the TX pair is being used is also a collision by definition, again, even if the checksum worked.

Figure 1-11 illustrates the methods for connecting workstations or end stations to Ethernet networks. It should be noted that 10Base-T or 100Base-TX is used almost universally at this time, due to their ease of installation and troubleshooting, as well as their low cost. When 100-meter twisted pair Gigabit Ethernet becomes widely available (and the price per port comes down), it is expected to join the first two technologies as the preferred implementations.

Ethernet Hubs   A hub simply repeats any data received from one of its ports to all other ports. Unlike other network devices, no filtering or addressing is possible with a hub. Because a hub operates this way, we can say that a hub operates on the physical layer of the OSI model. It's only concerned with the raw data itself, without any logic to handle the data in any special way. For this reason, hubs are inexpensive, but only suited to modestly sized networks.

Figure 1-11
A 10Base-T Ethernet
network

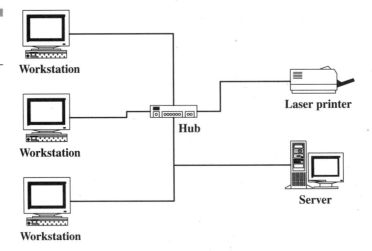

NOTE: *It should be noted that hubs do not weaken or split Ethernet signals. This is a common misapprehension. Instead, they amplify Ethernet signals, allowing them to travel for greater distances.*

In the most commonly used LAN types, the 10Base-T and 100Base-TX Ethernet network, hubs or repeaters are used to enable communications between stations. Typically, Ethernet hubs will have from four to 24 ports and will enable RJ-45-terminated Ethernet cables to be connected to ports located on the front or back. As these hubs are located in the center of an Ethernet network, this gives such networks a star topology. Each workstation is connected to the hub, rather than to other workstations. If it is necessary to use additional hubs, they are connected to each other in a daisy-chain fashion, with each end-station being connected to only one of the hubs. Thus, the star topology is maintained.

When using a hub, several factors must be taken into account. A repeated network shares the same bandwidth. If this were a 10-Mbps Ethernet network, then all workstations, servers, and printers would share the same 10 MB of bandwidth. Because all devices are sharing the bandwidth, a collision may occur. Collisions happen when multiple endstations attempt to transmit data at exactly the same moment. When this occurs, both stations will attempt to retransmit later after a random amount of time has occurred. This method of dealing with collisions is known as *Carrier Sense Multiple Access with Collision Detection* (CSMA/CD), as shown in Figure 1-12.

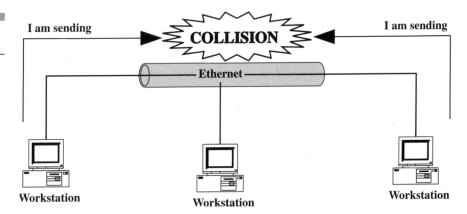

Figure 1-12
The collision process

The more endstations that exist in a repeated network, the more likely collisions are to occur. When the number of collisions starts to impact network performance, a switch is used to segment the LAN and prevent collisions. Switches operate at the second level of the OSI model, the data link layer.

NOTE: *We have more in-depth OSI Model information in the index if needed.*

Cisco Network Devices

Now that we have discussed the differences between the standard network devices, such as hubs, routers, and switches, let's examine the Cisco product line to see how their offerings might be used to build a network. Some important factors to consider when selecting network equipment are as follows:

- Manufacturer reputation
- Availability of technical support
- Cost
- Availability of an upgrade path
- Functionality
- Ease of use

Cisco Hubs

Although they are not the best-known manufacturers of hubs, Cisco has a full product line. As this is a rapidly evolving family of products, checking Cisco Connection Online (www.cisco.com) is highly recommended. Other manufactures such as 3Com (the market leader), Bay/Nortel (Netgear), and SMC also make excellent hubs.

Cisco has divided their family of hubs into two groups: MicroHubs, operating at 10 MB, and FastHubs, operating at 100 MB. For small offices, the MicroHubs are more than sufficient. However, higher bandwidth users, such as engineers and accountants or other professionals, may need more bandwidth. The FastHub series is certainly appropriate for these users. Additionally, heavy users of multimedia products would probably want to use the FastHub series. In most enterprises, a mix of 10 MB and Fast Ethernet is used, depending on the requirements. In larger enterprises, switches are also used, both for connecting hubs and for directly connecting large resource and demand nodes like servers.

Hubs require little administration or configuration; a few even have console ports or Web interfaces. They can be plugged in, wired up, and used. Some hubs have management capabilities, but this is rarely needed and is not recommended. This is because hubs offer little useful information through their management software but require a unique IP address and significant configurations if you want to use the management features. For that reason, the authors suggest leaving management to switches and routers.

Cisco Switches

Cisco also offers a line of LAN switches, known as *catalyst switches*. Although most of then were originally acquired from other companies, like Kalpana, Cisco has developed their switches into high-performance, feature-rich units. Key features include ISL trunking for connecting routers and switches together into coherent units, (which will be discussed later in the text) and full manageability through both Web and console interfaces. Catalyst switches (frequently called *cat switches* in the industry) have available speeds from 10 Mbps to 1,000 Mbps and many have a variety of ports and speed. The cat switches that Cisco offers are as follows:

- Catalyst 1912 or 1924 switches are access-layer switches with either 12 or 24 10-Mb Ethernet ports and two 100-MB Ethernet ports used for trunking. This is an excellent switch for a small- or medium-sized office. It is very similar in function to the 3Com Superstack 1100 switch. The Catalyst 2924XL is also an access-layer switch and is similar to the 1924, but has 24 100-MB ports. It is similar, though superior, to the 3Com Superstack 3300 switch. It can be used as an core-layer switch in a small network.

■ The Catalyst 5500 and 5000 series switches are designed as core-layer switches and can also act as routers with the installation of a *Route Switch Module* (RSM). These switches are expensive but are highly flexible and extremely fast.

■ The Catalyst 8500 family is Cisco's most powerful router offering layer 3 switching, *Asynchronous Transfer Mode* (ATM), and *Quality of Service* (QoS) offerings.

Cisco Routers

Cisco is best known for their award-winning routers. They offer an extremely wide array of routers, perhaps too large to be accurately discussed in this text (*The Cisco Router Handbook*, also from McGraw-Hill, examines each model in some detail). Suffice to say, several criteria must be evaluated when choosing a router:

■ *Port density*   The number of available Ethernet, Token Ring, serial, or ISDN ports

■ *Interface availability*   The ATM and Channelized DS3 interfaces are only available on certain models of routers. Additionally, the ISDN *Basic Rate Interface* (BRI) and *Primary Rate Interface* (PRI) are only available on certain models. Other routers are modular and can be fitted with almost any type of interface.

■ *Cost*   Cisco routers span the gamut of costs, with some being very affordable and others being those that only large enterprises could afford to own.

■ *Special capacities*   Some routers are capable of handling special payloads like voice or multimedia streams.

Cisco has divided its router families into three main groups:

■ *Access routers*, including the Cisco 1600 and 2600 are used to enable remote offices to communicate with large or main offices. The Cisco 2500 series is also in this group. The 2500s have been Cisco's most popular routers but are being phased out in favor of the modular 1600 and 2600 series. The Cisco 800 series is also in this category. It is used for SOHO access via ISDN and iDSL.

■ *Mid-level routers*, including the Cisco 3600, 4000 and AS5200 series, are used for large regional offices, as core routers for smaller networks, or as special-use routers, such as dial access servers. The 3600 series is highly modular and can exchange modules with the 1600 and 2600 series. It is currently Cisco's best-selling router. The 4000 series is also being phased out and should not be acquired.

■ *High-end routers*, including the Cisco 7200, 7500, and 12000GSR, are used as core routers for large enterprise and service provider networks. They can be used for extremely high-capacity data lines, such as OC48, and special connections, such as channelized DS3. The Cisco 7200 series has recently been enhanced to provide voice capacity and is available as the 7200VXR.

Chapter Summary

During the course of this chapter, we have covered a lot of territory. We have discussed two important ways of organizing networks and identifying requirements: the hierarchical model and the size and geography method. These techniques work together to enable us to design networks of increasing complexity. Additionally, they offer us a way to ensure that network topology and design dovetail with business requirements.

We also reviewed the structure of the OSI model, the basic building blocks of networking. We examined the upper layers of the OSI model and observed how they corresponded to application functions. We also looked at the transport, network, data link, and physical layers of the OSI model. We examined their structure and identified network devices such as hubs, switches, and routers that worked within their confines. During this discussion, we learned about collisions and broadcasts, and methods to contain both.

Finally, we examined Cisco networking products and the way they fit into the OSI model and network design. We also compared them with some competing vendors' products. The Cisco product line is vast, so any treatment in a textbook such as this can only be cursory. For more information, check out the Cisco System Web site, Cisco Connection Online, at http://www.cisco.com.

From the Real World

As senior engineers, we get to interview many network engineers and prospective network engineers. The first question we ask is, "What is the difference between a switch and a hub?" Those that answer "switches are faster" are usually shown the door. If they don't have an understanding of that basic level of internetworking, routing is probably beyond them. Most of these folks know the OSI model. They have memorized it, usually with a catchy mnemonic as they studied for their other certifications. True understanding of the OSI model typically eludes them, and they don't realize that it adversely effects their level of technical understanding. This is because the OSI model is also a great guide for troubleshooting, and understanding the operations of each layer will make you very effective.

This is why it's important to understand and be able to put into practice the principles of the OSI model. High-level network engineers know that this understanding is a prerequisite for their profession. Many of the concepts we deal with, such as routing, switching, network addressing, and network management, are closely tied with the OSI model. Our advice is this: (see Table 1-3) make a chart of the OSI model with the name of each layer, its function, the type of addressing that corresponds with each level, and the network devices that work at that level. Make sure you understand why each device and each type of addressing goes with each layer. At the network layer and transport layers, show how both IP and IPX are used. Also try to place the appropriate PDUs at each level: bits, frames, packets, and segments. This assignment may be difficult at this stage. If so, return to it when you have completed this text. This type of knowledge is often easier to understand in the light of concrete applications, rather than just dry theory, although we did try and make the theory a little wet.

Thomas M. Thomas II and Daniel L. Golding

Frequently Asked Questions (FAQ)

Question: What is a switching hub?

Answer: Several years ago when switches were still extremely expensive, several manufacturers introduced devices known as *switching hubs*. These were devices that typically had 24 ports with an internal four-port switch. They were essentially four six-port hubs, connected by a small switch, all in one unit. As switched ports became less expensive, these units were discontinued.

Question: What is a repeating hub?

Answer: This is a misnomer. All hubs are repeaters, and all repeaters are hubs. There isn't a different animal known as a repeating hub. Hubs and repeaters are also sometimes called Ethernet concentrators.

Question: Is a switch faster than a hub?

Answer: No, there are 10-MB switches and 10-MB hubs, as well as 100-MB switches and 100-MB hubs. Any performance increase is due to the fact that no collisions are possible, so the entire 10-MB bandwidth is available to all end devices.

Question: What is a non-blocking switch?

Answer: This is a switch that has sufficient internal bandwidth to prevent any backups on any of the ports. Typically, a non-blocking switch would have enough bandwidth to operate properly with all ports fully utilized.

Question: Since using a switch will get me better performance than using a hub, will using a router give me even better performance?

Answer: Usually not. Switches and hubs are typically wire-speed devices. They operate at the same speed as the media. Because routers function through software, they are typically slower than LAN wire speeds. Thus, using a router instead of a LAN switch can be a poor idea.

Question: How do I know when I need to move up to a switch from a hub?

Answer: Look for a collision light or indicator on the front of your hub. If it's on frequently during heavy network utilization periods, it's time to look into getting a switch. With today's switch prices, any network with 50 users should have a switch.

Questions

1. At which layer of hierarchical design model are dial access servers located?

   a. Access layer
   b. Distribution layer
   c. Core layer
   d. Transport layer

2. At which layer of the Cisco hierarchical design model are high-speed LAN switches located?

   a. Access layer
   b. Distribution layer
   c. Core layer
   d. Network layer
   e. Transport layer

3. By default, how many broadcast domains are there on a switch?

   a. None
   b. 1
   c. 2
   d. 24

4. How many broadcast domains are there on a hub?

   a. None
   b. 1
   c. 2
   d. 24

5. How many collision domains are there on a hub?

   a. None
   b. 1
   c. 2
   d. As many as there are ports on the device

6. How many collision domains are there on a switch?

   a. None
   b. 1
   c. 2
   d. As many as there are ports on the device

7. On which layer of the OSI model are connections between end stations established?

    a. Transport

    b. Network

    c. Data link

    d. Physical

8. At which layer of the OSI model is addressing of any kind *not* present?

    a. Transport

    b. Network

    c. Data link

    d. Physical

9. Which layer of the OSI model is responsible for the encryption and decryption of user data?

    a. Applications

    b. Presentation

    c. Network

    d. Data link

10. Which network devices operate exclusively on the physical layer of the OSI model? Choose two answers.

    a. Routers

    b. Switches

    c. Repeaters

    d. Hubs

    e. Switching hubs

11. Which network devices operate primarily on the network layer of the OSI model? Choose two answers.

    a. Routers

    b. Switches

    c. Repeaters

    d. Hubs

    e. Layer 3 switches

12. Which of the following Cisco products operates as a 100-MB hub?

    a. Catalyst switch
    b. Cisco MicroHub
    c. Cisco FastHub
    d. Cisco 12000 GSR

13. Access layer devices are primarily for

    a. Interfacing with end users and workstations
    b. Converting different network media types
    c. Providing the fastest switching possible
    d. Providing remote access

14. Which layer of the OSI model specifies line voltages and cabling types?

    a. Application
    b. Presentation
    c. Physical
    d. Data link

15. Which network devices operate primarily on the data link layer of the OSI model?

    a. Routers
    b. Switches
    c. Repeaters
    d. Hubs
    e. Layer 3 switches

16. Which type of address is also known as a Burned-In Address?

    a. IP addresses
    b. IPX addresses
    c. Port numbers
    d. MAC addresses

17. The two parts of a network-level address are (choose two)

    a. Network address
    b. MAC address
    c. Node address
    d. Router address
    e. Subnet mask

18. When using TCP/IP, the following splits an IP address into a network address and a node address:

    a. Subnet address
    b. Subnet mask
    c. Default gateway
    d. Port number
    e. MAC address

19. Port numbers are the addressing used to identify

    a. Individual nodes
    b. Separate networks
    c. Cisco routers
    d. Specific TCP/IP applications

20. These devices function to interconnect networks, rather than link together individual PCs or workstations:

    a. Bridges
    b. Routers
    c. Switches
    d. Repeaters
    e. Hubs

Answers

1. **b.** Distribution layer

   The distribution layer aggregates all different media types into a standard that is used in the core. Dial access is usually a significantly different media type than most of the access layer.

2. **c.** Core layer

   Although high-speed switches can exist at other points in the network, they will always comprise the network core, because of the need for high speed with little or no actual processing, filtering, or conversion.

3. **b.** 1

   Although a switch segments a network, it still propagates broadcasts to all of its ports. This is a requirement for all of the connected stations to be considered to be on the same LAN. If a switch didn't repeat these broadcasts, many LAN protocols would not function.

4. **b.** 1

   A hub will repeat any traffic sent to one of its ports, including broadcasts.

5. **b.** 1

   Because a hub repeats all traffic and has no buffering, intelligent switching, or collision-avoidance capability, it is always considered to be a single collision domain.

6. **d.** As many as there are ports on the device

   A switch will intelligently decide which traffic to forward to any given port. It also has buffering and memory to enable it to "hold on" to traffic before it transmits. For these reasons, a collision on one of its ports is not a collision on all ports.

7. **a.** Transport

   By definition, the transport layer controls and regulates connections between end stations.

8. **d.** Physical

   The physical layer is purely concerned with voltages, currents, and physical wiring.

9. **b.** Presentation

   The presentation layer is the arbiter between the computer's representation of data and the representation expected by the user. The process of mediating between these two expectations is essentially one of encryption and decryption.

10. **c.** Repeaters and **d.** Hubs

    Hubs and repeaters are exactly the same devices, although hub is now used in most discussions.

11. **a.** Routers and **e.** Layer 3 switches

    Remember that layer 3 switches are just very fast routers. All routers and layer 3 switches operate on the third level of the OSI model, the network layer.

12. **c.** Cisco FastHub

    A good reference for the Cisco product families is found at `www.cisco.com/univercd/cc/td/doc/pcat`.

13. **a.** interfacing with end users and workstations.

    The conversion of different media types and the provisioning of remote access occur at the distribution layer. The fastest switching possible is desired at the core, rather than at the edges of a network.

14. **c.** Physical

    By definition, these functions are performed at the physical layer. This enables a variety of protocols to run at higher layers without concern as to the exact physical media type.

15. **b.** Switches

    Switches utilize data link addressing and MAC addresses to make their switching decisions. Hubs and repeaters operate at the physical layer, while routers and layer 3 switches operate at the network layer.

16. **d.** MAC addresses

    MAC addresses are burned in at the factory.

17. **a.** Network address and **c.** Node address

    MAC addresses function at the data link layer. Subnet masks are ways of dividing the network layer address into network and node addresses.

18. **b.** Subnet mask

    Subnet masks perform this function. Port numbers identify specific network applications, and MAC addresses function at the data link layer. The default gateway is typically the network address of the router.

19. **d.** Specific TCP/IP application

    Port numbers are transport-level addresses used to enable network data streams to carry information for multiple applications. Network-level addresses identify specific networks, nodes, and routers.

20. **b.** Routers

    Because routers function on the network level, they are primarily concerned with interconnecting networks. They can identify and act on differences in network-level addressing, so that they can route information between networks. They are typically not as useful on a LAN as a switch, because they are slower and filter broadcasts.

Identifying, Cabling, and Attaching to Cisco Devices

Objectives

On completion of this chapter, the reader should be able to demonstrate a proficiency in the following:

- Understand and identify the various cables and connectors that facilitate connectivity at the physical layer.
- Have familiarity with the many flavors of Ethernet-based physical topologies.
- Understand the cabling requirements of Ethernet-based networks.
- Understand the cabling requirements of various serial connections.
- Understand the cabling requirements of ISDN networks.
- Identify and connect to both *Local Area Network* (LAN) and *Wide Area Network* (WAN) interfaces on Cisco routers.
- Differentiate between modular and fixed configuration routers.
- Connect to the console port of a Cisco router.

This chapter can also help you fulfill the following CCNA exam objectives:

- Describe Full and Half-Duplex Ethernet operations.
- Describe the features and benefits of Fast Ethernet.
- Describe the guidelines and distance limitations of Fast Ethernet.

This chapter focuses upon the physical layer of data communications networks. As noted in the first chapter, the physical layer represents the base of the OSI model and carries the primary responsibility for the raw transmission of bits over a medium. Over the years, LANs and WANs have been implemented in a variety of ways using various types of physical media. This chapter will identify and discuss many of the more common, physical layer implementations and their respective specifications. Beginning with Ethernet, the most dominant LAN specification, and then moving through various WAN specifications, the chapter will endeavor to provide the reader with a broad understanding and awareness of the many technologies at play in the physical layer. Following a look at the various specifications, the technologies as they present themselves in the Cisco equipment series will be discussed.

LAN Physical Layer Implementations

The LAN space has been occupied by a number of technologies over the years. Chief among them in recent years has been Ethernet and Token Ring. However, due to its lower cost of ownership and ease of installation and maintenance, Ethernet has won out as the LAN technology of choice for most organizations. Although many organizations still rely on technologies other than Ethernet for their LAN needs, the lion's share of the market has migrated into the Ethernet family. For that reason, this chapter will focus solely on Ethernet technology as it exists in the physical layer.

Ethernet

Ethernet today plays an extremely large role in networks of all sizes. Despite remaining constant in most of its functions, Ethernet at the physical layer has undergone many changes. Today Ethernet and Fast Ethernet exist in numerous forms, each with their own unique characteristics. One should remember that despite what the name implies, the physical layer represents more than just the physical composition of media. Many other facets of a transmission, including signaling types and rates as well as encoding schemes, are governed by physical layer definitions. As such, there is a tremendous opportunity for diversity within this layer.

As this point, we will begin to briefly investigate several of the physical-layer definitions of both Ethernet and Fast Ethernet technology. It should be noted that the names of the individual specifications themselves lend a great deal toward their being understood. For example, each specification is named first with its transmission rate in *megabits per second* (Mbps). The second part of the name indicates whether the signal is carried in a broadband or baseband method across the media. What is the difference between broadband and baseband? Baseband networks use a single channel for communication between stations, while broadband networks enable different services to communicate over different channels distinguished by a frequency across the same media, much like cable television. Finally, the last. For example, 10Base-F represents a 10-Mbps signal carrier baseband across fiber cabling digit(s) represent, for the most part, the media that the signal is carried on. However, it should be noted that the first few iterations of Ethernet technology used the last digit to represent the maximum network diameter in hundreds of meters.

NOTE: *Although all of the Ethernet information we cover in the chapter involves baseband transmissions, it should be noted that broadband versions do exist. 10Broad36, although seldom used, carries a 10-Mbps signal over coaxial cable with terminating equipment very much like that used in* Computer Antenna Television *(CATV).*

10Base2   10Base2, often described as Thin Ethernet or "Thinnet," represents the original design for a departmental or workgroup-sized Ethernet environment. It generally provides connectivity to the access layer. It is designed to be simple to configure, inexpensive, and offer a degree of flexibility to enable the movement of people and stations. The traditional 10Base2 network involves devices connected to a length of coaxial cable via a "T" connector. The coaxial cable itself is then terminated at both ends and the network runs a Bus topology. The diagram in Figure 2-1 depicts such an environment.

10Base2 networks use a 50-ohm coaxial cable (RG-58 A/U & RG-58 C/U) with a maximum length of 185 meters as the transmission media. The connector used to attach devices to a 10Base2 is called a BNC connector (short for British Naval Connector, Bayonet Nut Connector, or Bayonet Neill Concelman).

10Base5   10Base5, known as Thick Ethernet or "Thicknet," represents the original Ethernet backbone technology. The Thicknet reference was earned by the large (an approximately two centimeter or $^3/_4$ -inch diameter) 50-ohm cable that 10Base5 uses. Much less flexible than 10Base2, 10Base5 cabling

Figure 2-1
The 10Base2
network

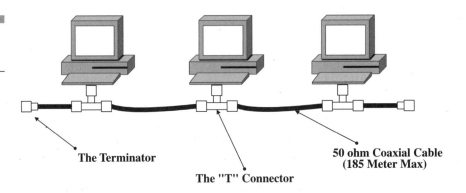

The Terminator

The "T" Connector

50 ohm Coaxial Cable
(185 Meter Max)

is typically used to serve a more permanent role, such as connecting fixed physical locations. The outer insulation (jacket) of the cable may be plain PVC (yellow in color) or Teflon (orange-brown in color). This composition has also earned 10Base5 cabling the nickname "garden hose." As with 10Base2, Thicknet uses a Bus topology. Figure 2-2 depicts a typical 10Base5 environment.

The most common way to connect devices to a 10Base5 segment involves the use of a transceiver/tap combination. The tap portion, often called a *vampire tap*, essentially pierces the outer jacket of the Thicknet cable and makes a direct physical (and electrical) connection to the ground sheath and center conductor of the cable. This form of tap can be done without disrupting the Ethernet segment and is thus known as *non-intrusive*. The transceiver portion is essentially the packaged electronics that provide access to the media. The transceiver is physically mated to the tap. The device then connects to *Data Terminal Equipment* (DTE) via an *Attachment Unit Interface* (AUI) cable. The AUI cable terminates into a DB15 connector.

NOTE: *Although you may come across Thicknet backbones very infrequently in your travels, it is not at all unlikely to find an AUI connection as your primary Ethernet interface on a device. For this reason, its advisable to keep an inexpensive AUI to a 10Base-T transceiver for those awkward moments.*

10Base-T Easily the most predominant flavor of Ethernet in use today, 10Base-T represents the first iteration of non-coaxial-cable-based Ethernet

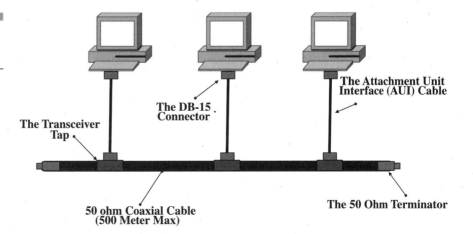

Figure 2-2
The 10Base5 network

The Transceiver Tap

The DB-15 Connector

The Attachment Unit Interface (AUI) Cable

50 ohm Coaxial Cable (500 Meter Max)

The 50 Ohm Terminator

on copper media. The "T" in 10Base-T indicates that the copper used is twisted pair. Specifically, 10Base-T uses a cable that consists of four individually twisted pairs of unshielded copper conductors rated at *Category 3* (CAT3) or above. This cable is most often referred to as *Unshielded Twisted Pair* (UTP). The twisting of the pairs enables Ethernet signals to travel distances of up to approximately 100 meters. More specifically, the Telecommunications Industry Association/Electronics Industry Association (TIA/EIA) recommends a wiring-closet-to-wall-jack distance of 90 meters, with the remaining 10 meters set aside for patch cables and any small intermediary losses incurred at connection points. Although capable of running over CAT3, voice-grade cable, most implementations of 10Base-T utilize *Category 5* (CAT5) cabling infrastructures.

10Base-T wiring differs from the previous copper iterations in that it uses a star wired topology. Traditional installations involve end nodes directly connected to network repeaters. Figure 2-3 illustrates a standard configuration.

10Base-T cabling terminates with an RJ-45 connector. This eight-pin connector is strategically pinned out to leverage the twists in the cable, thus minimizing crosstalk. Specifically, 10Base-T pairs the individual wires 1 and 2 and 3 and 6. The specifics for cabling this connector will be discussed later in the chapter.

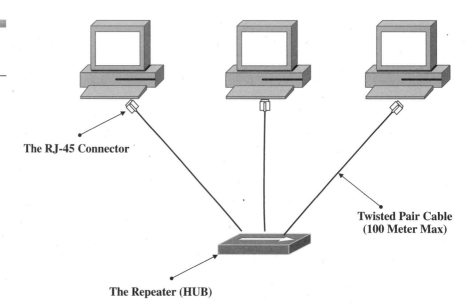

Figure 2-3
The 10Base-T
Network

The RJ-45 Connector

Twisted Pair Cable
(100 Meter Max)

The Repeater (HUB)

NOTE: *The TIA/EIA created a standard called the ANSI/TIA/EIA 568A. It should be noted that most references to the standard drop the ANSI and simply refer to it as TIA/EIA 568A. This highly recognized and often-referenced standard governs building cabling systems including aspects ranging from cable lengths, frequencies, and losses to wiring closet locations and configurations. The standard also contains the specifications for the various categories of cable, such as Category 3, 4, and 5. Extensive references will be made to these standards, but a detailed investigation into their specifics is beyond the scope of this text.*

10Base-F   10Base-F represents the implementation of Ethernet over a fiber optic medium. Fiber optics offer numerous benefits over copper media with the primary drawback being the cost of both the cable itself and the fiber interfaces on networking equipment. Fiber offers complete resistance to both *Electro-Magnetic Interference* (EMI) and *Radio Frequency Interference* (RFI). Further, much greater distances can be traversed via fiber than with copper due to significantly less signal loss. These characteristics leave fiber connectivity very well suited to play a role in connecting areas separated by large distances, such as wiring closets in an office building or buildings spread around a campus. In addition, very high signaling rates in the terabit range can be achieved with fiber.

The 10Base-F standard is actually a suite of three individual specifications. The first and most common, 10Base-FL, was developed to replace the original *Fiber Optic Inter-Repeater Link* (FOIRL) technology. Used end to end, 10Base-FL connections can span up to 2000 meters, effectively doubling the FOIRL maximum of 1000 meters. Another standard within the 10Base-F family is 10Base-FB. Like FL, FB links can stretch to 2000 meters and are traditionally used to connect repeaters. However, only a select few manufacturers chose to market technology based on the FB specification. The final member of the 10Base-F family is 10Base-FP. Never widely adopted, 10Base-FP specifies a passive fiber system capable of linking up to 33 computers via fiber optic cable without the use of a repeater. As 10Base-FL clearly remains the dominant version of the 10Base-F technology group, we will focus solely on it.

10Base-FL typically uses a *multi-mode fiber* (MMF) optic cable that consists of a 62.5-micron core and a 125-micron outer cladding (62.5/125). The wavelength of light used on the fiber link is 850 *nanometers* (nm). Communication over a 10Base-FL link takes place across two fibers: one to *transmit* (TX) and one to *receive* (RX). Traditionally, 10Base-FL is terminated with a ST-type fiber connector. This bayonet style connector (push and twist)

attaches by sliding the ST plug into the ST receptacle and twisting the connector into a locked state. Figure 2-4 displays the ST cable and connector.

NOTE: As a helpful reminder of the ST designation, I like to consider the mnemonic "Stick and Twist." Essentially, this describes the way that ST connections are made as the plug is stuck into the receptacle and twisted.

100Base-TX   Yet another variation of Ethernet on UTP is the 100Base-TX standard, which describes 100 Mbps signaling over UTP copper cable. Quickly becoming the dominant method of delivering higher speed connectivity in an internetwork, 100Base-TX offers numerous benefits to a variety of environments. Due to its high volume of sales, 100Base-TX offers a very attractive bandwidth-per-dollar ratio. Further, given that it performs almost exactly like 10Base-T, only 10 times faster, a very shallow learning curve is required before organizations can safely deploy the technology. Less tolerant of signal loss than its 10-Mbps ancestor, 100Base-TX requires a high quality UTP cabling system of a CAT5 (or higher) variety.

100Base-TX currently plays a number of roles in an infrastructure. Initially used to connect server farms to the core network layer and as a way to connect the access to the distribution layers, TX now sees use in many areas. Figure 2-5 depicts a typical 100Base-TX network.

As with 10Base-T, 100Base-TX uses an RJ-45 connector to terminate its cabling. Later in the chapter, we will discuss the specifics of the pinout for this connector. However, it can be noted that 100Base-TX uses two pairs of wires, the 1 and 2 and 3 and 6 combination, just like 10Base-T. The 100 meter (total) segment length of 10Base-T is also preserved in TX.

100Base-FX   100Base-FX represents a higher speed variety of Ethernet over fiber optic cabling. Again, a MMF fiber cable with a 62.5-micron fiber optic core and 125-micron outer cladding (62.5/125) is used. Unlike 10Base-FL, FX uses a light wavelength of 1350 nanometers (1350 nm). Given that 100Base-FX runs essentially over the same cabling as its lower speed

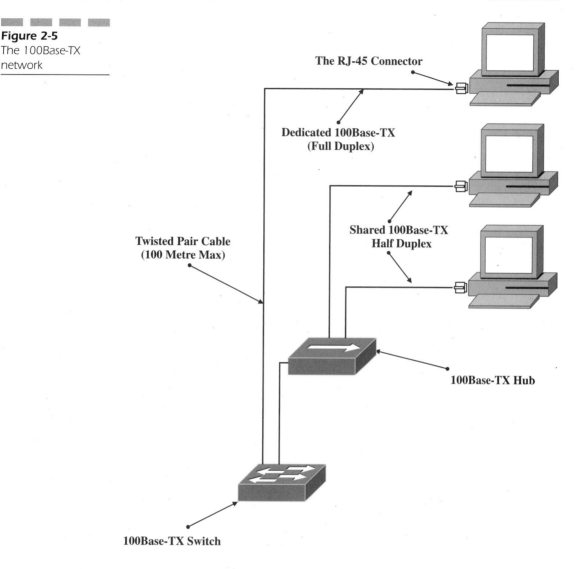

Figure 2-5
The 100Base-TX
network

The RJ-45 Connector

Dedicated 100Base-TX
(Full Duplex)

Twisted Pair Cable
(100 Metre Max)

Shared 100Base-TX
Half Duplex

100Base-TX Hub

100Base-TX Switch

ancestor, FL, it is not surprising to see many organizations upgrading to this faster technology. Overall, 100Base-FX now sees primary use providing high-speed connectivity from the access layer to the distribution layer. 100Base-FX can also be effectively used to connect workgroups or individual servers/workstations in areas that exhibit high amounts of EMI/RFI. A traditional use of 100Base-FX technology is presented in Figure 2-6.

Figure 2-6
The 100Base-FX
network

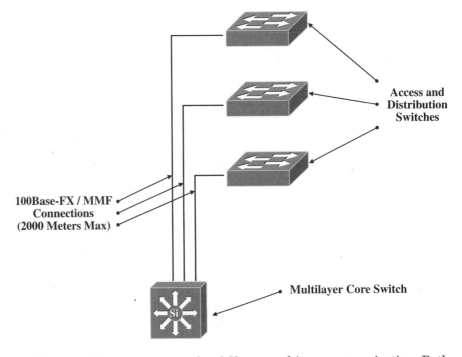

Access and
Distribution
Switches

100Base-FX / MMF
Connections
(2000 Meters Max)

Multilayer Core Switch

100Base-FX uses two strands of fiber to achieve communication. Both
the TX and the RX strand are normally terminated with a SC-type fiber
connector. The SC connector is keyed and easily connects by pushing the
plug directly into the receptacle. The quality of the connection and its ease
of use make SC the recommended connector type for most 100Base-FX terminations. Further, the EIA/TIA has made a push towards a global standardization of fiber optic cable termination. To support this decision, North
American organizations have been asked to move toward SC to harmonize
with European organizations. 100Base-FX connections can stretch to 400
meters over the above described MMF cable.

NOTE: *Upon making the connection, an SC connector emits an audible
click. This click lends justice to the mnemonic "Stick and Click."*

It should be noted that three other ways currently exist for terminating
a 100Base-FX fiber cable. A newer, less prevalent connector type can be
found on some popular equipment (Cisco, for example). This is the MTRJ

connector, which provides the same benefits of the SC, but incorporates two strands of fiber (the TX and RX strands) into a single "hood." This enables a higher density of fiber interfaces to reside in a smaller space, which is an important fact for equipment manufacturers as it enables the port densities of modules to be significantly increased. Another, the FDDI MIC connector, traditionally used for the FDDI networking technology, uses ends that can be physically keyed as A, B, M, and S types. These aptly differentiate between the various types of FDDI connections but have little relevance to 100Base-FX. Should a MIC connector be used to terminate FX, it is recommended that the keyed position be set to M. Finally, 100Base-FX can also be terminated with the ST connector as with 10Base-FL.

100Base-T4 Prior to the market settling, many debates took place about which of the 100-Mbps-over-copper standards would become the industry choice. 100Base-T4 offers a distinct advantage over 100Base-TX, that being the capability to run over voice-grade, CAT3 cabling. The T4 in 100Base-T4 represents the fact that the signal is carried over four pairs of copper wire (as opposed to two pairs in TX). As with 100Base-TX, segment lengths are limited to 100 meters, but it is likely that T4 could run at distances up to approximately 150 meters due to its increased tolerance to signal loss. However, networking "best practices" always advise a strict adherence to cabling and signaling standards. Despite some of its advantages over 100Base-TX, T4 has never been widely adopted and remains somewhat of a fringe technology.

100Base-T4 terminates with an RJ-45 connector. As previously mentioned, all eight wires in the connector are used for communication. Table 2-1 illustrates the pinning and functions for the RJ-45, 100Base-T4 connection. Within the four pairs, two are used for transmitting and receiving, and two are bidirectional.

Identifying Ethernet Connectors on Cisco Routers

Cisco routers present a number of different LAN interface connector types. The format of the various connectors tends to depend on the legacy of the equipment in question. In the upcoming sections, we will identify some of the more common LAN interface connectors.

Table 2-1

The RJ-45,
100Base-T4
connection's
pinning and
functions

100B-T4			
Pin	Function	Pair	Polarity
1	Transmitting	One	+
2	Transmitting	One	−
3	Receiving	Two	+
4	Bidirectional	Three	+
5	Bidirectional	Three	−
6	Receiving	Two	−
7	Bidirectional	Four	+
8	Bidirectional	Four	−

Figure 2-7
The RJ-45 jack

Cisco 1601 Router

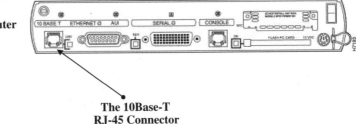

The 10Base-T
RJ-45 Connector

RJ-45

The RJ-45 jack is the most common method for presenting a 10Base-T or
100Base-TX connection. The diagram in Figure 2-7 portrays the rear panel
of a Cisco 1601 and indicates a standard RJ-45 Ethernet connector. Cisco
will typically print a description of the technology and the module number
alongside the connector for identification purposes.

AUI

Many devices, specifically those of some legacy, incorporate the AUI connector as a LAN interface. The AUI LAN interface consists of a female DB-
15 connector. As discussed earlier, AUI was a common interface used in

10Base5 LAN technology. Given that most networks no longer use 10Base5, it becomes necessary to use a device to convert the AUI into a more common RJ-45 connection. A typical AUI-to-10Base-T micro-transceiver does very well for these cases.

Fiber Connector

Fiber connectors on Cisco routers generally come in two flavors. For 10-Mbps Ethernet (10Base-F) connectivity, the connector is most often a ST style. For 100-Mbps Ethernet (100Base-FX), the connector type is most often a SC variety. Figure 2-8 illustrates both options.

NOTE: *Cisco has now begun to incorporate the MTRJ type of connector on various types of equipment. The MTRJ resembles the SC connector but incorporates both the transmit and receive fiber pair in a single element.*

Full Duplex/Half Duplex

When configuring Ethernet interfaces of all varieties, the duplex of the connection is a vital component to consider. The terms half- and full-duplex deal with the nature of the communication taking place on a point-to-point or point-to-multipoint link (see Figure 2-09). Full-duplex indicates that traffic can flow simultaneously in both directions across a link. A telephone conversation is an excellent example of a full-duplex conversation as both parties can talk at the same time. Half-duplex conversations occur in one

Figure 2-8
The ST and SC connectors

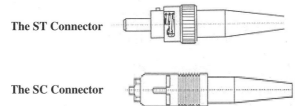

The ST Connector

The SC Connector

Figure 2-9
Full- and half-duplex

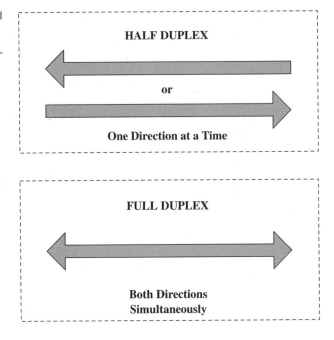

direction at a time. A walkie-talkie is a good example of half-duplex communications as there is only the capability for one party to talk at any one moment.

Recalling from Chapter 1, "Network Concepts Review," Ethernet is based on the *Carrier Sense Multiple Access with Collision Avoidance* (CSMA/CD) algorithm. The CD aspect, that being collision detection, is essential to this contention-based technology. Consider a group of nodes on an Ethernet segment. When one is transmitting, all the others are receiving. While the node is transmitting, it is also listening to traffic on the medium to ensure that it remains the only node transmitting. Should it receive any traffic during that period, it will signal a collision and move through the collision algorithm. As noted above, full-duplex conversations require two parties to send and receive at the same time. In order for this to work, the parties must disable their collision detection algorithms. However, with any more than two parties in conversation, disabling collision detection would render the communication ineffective. It is for this reason that full-duplex communication in the Ethernet world is strictly limited to two-party, point-to-point communication.

Given the point-to-point nature of full-duplex Ethernet, one must be careful when deploying it. For example, enabling full-duplex connectivity makes sense for switch-to-switch connections. Also, nodes that are connected directly to a switch port can utilize the additional bandwidth provided by full-duplex connectivity.

NOTE: *A cautionary word about duplex must be made at this point. Be very wary of incorrect duplex settings, that being one side is running full and the other is running half. There will be no obvious signs of this misconfiguration. No red or amber lights will warn you. However, as you can imagine, you will achieve a drastically suboptimal performance. A general indicator of this error will be overall slowness in the connectivity and a high degree of errors noted by the switch. As a rule, it is advantageous to allow the device to autonegotiate the duplex. In case of a disagreement over full-duplex connectivity, auto-negotiating devices will fall back to a functional half-duplex setting. In the event that it becomes necessary to hard code devices for duplex, these settings should be set on both ends of the connection and fully documented to prevent issues in the future.*

Cabling Ethernet

The most common way to cable Ethernet involves the use of UTP cabling with RJ-45 connectors (in the copper world) and multimode 62.5/125 ST/SC fiber (in the fiber world). For that reason, this text will limit its description to those methods. A very important issue to keep in mind when dealing with cabling is the relationship of transmit and receive signals. For example, if every device interface and cable were "pinned out" exactly the same, the transmit portion of the device interface would end up pointing directly to the transmit portion of other devices and likewise for the receive side of things. Obviously, this would disable any sort of communication. For that reason, certain devices have their transmit and receive pins in one position, and other types of devices use the opposite configuration. When connecting like devices together, we need to compensate with our cabling infrastructure by using cables known as *crossover cables*. We will investigate which devices fall on each side of that differentiation shortly when we consider *Data Terminal Equipment* (DTE) and *Data Circuit-terminating Equipment* (DCE) terminology. For the moment, consider that workstations, servers, and routers fall on one side, while hubs and switches fall on the other.

Cat 3, 4, 5

Each of the cabling performance categories (type 3, 4, and 5) is configured exactly the same. When creating a straight-through pinned cable, one that doesn't need to compensate for like devices at both ends, we simply map out the individual cable conductors in a one-to-one relationship. UTP Ethernet cables use pins 1, 2, 3 and 6 for communication. As described in Table 2-2 and Figure 2-10, the pins are paired to create the transmit and receive channels for communication. Of the two cables per pair, one receives a positive electrical signal and the other a negative.

Theoretically, all we need to do is pin our connectors the same on both sides. However, twisted pair cable is strategically constructed with certain pairs twisted at certain intervals to minimize electrical crosstalk on the cable. Crosstalk occurs when one conductor imparts an amount of its electrical signal onto another by virtue of *electromagnetic interference* (EMF). To take advantage of this strategic twisting of pairs, we need to pin our cabling connectors according to TIA/EIA standards.

Color coding on the plastic coating of each individual conductor in a UTP cable can help you identify the conductors end to end. You will find that the paired cables have one wire in a solid color and the other is white with the striping of the same color. As an example, one pair would be blue and blue/white. Table 2-2 indicates the pinning and color scheme to be used when pinning out a straight-through Ethernet cable. Two TIA/EIA standards are used for cabling an RJ-45 connector, the T568A and the T568B. As T568a is the stated preference of the two, the figures will use it.

As described in the table, the wires on both cable ends directly connect to each other in a one-to-one mapping. You can quickly verify if you are dealing with a straight-through cable by holding the ends side by side and verifying that the conductor colors are in the same order (see Figure 2-10).

Figure 2-10
RJ-45 straight-through

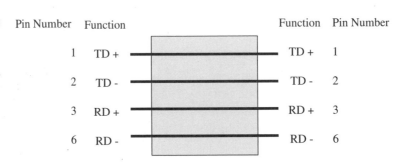

Pin Number	Function		Function	Pin Number
1	TD +		TD +	1
2	TD -		TD -	2
3	RD +		RD +	3
6	RD -		RD -	6

Table 2-2	Hub/Switch			Server/Router		
The pinning and color scheme for a straight-through Ethernet cable	Pin	Function	Color	Pin	Function	Color
	1	RD+	W/Green	1	TD+	W/Green
	2	RD–	Green	2	TD–	Green
	3	TD+	W/Orange	3	RD+	W/Orange
	4	NC	Blue	4	NC	Blue
	5	NC	W/Blue	5	NC	W/Blue
	6	TD–	Orange	6	RD–	Orange
	7	NC	W/Brown	7	NC	W/Brown
	8	NC	Brown	8	NC	Brown

NOTE: *You may be wondering why the standard uses the RJ-45 pins of 1, 2, 3, and 6 instead of the more logical 1, 2, 3, and 4? When Ethernet was first developed for UTP cable, it was thought that it could run on the same cabling infrastructure as the existing telephone system. Given this setup, if you plugged an RJ-11 (telephone plug) into an RJ-45 jack, the middle pins, 2 and 3, would connect to pins 4 and 5 on the RJ-45 and enable the phone to work. Similarly, a connected Ethernet RJ-45 data cable plugged into the same jack would connect to the 1, 2, 3, and 6 pins.*

Crossover Cables

When connecting like devices together, such as a LAN switch to another LAN switch or a router to a router, one needs to compensate for the fact that the transmit and receive pins contained in RJ-45 Ethernet interfaces found on the devices are in the same order on both sides. To direct the transmit pairs to the receive pairs, one needs to layout the cabling accordingly.

Referring to Table 2-3, we can see that the pinout on one side differs from the other. Specifically, pins 1 and 2 on the left now connect to 3 and 6 with the other pairs reversed as well. Again, this aligns the transmitters with the receivers to properly enable communication.

Looking at the table, we see that pins 1 and 2 now connect with 3 and 6 in both directions.

Table 2-3

Connecting the
transmit and
receive pins

Router				Router		
Pin	**Function**	**Color**		**Pin**	**Function**	**Color**
1	RD+	W/Green		1	TD+	W/Orange
2	RD–	Green		2	TD–	Orange
3	TD+	W/Orange		3	RD+	W/Green
4	NC	Blue		4	NC	Blue
5	NC	W/Blue		5	NC	W/Blue
6	TD–	Orange		6	RD–	Green
7	NC	W/Brown		7	NC	W/Brown
8	NC	Brown		8	NC	Brown

Fiber, SC/ST

Wiring a fiber connection is relatively simple. In this section, we will
assume that our cabling has been terminated properly with the appropriate
connectors. Whether SC or ST, we are simply concerned about mapping the
transmit port to the receive port. If you recall, fiber optic connections use
one strand of fiber for each signal.

The DTE/DCE issues involved with pin-outs on RJ-45 connectors are of
no concern when dealing with fiber cabling. All that you need to ensure is
that you cross-over the cable at some point in the point-to-point fiber connection to ensure that the transmit interface connects to the receive interface. For example, if you have color-coded cabling ends and you use red/blue
at one side, make sure you connect blue/red at the other. The easiest way to
know if you have connected the cable correctly is to activate the devices and
look for a link light on the interface. Connecting them backwards typically
does not harm the equipment.

WAN Physical Layer Implementations

Cisco has many options when it comes to making connections to WANs. However, we can break down these many interfaces into two general categories: those that use serial ports, and those that do not. As WAN technologies vary greatly from one to the next, it's not surprising that the devices required to leverage them vary accordingly. In many cases, Cisco provides for direct support of a particular WAN technology by incorporating the connectivity requirements directly in the router. Good examples of this include the integrated ISDN terminal adapter and the integrated DSU/CSU. For the cases where integrated functionality does not exist, Cisco offers the serial port. Serial ports can make connections to intermediary devices to ensure connectivity to a multitude of WAN technologies.

Cisco Serial ports

The serial port represents somewhat of a WAN-technology-independent port. For example, you can use a serial port to connect to practically any technology on the market from traditional T1/E1 or ISDN to newer technologies like DSL. The reason behind this is that you will always use an intermediary device between the router and the wide area. Some of these devices include DSU/CSUs, ISDN terminal adapters, and various types of modems. For this reason, the Cisco serial port represents a very versatile interface and one of which you should have a good understanding.

Although it would be nice to have a singular connector and cable to attach to every serial device, this is simply not the case. Cisco adheres to a number of physical layer standards when making connections to serial-attached devices. The variations deal with a number of qualities including signaling and connector types, supported speeds, and cable lengths. The following sections describe most of the more common variants.

NOTE: *To offer some serial port flexibility, Cisco router serial ports are often offered in a five-in-one module. The five-in-one module indicates that the port has support for each of the serial connection types (EIA / TIA-232, EIA / TIA-449, EIA-530, V.35, X.21). The serial port is typically terminated with a high-density, 60-pin connector. For that reason, it is generally necessary to purchase the specific Cisco serial cable for a given serial connection to ensure connectivity to this five-in-one interface.*

EIA/TIA-232   EIA/TIA-232-E, commonly known as RS-232C, is a mature standard for providing an electrical interface between DTE and DCE. Most commonly used to connect to asynchronous modems, EIA/TIA-232 can also operate in a synchronous mode. The standard describes two primary interfaces to be used for serial connections, a 25-pin, D-type connector (DB-25) and a nine-pin, D-Type connector (DB-9). These interfaces are shown in Figure 2-12.

The standard generally restricts cable lengths to 15 meters and speeds to 20 kbps. However, in practice, EIA/TIA-232 has proven reliable at speeds approaching 200 kbps on cable of lengths approaching 30 meters.

The primary element that defines the EIA/TIA-232 in the electrical sense is that the signals carried on the line are compared with respect to electrical ground to determine their high and low logic states. However, if you consider that everyone's ground is relative to his or her individual location, you may gain some valuable insight into the EIA/TIA-232's primary weakness. Should the ground voltage level at one side of a connection be different from that of the other side, communication can be significantly influenced.

EIA/TIA-449   EIA/TIA-449, also known as RS-449 as well as V.11, is one of many standards introduced to provide serial connectivity through the DB style connector using a two-line, balanced interface. Balanced-line interfaces calculate the high and low logic states based on comparisons of the two lines within a connection. Figure 2-13 illustrates the two-line, balanced operation of EIA/TIA-449. This balanced operation eliminates any depen-

Figure 2-12
RS-232 connectors

dence on ground voltage levels and thus avoids some of the issues that EIA/TIA-232 suffers from. Using a twisted pair cable, EIA/TIA-449 is capable of transmitting signals of various frequencies up to distances approaching 1000 meters. EIA/TIA-449 is traditionally terminated with a DB-37 type connector, as depicted in Figure 2-13.

X.21 The X.21 interface is an *International Telecommunications Union* (ITU-T) standard for providing serial communications over synchronous digital lines. This standard is primarily used in Europe and Japan. Typically terminated with a DB-15 connector, X.21 serial connections can be made to a number of devices including synchronous modems and DSU/CSUs. Figure 2-14 describes the X.21 interface.

V.24 The V.24 interface is essentially the ITU-T version of the EIA/TIA-232 standard for a physical layer interface between DTE and DCE devices. The two standards are fully interoperable and for this reason we will not investigate V.24 any further than mentioning its existence.

V.35 The V.35 interface was originally specified by the ITU-T (formerly the CCITT) as an interface for 48-kbps line transmissions. Since that time, the interface has been very well received and is now in general use for line speeds above 20 kbps. Among the serial interface family, V.35 represents the most widely used interface. V.35 interfaces connect to practically every intermediary device available when dealing with traditional WANs including ISDN, T carrier, and Frame Relay.

Figure 2-13
DB-37 Connector

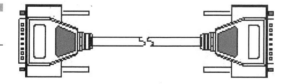

Figure 2-14
The X.21 connector

Electrically, V.35 connections use a mixture of balanced and unbalanced signals to transmit both data and control information across synchronous links. As you might expect, the high-frequency signals are carried over two wires in a balanced form. The standard connector used in V.35 is the Winchester style 34 pin, as shown in Figure 2-15.

HSSI The *High-Speed Serial Interface* (HSSI) is a DTE/DCE interface that was developed by Cisco and T3plus Networking. As WAN speeds continued to rise, the need for a higher speed interface became evident. HSSI was developed to meet this need.

The HSSI standard governs both the physical and electrical characteristics of the interface. Functionally, this serial type of connection is capable of data rates of up to 52 Mbps over shielded twisted pair cable with lengths of up to 50 feet. Physically, HSSI uses a subminiature, FCC-approved, 50-pin connector that looks exactly like a SCSI-2 connector for those familiar with it. The connector is shown in Figure 2-16.

The high data rate that HSSI supports makes it ideal for connecting to T3-based (45-Mbps) WANs. In addition, the interface is used connecting routers back to back in certain cases to provide for high-speed connectivity.

Figure 2-15
V.35 Winchester connector

Figure 2-16
The HSSI connector

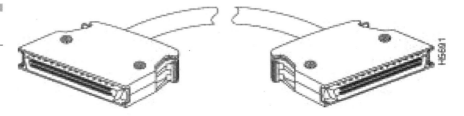

ISDN Connections

ISDN connections come in two flavors. The difference between the two depends on the role that the device is playing within the ISDN architecture. ISDN and its architecture are covered in detail in Chapter 12, "ISDN." However, for the purposes of understanding the connectivity requirements of an ISDN router interface to an ISDN network, we need to understand what is known as the *reference point*.

Essentially, an ISDN network consists of a "cloud" of ISDN switching services with end points (or demarcation points) located on the customer premises. From a device perspective, ISDN services can be considered as being similar to analog modem services or *plain old telephone services* (POTS). For example, to connect routers together over an analog modem circuit, you require a serial cable from the router to the modem, and a RJ-11 from the modem data port to the service provider's (telco) point of demarcation. ISDN technology involves the very same concepts, albeit with a significantly different underlying technology. In the ISDN world, the modem is referred to as an *ISDN Terminal Adapter*, which most people call the ISDN TA. Cisco offers the opportunity to build the ISDN TA into the router as an integrated module, thus eliminating the need to use a serial interface and associated cable. It is this type of connection that we are interested in.

As mentioned above, the concept of ISDN reference points are crucial toward the understanding how to connect our ISDN configured router to the telco's point of demarcation. The reference points define logical interfaces between devices of differing functionality within an ISDN network. Described below are the reference points relevant to this discussion:

- *S:* The reference point between user terminals and the NT2. A *network-terminating device type 2* (NT2) is a *Customer Premises Equipment* (CPE) device that converts the two-wire local loop connection into a four-wire connection and presents the interface to a *Private Branch Exchange* (PBX). This device would be irrelevant to this discussion if the S interface was not typically grouped together with the T.

- *T:* The reference point between NT1 and NT2 devices. A *network-terminating device type 1* (NT1) is a CPE device that converts the local loop two-wire interface into a four-wire interface usable by ISDN TAs.

■ *U*: The reference point between NT1 devices and line-termination equipment in the carrier network. The U interface describes the way that a North American Telco demarcates ISDN circuits. It presents a two-wire interface.

The reference points are identified alphabetically and start at the farthest point away from the ISDN switched network and move toward it. An essential element in the ISDN world that does not exist in the analog world would be the network-terminating device. As described above, two forms of NT devices exist: NT1 and NT2. NT2 devices involve a great deal more functionality specifically related to digital PBX systems, which are not relevant in this data-only discussion. The NT1 device, however, is an essential component to any ISDN installation. Figure 2-17 illustrates a typical ISDN-based router-to-router connection and the relevant reference points.

As shown in Figure 2-17, we need to consider a few distinct points of functionality. These include the router, the ISDN TA, and the NT1 device. As mentioned previously, in many cases the ISDN TA function is integrated within the router itself, and thus there is no physical device or cabling requirement to consider. Further, most newer ISDN-based equipment now incorporates the NT1 device as well. What this means is that the telco will present a U interface, the router will present a U interface, and all that is left is to connect the two with a straight-through pinned RJ-45 cable. The signal runs on the 4/5 pairing within the RJ-45 cable. Should a router not

Figure 2-17
The ISDN network

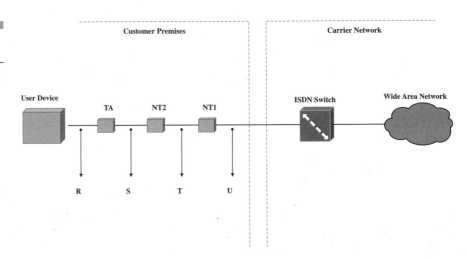

have a U interface built in, it will require the services of an external NT1. In this case, the router's interface will be referred to as S/T, and the external NT1 will have both a U and an S/T (sometimes 2) port. The S/T port also uses a straight-through cable with the signal running on pairs 3 and 6, and 4 and 5.

WARNING:　*The data communications world tends to be very friendly when it comes to cabling. For example, if you connect a straight-through cable between Ethernet switches, usually the worst thing that will happen is that your connection will not work. However, ISDN is not so forgiving. The electrical characteristics of an ISDN connection versus a non-ISDN device vary to such a degree that should you plug non-ISDN equipment into an ISDN port, you will more than likely damage your ISDN equipment. For example, should you accidentally plug an Ethernet device into an ISDN port (which is not at all unlikely, given they are both RJ-45-type connectors), you may damage your ISDN port, which will generally involve equipment replacements.*

DTE/DCE

Two terms used often in the data communications world are DTE and DCE. Usually referenced in their acronym form, DTE and DCE represent two distinct roles to be played in electronic communications. The two together provide for the user-to-network interface into a WAN, be it Frame Relay, analog modem-based, or any other format.

A DTE device generally represents the end points of a communication link. Devices like routers and computers typically play DTE roles. Essentially, a DTE device presents the user or data interface and connects to a DCE device. Cisco describes this functionality as being the "user end" of the user-to-network interface. From a signaling standpoint, the DTE device usually accepts the clocking signal from the DCE device to which it is connected.

A DCE device sits at the edge of a particular WAN service and presents an interface into that WAN to a DTE device. Cisco describes this as being on the "network end" of the user-to-network interface. Modems and CSU/DSUs are both good examples of DCE devices. The DCE device is responsible for providing the clocking for the communication to the DTE end of the connection.

Physically, DTE and DCE cabling can take many different forms. The relationship itself in no way dictates any specific physical attributes, outside of being able to provide a clocked data transfer. For example, when connecting a Cisco 2501 router to a CSU/DSU, you would normally use a male DTE cable, but the connection could very well take place with a female DTE cable. For this reason, it is wise to pay very close attention to the cabling requirements of all DTE/DCE devices to ensure that gender and pin out issues do not pose connectivity problems. Of all the reasons for a router installation to go poorly, cabling is about the most common and the easiest to avoid.

TIP: *Given two routers with serial interfaces, it is possible to connect them in a back-to-back configuration with the correct setup. This setup includes two key elements, cabling and clocking. If you have both a DTE and a DCE cable, you can connect the two together and create a physical path upon which you can communicate (in effect, simulating a WAN circuit). However, you may recall that the DCE in this situation needs to provide for clocking. This can be accomplished by simply configuring the DCE router's serial interface with DCE-terminal timing and adding the clock rate (say 2000000), which will bring the link up with a two-Mbps data rate.*

Cisco Routers with Fixed Ports

Cisco routers come in two general flavors: those with fixed ports and those that are modular. As the name implies, the fixed version routers contain interfaces that cannot be changed. When you order a specific router model with fixed ports, it arrives with the type and quantity of interfaces as described. Further, there is no opportunity to increase port densities or modify technologies within the router. Figure 2-18 illustrates a 2513 series router, which is a good example of such a router. Cisco provides a number of fixed configuration routers that fit into various price/performance needs. The 800, 1000, and 2500 series routers are good examples of such families. Within the family, there is generally a good deal of flexibility with respect to which LAN and WAN interfaces will be built into the unit. The model numbers represent the differentiation of one from the next. For example, a 2501 offers two serial WAN interfaces and one Ethernet LAN interface, while a 2502 offers two serial WAN interfaces and one Token Ring LAN interface.

Figure 2-18
The 2513 router

Obviously, purchasing fixed configuration routers has some benefits, the most significant of which is a lower cost. Another less obvious benefit is the isolation of services for redundancy and organizational reasons. Throughout the core, distribution, and access layers of a network, it may be necessary to use multiple, small, specific function routers instead of larger modular routers. This can be attributed to any number of reasons, including but not limited to security, administration, and performance. For these reasons, the fixed function router is alive and well and is likely to be seen on a regular basis throughout internetworks.

Cisco Routers with Modular Ports

Cisco offers modularity throughout much of its router product line. A modular router is one that enables the core functionality of the router itself to be purchased separately from the specific LAN and WAN technology options. For example, you can purchase a 3600 series router and then populate it with a variety of LAN/WAN modules to suit a particular situation. An important point to remember is that modular routers typically do not come ready to communicate by themselves and tend to depend on the use of add-on modules.

Coming in at a higher price point than the fixed-configuration-style routers, modular routers offer tremendous flexibility. Investments in routing functionality within an infrastructure can be protected from many aspects by a modular router. Primarily, a router with some additional slots available for extra modules offers some scalability for growth, whether foreseen or unforeseen. Further, since much of the investment in a modular router is in its core functionality, should criteria dictate the use of a different LAN or WAN technology, the modular router offers the capability to adapt without having to resort to a complete replacement of the unit. Finally, although many modular routers are now fulfilling roles in the access layer, many of the modular router platforms are used in high-performance and high-availability roles within the core and distribution layers. For that reason, the higher end modular routers tend to offer more options for redundancy, including redundant power supplies or redundant processors.

Examples of Cisco modular routers include the 2600 series, the 3600 series, the 4000/4500 series, and the 7000/7500 series. Depicted in Figure 2-19 is a 3640 router with two modules inserted and two slots available.

Connecting to Cisco Devices via the Console Port

In order to work with the *command-line interface* (CLI) on a Cisco device, one must attain some form of access to that device. The methods for doing so include the *in-band* and *out-of-band* options. In-band management involves using a traditional data port, and the technology that it provides to carry your normal data flow, as your access into the router. Hence, you are managing the device within the band that is also carrying your normal traffic. A Telnet session represents the most common way to manage a router in-band.

Out-of-band management involves using an isolated connection that is not dependent on any other technologies to facilitate access. Out-of-band access to a Cisco router can take place through one of two interfaces present on all Cisco devices. Two ports, as indicated in Figure 2-20, provide access to the router's CLI and are labeled CON and AUX. The CON port, short for

Figure 2-19
The 3640 router

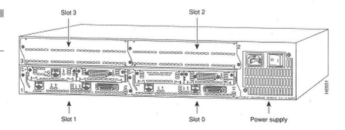

Figure 2-20
The CON/AUX ports

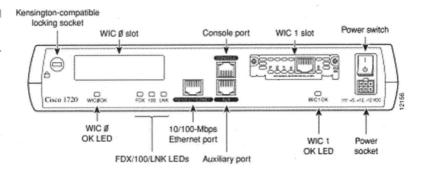

Console, represents the purest way of accessing the CLI. Along with being the first interface one needs to access in order to work with a new router, it is also the only port that offers complete access to the router independent of any other technology. The AUX, or auxiliary, offers access to the CLI typically through an analog modem or similar connection, and as such provides an excellent and highly recommended way to gain access to a router when an in-band connection is not possible. Both of the CON and the AUX ports are RJ-45 female on the router itself, as shown in Figure 2-21.

The cable used to connect to the console port is known as a *rollover cable*. It is known as such because one end of the cable is essentially pinned opposite to the other or is a rolled-over version of the other. Specifically, the pinouts are shown in Table 2-4.

To access the CLI, a standard VT100 terminal emulator is required. HyperTerminal from Microsoft is a good example of such software. The console port is a serial-based interface and, as such, we need to be aware of some items in order to connect our PC to it properly. First off, most PCs ship with DB-9 or DB-25 serial ports and the rollover cables supplied with the routers are RJ-45. To connect the two, the use of an RJ-45–to–DB-9 or RJ-45–to–DB-25 adapter is required. These adapters also ship with a rollover cable, so finding one should not be difficult. From there, we need to consider the signaling characteristics of the serial connection. The router, by default, uses a baud rate of 9600 with eight data bits and one stop bit with no parity or flow control. By setting your terminal application to these settings and properly cabling the PC to the router, a press of the Enter key should bring up the CLI.

Table 2-4

Pinouts for rollover cable

Side A Pin	Side B Pin
1	8
2	7
3	6
4	5
5	4
6	3
7	2
8	1

Chapter Summary

In this chapter, we have covered in some detail the many physical requirements that LAN and WAN technologies place upon Cisco devices. Specifically, at this point you should have a good understanding of the different flavors of Ethernet technology and the cabling requirements that each demands. To support this, Table 2-5 offers a quick summary of those technologies and some of their key attributes. You should also have a good feeling for the difference between full- and half-duplex communications and where each can fit in an organization's network.

On the WAN side of things, we covered each of the predominant serial interfaces and their respective uses in an infrastructure. A quick summary of those interfaces is provided in Figure 2-21. You should have a general feeling for when and if you should use each, as well as a solid understanding of the cabling requirements for each. The roles of DTE and DCE within a communication were also described in some detail. Finally, a brief introduction into ISDN technology and specifically its cabling requirements were covered (though ISDN will receive its full coverage in Chapter 12.)

This chapter also covered Cisco's fixed and modular router families and some of the issues surrounding their use in a network. Also, the methods for using Cisco's out-of band management through the console and auxiliary ports were described.

Table 2-5

The different flavors
of Ethernet
technology and
their cabling
requirements

Quality	10Base2	10Base5	10Base-T	100Base-TX	100Base-T4	100Base-FX
Media	50-Ohm Coaxial	50-Ohm Coaxial	Twisted Pair CAT 3/4 /5	Twisted Pair CAT 5	Twisted Pair CAT 3/4 /5	62.5/125 Micron MMF
Connector	BNC	AUI	RJ-45	RJ-45	RJ-45	ST/SC/MIC
Diameter	185 m	500 m	100 m	100 m	100 m	400 m
Technology	Bus	Bus	Star	Star	Star	Point to Point

Figure 2-21

Serial interface
summary

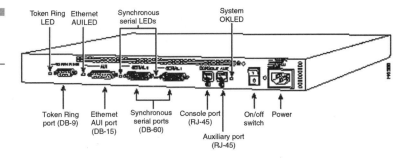

At this point, should you be presented with a Cisco router, you should feel
comfortable answering the following questions:

- What are its LAN interfaces?
- What are its WAN interfaces?
- Where is the CON and AUX port?
- Is the router fixed or modular?
- How would I connect to the CLI?

From the Real World

Here is a quick piece of advice: never underestimate the significance of cabling. This may seem obvious since we are dealing with the physical layer, the platform upon which all else is built. However, time and again, I and many others lose time, money, and patience over cabling issues.

For example, nothing can stop an installation dead in its tracks quicker than using the wrong serial cable. No amount of collective experience is ever going to get a Winchester-terminated serial cable into the DB-25 on the CSU/DSU. I cannot stress enough the value in doubling-checking all the physical layer aspects of an installation or modification prior to arriving onsite.

Cabling can also eat into your time when troubleshooting. Often, particularly in installations of some complexity, when things go wrong, the collective brain tends not to trust the complex. Much time and effort can be spent troubleshooting high-layer issues before a faulty cable is found. As a general rule, if you are performing a new installation and everything seems to be set up correctly yet things are still not functional, check out your cabling before entering into complex troubleshooting procedures.

As a final note, I would like to draw attention to two important items that can play a large role in a well-designed and managed cabling infrastructure. The first would be cable management itself. Contrary to popular belief, this stuff was not designed just to make the equipment rack look pretty. When the network is down and time is money, good cable management can truly expedite your troubleshooting procedures. The second component would be the use of colored and labeled patch cables for UTP connections. Because you can now buy cables in just about any color, there is very little reason not to define a company-wide standard for patch cable coloring and labeling, and adhering to it. Simply using one color for a WAN, one color for a straight-through LAN, and one color for crossed-over LAN can make a world of difference. You only have to get snagged by one blue crossover cable hanging in a mess of blue straight-through cables before you completely buy into this ideal.

Peter A. Van Oene

Frequently Asked Questions (FAQ)

Question: Will I damage my fiber ports if I plug the patch cords in backwards (transmit to transmit)?

Answer: No damage will be done in this event, and in many cases this is a necessary procedure. For one reason or another, there seem to be a fair amount of fiber patch cords that do not differentiate one end from the other. This leaves the installer some guesswork when patching.

Question: The text says that cabling similar devices together requires a crossover cable, yet my hubs and switches are connected together with a straight-through cable.

Answer: Many hubs and switches have a special port (usually the last port or the first) that is labeled MDI/MDIX or simply X. This port will have the capability to alter which pairs of wire it uses for transmitting and receiving and thus achieve the same goal as the crossover cable. These ports usually are selectable with a small switch or button.

Question: What will happen if I didn't use the 568A color scheme for pinning out my RJ-45 cables?

Answer: Assuming the cables are pinned one to one at both ends, this scenario can be very misleading. Very likely, all evidence will point toward your having made a good connection and in many cases, specifically those over short cable runs, you may be fine. However, the twisted cables are paired strategically to avoid crosstalk and unless you pin them accordingly, you may encounter signal degradations that will eventually lead to a packet loss on your cable runs.

Question: How do I know if my ISDN BRI connection requires an NT1?

Answer: When ordering Cisco routers, you can specify whether or not to use an external NT1. Generally, I find it cleaner to use an integrated version. However, whether you are ordering a new router or working with an existing one, the S/T or U indicator silk-screened on the router will enable you to answer this question. Again, the U interface signifies an integrated NT1, while the S/T will require the use of an external one.

Question: I've connected my routers back to back with a DTE/DCE cable, but the line protocol is still down. Why is that?

Answer: Recalling from the text, the DCE end of this connection must provide the clocking for the signal. Without it set, communication cannot take place. From the config mode for the DCE serial end, you must enter the `clock rate 2000000` command. The two Mbps, is a user selected rate and can actually be any of the listed available values.

Questions

1. The BNC terminology used to describe a 10Base-2 connector is the acronym for which of the following?

   a. British Naval Connector
   b. Bayonet Nut Connector
   c. Bayonet Neill Concelman
   d. All of the above

2. The 10Base-5 Tap is often referred to as which of the following?

   a. Clamp Tap
   b. Vampire Tap
   c. Converter Tap
   d. Electrical Tap

3. An AUI interface uses which of the following connectors?

   a. The Winchester
   b. A DB-15
   c. A DB-25
   d. A DB-9

4. The "T" in 10Base-T refers to which of the following?

   a. Ten Mbps
   b. Two Hundred Meters
   c. Two Pairs
   d. Twisted Pair

5. The most popular 10-Mbps Ethernet over fiber standard is which of the following?

   a. 10Base-FL
   b. 10Base-FB
   c. 10Base-FX
   d. 10Base-FC

6. 100Base-TX can run over which of the following cable types?

   a. Category 3 (CAT3)
   b. Category 4 (CAT4)
   c. Category 5 (CAT5)
   d. All of the above

7. If the FDDI MIC connector is used to terminate 100Base-FX, which key position should be used?

   a. M
   b. A
   c. B
   d. S

8. 100Base-T4 runs over how many wires?

   a. Two
   b. Four
   c. Six
   d. Eight

9. When pinning out an Ethernet Twisted pair RJ-45 connector, which of the following pairs are used?

   a. 1 and 2, 4 and 5
   b. 1 and 3, 2 and 6
   c. 3 and 6, 4 and 5
   d. 1 and 2, 3 and 6

10. When a switch is connected to a router and the two have different duplex settings hard-coded, what will be the indication of this misconfiguration?

    a. The link status *light-emitting diode* (LED) on the switch will be off.
    b. The link status LED on the switch will be amber.
    c. The link status LED on the switch will be flashing.
    d. No visual indication will be present.

11. The EIA/TIA-232 specification dictates a maximum signal rate of which of the following?

    a. 20 kbps
    b. 1.544 Mbps
    c. 384 kpbs
    d. 9.6 kpbs

12. The V.24 standard is fully interoperable with which of the following?

    a. EIA/TIA-232
    b. V.35
    c. X.21
    d. HSSI

13. EIA/TIA-449 serial connections have which of the following qualities?

   a. Balanced mode

   b. Unbalanced mode

   c. A combination of the above

   d. Neither of the above

14. A telco's ISDN demarcation point in the United States signifies which of the
following reference points?

   a. R

   b. S

   c. T

   d. U

15. NT1 is the acronym for which of the following?

   a. Network Testing Device Type One

   b. Negative Terminal Device Type One

   c. Network Termination Device Type One

   d. Normal Terrestrial Device Type One

16. A router with an integrated NT1 will have which of the following ISDN
interfaces?

   a. R

   b. S

   c. S/T

   d. U

17. Connecting a router serially to a CSU/DSU normally involves which of
the following serial cables?

   a. Male DCE

   b. Female DCE

   c. Male DTE

   d. Female DTE

18. In a DTE/DCE connection, which device provides the clocking for the
signal?

   a. The DTE side

   b. The DCE side

   c. Neither, as clocking is irrelevant in serial connections

   d. Neither, as clocking is provided by the WAN network

19. Which of the following ports offer in-band access to a router?

    a. The CON port

    b. The Ethernet Port

    c. The AUX Port

    d. All of the above

20. The CON port on a Cisco router requires the use of which cable?

    a. A rollover cable

    b. A straight-through cable

    c. A crossover cable

    d. A null modem cable

Answers

1. **d.** All of the above

   The BNC connector can be referred to with any of the above descriptions.

2. **b.** Vampire Tap

   When making a tap connection to a 10Base-5 cable, the tap almost "bites" into the cable, and hence the term Vampire Tap is often used to describe this connector.

3. **b.** A DB-15

   A Female DB-15 connector is most often used as the Ethernet interface on legacy routers.

4. **d.** Twisted Pair

   The T signifies the use of four-pair twisted pair cabling.

5. **a.** 10Base-FL

   Most 10-Mbps Ethernet fiber connections will utilize the 10Base-FL standard.

6. **c.** Category 5 (CAT5)

   Unlike 100Base-T4, the TX requires the use of Category 5 rated cabling due to its higher sensitivity to signal losses through crosstalk.

7. **a.** M

   Although seldom encountered if terminated, a 100Base-FX connection with a MIC connector, the M key position, for Master, is recommended.

8. **d.** Eight

   The 4 in T4 refers to the use of four pairs of cable or eight physical wires.

9. **d.** 1 and 2, 3 and 6

   The pairs are pinned into the 1 and 2 and 3 and 6 pin locations on an RJ-45 connector.

10. **d.** No visual indication will be present.

    A challenging thing to troubleshoot, this form of misconfiguration will exhibit no visual indicators. In this scenario, high amounts of collisions indicated by the switch or router's software will be the best indicator.

11. **a.** 20 kbps

    Although practically capable of higher speeds, the EIA/TIA-232 specification signifies a maximum rate of 20 kbps.

12. **a.** EIA/TIA-232

    The V.24 is fully interoperable with the EIA/TIA-232 standard, often referred to as RS-232.

13. **a.** Balanced mode

    A significant improvement over EIA/TIA-232, 449 runs in balance mode.

14. **d.** U

    The telco's point of demarcation is the two-wire U interface.

15. **c.** Network Termination Device Type One

    An NT1 refers to a Network Termination Device Type One, which is used to convert a U to an S/T interface.

16. **d.** U

    The router's ISDN interface will be at the U reference point.

17. **c.** Male DTE

    Generally, a Male DTE cable will be required for this connection. However, one should always verify this prior to ordering any cabling.

18. **b.** The DCE side

    The DCE side of this connection provides the clocking.

19. **b.** The Ethernet Port

    Although all of the listed answers can provide access to the router's CLI, only the Ethernet interface will do so in-band.

20. **a.** A rollover cable

    A rollover cable is typically used to connect to a Cisco router.

The Basics of Cisco Configuration and Operations

Objectives

Upon completion of this chapter, you will be able to do the following:

- Understand and perform the start-up sequence on both Cisco routers and switches.

- Be able to correctly enter an initial configuration for a Cisco switch.

- Properly navigate the initial setup dialog on Cisco routers.

- Be able to identify the various user modes on Cisco equipment.

- Have the ability to switch between user modes on Cisco equipment.

- Understand and be able to issue basic Cisco IOS commands.

- Be able to use the basic navigation and help facilities of Cisco IOS.

- Understand various router interfaces and their configurations.

- Utilize basic Show commands to determine the status of Cisco routers and switches.

An Introduction to the Cisco Internetwork Operating Systems (IOS)

One of the precepts of computer science is that all computers require an *operating system* (OS). OSs function by providing an interface between the user and the hardware, as well as by regulating the operation of the hardware. Familiar OSs to the reader may include Windows, Unix, Linux, or the Macintosh OS. The Cisco OS, known as IOS (for Internetwork Operating System), functions in a similar fashion. It enables the user (network engineer) to interface with a computer (a Cisco router or switch) and regulates the operating of hardware (in this case, routing or switching). The primary differences between the more commonly used OSs and Cisco IOS are as follows:

- Cisco IOS is text-based, rather than employing a *Graphical User Interface* (GUI). In this, it is similar to Unix or Linux.

- Cisco IOS is proprietary. It will only run on hardware approved or manufactured by Cisco systems. This is similar to the Macintosh OS.

- Cisco IOS is special purpose. It will not run user applications. The IOS is an extremely complicated application within itself.

■ Many different versions of Cisco IOS exist. Unlike a standard OS, where you simply buy an applications program to increase functionality, the many different versions of Cisco IOS each have a different level of functionality.

Another big difference between Cisco's IOS and a standard OS is the manner in which it is stored. A normal OS resides on a hard disk drive and is loaded into memory for execution. A Cisco IOS resides in special Flash memory, similar to the type used in digital cameras. This Flash memory retains its contents even when power is removed, but it is far slower than normal RAM. For this reason, the IOS is loaded into normal RAM, just like a PC operating system, before it is executed.

Cisco IOS has several functions in addition to providing a user interface to us. These include the following:

■ Supporting a large number of network protocols including TCP/IP, IPX/SPX, AppleTalk, DECNet, Banyan Vines, and others. In this text, we will only examine the methods for configuring routers for TCP/IP and IPX/SPX.

■ Working with a variety of different network media types, *Local Area Networks* (LANs), and *Wide Area Networks* (WANs). These include Ethernet, Fast Ethernet, ISDN, synchronous and asynchronous serial ports, modems, *Asynchronous Transfer Mode* (ATM), and Token Ring. We will focus on Ethernet, ISDN, and synchronous serial in this text.

■ Providing network security in the form of access lists, content-based access control, *Terminal Access Controller Access Control System* (TACACS+), and Radius authentications.

As previously stated, the Cisco IOS has no GUI. Three direct methods exist for entering IOS commands:

■ *A serial connection through the console port* You can use a PC with a serial cable and a program such as HyperTerminal to access the Cisco IOS command line. This is normally known as *consoling in*. This is the method that you will typically use when configuring a router for the first time.

■ *A Telnet connection through a LAN or WAN* Using a PC with Telnet or a similar utility, you can connect to the router through an IP address. This is known as *telnetting in*.

■ *An HTTP connection through a Web browser* Limited functionality is available by using a Web browser such as Netscape Navigator or Microsoft Internet Explorer. Although commands can be issued this way, it's cumbersome and not recommended. However, Cisco is making a concerted effort to change these negatives. So your mileage may vary.

When initially configuring a Cisco router or switch (out of the box or in an unknown state), it is usually only possible to perform a configuration via the Console port. A couple of "indirect" methods for entering configuration commands into Cisco routers and switches also exist:

- *Cisco Fast Step* This is a program distributed by Cisco Systems that will auto-configure selected lower-end routers and switches.
- Trivial File Transfer Protocol *(TFTP)* Router configurations can be stored on a TFTP server as a backup.

The Cisco Boot Process

Just as with Microsoft Windows and most OSs, the Cisco devices undergo a boot process when they start up. A Cisco IOS boot has three phases:

1. *The* Power-On Self-Test *(POST)* When you start a PC, it always checks its memory and internal hardware before proceeding to load the OS. Cisco equipment does exactly the same thing, testing all hardware before proceeding. Often, the hardware will report its condition (good or bad) by using front- or rear-panel *light-emitting diodes* (LEDs).

2. *OS load* This is the equivalent of a Windows 98 boot-up splash screen. The IOS software is loaded from the router's Flash memory into its RAM. As the IOS image in Flash is compressed, this may take up to 30 seconds for decompression and loading.

3. *Configuration load* The current configuration of the router is loaded into RAM. Normally, the configuration is kept in a special type of memory known as *non-volatile RAM* (NVRAM), which retains its contents when power is off. Just like the IOS from the Flash, configuration is loaded into RAM from the NVRAM.

The obvious question this raises is, "How does step 3 happen with a new router or switch? There isn't any configuration, is there?" The answer is "it depends." For Cisco routers, no initial configuration takes place. Instead of the normal loading process, a special initial configuration (setup) dialog text is brought up. This is a long series of questions, specially tailored to the detected physical configuration of the router. At the end of this process, a configuration is generated from your responses and loaded.

TIP: *It's possible to get to this initial configuration dialog at any time, not just the first time you turn on the router. The command to do this is "Setup," although this is not recommended for use on a production router.*

For Cisco switches, things are a little different. Rather than an initial configuration dialog, a default configuration is entered into every switch at the factory. This configuration is fine for basic operations, enabling these switches to be used out of the box for many applications.

Cisco Device Startup

There are two main types of Cisco Devices—Routers & Switches. We will look at how they both start up and the importance of each step.

Catalyst 1900 Series Switches: POST

Here is a good procedure to follow for setting up a Catalyst switch:

1. Remove the switch from the box, but be careful to retain the mounting brackets. Even if you are not going to use these immediately, be sure to keep them. They are expensive to replace.

2. Mount the switch in a rack or clear area. Be sure not to block the surfaces of the switch in such a way that you would have trouble seeing either the front or back. Also, be sure not to interfere with the fan or cooling ports. One of the most common sources of failure for Cisco network devices is overheating due to environmental conditions or poor placement. Catalyst switches are not made for placement in outside environments.

TIP: *This may seem like an obvious point, but you might be surprised at the number of people who think that they are getting away with something by mounting a network device in a hostile environment. It will almost certainly fail. Liebert makes a series of special self-contained equipment racks that can be used to provide conditioned environments in non-conditioned spaces like warehouses.*

3. Plug in the console cable to the console port (the rear of the switch). Also plug in any necessary network cables and the power cord. You can't hurt anything by plugging and unplugging network cables during operation so long as you are in a test environment. The console cable should be connected to a laptop or desktop PC running a terminal emulation software package like HyperTerminal or Procomm Plus. Which program you use is a matter of personal preference. The settings should consist of eight data bits, one stop bit, no parity, and a speed of 9600 BPS.

4. As the switch starts, you will see the LEDs of the front of the switch going through a series of changes. These changes are telling you something!

The Front Panel LEDs

All front-panel LEDs start out solid green. Ensure that this happens. It is a good way to ensure all of the LEDs are functioning and will prevent any false positives. As the switch proceeds with the POST, each of the LEDs will shut off in sequence. If any of the LEDs turns amber, it is because of a problem with the switch. This happens very infrequently in actual operations, but the first time you start a switch, careful attention should be paid to the POST. If it's going to fail, chances are that it will fail right out of the box.

The POST can return with one of two possible types of errors: fatal or non-fatal. With a fatal error, the switch stops at that point in the POST and freezes up. On the other hand, a non-fatal error permits operation of the switch (with limitations). In either case, the error should be carefully noted for Cisco technical support. Table 3-1 outlines the Catalyst 1900's POST errors.

For more information on switch POST failures, refer to www.cisco.com/univercd/cc/td/doc/product/lan/28201900/1928v8x/19icg8x/19ictrbl.htm#12942.

If you are using a Catalyst 2900XL instead of a Catalyst 1924, the POST will seem very similar. All of the LEDs will turn green and go off one by one. However, the tests are different. Only eight tests are done, as shown in Table 3-2.

Cisco claims that all POST failures on 2900XL series switches should be considered fatal and require repairs by Cisco technical support.

After the POST has been completed successfully, it is time to look at the output on the console port. A good initial switch boot-up should look something like this:

Table 3-1

Catalyst 1900
POST errors

LED	Component being referenced	Fatal/non-fatal
1	Port loopback, which indicates a failure of one or more specific ports. The actual failed ports are specified on the console.	Non-fatal
2	Burned-in address, which indicates a problem with the switch's MAC address.	Non-fatal
3	*Content Addressable Memory* (CAM), a problem with the CAM table memory.	Fatal
4	Console port, which indicates that the console port is non-functional. The switch may still be manageable through Telnet or the Web interface if an IP address has already been set.	Non-fatal
5	*Real Time Clock* (RTC). The switch will function without the RTC but will have problems performing a soft boot or automatic restart in case of an error. This may cause the switch to hang during operation.	Non-fatal
6	*Content Addressable Memory* (CAM) SRAM, a problem with the CAM SRAM memory.	Fatal
7	System timer interrupt	Fatal
8	Port control/status	Fatal
9	ISLT ASIC	Fatal
10	Packet DRAM	Fatal
11	Forwarding engine SRAM	Fatal
12	Forwarding engine	Fatal
13-15	Unused	NA
16	ECU DRAM	Fatal
18-24	Unused	NA

```
Catalyst 1900 Management Console
Copyright (c) Cisco Systems, Inc. 1993-1998
All rights reserved.
Enterprise Edition Software
Ethernet Address:        00-D0-C0-6B-ED-40

PCA Number:              73-3122-03
PCA Serial Number:       FAB03183BMA
Model Number:            WS-C1912-EN
System Serial Number:    FAB0320V0W3
Power Supply S/N:        PHI031305AD
```

Table 3-2

Catalyst 2900XL
POST errors

LED	Component being referenced	Fatal/non-fatal
1	DRAM	Fatal
2	Flash memory	Fatal
3	Switch CPU	Fatal
4	System board	Fatal
5	CPU/Interface ASIC	Fatal
6	Switch/core ASIC	Fatal
7	Ethernet controller ASIC	Fatal
8	Ethernet interfaces	Fatal
9-24	Unused	NA

```
Power Supply P/N:
PCB Serial Number:      FAB03183BMA,73-3122-03
---------------------------------------------

1 user(s) now active on Management Console.

        User Interface Menu

    [M] Menus
    [K] Command Line
    [I] IP Configuration
Enter Selection:
```

Of course, the serial numbers and MAC address will be different on other switches. This completes our examination of Cisco switch startup procedures. It would be easy to assume a similar startup procedure for Cisco routers, but unfortunately this would be a more or less incorrect assumption. Although Cisco switches are mostly acquired from other companies during Cisco's rapid expansion, their routers are "home-grown" and have significantly different characteristics.

Cisco Routers

When setting up your Cisco router, you should follow a similar procedure to that used when setting up your switch:

1. Remove it from the packing material, being careful to keep the mounting hardware.

2. Many newer Cisco routers are modular. If your router is a 1600, 2600, or 3600, install any network or WAN modules that came with your router. Care should be taken to ensure that the modules are firmly seated inside the router. These modules should never be inserted or removed during operation. If your router is a 7000 series or greater, stop and get a new router. Higher end routers have significant complexities that are not conducive to a learning environment.

3. Mount or place the router in an area where the front and rear panels can be conveniently accessed and where cooling is not impeded.

4. Plug your router into the wall outlet. Unlike Catalyst switches, Cisco routers do not start upon being plugged in. They have a separate power switch. Connect your console cable and any applicable network cables, and then turn the router on. It may take some hunting to find where to plug the console cable in. Although this location is always on the back of a Catalyst 1900/2900 XL switch, it can be in many different places on a router. Here are some ideas of where to look depending upon the model of router:

   - *3600 Series Routers*   At the lower part of the front panel.
   - *1600/2600 Series Routers*   At the back of the router, usually next to the Ethernet port. Take care not to plug the console cable into the Ethernet port. Although I have heard no tales of damaging routers (or serial ports) due to this error, it could occur.
   - *800 Series Routers*   Between the WAN port (ISDN or serial) and the Ethernet ports.

On Cisco routers, as opposed to Catalyst switches, usually two similar-looking ports can be spotted: the console port and the auxiliary port. Be sure to plug your console cable into the console port. The auxiliary port is similar but is wired differently. It is generally used to connect the router to a modem for "out-of-band management":

TIP: *Out-of-band versus in-band management. These are terms much ballied about the network world. In-band management is a method of managing your switches and routers over your production network, usually via Telnet or a Web interface. This raises the question, what if the network goes down and you need to manage the switch or router to bring it back up again? It's a Catch-22 situation. You can't manage the device without the network, and the network won't function until you manage the*

device. With a small network, this isn't a problem. You could walk over to the wiring closet or server room and plug your console cable in. But what if the device is in the next state? If all you have is in-band management, it's time to polish up that resume; you are going to need it. The smart network engineer has another solution: out-of-band management. He has modems connected to each of his routers, with each modem connected to a direct-dial phone line. In case of problems, he can use the modem in his workstation to dial the router directly and bypass the network. He can then solve the problem and bring the network back up, a hero.

Unlike a Catalyst switch, where much of the fireworks occur on the front panel of the device, Cisco routers take a different approach. While the router starts up, don't look on the front panel. Due to the almost total lack of indicator lights, it won't be an enlightening experience, please pardon the pun. Instead, keep your eyes on the output from the router's console port. That's where the action is. The output will look something like this, in a properly functioning router:

```
TinyROM version 1.0(3)
Fri Apr 30 18:22:12 1999
Copyright (c) 1998-1999 by Cisco Systems, Inc.
All rights reserved.

POST ........ OK.   4MB DRAM, 8MB Flash.


Booting "c800.bin" ...,
              Restricted Rights Legend

Use, duplication, or disclosure by the Government is
subject to restrictions as set forth in subparagraph
(c) of the Commercial Computer Software - Restricted
Rights clause at FAR sec. 52.227-19 and subparagraph
(c) (1) (ii) of the Rights in Technical Data and Computer
Software clause at DFARS sec. 252.227-7013.

              Cisco Systems, Inc.
              170 West Tasman Drive
              San Jose, California 95134-1706


Cisco Internetwork Operating System Software
IOS (tm) C800 Software (C800-OSY6-MW), Version 12.0(5)T,   RELEASE
SOFTWARE (fc1)

Copyright (c) 1986-1999 by Cisco Systems, Inc.
Compiled Fri 23-Jul-99 03:38 by kpma
Image text-base: 0x000E9000, data-base: 0x006E1000

Cisco C804 (MPC850) processor (revision 1) with 43876K bytes of
virtual memory.
```

```
Processor board ID JAD02521746
CPU part number 33
X.25 software, Version 3.0.0.
Bridging software.
Basic Rate ISDN software, Version 1.1.
1 Ethernet/IEEE 802.3 interface(s)
1 ISDN Basic Rate interface(s)
4M bytes of physical memory (DRAM)
8K bytes of non-volatile configuration memory
8M bytes of flash on board (4M from flash card)


Press RETURN to get started!
```

If your router output doesn't look exactly like this, don't worry; it almost certainly won't. Router boot-up output looks different on every different model of router. However, some elements will be the same; look for the proper amounts of memory and Flash. Incorrect amounts could mean that the appropriate memory chips are not seated correctly. Also, ensure that all of your interfaces are listed. Missing interfaces usually mean that the version of the Cisco IOS is too old to support all of your interfaces. Although it may be hard to believe that Cisco ships devices with software that is too old to support the hardware it ships with, it happens all of the time. Finally, keep your eyes out for any errors that may be displayed or for a "boot loop" where the router will crash and cycle through the boot sequence again. These are good signs that it may be time to get Cisco technical support, or the *Technical Assistance Center* (TAC), involved.

NOTE: *Throughout this course, my advice on unexpected errors, particularly of the hardware variety, will be to call Cisco for support. If you have a support contract, or the router is still under warranty, this is a fine idea. However, Cisco is not the only place you can go for help. Other sources of assistance may be more experienced network professionals inside your organization, Usenet newsgroups, Cisco Certified Network Professionals (CCNPs) or Cisco Certified Internetwork Experts (CCIEs).*

Methods of Interacting with Cisco Devices

As we have previously discussed, the IOS interface is text-based. This is similar to the MS-DOS prompt that many readers are familiar with. The IOS interface can differ from device to device, but its core functionality and method of operation is similar from a small Cisco 800 router up to a Cisco 12000GSR.

Cisco IOS has three primary modes of operation, each with its own identifying prompt and behavior. The first mode is known as *user mode* or *user exec mode*. This is the mode you use by default upon consoling or telneting into a router, as shown here:

```
User Access Verification

Password:
Router>
```

TIP: *When you enter a router password, it will not appear on the screen. In many OSs, passwords appear as a series of asterisks (*). This is not the case with Cisco IOS.*

The purpose of the user mode is to allow for basic router commands that do not alter the configuration and enable the router to be used as a "jumping-off point" to other devices; other devices can be telneted into from user mode. Basic network troubleshooting commands like trace route and ping can also be executed from user mode.

NOTE: *In practice, user-level access is rarely used in small- or medium-sized enterprises. It is far more common to see it used in* Network Operations Center *(NOC) environments at large enterprises or* Internet Service Providers *(ISPs) for first-level support staff.*

The second mode used for interacting with IOS is the *privileged mode*, also known as the *privileged exec mode*. This mode is used to give access to all router configuration and management commands. It enables a detailed examination of the equipment's condition and operations. It also enables the use of debugging commands to monitor ongoing equipment activity.

```
User Access Verification

Password:
Router>enable
Password:
Router#
```

As seen in the previous code, the `enable` command changes the IOS from user mode to privileged mode. The password to enter privileged mode is called the *enable password* or *enable secret*, and is almost always different from the normal login password. Just as with the login password, the enable password does not appear on the screen as you type it, nor do asterisks appear.

NOTE: *Because the enable command is used to enter privileged mode, it is colloquially known as "enable mode" amongst network engineers. However, on a Cisco exam, it's best to use its proper name, privileged mode.*

The primary method of knowing which mode you are in is by looking at the prompt. Notice the difference between the user and privileged mode prompts:

User mode: Router>

Privileged mode: Router#

The method for moving back to user mode from privileged mode is the disable command:

```
User Access Verification

Password:
Router>enable
Password:
Router#disable
Router>
```

The final mode of IOS operation that we'll look at is called *configuration mode*. Although privileged mode can be used to examine any router setting or problem, actually making changes to the router's running configuration is done through the configuration mode. It is entered by using the `configure` command. This command will be examined in greater depth later in this chapter, but suffice it to say, it shifts the router or switch into configuration mode. Anything typed in that mode will change the router's current, running configuration. When discussing router configuration, people often speak of router programming. Indeed, there is much in common between programming in some languages like C++ and doing IOS configurations. However, there is one important difference: Any command typed in configuration mode takes effect immediately. There is no compiler, nor a command to trigger an interpreter such as Perl. This caution should be kept in mind when making configuration changes to production routers and switches.

```
User Access Verification

Password:
Router>enable
Password:
Router#configure
Configuring from terminal, memory, or network [terminal]? terminal
Enter configuration commands, one per line. End with CNTL/Z.
Router (config)#
```

Notice in the previous example that the prompt changes from privileged mode to configuration mode. In order to leave configuration mode and re-enter privileged mode, simply use the command `exit` at the configuration mode prompt.

Catalyst 1900 Switch: Basic IOS Commands

We will now cover some basic IOS commands. Although most IOS commands are common across router and switch platforms, the output and the behavior induced can differ. For this reason, we will start out with the Catalyst 1900 switch. The commonality of IOS commands across Cisco devices is one of the most powerful features and benefits available. Throughout the next several sections, as we examine IOS commands, the command syntax will be given first, followed by a brief explanation and then a sample output. It is extremely important that you follow along on an actual router or switch, entering the commands, and observing the output. Although it is possible to simply memorize the commands, hands-on learning is far more effective in turning out a good network engineer.

We will start out with a command that should be familiar from the last section, the `enable` command:

```
Switch> enable
```

As you can see from this syntax example, the `enable` command is issued from user mode. Throughout this section, each syntax example will show you which mode a command is generally issued in. For reasons of simplicity, most of the commands we will use are issued in privileged or configuration mode. Some of the privileged mode commands can also be issued in user mode, such as some of the show commands. It is left as a learning exercise for you to determine which commands fall into this category.

As previously discussed, the `enable` command causes the routers to change modes, from user mode to privileged mode. The same is true for switches:

```
Switch>enable
Password:
Switch#
```

NOTE: *From this point forward, we will refer to privileged mode as enable mode (even though it would be a simple thing to use privileged mode instead of enable mode). Although this is not technically correct, it is the common usage amongst working network engineers, a category that the authors of this text generally fall into. However, if you are pursuing a Cisco career certification, be sure to remember that privileged mode is the correct answer for test purposes. However, don't worry that a Cisco exam will ask you to make any distinction. There isn't any.*

Show Version

```
Switch# Show Version
```

`Show Version` is a command that tells you a lot more than just the version of IOS that the switch is running, although that is its primary function. It also lists the exact configuration of the switch:

```
Switch#Show Version
Cisco Catalyst 1900/2820 Enterprise Edition Software
Version V8.01.02     written from 209.049.143.005
Copyright (c) Cisco Systems, Inc.  1993-1998
Switch uptime is 99day(s) 07hour(s) 50minute(s) 16second(s)
Cisco Catalyst 1900 (486sxl) processor with 2048K/1024K bytes of
memory
Hardware board revision is 1
Upgrade Status: No upgrade currently in progress.
Config File Status: No configuration upload/download is in progress
27 Fixed Ethernet/IEEE 802.3 interface(s)
Base Ethernet Address: 00-E0-A3-FC-69-80
```

Let's take a closer look at this output. Although this looks like a clutter of arcane information, and some of it is certainly arcane, there is a significant amount of useful information that can be extracted:

- *Software Version*   This switch is running version 8.01.02. For troubleshooting purposes, this information is invaluable.

- *Written from*   This is the IP address of the server that the IOS software was downloaded from if applicable.

- *Uptime*   This can be traced back to show the time of the last reboot or crash.

- *Hardware configuration*   Most of this information is only useful from a troubleshooting perspective. Take note of "Base Ethernet Address." This is the switch's MAC address or burned-in address.

- *Hardware model*   Although it doesn't say so explicitly, this is a Catalyst 1924 switch. We can determine that because it is identified as a Catalyst 1900 with 27 fixed Ethernet ports. A Catalyst 1912, the other choice, has only 15 ports.

Show Running-Configuration

```
Switch# Show Running-Configuration
```

This command will show you the current switch configuration loaded in RAM and being used to determine the switch's current state of operation. The following configuration is fairly common for a production switch. It's not necessary to fully understand all of it now. However, as we begin to configure your switch, it's important to refer back to this command often. It will be a good way for you to determine which configuration mode you are in.

It has often been said that the best way to learn switch and router configuration, once certain basics have been covered, is to sit down with a series of Show Running-Configuration outputs of increasing complexity. Studying these configurations line by line will enhance your understanding of this area significantly. Show Running-Configuration is one of the two most important basic IOS commands. The other is Show Interfaces.

```
Switch#Show Running-Configuration
Building configuration...
Current configuration:
!
hostname Switch
!
ip address 216.230.68.42 255.255.255.248
ip default-gateway 216.230.68.41
!
enable password level 15 XXXXXX
!
interface Ethernet 0/1
!
interface Ethernet 0/2
!
interface Ethernet 0/3
!
interface Ethernet 0/4
!
<Text Omitted>
```

```
!
interface Ethernet 0/24
!
interface Ethernet 0/25
!
interface FastEthernet 0/26
  duplex full
  trunk On
  description "ISL Trunk to Router"
!
interface FastEthernet 0/27
!
line console
 time-out 480
end
```

Show Interfaces

```
Switch# Show Interfaces
```

This is the single most important command for debugging and troubleshooting. Although `Show Running-Configuration` will tell you what's supposed to be happening (what you or the person who configured the switch intended), `Show Interfaces` will tell you the current condition of your switch. It should be noted that our sample contains the output that relates to just one of the ports on the switch. In an actual output from this command, information on all ports will be displayed, one after the other. If we wanted to display the output from just one port, we would use the following syntax:

```
Switch# Show Interfaces Ethernet0/<PORT NUMBER>
```

or

```
Switch# Show Interfaces FastEthernet0/<PORT NUMBER>
```

Which of these two syntaxes you utilize depends on what type of port you are querying. On a Catalyst 1912, ports 1 through 12 and 25 are Ethernet, while on a Catalyst 1924, ports 1 through 25 are Ethernet. On both models of the switch, ports 26 and 27 are always Fast Ethernet.

Let's take a look at a sample output from a `Show Interfaces` and try to sort it out.

```
Switch#Show Interfaces Ethernet 0/1

Ethernet 0/1 is Enabled
Hardware is Built-in 10Base-T
Address is 00E0.A3FC.6981
MTU 1500 bytes, BW 10000 Kbits
```

```
802.1d STP State:  Forwarding      Forward Transitions:  1
Port monitoring: Disabled
Unknown unicast flooding: Enabled
Unregistered multicast flooding: Enabled
Description:
Duplex setting: Half duplex
Back pressure: Disabled


        Receive Statistics                    Transmit Statistics
   ------------------------------------       --------------------------
   Total good frames           3119825   Total frames
   7834852
   Total octets              438204061   Total octets
   1492402933
   Broadcast/multicast frames     85484   Broadcast/multicast frames
   6206746
   Broadcast/multicast octets  11147541   Broadcast/multicast octets
   429486314
   Good frames forwarded        1656025   Deferrals
   2391
   Frames filtered             1463800   Single collisions
   310
   Runt frames                       0   Multiple collisions
   263
   No buffer discards                0   Excessive collisions
   0
                                         Queue full discards
   0
   Errors:                               Errors:
     FCS errors                      0     Late collisions
   0
     Alignment errors                0     Excessive deferrals
   0
     Giant frames                    0     Jabber errors
   0
     Address violations              0     Other transmit errors
   0
```

The `Show Interfaces` command has earned a reputation as IOS's scariest command. The amount of data it outputs is significant, and even some network engineers shrink from using it because they don't understand everything that is included within the output. This is a significant mistake on their part. It is extremely difficult to troubleshoot without this command, and several difficult-to-troubleshoot problems become trivially easy to solve if you can read the output. That having been said, let's extract some basic information from the above output:

■ *Port status*   The output shows that Ethernet0/1 (Port #1 on the switch) is enabled. Another possible port static is "Suspended - No Linkbeat." Enabled should be self-explanatory: the port is hooked up to another Ethernet device and is running properly. "Suspended - No Linkbeat" means that the port is not attached to a functioning

Ethernet device. This is caused by several things. The most common is that there isn't a cable plugged into that port. Other reasons may include a cable cut or a loss of power to the other device. Turning off a workstation that is directly attached to a switch will also cause this message.

- *Hardware* In the above output, the hardware is listed as Built-In 10BaseT. This simply means that port #1 is a 10-MB/second twisted pair Ethernet port. There are also several other possibilities. One is that the hardware is Built-In 100BaseT, which denotes a Fast Ethernet port. The other is Built-In AUI, which indicates that the port is a 10-MB/second AUI port, always located on the rear of the switch. Unlike some other manufacturer's switches, on a Catalyst switch the AUI port is not tied to one of the normal 10BaseT ports. It can be used even when all other ports are utilized. All that is needed is an Ethernet transceiver.

- *Address* This is the MAC address of the port. Each port has its own MAC address, distinct from that of the switch itself. Compare the MAC addresses of each port and you will discover that they are assigned in sequence, one after the other.

- *MTU* This stands for Maximum Transmission Unit and is the largest physical packet size, measured in bytes, that a network can transmit. Any messages larger than the MTU are divided into smaller packets before being sent. Every network has a different MTU, which is set by the network administrator. On Windows 2000, you can also set the MTU of your machine. This defines the maximum size of the packets sent from your computer onto the network. Ideally, you want the MTU to be the same as the smallest MTU of all the networks between your machine and a message's final destination. Otherwise, if your messages are larger than one of the intervening MTUs, they will get broken up (fragmented), which slows down transmission speeds. Trial and error is the only sure way of finding the optimal MTU, but some guidelines can help. For example, the MTU of many PPP connections is 576, so if you connect to the Internet via PPP, you might want to set your machine's MTU to 576 too. Most Ethernet networks, on the other hand, have an MTU of 1500, which is the default MTU setting for Windows 2000. Furthermore, at the *Logical Link Control* (LLC), it is the size of the entire message, but at the MAC layer, the MTU only specifies the data field size.

- *BW* This stands for bandwidth and will be 10,000 Kbits for an Ethernet port and 100,000 Kbits for a Fast Ethernet port.

■ *802.1d STP State*   This indicates the port's Spanning Tree protocol status. Spanning Tree will be discussed later in this text.

■ *The receive and transmit statistics*   These show the number and type of frames being sent through the port. In a functioning switch, the numbers may change each time the command is issued. If the statistics for transmit change but the numbers for receive remain static, this is generally indicative of a cabling problem.

TIP: What is an AUI port anyway? Back in the day when many different types of Ethernet were being used, such as Thicknet (10Base5), Thinnet (10Base2), and twisted pair (10BaseT), it was thought to be a good idea that network cards and network devices should be able to work with any of those types of media. This was a fine idea in theory, because no one wanted to keep several different types of network cards or other devices around. They wanted "one size fits all." Unfortunately, it was more expensive to go with the universal AUI ports, because they required somewhat expensive transceivers to convert them into anything useful. The introduction of "combo" network cards with both BNC (10Base2) and RJ-45 (10BaseT) connectors spelled the end of AUI. It is still found on some types of network gear to assist in connecting legacy networks. Although it can be found on Catalyst 1900 series switches and Cisco 2500 series routers, newer Cisco devices omit the once-ubiquitous AUI port as unnecessary. However, if you want to hook your Catalyst up to a 10Base2 network, that AUI port could come in handy. If not, just get a 10BaseT transceiver and use it as an extra port.

Show IP Command

```
Switch# Show IP
```

This command will display the switch's current IP address as well as its subnet mask and default gateway. Other information includes name servers, which are analogous to *Domain Name Server* (DNS) entries. HTTP Server refers to the capability to manage the switch through a Web browser. If it is enabled, entering the IP address of your switch in a Web browser's URL window will give you the opportunity to enter the Web-based management interface. Many of the same manipulations we accomplish on the command line using IOS can be done through the Web interface. Additionally, the Web interface will give you a "virtual" view of the switch front panel

Figure 3-1
Switch Web interface

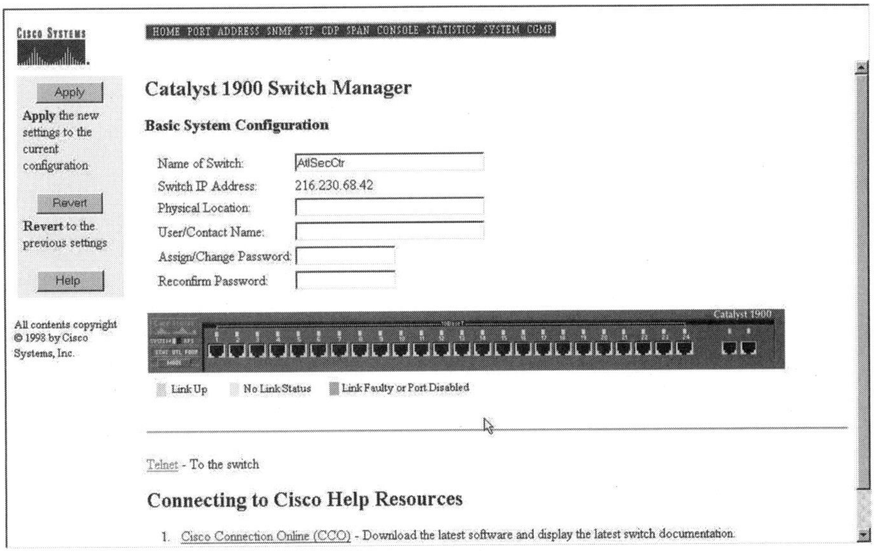

(see Figure 3-1), which is useful if you aren't conveniently located near the switch.

```
Switch#show ip
IP Address: 216.230.68.42
Subnet Mask: 255.255.255.248
Default Gateway: 216.230.68.41
Management VLAN:  2
Domain name:
Name server 1: 0.0.0.0
Name server 2: 0.0.0.0
HTTP server : Enabled
HTTP port :  80
RIP : Enabled
```

Configure Terminal

```
Switch# Configure Terminal
```

This command should be familiar from the last section. It changes the state of the switch from enable mode (privileged mode) to configuration mode. Two important things must be remembered here: Enable mode commands don't work in configure mode (and vice versa), and any command you issue in configure mode will have an immediate effect on the operation of the switch. There is no compile or any delay in effect; all changes happen immediately. A common mistake is to think that the changes won't take effect until you leave configuration mode using the `Exit` command; this is not so, as a good many network engineers have found to their detriment.

```
User Access Verification

Password:
Switch>enable
Password:
Switch#configure Terminal

Enter configuration commands, one per line.  End with CNTL/Z.
Switch(config)#
```

It isn't necessary to "End with CNTL/Z," although that will work. Most folks just use the `Exit` command, which works nicely. Now let's try out a few basic configuration mode commands, `Hostname` and `IP Address`.

Hostname

```
Switch(config)# Hostname <NAME>
```

You may have noticed during the course of this chapter that some examples have a prompt like this:

```
Switch#
```

while others have a prompt like this:

```
Third-Floor-Wiring-Closet#
```

The `Hostname` command lets you change the name of the switch and thus the prompt. The change is also reflected in the `Show Running-Configuration` command, as most configuration mode commands are. Let's try it out:

```
Switch# Configure Terminal
Enter configuration commands, one per line.  End with CNTL/Z.
Switch(config)#Hostname WiringCloset
WiringCloset(config)#
```

As you can see, the change took effect immediately, but the next prompt is different. Any alphanumeric characters will work fine in a `Hostname` command. However, it is recommended that you limit yourself to letters, numbers, and the dash character. Although other characters will work, you may regret using underscores or other characters, as they are not supported by the DNS and you may want to create DNS entries for your switches. In other words, you would have to use a different name for the DNS entry for the stated reasons in the preceding section.

IP Address

```
Switch(config)# IP Address <ADDRESS> <NETMASK>
```

As we have previously discussed, an IP address is not necessary for the operation of a switch. A switch operates on layer 2, the data link layer, so that an IP address is superfluous. However, several good reasons exist for assigning an IP address to your switches. Although not required, the management of switches becomes much easier with an IP address. Although we are currently using a console cable to administer your switch, that will become much more difficult with a production switch, which may be in an out-of-the-way area, if not out of state. For that reason, we need alternative ways to administer switches, such as the Web interface shown earlier. The most commonly used method is Telnet, which is a text-based "Teletype" protocol that utilizes TCP/IP as its method of transport. In order to use Telnet or the Web interface, the switch requires an IP address:

```
Switch# Configure Terminal
Enter configuration commands, one per line.  End with CNTL/Z.
Switch(config)#IP Address 10.10.0.100 255.0.0.0
```

In order to administer this switch through Telnet, the command `Telnet 10.10.0.100` could be issued from a Windows or Unix command line after you have given the switch that IP address, of course!

Now that we have discussed some basic switch commands, we will move our focus over to Cisco routers. Although many of the commands are similar and most are identical, several important differences must be discussed.

Cisco Routers: The Initial Configuration Dialog

When a Cisco switch is started for the first time, it contains a basic configuration, which is generally sufficient for initial operations. This is fairly easy to do. The basic operating mode of a switch is to forward frames. However, things are different for routers. As routers require network-level addressing, it's simply not possible to ship them with a working, initial configuration.

However, Cisco routers do start with a tool to assist their initial configuration, the Initial Configuration dialog. This is a question and answer session or an interrogatory dialog that will generate a basic router configuration for you. As there is a limit on the number of questions that can (or should) be asked, this dialog is only for creating basic functionality. For more advanced settings, configuration mode should be used.

After booting a router for the first time, the following dialog will appear:

```
-- System Configuration Dialog --

Continue with configuration dialog? [yes/no]: yes

At any point you may enter a question mark '?' for help.
Use ctrl-c to abort configuration dialog at any prompt.
Default settings are in square brackets '[]'.


Basic management setup configures only enough connectivity
for management of the system, extended setup will ask you
to configure each interface on the system

Would you like to enter basic management setup? [yes/no]: yes
```

This dialog can also be triggered through the use of the Setup command in enable mode. It should be noted that all the questions would have bracketed answers immediately after them. A single answer in brackets denotes the default answer, which can be accepted by pressing the <Enter> key. Typing <CTRL>-<C> at any time during the Initial Configuration dialog will enable you to exit back to the router prompt.

Basic Management Setup

The first question, "Would you like to enter basic management setup?" is used to determine if you would like to enter a dialog to determine basic router information, like hostname, passwords, and other basic information:

```
Would you like to enter basic management setup? [yes/no]: yes
Configuring global parameters:

  Enter host name [Router]:

  The enable secret is a password used to protect access to
  privileged EXEC and configuration modes. This password, after
```

```
entered, becomes encrypted in the configuration.
Enter enable secret [<Use current secret>]:

The enable password is used when you do not specify an
enable secret password, with some older software versions, and
some boot images.
Enter enable password [XXXXXXX]:

The virtual terminal password is used to protect
access to the router over a network interface.
Enter virtual terminal password [XXXXXXX]:
Configure SNMP Network Management? [no]:
```

Certain entries require some explanation:

- *Hostname*   This is the name of the router. This question generates a configuration mode command of the form `Hostname <Name>`.

- *Enable secret*   This is simply the password you enter after typing the Enable command. It gives you entry into the privileged exec mode (enable mode).

- *Enable password*   This is a backup password for entry into privileged exec mode. In older versions of Cisco IOS, this was the primary password, but it has been superseded. The primary difference is that the enable secret is encrypted, preventing anyone from learning the password, even if they do a `Show Running-Configuration` command. The enable password is still used for some purposes, namely if you have to recover from certain types of problems or crashes. It's still a good idea to set an enable password. Generally, the Initial Configuration dialog will not let you set the enable password to be the same as the enable secret. This can be done through the configuration mode, however.

- *Virtual terminal password*   This is the login password that is requested when you use Telnet to administer a router. As most routers are reachable through the Internet, this password is your first line of defense, so it should be suitably obscure and incorporate numbers, letters, and capitalization.

- *SNMP network management*   This is a setting that will determine if the router can be managed by special network management software utilizing the *Simple Network Management Protocol* (SNMP). These software packages include HP Openview and CiscoWorks. As a rule, this should not be enabled, unless you are using such software. If you enable this option, certain default SNMP community names, or passwords, should be used. This may cause your router to be insecure.

Protocols

After the basic management setup, the dialog shifts to network protocols. The exact list of protocols asked about may vary with your router's IOS version. Cisco typically ships routers that support only TCP/IP. Additional protocols require updated IOS versions, which are available for a fee. For the purposes of this text, we will look at a Protocols dialog for TCP/IP and IPX/SPX, the two protocols we will be discussing:

```
Configure bridging? [no]:
  Configure IP? [yes]:
    Configure IGRP routing? [yes]: no
    Configure RIP routing? [no]:
  Configure IPX? [no]:
```

Bridging causes the router to function in a manner similar to but slower than a switch. IGRP and RIP are routing protocols; they are a means for routers to communicate routing information to each other. When initially experimenting with routers, it is typically a good idea to only configure IP and to turn off all other configuration options. Your router may have many more protocols, such as Vines, DECnet, AppleTalk, and others. Although some of these protocols are still used, they are advanced topics and outside the scope of this text.

NOTE: In the previous output, you can see that many values are enclosed by brackets. Whenever you see them on a Cisco device, you should know the value the brackets contain is the default entry if you were to press the enter key. That is why you only see us answering no to one question!

Interfaces

Finally, the Initial Setup dialog will ask you a series of questions on how to configure each router interface. Some possible router interfaces include ISDN *Basic Rate Interface* (BRI), Ethernet, Fast Ethernet, Serial (for Frame Relay or Leased Line), and Token Ring. The router used in the following Interfaces dialog has one ISDN BRI interface and one Ethernet Interface; thus, we will be prompted to configure those interfaces:

```
BRI interface needs isdn switch-type to be configured
  Valid switch types are:
```

```
                              [0]   none.........Only if you don't want to
              configure BRI.
                              [1]   basic-1tr6....1TR6 switch type for Germany
                              [2]   basic-5ess....AT&T 5ESS switch type for the
              US/Canada
                              [3]   basic-dms100..Northern DMS-100 switch type for
              US/Canada
                              [4]   basic-net3....NET3 switch type for UK and
              Europe
                              [5]   basic-ni......National ISDN switch type
                              [6]   basic-ts013...TS013 switch type for Australia
                              [7]   ntt..........NTT switch type for Japan
                              [8]   vn3..........VN3 and VN4 switch types for
              France
                Choose ISDN BRI Switch Type [2]: 5

              Configuring interface parameters:

              Do you want to configure BRI0 (BRI d-channel) interface? [yes]:
                Configure IP on this interface? [no]: no

              Do you want to configure Ethernet0  interface? [yes]: yes
                Configure IP on this interface? [yes]:
                  IP address for this interface [10.10.30.1]:
                  Subnet mask for this interface [255.0.0.0] :
                  Class A network is 10.0.0.0, 8 subnet bits; mask is /8
```

As you can see, we first selected a ISDN Switch Type (which is specified by your telecommunications provider). ISDN switches are discussed at a later point in this text. We also decided not to give the ISDN interface an IP address, but we did give an IP address to the Ethernet interface.

Script Review

After all sections of the Initial Configuration dialog have been completed, a Cisco IOS configuration is generated that matches the responses you have. The configuration that follows is a good example:

```
The following configuration command script was created:

hostname Router
enable secret 5 XXXXXX
enable password XXXXXX
line vty 0 4
password XXXXXX
no snmp-server
!
no bridge 1
ip routing
isdn switch-type  basic-ni
!
interface BRI0
```

```
no ip address
!
interface Ethernet0
ip address 10.10.30.1 255.0.0.0
dialer-list 1 protocol ip permit
dialer-list 1 protocol ipx permit
!
router igrp 1
redistribute connected
network 10.0.0.0
!
end


[0] Go to the IOS command prompt without saving this config.
[1] Return back to the setup without saving this config.
[2] Save this configuration to nvram and exit.

Enter your selection [2]: 0
% You can enter the setup, by typing setup at IOS command prompt
```

Although you can use the Initial Configuration dialog to create the skeleton of a configuration, as shown previously, the authors do not recommend it. The only way to actually learn Cisco IOS along with the means and methods of configuration is to perform the configurations manually through the configure mode. Not only is it faster, but it permits much better control of the eventual configuration. The proof of this lies in the reality of current practice; very few experienced network engineers will ever use the Initial Configuration dialog. In the next few sections, we will cover the command necessary to do this configuration yourself.

Cisco Routers: Basic IOS Commands

The manner of logging into and using a Cisco router is similar to that of a Cisco switch. The biggest difference is that the router will not ask you if you want to use menu interface. It will simply ask you for a password and immediately put you into user mode:

```
User Access Verification

Password:
Router>
```

From this point, we can issue the enable command to place us into privileged exec mode, so we can start issuing commands:

```
Router>Enable
Password:
Router#
```

As you have had some familiarity entering IOS commands, as we worked on your switch, let's go over some more advanced techniques as we move to the router.

Keyboard Help and Command Completion

Over time, Cisco IOS has grown to incorporate thousands of commands. Luckily, several facilities have been built in to your router to help you. Two primary help facilities are used.

The first is Command List Help. This type of help will give you a list of commands or subcommands that are appropriate for your router and IOS mode. Command List Help is triggered by typing a ? at the command line. This will list all the appropriate commands.

```
router#?
Exec commands:
  <1-99>            Session number to resume
  access-enable     Create a temporary Access-List entry
  access-profile    Apply user-profile to interface
  access-template   Create a temporary Access-List entry
  archive           manage archive files
  bfe               For manual emergency modes setting
  cd                Change current directory
  clear             Reset functions
  clock             Manage the system clock
  configure         Enter configuration mode
  connect           Open a terminal connection
  copy              Copy from one file to another
  debug             Debugging functions (see also 'undebug')
  delete            Delete a file
  dir               List files on a filesystem
  disable           Turn off privileged commands
  disconnect        Disconnect an existing network connection
  enable            Turn on privileged commands
  erase             Erase a filesystem
  exit              Exit from the EXEC
  help              Description of the interactive help system
 —More—
```

Some commands have options or subcommands. A good example of this is the Show command. In order to list various options to use with the Show command or another command, simply type the command name followed by a ?.

```
router#Show ?
  access-expression  List access expression
  access-lists       List access lists
  accounting         Accounting data for active sessions
  aliases            Display alias commands
  arp                ARP table
  async              Information on terminal lines used as router
interfaces
  bridge             Bridge Forwarding/Filtering Database [verbose]
  buffers            Buffer pool statistics
  cdp                CDP information
  class-map          Show QoS Class Map
  clock              Display the system clock
  cls                DLC user information
  compress           Show compression statistics
  configuration      Contents of Non-Volatile memory
  controllers        Interface controller status
  debugging          State of each debugging option
  dhcp               Dynamic Host Configuration Protocol status
  dial-peer          Dial Plan Mapping Table for POTS  Peers
  dialer             Dialer parameters and statistics
  dnsix              Shows Dnsix/DMDP information
  entry              Queued terminal entries
  exception          exception information
—More—
```

Command Completion Help will assist you in completing commands. For example, typing Sh? at the router command line will produce the following:

```
router#Sh?
show

router#Sh
```

At this point, you can simply complete the command by typing the remainder or use the <TAB> key to complete the command for you:

```
router#Sh <TAB>
router#Show
```

If multiple possible commands are listed, the <TAB> key won't work and you must complete the command manually:

```
router#S?
*s=show  send    set         setup   show
slip     squeeze  start-chat  systat

router#S <TAB>
router#
```

Additionally, IOS will let you abbreviate commands. This means that instead of using Show Interfaces, you can use Sh Int or Sh Inter:

```
router#Show Interfaces
BRI0 is up, line protocol is up (spoofing)
```

```
     Hardware is BRI with U interface and POTS
     MTU 1500 bytes, BW 64 Kbit, DLY 20000 usec,
        reliability 255/255, txload 1/255, rxload 1/255
     Encapsulation PPP, loopback not set
     DTR is pulsed for 1 seconds on reset
     Last input 00:00:04, output 00:00:04, output hang never
     Last clearing of "show interface" counters 3d23h
     Queueing strategy: fifo
     Output queue 0/40, 0 drops; input queue 0/75, 0 drops
     5 minute input rate 0 bits/sec, 0 packets/sec
     5 minute output rate 0 bits/sec, 0 packets/sec
        26313 packets input, 113864 bytes, 0 no buffer
        Received 0 broadcasts, 0 runts, 0 giants, 0 throttles
        89 input errors, 0 CRC, 87 frame, 0 overrun, 0 ignored, 2 abort
        26302 packets output, 116911 bytes, 0 underruns
        0 output errors, 0 collisions, 6 interface resets
        0 output buffer failures, 0 output buffers swapped out
        1 carrier transitions

router#
router#Sh int
BRI0 is up, line protocol is up (spoofing)
   Hardware is BRI with U interface and POTS
   MTU 1500 bytes, BW 64 Kbit, DLY 20000 usec,
      reliability 255/255, txload 1/255, rxload 1/255
   Encapsulation PPP, loopback not set
   DTR is pulsed for 1 seconds on reset
   Last input 00:00:08, output 00:00:08, output hang never
   Last clearing of "show interface" counters 3d23h
   Queueing strategy: fifo
   Output queue 0/40, 0 drops; input queue 0/75, 0 drops
   5 minute input rate 0 bits/sec, 0 packets/sec
   5 minute output rate 0 bits/sec, 0 packets/sec
      26313 packets input, 113864 bytes, 0 no buffer
      Received 0 broadcasts, 0 runts, 0 giants, 0 throttles
      89 input errors, 0 CRC, 87 frame, 0 overrun, 0 ignored, 2 abort
      26302 packets output, 116911 bytes, 0 underruns
      0 output errors, 0 collisions, 6 interface resets
      0 output buffer failures, 0 output buffers swapped out
      1 carrier transitions
```

The rule on abbreviations is that you must have enough of the command listed to avoid any ambiguity. For this reason, Sh Int would be equivalent to Show Interfaces, but S Int would not. This is because several commands begin with S, making S Int ambiguous. Experimentation is the best way to learn IOS's built-in help and keyboard shortcut techniques.

Command History

IOS also has a command history facility that is of significant assistance to those using it. A command history is a list of the last several commands given to the router. If you want to see what's in your router's current command history, just use the Show History command:

```
router#show history
   en
   Show Interfaces
   Sh int
   show history
router#
```

This shows that the last four commands given were enable (en is an acceptable abbreviation), Show Interfaces, Sh int (an abbreviation for Show Interfaces), and show history. Sometimes it is desirable to issue commands several times, particularly long or difficult to remember commands. When this happens, the command history can save you significant typing. Simply use the <Up Arrow> key on your terminal emulator to move back through the history. The <Down Arrow> will move to more recent commands. Here's an example of the router command history:

```
router#show history
   en
   Show Interfaces
   Sh int
   show history
router# <Up-Arrow>show history<Up-Arrow>Sh Int
```

In this example, we didn't actually type the show history or Sh Int commands. They simply appeared after using the <Up Arrow>. Although it is difficult to show in text, the Show History command disappeared as soon as the <Up Arrow> was pressed a second time. In this manner, you can scroll through the command history.

```
Router# Terminal History Size n
```

By default, the last 10 commands are included in the command history. In order to increase or decrease the size of the history, use the Terminal History Size command:

```
router#Terminal history Size 20
router#
```

That increased the size of our router's command history to 20 commands. The maximum number of commands that can be stored in the command history is 256.

Now that we have explored some of the advanced features of the IOS command line, let's jump into some commands for managing and configuring routers.

Show Version

```
Router# Show Version
```

This command should be familiar from switch configuration. The command syntax is exactly the same, but the output is significantly different:

```
router#Show Version
Cisco Internetwork Operating System Software
IOS (tm) C800 Software (C800-OSY6-MW), Version 12.0(5)T,   RELEASE
SOFTWARE (fc1)
Copyright (c) 1986-1999 by Cisco Systems, Inc.
Compiled Fri 23-Jul-99 03:38 by kpma
Image text-base: 0x000E9000, data-base: 0x006E1000

ROM: TinyROM version 1.0(3)
router uptime is 4 days, 6 minutes
System returned to ROM by power-on
System image file is "flash:c800.bin"

Cisco C804 (MPC850) processor (revision 1) with 43876K bytes of
virtual memory.
Processor board ID JAD02521746
CPU part number 33
X.25 software, Version 3.0.0.
Bridging software.
Basic Rate ISDN software, Version 1.1.
1 Ethernet/IEEE 802.3 interface(s)
1 ISDN Basic Rate interface(s)
4M bytes of physical memory (DRAM)
8K bytes of non-volatile configuration memory
8M bytes of flash on board (4M from flash card)

Configuration register is 0x2102
```

Let's take a look at some of the pertinent information from Show Version:

- *IOS version*   This is listed above as Version 12.0(5)T. This is extremely important information for Cisco Technical Support, as certain features are only supported in specific versions.
- *Router uptime*   This lists the amount of time since the last router power cycle or restart.
- *Method of restart*   This shows that a power cycle, rather than a crash, restarted the router. This is obviously important diagnostic information, as action is called for if a router should restart via a crash. Also, this can show you if a router has been tampered with or if electrical power was lost in a remote location.
- *Router mode*   This is a Cisco 804 router, as the output reflects.

■ *Interfaces*   The output lists the router's two interfaces: an Ethernet port and an ISDN BRI port. If all physical interfaces do not appear in the Show Version output, it could mean that there is a hardware malfunction or that the version of IOS you are using does not support that specific interface and should be upgraded.

■ *Memory*   The output shows that this router has eight MB of RAM memory used for router operations and holding the currently active configuration. It also has four MB of flash memory used for holding the IOS image. Finally, it has eight KB of *Non-Volatile RAM* (NVRAM) used for holding the stored configuration.

■ *Configuration register*   This is a value that determines how the router starts up and some of its basic operational parameters. It should not be altered unless you are absolutely sure that you know what you are doing. A good introduction to the configuration register is contained in *The Cisco TCP/IP Professional Reference* by Chris Lewis, also from McGraw-Hill.

Methods of Viewing the Configuration

As we discussed in the section on configuring switches, Show Running-Configuration will display a switch or router's current configuration. On a Cisco switch, that running configuration is the only configuration. As soon as you make any changes to the configuration, it is permanently stored. This is not the case with Cisco routers. With routers, two copies of the configuration are kept: the running configuration and the stored configuration (see Figure 3-2).

The stored configuration is always present, regardless of whether the router is on or off. It is the equivalent of an OS configuration file, stored on a mass-storage device. The stored configuration is loaded into RAM when the router is booted. This copy in RAM is called the running configuration. Every time you make a change to the configuration by issuing an IOS command, the running configuration is changed, but the stored configuration is not. This is a good thing, as it keeps a "clean" copy of your configuration present in case you want to fall back to your last saved version. Just like in a conventional PC OS, commands can be used to copy the running configuration to the NVRAM, overwriting the startup or stored configuration. Also, commands can be used to copy the stored configuration into RAM, canceling out any changes you may have made since the last time the configuration was saved.

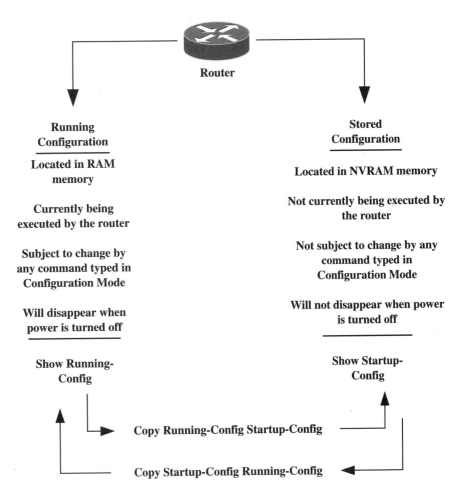

Figure 3-2
Running
configurations versus
stored configurations

The `Router# Show Startup-Config` command displays the configuration stored in NVRAM. Note that the output states, "Using x out y bytes." This corresponds to the amount of NVRAM in the router. Note in the following example a total of 8072 bytes, which matches the amount of NVRAM reported in the `Show Version` listed earlier. The `Show Configuration` command is an obsolete syntax for the `Show Startup-Config` command. Because it is far more specific, `Show Startup-config` should be used instead.

```
router#show startup-config
Using 2079 out of 8072 bytes
!
version 12.0
no service pad
```

```
service timestamps debug uptime
service timestamps log uptime
no service password-encryption
!
hostname dan
!
boot buffersize 8064
boot system flash c800.bin

!
!
(MORE)
```

The `Router# Show Running-Config` command is similar to `Show Startup-Config`, except that it displays the copy of the configuration in RAM, rather than the copy in NVRAM. This is the working copy and is being used by the IOS image to control the router. Note that the following output doesn't have any figures for the amount of NVRAM used but does note that it is the current configuration:

```
router#Show Running-Config
Building configuration...

Current configuration:
!
version 12.0
no service pad
service timestamps debug uptime
service timestamps log uptime
no service password-encryption
!
hostname router
!
boot buffersize 8064
boot system flash c800.bin
```

Every time the router is started, a copy of the Startup-Config is loaded into RAM and becomes the Running-Config. It is possible to affect such a copy within IOS as well.

The `Router# Copy Running-Config Startup-Config` command writes a copy of the currently running configuration in RAM over the startup configuration in NVRAM. This has the effect of erasing the old startup configuration and replacing it. `Write Memory` is another IOS command used for this purpose, but it is considered obsolete:

```
Router#Copy Running-Config Startup-Config
Destination filename [startup-config]? <ENTER>
Building configuration...

Router#
```

It may take some time to build the configuration, as much as 30 seconds for some older routers. It is important to wait through this time; cycling the router's power during this period could result in a corrupted NVRAM.

Similarly, the Router# Copy Startup-Config Running-Config command copies the current contents of NVRAM over the running configuration. As with the previous command, this process can take some time to complete and should not be interrupted:

```
Router#copy startup-config running-config
Destination filename [running-config]?
2102 bytes copied in 5.504 secs (420 bytes/sec)
Router#
```

Cisco Routers: Configuration Mode

Now that we have covered how to save configurations to NVRAM, it's time to start doing some hands-on router configuration in IOS. We will cover several topics including how to set your router's hostname, setting passwords, console settings, and how to do basic interface configurations.

Hostname

```
Router(config)# Hostname <NAME>
```

This configuration mode command is exactly the same as the switch's Hostname command. However, when performing this command on a router, remember to exit from configuration mode and do a Copy Running-Config Startup-Config to make the change permanent:

```
Router#config t
Enter configuration commands, one per line. End with CNTL/Z.
Router(config)#Hostname Router
Router(config)#exit
Router#copy running-config startup-config
```

Remember that while Hostname and the other configuration mode commands we will discuss are performed in configuration mode, Copy is a privileged exec mode command.

Changing the Login Password

```
Router(config)# Line vty 0 4
Router(config-line)# Login
Router(config-line)# Password <PASSWORD>
Router(config)# Line Console 0
Router(config-line)# Login
Router(config-line)# Password <PASSWORD>
```

Most of the time during production operations on an internetwork, it is desirable to have passwords assigned to prevent unauthorized access. In order to assign login passwords for Telnet access, it is necessary to perform the following steps:

1. Enter configuration mode. This is accomplished through the use of `Configure Terminal`.

2. Select all Virtual Terminal Line. This is done by issuing the command `Line vty 0 4`. This places the router into line configuration mode. Any commands done in this mode will affect the specified terminal lines, in this case *Virtual Terminals* (VTs) 0 through 4. Furthermore, in open systems, VTs (which are considered to be an application service) enable host terminals on a multi-user network to interact with other hosts regardless of the terminal type and characteristics. They also enable remote logons by LAN managers for management purposes, enable users to access information from another host processor for transaction processing, and serve as a backup facility.

3. Set the password. This is done by using the `password` command, followed by the desired password:

```
Router#config t
Enter configuration commands, one per line.  End with CNTL/Z.
Router(config)#line vty 0 4
Router(config-line)#login
Router(config-line)#password ABC
Router(config-line)#exit
Router(config)#exit
Router#
```

This password only affects any attempts to use Telnet to manage the router. If you want to apply a password to the console line, a similar procedure is used that replaces `Line vty 0 4` with `Line Console 0`:

```
Router#config t
Enter configuration commands, one per line. End with CNTL/Z.
Router(config)#line Con 0
```

```
Router(config-line)#login
Router(config-line)#password XYZ
Router(config-line)#exit
Router(config)#exit
Router#
```

As we have shown previously, it is not necessary for these passwords to be the same.

Changing the Enable Secret and Enable Password

```
Router(config)# Enable Secret <PASSWORD>
Router(config)# Enable Password  <PASSWORD>
```

As we have discussed earlier, the `enable secret` and `enable password` are important means of securing the router. As noted in the Initial Configuration Dialog section, the `enable secret` has generally superseded the `enable password`. However, it's still good practice to set them both. It is recommended that they be set to different values. The `enable secret` is encrypted, while the `enable password` is not. It doesn't do much good to have an encrypted password if an unencrypted password listed next to it has the same value.

```
Router#Config t
Enter configuration commands, one per line.  End with CNTL/Z.
Router(config)#enable secret YYY
Router(config)#enable password XXX
Router(config)# Service Password-Encryption
```

If you desire an additional level of security, it is possible to make all router passwords encrypted, including console and Telnet passwords. This is accomplished by using the `Service Password-Encryption` command. It should be noted that only passwords entered after this command is issued would be encrypted. It will not encrypt existing passwords in your configuration. Similarly, turning this command off using the `No Service Password-Encryption` command does not decrypt router passwords. Although it is possible to decrypt router passwords, this is left as an exercise for the reader, as it is an advanced topic.

Console and VTY Settings

```
Router(config-line)# Exec-Timeout m n (m = Minutes, n = Seconds)
Router(config-line)# Logging Synchronous
```

Earlier in this chapter, we discussed line configuration mode, where we could change the settings for the console and virtual terminal (for Telnet sessions). Several other settings can be changed in addition to passwords. Exec-Timeout sets the timeout for console and Telnet sessions. This is a valuable security tool in production environments, similar to a feature on some servers that automatically locks the console after a certain amount of time elapses. This prevents the curious or malicious from tampering with an active router configuration session. However, this feature can be somewhat irritating in a training environment. Use Exec-Timeout 0 0 to disable this feature. Alternatively, experiment with it utilizing longer and shorter timeouts, being careful not to make the timeout too short, which could make control of the router difficult.

During the course of router configuration, the router will supply us with a variety of messages to inform us of the state of the router. Because the router is really a computer running its own multithreaded OS (that is, IOS), these messages can appear in the middle of your input. This has the unfortunate effect of making the router output extremely difficult to read as well as making input challenging. The Logging Synchronous command has the effect of cleaning up this output and replacing your partially finished input. Its use is highly recommended.

```
Router(config)#line vty 0 4
Router(config-line)#Exec-Timeout 0 0
Router(config-line)#Logging Synchronous
Router(config-line)#Exit
Router(config)#line con 0
Router(config-line)#Exec-Timeout 0 0
Router(config-line)#Logging Synchronous
Router(config-line)#Exit
```

Interface Configuration

```
Router(config)# Interface Ethernet n (n = Interface Number)
Router(config)# Interface BRI n (n = Interface Number)
Router(config)# Interface Serial n (n = Interface Number)
```

We have discussed line configuration mode where we can issue commands that affect specific console or terminal lines. We will now discuss the interface configuration mode, which is used to issue commands to configure specific interfaces. This mode is necessary because we often must define properties or settings by specific interfaces:

```
Router#config t
Enter configuration commands, one per line. End with CNTL/Z.
```

```
Router(config)#interface Ethernet0
Router(config-if)#
```

As you can see from the previous example, entering interface config mode changes the prompt. This example holds true for lower end routers of the type that you are probably using for training, such as the Cisco 800, 1600, and 2500 series routers. For higher end routers, such as the Cisco 2600, 3600, 4000, and 7200, some subtle differences exist. The most important one is that these are modular routers with their interfaces on removable modules or cards. Instead of referring to Interface Ethernet 0, you may refer to Interface Serial 2/3, which means the third serial interface on the second module. Even if one of these routers has only a single interface, the module/port notation must still be used.

TIP: *(for the practitioner) All professions come up with their own vocabulary and network engineering is no different. Modules or cards in higher-end Cisco routers are typically called blades, just as memory modules are usually called sticks.*

At this point, you can issue some additional commands to apply to these interfaces:

```
Router(config-if)# Description <TEXT>
Router(config-if)# IP Address <Address> <Mask>
```

We can use these commands to assign text descriptions to each interface as well as to assign a unique IP address to each:

```
Router(config)#interface Ethernet0
Router(config-if)#Description This is an Ethernet Interface
Router(config-if)#IP Address 10.10.30.1 255.255.255.0
Router(config-if)#exit
```

This can be repeated for each interface, with unique descriptions and IP addresses.

```
Router(config-if)# Shutdown
```

We can also disable specific interfaces for maintenance or other reasons. This is common on production networks and is frequently used for troubleshooting. It is helpful for problem isolation and as a means of "resetting" a troublesome interface without rebooting the entire router. This command is reversed by using the no shutdown command on the interface. Care should be taken using this command. If you shutdown the interface that connects you to the router, you are immediately disconnected. The only recourse is to either connect via another interface (which is usually quite difficult) or console into the router to reverse the shutdown.

Most versions of IOS automatically place interfaces in a shutdown status when first started. It is necessary to issue a `no shutdown` command on each port you want to use in order to enable the interfaces.

```
Router(config)#int BRI0
Router(config-if)#shutdown
Router(config-if)#no shutdown
Router(config-if)#exit
```

Cisco Routers: Show Interfaces Commands

Now that we have examined some commands used to configure routers, we should also examine some basic troubleshooting commands. The single most important troubleshooting command is `Show Interfaces`:

```
Router# Show Interfaces
```

This command will display in-depth troubleshooting information on all router interfaces in a very similar manner to the switch IOS show interface command. Let's examine a sample output from this command:

```
Ethernet0 is up, line protocol is up
  Hardware is PQUICC Ethernet, address is 0050.0f02.6045 (bia
    0050.0f02.6045)
  Description: This is an Ethernet Interface
  Internet address is 10.10.30.1/24
  MTU 1500 bytes, BW 10000 Kbit, DLY 1000 usec,
    reliability 255/255, txload 1/255, rxload 1/255
  Encapsulation ARPA, loopback not set
  Keepalive set (10 sec)
  ARP type: ARPA, ARP Timeout 04:00:00
  Last input 00:00:00, output 00:00:00, output hang never
  Last clearing of "show interface" counters never
  Queueing strategy: fifo
  Output queue 0/40, 0 drops; input queue 0/75, 0 drops
  5 minute input rate 0 bits/sec, 1 packets/sec
  5 minute output rate 1000 bits/sec, 1 packets/sec
```

```
65866 packets input, 6868174 bytes, 0 no buffer
Received 303 broadcasts, 0 runts, 0 giants, 0 throttles
0 input errors, 0 CRC, 0 frame, 0 overrun, 0 ignored
0 input packets with dribble condition detected
122591 packets output, 80167700 bytes, 0 underruns
0 output errors, 31 collisions, 1 interface resets
0 babbles, 0 late collision, 62 deferred
0 lost carrier, 0 no carrier
0 output buffer failures, 0 output buffers swapped out
```

Although the output is different for each type of interface, be it Ethernet, BRI, or Serial, this provides us a good starting point to discuss how to interpret the output:

- *Ethernet0* This indicates whether the Ethernet port can be up, down, or administratively down. If up, the port is operating properly. If down, this indicates that the interface hardware is not in operation for some reason, like not being able to see another Ethernet end station. Administratively down indicates that the interface has been turned off using the shutdown command.

- *Line protocol* This indicates whether the protocol can be up or down. Generally, this will match the port status on an Ethernet port. On a serial port, it is entirely possible to have a port up with the line protocol down, which generally indicates a misconfiguration or downed connection.

- *Hardware* This shows the interface's hardware (MAC) address.

- *Internet Address* This is the IP address. It is followed by a prefix, such as /24, which indicates a subnet mask of 255.255.255.0. Masks and prefixes are discussed elsewhere in this text.

- *MTU* The Maximum Transmission Unit for the interface. Generally, this is the maximum frame size, which would be 1518 bytes for Ethernet interfaces (including the headers). This corresponds to the maximum Ethernet data field size. At the LLC, it is the entire message after the Ethernet headers (the MAC layer stuff) have been removed. BW signifies the interface's bandwidth. A Fast Ethernet port's BW value would be 10 times greater than that listed in the above output, that is, 100,000 Kb. Nevertheless, some users have run into problems with this particular BW setting and network management stations. This does not actually change the port configuration; it only changes what the device tells other devices about itself. That can be an important distinction. In any event, this value can be changed in interface configuration mode with the bandwidth command. It is used to provide data to routing protocols, so that they can determine which connections are most desirable.

- *DLY, reliability, and load* These are line delays (in microsecond), the line reliability (in a percentage), and transmit and receive loads. As with bandwidth, these values provide data to routing protocols.

- *Output queue, input queue, drops* These indicate how full the interface's input and output queues are. This is of particular concern if that interface is being overloaded with traffic, which could cause the number of drops to increase.

- *5 minute rates* This shows the average bandwidth utilization of the interface, as a running average over the last five minutes.

- *Input and output errors* These values can be useful while troubleshooting, and large increases in these values can indicate problems with the interface, media, or other end stations.

- *Carrier* Lost carrier and no carrier can also be sources of concern. However, keep in mind that simply unplugging the router from its Ethernet feed will cause these values to increase.

Chapter Summary

During the course of this chapter, we have covered some significant ground. Although much of this chapter may seem basic, this information is extremely important. At this point, it's a good idea to go back and review the objectives at the beginning of the chapter. Ensure that you can answer all of them. For those preparing for Cisco certification exams, your ability to answer all exam objectives is the key to success. If you have trouble with any of the objectives, go back and review the pertinent material. Pay particular attention to the following:

- *The start-up procedures and self-tests for switches and routers* It is not important to memorize each self-test; that's what reference books are for. However, it is important to have a good grasp of the general steps that various Cisco devices go through as they start up.

- *Various modes of interacting with Cisco devices* In particular, be very familiar with the differences between user mode, privileged mode, and the various configuration modes. Know how to navigate between them.

- *Some of the common IOS commands* Be sure that you are familiar with the various commands for managing configurations. Also know how to assign IP addresses and descriptions to various interfaces. Some familiarity with the Show Interfaces command is also very important.

From the Real World

In the world of network engineering, many lower level engineers treat routers like magic wands. They endeavor to memorize as many commands as possible but do not truly understand how they operate. Once when I was starting a new job at a small ISP, one of the junior engineers asked for my assistance in debugging a problem. Wanting to evaluate his troubleshooting skills, I observed his actions. He kept using the `Show Running-Config` command and staring at the router configuration. I asked him if he had changed the router configuration at any time before the problem was called in. He replied that it had not changed for weeks. I introduced him to the `Show Interfaces` command, which quickly isolated our problem: a bad T-1 line between two locations. His response to seeing this command was, "That's a pretty neat trick. I'm going to have to remember that one." He didn't seek to understand the output that the router was giving him, only the way he had gotten to the impressive-looking debugging information. The moral of this tale is that while it may be necessary to learn some commands by rote in the beginning, it's far more important to understand the router's output and be able to interpret it. You can't always simply solve a problem by following a list of instructions; analytical thought is required. The junior engineer in question soon left the ISP. He went into the LAN/server consulting business, installing Windows NT servers, where problems popped up in pastel dialog boxes and could be easily fixed by clicking yes or no . . .

Thomas M. Thomas II and Daniel L. Golding

Frequently Asked Questions (FAQ)

Question: We talked about various kinds of memory in this chapter. My PC gets faster if I add more memory. What about my router?

Answer: Your PC uses something called virtual memory, where portions of active memory are paged out to a mass storage device. This paging is slow, so adding more RAM speeds things up. Few routers use any type of mass storage or virtual memory, so adding more memory won't make your router any faster.

Question: Then why would I add more memory?

Answer: As we discussed in this chapter, many different versions of the Cisco IOS software exist. Most of them add features, so they end up requiring more Flash to hold the image and more RAM to execute it.

Question: What if I need to add more NVRAM to hold a really big configuration?

Answer: In practice, this is a non-issue. NVRAM is almost always large enough to hold a configuration. Large routers have more NVRAM, so if you run into a situation where you have a monstrous configuration, it may be time to look at a larger router.

Question: We talked about having a copy of the configuration in NVRAM as a clean backup. But what if I want to make a backup of my configuration and put it on a server or off-site?

Answer: Several good methods exist for doing this. One is simply to do a `Show Running-Config` while your terminal program captures the resulting text file. Another is to set up a TFTP server and then use the command `Copy Startup-Config TFTP` to copy your configuration there. This can also work in reverse to restore configuration from a TFTP server.

Question: Some of my coworkers laugh when I use `Copy Running-Config Startup-Config`. They say that real engineers use `Write Memory`. What's up with this?

Answer: For the past several years, Cisco has been teaching the new usage. Although it's still common to run across the old usage, either is correct. At some point, Cisco may decide to phase out the older usage. Who will be laughing then?

■ ■ ■ # Case Study

For this practical exercise, you will perform an initial configuration on a switch and a router. The required equipment is as follows:

■ One Cisco router with at least one Ethernet port

■ One Catalyst 1912 or 1924 switch

The router configuration is as follows:

1. Connect your router to a console cable, and then connect the cable to a PC running a terminal program.

2. Apply power to the router.

3. Observe the router start-up sequence.

4. Enter the Initial configuration dialog.

5. Assign the following information to your router:

   ▪ Hostname: Lab1

   ▪ Ethernet0 IP address: 10.10.0.1

   ▪ Ethernet0 Subnet Mask: 255.255.255.0

   ▪ Do not enable RIP, IGRP, or SNMP.

   ▪ Give the router an enable secret and password of your choice.

6. When the router asks you if it should save the configuration, answer Yes.

7. Examine the configuration you are given and compare it with the information entered.

8. When you reach the router prompt, try each of the following IOS commands at least once:

   ▪ `Show Running-Config`

   ▪ `Show Version`

   ▪ `Show Interfaces`

   ▪ `Copy Running-Config Startup-Config`

   ▪ `Configuration Terminal`

9. Also make use of configuration mode to make a description line for Ethernet0.

10. View the revised configuration with `Show Running-Config`.

11. Save the revised configuration to NVRAM.

Switch Configuration

1. Connect your switch to a console cable and then connect the cable to a PC running a terminal program.

2. Apply power to the switch.

3. Observe the switch start-up sequence, paying particular attention to the front panel LEDs.

4. Go to the `Switch` command prompt.

5. Enter privileged exec mode and do a `Show Running-Config`.

6. Enter configuration mode and perform the following steps:

   a. Change the name of the switch to Lab2.

   b. Give the switch an IP address of 10.10.0.2 with a subnet mask of 255.255.255.0.

   c. Give the switch an enable password of your choice.

   d. Exit configuration mode.

7. Do the following commands:

   a. `Show Interfaces`. Compare the output with that of the router you just configured.

   b. `Show IP`.

   c. `Show Version`. Compare the output with that of the router you just configured.

8. Turn the switch off and on. Observe that the switch's configuration stayed the same.

■ ■ **Questions**

1. The command to enter configuration mode from privileged exec mode is

   a. `Disable`

   b. `Enable`

   c. `Interface Ethernet0`

   d. `Configure Terminal`

2. The command to leave privileged exec mode and enter user mode is

   a. `Disable`

   b. `Enable`

   c. `Exit`

   d. `Shutdown`

3. During Catalyst Switch POST, a LED that stays on after all others have gone out indicates:

   a. A problem with that LED

   b. A failure of a specific POST test

   c. Normal behavior, the POST passed

   d. That specific port being inoperable

4. During Catalyst Switch POST, if an LED fails to light at all, this indicates:

   a. A problem with that LED

   b. A failure of a specific POST test

   c. Normal behavior, the POST passed

   d. That specific port being inoperable

5. Switches have how many MAC addresses?

   a. One

   b. None, only Endstations have MAC Addresses

   c. As many as you want to define

   d. One for each port

6. Which command will give basic information for each port or interface on a switch or router?

   a. `Show Ports`

   b. `Show Interfaces`

   c. `Show Config`

   d. `Show Version`

7. Which command will show you how much Flash and RAM a switch or router has?

   a. Show Memsize
   b. Show Config
   c. Memory
   d. Show Version

8. Which commands will copy the currently running configuration in RAM into NVRAM? Choose all that apply.

   a. Write RAM
   b. Write Flash
   c. Copy RAM NVRAM
   d. Copy Startup-Config Running-Config
   e. Copy Run Start
   f. Write Memory

9. Which commands or actions will copy the stored configuration in NVRAM into RAM?

   a. Power Cycle the Router
   b. Copy RAM NVRAM
   c. Copy Startup-Config Running-Config
   d. Copy Run Start
   e. Write Memory
   f. Write Now

10. Which keys will generally enable you to scroll through the command history buffer? Choose all that apply.

    a. PageUp
    b. PageDown
    c. Up Arrow
    d. Down Arrow
    e. Home
    f. End
    g. Escape

11. How many IP addresses will a Cisco switch generally have if you want it to be manageable through Telnet?

    a. None
    b. One
    c. As many IP addresses as there are ports
    d. As many IP addresses as there are ports, plus one

12. If you want to route TCP/IP, how many IP addresses will a router generally have?

   a. None

   b. One

   c. As many IP addresses as there are interfaces

   d. 255

13. Which command sets the login password to be used for Telnet sessions to a router?

   a. Enable

   b. Secret

   c. Password

   d. Service Password-Encryption

   e. Line Con 0

14. Which command will let you change the router's name and prompt?

   a. Name

   b. Prompt

   c. Banner

   d. Description

   e. Hostname

15. In order to set the console timeout to five minutes and 30 seconds, the following commands are used:

   a. Line vty 0 4
      Console Time-out 5 30

   b. Line Con 0
      Exec-timeout 0.0

   c. Line vty 0 4
      Exec-timeout 5:30

   d. Line Con 0
      Exec-timeout 5 30

16. In order to disable a specific interface, the shutdown command is used in which IOS mode?

   a. User mode

   b. Privileged exec (enable) mode

   c. Configuration mode

   d. Interface configuration mode

   e. Line enable mode

17. In order to determine the cause of the last router reset, the following command is used:

    a. `Show Reset`
    b. `Show Reload`
    c. `Show Version`
    d. `Show Running-Config`
    e. `Debug Reload`

18. Which of the following types of memory retain their content when the router is powered off? Choose all that apply.

    a. Flash
    b. NVRAM
    c. RAM
    e. ROM
    f. All of the above

19. On a Cisco switch, the Initial Configuration dialog appears when?

    a. Each time the switch is started
    b. Never
    c. By using the M option at bootup
    d. When the POST fails
    e. By using the setup command

20. IOS user mode is for

    a. End users to configure their workstations to function with routers or switches
    b. No use. It's an obsolete hold-over from an earlier IOS version.
    c. Setting router configuration settings
    d. Viewing basic router operational data, but not changing or viewing configurations
    e. Performing the initial router setup

Answers

1. **d.** `Configure Terminal`

   `Enable` and `disable` control the entry and exit from privileged exec mode into user mode. Interface commands regulate entry into the interface configuration mode.

2. **a.** `Disable`

   `Exit` is only used in configuration mode to go back to privileged exec mode. `Shutdown` is used to administratively disable an interface. `Enable` enters privileged exec mode.

3. **b.** A failure of a specific POST test

   Each LED corresponds to a specific failed POST test.

4. **b.** A failure of a specific POST test

   All LEDs should light during the POST. If they don't, chances are that one of them is burnt out.

5. **d.** One for each port

   Because each port is acting like its own separate bridge on an individual segment, the switch requires that each port have its own MAC address.

6. **b.** `Show Interfaces`

   `Show Ports` is not an IOS command. `Show Config` will show the stored configuration for the entire router. `Show version` provides a summary of information on the current IOS version and the router.

7. **d.** `Show Version`

   `Show Config` will show the router configuration but not the memory size. `Show Memsize` and `Memory` are not IOS commands.

8. **e.** `Copy Run Start` and **f.** `Write Memory`

   `Copy Run Start` and `Write Memory` will accomplish the task. `Copy Start Run` will copy the NVRAM config to RAM, the reverse of what is being asked. The other answers are not IOS commands.

9. **a.** `Power Cycle the Router` and **c.** `Copy Startup-Config Running-Config`

   `Write Memory` and `Copy Run Start` will do the opposite. They will copy the Config in RAM to NVRAM.

10. **c.** Up Arrow and d. Down Arrow

    The other keys will have no effect on an IOS session.

11. **b.** One

    Because a switch operates on the data link layer, rather than the network layer, it doesn't need an IP address for normal operations. It only needs an IP address so that the administrator can Telnet in for management. Only one IP address is required for that purpose.

12. **c.** As many IP addresses as there are interfaces.

    A router operates on the network layer. In order to route packets between networks, each interface must be capable of communicating with other TCP/IP end stations in their respective networks. This requires each interface to have an IP address from each network's range. The only exception to this requirement is a feature called IP Unnumbered, which is covered in the Advanced course.

13. **c.** Password

    The enable command is used to set the enable password, rather than the login password. Service Password-encryption turns on the auto-password encryption feature.

14. **e.** Hostname

    Description is used to place comments on interfaces. Banner is used to create login banners. The other answers are not IOS commands.

15. **d.** Line Con 0

    Exec-timeout 5 30

    Choice d will result in a Telnet timeout of 5:30. Choice b will result in no timeout at all for the console. Choice c will result in a syntax error; the ":" should be omitted. Only choice d provides a 5:30 timeout for console sessions.

16. **d.** Interface configuration mode

    Shutdown can only be applied to a specific interface, and the only way to apply any IOS command to an interface is through interface configuration mode.

17. **c.** Show Version

    Show Reload is an IOS command, but it shows scheduled future reloads, not past ones. Show Reset and Debug Reload are not IOS commands. Show Running-Config will not display the cause of the last reset, only the currently running configuration.

18. a. Flash, b. NVRAM, d. ROM

RAM loses all of its contents when power is removed. All of the other forms of memory are static in the case of a loss of power.

19. b. Never

The Initial Configuration dialog only appears on routers and generally only the first time the router is started.

20. d. Viewing basic router operational data, but not changing or viewing configurations

End users have little or no reason to be logging into any mode on a router. User mode is still highly useful for network operation center and help desk personnel, who may use it to perform basic troubleshooting tasks without fear that they could alter the operations of the router.

4

Network Management

Objectives

On completion of this chapter, you will be able to do the following:

- Understand the uses of the Cisco Discovery protocol configuration.
- Understand the uses of Telnet, ping, and traceroute.
- Understand how the router initialization takes place.
- Know the default locations of router files.
- Be able to change the location of router files.
- Save changes of the configuration to several locations.

    This chapter can also help you fulfill the following CCNA exam objectives:

- Manage configuration files from the privileged exec mode.
- Identify the main Cisco IOS commands for router startup.
- Copy and manipulate the configuration files.
- List the commands to load Cisco IOS software from flash memory, a TFTP server, or *Read-Only Memory* (ROM).
- Prepare to back up, upgrade, and load a Cisco IOS Image.
- Identify the functions performed by ICMP.

Cisco Discovery Protocol

Cisco equipment runs a proprietary protocol called the *Cisco Discovery Protocol* (CDP). CDP runs by default on all routers with IOS versions 10.3 or later and enables equipment to learn about their neighbors connected directly through the *Local Area Network* (LAN) or *Wide Area Network* (WAN).

Because you have no guarantee that neighboring routers will be running the same Network-Layer protocol, Cisco runs CDP at the Data-Link layer level of the OSI model. Utilizing a *Subnetwork Access Protocol* (SNAP) frame at the Data-Link Layer removes any requirement that both pieces of equipment run the same Network-Layer protocol. This will enable, for example, equipment running only IPX to communicate with equipment running only IP.

The CDP process starts by issuing Data-Link broadcasts out all active interfaces. These broadcasts contain information concerning the equipment, IOS version, and other information that we will display through CDP commands. When a Cisco router or switch receives a CDP packet from a neighbor, an entry is made in the CDP cache table. The cache table is updated as the information received changes. The CDP cache table only holds information about directly connected neighbors. For example, in Figure 4-1, RouterA only learns about RouterB through CDP. RouterB learns about both RouterA and RouterC. RouterC only learns about RouterB.

The first command associated with CDP is the `show cdp` command. When used by itself, it shows how often CDP packets are sent out interfaces and the setting for the holdtime. In the following example, the default times are shown. Although it is possible to change these defaults, this should only be done after careful consideration of the consequences. Additionally, if the default times are changed for one device, it is usually necessary to change the times on all connected devices.

```
RouterA#show cdp
Global CDP information:
        Sending CDP packets every 60 seconds
        Sending a holdtime value of 180 seconds
```

`show cdp`, like many other commands, has optional keywords. By typing `show cdp ?`, we can see the available keywords.

```
RouterA#show cdp ?
  entry          Information for specific neighbor entry
  interface      CDP interface status and configuration
  neighbors      CDP neighbor entries
  traffic        CDP statistics
```

The first optional command we will explore is the `neighbor` keyword. This command is used more often than any of the other optional keywords. Typing `show cdp neighbor` gives us a summary of the directly connected equipment. An example is shown here:

```
RouterA#show cdp neighbor
Capability Codes: R - Router, T - Trans Bridge, B - Source Route
Bridge
                 S - Switch, H - Host, I - IGMP, r - Repeater
Device ID       Local Intrfce      Holdtme     Capability  Platform
Port ID
```

Figure 4-1
CDP neighbors

CDP Neighbors

Router A   Router B   Router C

```
RouterB             Eth 0              134           R      1602
Eth 0
RouterC             Ser 0              149           R      1602
Ser 0
```

The capability codes indicate that a number of differing types of equipment will be shown with this command. We need to remember that CDP is used on bridges, switches, and repeaters, not only routers. Cisco manages to include all of these equipment types by not relying on Network-Layer protocols. Other items shown include the following:

- The name of the remote device
- The local interface used for connections
- The current holdtimes for each connected neighbor
- The capability of the remote device
- The platform (model number) of the remote device
- The connected interface on the remote equipment

If more than one connection exists between the local and remote devices, multiple CDP entries will be shown for that remote device. This is a quick way to check how a remote device is connected, which interfaces are used for a connection, and the model number of the remote equipment. If more detail is required, add the keyword detail to a show cdp neighbor command:

```
RouterA#show cdp neighbor detail
─────────────────────
Device ID: RouterB
Entry address(es):
  IP address: 199.199.9.19
Platform: cisco 1602,  Capabilities: Router
Interface: Ethernet0,  Port ID (outgoing port): Ethernet0
Holdtime : 135 sec

Version :
Cisco Internetwork Operating System Software
IOS (tm) 1600 Software (C1600-Y-L), Version 11.2(10a)P, RELEASE
SOFTWARE (fc1)
Copyright (c) 1986-1997 by cisco Systems, Inc.
Compiled Wed 03-Dec-97 00:21 by ccai

─────────────────────
Device ID: RouterC
Entry address(es):
  IP address: 199.199.251.6
Platform: cisco 1602,  Capabilities: Router
Interface: Serial0,  Port ID (outgoing port): Serial0
Holdtime : 150 sec

Version :
Cisco Internetwork Operating System Software
```

```
IOS (tm) 1600 Software (C1600-Y-L), Version 11.2(10a)P, RELEASE
SOFTWARE (fc1)
Copyright (c) 1986-1997 by cisco Systems, Inc.
Compiled Wed 03-Dec-97 00:21 by ccai
```

Shown previously, adding the keyword `detail` has changed the display and added information. The additional information includes the following:

- The network address of the remote device
- The operating system (IOS)
- The IOS version of the remote device
- The compile date of the IOS

The network address is expressed in a format consistent with the Network-Layer protocol running on the remote device. In this instance, both neighbors are running IP as their Network-Layer protocol. Therefore, their network addresses are expressed in a TCP/IP format. If the remote device is running IPX, the network address would be expressed in the IPX format. If the remote routers are running DecNet, the network address would be expressed as a DecNet address, and so on.

The same output can be obtained through the use of the `show cdp entry` command. This command has a required keyword. This keyword can be either * or `WORD`. Using * will show all the neighbors. Substituting the name of a neighbor for `WORD` will show data for that neighbor only.

A quick way to check which interfaces have neighbors running CDP is by using the `show cdp interface` command. This will show all the interfaces on the local router that are receiving CDP packets, the link state of the interfaces, the encapsulation used for each interface, and the timings for the CDP packets and holdtime.

```
RouterA#show cdp interface
Ethernet0 is up, line protocol is up
  Encapsulation ARPA
  Sending CDP packets every 60 seconds
  Holdtime is 180 seconds
Serial0 is up, line protocol is up
  Encapsulation HDLC
  Sending CDP packets every 60 seconds
  Holdtime is 180 seconds
```

The final CDP command we will explore is the `show cdp traffic` command. This is used to check errors between CDP neighbors and the number of packets entering and leaving the device interfaces. A sample output is shown:

```
RouterA#show cdp traffic
CDP counters :
        Packets output: 22932, Input: 22675
        Hdr syntax: 0, Chksum error: 0, Encaps failed: 0
        No memory: 0, Invalid packet: 0, Fragmented: 0
```

We have looked at the uses and commands associated with CDP. A summary of the characteristics CDP follows:

- It is a proprietary protocol.

- CDP uses SNAP and the Data-Link Layer (Layer 2) of the OSI model.

- Its entries are held in a cache.

- It only knows about directly connected neighbors who are also running CDP.

- Neighbors can be any Cisco CDP-enabled device.

- The default time for sending packets is 60 seconds.

- The default holdown time is 180 seconds.

- The major CDP commands include

    - show cdp

    - show cdp neighbors

    - show cdp neighbor detail

    - show cdp entry

    - show cdp interface

    - show cdp traffic

Network Troubleshooting Commands

This section outlines the various troubleshooting commands. We'll cover the Telnet protocol, ping commands, traceroute commands, and router management.

Telnet Protocol

Telnet is a virtual terminal protocol that connects to remote hosts. The connection can be made over virtually any connection type including Serial,

Frame Relay, Ethernet, and X.25. As part of the TCP/IP protocol suite, Telnet uses source port 23 for originating connections. Cisco equipment uses a virtual terminal connection to support up to five simultaneous Telnet sessions on VTY 0 through 4.

Troubleshooting benefits can be gained due to the layers of the OSI model used by Telnet. The Telnet protocol uses Layers 2 (Data-Link) through 7 (Application). Telnet, in effect, enables the user to directly troubleshoot six of the seven layers of the OSI model with a single command. In addition, Telnet starts at the Data-Link level and will also check if the physical level is running properly. Telnet will only run successfully if all the seven layers work correctly.

NOTE: *When troubleshooting any issue, it is imperative that the troubleshooter understands the basic principles of the OSI model. In order for any layer to work properly, the layer below must first work properly. For example, assume that you are working on a problem where a connection to a remote site has died. No amount of configuration changes to static routes, IGRP routing tables, or update intervals will have any effect if a physical connection issue is causing the problem. If Layer 1 (Physical) is not working properly, changes to the Layer 3 (Network) configuration can never resolve the problem. We advise that while troubleshooting you work in a manner that ensures that the lower layers are working before attempting any changes on upper layer configurations.*

Entering the command `telnet` followed by the `host` and optionally a `port` starts a Telnet session. The host may either be the network address of a host or the name of a host if provisions have been made to translate that host name to a network address. Assuming we know the IP address we want to telnet to, we would enter the command and receive the output as follows:

```
RouterA#telnet 199.199.9.19

Trying 199.199.9.19... Open

User Access Verification

Password:

RouterB>exit
```

If we do not know the IP address of the router, but do know the name of the router and have enabled a method of resolving the host names (to be discussed shortly), we can substitute the host name for the IP address as follows:

```
RouterA#telnet RouterB

Trying 199.199.9.19... Open

User Access Verification

Password:

RouterB>exit
```

We can enable host name resolution in one of two ways. The quickest way to enable resolution for a small number of hosts is through the `ip host` command. Here is an example:

```
RouterA#config t
Enter Configuration commands, one per line. Rend with CNTL/Z.
RouterA(config)# ip host RouterB 199.199.9.19
RouterA(config)#^Z
RouterA#
```

The second way to resolve host names requires a *Domain Name System* (DNS) server. If you have a DNS server available, you can tell the router to look to this server for resolving host names. In order to do this, we need to enable domain lookup and assign a name server. The following is an example:

```
RouterA#config t
Enter Configuration commands, one per line. Rend with CNTL/Z.
RouterA(config)# ip domain-lookup
RouterA(config)# ip name-server 199.199.9.77
RouterA(config)#^Z
RouterA#
```

In the previous example, the first configuration line tells the router to use a name server. The second line specifies the address of the name server to use. A router can use a maximum of six name servers.

The advantage of using domain lookup, which is enabled by default, is that you can now enter a Telnet session simply by specifying a router name. For example, if we want to Telnet to a remote device, we would merely have to type the name of that device:

```
RouterA#RouterB

Trying 199.199.9.19... Open

User Access Verification

Password:

RouterB>exit
```

NOTE: *One disadvantage of enabling domain lookup on a router is that many incorrectly entered commands are interpreted as a request to open a Telnet session. For example, assume that we are not paying close attention and falsely assume we are in configuration mode. If we try to change something, it may be interpreted as a request to open a Telnet session. Look at this example:*

```
RouterA#eigrp
Translating "eigrp"...domain server (255.255.255.255)
%unknown command or computer name, or unable to find computer
address
RouterA#

Because we attempted to resolve the word eigrp to a host name, we
will need to wait until the resolution times out, as shown above.
This may take much longer than you are willing to wait. We can
disable domain lookup with the following:

RouterA#config t
Enter Configuration commands, one per line. Rend with CNTL/Z.
RouterA(config)# no ip domain-lookup
RouterA(config)#^Z
RouterA#
```

It is possible to switch between a remote Telnet session and the original Telnet session used to configure your router. It is also possible to have multiple Telnet sessions running at the same time. The ability to connect to several routers and switch between these sessions is an invaluable asset in the troubleshooting process. Using multiple sessions, you can make a change on a remote router and then check that the desired affects are seen on a different router. Using the key combinations of Ctrl+Shift+6 and then X enables us to suspend a session. We will use the show sessions command to see all of our active Telnet session, and then move between the sessions. In the following example, we will open up two Telnet sessions and move between them:

```
RouterA#telnet 199.199.9.19

Trying 199.199.9.19... Open

User Access Verification

Password:

RouterB>
(Here we type CNTRL+SHIFT+6, then X, which will not show on the
screen. This brings us back to the original router - RouterA)
```

```
RouterA#telnet 199.199.251.6

Trying 199.199.251.6... Open

User Access Verification

Password:

RouterC>
(Again, we type CNTRL+SHIFT+6, then X, which will not show on the
screen. This brings us back to the original router - RouterA.)

RouterA#show sessions
Conn Host          Address         Byte    Idle    Conn Name
*   1 RouterB        199.199.99.19   0       0       RouterB
*   2 RouterC        199.199.251.6   0       0       RouterC

RouterA#2 (by entering '2', we are choosing to go to connection
number 2- RouterC)
[Resuming connection to RouterC ...]
RouterC#
```

Using Ctrl+Shift+6 and then X enables us to move between all of the active Telnet session, as shown earlier. The `show sessions` command shows which sessions are available. Entering the number of the session moves us to that session.

NOTE: *A few words need to be said about the traffic generated by Telnet. It is easy to assume that Telnet sessions do not generate much traffic because you are only typing commands instead of transferring files as in FTP. However, a closer look at a Telnet session will reveal exactly how much traffic is generated.*

Every character within a Telnet session is encapsulated individually and sent to the remote host. The host then interprets the character. If the character should be shown on the screen, then the character is encapsulated and sent back to the remote user. Take a moment and look at Figure 4-2, a dump from a protocol analyzer. The only end-user data in this whole frame is the letter "m." This frame was captured as it was being echoed back to the local router.

Multiple Telnet sessions, especially those using large amounts of data, such as remotely downloading configurations, can quickly tax a connection. Do not open Telnet sessions unnecessarily on lines that have low bandwidth or are already heavily utilized.

Figure 4-2
Telnet return

```
IEEE 802.3/Ethernet DIX V2 Header
            Decode Status : -
             Frame Length : 64
      Destination Address : AA-00-04-00-FA-BA,  DECNET    00-FA-BA ( OUI = DECNET, Individu
           Source Address : AA-00-04-00-8C-C7,  DECNET    00-8C-C7 ( OUI = DECNET, Locally
             Frame Format : Ethernet DIX V2
                Ethertype : 0x800 (IP)
           Frame Checksum : Good,   Frame Check Sequence : 34 BE 11 87

IP - Internet Protocol
            Decode Status : -
                  Version : 4,  Header length : 20
          Type of Service : 0x00
                            000. .... = Routine Precedence
                            ...0 .... = Normal Delay
                            .... 0... = Normal Throughput
                            .... .0.. = Normal Reliability
                            .... ..00 = Reserved
             Total length : 41 bytes
           Identification : 1548
         Fragment Control : 0x00
                            0... .... ....  .... = Reserved
                            .0.. .... ....  .... = May Fragment
                            ..0. .... ....  .... = Last Fragment
                            ...0 0000 0000 0000 = Fragment Offset = 0 bytes
             Time to Live : 58 seconds/hops
                 Protocol : 6 (TCP)
                 Checksum : 0x4251 (Checksum Good)
           Source Address : 137.28.1.2
      Destination Address : 128.52.46.32
No IP options

TCP - Transmission Control Protocol
            Decode Status : -
              Source Port : 28264 (Unknown)
         Destination Port : 23 (Telnet)
          Sequence Number : 45416955
    Acknowledgement Number : 3654446334
              Data Offset : 0x50
                            0101 .... = Header length = 20
                    Flags : 0x18
                            ...0 .... = No Urgent pointer
                            .... 1... = Acknowledgement
                            .... .1.. = Push
                            .... ..0. = No Reset
                            .... ...0 = No Synchronize Sequence numbers
                            .... ...0 = No End of data flow from sender
                   Window : 4078
                 Checksum : 0x406A (Checksum Good)
           Urgent pointer : 0
No TCP options

Telnet - The Telnet Protocol
            Decode Status : -
              Telnet Text : m
```

NOTE: *We have looked at the uses and commands associated with Telnet. A summary of Telnet follows:*

- *Telnet enables virtual terminal sessions over a number of different connection types.*
- *Telnet is part of the TCP/IP protocol suite.*
- *Telnet uses source port 23.*
- *Five simultaneous connections to a single router can be maintained. This utilizes VTY ports 0 through 4.*
- *Host names can be specified with the ip host command.*

- *Host names can be resolved with a DNS server. This requires the following lines:*
  - *Ip domain-lookup*
  - *Ip name-server [ip-address]*
- *Multiple Telnet sessions are possible:*
  - *Use Ctrl+Shift+6 and then X to return to the original session.*
  - *Use the show sessions command to show the session.*
  - *Use the session number to go to that session.*
- *Telnet creates more traffic than is readily apparent.*

Ping Commands

Packet Internet Groper (`ping`) is a command that can be used with various protocols to check the connectivity to remote hosts. Ping is not only useful for IP, but can also be used with Apollo, AppleTalk, CLNS, DECnet, IPX, Vines, and XNS. To fully realize the potential uses of ping, we must remember not only the different protocols useable with ping, but also the two differing forms of ping. The first form, called the *user form*, is a single-line command. The second form, called *privileged* or *extended*, is a series of commands. For the remainder of this chapter, we will refer to the former as merely ping and the later as an extended ping. We will look at how ping operates before we explore the uses, tricks, and traps associated with ping.

Because ping relies upon the *Internet Control Message Protocol* (ICMP) functions of `echo-request` and `echo-reply` messages, it is necessary for us to look at how ICMP works before we delve into Cisco's implementation of ping.

ICMP   We know that we can have unreliable, connectionless deliveries of data within our network. We need a method to see if the receiving host is available before flooding the network with information sent to a host that is not available. We also must have some way in which a connecting device, such as a router, tells the sending device that the receiving host is not available. Generally speaking, routers use the ICMP services to report that a destination is unreachable, while hosts use the ICMP services to check if the destination is reachable. In other words, routers tell and hosts ask about the availability of destinations.

The purpose of ICMP is to report a delivery error back to the original source of the ICMP request. Figure 4-3 shows a hypothetical network with three routers, A, B, and C. Assume that we are sending an ICMP packet

Figure 4-3
ICMP flow

ICMP Routes

Router A   Router B   Router C

from router A to router C. If router B is not able to connect to router C, an ICMP message is sent back to router A.

ICMP does not know or care what route has been taken, except when the record route option is used. Reporting the error back only to the originator makes sense in an internetworking environment. Routers are autonomous devices. Router A usually has no control over Router B. The most that ICMP can and should do is to tell Router A that Router B does not know how to forward the packet. Now that we know what ICMP is trying to accomplish, we will look at how it goes about reaching its goal.

ICMP messages are encapsulated within IP packets. Usually, only higher level protocols are encapsulated within another protocol. However, ICMP is an integral part of the IP protocol suite but is still encapsulated within an IP packet. With one exception, ICMP packets are treated like all other IP packets. This exception occurs when an error is detected on sending or receiving an ICMP packet. Because an ICMP message is used to report errors, we should not report errors on the ICMP messages themselves. Assume that we have a serious issue with connectivity where every other packet has an error. If we needed to send out messages that the ICMP messages are not flowing, we would quickly flood the network with ICMP notifications that ICMP is not working properly. Therefore, the IP specifications for ICMP state that ICMP error messages are not generated for errors caused by ICMP messages.

Now that we have reviewed how the ICMP messages work, we are ready to continue with the uses, tricks, and traps associated with ping.

Ping   Ping is an extremely useful tool for testing connectivity. However, several cautions should be considered before relying on the ping command to decisively tell us if a remote host is available. We will look at several items that can affect the capability of ping to accurately judge host availability before looking at the syntax of both ping and extended ping.

A host or router sends the ICMP echo-request to a remote host or router for the purpose of establishing if the remote is reachable. The last router that is unable to forward the packet or the destination host sends back an

Table 4-1

The Ping or
Traceroute
command
responses received
by a Cisco router

Ping or Traceroute Response	Meaning
U	Unreachable (unreachable port for traceroute, unreachable destination for ping)
P	Protocol unreachable (traceroute)
?	Packet type unknown (ping)
C	Congested connection (Used in FECN and BECN) (ping)
|	Interrupted ping
&	Time-to-Live (TTL) exceeded (ping)
.	Time out
!	Success
!H	Administratively prohibited (usually an access list issue)
N	Network unreachable (traceroute)

echo-reply. Remember that this ICMP message is imbedded within the data portion of an IP packet, which is in turn encapsulated within another protocol such as Ethernet. Table 4-1 lists the responses a Cisco router may receive through the use of either ping or traceroute commands.

If sufficient resources and time enable you to reply to the ping, the host will reply. If not enough resources or time exist, the ping request gets put into the queue and will be answered when there is time. When the host finally gets a chance to reply to the ping, it may be too late. In the same way that a phone will eventually stop ringing if it is not answered, a ping may have timed out by the time a response is sent. If ping does not receive a response within the time specified (two seconds by default), ping will act as if it had received an ICMP time-exceeded message. Timing out does not necessarily mean that the host is not available. It may merely mean that the host is too busy to answer within the time allowed. Because the default time in which a reply is expected from a ping is only two seconds, it is likely that during periods of high congestion hosts may appear to lose connectivity if ping is the only test used for connectivity.

A ping may not work when IP connectivity is available for a number of reasons. One of the most common reasons is access lists. Assume that you have the following lines in an access list that is activated on the inbound serial port of your router:

```
Deny icmp any any echo-reply
Permit icmp any any echo-request
```

Here the echo-request will be sent out, but no replies will be let in. The pings will eventually time out. Hosts on other networks will be able to ping your hosts, but your hosts will never be able to successfully ping a host across this interface. Knowing exactly what your access lists do and do not permit is critical to knowing whether a ping should or should not succeed to a given host.

One other caution should be given about ping. By default, the user form of ping sets the TTL to 32. Each router the ping encounters decrements this by one. If the TTL becomes zero, the last router will send back an ICMP time-exceeded message. If you have extremely long paths, this may be insufficient. On a very large network, it may be necessary to use the extended ping to check connectivity. Now that we have discussed some of the more common assumptions made while using ping, we are ready to look at how to use the ping command in the user form.

User Ping   The user form of ping is actually quite a simple global command. The form is

```
Router#ping [protocol] {host | address}
```

Using this form, we can ping by typing

```
Router#ping 172.30.1.1
```

Our Cisco router will assume we mean to use the IP protocol and sends five ICMP echo-request packets to the remote host at IP address 172.30.1.1. Instead of using an IP address, the name of a device can be used if the router is able to resolve that name to an IP address. Or, if we want to check an AppleTalk host, we would use "apple" instead of the implied "ip" and use a valid AppleTalk address, such as

```
Router#ping apple 12.164
```

Similarly, we can use any other protocol that ping supports, including Apollo, AppleTalk, CLNS, DECnet, IPX, Vines, and XNS. In each case, the host address must be in the proper format, as specified by the protocol. We can also use a host name instead of an address as long as name resolution for the protocol chosen has been enabled.

Let's spend a few minutes looking at the outputs we get from a ping. Here we show a typical ping to an IP host:

```
Router#ping 172.31.118.1
Type escape sequence to abort.
Sending 5, 100-byte ICMP Echos to 172.31.118.1, timeout is 2
seconds:
.!!!!
Success rate is 80 percent (4/5), round-trip min/avg/max = 48/49/52 ms
```

Notice that five packets were sent out. However, we received a timeout on the first packet, while all the other packets only took 49 milliseconds on average to get a response. This is not necessarily a problem. As a matter of fact, this is very common. The reason the first packet timed out is easy to explain. Ethernet works on Layer 2 of the OSI model. IP and ICMP are working at Layer 3. We have to convert the Layer 3 address to a Layer 2 address before we can talk to the remote host. This will take time. The default timeout for ping is only two seconds. We did not resolve the IP address to a MAC address fast enough to prevent the first packet from timing out. Subsequent packets did not need to resolve the MAC address because it was already held in the ARP table. If we try the very same ping immediately after the first ping, we should not see the first packet timeout because the ARP cache still holds the MAC address of the remote host.

Here is an example of the same command executed immediately after the first ping:

```
Router#ping 172.31.118.1

Type escape sequence to abort.
Sending 5, 100-byte ICMP Echos to 172.31.118.1, timeout is 2
seconds:
!!!!!
Success rate is 100 percent (5/5), round-trip min/avg/max =
48/50/55 ms
```

Notice that this time all of the packets were received. Circumstances will occur where several packets might not be received. One that immediately comes to mind is an ISDN connection. If the ISDN link happens to be down when the ping is sent, all five packets may timeout before the connection becomes established. The connection may also be made by modem, which may take 30 seconds or longer to connect. This means that it may take numerous attempts before any are successful. Additionally, if a dial connection is not up at the time the ping is initiated and a ping has not been specified as "interesting traffic," the ping command will not activate the line. In this case, you can either change the definition of interesting traffic or you can bring the line up by another means before trying a ping.

Now that we have looked at the user form of ping, we are ready to move toward a more sophisticated form of ping, the extended ping.

Extended Ping   Extended ping differs from user ping in three ways. The first difference is that we need to be in enabled mode to use extended ping. The second difference is that extended ping is only supported by IP, AppleTalk, and IPX. There is no support for extended ping while using Apollo, CLNS, DECnet, Vines, or XNS. The third and most important difference is that extended ping enables us to change the defaults that ping uses. Changing these defaults gives us the ability to run a number of different tests with the same utility. Before we go into how extended ping can be more useful than user ping, we will walk through an extended ping. An extended ping is started by typing `ping` while in enabled mode and then hitting return. You will then be prompted for variables by the ping utility.

```
Router#ping
Protocol [ip]:
Target IP address: 172.30.1.1
Repeat count [5]:
Datagram size [100]:
Timeout in seconds [2]:
Extended commands [n]: y
Source address or interface: 172.30.1.3
Type of service [0]:
Set DF bit in IP header? [no]:
Validate reply data? [no]:
Data pattern [0xABCD]:
Loose, Strict, Record, Timestamp, Verbose[none]:
Sweep range of sizes [n]:
Type escape sequence to abort.
Sending 5, 100-byte ICMP Echos to 172.30.1.1, timeout is 2 seconds:
!!!!!
Success rate is 100 percent (5/5), round-trip min/avg/max = 1/2/4 ms
```

Notice in the previous output what parameters are available to us. First, we are asked which protocol to use. Pressing the return key chooses the default, which is IP. The next item is the target IP address. If we had chosen AppleTalk as our protocol, we would have been prompted for the target AppleTalk address. The same holds true for IPX.

The next parameter is the repeat count. We can set this to any reasonable integer. If we are experiencing an intermittent loss of connection, setting this value high will allow ping to keep running long enough for you to see when the connectivity is lost. This may also allow you to continuously run a ping, while on another host you run an application that appears to be losing connectivity. If both the application and ping lose connectivity at the same time, it is usually safe to assume that there is a problem with connectivity. However, if the application loses connectivity while ping does not, this would indicate a problem within the application.

The datagram size can also be changed from the default of 100 bytes. This is useful for checking the state of a connection under larger loads. Many times, a ping with the default size of 100 bytes will not reveal any anomalies in your network. However, when you raise the packet size to 500 bytes, you may see a significant loss of connectivity or a significant change in the response time. During your baseline analysis of your network, you should document the throughput speeds of large-, medium-, and small-sized pings. This will help paint an accurate picture of how your network performs under differing loads.

The next parameter we can adjust is the timeout parameter. If we have made the datagram size larger than the default, we will probably want to also change the timeout parameter because larger packets take longer to send and receive. Setting the timeout too low will result in what looks like either an intermittent loss of connectivity or a total loss of connection. In reality, it may merely be that the packets are arriving after the ping has timed out. If you are experiencing what looks like an intermittent or total loss of connectivity, double the timeout and see how the results change:

```
Router#ping
Protocol [ip]:
Target IP address: 172.30.1.1
Repeat count [5]:
Datagram size [100]: 18024
Timeout in seconds [2]: 4
Extended commands [n]: y
Source address or interface: 172.30.1.3
Type of service [0]:
Set DF bit in IP header? [no]:
Validate reply data? [no]:
Data pattern [0xABCD]:
Loose, Strict, Record, Timestamp, Verbose[none]:
Sweep range of sizes [n]:
Type escape sequence to abort.
Sending 5, 18024-byte ICMP Echos to 172.30.1.1, timeout is 4
seconds:
!!!!!
Success rate is 100 percent (5/5), round-trip min/avg/max =
40/40/40 ms
```

Extended ping also enables you to enter variables that are not available with the user form of ping, hence the term "extended ping." These can be used for a number of differing reasons. The most interesting of these variables for our purpose is the source address variable.

It is possible to set the source address of a ping to be a different interface than the interface over which you Telnet into the router. By default, if you Telnet into a router on the Ethernet interface, your pings will have a source address of that Ethernet interface. Sometimes it is useful to use a different interface than the one you have chosen for Telnet. For example, you may have access lists set so that only one of your Ethernet interfaces has access to a given network and that you cannot Telnet to that interface. You can still test connectivity by answering "Y" to the extended command's prompt. This will cause the router to ask for the source interface address. Putting in the address of the previously unavailable interface will cause the ping to travel out of that interface. This way you can test connectivity without changing the very access list that may be the cause of your problems.

Windows Ping   Within Microsoft Windows 95/98 and Windows NT, ping and traceroute work very similarly to how a router operates. A few differences and similarities are worth mentioning.

The first difference is how they check the current the current IP configuration. On a Windows 95 system running the `winipcfg.exe` program may check the IP configuration. On a Windows NT system, the equivalent command is `ipconfig.exe`. The second difference is that traceroute and ping enable options to be entered on the command line instead of interactively.

Although the output from a ping in the Windows environment is different than a router, the basic information received is the same. The following is a sample ping from a Windows 95 host:

```
C:\>ping 172.30.100.1

Pinging 172.30.100.1 with 32 bytes of data:
Reply from 172.30.100.1: bytes=32 time=242ms TTL=252
Reply from 172.30.100.1: bytes=32 time=239ms TTL=252
Reply from 172.30.100.1: bytes=32 time=239ms TTL=252
Reply from 172.30.100.1: bytes=32 time=239ms TTL=252
```

In both Windows systems and routers, there is a definite methodology to using ping when you cannot reach the end destination. Following this order will enable you to quickly find where the problem resides. The following is the recommended order of troubleshooting using the ping command:

1. Look at the current IP configuration using `winipcfg`, `ipconfig`, or `show run`. Ensure that the IP address, subnet mask, and default gateway are all correct.

2. Ping 127.0.0.1. This tests the network interface on the equipment. If this does not produce a reply, the issue is almost certainly that your IP protocols are not correctly installed. In a Windows system, this is indicative of an issue within the IP stack.

3. Ping the default gateway. If there is a reply, the issue is probably related to the default gateway, either in the routing tables or in the connections through the WAN.

4. Ping another host on the local subnet. If a response is received, this confirms the issue is with the default gateway. If no response is received, continue to the next step.

5. Move to another workstation and try to ping through the default gateway. If this station works, the issue is on the original station. If it does not work, the issue is with the default gateway.

Following this methodology when a ping to a remote host is not successful will help you locate the origination point of the problems at least 95 percent of the time.

Now that we have seen what ping can do as well as some common traps within ping, we will look at the traceroute command that not only gives the same information as ping, but also shows the route a packet follows.

Traceroute Commands

Traceroute, like ping, is used to test connectivity. You can use traceroute instead of user ping in almost every circumstance. The disadvantage of doing this is that a traceroute takes significantly longer to process than a ping. The reason for the longer response times is that traceroute works differently and gives you additional information. Traceroute, like ping, also has an extended mode.

Ping and traceroute are both based on ICMP messages. Although they use the same underlying principles, the data received and the actual mechanisms used differ. Ping sends an ICMP echo-request with the TTL set to 32. Traceroute starts by sending three ICMP echo-request messages with the TTL set to 1. This causes the first router that processes these packets to send back ICMP time-exceeded messages. Traceroute looks into the ICMP time-exceed message and displays the router that sent the messages on the console. Then, traceroute sends another set of echo-request messages, this time with the TTL increased by one more than the last TTL. The request passes through the first router to the second router. Since both routers decrement the TTL, the second router sends back a set of time-exceeded messages. The second router's information is shown on the console. This process continues until the remote host responds, or it is determined that the path cannot be found. By the time the remote host responds, traceroute will have displayed the complete path with the time between each router. If the remote host does not respond, we are still told the path the messages took in an attempt to reach the host. This is the real value of traceroute.

A typical traceroute will look similar to the following traceroute.

```
Router#traceroute 172.28.237.1

Type escape sequence to abort.
Tracing the route to 172.28.237.1

  1 172.30.100.2 0 msec 0 msec 4 msec
  2 172.31.252.13 92 msec 92 msec 92 msec
  3 172.31.252.6 100 msec 100 msec 100 msec
  4 172.28.233.53 140 msec 140 msec  140 msec
```

Because we have no indication through traceroute of which interface sends out the packet, we need to know where we expect to send packets. Figure 4-4 shows the interfaces that will respond to a traceroute. Notice that the first interface encountered is the one that replies to the traceroute.

Extended Traceroute   Traceroute, like ping, also has an extended mode. Many of the extended mode options of ping are available with the extended traceroute. In the following extended traceroute, a few items require a little explanation. First, settings exist for both the minimum and maximum

Figure 4-4
Traceroute flow

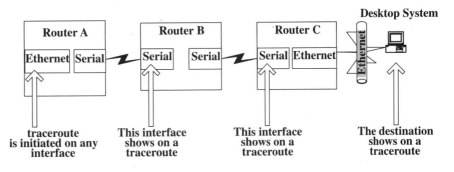

INTERFACES
RESPONDING
TO A
TRACEROUTE

TTL. Traceroute will not accept an echo-reply that occurs before the minimum TTL. In the following example, we have increased the maximum TTL to 60 seconds. Second, we can also adjust the number of echo-requests sent from the default of three. In the example, we have raised this value to five. Third, the port number is definable. By default, traceroute sends the echo-request to an arbitrary port number. We are allowed to change this number in case only certain ports are allowed to receive traffic, such as in an access list.

```
Router#traceroute
Protocol [ip]:
Target IP address: 172.28.237.1
Source address: 172.30.100.1
Numeric display [n]: y
Timeout in seconds [3]: 3
Probe count [3]: 5
Minimum Time to Live [1]:
Maximum Time to Live [30]: 60
Port Number [33434]:
Loose, Strict, Record, Timestamp, Verbose[none]:
Type escape sequence to abort.
Tracing the route to 172.28.237.1

  1 172.30.100.2 4 msec 4 msec 4 msec 0 msec 4 msec
  2 172.31.252.13 88 msec 92 msec 92 msec 88 msec 92 msec
  3 172.31.252.6 104 msec 100 msec 100 msec 100 msec 104 msec
  4 172.28.233.53 136 msec 180 msec 140 msec 150 msec 136 msec
```

Another potential issue that is easily solved with a traceroute is a circular route. A circular route occurs when Router A thinks that Router B knows the path to a destination at the same time that Router B thinks Router A knows the destination. Using a ping command will merely result in receiving time-exceeded errors, while with traceroute, the issue is almost instantly detectable. Looking at the following traceroute, notice where the packets travel:

```
Router#traceroute 172.28.12.1

Type escape sequence to abort.
Tracing the route to 172.28.12.1

  1 172.30.1.1 4 msec 0 msec 4 msec
  2 172.30.1.3 4 msec 0 msec 4 msec
  3 172.30.1.1 4 msec 0 msec 4 msec
  4 172.30.1.3 4 msec 0 msec 4 msec
```

The packets travel from one router to the second and then back to the first. Any time that a traceroute shows the same interface two or more times, you have a routing loop. Sometimes the loop will not become apparent until the packets have traveled through several different routers. Static routes improperly used or redistributed generally cause this and therefore should be one of the first things that are checked when encountering this problem.

Windows Tracert   A Windows system will produce similar output on a tracert command. The following is a sample from a Windows 95 machine:

```
C:\>traceroute 172.30.100.1
Tracing route to 172.30.100.1 over a maximum of 30 hops
  1    164 ms    164 ms    166 ms   172.30.2.200
  2    159 ms    156 ms    152 ms   172.30.1.3
  3    239 ms    250 ms    247 ms   172.31.252.14
  4    245 ms    247 ms    254 ms   172.30.100.1
Trace complete.
```

We have looked at the uses and options associated with ping and traceroute. Here is a summary of them:

- Ping and traceroute rely on ICMP echo-request and echo-reply messages.

  - Ping sends a series of five echo-requests.
  - Traceroute starts by sending three echo-requests with the TTL set to one. The TTL is increased by one every time a router is traversed.

- Ping will tell you if a connection is good.
- Traceroute will tell you where a connection dies.
- Both ping and traceroute have extended modes. Extended mode enables you to change the default timings, size, and so on.

Router Management

Routers have four different types of memory, each one with a different purpose. We'll briefly outline them before we explore how each type is used during the startup process. The four types of memory within a router are as follows:

- *ROM*   This stores the *Power On Self Test* (POST) program, bootstrap program, and operating system.
- *Flash*   A reprogrammable and erasable ROM containing the operating system image and microcode.

- *RAM* This holds the running operating system, buffers, caches, and routing tables.
- *NVRAM* *Non-Volatile RAM* (NVRAM) storing the startup configuration.

Startup Sequence

The startup sequence starts with the POST. During the POST, the hardware is checked for issues that would prevent proper operation. The CPU, memory, and interfaces are checked for integrity. If a hardware condition situation that makes the router unusable is detected, the startup sequence is ended. The final portion of the POST loads and executes the bootstrap program.

The bootstrap program, residing and executing within the ROM, searches for a valid IOS. Flash memory is the default location for the IOS. Other valid locations include a TFTP server or ROM. A TFTP server, also called a *network load*, is the second most common load source. ROM is the least often used because the ROM chips usually contain the oldest of all versions of the IOS. The source of the IOS is determined by configuration register settings.

After a valid IOS is located and loaded into lower memory, a search is made for a configuration file. The configuration file may be located in NVRAM or on a TFTP server. If no configuration file is located, the console will prompt the user to start configuring the router through the System Configuration dialog box, also known as the Setup dialog box.

Where a router finds the configuration file and IOS image depends on the configuration register settings. To view the current settings, use a show version command:

```
RouterA#show version
Cisco Internetwork Operating System Software
IOS (tm) 1600 Software (C1600-Y-L), Version 11.2(10a)P, RELEASE
SOFTWARE (fc1)
Copyright (c) 1986-1997 by cisco Systems, Inc.
Compiled Wed 03-Dec-97 00:21 by ccai
Image text-base: 0x0801BFA8, data-base: 0x02005000

ROM: System Bootstrap, Version 11.1(10)AA, EARLY DEPLOYMENT RELEASE
SOFTWARE (f)
ROM: 1600 Software (C1600-BOOT-R), Version 11.1(10)AA, EARLY
DEPLOYMENT RELEASE

Router uptime is 8 hours, 35 minutes
System restarted by power-on
```

```
System image file is "flash:c1600-y-1.112-10a.P", booted via flash

cisco 1602 (68360) processor (revision C) with 1536K/512K bytes of
memory.
Processor board ID 07082664, with hardware revision 00000000
Bridging software.
X.25 software, Version 2.0, NET2, BFE and GOSIP compliant.
1 Ethernet/IEEE 802.3 interface(s)
1 Serial network interface(s)
On-board Switched 56K Line Interface.
System/IO memory with parity disabled
2048K bytes of DRAM onboard
System running from FLASH
8K bytes of non-volatile configuration memory.
4096K bytes of processor board PCMCIA flash (Read ONLY)

Configuration register is 0x2102
```

The last line in a show version output displays the current configuration register settings. In this example, the setting is 0x2102. Use the config-register command from the enabled mode to change the settings. This changes how the router acts the next time it boots. There is no need to save the configuration after changing the register settings.

The most common reason for wanting to change the configuration register is during the password recovery process. At the end of this chapter is an exercise for recovering a password. Working through this exercise when it is not an emergency will help when you really need to recover a password quickly.

As shown in the output from a show version command, the flash can hold a copy of the IOS. You will occasionally be required to upgrade the flash with new images. The second exercise at the end of this chapter will walk you through how to upgrade a flash memory.

Unless you have a specific reason for upgrading your IOS, there is no advantage in using the latest version available. Using a version that has been tested by other users for the last six months or a year helps you avoid becoming a "beta site" for the newest versions available.

Caution should also be used to avoid lagging too far behind in upgrading your IOS. Most, if not all, new versions of IOS improve performance and stability. It is also easier to debug a problem on a current version of the IOS. The *technical assistance center* (TAC) personnel are usually very adept on both the latest and the previous versions. If you call the TAC with an old version of the IOS installed, one of the first things they may request is that you upgrade to a newer version. For these reasons, we suggest sticking to a newer yet tested version of the IOS on your routers.

Boot Command

We can change the default place a router looks for the IOS and the startup configuration file with the boot command, as we will soon see. In the following example, we will show the options available with the boot command. It is important to note that the default location of the startup configuration file as well as the IOS file can be set using the boot command. Storing the IOS and startup configuration files on a server allows these files to be backed up with all of the other corporate data. Since routers are seldom booted, few real traffic bandwidth penalties are related to this technique.

```
RouterA(config)#boot ?
bootstrap       Bootstrap Image file
buffersize      Specify the buffer size for netbooting a config file
host    Router-specific config file
network Network-wide config file
system  System image file
```

Under the bootstrap option, we have several other options:

```
RouterA(config)#boot system
WORD    System image filename
flash   Boot from flash memory
mop     Boot from a Decnet MOP server
rcp     Boot from a server via rcp
rom     Boot from rom
TFTP    Boot from a TFTP server
```

We can also set the order in which the router will search for IOS files. For example, assume we want the router to look for IOS images in the following order: TFTP server, flash, then rom. Using the boot command, we will tell the router the order in which to search for valid IOS files multiple times. In the following example, we tell the router to first look on the TFTP server at IP address 10.1.1.1 for a file called c1600-y-1.112-10a.P. If that file is not found, look on the flash memory for the file called c1600-y-1.112-10a.P. If the flash does not contain this file, then boot from ROM. Because ROM is considered a last resort and can only hold a single file, no filename is required.

```
RouterA(config)#boot system TFTP c1600-y-1.112-10a.P 10.1.1.1
RouterA(config)#boot system flash c1600-y-1.112-10a.P
RouterA(config)#boot system rom
```

NOTE: *Cisco IOS filenames tend to be long and complicated. This is because the filename contains the model number, the major and minor releases of the IOS, and the IOS feature set.*

It may be tempting to shorten the name of the IOS when saving to a server. However, we strongly urge you to keep the default name. Changing the name to anything other than the official Cisco name will tend to cause problems while obtaining support from Cisco.

Running and Startup Configurations

It is important to know the difference between the current (running-config) configuration and the configuration run when the router first starts (startup-config). A few rules must be remembered when working with these configurations:

- The running configuration is stored in RAM. This information is lost every time the router is rebooted.
- The startup configuration is stored in NVRAM by default. It is copied into the running configuration when the router boots.
- The configurations have no relation to each other unless you tell them that they are related.
- The startup configuration is run every time the router is rebooted either by applying power or through use of the `reload` command.
- The running configuration includes all of the commands within the startup configuration plus all of the changes made to the router since the last reboot.
- Copying from the running configuration to the startup configuration will overwrite the startup configuration.
- Copying from the startup configuration to the running configuration will combine the two configurations, overwriting lines already present and adding those lines that are not present.

You can see the current running configuration with the `show running-config` command. The startup configuration can be seen with the `show startup-config` command. Try both of these commands and see if any difference exists between the two outputs. If there is no difference, change the IP address of an interface and then do both commands again. The startup configuration should show the old IP address while the running configuration will show the changes you just made. Now reboot the router. Once the router is rebooted, do a `show running-config` command. We have reloaded from the NVRAM back into the RAM that was erased during the boot process. To make the changes permanent, issue the following command:

```
RouterA#copy running-config startup-config
```

The `copy` command has two arguments as shown earlier, `source` and `destination`. In the example, we were copying from the running configuration to the startup configuration. We can also choose other sources and destinations, as we will see in a little while. This will take a few seconds. The NVRAM (startup-config) now has the same configuration as the RAM (running-config). Try this mini-lab:

1. Start up the router.

2. Connect to the router.

3. Enter configuration mode with the `config-t` command and move to Ethernet interface E0 with the `int e0` command. Add a helper address with `ip helper-address 10.1.1.1`.

4. Change the IP address of the interface with `ip address 10.3.3.3`.

5. Save the configuration to the NVRAM with the `copy running-config startup-config` command.

6. Issue the `show running-config` and `show startup-config` commands to verify that the helper address and the IP address are the same in both configurations.

7. Enter configuration mode with the `config-t` command and move to the same Ethernet interface with an `int e0` command.

8. Change the IP address with an `ip address 10.4.4.4` command.

9. Remove the old helper address with the `no ip helper-address 10.1.1.1` command.

10. Add a different helper address with an `ip helper-address 10.2.2.2` command.

11. Issue the `show running-config` and `show startup-config` commands to verify that the running configuration has a different helper address and IP address than the startup configuration.

12. Copy from the startup configuration to the running configuration with a `copy startup-config running-config` command.

13. Issue a `show running-config` command.

At this point, you should see two helper addresses in the running configuration. You should also see only one IP address on the interface, set to 10.3.3.3. Steps 1 through 4 set up our scenario. Steps 7 through 10 made sure that our running configuration was different than the startup configuration. When we copied from the startup configuration in step 12, those lines that are unique (such as the IP address) were overwritten. The lines that are not unique, such as the helper addresses, were added to the running configuration. When copying from a saved configuration, unique lines are overwritten and non-unique lines are added. When saving to a configuration file, all lines are overwritten. Next we will explore other places to load and store configurations.

We have another place from where we can run and load configurations. A TFTP server can also be used if available. The TFTP server must be accessible through TCP/IP and the user must have the rights to either save or read files on that server. Normally, a ping is run to the TFTP server before attempting to save or load a file in order to check connectivity.

In the following example, we will copy from the running configuration to a TFTP server:

```
RouterA#copy running-config tftp
Remote host[]? 10.1.1.1
Name of configuration file to write [routera-confg]? <ENTER>
Write file routera-confg on host 10.1.1.1?
[confirm] <ENTER>
Building configuration...
OK
```

Notice that the router did two things to the name of the configuration file. First, the router added "-confg" to the end of the router name. Second, the name of the file was made lower case. In order to load from a TFTP server to a running configuration, simply reverse the `source` and `destination` arguments, as in `copy tftp running-config`.

As shown earlier, we can boot a router's IOS from a TFTP server. We can also copy from a TFTP server to flash memory or from flash memory to a TFTP server. The syntax for the copy command does not change. The *source* and *destination* merely change. To copy the IOS from a TFTP server to flash memory, our syntax would be

```
RouterA#copy TFTP flash
```

To copy from flash memory to a TFTP server, our command looks like this:

```
RouterA#copy flash TFTP
```

In both cases, we will be prompted for the IP address of the TFTP server and the filename for the IOS image. While we are copying to the flash, we will be presented with the option to erase the current IOS on the flash. If we have room on the flash (not usual), we can answer "no" to the prompt and then have two IOS files on the flash. In this case, we need to run the `boot system flash` command with the appropriate file name.

Here is a summary of the management aspects of routers and the locations of the IOS and configuration files:

- The default startup sequence is

  - POST
  - Bootstrap
  - IOS
  - Configuration

- The default IOS locations and order are

  - Flash
  - ROM

- You can store both the IOS and configuration files on the router or on a network server.
- `COPY` moves from `source` to `destination`.

Chapter Summary

This chapter has looked at the *Cisco Discovery Protocol* (CDP) and its usefulness. We have discussed the troubleshooting tools of Telnet, ping, and traceroute in routers and within a Windows system. Finally, we looked at the boot process and the location and manipulation of files. Take your time and work on the exercises before moving on to the next chapter.

From the Real World

Whenever I am hiring a new network engineer, the first technical question I ask them is about a problem they would know little about. For example, if I know the person is a *Cisco Certified Network Associate* (CCNA), I will usually ask them a complex question about the *Border Gateway Protocol* (BGP) or *Open Shortest Path First* (OSPF). If they successfully answer this question, I will keep asking about more and more obscure subjects until I am sure they do not have a clue. I am not trying to be cruel. My purpose here is threefold.

First, I want to see how well the person works under pressure. The daily routine of a network engineer is filled with hard questions and emergencies. It is imperative that the engineer remain calm when situations go poorly.

Equally important is finding out if the engineer is willing to admit when they are in trouble. The real world is not like a test. If you do not know how to do something, guessing will generally only cause problems. Knowing when to yell for help is a valuable trait. Admitting you do not know is better than trying to fake an answer.

The final reason I ask these types of questions is to see how the applicant will approach a problem. The way a problem is analyzed shows a lot more about a person's ability to work in the real world than any resume, job description, or certification can tell. I always treat a solid approach to a problem as if it were a correct answer.

So, what do you do if you are unfortunate enough to have someone like me as your interviewer? The first thing to remember is that no one person can possibly know all the answers. A single incorrect answer should never preclude you from getting a job. If it does, you probably do not want to work there. Stay calm. Be honest. Tell the interviewer that you do not have any experience with that subject. Then, in the same breath, tell the interviewer how you approach the problem based on the limited knowledge you do posses.

Although all hiring managers ideally want someone needing no training, the second choice is almost always the person who can analyze a problem. I have received calls from hiring managers regarding applicants they knew that were bright but did not have the specific skills required for the immediate opening. They routinely ask if there is an opening where I work that the applicant can fill. I am always interested in talking to someone who knows how to approach a problem.

Mark J. Newcomb

Frequently Asked Questions (FAQ)

Question: Why is ROM the last place the router will look for an IOS image?

Answer: The ROM can only be upgraded by replacing the chips on the motherboard. This is usually only done when the router is in a shop for other reasons. The ROM is the least likely place to have the latest version of the IOS.

Question: Earlier in the chapter, it stated that more than one connection between devices would cause CDP to show a neighbor more than once. Why would you ever want more than one connection between two devices?

Answer: Although there is usually only one connection between devices, it is sometimes possible and preferable to have more than one connection. The first situation where this commonly occurs is with bandwidth-on-demand dial-up routing. The second area this could occur is with EtherChannel connections. EtherChannel is a Cisco proprietary protocol that enables multiple Ethernet ports to act as a single Ethernet port, providing additional bandwidth and redundancy. CDP still sees every port as an individual port and therefore reports each port individually.

Question: Which is better for testing connectivity, ping or traceroute?

Answer: Both are equally useful in their own way. To simply test if a connection exists, ping is the quicker. To test where a connection fails, traceroute is more useful.

Question: How long should it take to receive a response from a ping?

Answer: That depends on many factors. How the links are that the ping must travel over is probably the greatest factor. Any individual slow link between the source and destination will cause the response times to drop.

Case Study #1

For this practical exercise, you will recover the password on a router.
Required Equipment: One Cisco router

1. Connect your router to a console cable and then connect the cable to a PC running a terminal program.

2. Apply power to the router.

3. Within the first 60 seconds of the boot process, press the BREAK key.

4. You will come to a > prompt.

5. Type `e/s 2000002` and then `<ENTER>`. Note that some systems may not respond to the `e/s` command. In this case, enter `o`. Which is accepted depends on the model number.

6. This will show the configuration register settings. Write them down. This is a critical step.

7. Use the O/R command to change bit 6 to ignore the NVRAM at startup. In other words, you should enter `o/r 0x**4*`, where * is the original value shown through the `e/s` or `o` command. So, if you received an output of `0x2102` from Step 6, you should enter `0x2142`.

8. At the > prompt, type `I` and then `<ENTER>`.

9. Answer "No" to all of the setup questions.

10. Enter privileged mode with the `enable` command.

11. Load NVRAM into memory with a `configure memory` command.

12. Restore the configuration register to the received in Step 6 with the following:

```
Config Term
Config-register 0x****
```

Note: * is the value received in Step 6. So, if you received an output of `0x2102` from Step 6, you should enter `0x2102`. This sets the register back to its original value. Press CTRL1Z to exit configuration mode.

13. Load the startup configuration into the running configuration with a `copy startup-config running-config` command.

14. Go back into configuration mode with `config term`.

15. Change the password with

```
Line console 0
Login
Password newpassword
CTRL-Z
```

*Note: newpassword is the new password you want to assign to the router.

16. Save the new configuration with a copy running-config startup-config command.

17. Log off the router

18. Reboot the router.

19. Log on using the new password.

Case Study # 2

For this practical exercise, you will save the IOS to a TFTP server and then copy the IOS back to the flash card within your router.

Required Equipment: One Cisco router connected to a LAN and a TFTP server on the same LAN

1. Connect your router to a console cable and then connect the cable to a PC running a terminal program.

2. Apply power to the router.

3. Ensure that the TFTP server will accept file transfers.

4. Log onto the router.

5. Enter enable mode.

6. Issue a `show flash` command.

7. Write down the name of the IOS file exactly as it appears. Make notes regarding the upper- and lowercase letters. Keep this in a safe place. This is a critical step.

8. Issue a `copy flash tftp` command.

9. You will be asked the IP address of your TFTP server. Enter the IP address.

10. You will be asked the source file name. Enter the name exactly as you wrote it down in Step 7.

11. You will be asked for the destination file name. Enter `icndtest`. If you had simply pressed <ENTER> at this point, the destination file name would default to the same as the source file name.

12. You will see a number of exclamation points appear onscreen. These (like ping) indicate a successful transfer of data. An `O` indicates a lost packet. Unless you receive numerous `O`s, do not worry about some lost packets. They will be retransmitted.

13. Wait until this portion is completed. This may take up to one hour. Get some coffee.

14. When you see `upload to server done`, you have successfully loaded the IOS to the server.

15. Check that the server contains the file `icndtest`.

16. If the server contains this file, go to Step 17. If not, go back to Step 1.

17. We are now ready to copy from the server to the router.

18. Issue a `copy tftp flash` command. This will start the process of moving the file from the TFTP server to the router flash.

19. You receive a warning about loosing connectivity and are asked to confirm. Press <ENTER>.

20. You are prompted to enter the IP address of your TFTP server. Enter the IP address.

21. You are asked to enter the source file name. Enter `icndtest` and then press <ENTER>.

22. You will be asked the destination file name. Enter the name you wrote down in Step 7. Enter the exact file name, including upper- and lowercase letters.

23. The router will check the availability of the file.

24. You will be asked if you want to confirm the erase of the flash memory. Press <ENTER>, indicating to erase the flash.

25. The flash will be erased.

26. You will see a number of `!`s appear onscreen. These (like ping) indicate a successful transfer of data. An `O` indicates a lost packet. Unless you receive numerous `O`s, do not worry about some lost packets. They will be retransmitted.

27. Wait until this portion is completed. This may take up to one hour. Get some more coffee.

28. The router will reboot after the IOS is downloaded.

Questions

1. Which command is used to show the name of the image stored in the flash?

   a. show files
   b. show nvram
   c. show flash
   d. show files:nvram

2. When a host initiates a ping, how many ICMP echo replies are sent?

   a. 5
   b. 10
   c. 7
   d. none

3. Name two advantages of extended ping over user ping.

   a. The number of packets cannot be increased.
   b. The time-out period can be increased.
   c. The sending interface can be changed.
   d. No echo-requests are sent.

4. Which command can be used to obtain the current configuration on a router?

   a. show nvram
   b. show running-config
   c. show controllers
   d. show modules

5. A ping command shows three exclamation points (!) and two periods (.) in the output. What does this mean?

   a. The connection is experiencing intermittent problems.
   b. The remote host is not available.
   c. There is a connection to the remote host.
   d. The remote host has been shut off.

6. From which interface will a remote device respond to an ICMP echo-request?

   a. The last interface encountered
   b. The first interface encountered
   c. The interface with the highest IP address
   d. The interface with the highest MAC address

7. What is the syntax to copy to a TFTP server from flash?

    a. `copy tftp flash`

    b. `copy NVRAM TFTP`

    c. `copy flash TFTP`

    d. `copy to flash from TFTP`

8. By default, what is the holdtime for CDP?

    a. 180 seconds

    b. 240 seconds

    c. 90 seconds

    d. 60 seconds

9. How often are CDP packets exchanged?

    a. 180 seconds

    b. 240 seconds

    c. 90 seconds

    d. 60 seconds

10. Which command is used to show the names associated with IP devices?

    a. `show names`

    b. `show named addresses`

    c. `show hosts`

    d. `show name`

11. What happens if you type `10.1.1.1` at a router prompt?

    a. You will ping the router at 10.1.1.1.

    b. You will Telnet to the device at 10.1.1.1.

    c. You will Telnet to the router at 10.1.1.1.

    d. You will receive an error.

12. Which command will prevent DNS lookups from occurring?

    a. `no ip dns-lookup`

    b. `no ip domain-lookup`

    c. `ip domain-lookup`

    d. `no ip lookup`

13. How many entries will be made into the CDP table for a neighboring router that is directly connected through both a serial and an Ethernet port?

    a. two

    b. one

    c. You can only connect a neighboring router through one connection.

    d. None

14. Which of the following Cisco devices can run CDP?

    a. routers

    b. switches

    c. hubs

    d. all of the above

15. Which command will show all of the active Telnet sessions?

    a. `show telnet`

    b. `show sessions`

    c. `show telnet sessions`

    d. `show sessions telnet`

16. Which keystroke combination will suspend a Telnet session and return you to the original session?

    a. Shift+Break

    b. Shift+6+X

    c. Ctrl+Shift+6, then Break

    d. Ctrl+6, then Break

17. Which OSI Layer does CDP operate at?

    a. Physical

    b. Data-Link

    c. Network

    d. Transport

18. How much data is transferred over an Ethernet LAN for each character entered in a Telnet session?

    a. 1

    b. 2

    c. 64

    d. 128

19. What is special about a CDP packet?

    a. CDP uses a TCP header.

    b. CDP uses a SNAP frame.

    c. CDP does not need to conform to Ethernet standards.

    d. CDP has no special properties.

20. What is a requirement of running the `copy tftp flash` command?

    a. TCP/IP must be running.

    b. The flash must be large enough to hold the image.

    c. There must be an Ethernet connection.

    d. The flash IOS Image must be older than the TFTP IOS image.

Answers

1. **c.** The `show flash` command is used to display the contents of the flash memory. This is where the router images are stored.

2. **d.** A ping sends out five ICMP echo-request packets. ICMP echo-reply packets are sent back to the initiator.

3. **b.**, and **c.** Extended ping enables the timeout period to be increased. This helps when pinging very busy hosts and pinging hosts over very busy lines. The sending interface can be changed, which may help overcome issues such as access lists.

4. **b.** `Show running-config` shows the current configuration of the router.

5. **c.** A ping that shows three exclamation points (!) and two periods (.) in the output confirms that there is a connection to the remote host. A single set of pings where two echo-replies are not received in time does not necessarily show a connection problem.

6. **b.** A remote device will respond to an ICMP echo-request from the first interface receiving that request.

7. **c.** Remember the syntax is `copy source destination`. This is the same as in DOS and Unix.

8. **a.** The default holdtime for CDP is 180 seconds.

9. **d.** By default, CDP packets are exchanged every 60 seconds. Assume a test question means "by default" unless it specifies differently.

10. **c.** `Show hosts` is the correct command.

11. **b.** Although "c" looks correct, there is no guarantee that the device at 10.1.1.1 is a router. Telnet does not care what type of device is at a given IP address. Answer B is the *most* correct.

12. **b.** `no ip domain-lookup` will prevent the router from attempting name-to-IP address resolution.

13. **a.** CDP will show one entry for every direct connection to another Cisco device.

14. **d.** CDP is used by routers, switches and hubs.

15. **b.** `show sessions` will show all of the active Telnet sessions.

16. **c.** Ctrl+Shift+6 and then X will move you back to the original session.

17. **b.** CDP uses the Data-Link layer of the OSI model. This enables devices running dissimilar Network-Layer protocols to talk.

18. **d.** On Ethernet, the minimum packet size is 64 bytes. Since the character entered must be encapsulated and travel to the host and back again, a total of 128 bytes are transferred for each character.

19. **b.** CDP uses SNAP frames. SNAP frames have the DSAP and SSAP both set to AA.

20. **a.** `copy tftp flash` requires TCP/IP to be running. TFTP is part of the TCP/IP protocol suite. Therefore, TCP/IP must be running before TFTP will work. You don't need enough flash to start the TFTP command, but you do to finish!

Catalyst 1900 Switch Operation

Objectives

On completion of this chapter, you will be able to do the following:

- Understand the role of layer-two switching in a network.
- Differentiate between bridging and switching technologies.
- Comprehend the switching process including filtering and forwarding mechanisms.
- Understand the differences between the various switching methodologies.
- Understand how broadcast and multicast frames are handled by switches.
- Be aware of the complexity switching may bring to a network.
- Understand the role and reasoning behind the *Spanning Tree Protocol* (STP).
- Describe the Spanning Tree algorithm.
- Understand the various Spanning Tree-related modes that switch ports can be in.
- Be familiar with the various ways to configure a 1900 series switch.
- Be able to perform a number of configuration and maintenance tasks on the 1900 switch.

This chapter can also help you fulfill the following CCNA exam objectives:

- Describe the advantages of *Local Area Network* (LAN) segmentation.
- Describe LAN segmentation using bridges.
- Describe LAN segmentation using switches.
- Name and describe two switching methods.
- Describe the benefits of network segmentation with bridges.
- Describe the benefits of network segmentation with switches.
- Distinguish between cut-through and store-and-forward LAN switching.
- Describe the operation of STP and its benefits.
- Define and describe the function of a *Media Access Control* (MAC) address.

Introduction

Layer-two switching in the Ethernet world has grown to play an extremely significant role in almost all networks. Due primarily to its blend of high functionality and low cost, the layer-two switch has come to represent a soon-to-be ubiquitous form of LAN access.

This chapter will investigate the roles and responsibilities of a layer-two switch as well as some design concerns surrounding the deployment of this technology. As well, the Cisco 1900 series switch will serve as an example of the manifestation of this technology and both its operation and management will be closely examined.

The first half of the chapter will be dedicated to the technology behind the LAN switch and its operation. Topics including the standards, methods, and modes of switching will be covered as well as an in-depth look at STP. The latter half of the chapter will delve into the Cisco 1900 switch and the relevant aspects of its use and configuration.

Understanding Layer-Two Switching Fundamentals

Today's OSI layer-two LAN switch plays a role not unlike its ancestor, the LAN bridge. Essentially a layer-two device, the layer-two switch is tasked with the intelligent forwarding of packets throughout an internetwork based on fields contained within the data link layer header. Due to its capability to provide segmentation of the collision domain with minimal latency, the layer-two switch has become a widely deployed technology throughout the industry.

Many forms of bridging take place at layer two. Depending on the layer-two technologies in play, one may encounter source route bridging, source route/translational bridging, source route/transparent bridging, or the more basic transparent bridging. Although each of these technologies strives toward the same basic ends, they differ in a number of significant ways. In order to achieve some clarity, this chapter will focus on transparent bridging in Ethernet-based environments. Hence, from this point forward, all references to bridging should be understood as transparent bridging.

The switch serves one essential purpose; it segments the collision domain. The collision domain is comprised of the group of nodes that contends for access to the medium in a shared media environment. For example, in a traditional Ethernet environment where devices are connected to an Ethernet repeater (or hub), each connected device needs to make use of the same media or, more simply, the same bandwidth. When devices attempt to use the bandwidth simultaneously, a collision occurs. Obviously, as the number of devices added to the collision domain increases, the likelihood of collisions occurring does as well. At a certain point, the overall efficiency of the network can be severely impacted as the media simply becomes too congested. The switch, or historically the bridge, strives to alleviate this congestion. Where a repeater can be seen as one wire, the bridge can been seen as a number of wires where each port represents an individual wire. Hence, multiple devices can have access to the wire(s), or more specifically the medium, at the same time. Given some buffering capabilities, the switch can then facilitate multiple simultaneous transmissions, thus augmenting the amount of available bandwidth in a network. To accomplish this, the switch is responsible for three basic functions: to learn layer-two addresses, to make forwarding and filtering decisions, and to look for and prevent loops in the network. By doing so, the switch enables a level of segmentation at the data link layer and provides for some redundancy when deployed correctly. Each of these tasks is handled by various methods and protocols that serve as the basis for the study in the early part of this chapter.

Bridging versus Switching

As previously mentioned, bridging and switching technologies are very similar, so much so that the two terms are often used synonymously throughout the industry. In many respects, the two terms represent identical functionality. For example, the specifications that define the functionality of a layer-two bridge, as defined by IEEE 802.1D, are used for both switches and bridges. In fact, for the purposes of technical discussion, these two terms are interchangeable.

The differentiation that can be made is somewhat subtle. Historically, bridges existed in low-port densities with limited functionality and introduced a level of delay or latency. As such, these devices were used simply when the congestion within a collision domain became too great or when the physical size of the collision domain spanned too great a distance. The bridging algorithms were generally run from software within the bridge and as such were not optimized for performance. However, as the cost of *Application-Specific Integrated Circuits* (ASIC) continued to drop over time,

Figure 5-1
Bridging versus
switching

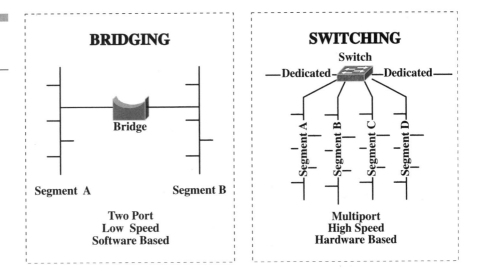

the price point for developing hardware-based bridges became tolerable. Today's bridge exists as a high-port density, high-functionality, wire-speed device capable of playing a much larger role in the network. For that reason, these new bridges have been marketed as switches. Figure 5-1 illustrates this contrast in functionality and the corresponding change in roles from bridging to switching technologies.

From this point forward, the term *switch* will be used to represent either device unless otherwise stated.

How Layer-Two Switches Learn MAC Addresses

Transparent switching involves the intelligent forwarding of packets without the involvement of the end nodes themselves. For a switch to succeed, it must pay attention to or, more specifically, store and process every packet it sees on every one of its interfaces. Given that the nodes in a network will be spread among many of the switch's interfaces, the switch endeavors to intelligently direct frames to the interfaces where their destination node exists. The switch also attempts to do this transparently to both the source and destination. The process involves the switch reading a frame off an interface and making a decision whether to forward that frame out of another interface or ignore the frame. To do so requires the capability to identify a particular node attached to a particular interface of the switch. To

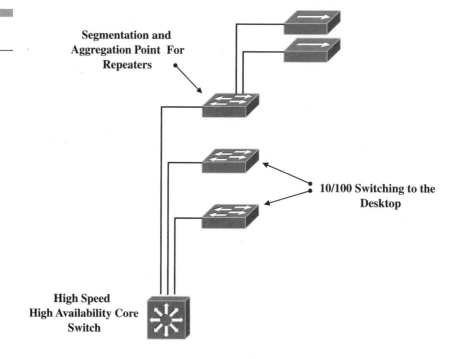

Segmentation and
Aggregation Point For
Repeaters

10/100 Switching to the
Desktop

High Speed
High Availability Core
Switch

enable this intelligence, the switch must build a table consisting of end-node MAC addresses matched to switch interfaces so that the table can correctly identify every device connected to each interface. It should be noted that the MAC address is a six-byte, globally unique identifier used to address Ethernet network nodes.

Figure 5-2 depicts a typical switch in a LAN environment. When initially powered on, a switch will have no awareness of where the various MAC addresses are located. During this period it will rely on the default rule that instructs the switch to flood incoming frames destined for unknown MAC addresses out all of the ports except to the port from which it came. However, by paying attention to the source MAC addresses of all of the frames it receives, the switch quickly builds a table of MAC address/interface mappings. This table is often referred to as the *Content Address Memory* (CAM) table in many Cisco switches. In Figure 5-3, the process of MAC table development is traced systematically. Notice that when Node A first transmits a frame to Node B, Node B's MAC address is unknown. As prescribed, this first frame is flooded out each port of the switch. However, during this process the switch reads Node A's MAC address and enters its location of E1

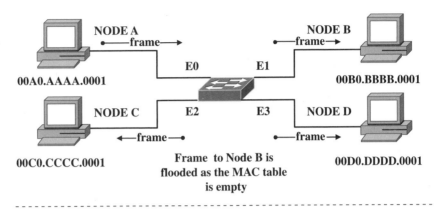

Figure 5-3
MAC table
development

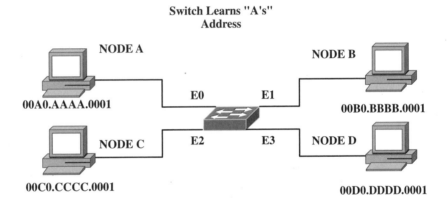

into its MAC table. By doing so, the switch will soon develop a MAC address to interface mapping for most, if not all, of the active nodes on a LAN.

Once this table is built, the amount of frames that will require flooding out of all the ports is reduced to a minimum. At this point the switch is providing its optimal benefit to the network. However, as very few environments are static, the switch must be ready to adapt to changes in network composition. For example, if the switch maintains its addresses permanently and a node is moved from one port to another, that node would experience a loss of connectivity to the network. Examining Figure 5-4, we can observe exactly this issue. When Node A is moved from port E0 to port E2, the switch remains unaware of this and the MAC table becomes invalid.

Figure 5-4

Invalid MAC tables

Node B Transmits Frame to Node A

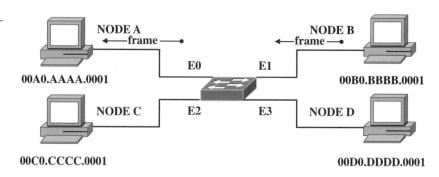

Node B Transmits Frame to Node A

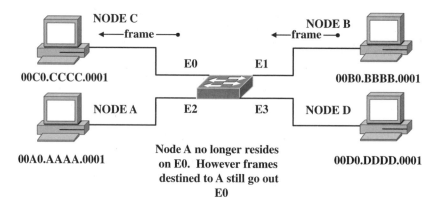

Because of this, all of the traffic destined for Node A is still directed to port E0 until Node A transmits a packet and the switch modifies its MAC table.

To address this issue, the switch issues each newly learned address an *age value*, typically 300 seconds, when they are added to the table. Should traffic from that MAC not occur within the age interval, the address will be removed from the table. This age value can be changed to suit the needs of a particular environment. The value is refreshed each time the MAC address is seen and thus in a stable environment, the table will remain accurate at all times.

It should be noted that the size of the MAC tables in different switches varies from switch to switch. Ranges from 1024 to well into the thousands can be seen throughout the Cisco product line. These sizes are a good indicator of where a specific switch should play a role within an internetwork. As such, good design practices dictate that these values are considered as key criteria when designing internetworks.

NOTE: *The concept of delivering dedicated or switched bandwidth to the desktop has brought forth a series of switches designed purely around this market space. The desktop switch, as it is often called, has one key limiting quality that must be clearly understood. These switches are often designed to support only a few MAC addresses per port (in the range of two to five) and carry a low per-port cost that makes them ideally suited for their designed use. However, any attempts to misuse these switches by placing them in distribution roles where hubs or other switches are collapsed into them quickly results in the MAC table becoming oversubscribed. At this point, a serious lack of connectivity occurs, which at times can be troublesome to identify. This simply underscores the need to be diligent in understanding the capacity of a particular switch before positioning it within a network.*

The Switching Process within the Switch

To effectively switch frames, a switch needs to read two key items from the data link header of each frame it receives: the *source MAC address* (SMAC) and the *destination MAC address* (DMAC). Both of these items are contained in the Ethernet frame header. Figure 5-5 describes the complete Ethernet frame. However, as is evident in the figure, the SMAC and DMAC are only a small portion of the entire frame. In the continuous effort to increase the speed at which switches can forward packets, engineering teams have taken note of this fact and have designed switching algorithms to exploit it. At this point in time, switches can operate in three conventional modes. Those modes are known as cut-through, store and forward, and fragment-free. The following sections describe the three variations.

Figure 5-5
The Ethernet frame

6 Bytes	6 Bytes	2 Bytes	46-1500 Bytes	4 Bytes
Destination (DMAC)	**Source (SMAC)**	**Protocol**	**Data**	**FCS**

> **NOTE:** *When the IEEE standardized Ethernet as IEEE 802.3, it made some slight modifications to Xerox's proposed Ethernet header. As a result, two frame types are now referred to as Ethernet and 802.3. The difference lies in a two-byte field that Ethernet uses to identify the layer-3 protocol and 802.3 uses to signify frame length. For this reason, all protocol types use numbers above 1500 (the maximum length of an Ethernet frame) so that one can easily distinguish between the two versions.*

Cut-Through Switching   The fastest form of switching available today is cut-through switching. This mode takes into consideration that the switch merely requires the knowledge of the DMAC in order to successfully forward the frame to its destination. As shown in Figure 5-6, as soon as the switch has read enough of the frame to recognize the DMAC, it immediately begins to transmit the frame out the destination port.

Despite being very fast, this mode does have its drawbacks, the most significant of which is the fact that many frames may be malformed and thus invalid on the wire. This mode of switching does not validate a frame prior to transmission, and thus will tend to forward invalid frames and consume bandwidth unnecessarily. On a network with many repeaters or suspect wiring where errors and congestion tend to be the norm, this may not represent an ideal switching methodology.

Store and Forward   At the expense of performance, store and forward switching endeavors to reduce the amount of invalid frames throughout a network. In this switching method, as depicted in Figure 5-7, the switch reads the entire frame and validates the *Cyclic Redundancy Check* (CRC) value before beginning to forward the frame. By doing so, the amount of invalid frames on the network can be significantly reduced. Many newer

Figure 5-6
Cut-through
switching

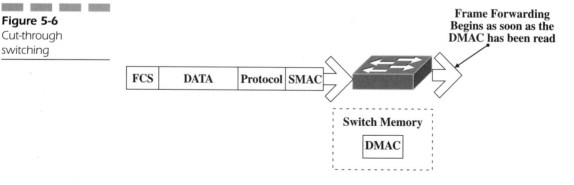

Figure 5-7
Store and forward
switching

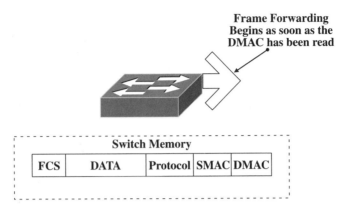

Frame Forwarding
Begins as soon as the
DMAC has been read

Switch Memory

| FCS | DATA | Protocol | SMAC | DMAC |

switches can perform this full frame check in very short order due to increased ASIC and processor speeds, and thus this form of switching may prove ideal in all cases. This value of this method of frame forwarding may be evident to many, given that it represents the methodology used by the traditional, pre-ASIC bridges. The underlying benefit is the complete isolation of the collision domain, as only valid frames are ever forwarded.

NOTE: The CRC process is essentially a mathematical process used to verify if any of the bits in a transmission have changed during that transmission, thus indicating a loss of frame integrity. To perform this check, the sender sums the bit total of the frame to be transmitted and divides it by a 32-bit prime number. The remainder of this division is sent along with the frame. Upon reception of the frame, the receiver performs the same calculation and checks the value of its remainder with the sender's version that was appended to the end of the frame. A match in these numbers indicates with very high accuracy the success of the transmission.

Fragment-Free Switching   Fragment-free switching represents a compromise of the above two techniques. This methodology understands that the key to faster switching lies in reducing the time it takes to read the frame before it begins to transmit. However, unlike cut-through mode, which takes this idea to the fullest, fragment-free switching attempts to eliminate some invalid frames. Valid Ethernet frames can range from 64 bytes to approximately 1500 bytes. As shown in Figure 5-8, fragment-free switching takes into consideration this 64-byte minimum and optimizes its performance around it. More specifically, a fragment-free switch will read

Figure 5-8
Fragment-free
switching

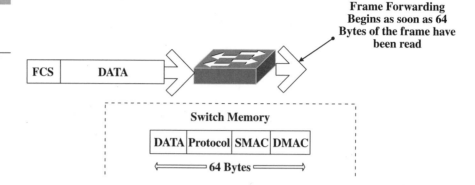

the first 64 bytes of any frame before it begins to forward it. Doing so enables engineers to optimize their code around the fixed length of 64 bytes and enables the switch to rid networks of any packets that do not meet the minimum criteria for validity. These types of packets, often called *runts*, are generally produced when collisions occur on a segment and transmission is halted midway. Figure 5-8 illustrates the fragment-free switching methodology.

NOTE: *A fourth switching methodology exists and is widely used in the industry. This last methodology operates using a hybrid of the cut-through and store and forward techniques. The technology is often called adaptive or error-sensing, as it tries to adapt to the health of the medium. In situations where few errors exist on the network, the switch will forward in a cut-through mode for the fastest performance. However, should error rates reach a specific threshold, the switch will dynamically adjust to the store and forward technique, ensuring optimum use of the media. The 1900 switch used for the examples in the chapter does not support this mode of switch within the selected version of software.*

How Switches Filter Frames

As mentioned at the beginning of the chapter, switches use three processes to accomplish their tasks. As this point the first of those tasks, that being the learning of MAC addresses and the development of the MAC to interface relationship tables or forwarding tables, should be understood. The next essential element in the process involves the intelligent use of those tables to strategically filter and forward frames. The switch is considered to filter a frame when it chooses not to forward the frame. This is usually because the switch realized that the interface from which it heard the frame is the same interface where the destination node resides.

In order to alleviate congestion on a network, the switch must minimize the amount of traffic that is forwarded from one port to another. To do so, the switch must monitor the destination address of every frame transmitted on the segments to which its ports connect. The switch accomplishes this by reading every frame heard on every interface into stored memory and processing the relevant fields in the data link header. Each time the switch sees a DMAC for a node, it must decide whether to do one of three things:

- Ignore the frame (filter it).
- Forward the frame out a specific interface.
- Flood the frame out all interfaces.

If the switch recognizes that the DMAC in a frame identifies a node that exists on the same interface on which it heard the frame, it can add no value by handling the frame because the destination node will be hearing the same frame at the same time. In this case, the frame is ignored. However, should a check of the forwarding table indicate that the DMAC signifies a node that lies on another segment, the switch will forward that frame out of the appropriate port. The last case comes into play in a number of instances. As discussed previously, when a switch is unsure of the location of a DMAC, it will flood all traffic it sees destined for that location out all of the ports to ensure the end node will receive the traffic. However, this is not the only time that a switch is called upon to flood packets out all of its interfaces. Special communications including broadcast and multicast packets also call for a similar action and are discussed in the upcoming section.

Broadcast and Multicast Frames

Many protocols involve communication that is not strictly of a point-to-point or unicast variety, where there is one sender and one receiver. Numerous protocols utilize one or both broadcast and multicast transmissions in order to accomplish their goals. The two processes are very similar in that they involve one sender and more than one recipient.

The broadcast packet involves a transmission from one node to the full set of all other listening nodes. This form of transmission is heavily used in most protocol stacks, including TCP/IP and IPX/SPX among many others.

Many times, a node simply needs to announce a particular item to the group of nodes to which it maintains a logical association. A Novell NetWare server announcing the availability of a print service is a good example of such a need. As it would be very challenging for a device to know the MAC address of all connected devices and, furthermore, very inefficient to attempt to send a unicast to each of those devices, the value of broadcast functionality is quite evident. When the broadcast frame is transmitted, every node that receives it will fully process the frame.

From a MAC address perspective, the broadcast packet can be identified by its all-ones destination MAC. MAC addresses are generally displayed in hexadecimal format due to their length. Hence, the all ones MAC in HEX is represented by all Fs. The Ethernet broadcast address is shown here:

```
FF-FF-FF-FF-FF-FF
```

The switch understands that the intent of the all-ones destined packet is to ensure that all nodes receive the transmission. Accordingly, it will flood the packet out all of its interfaces, as shown in Figure 5-9. Just as the term

Figure 5-9
The broadcast
transmission

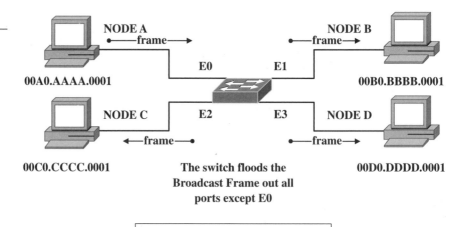

NODE A TRANSMITS A BROADCAST FRAME

NODE A
—frame→
NODE B
—frame→

E0   E1

00A0.AAAA.0001   00B0.BBBB.0001

NODE C   E2   E3   NODE D
←frame—   ←—frame→

00C0.CCCC.0001   The switch floods the
Broadcast Frame out all
ports except E0   00D0.DDDD.0001

Frame Information
DMAC: FFFF.FFFF.FFFF
SMAC: 00A0.AAAA.0001

collision domain signified the set of all nodes contending for the same medium, the broadcast domain signifies the set of all nodes that receive the same broadcast frames.

Another type of transmission, the multicast, also requires assistance from the switch. The multicast is very much like a broadcast except that its destination is not all nodes, but a group of nodes. Hence, it remains a one-to-many transmission and thus the switch must flood the multicast in order for it to be successful. As mentioned above, every node must process each broadcast packet on the network. This involves processor cycles on those nodes and as the rate of broadcasts increases, the load on end node processors can become quite significant. Multicast capabilities address the need for one-to-many communications when one-to-all is not necessary. For example, as we will see shortly, switches using the Spanning Tree algorithm need to communicate to ensure that loops in the network are avoided. To do so, a bridge needs to send frames to the set of all other bridges on the network. Although it could simply send a broadcast frame, this frame would need to be processed by each device, including workstations, servers, and printers, all of which would have no use for the frame. By using a multicast frame, the bridge can send to an address that will only have meaning to other devices looking for that address.

The multicast address used in those frames can be identified by its bit pattern. Specifically, the eighth bit in the DMAC is designated as the multicast bit. If this bit is one, the frame is a multicast frame. Just as MAC addresses require registration, so do multicast addresses. Below are two relevant multicast addresses in their six-byte hexadecimal format:

01-00-0C-CC-CC-CC   *Cisco Discovery Protocol* (CDP)

01-80-C2-00-00-00   Spanning Tree

Examining the first byte, 01, in either frame illustrates that the eighth bit is indeed set to one.

0000 0001   Binary representation of 01 in Hex

As mentioned, when the switch receives a multicast frame, it floods it out all ports to ensure that every device has an opportunity to receive it. One should note that since several of the switch interfaces may not contain devices that are interested in the multicast, this flooding still leads to a sub-optimal use of the medium. Figure 5-10 displays the flow of the multicast frame. Although all nodes will see the multicast, only those nodes that have been expressly configured to do so will process the frame.

Figure 5-10
The multicast
transmission

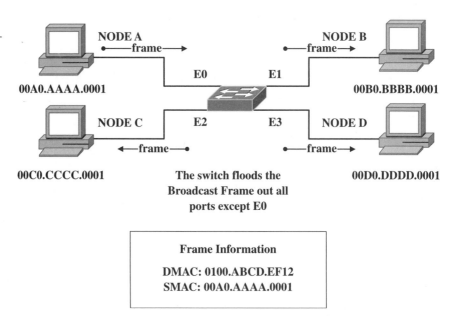

NODE A TRANSMITS A MULTICAST FRAME

How Switches Complicate LANs

Although it may superficially look like switches can act transparently in a network, one must be aware of the complexity they add to an infrastructure. As intelligent devices, switches require a certain amount of configuration and control to ensure than they have the desired effect on the network. Misconfiguring a switch or positioning it incorrectly within a topology can have instant and dramatic ramifications. The following sections cover the more common obstacles.

Broadcast Storms

In some topologies, as described in the following series of figures, the opportunity for a broadcast frame to loop throughout a network can be very real. For example, with two switches providing a redundant connection from one segment to another, the default switching action will force all broadcast frames to loop endlessly throughout the network at close to wire speed.

Unlike many types of transmissions, there is no *Time to Live* (TTL) field in the Ethernet frame, and thus there is no way to halt this endless forwarding. Needless to say, unbounded, this issue will bring a network to its knees. Figures 5-11a through 5-11c illustrate how a looped topology can create an opportunity for a broadcast storm.

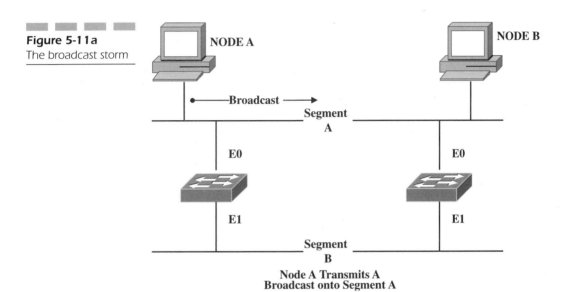

Figure 5-11a
The broadcast storm

Node A Transmits A
Broadcast onto Segment A

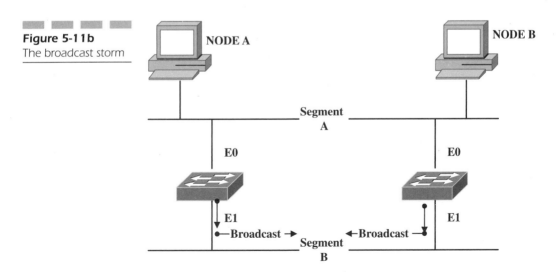

Figure 5-11b
The broadcast storm

Both Switches hear the broadcast on Segment
A and try to forward it to Segment B

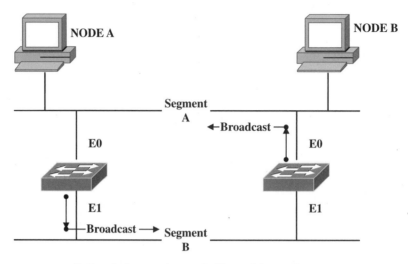

Figure 5-11c
The broadcast storm

Both switches continue to buffer and forward
the same broadcast over and over

NOTE: *Most switches have a broadcast threshold value that can be set to address the too-many-broadcasts issue. This threshold enables the switch to recognize circumstances that may be indicative of a broadcast storm and to proactively disable the port during those times. The specific implementation of the broadcast thresh tends to vary from switch to switch and it is wise to read and understand the documentation surrounding the functionality before enabling it to ensure the desired result occurs.*

Multiple Frame Copies

In topologies where redundant switches have been provisioned to provide connectivity from one segment to another, certain circumstances can lead to the duplication of frames. As shown in Figure 5-12, when a frame is transmitted to a destination address whose DMAC is not already active in either of the switches' forwarding tables, both switches will attempt to flood the frame. However, given that both segments are shared media, due to the *Carrier Sense Multiple Access with Collision Detection* (CSMA/CD) architecture, only one of the switches can gain access to the wire on the second segment at any given instant. The switch that does will transmit the frame onto the segment.

Figure 5-12

Multiple frame
copies: transmit

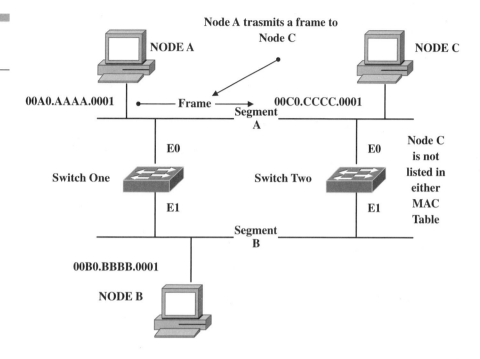

Node A transmits a frame to Node C. Node C's MAC address
is not in either MAC address table

At this point, as shown in Figure 5-13, two copies of the frame exist in the network. Node C has also already accepted delivery of the original frame and thus the goal of Node A has been achieved.

However, the second copy of the frame on segment two is now being read by the second switch. Assuming that this switch hadn't already queued the original frame for transfer to a particular port, it will now assume that Node A has moved across to segment two and it will forward the frame back onto segment one, as shown in Figure 5-14.

Hopefully by now, the first switch has learned where Node C is located or this process will be reiterated when it sees the second copy of the frame. In some cases, this looping of traffic can continue endlessly due to the fact that there is no way for a switch to determine whether a frame is the original or a copy due to the absence of any type of TTL field in the data link header. Although this scenario takes place over a very brief period of time and relies on some key characteristics, the opportunity for traffic duplication with this type of uncontrolled topology should become more obvious.

Figure 5-13
Multiple frame
copies: two copies

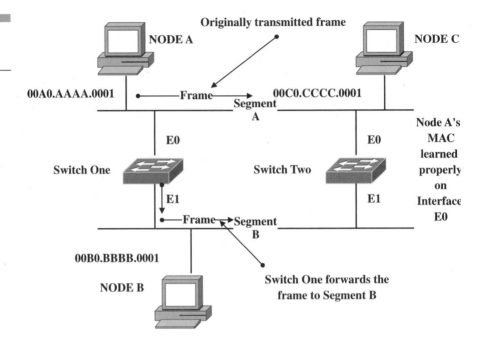

Two Copies of the Frame now exist on the network

Figure 5-14
Multiple frame copies
duplicate the
reception

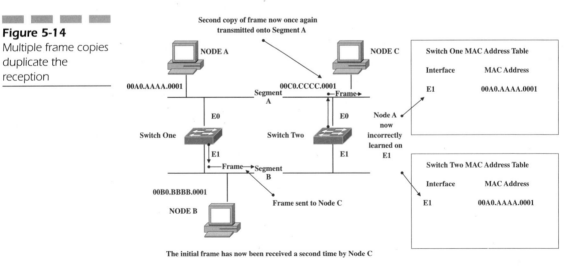

The initial frame has now been received a second time by Node C

MAC Database Instability

As alluded to earlier, the opportunity for a switch configured in a redundant fashion to misrepresent the physical location of nodes can cause serious grief. As shown in Figure 5-14, when switches flood frames due to unknown destinations, the duplicate frames created can cause other switches to modify their forwarding tables. For example, referring to Figure 5-15, assume that neither switch has Node C's MAC address in their forwarding table. When Node A transmits to Node C, as we previously encountered, a duplicate frame is placed on segment two.

This duplicate frame will trick the second switch into thinking that Node A has actually moved across to segment two. Until that switch hears another packet from Node A on segment one, it will begin to forward all traffic destined to Node A onto segment two. As one can imagine, the effect of this instability on network performance can be very severe.

Multiple Loop Problems

The previous examples have examined situations where two switches have been placed between two segments creating in effect one single loop. Although the previous situations led to a definite degradation in performance, their effect pales in comparison to what can happen when multiple loops take place in a layer-two network. Again, the fact that no timeout values exist in data link frames, and that switches cannot differentiate

Figure 5-15
MAC database
instability

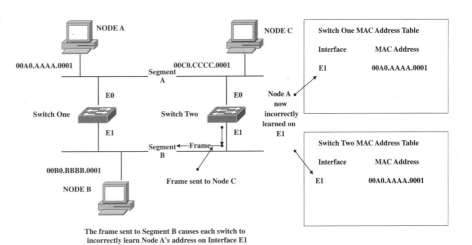

The frame sent to Segment B causes each switch to
incorrectly learn Node A's address on Interface E1

Figure 5-16
Multiple network
loops

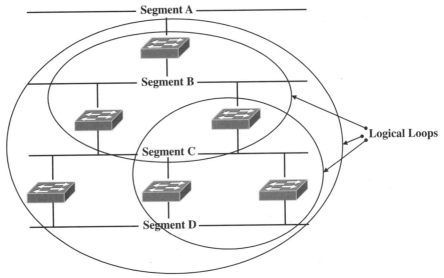

Multiple loops exist throughout the topology

whether they are looking at frames for the first or the tenth time, leads to the complete inability to control these looped topologies. Tracing the packet flow in a network like the one depicted in Figure 5-16 will quickly provide the realization that exponential frame multiplication and a corresponding increase in traffic levels are the net effect of such a topology.

NOTE: *A looped network is a very easy thing to diagnose. Due to the extremely high level of traffic, the activity- or traffic-indicating LEDs on any connected hubs or switches will simply remain lit. It should be noted, however, that many end nodes might have adverse reactions to the level of traffic offered while the network is looped which may not be immediately evident, and may require attention beyond rectifying the looped topology.*

Spanning Tree

Considering the disastrous effects that looped topologies seem to cause, one might imagine that they reflect a poor design. However, when properly controlled, the looped topology can provide an active, self-policing, redundant layer-two infrastructure. What makes this possible is the STP algorithm.

Specified in IEEE 802.1D, the STP algorithm is a relatively simple process that enables a number of bridges to identify and eliminate loops in a network in a dynamic fashion. It should be noted that the acronym STP is not an industry-recognized term with respect to its relation to the Spanning Tree algorithm, but it is heavily used throughout Cisco's documentation and will be used in this text.

The term *Spanning Tree* depicts the underlying concept of the algorithm. In reverse order, the Tree portion refers the process of identifying the topology of a LAN and configuring it in the form of a tree so that network loops are eliminated. Spanning refers to the protocol's capability and need to span across multiple LAN segments in order to build that tree. The protocol uses various methods and metrics to identify loops and prune connections so that in the end a tree topology exists where there is only one path from each segment to another. Once built, the validity of the tree is confirmed on an active basis to ensure that all links remain active. The STP process is covered in more detail within the following sections.

The following sections will describe in detail how the algorithm accomplishes the goal of loop-free connectivity. However, to keep the complexity in perspective, it is key to remember that the algorithm is purely attempting to build a single path from one point to another throughout the tree. Hence, when examining the roles of the root and designated bridges as well as the root and designated ports, keeping in mind that the algorithm is simply attempting systematically to build this single path from one point to another should enable one to quickly grasp these concepts.

How Spanning Tree Works

For switches to effectively build a tree through pruning various links, they must first establish a method of communication between one another. The STP algorithm specifies the use of a special message called the *Configuration Bridge Protocol Data Unit* (BPDU), which is multicasted throughout the network in a regular data link frame for most of its operation. The Configuration BPDU has the appropriate fields to facilitate all of the communication relevant to the use of the STP algorithm. Table 5-1 describes the Configuration BPDU message.

A second message, shown in Table 5-2, the Topology Change BPDU, is used to communicate changes in the topology.

In their initial state, switches transmit and receive the configuration BPDUs in order to gain an understanding of the topology of the segments

Table 5-1

The Configuration
BPDU

Number of Bytes	Field
2	Protocol Identifier
1	Version
1	Message Type
1	Reserved
8	Root ID
4	Cost of Path to Root
8	Bridge ID
2	Port ID
2	Message Age
2	Maximum Age
2	Hello Time
2	Forward Delay

Table 5-2

The Topology
Change BPDU

Number of Bytes	Field
2	Protocol Identifier
1	Version
1	Message Type

to which their interfaces are connected. Shortly thereafter, the process of tree building begins.

The key to building a valid tree lies first in the election of a *root bridge*. The root bridge serves as the top or center of the tree and the rest of the topology branches out from it. Once a root bridge has been selected, all other switches in the network will calculate their position with respect to that bridge. From there, the shortest paths from each bridge to the root bridge are selected for use and all other redundant, loop-forming connections are temporarily disabled to ensure that there is only one path from any point to another within the network.

The Spanning Tree process can be summarized into the following steps undertaken by connected bridges within an internetwork:

1. Elect one bridge out of the group to serve as the root bridge.
2. Calculate the distance to the root bridge from each interface.
3. Elect a designated bridge for each segment in the network.
4. Choose the port with the shortest path to the root called the root port.
5. Select the root port and any ports that have been elected as designated bridges and set them to forward. Disregard incoming data on all other ports.[1]

This process and the elements that play a part in it are described in more detail within the upcoming sections.

Root Bridge   The root bridge is a bridge that has been elected through a process that involves all other bridges in a network. This particular bridge then serves as the central point of reference from which the tree is built. Essentially, all other bridges branch out from the root. As such, there can and will be only one root bridge chosen per network of bridges. Fully described in the following section, the bridge having the lowest bridge ID is elected as the root bridge via the selection process.

Root Bridge Selection   As previously discussed and depicted in Table 5-1, bridges use multicasted Configuration BPDUs to communicate the relevant details of their configurations and statuses. Within the BPDU is a bridge ID number, which consists of a two-byte bridge priority followed by the bridge's MAC address. However, as you may have inferred, the bridge will have one MAC address per port so that it may participate validly in connectivity on every segment. However, the MAC used in the bridge ID can be either one of those connected interface MACs or a separate MAC used to identify solely the bridge as a whole. In either event, which MAC is used tends to be somewhat irrelevant.

Initially, bridges assume that they are the root bridge and report themselves accordingly via the multicasted BPDUs. However, as soon as a bridge sees a BPDU from another bridge, which has a lower bridge ID, it sets that bridge as the root and stops forwarding the Configuration BPDUs. Through

---

[1] From *Interconnections, Second Edition: Bridges, Routers, Switches, and Internetworking Protocols*, Radia Perlman, Addison-Wesley.

a process of step-by-step elimination, eventually only the bridge with the lowest bridge ID will remain forwarding Configuration BPDUs and that bridge will be the root bridge. Unlike the other bridges in the network, the root bridge will forward packets on all of its interfaces at all times. An example of the results of a root bridge election is shown in Figure 5-17.

The previously mentioned bridge priority is a settable item in every bridge configuration. Using this variable, it is possible to influence the outcome of the root bridge election. Doing so enables the logical configuration of the tree to be mated with the designed functionality of the network. Left unset, the opportunity for suboptimal trees to be built is very likely.

NOTE: *Although not fully covered in this text, the settable attributes including the maximum age, the forward delay, and hello times are all designated by the root bridge. These attributes define the functionality of the Spanning Tree topology and it is critical that all bridges agree on their values. Having one bridge set them is an ideal way to accomplish this. This aspect also further illustrates the value in manually adjusting the priorities of bridges or switches in a network to define which will win the root bridge election.*

Root Port Just as a root bridge is selected from the entire set of bridges, each bridge must itself have an election of sorts among its individual interfaces. Should a bridge find that it has two paths to the root bridge through

Figure 5-17
The root bridge
election

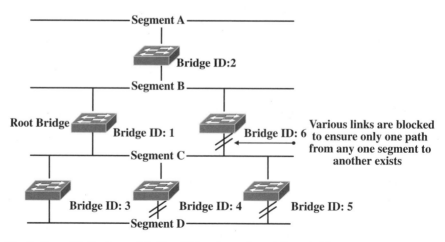

The Bridge with the Lowest Bridge ID has been elected Root Bridge

two of its interfaces, it must make a decision upon which of those two to use. Also contained in the Configuration BPDU and examined in this process is the cost of the path to the root. In this case, the root port that the bridge selects will be the port with the lowest path cost to the root bridge. The path cost is a summed total of the various link speeds of the links leading up to the current bridge. Figure 5-18 indicates a typical example of such a path. The values used to represent the link speeds are designated by the preset values based on the interface speed as assigned by the IEEE. Those values have recently been modified by the IEEE and are listed along with the older values below. The newer values tend to reflect the recent advances in technology, which have made speeds of this nature feasible. Table 5-3 lists both the older and newer high values for costs of the various interfaces.

Figure 5-18
Path cost

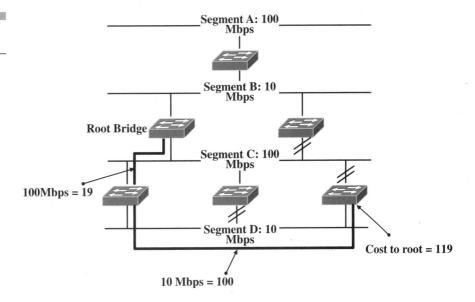

Table 5-3

First and second revision port costs

Link Speed	First Revision Cost	Second Revision Cost
10 Gbps	1	2
1 Gbps	1	4
100 Mbps	10	19
10 Mbps	100	100

As it is possible for two ports to have the same cost to the root bridge, a tiebreaker value, the port ID is used. The port ID is also contained in the Configuration BPDU and contains a value that the transmitting bridge applies to the specific port from whence it transmitted the frame. This port ID is somewhat of an arbitrary value in that it can be left to default or set to reflect a priority, should one want to influence the root port selection process. The port ID is a two-byte field that is generally divided into one byte for priority and one byte for the port number. As with the root bridge, it is the lowest of the reported port IDs that the switch will designate as the root port.

Designated Port Per Segment Each segment in a network requires a single path towards the root bridge to ensure that network loops are not present. To that end, in segments that contain multiple paths back toward the rout, one port from one bridge will be designated as the path toward the root. This particular port is generally called the *designated port*. As with the bridge's selection of a root port, the segment's selection of a designated port is based on choosing the lowest advertised path to the root bridge. As previously mentioned, the cost of the path to the root field of the Configuration BPDU is used by the bridges to select who will forward frames off the segment. To that end, any bridge that notices a lower cost to root advertised on a particular segment will not forward that segment. The bridge's port that has been designated as the closest port to the root bridge is often referred to as the *designated bridge*.

STP Port States As the spanning tree is built and utilized, the interfaces on a switch move through various stages. Understanding these stages is an essential part of understanding the status of STP switches in an internetwork. The following sections touch on the four possible modes that interfaces on switches running the Spanning Tree algorithm can be in.

Blocking The blocking mode signifies that traffic is not flowing through the interface. Blocked ports are ports that have not been elected to forward traffic in any phase in the Spanning Tree algorithm. However, these ports are not disabled and continue to listen to traffic present on the segment. The blocked state specifies that the port is in a receive-only mode. Being in such a mode enables the interface to process incoming STP frames and thus remain advised of the current status of the Spanning Tree topology.

Listening The listening state is the initial state a bridge will enter when the STP algorithm is reset or first enabled. During this phase, the bridge is forwarding only Configuration BPDUs that it originates itself. Another essential element in this state is that the bridge is not learning any MAC addresses. As previously discussed, one of the core functions of a switch is to learn and cache the locations of MAC addresses in a forwarding table. However, to minimize the chances of incorrect address learning during the initial setup of the Spanning Tree, the switch will not learn any addresses in this state. This state is generally set to a 15-second duration.

Learning At this state, directly following the listening state, it is generally felt that some stability should exist within the network. Hence, the switch will begin to build its MAC table. However, the switch is still only forwarding its own Configuration BPDUs (assuming it has not already heard a better root value and ceased transmitting). The rest of the network's bridgeable traffic is still being fully filtered. As with listening, this state generally takes place in a 15-second interval.

Forwarding After the first two states have been completed, or 30 seconds after the Spanning Tree has been reinitialized, the switch will be capable of deciding whether or not it needs to forward traffic. Interfaces that are root ports or the designated bridge for the segment will forward traffic. Interfaces in this state are fully functional and forward all traffic that meets the criteria for forwarding.

Topology Changes

The previous sections have covered the creation of a stable Spanning Tree topology. However, as mentioned, STP is a dynamic protocol. Using various mechanisms, each switch maintains an awareness of the stability of the tree and can act in a preventative nature, should things change. Aside from the Configuration BPDU, another type of BDPU exists. The Topology Change BPDU is used to indicate that a bridge port has transitioned from a blocked to a forward state or vice versa.

Depending on where the change occurs, the impact of the change can be more or less dramatic for the end nodes connected. In the worst case, should the topology change affect the root bridge and a new election becomes necessary, all ports in the network will move to a non-forwarding state for 30 seconds (to accommodate the listen and learn stages). These transitions will cause a loss of connectivity between segments for that 30-second period of time. The time it takes for all bridges to move through the listen and learn stages into either a blocked or forwarding stage is referred to as the *convergence time*. Convergence is a common networking term that typically refers to the amount of time it takes for all entities within a system to synchronize their awareness of a set of criteria, which in this case is Spanning Tree topology.

Should the root remain constant during a change, a less dramatic effect will be seen. Should a bridge in a branch of the tree undergo a transition, it will simply act to inform the root bridge so that the root understands the current topology. To do so, the bridge in question forwards a Topology Change BPDU out its root port. From there, the designated bridge per segment passes along the frame until it reaches the root. The root then forwards an acknowledgement back along the same path to the instigating bridge, indicating that the root is now aware of the change in topology.

Configuring the 1900 Switch

The Cisco Catalyst 1900 series switch is an excellent example of the many switching topics that have been covered thus far in the chapter. A fully IEEE 802.1D-compliant switch, the 1900 represents not only good value as an example, but is at the same time a very widely deployed switch in the industry. As such, a solid understanding of the 1900's configuration and behavior should prove valuable on multiple levels.

The switch itself comes in a number of flavors essentially providing either 12 or 24 ports of 10-Mbps Switched Ethernet along with two 100-Mbps Switched Fast Ethernet ports carried via fiber or copper. As such, the switch finds its place traditionally providing connectivity to desktop or end-node locations in the access layer while providing a high-speed connection upward to the distribution layer.

User Interfaces

In order to work with or manage the 1900 switch, one must gain access to the switches' command interpreter. Cisco provides a number of ways to accomplish this, including the traditional *command line interface* (CLI) through either a console program or in-band through a Telnet application, along with a Web-based *graphical user interface* (GUI). Further, the CLI version is supported in two varieties: a menu-based program or an IOS-like CLI. Each of the three methodologies is examined below. For clarity, the IOS CLI will be used throughout the chapter to provide examples where relevant.

Menu-Driven The menu-driven CLI represents more of an industry standard between the two CLIs. Essentially, access to the various pieces of viewable information and settable configurations is provided via a menu system. The user can navigate through a logical set of menus that provide information on current settings along with the ability to modify those settings. The main menu is depicted in Figure 5-19.

The menus themselves tend to follow a specific format. In many cases, the menus are comprised of a number of sections delineated by hyphen lines. The following represent some of those sections:

- *Information* A read-only display of currently configured relevant values.
- *Settings* Commands to modify relevant individual settings.
- *Actions* Tasks to be carried out by the switch (including resets/reloads and so on).
- *Related menus* Access to menus with commands of a related nature.

It should be noted that menus might tend to use all, some, or none of the above sections. The composition of one menu to the next will tend to vary, depending on the number or type of commands and actions relevant to the menu.

Figure 5-19

The 1900 menu-driven main menu

```
Catalyst 1900 - Main Menu
   [C] Console Settings
   [S] System
   [N] Network Management
   [P] Port Configuration
   [A] Port Addressing
   [D] Port Statistics Detail
   [M] Monitoring
   [V] Virtual LAN
   [R] Multicast Registration
   [F] Firmware
   [I] RS-232 Interface
   [U] Usage Summaries
   [H] Help
   [K] Command Line
   [X] Exit Management Console
Enter Selection:
```

Web-Based Virtual Switch Manager The Web-based *Virtual Switch Manager* (VSM) enables access to the switch's command interpreter via a Web browser. Included in the 1900 switch is an HTTP server that by default is enabled. Once the switch is furnished with a valid IP configuration and is connected to the network, the VSM can be accessed out of a standard Internet browser. From there, relevant aspects of the switch's configuration and performance can be changed or monitored via this GUI interface. For example, to change the duplex on a port, one would simply click on the desired port and from the next screen, select the appropriate duplex setting for that port.

Unlike the CLI access methods where configuration changes take place immediately, the VSM enables the configuration to be modified passively, setting by setting, and then sent in whole to the switch. As the configuration is changed in the VSM, the to-be-changed settings are simply saved in the VSM and are not enacted live on the switch. When the desired configuration has been achieved, one can select the Apply option from the left-hand side, which will then apply each of the changed settings. Further, should one want to reset the VSM to the currently configured settings, the Revert button can be used.

The VSM also provides links to *Cisco Connection Online* (CCO) as well as the Cisco *Technical Assistance Center* (TAC) along with built-in documentation. Further, the CLI can be quickly accessed via the Telnet link, should one so desire.

IOS CLI The IOS CLI is based on Cisco's IOS architecture and offers a Cisco standard interface. As with standard IOS, one can enter the enable mode and perform numerous live commands along with modifying the running and stored configurations with the configure command. For those that are familiar with Cisco products and routers in particular, this form of access will prove the easiest to digest.

Figure 5-20 depicts the IOS CLI. More specifically, one can tell from the [#] prompt that the user is in the enable mode and has typed `show version` to display the hardware, software, and memory details of the switch.

Default Configuration

The 1900 switch comes preconfigured with a number of essential settings that one should be aware of. Those settings are covered one by one in the following sections.

IP Address for Management   Because the IP address assigned to the switch will be unique to the network upon which it is installed, the default is set to 0.0.0.0. Doing so ensures that it will not overlap with any other addresses. The IP address 0.0.0.0 will render the switch unmanageable from in-band via any IP based programs like Telnet or *Simple Network Management Protocol* (SNMP) and thus will need to be changed before these activities can take place.

CDP   By default, the *Cisco Discovery Protocol* (CDP) is enabled on the 1900 switch. It should be noted that CDP is controlled in two areas, both on the switch as a whole and on a port-by-port basis. Hence, it is advisable to leave CDP enabled on the entire switch and then control its use port by port. Although it may seem easiest to leave CDP enabled on all ports, the CDP multicasts may cause issues with specific end stations. Hence, it is advisable to disable CDP on ports where Cisco devices do not reside.

Switching Mode   The 1900 chooses to switch frames using the fragment-free methodology. As previously discussed, this method involves the switch ensuring that it forwards only those packets that meet the 64-byte minimum size in Ethernet while beginning to forward the frame as soon as the first 64 bytes have been received, regardless of the outcome of the CRC check. Depending on the nature of the network in which the 1900 will play a role, this may or may not be the best setting, but it likely serves the best balance between performance and integrity.

Figure 5-20
The output from a show version in the IOS CLI

```
#show version
Cisco Catalyst 1900/2820 Enterprise Edition Software
Version V8.01.02
Copyright (c) Cisco Systems, Inc.  1993-1998
 uptime is 9day(s) 16hour(s) 14minute(s) 52second(s)
cisco Catalyst 1900 (486sxl) processor with 2048K/1024K bytes of
memory
Hardware board revision is 5
Upgrade Status: No upgrade currently in progress.
Config File Status: No configuration upload/download is in
progress
27 Fixed Ethernet/IEEE 802.3 interface(s)
Base Ethernet Address: 00-D0-06-92-64-00
#
```

Auto-Negotiation of Duplex and Speed   The auto-negotiation of speed and duplex are set on a per-port basis where applicable. The 100BaseX ports (TX or FX) come set to autonegotiate both speed and duplex by default. The 10Base-T ports are set to half-duplex. The 10Base-T settings are very safe and likely will not need to be changed. However, depending on what connects to the 100BaseX ports, a hard-coded setting would probably prove appropriate.

Enabling/Disabling Spanning Tree   The Spanning Tree algorithm is enabled on the 1900 switch by default. However, it must be noted that as with CDP, STP is enabled on the switch as a whole as well as on a port-by-port basis. Again, it is advisable to leave STP running on the entire switch and configure the ports one at a time to control the use of the STP protocol. Even in networks that will not rely on STP for redundancy, enabling the protocol can provide protection against any misconfigurations in cabling that may occur.

Console Passwords   The console passwords are set to none by default. It is advisable to change these as soon as the switch goes into service.

Ports on the 1912/1924

As previously mentioned, the 1900 series comes in a 12-port and a 24-port Ethernet version. The main difference between the two is purely port density. It should also be noted that both of these switches have a 10Base5 or AUI port available on the back of the unit to provide for integration into legacy networks. This port is always identified as 0/25 within the switch. When configuring the switch, ports are often referred to as interfaces as well as ports

10Base-T Ports   The 1900 switch provides either 12 or 24 ports of RJ-45 female terminated 10Base-T Ethernet in the 1912 and 1924 respectively. Each of these ports represents a fully switched, often called *dedicated*, 10 Mbps of bandwidth. Within the switch configuration utilities, these ports are identified as 0/1–0/12 or 0/1–0/24 depending on the port density of the switch.

100Base-TX Ports The 1900 switch offers up to two 100Base-TX ports that terminate in RJ-45 female jacks on the front of the switch. These ports are ideal for the connection to either servers or additional switches. Within the switch's configuration, these ports are identified as either 0/26 or 0/27.

100Base-FX Ports The 1900 switch offers up to two 100Base-FX ports that terminate in SC jacks on the front of the switch. The ports are ideal for long connections between switches or uplinks into core or distribution closets in a network. As with the TX ports, these ports are identified as either 0/26 or 0/27 within the switch's configuration.

NOTE: *The leading 0 in the port or interface notation may seem confusing. However, one must recall that the software used on the 1900 switch is software that is also used for a great number of other switches with differing compositions. In a modular device, ports are labeled with a slot / port or module / port-number style notation. This format has been maintained for the 1900, but no slots or modules differentiate them. Hence, the 0 placeholder is used with the result being all ports labeled with a leading 0 / port-number.*

Configuring the Switch

When initially deploying a switch, a number of essential elements need to be configured. These elements represent those that are critical to the performance and management of the switch within the network. The following sections will describe and provide examples of the configuration of these elements. As previously mentioned, the IOS CLI will be used in the examples.

One key difference in the IOS used on the 1900 switch and that of a router IOS lies in storage of the configuration. Unlike a router IOS, there is no need to save the running configuration to a more permanent startup configuration. All configuration changes made to the switch will remain and can be considered set. Hence, there is no need to save the configuration to the switch itself upon configuration completion. However, it should be noted that the configuration could still be saved to disk or a TFTP server for backup reasons.

IOS offers a number of modes from which to configure the switch. The first mode that one enters is known as the global configuration mode. It can be recognized by the word `config` in brackets following the hostname. Figure 5-21 depicts entry into the global configuration.

The config indicates that the commands entered will be applied to the global configuration. From the global configuration, one can enter more specific areas including interface configuration or line configuration modes. For example, should the administrator want to modify the interface configuration (also known as a port configuration) for the first Ethernet port, one would enter the interface configuration mode for that port. Figure 5-22 illustrates how this is accomplished. It should be noted that commands can be abbreviated as long as they remain unique. One often abbreviated command is the `configure terminal` command, which can be represented by the shorter `conf t`. The use of abbreviated commands can significantly enhance one's efficiency at the terminal.

As noted in Figure 5-22, the interface configuration mode is accessed from the global configuration mode and can be identified by the `-if` listed beside the `config` in the parentheses.

Hostname   Setting the hostname of the switch to a unique and identifiable string provides a number of benefits. The hostname variable is used both as the prompt for the switch in a CLI mode as well as the SNMP hostname for the switch. Depending on the size of the network and the number of devices employed, using strategic names for devices can significantly improve the productivity of those tasked with the remote management of those devices.

Figure 5-21
Entering global configuration mode in the IOS CLI

```
sw1924_A#configure terminal
Enter configuration commands, one per line. End with CNTL/Z
sw1924_A(config)#
```

Figure 5-22
Entering the interface configuration mode in the IOS CLI

```
sw1924_A(config)#interface ethernet0/1
sw1924_A(config-if)#
```

The hostname is simply a string of alphanumeric text that can range from one to 255 characters in length and is entered in the global configuration. The example in Figure 5-23 indicates that the hostname is set to sw1924_A.

Notice in Figure 5-23 that as soon as the new hostname is entered, the prompt for the CLI changes. Although it is unnecessary, one can further verify the hostname using a show command. The syntax and result is shown in Figure 5-24.

Management IP Configuration A number of switch management functions take place in-band. That is to say, one can access the switch through an Ethernet port over the network instead of through the console port. This facilitates the switch being managed remotely. All forms of remote management or in-band management take place using the IP protocol, and thus the switch itself must be a valid IP node on the network. As such, the switch must have a full IP node configuration including the IP address, subnet mask, and default gateway. Keep in mind, however, that the switch is purely a layer-two device and will continue to switch packets whether it has an IP address or not. The IP address is only installed to facilitate in-band management.

All of the commands related to IP addressing are implemented from the global configuration mode. In the following example, an IP address of 10.1.1.2 with a subnet mask of 255.255.255.0 or 24 bits is entered for the switch address. The TCP/IP protocol is fully covered in upcoming chapters, but at this point it can be said that the address and mask combination indicate that the switch will participate in a subnet of the 10.0.0.0 network, which is described as 10.1.1.0, and its node address will be 2. Figure 5-25 depicts this configuration.

Figure 5-23
Changing the
hostname

```
#conf t
Enter configuration commands, one per line.  End with CNTL/Z
(config)#hostname sw1924_A
sw1924_A(config)#exit
sw1924_A#
```

Figure 5-24
Viewing the
hostname

```
sw1924_A#show snmp hostname
sw1924_A
sw1924_A#
```

At this point, it is recommended that a default gateway address be entered to enable the switch to communicate with nodes on other subnets. This address represents the router or routing device on the same subnet as the switch that should be used by the switch when it needs to communicate with devices outside of the subnet. In this example, the default gateway address will be 10.1.1.1. Figure 5-26 describes the necessary syntax.

In order to verify that the IP configuration has been entered successfully, one can use a show command. Specifically, the command show ip will provide all of the details relevant to the switch's IP configuration, including those that have been entered in the previous example. Figure 5-27 shows the command and its result.

The meaning of several of the values in Figure 5-27 will be addressed in upcoming sections. However, one can see that the correct IP address, subnet mask, and default gateway have been entered into the switch.

Enable Password

In order to control access to the enable mode, also known as the supervisor mode, one can set an enable password. Knowledge of this password will be required for one to gain access to the more secure or read/write-oriented

Figure 5-25
Setting the IP address

```
sw1924_A#conf t
Enter configuration commands, one per line.  End with CNTL/Z
sw1924_A(config)#ip address 10.1.1.2 255.255.255.0
sw1924_A(config)#exit
sw1924_A#
```

Figure 5-26
Assigning a default
gateway address

```
sw1924_A#conf t
Enter configuration commands, one per line.  End with CNTL/Z
sw1924_A(config)#ip address 10.1.1.2 255.255.255.0

sw1924_A#conf t
Enter configuration commands, one per line.  End with CNTL/Z
sw1924_A(config)#ip default-gateway 10.1.1.1
sw1924_A(config)#exit
sw1924_A#
```

aspects of the configuration. The enable password is set from the global configuration mode, as shown in Figure 5-28.

As shown in Figure 5-28, the `enable password` command also contains another parameter called *level*. The level enables an administrator to assign different functions different passwords and, as such, create multiple levels of access controlled by passwords. Although a detailed look at the level parameter is beyond the scope of this text, it can be noted that a level of 15 represents full administrative access to the switch.

Once a password has been set, the next time a user wants to enter the enable mode, that user will be prompted for the password, as shown in Figure 5-29.

Figure 5-27
Viewing the IP configuration of the switch

```
sw1924_A#show ip
IP Address: 10.1.1.2
Subnet Mask: 255.255.255.0
Default Gateway: 10.1.1.1
Management VLAN:  1
Domain name:
Name server 1: 0.0.0.0
Name server 2: 0.0.0.0
HTTP server : Enabled
HTTP port :  80
RIP : Enabled
sw1924_A#
```

Figure 5-28
Setting the enable password

```
sw1924_A#conf t
Enter configuration commands, one per line.  End with CNTL/Z
sw1924_A(config)#enable password level 15 cisco
sw1924_A(config)#exit
sw1924_A#
```

Figure 5-29
Entering the enable mode

```
sw1924_A>enable
Enter password:  *****
sw1924_A#
```

Setting Duplex

The duplex setting on each port is fully configurable. As previously mentioned, the switch will default to half-duplex on its 10-Mbps ports and autonegotiate on its 100-Mbps ports. Incorrectly set duplexes can lead to serious network performance issues that may prove challenging to troubleshoot in larger networks. Some of these issues are highlighted in an upcoming section. However, for these reasons, it is wise to consider and modify, where necessary, the duplex settings on a switch before it is deployed.

In order to change a duplex setting, one must enter the interface mode for the desired port. Figure 5-30 illustrates both the methods for setting the duplex as well as the options available for the setting.

As shown in Figure 5-30, four options are available to the administrator for the duplex setting on a particular port. In auto mode, a port will attempt to negotiate for full-duplex and failing that will resort to half-duplex. Along with the half and full settings, Cisco also offers a full-duplex setting with flow control enabled. Because a full-duplex connection removes the inherent flow control provided in half-duplex (that being the fact that only one device can transmit at any one time), the opportunity for a receiver to become congested is much higher in full-duplex connections. To offset this risk, the full-flow-control setting may be used.

In order to check the duplex settings on a port or a number of ports, the show interfaces command can be used. Typing show interfaces ? will reveal that one can view a list of all interfaces or a specific one. Figure 5-32 illustrates the use of the command for the Ethernet 0/1 interface.

As shown in Figure 5-31, the show interface command displays far more than just the duplex settings on the port. The output of the command is very telling in a number of ways and can be relied upon to provide a great deal of relevant information.

Figure 5-30

The duplex options for Ethernet 0/1

```
sw1924_A#conf t
Enter configuration commands, one per line.  End with CNTL/Z
sw1924_A(config)#int ethernet 0/1
sw1924_A(config-if)#dup
sw1924_A(config-if)#duplex ?
  auto                     Enable auto duplex configuration
  full                     Force full duplex operation
  full-flow-control        Force full duplex with flow control
  half                     Force half duplex operation
sw1924_A(config-if)#
```

Figure 5-31
The output of the
show interface
command

```
sw1924_A#show interface ethernet 0/1

Ethernet 0/1 is Suspended-no-linkbeat
Hardware is Built-in 10Base-T
Address is 00D0.0692.6401
MTU 1500 bytes, BW 10000 Kbits
802.1d STP State: N/A     Forward Transitions:  0
Port monitoring: Disabled
Unknown unicast flooding: Enabled
Unregistered multicast flooding: Enabled
Description:
Duplex setting: Half duplex
Back pressure: Disabled

    Receive Statistics              Transmit Statistics
 --------------------------      --------------------------
Total good frames           0   Total frames              0
Total octets                0   Total octets              0
Broadcast/multicast frames  0   Broadcast/multicast frames 0
Broadcast/multicast octets  0   Broadcast/multicast octets 0
Good frames forwarded       0   Deferrals                 0
Frames filtered             0   Single collisions         0
Runt frames                 0   Multiple collisions       0
No buffer discards          0   Excessive collisions      0
                                Queue full discards       0
Errors:                         Errors:
  FCS errors                0   Late collisions           0
  Alignment errors          0   Excessive deferrals       0
  Giant frames              0   Jabber errors             0
  Address violations        0   Other transmit errors     0
sw1924_A#
```

Problems with Duplex Mismatches   A duplex mismatch occurs when one side of a connection has a different duplex setting than the other side. As noted in Chapter 2, "Identifying, Cabling, and Attaching to Cisco Devices," few obvious ways exist for detecting this misconfiguration, and thus the value of setting it correctly during the initial configuration is great. Obviously, a duplex mismatch will occur when two sides are expressly configured in opposite ways, such as when one side is set to full-duplex and the other is half. However, duplex mismatches may also occur as a result of one side or another failing to autonegotiate its duplex correctly. This second method is even more challenging to detect, as the configurations will seem valid on paper yet not function properly.

Late-Collisions and What They Mean   A late collision is somewhat of an anomaly in an Ethernet network and is a real indicator of issues on the network. CSMA/CD, the algorithm used for Ethernet, signifies that before a node transmits, it must first listen to the medium to ensure than someone else isn't currently transmitting. This behavior would lead a system to a situation in which collisions only occur when two nodes try to transmit simultaneously because at all other times the medium would contain an active transmission. A late collision signifies that a node has begun to transmit during the later stages of another node's transmission. This signifies that the second node for one reason or another did not detect an active transmission and began to transmit freely. This error may be due to an oversized Ethernet collision domain or a defective node on the network. Of the errors listed in Figure 5-31, the late collision is one of the strongest indicators of a defective network.

Maintaining the Switch

After a switch has been successfully integrated into a network, Cisco offers a number of important tools that enable one to gain valuable insights into the performance and health of the switch and the network itself. A user or administrator can take advantage of a number of `show` commands from the switch's CLI that will display all relevant aspects of the switch's configuration and its performance. A few of the more critical items are highlighted in the upcoming sections.

The complete set of show commands can be displayed at any time by typing `show ?` at the command line. Figure 5-32 describes the output of this command.

Using the Show Commands

The following sections describe some of the more critical `show` commands and their corresponding output.

Running-config The command `show running-config` will display a textual version of the switch's current configuration. As with traditional IOS, this textual version can be archived and pasted back into the switch

Figure 5-32
The list of items that
can be seen with the
show command

```
sw1924_A#show ?
  bridge-group          Display port grouping using bridge groups
  cdp                   cdp information
  cgmp                  Cgmp information
  history               Display the session command history
  interfaces            Interface status and configuration
  ip                    Display IP configuration
  line                  Display console/RS-232 port configuration
  mac-address-table     MAC forwarding table
  port                  Display port information
  running-config        Show current operating configuration
  snmp                  Display snmp related information
  spantree              Spanning tree subsystem
  spantree-option       Show STP port option parameter
  spantree-template     Show STP bridge template parameters
  storm-control         Show broadcast storm control configuration
  tacacs                Shows tacacs+ server configuration
  terminal              Display console/RS-232 port configuration
  tftp                  TFTP configuration and status
  trunk                 Display trunk information
  uplink-fast           Uplink Fast
  usage                 Display usage summaries
  version               System hardware and software status
  vlan                  Show VLAN information
  vlan-membership       Show VLAN membership information
  vtp                   VLAN trunk protocol
sw1924_A#
```

later, should a backup become necessary. Additional notes on backups are provided later in the chapter. Figure 33 contains the output of the show running-config command, which is a full configuration for a 1900 switch.

Interface Statistics Previously mentioned, the show interfaces command displays a number of highly useful values. Included in the output are such key items as the interface's MAC address, its STP status, and the operational status of the port itself. Further, beneath the configuration details, counters relevant to Ethernet traffic and errors are provided and can be useful in many ways (see Figure 5-34).

Figure 5-33

The output of the
show run
command

```
sw1924_A#show running-config
Building configuration . . .
Current configuration:
!
!
!
vlan 2 name "VLAN0002" sde 100002 state Operational mtu 1500
vlan 3 name "VLAN0003" sde 100003 state Operational mtu 1500
vlan 4 name "VLAN0004" sde 100004 state Operational mtu 1500
vlan 5 name "VLAN0005" sde 100005 state Operational mtu 1500
vlan 6 name "VLAN0006" sde 100006 state Operational mtu 1500
vlan 7 name "VLAN0007" sde 100007 state Operational mtu 1500
vlan 8 name "VLAN0008" sde 100008 state Operational mtu 1500
vlan 9 name "VLAN0009" sde 100009 state Operational mtu 1500
vlan 10 name "VLAN0010" sde 100010 state Operational mtu 1500
vlan 11 name "VLAN0011" sde 100011 state Operational mtu 1500
vlan 12 name "VLAN0012" sde 100012 state Operational mtu 1500

—More—
vlan 13 name "VLAN0013" sde 100013 state Operational mtu 1500
no cgmp
!
no spantree 1 2 3 4 5 6 7 8 9 10
no spantree 11 12 13 14 15 16 17 18 19 20
no spantree 21 22 23 24 25 26 27 28 29 30
no spantree 31 32 33 34 35 36 37 38 39 40
no spantree 41 42 43 44 45 46 47 48 49 50
no spantree 51 52 53 54 55 56 57 58 59 60
no spantree 61 62 63 64
!
hostname "sw1924_A"
!
!
ip address 10.1.1.2 255.255.255.0
ip default-gateway 10.1.1.1
!
enable password level 15 "CISCO"
!
interface Ethernet 0/1
  no cdp enable
!
interface Ethernet 0/2
  no cdp enable
!
interface Ethernet 0/3
  no cdp enable
!
interface Ethernet 0/4
  no cdp enable
!
interface Ethernet 0/5
  no cdp enable
!
interface Ethernet 0/6
  no cdp enable
!
```

```
interface Ethernet 0/7
  no cdp enable
!
interface Ethernet 0/8
  no cdp enable
!
interface Ethernet 0/9
  no cdp enable
!
interface Ethernet 0/10
  no cdp enable
!
interface Ethernet 0/11
  no cdp enable
!
interface Ethernet 0/12
  no cdp enable
!
interface Ethernet 0/13
  no cdp enable
!
interface Ethernet 0/14
  no cdp enable
!
interface Ethernet 0/15
  no cdp enable
!
interface Ethernet 0/16
  no cdp enable
!
interface Ethernet 0/17
  no cdp enable
!
Interface Ethernet 0/18
  no cdp enable
!
interface Ethernet 0/19
  no cdp enable
!
interface Ethernet 0/20
  no cdp enable
!
interface Ethernet 0/21
  no cdp enable
!
interface Ethernet 0/22
  no cdp enable
!
interface Ethernet 0/23
  no cdp enable
!
interface Ethernet 0/24
  no cdp enable
!
interface Ethernet 0/25
  no cdp enable
```

```
!
interface FastEthernet 0/26
 no cdp enable
!
interface FastEthernet 0/27
  no cdp enable
!
!
line console
end
sw1924_A#
```

Figure 5-34
The output of the
show interface
command

```
sw1924_A#show ?

sw1924_A#show interface ethernet0/24

Ethernet 0/24 is Enabled
Hardware is Built-in 10Base-T
Address is 00D0.0692.6418
MTU 1500 bytes, BW 10000 Kbits
802.1d STP State:  N/A      Forward Transitions:  0
Port monitoring: Disabled
Unknown unicast flooding: Enabled
Unregistered multicast flooding: Enabled
Description:
Duplex setting: Half duplex
Back pressure: Disabled

      Receive Statistics                Transmit Statistics
---------------------------------      ----------------------------
Total good frames       25692       Total frames           20561
Total octets            2782859     Total octets           10995881
Broadcast/multicast                 Broadcast/multicast
frames                  2824        frames                 2
Broadcast/multicast                 Broadcast/multicast
octets                  613810      octets                 128
Good frames forwarded   25444       Deferrals              125
Frames filtered         248         Single collisions      0
Runt frames             0           Multiple collisions    0
No buffer discards      0           Excessive collisions   0
Queue full discards     0
Errors:                 Errors:
  FCS errors            0           Late collisions        0
  Alignment errors      0           Excessive deferrals    0
  Giant frames          0           Jabber errors          0
  Address violations    0           Other transmit errors  0
sw1924_A#
```

Version Information   As the performance attributes of the switch are governed by the revision of software that is controlling it, an understanding of the details of that revision can be very important. The `show version` command can be used to provide those software details. In addition to outputting the current type and version of software running on the switch, the `show version` command can also provide some other hardware-oriented details, including the revision of the hardware boards as well as the memory configuration of the unit. Further, the hardware configuration details including port counts and types are also provided; they can be very useful when working remotely. Figure 5-35 displays the syntax and output of the `show version` command.

Managing the MAT

The *MAC Address Table* (MAT) is the forwarding table that the switch uses to make its filter or forward decisions. The table has also been referred to as the *Content Address Memory* (CAM) table. The 1900 switch enables a user to view and an administrator to modify the contents of the MAT. Using the `show mac-address-table` command, as shown in Figure 5-36, one can view the entire contents of the MAT. As shown in the figure, the first few lines indicate the number of permanent, restricted, and dynamic addresses that the switch is aware of. A dynamic address is one that has been learned through the normal switching process, and will include any address that the switch has heard traffic from within the age interval will be listed in the MAT.

The MAT describes a number of key items. Primarily, the table lists individual MAC addresses and the corresponding interface upon which the addresses were learned. This interface is known as the *destination interface* because it represents the interface that the switch will forward traffic out of for each of the MAC addresses that are assigned to it. Hence, if the MAC address of 0000.0000.0001 has been learned on destination interface Ethernet0/1, the switch will forward all traffic destined to 0000.0000.0001 out of Ethernet0/1. The MAT also lists a source interface that is set to "all" in every case, except for when a restricted static address has been configured. The restricted static address is covered in a following section.

Figure 5-35
The output of the
show version
command

```
sw1924_A#show version
Cisco Catalyst 1900/2820 Enterprise Edition Software
Version V8.01.02
Copyright (c) Cisco Systems, Inc.  1993-1998
sw1924_A uptime is 10day(s) 14hour(s) 40minute(s) 17second(s)
cisco Catalyst 1900 (486sxl) processor with 2048K/1024K bytes of
memory
Hardware board revision is 5
Upgrade Status: No upgrade currently in progress.
Config File Status: No configuration upload/download is in
progress
27 Fixed Ethernet/IEEE 802.3 interface(s)
Base Ethernet Address: 00-D0-06-92-64-00
sw1924_A#
```

Figure 5-36
Viewing the entire
contents of the MAT

```
sw1924_A#show mac
Number of permanent addresses : 0
Number of restricted static addresses : 0
Number of dynamic addresses : 2

Address                 Dest Interface     Type        Source
Interface List
----------------------------------------------------------------
0010.4B2A.A203          Ethernet 0/1       Dynamic     All
0800.0999.BA3E          Ethernet 0/1       Dynamic     All
sw1924_A#
```

The MAC Address Table

Given the significance of this table, one can infer that managing it may
prove beneficial. Beyond simply ensuring that the table is correct and that
frame switching is working as desired, management of the MAT can provide a number of additional benefits.

Setting Permanent MAC Addresses   Permanent addresses represent
those that have been statically configured in the switch's configuration.
These addresses are not subject to the age limit and thus do not time out.
These addresses are also not cleared if the switch happens to reboot or have
its MAT table cleared. Certain unique situations may require the use of permanent MAC addresses. In order to add a permanent entry to the MAT, the
global command mac-address-table is required. The syntax is as follows:

```
sw1924_A(config)#Mac-address-table [Type] [Address] [Interface]
```

The type can be either permanent or restricted. The address is the 48-bit MAC address that is entered in Hex in the H.H.H format where each H represents 16 bits or two bytes of an address. The interface is the destination interface on the switch or, more specifically, the port on the switch that the device is connected into. In Figure 5-37, a MAC address of 0000.0000.0001 is entered into the MAT with a destination address of Ethernet 0/1.

Displaying the MAT again indicates the addition of the now-permanent entry to the table (see Figure 5-38).

Setting Restricted Static Addresses   Restricted addresses are a variation on the permanent theme. Where the permanent entry enables the static configuration of the destination interface for specific MAC addresses, the restricted static entry enables both the source and destination interface to be specified. Doing so enables an administrator to restrict which ports are able to communicate to specific addresses on other ports. For example, if a user or group of users connect to port 4 of the switch where the only users are allowed to communicate with a certain file server on port 1, the administrator could hard-code this functionality into the switch using a restricted static entry in the MAT.

Figure 5-37
Permanent MAT table entry

```
sw1924_A(config)#mac-address-table permanent 0000.0000.0001
Ethernet0/1
```

Figure 5-38
The updated MAT

```
sw1924_A#show mac-address-table
Number of permanent addresses : 1
Number of restricted static addresses : 0
Number of dynamic addresses : 2

Address              Dest Interface    Type        Source
Interface List
-------------------------------------------------------------
0000.0000.0001       Ethernet 0/1      Permanent   All
0010.4B2A.A203       Ethernet 0/1      Dynamic     All
0800.0999.BA3E       Ethernet 0/1      Dynamic     All
sw1924_A#
```

In the example in Figure 5-39, a MAT table entry signifies that only the user or users on port 4 will be able to send traffic to the MAC address 0000.0000.0002 on port 1 of the switch.

Viewing the MAT after this command has been entered indicates the desired effect has been achieved and a static entry has been added to the MAT. This output is shown in Figure 5-40.

Port Security The MAT table has the capability to offer a level of security to the network. As connectivity through the switch depends on the MAT table, by specifying a list of MAC addresses on a port, one can ensure that only those MAC addresses receive traffic. However, setting permanent MAC addresses on every port on every switch throughout a network would be an extremely laborious task. Port security offers this functionality with much less time investment.

When port security is enabled on a port, that port will permanently learn every MAC address that it hears up to a user-designated number of addresses. For example, if there is a single node connected to a port, port security would ensure that that single node's MAC address is permanently

Figure 5-39

Setting a restricted destination MAC address

```
sw1924_A(config)#mac-address-table restricted static
0000.0000.0002 Eth0/1 Eth0/4
```

Figure 5-40

Viewing the MAT to identify the static entry

```
sw1924_A#show mac
Number of permanent addresses : 1
Number of restricted static addresses : 1
Number of dynamic addresses : 2

Address                 Dest Interface    Type         Source
Interface List
-----------------------------------------------------------------
0000.0000.0001          Ethernet 0/1      Permanent         All
0000.0000.0002          Ethernet 0/1      Static          Et0/4
0010.4B2A.A203          Ethernet 0/1      Dynamic     All
0800.0999.BA3E          Ethernet 0/1      Dynamic         All
sw1924_A#
```

learned on the port as soon as the node transmits a frame. From that point onward, the switch will not learn any additional addresses on the port. Hence, only that single node is capable of using the port. The term "sticky-learn" is sometimes used to describe this form of address learning due to the fact that the addresses are still dynamically learned, but they are not forgotten. As permanent addresses, these "sticky-learned" MACs are not subject to the age value and thus do not timeout.

The command to enable port security is an interface command with the following syntax:

```
sw1924_A(config-if)#port secure [max-mac-count] count
```

The `max-mac-count` option enables the administrator to define how many MACs the switch should sticky-learn. For example, if a 12-port repeater is attached to the port, it may be useful to set the count to 12 to ensure that all but not more than those 12 ports can have access to the network. The default number of addresses assigned is 132, which is also the maximum number one can assign to a single port. In the example in Figure 5-41, port security is applied to port one of the switch with a `max-mac-count` of 5.

A view of the MAT at this point indicates that the two dynamic addresses previously learned on port one are now permanent entries (see Figure 5-42).

Managing the Configuration File

The configuration of the 1900 switch exists as a text file stored on the switch itself. This text file can be easily backed up by a number of means. Although it is possible to simply cut and paste the configuration to a text file, the 1900 switch also offers the more scalable option of using a TFTP

Figure 5-41
The syntax for the port secure command

```
sw1924_A#conf t
Enter configuration commands, one per line.  End with CNTL/Z
sw1924_A(config)#interface ethernet 0/1
sw1924_A(config-if)#port secure max-mac-count 5
```

Figure 5-42
Viewing the result of
the port secure
command

```
sw1924_A#show mac-address-table
Number of permanent addresses : 3
Number of restricted static addresses : 1
Number of dynamic addresses : 0

Address               Dest Interface  Type         Source Interface
                                                   List
-----------------------------------------------------------------------
0800.0999.BA3E        Ethernet 0/1    Permanent    All
0010.4B2A.A203        Ethernet 0/1    Permanent    All
0000.0000.0001        Ethernet 0/1    Permanent    All
0000.0000.0002        Ethernet 0/1    Static
```

server to store configuration files. On the switch itself, the configuration file is stored in the switch's *Non-Volatile Random Access Memory* (NVRAM).

Copying to a TFTP Server   Copying the configuration file to a TFTP server is a relatively simple process involving a copy command with the source being the switch's NVRAM and the destination being a functional TFTP server. The syntax of the command is as follows:

```
sw1924_A#copy nvram tftp://[server address]/[filename]
```

The server address represents the IP or DNS address of the TFTP server. The filename represents the name of the file that will be created on the TFTP server for the configuration. In Figure 5-43, the TFTP server address is 10.1.1.1 and the filename for the configuration is 1924a_cfg.

Restoring from a TFTP Server   Because a valid configuration lies on a TFTP server, one can load that configuration onto a switch via the TFTP protocol. Doing so enables the efficient configuration of a switch from a remote location. Naturally, as the TFTP protocol is an IP-based protocol, the switch must be connected to the network and possess a viable IP configuration to enable it to communicate with the TFTP server. Given that those aspects are in place, a simple command will transfer the configuration file from the TFTP server to the switch. The syntax for the command is as follows:

```
sw1924_A#copy tftp://[server address]/[filename nvram
```

As with the previous command, the server address represents the IP or DNS address of the TFTP server, and the filename represents the configuration file. In Figure 5-44, the previously stored configuration file, `sw1924a_cfg`, is restored to the switch.

Clearing NVRAM As previously described, the NVRAM contains the switch's configuration. Often, it may become necessary to eliminate the configuration and start fresh. For example, should one need to redeploy a switch somewhere else in the network, it stands to reason that the switch should be completely reconfigured. By deleting the contents of the NVRAM, the switch is essentially reset to factory defaults. The syntax of the command used to clear the NVRAM is as follows:

```
sw1924_A#delete nvram
```

When the command is entered, as shown in Figure 5-46, the switch will prompt the administrator to verify that the command was not entered in error. Answering "Yes" to the prompt will erase the switch's configuration and thus reset it to factory defaults.

Figure 5-43
Copying to a TFTP server

```
sw1924_A#copy nvram tftp://10.1.1.1/1924a_cfg
Configuration upload is successfully completed
sw1924_A#
```

Figure 5-44
Restoring from a TFTP server

```
sw1924_A#copy tftp://10.1.1.1/1924a_cfg nvram
TFTP successfully downloaded configuration file
```

Figure 5-45
Clearing the NVRAM

```
sw1924_A#delete nvram
This command resets the switch with factory defaults.  All system
parameters will revert to their default factory settings.  All
static
and dynamic addresses will be removed.

Reset system with factory defaults, [Y]es or [N]o?  Yes
```

Chapter Summary

This chapter covered a fair amount of ground in the area of layer-two switching. At this point, you should have a strong feel for a number of topics. As always, it is recommended that you go back to the beginning of the chapter and reaffirm that you have successfully achieved the chapter's objectives as well as those required for the CCNA exam, should that be your direction.

A number of essential things should be evident after studying this chapter: First and foremost being the fact that bridges and switches are implemented with the primary goal being the segmentation of the collision domain. Today's networks simply require the increased, available bandwidth that switching technology provides. When tasked with differentiating between bridges and switches, understand that they are essentially the same device, as both are governed by the IEEE 802.1D protocol. The key area where it can be said that they differ is in port density and speed. Today's bridges have much higher port densities, forward frames at much higher rates, and are referred to as layer-two switches. Another key item of note would be the three flavors of switching described in the chapter. They are as follows:

- Store and forward: Latency high, retransmission of errors low
- Cut-through: Latency low, retransmission of errors high
- Fragment-free: Latency low, retransmission of errors low

Also covered in the chapter was STP. STP plays a significant role in today's internetworks and, as such, should be a protocol you are familiar with. Specifically, the role of the root bridge and the generation of the tree topology are of high importance. Also, a good understanding of the meaning of the port states listen, learn, forwarding, and blocking will serve you well.

The second half of the chapter focused on implementing many of the theoretical aspects discussed in the first half using the Cisco 1900 series switch. At this point you should feel comfortable obtaining access to the switch using either the Web-based VSM or one of the CLI modes. Setting up IP addresses and configuring ports properly for speed and duplex settings should not present a significant challenge. As a guide, a brief practical exercise is provided in an upcoming section.

From the Real World

In my role as a network engineer, I am often called upon to troubleshoot some very odd issues in very large networks. This can often be a very daunting challenge. In rare circumstances, I am provided with the results of accurate and relevant first-level troubleshooting details that enable me to quickly rule out a number of potential problems. However, this is surely not the norm. In most situations, I find success by relying on a good, logical troubleshooting methodology that works layer by layer. Following such a sequential process enables me to isolate issues quickly and begin more focused diagnostic efforts.

Hand in hand with a good process, one must have a good theoretical understanding of the normal operation of devices. The key to troubleshooting lies in one's ability to understand what should be happening. When you know what the traffic should look like, you can tell when it's misbehaving.

This brings me to the material covered in this chapter. On a previous troubleshooting effort, the staff of a large, switched network complained of extreme slowness on the network and described packet captures that seemed to indicate the flooding of unicast packets. Unicast floods are extremely rare and at the time were a phenomenon I hadn't seen. Generally in cases like these, I am skeptical of the accuracy of the information provided by the client and feel compelled to verify it. Sure enough, the network was exhibiting an end-to-end flood of one particular unicast frame. Recalling the discussion earlier in the chapter, a switch will flood any unicast that it does not have an entry for in the forwarding table. However, normally in a conversation, the first frame or two will be flooded, but as soon as the receiver responds, all of the switches in the network learn its location and the flooding stops. Further, additional knowledge told me that if a sender doesn't hear from its receiver in good time, upper layer protocols would halt the transmissions. The fact that both of these rules were being broken enabled me to make the hypothesis that there may be an application error causing this problem. In the end, that hypothesis allowed me to bring a timely resolution to a rather odd problem.

The moral of the story, if you will, is the value of theoretical knowledge. It was the knowledge of ordinary switch operation that enabled me to quickly narrow my diagnostic efforts and solve this problem. Given the pervasiveness of switching technology today, I cannot overemphasize the value of having a good understanding of normal switch behavior.

Peter A. Van Oene

Frequently Asked Questions (FAQ)

Question: After installing switches, why do my Microsoft Windows clients have trouble logging in when they first boot up?

Answer: This is a very common issue that involves STP. If you recall, when a switch port becomes active, it moves the listen and learn stages of STP before it begins to forward packets. This process takes approximately 30 seconds. When a PC is turned on, it will likely boot up and attempt to begin the logon process before this 30-second window has elapsed. However, when it attempts to do so, the switch port will not yet forward traffic and thus the logon process will fail, as the PC will not be able to communicate with the rest of the network.

To address this issue, you can modify the delta time between initialization and forwarding for a switch port. Cisco offers an setting called *Port Fast* that instructs a switch port to begin forwarding packets immediately instead of waiting the 30 seconds for full listen and learn stages. This mode should be enabled on all switch ports that connect to end nodes to eliminate the above symptoms.

Question: How can I use my packet analyzer to monitor the network now that I have switches installed?

Answer: Packet analyzers, including packet capture utilities, have lost some of their value due to the implementation of switches. The segmentation that a switch provides serves to help the network, but at the same time limits the amount of traffic that an analyzer connected to a specific port would have access to. As analyzers tend to be passive devices, they simply listen to any traffic that is present on the segment to which they are attached. As the switch will only forward traffic to the specific end nodes attached to a port along with broadcasts and multicasts, this traffic is all that an analyzer will be able to capture and analyze. Hence, unlike in the days when networks consisted of a single collision domain, analyzers can no longer capture all traffic present on the network.

Although this changes the role of the analyzer, it does not diminish the value of packet and frame analysis. One simply needs to leverage the tool within the constraints provided. Further, switch manufactures include the ability in many switches to mirror traffic from one port to another or from groups of ports or VLANs onto single ports to offset this limitation. Also, additional tools like RMON-enabled switches and advanced network analyzers provide a means of providing a kind of end-to-end view of the network.

Case Study: Configuring a New Switch

The exercise will build on the knowledge gained in Chapter 3, "The Basics of Cisco Configuration and Operations," by including some of the topics learned in this chapter. The required equipment is as follows:

- One Catalyst 1900 series switch
- One PC with a terminal program
- One TFTP server

The steps for the switch configuration are as follows:

1. Connect to the switch via the console port.
2. Log in and enter the enabled mode of the IOS CLI.
3. Clear the contents of the NVRAM.
4. Input the following basic configuration:
   a. Hostname: Labswitch
   b. IP address: 10.1.1.1
   c. Subnet mask: 255.255.255.0
   d. Default gateway address: 10.1.1.254

5. Set the duplex on the 100BaseX (TX and/or FX) ports to half.
6. View the interface to verify the duplex on the above ports.
7. Add a static MAT entry for 0000.0000.0001 on port 0/1.
8. View the MAT table to verify this entry.
9. Save the config file to the TFTP server (note the TFTP server must be reachable by IP).

For an advanced configuration, do the following:

1. Clear the contents of the NVRAM.
2. Restore the above configuration of the switch from the TFTP server.

Questions

1. The transparent switch requires involvement from the end nodes for it to function.

   a. True

   b. False

2. In the MAT or forwarding table, dynamic MAC addresses are maintained for what period of time?

   a. Until the switch is rebooted

   b. For the period of time designated by the age value

   c. For the period of time designated by the forward delay value

   d. Permanently

3. The default value for the age parameter is how many seconds?

   a. 100

   b. 200

   c. 300

   d. 400

4. Which of the following is not a valid Cisco switching methodology on the 1900 switch?

   a. Store and forward

   b. Fast-forward

   c. Fragment-free

   d. Cut-through

5. Bridging and switching are both governed by what standard?

   a. ANSI 802.1D

   b. IEEE 802.1D

   c. IETF 802.1D

   d. ITU/T 802.1D

6. Which of the following does not represent an option a switch has when deciding how to process a frame?

   a. Forwarding the frame out a set of interfaces

   b. Filtering the frame

   c. Flooding the frame out all interfaces

   d. Forwarding the frame out of a single interface

7. Which of the following transmissions represents one-to-many valid Ethernet transmissions?

   a. Simulcast
   b. Multicast
   c. Unicast
   d. Broadcast

8. What is the size of a MAC address?

   a. Six Bytes
   b. Eight Bytes
   c. 16 Bytes
   d. 32 Bytes

9. What is the first bridge elected in the Spanning Tree process?

   a. Designated bridge
   b. Bridge elect
   c. Root bridge
   d. Segment bridge

10. During a root bridge election the bridge exhibiting which quality will be elected?

    a. The lowest MAC address
    b. The highest MAC address
    c. The lowest bridge ID
    d. The highest bridge ID

11. What does the acronym BPDU stand for?

    a. Bridge packet data unit
    b. Base protocol data unit
    c. Binary packet data unit
    d. Bridge protocol data unit

12. The listen and learn stages of the Spanning Tree process take place over what time interval each?

    a. 10 seconds
    b. 20 seconds
    c. 30 seconds
    d. 15 seconds

13. The 1900 switch can be managed by which of the following methods?

    a. ISO CLI

    b. IOS CLI

    c. Web-based VSM

    d. Menu-based CLI

    e. All of the above

14. What is the default switching mode on the 1900?

    a. Store and forward

    b. Fast-forward

    c. Fragment-free

    d. Cut-through

15. By default, Spanning Tree is disabled on the 1900 switch.

    a. True

    b. False

16. By default, the 10Base-T ports on the 1900 are set to which duplex?

    a. Autonegotiate

    b. Full-duplex

    c. Half-duplex

17. The `show interfaces` command will display which of the following?

    a. The MAC address of the interface

    b. The duplex of the interface

    c. The STP state of the interface

    d. All of the above

18. Which of the following are representative of possible cabling or adapter issues on a shared segment?

    a. Normal collisions

    b. Late collisions

    c. Both of the above

    d. Neither of the above

19. Which IOS command will display the configuration of a switch?

    a. `show startup-config`

    b. `show running-config`

    c. `show config`

    d. `show switch-config`

20. Which of the following IOS commands will reset the switch to factory defaults?

    a. `clear config`
    b. `reset config`
    c. `delete nvram`
    d. `erase nvram`

Answers

1. **b.** False

   The true value in the transparent switch is exactly that, transparent to the end nodes in a network.

2. **b.** For the period of time designated by the age value

   MAC addresses remain in the MAT until they have not been heard from for a period of time dictated by the age value.

3. **c.** 300

   Cisco uses 300 seconds as a default age value.

4. **b.** Fast-forward

   Fast-forward is not a valid term for any switching methodology. However, it does represent the terminology used by some manufacturers to signify that the 30-second interval for Spanning Tree listen and learn stages is being skipped.

5. **b.** IEEE 802.1D

   Bridging and switching are both governed by the IEEE committee under the 802.1D standard.

6. **a.** Forwarding the frame out a set of interfaces

   A switch will not forward a frame out a set of interfaces. It will either filter, flood, or forward out a single interface.

7. **b.** Multicast and **d.** Broadcast

   Both broadcasts and multicasts represent one to many transmissions.

8. **a.** Six bytes

   A MAC address is six bytes or 48 bits in length.

9. **c.** Root bridge

   The first election in the Spanning Tree process elects a root bridge.

10. **c.** The lowest bridge ID

    The bridge with the lowest bridge ID will always win the root bridge election. The bridge ID contains a two-byte priority along with a six-byte MAC address.

11. **d.** Bridge protocol data unit

    BPDU stands for Bridge Protocol Data Unit.

12. d. 15 seconds

Both the listen and learn stages take place over 15-second windows.

13. e. All of the above

A 1900 switch can be managed by any of the listed methods.

14. c. Fragment-free

By default, the 1900 switch forwards with the fragment-free methodology.

15. b. False

Spanning Tree is enabled by default on the 1900 switch.

16. c. Half-duplex

All of the 10-Mbps ports on the 1900 switch come set to half-duplex.

17. d. All of the above

Each of the above items can be verified with the `show interfaces` command.

18. b. Late collisions

Normal collisions are to be expected in a shared media topology. However, late collisions are indicative of possible design or hardware faults in a network.

19. b. `show running-config`

The command `show running-config` will display the configuration on a 1900 switch.

20. c. `delete nvram`

As the configuration for the switch is contained in the NVRAM, deleting the NVRAM causes the switch to reset to the defaults.

Extending Switched Networks with VLANs

Objectives

On completion of this chapter, you will be able to do the following:

■ Differentiate clearly between collision and broadcast domains

■ Define *Virtual Local Area Network* (VLAN) technology and its industry drivers

■ Describe the role of VLAN technology in an internetwork

■ Configure VLANs in a 1900 switch

■ Understand to the role of the *Virtual Terminal Protocol* (VTP) in a network

■ Differentiate between the various VTP modes

■ Understand the role and use of VLAN trunking mechanisms

■ Describe the use of Spanning Tree in VLAN-enabled networks

This chapter can also help you fulfill the following CCNA exam objectives:

■ Describe the advantages of LAN segmentation

■ Describe LAN segmentation using bridges

■ Describe LAN segmentation using routers

■ Describe LAN segmentation using switches

■ Describe network congestion problem in Ethernet networks

■ Describe the benefits of VLANs

The Domains of a LAN

In order to have an informative discussion about the concepts involved in VLAN technology, two essential qualities of a LAN need to be understood. Those qualities represent what are called the *domains* of a LAN. Both the collision domain and the broadcast domain represent important sets of nodes within a LAN and also possess some performance-oriented and potentially inhibiting characteristics. In order to understand and architect well-designed LANs, one must have a strong understanding of both of these concepts. The previous chapters have touched on these concepts in a number of contexts and the following sections will dig into each a little deeper.

The Collision Domain

The collision domain identifies the set of Ethernet nodes that contend for the same bandwidth. It can also be said that this domain represents the area in which collisions occur and are propagated. This area or domain can also be thought of as a shared segment. Within the OSI model, the collision domain can be considered as a layer-one area. As such, the devices that continue to the collision domain are hubs or repeaters, or any device that purely repeats the Ethernet signaling. Hence, it can be said that every device connected to the same repeater, or group of repeaters, is a member of the same collision domain. As discussed in the previous chapter, collision domains are divided or segmented at layer two by devices like bridges and layer-two switches. However, just as the switch segments the collision domain, it also provides the connectivity between collision domains. Figure 6-1 depicts the collision domain graphically.

How Collisions Affect the Performance of the LAN The CSMA/CD methodology that Ethernet employs is contention-based. That is to say that the nodes participating in the algorithm must contend for access to the medium. As one can imagine, as the number of nodes contending for the same medium increases, the individual probability of any one of those nodes successfully accessing the medium decreases. Also, during this

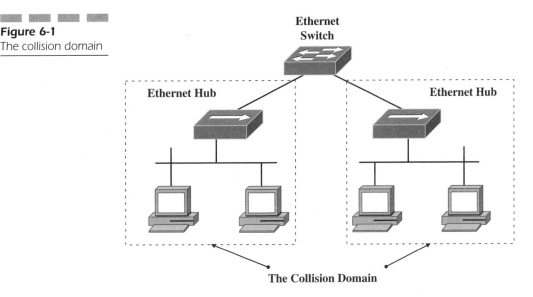

Figure 6-1
The collision domain

increase in the number of nodes in contention, a similar increase in the amount of collisions is also likely to occur. Generally, a very high rate of collisions leaves Ethernet ineffective due to an overwhelming amount of contention and collision activity.

However, the topic of collision rates and utilization levels in CSMA/CD networks represents an opportunity for much theoretical discussion and debate. One of the most notable studies on this topic, "The Measured Capacity of an Ethernet: Myths and Reality," by Boggs, Mogul, and Kent (WRL Research Report 88/4), brings to light a common mythology in Ethernet networks. The myth surrounds the concept that all Ethernet, CSMA/CD networks operating at or above 37 percent utilization exhibit high collision rates and poor performance, which is not necessarily true. In fact, tests done within the study indicate in many cases that Ethernet is a viable technology at up to 85 percent utilization. The study brought to light the need for considering both the utilization rate and collision rate of an Ethernet as they relate to a network's capability to effectively deliver data. When designing CSMA/CD networks, it is wise to pay careful attention to certain qualities including the number of nodes per segment, the data rates, the collision domain diameter, the number and type of repeaters per segment, and the applications and protocols in use, to name a few.

Without delving further into this topic, it can be said that utilization rates at or above 40 percent coupled with collision rates at or above five percent may represent an area for concern. However, in all cases it is essential to examine both the utilization rate and the collision rate before rendering an opinion on the relative health of a network. Although many will ask what the optimum size of a collision domain is, measured in the number of nodes, no definite answer can satisfy this question. A small number of active nodes can easily congest a collision domain and an inactive large group of nodes may be adequately served. It should be noted, however, that the trend toward the continued deployment of switching technology through the core of the network to the desktop is slowly eliminating many of these CSMA/CD-related design considerations.

The Broadcast Domain

The broadcast domain can be considered the set of nodes that receives the same broadcasts. For example, if any one node within the set transmits a broadcast frame, all other nodes that hear that broadcast frame can be considered part of the broadcast domain. Many devices in the network, including workstations, routers, and servers, originate broadcast and multicast frames. The broadcast domain is in many ways a layer-two area, as devices like bridges and switches simply continue the broadcast domain by forwarding all broadcast and multicast frames. The layer-three device that bounds or segments the broadcast domain is traditionally a router or a layer-three switch. Figure 6-2 illustrates the broadcast domain. Just as a switch provides connectivity between collision domains, the router or layer-three switch also provides connectivity between different broadcast domains.

How Broadcasts Affect the Performance of the LAN   In an Ethernet network, end nodes must process all frames that are either uniquely addressed to them or broadcasted to the entire broadcast domain. Processing a frame can be an intensive activity for an end node. Furthermore, in many networks, most broadcast frames have little value to a great number of those end nodes; thus, the processing that does occur represents a waste of processor resources. However, as all prevalent networking protocols are broadcast-intensive, this processing tends to be inevitable. For that reason, well-designed networks need to pay close attention to the size and substance of broadcast domains in order to balance functionality with performance. As mentioned above, this is done through the effective use of layer-three devices to segment the broadcast domain into smaller sizes. The optimum size of a broadcast domain depends on the types of protocols in use within the domain. Each of the major protocols, including TCP/IP,

Figure 6-2
The broadcast
domain

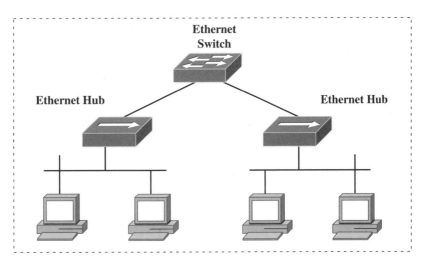

The Broadcast Domain

IPX/SPX, and AppleTalk, possess somewhat different broadcast-oriented characteristics. In general, it is recommended that one keep the percentage of broadcast traffic on a particular segment somewhere around or beneath 20 percent of the total traffic.

NOTE: *When considering broadcast rates, one must remember that a switch port will only forward traffic destined to* Media Access Control (MAC) addresses *located off the port, unknown MAC addresses, and all broadcasts and multicasts from the broadcast domain. Thus, when one attaches a network analysis device to a switch or views the traffic on a particular switch port via the span command, the traffic shown on the port will seem to contain an extremely high percentage of broadcast traffic. This is due to the fact that the switch has filtered most unicasts, as they are not relevant on the particular segment. Naturally, this fact tends to misrepresent the broadcast rate of a broadcast domain. For that reason, it is essential to also consider the utilization rate on an interface when examining the broadcast rate in order to keep things in perspective.*

Virtual Local Area Networks

The term VLAN is certainly one that is used very often in the industry. However, in many respects, there is also a certain degree of mythology that surrounds the term. VLAN technology is certainly not an overly complex topic when compared with many other technologies. Despite that, VLANs tend to be often misunderstood by many. This misunderstanding is likely due to the overwhelming amount of ambiguous marketing collateral that surrounds VLAN technology.

The first essential concept one needs to understand is that a LAN is a broadcast domain. Recalling that broadcast domains are bound by routers and comprised of switches and repeaters, we can quickly conceptualize the LAN. Figure 6-3 illustrates this concept once again. A quick look at the figure indicates that the hardware that comprises the LAN, that being the switches and repeaters along with the router boundaries, presents somewhat of a physical dependency on the size and scope of the LAN. More specifically, it can be seen that all devices that connect to the switches and repeaters participate in the same broadcast domain or the same LAN. It is specifically this physical dependency that VLAN technology is designed to overcome.

Figure 6-3
The LAN

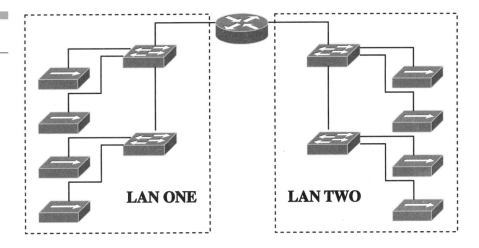

LAN ONE   LAN TWO

VLAN Defined

A VLAN is nothing more than a LAN itself. Given that a LAN is a broadcast domain, it can be said that a VLAN is also simply a broadcast domain. However, the broadcast domain in a VLAN-enabled network is not bound by the same physical dependencies, as found in traditional LANs. Today's LAN infrastructure has the capability to strategically propagate broadcast traffic to specific end nodes as defined by network administrators, as opposed to dictated by physical location.

For example, in Chapter 5, "Catalyst 1900 Switch Operation," it was noted that a switch will forward a broadcast out of all of its interfaces, making it simply one broadcast domain. However, when configured to enable VLANs, that same switch has the capability to group various interfaces together and maintain multiple broadcast domains. In Figure 6-4, this capability is depicted. As shown in the VLAN-enabled switch, more than one broadcast domain can exist in a single switch and the switch ensures that there is no cross-pollination of broadcasts.

Essentially, this multiple broadcast domain capability is very much like having parallel but not interconnected devices. For example, if an area requires two broadcast domains or two LANs for one reason or another, one would traditionally use two isolated switches to provide for this connectivity. Given that the two switches are not interconnected, the network would consist of two separate broadcast domains, thus meeting the area's needs. However, this may not represent the most efficient use of resources. Consider that only 12 nodes require connectivity with, say,

Figure 6-4
Multiple broadcast
domains

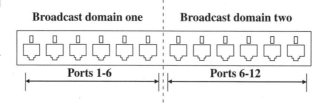

Broadcast domain one | Broadcast domain two

Ports 1-6 | Ports 6-12

**Through isolating ports, two broadcast domains have
been created**

Figure 6-5
VLANs isolate traffic

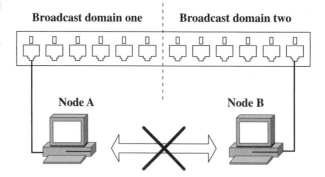

Broadcast domain one | Broadcast domain two

Node A | Node B

Node A cannot communicate with Node B

six per each broadcast domain. The legacy solution would most likely have to be made up of two 12-port switches, thus wasting 12 ports, or being 50 percent efficient. With VLAN technology, a single switch could be configured with two VLANs and provide the same connectivity as the two previous switches without the same penalty in efficiency. Figure 6-5 describes these two solutions. In this way, defining or using multiple VLANs on a switch can be seen as logically creating multiple switches within a single switch.

A key point to remember is that VLANs, as broadcast domains, require a layer-three capability in order to communicate with each other. The devices from the different VLANs in Figure 6-5 will not communicate with other, even though they are physically connected to the same switch. This will become clearer as later chapters describe the relationship of IP subnets an IPX networks to VLANs.

VLAN Transparency

End-node participation is not required for functional VLAN-oriented networks. Ideally, the administrator of a network can, through some means, define the VLAN characteristics of the network within the network's switching devices and thus enable the switches to maintain all of the VLAN properties. In this environment, end nodes interact with the network as normal, while the network ensures the desired connectivity with respect to the separation of broadcast domains. In the end, the switch needs only to ensure that each port designated for end-user connectivity is set to participate in the correct VLAN.

VLAN Membership Techniques

As previously mentioned, the key to constructing and maintaining functional VLANs is ensuring that the individual switch ports know which VLANs they are a part of. This knowledge ensures that the broadcast domains remain isolated and that each end node has access to the correct broadcast domain.

A number of different techniques are available that enable the ports to map to VLANs in switches. The most functional and currently the most employed methodology involves the manual and static configuration of VLAN ports in each switch used in a network. Although laborious to initially set up, this form of VLAN construction is very accurate and provides few, if any, areas for concern. It should be noted, however, that some dynamic ways exist for assigning ports to a VLAN. One such methodology includes the use of VLAN servers that use static MAC address-to-VLAN relationship tables to dynamically assign a port to a VLAN, based on the MAC address learned on the individual port. For example, if the VLAN server indicates that MAC address 0000.0000.0001 is a member of VLAN2, the switch that learns that MAC address in its forwarding table will automatically assign the port to VLAN2.

Another technique enables the port to detect which protocol the end node is using and dynamically assigns the port to a protocol-specific VLAN. However, these more dynamic methods have proven unstable or unscalable and simply have not achieved the widespread use that port-based static configuration has. As such, in the configuration sections of this chapter, the focus will be on static port assignment.

VLAN Technology Drivers

VLAN technology, though relatively simple, can provide a great number of benefits to a network. The upcoming sections describe some of the more prevalent reasons why VLANs are becoming such a pervasive element in today's network design.

Performance   As discussed previously, high levels of broadcast traffic on a network can have a detrimental impact on the performance of the nodes within the broadcast domains. Thus, the segmentation of broadcast domains tends to provide an increase in overall performance on a network. Although VLANs do not inherently impact the size of broadcast domains, what they do provide is a greater flexibility for segmentation. Network administrators who possess VLAN-capable devices have an excellent opportunity to leverage that functionality to more easily reduce the size of their broadcast domains and thus positively impact network performance. Hence, the network administrator can impact performance simply by switch reconfiguration instead of hardware replacements.

NOTE: *One should be aware that although VLANs can quickly alter a broadcast domain's composition in a network, other elements like network layer addressing and routing will be affected in the process. Further chapters will touch on this dependency, but for now suffice it to say that VLAN reconfiguration requires a strategic approach to ensure that all layers of the OSI model are properly addressed.*

Cost-Efficiency   In networks where broadcast domain isolation is necessary for one reason or another, VLAN technology can enable this isolation without the costly replication of hardware. The brief previous example indicated a segment with a small amount of users that could be served with one VLAN-capable switch instead of two separate switches. Economies of this type can be found throughout large and small internetworks where a single VLAN-capable set of networking devices can provide flexible connectivity to the user base. This enables the network to flex via a logical configuration, as opposed to a more costly physical alteration or duplication.

Network Security   Consider a typical corporate network like the one described in Figure 6-6. It can be seen that the company is comprised of a number of functional business units that are generally grouped together physically throughout the network.

Figure 6-6
Sample corporate
network

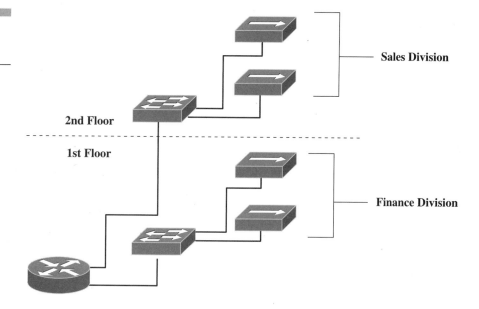

2nd Floor

Sales Division

1st Floor

Finance Division

However, in some cases, the physical topology and the logical topology of the users do not align. In other words, just because a group of people sit close to each other does not mean that they should ideally share a broadcast domain. In cases like this where traffic isolation is necessary from a security perspective, this mismatch in topologies can become a challenge. For example, consider an area like the one depicted in Figure 6-7 where users from both the finance and sales divisions are physically located together. Normally, this physical quality would dictate that both of these user groups share a broadcast domain.

However, this sharing can represent somewhat of a security risk. VLAN technology enables the traffic presented by the two groups to become fully isolated one from the other. Should the two groups need to communicate, security can be deployed between the two broadcast domains in the form of packet-filtering routers or firewalls.

Protocol Dependencies   Network-layer protocols like TCP/IP, IPX/SPX, and AppleTalk rely on the broadcast functionality provided by Ethernet networks. However, in many cases, specifically those related to TCP/IP, certain relationships between the protocol and the broadcast domain can prove limiting. For example, as will be discussed in upcoming chapters, TCP/IP demands that each network node within a broadcast domain have the same IP network number. Thus, should a node move from one broadcast domain

Figure 6-7
Mixed users

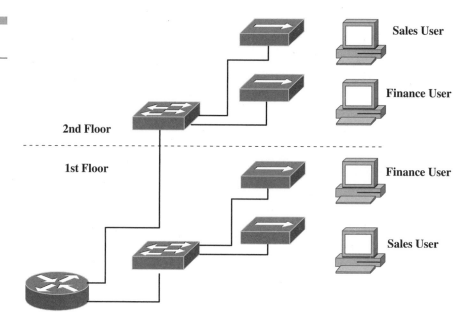

to another, that node would require reconfiguration. This dependency can prove laborious in a situation where moves, adds, and changes in a network occur frequently. VLAN technology enables the broadcast domain to be flexible with respect to a device's physical location and thus avoids the time-consuming reconfiguration of nodes that move from one location to another.

NOTE: *The* Dynamic Host Control Protocol *(DHCP) enables the dynamic reconfiguration of IP properties on an end node and thus helps mitigate the above constraints. However, these two technologies are not in competition with each other and, in fact, the proper integration of DHCP and VLAN technology provides the optimum network solution for IP-based networks.*

VLAN Configuration

As described previously in the chapter, VLAN topologies are most often enabled on a port basis. Hence, in order to deliver VLAN functionality to a network, one must configure the individual switches that comprise the network. Cisco supports not only the ability to assign ports to VLANs, but also provides a number of additional features to aid in the configuration and management of both large and small internetworks. The following sections will describe these features in some detail and present some examples using the Cisco 1900 series switch.

VLANs and Switch Support

VLAN capability is a feature that is not present in all switches. Further, certain aspects of VLAN functionality, including features like VTP or ISL/802.1q trunking, may or may not be supported in a particular switch. Hence, when selecting a switch for a network or considering the design of an existing network, one must have a good understanding of the VLAN-oriented capabilities of the switches in question. Further, many switches have feature sets that are enacted via a software code. In situations where multiple versions and types of code exist, one must again be aware of the VLAN capabilities of each of the software sets. In all, it proves wise to read the fine print when working with switches in VLAN environments in order to ensure that the required functionality will be there when it's needed.

VLAN Trunking Protocol

In large internetworks where many switches exist, enabling and managing VLANs on a network-wide basis can become challenging. Consider a simple network that has a need for two VLANs, one for lawyers and one for legal secretaries, for example. The challenge surrounds ensuring that every switch in the network maintains these two VLANs and their related characteristics. With two switches, one would have to configure the VLANs twice (once per switch) and ensure that they properly integrate with the right amount of availability and security. With 20 switches, the opportunity for misconfiguration increases tenfold. This becomes further complicated when the number of VLANs increases. In large networks with many switches and many VLANs, the task of ensuring the consistency, availability, and security of each VLAN on each relevant switch is administratively daunting.

To address this issue, Cisco has developed a proprietary protocol called the *VLAN Trunking Protocol* (VTP). VTP enables the centralized control and administration of VLAN instances and properties. Within a VTP-enabled network, an administrator can centrally manage the addition, deletion, or modification of VLANs as well as their related properties and benefit from those modifications being propagated across the network. VTP is a layer-two messaging protocol that switches use to communicate information related to VLAN configuration. Using VTP minimizes the opportunities for the misconfiguration of VLAN information that can lead to issues such as a lack of VLAN capability, a loss of connectivity, and a breach of security.

Creating a VTP Domain   To enable VTP connectivity, one must first create a VTP domain. Every switch that needs to participate in VTP conversations must belong to this VTP domain. Hence, if one is configuring a network for ABC Company, one might chose ABC as the VTP domain name. From there, each switch in the network that has its VTP domain name set to ABC would participate in the VLAN management provided by the VTP protocol.

VTP advertisements are transmitted out all the interfaces that are set to trunk mode. Trunked interfaces are those that use protocols like the *Inter-Switch Link* (ISL), IEEE 802.1Q, IEEE 802.10, and *ATM LAN Emulation* (LANE). These interfaces enable multiple VLANs to exist on a single interface and provide a mechanism for the switches to differentiate between each VLAN. Trunked interfaces will be covered in more detail further into this chapter.

In the 1900 switch, the VTP domain name is set as a global parameter. The following command adds the switch to the VTP domain ICND.

```
sw1924_A(config)#vtp domain ICND server
```

In the previous command, the parameter *server* indicates that the switch will play the role of server within the VTP domain. Each of the available VTP roles are described in the following sections.

VTP Modes   The VLAN trunking protocol works in a client/server arrangement. This relationship enables VLANs to be created or modified on a server and have the changes then propagated out to each client.

Server   The VTP server acts as the source of VLAN information within a VTP domain. As such, this switch is where a network's VLAN information should be managed. Within the domain, the VTP server is responsible for transmitting the most current VLAN-oriented details to the rest of the network. Hence, an administrator uses the VTP server to create, modify, or delete VLANs from a network. The server then advertises those details outward to the network so that each switch is aware of the current VLAN configuration. The details of the VLAN configuration are stored in the *Non-Volatile Random Access Memory* (NVRAM) on the server so that if the server or switch loses power, the details of the VLAN configuration will be maintained.

Client A VTP client operates on VLAN information provided to it by a VTP server. As such, its role is to synchronize its VLAN configuration with that of the server and maintain the integrity of that configuration though various advertisement processes. The VLAN configuration on a VTP client is not stored in NVRAM and thus must be obtained dynamically from a VTP server upon bootup.

Transparent A switch operating in VTP transparent mode acts as neither a client nor a server. In fact, the switch is almost purely autonomous with respect to its VLAN configuration. The VLAN configuration on this type of switch is stored and manipulated locally, that is to say on the switch itself, as opposed to as dictated by a VTP-provided configuration. This switch does not synchronize its VLAN configuration with any other switch on the network. If it were not for one key function, this switch would not need to participate in the VTP domain whatsoever. However, certain network designs may dictate that an autonomous switch not fully participating in the VTP domain may separate a VTP client from a VTP server. Such a topology is illustrated in Figure 6-8. In these situations, instead of orphaning the VTP client, the intermediary switch can be brought into the VTP domain in transparent mode. In this mode, the switch will listen for and forward VTP advertisements, ensuring that VTP traffic transits through the switch so that connectivity to orphaned VTP clients can be maintained. It should be noted that the transparent switch's VLAN configuration and that of the VTP domain would remain fully separate entities.

How VTP Works

As described in the earlier sections, VTP is a layer-2 messaging protocol and thus uses the services of layer-two addressing to perform its responsibilities. Essentially, the VTP protocol needs to ensure that all switches operate with a consistent VLAN configuration and that any modifications are accurately communicated throughout the network. The following sections describe the functionality of VTP in more detail.

Figure 6-8
VTP transparent mode

VTP Server   VTP Transparent   VTP Client

The VTP Transparent Switch forwards VTP traffic between the client and server

VTP Advertisements   VTP advertisements are used by the VTP protocol for two reasons: to enable clients to request VLAN information on
bootup, and for servers to advertise VLAN information. The advertisements
are sent via a layer-two multicast and are ignored by routers, as they only
pertain to VTP-enabled switches. The server-side advertisements include a
VLAN summary sent every five minutes or when changes occur, along with
subset advertisements that provide more specific information on individual VLANs.

VLAN Synchronization   In order for VTP to be effective, every switch
in the VTP domain must process the same information and thus maintain
synchronization with each other. As more than one VTP server may exist
within a VTP domain, in order to maintain consistency, VTP advertisements contain a revision number. Each time the VLAN configuration is
modified, the VTP revision number is incremented by one. Within the
domain, the VTP server with advertisements that contain the highest
numerical revision number will be considered accurate. Hence, should a
client process a VTP advertisement with a revision number lower than the
previous one, that advertisement will be ignored, as generally this will indicate an out-of-date advertisement. Figure 6-9 illustrates the role of the VTP
revision number.

   This functionality ensures that, should a new VTP server enter into the
domain, its configuration will not take precedence over the domain's current configuration, assuming that it has a lower VTP revision number.
However, one should be aware of the current VTP revision number of any
VTP server before introducing it to a domain to ensure that one's current
VLAN configuration isn't overwritten by a VTP server that happens to have
a higher revision number.

   In order to verify the current VTP revision number within a domain, one
can use the following command:

Figure 6-9
The VTP revision
number

The Client will choose the Revision 17 Broadcast and Synch its VLAN
configuration with that Server

```
sw1924_A#show vtp
      VTP version: 1
      Configuration revision: 13
      Maximum VLANs supported locally: 1005
      Number of existing VLANs: 18
      VTP domain name         : ICND
      VTP password            :
      VTP operating mode      : Server
      VTP pruning mode        : Disabled
      VTP traps generation    : Enabled
      Configuration last modified by: 10.1.1.3 at 00-00-0000
00:00:00
```

In the above display, one can see that the current VTP revision number is 13 on this VTP server.

VTP Pruning   In a network with a number of VLANs, it may be quite likely that not all VLANs are represented on all switches. Therefore, forwarding a particular VLAN's traffic to a switch that does not have any ports within that VLAN would prove an inefficient use of bandwidth. The diagram in Figure 6-10 illustrates such a situation.

In order to address this inefficiency in bandwidth usage, Cisco has introduced the concept of VTP pruning. This technique enables switches to indicate which VLANs they do not have ports attached to. This information is then used to optimize the flooding of traffic throughout a network. Figure 6-11 describes this VTP pruning optimization.

It should be noted, however, that all switches in a network must be enabled for pruning before pruning will take effect. In order to enable pruning on the VTP-configured switch, the following command is used:

```
sw1924_A(config)#vtp pruning enable
sw1924_A(config)#
```

Figure 6-10
VTP pruning before

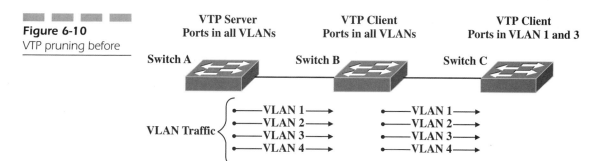

Traffic from VLANs 2 and 4 is forwarded onto Switch C despite Switch C
having no destination ports in those VLANs

Figure 6-11
VTP pruning after

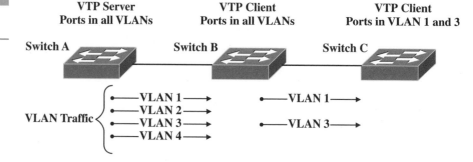

**Traffic from VLANs 2 and 4 has been "pruned" at switch B as Switch C
has no destination ports in those VLANs**

Another look at the overall VTP configuration summary indicates that
pruning has been enabled on the 1900 switch:

```
sw1924_A#show vtp
    VTP version: 1
    Configuration revision: 14
    Maximum VLANs supported locally: 1005
    Number of existing VLANs: 18
    VTP domain name        : ICND
    VTP password           :
    VTP operating mode     : Server
    VTP pruning mode       : Enabled
    VTP traps generation   : Enabled
    Configuration last modified by: 10.1.1.3 at 00-00-0000
00:00:00
```

The Significance of VLAN1

Within a VTP-enabled network, the first VLAN, VLAN1, plays an important role. This VLAN can be considered the management or administrative
VLAN. Due to its importance, VLAN1 must always exist and be available
network-wide. For this reason, one cannot remove this VLAN from a VTP-
enabled switch.

CDP and VTP Advertisements Sent on VLAN1   Among the manage-
ment-oriented protocols that use VLAN1 are CDP and VTP. Both of these
protocols require network-wide connectivity to be successful in providing
their functionality and thus work well on VLAN1.

Management IP Address in VLAN1   As VLAN1 carries the above-
mentioned management protocols and is guaranteed to be network-wide, it

also makes sense for IP-based network management to occur here. For this reason, the IP assigned to the switch resides on VLAN1.

NOTE: *Many Cisco switches, particularly those from the Catalyst 5000/6000 family, enable one to move the management IP to another VLAN. However, due to the reasons described above, it is advised that the management IP be left in the default VLAN, VLAN1.*

Managing VLANs

The following sections describe some of the more common tasks an administrator would perform when working with a VLAN configuration.

Naming a VLAN   When dealing with a number of VLANs, it becomes difficult to differentiate one from the next. In order to create some clarity, one can name the individual VLANs. VLAN names can be a combination of numbers and letters and cannot include spaces. The VLAN names are fully propagated throughout the VTP domain as well, so that easy enterprise-wide identifications can be achieved. The following command shows the syntax for naming a VLAN on the 1900 switch:

```
sw1924_A(config)#vlan 2 name 1stFloor
```

This command adds the name 1stFloor to the second VLAN. It is generally recommended that when many VLAN names are going to be used, a standard way of describing them should be used to ensure that the goal of creating recognizable names is reached.

The following command shows that the VLAN name of 1stFloor has been successfully added to the second VLAN:

```
sw1924_A#show vlan
VLAN Name              Status      Ports
----------------------------------------
1    default           Enabled     1-24
2    1stFloor          Enabled
3    VLAN0003          Enabled
4    VLAN0004          Enabled
5    VLAN0005          Enabled
6    VLAN0006          Enabled
7    VLAN0007          Enabled
8    VLAN0008          Enabled
9    VLAN0009          Enabled
10   VLAN0010          Enabled
11   VLAN0011          Enabled
```

```
12    VLAN0012          Enabled
13    VLAN0013          Enabled    A, B
20    VLAN0020          Enabled
1002  fddi-default      Suspended
1003  token-ring-defau  Suspended
1004  fddinet-default   Suspended
1005  trnet-default     Suspended
```

Assigning Switch Ports to a VLAN As VLANs are port-based, one must add those ports to their respective VLANs. By default, all switch ports begin in VLAN1. One should recall from previous chapters that the ports on the 1900 switch are referred to as *interfaces*. As such, the command to add switch ports to VLANs is an interface command. The following command moves port 2 into the second VLAN:

```
sw1924_A(config)#int ethernet0/2
sw1924_A(config-if)#vlan-membership static 2
```

The static parameter indicates that the port will operate in a static VLAN. As described previously, dynamic methods for VLAN assignments do exist but are rarely used. For further information on this topic, one could research the VMPS protocol.

Verifying VLAN Membership In order to ensure that the ports of the switch are properly assigned to their respective VLANs, one can use the following command

```
sw1924_A#show vlan-membership
   Port    VLAN Membership   Type    Port   VLAN   Membership Type
   ------------------------------------------------------------------
     1     1                 Static   13     1      Static
     2     2                 Static   14     1      Static
     3     1                 Static   15     1      Static
     4     1                 Static   16     1      Static
     5     1                 Static   17     1      Static
     6     1                 Static   18     1      Static
     7     1                 Static   19     1      Static
     8     1                 Static   20     1      Static
     9     1                 Static   21     1      Static
    10     1                 Static   22     1      Static
    11     1                 Static   23     1      Static
    12     1                 Static   24     1      Static
   AUI     14                Static
     A     13                Static
     B     13                Static
```

Defining Trunks

The concept of a trunk port is one that is integral to VLAN-enabled networks. Thus far, ports have been configured to exist in one VLAN or another. However, many times, specifically in the case of links between switches, it is advantageous to have a port exist in more than one VLAN. For example, consider the network described in Figure 6-12.

The depicted network consists of one core switch and two access switches. This network clearly has a need for two VLANs with those VLANs being present on each of the two access switches. In this case, were one limited to one VLAN per port, the connections between the core switch and each of the access switches would need to be doubled so that one link exists for each VLAN, as shown in Figure 6-13. In many cases, this limitation represents a very inefficient use of bandwidth in that one link would likely have sufficed for the two VLANs.

Furthermore, in networks where tens or hundreds of VLANs exist enterprise-wide, the cost of this duplication of cabling and port density would be overwhelming. To remedy this situation, the concept of VLAN trunking has been introduced. Essentially, this technology enables multiple VLANs to be multiplexed across a single link. Figure 6-14 illustrates this more clearly.

However, careful consideration of this multiplexing yields a valid question: "How can you differentiate one VLAN's traffic from another's?" Consider the Ethernet Frame in Figure 6-15.

Figure 6-12
A VLAN-enabled
network

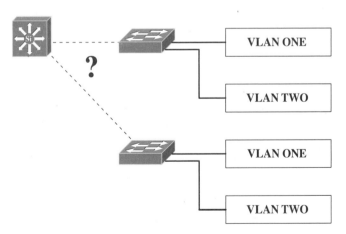

Both Access Switches have ports in each of VLAN ONE and TWO.

Figure 6-13
One VLAN per port

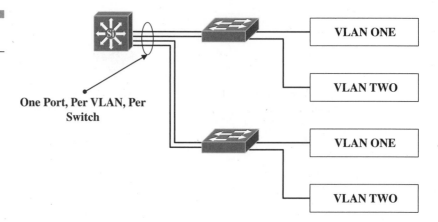

One Port, Per VLAN, Per Switch

VLAN ONE

VLAN TWO

VLAN ONE

VLAN TWO

To allow for connectivity between the two VLANs throughout the network, two links must be made from the core to each access switch

Figure 6-14
The VLAN trunk

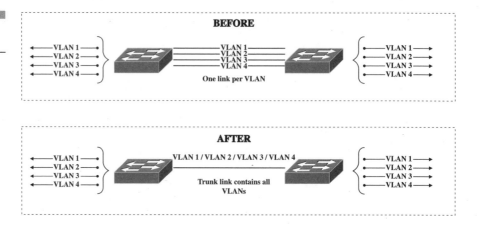

6 Bytes	6 Bytes	2 Bytes	46-1500 Bytes	4 Bytes
Destination (DMAC)	Source (SMAC)	Protocol	Data	FCS

Figure 6-15
The Ethernet frame

As one can see, no field within the standard frame indicates membership in any VLAN. Hence, when frames from different VLANs are combined on a single link, some method must be in place to ensure VLAN integrity. That is to say, when traffic goes into a trunk port from VLAN5, it exits the trunk and heads for VLAN5.

To support this requirement, Cisco employs two similar methodologies. Both of these methodologies involve addressing the standard Ethernet header to either include or be encapsulated by a field that designates the VLAN. This methodology is often referred to as *tagging* due to the fact that the frames are tagged upon entry into a trunk port. The tagging process is generally handled by an *Application-Specific Integrated Circuit* (ASIC) and thus occurs at wire speed.

Of the two methodologies employed, one, ISL, is proprietary, and the other, IEEE 802.1Q, is a recognized standard. In both cases, frames are tagged at the ingress point of the trunk and have the tag removed at the egress. This ensures that the tagging process occurs transparently to both end nodes and other intermediary nodes. Beyond simple inter-switch connections, VLAN tagging can prove advantageous in some cases for connections to routers or servers. For example, some internetwork designs incorporate a single, high-speed link to a router that provides inter-VLAN routing. Such a network is depicted in Figure 6-16.

NOTE: *Routers between ISL VLANs will use the fast-switching algorithm. Hence, when considering this type of implementation, one must also investigate the fast-switching characteristics of the router(s) involved, along with any performance-related impacts this may involve.*

The following sections will describe in some detail each of the two tagging methodologies.

ISL   ISL is a Cisco proprietary VLAN tagging protocol. Essentially, the technology involves the encapsulation of a normal Ethernet frame into a

Figure 6-16
A trunked router
connection

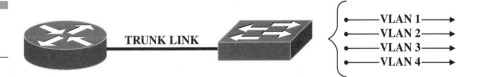

The Router provides interVLAN routing for all VLANs using a single
connection to the network

Figure 6-17
The ISL header

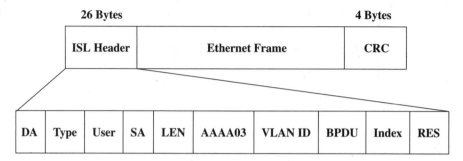

30-byte ISL header. The header, as shown in Figure 6-17, incorporates a two-byte VLAN-ID field that enables the switch to designate and differentiate VLAN membership.

Another key item to consider in the ISL header is the Configuration *Bridge Protocol Data Unit* (BPDU) field. Using this field, Cisco can support one instance of Spanning Tree per VLAN. This technique is called *Per VLAN Spanning Tree* (PVST). Leveraging this capability, one can build fully redundant switched networks with Spanning Tree without having to pay the traditional penalty of leaving half the network idle due to STP's failover-like algorithm. By altering the STP settings on half the VLANs, one can have a particular link block for one VLAN and forward for another, thus allowing for load balancing.

Enabling ISL To enable trunking using the ISL, one must enter the interface configuration mode of one of the trunk-capable ports. Generally, only ports that run at 100 Mbps in the Ethernet world are capable of becoming trunk ports. On the 1900, the Fast Ethernet interface is capable of trunking via the *Dynamic Inter-Switch Link* (DISL) protocol. It enables the negotiation of ISL properties to ensure that Fast Ethernet links are either in trunking or non-trunking mode. When enabling trunking, a few options need to be considered. Consider the following:

```
sw1924_A(config)#int FastEthernet0/26
sw1924_A(config-if)#trunk ?
        auto          Set DISL state to AUTO
        desirable     Set DISL state to DESIRABLE
        nonegotiate   Set DISL state to NONEGOTIATE
        off           Set DISL state to OFF
        on            Set DISL state to ON
```

Table 6-1 indicates the functionality of each of the above-listed options for the trunk mode.

Choosing trunk mode auto, for example, looks like the following:

Table 6-1

The functionalities of the trunk mode options

Mode	Functionality
Auto	Places the interface in trunk mode only if the other end is set to On or Desirable.
Desirable	Places the interface in trunk mode only if the other end is set to On, Desirable, or Auto.
No-negotiate	Sets the port to trunk mode and disables the sending/processing of the DISL frames. Used when connecting to a non-DISL supporting device.
Off	Sets the interface to non-trunk mode even if the other end is set to trunk mode.
On	Sets the interface to trunk mode, even if the other end is set to non-trunk.

```
sw1924_A#conf t
Enter configuration commands, one per line.   End with CNTL/Z
sw1924_A(config)#int FastEthernet0/26
sw1924_A(config-if)#trunk auto
```

802.1Q The IEEE finalized the 802.1Q standard in 1998. This standard is similar to ISL in that it enables the tagging of VLAN IDs to frames transiting trunk links. The implementation, however, is different in a few regards. The 802.1Q standard involves the insertion of 16 bits into the Ethernet header. These 16 bits are arranged such that 12 bits are available for the VLAN-ID and three bits for Priority. IEEE 802.1p governs the use and meaning of the priority bits. For this reason, one often sees the two standards listed together, such as IEEE 802.1P/Q. The following diagram in Figure 6-18 illustrates the 802.1Q and 802.1P structure. The 1900 series switch does not support tagging via the 802.1Q protocol at the time of this writing.

It should be noted that ISL and 802.1Q are not at all compatible with each other. Hence, when designing internetworks, one must pay careful attention to the tagging support of the switches in use.

NOTE: *Both ISL and 802.1Q tagging methods involve adding additional information into a standard Ethernet frame, whether by tag insertion in the case of 802.1Q or by frame encapsulation in the case of ISL. These additions, however, can sometimes increase the frame size of an Ethernet packet slightly beyond the maximum allowable size. In a network where two VLAN-enabled switches running a trunking protocol are separated by*

Figure 6-18
IEEE 802.1Q
insertion

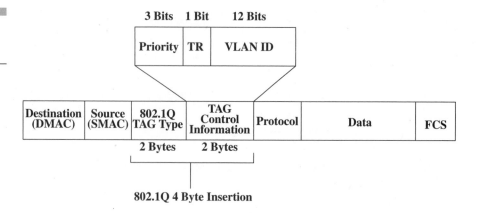

a switch or bridge that is not aware of the tagging protocols at play, the intermediary switch would tend to discard any of these packets, as they would appear illegally large. This is an important design consideration to keep in mind, particularly when considering extending VLAN trunking over wide areas where third-party bridged networks may exist.

Verifying Trunks As mentioned previously, the 1900 switch offers trunking support on its Fast Ethernet interfaces. These are represented as FastEthernet 0/26 and FastEthernet 0/27. Hence, when attempting to verify the trunking state on a 1900, one must focus on these two interfaces. The command structure of the IOS also takes this into consideration. When checking the trunk state of a port on the 1900, the command syntax includes a choice of Trunk A or Trunk B. These two choices relate to the FastEthernet interfaces as follows:

Trunk A = FastEthernet 0/26

Trunk B = FastEthernet 0/27

Given this information, the syntax for verifying the state of a trunk interface looks like the following:

```
sw1924_A#show trunk a
DISL state: Auto, Trunking: Off, Encapsulation type: Unknown
sw1924_A#show trunk b
DISL state: Desirable, Trunking: Off, Encapsulation type: Unknown
```

The previous commands indicate that for the 1900 switch, neither FastEthernet is currently in a trunking mode. However, FastEthernet 0/26 is set to auto, while FastEthernet 0/27 is set to desirable.

VLANs and Spanning Tree

As described in the previous chapter, the *Spanning Tree protocol* (STP) creates and manages a loop-free topology with a LAN. Given that a LAN is a broadcast domain, it would seem beneficial that Spanning Tree would also provide the same functionality within a VLAN. Further, that functionality should be unique on a VLAN-to-VLAN basis. To address this requirement, Cisco enables the propagation of STP BPDUs, which are the basis of STP communication, to traverse not only through VLAN-configured ports, but also through ISL-configured trunk ports. Doing so enables PVST, which enables a network architect to balance the load through a redundant network by altering the STP parameters on a VLAN-to-VLAN basis.

Along with enabling a more efficient use of bandwidth in a VLAN-configured network, PVST adds a number of other advantages. Primarily, simply having separate STP processing distributes the risk within a network, as failure in one VLAN will not influence another. Further, in some cases there may be reasons for enabling STP with varying parameters due to the unique needs of each VLAN, and PVST will enable this diverse configuration.

Configuring Spanning Tree   On the 1900 switch, Spanning Tree is enabled by default on all VLANs. To add or remove the STP protocol from a particular VLAN, one uses the following command:

```
sw1924_A(config)#(no) spantree (VLAN)
```

In the following example, the STP protocol is removed from VLAN2. The show span command enables one to verify the state of the STP protocol on either all VLANs or one in particular.

```
sw1924_A(config)#no spantree 2
sw1924_A(config)#exit
sw1924_A#show spantree 2
Error: STP is not enabled for VLAN 2
```

As shown in this example, when one tries to view the STP properties of a VLAN that is not currently running the STP protocol, an error occurs.

In the following example, the STP protocol is enabled for VLAN2 and another show span is executed to verify the results:

```
sw1924_A(config)#spantree 2
sw1924_A(config)#exit
sw1924_A#show spantree 2
VLAN2 is executing the IEEE compatible Spanning Tree Protocol
```

```
    Bridge Identifier has priority 32768, address 00D0.0692.6400
    Configured hello time 2, max age 20, forward delay 15
    Current root has priority 32768, address 00D0.0692.6400
    Root port is N/A, cost of root path is 0
    Topology change flag not set, detected flag not set
    Topology changes 0, last topology change occurred 0d00h00m00s ago
    Times:  hold 1, topology change 8960
            hello 2, max age 20, forward delay 15
    Timers: hello 2, topology change 35, notification 2
Port Ethernet 0/2 of VLAN2 is Forwarding
    Port path cost 100, Port priority 128
    Designated root has priority 32768, address 00D0.0692.6400
    Designated bridge has priority 32768, address 00D0.0692.6400
    Designated port is Ethernet 0/2, path cost 0
    Timers: message age 20, forward delay 15, hold 1
sw1924_A#
```

As shown here, the STP protocol is functional on VLAN2. Pay particular attention to the format of the show span results. The first few lines describe the global parameters of the STP process for the VLAN in question. Included in the display are such things as the bridge ID, along with the current root bridge. Following the global STP settings, the results display the particulars for every port currently active in the given VLAN. In this case, only port 2 or interface Ethernet 0/2 exists in VLAN2. Included in the port results are the bridge ID of the designated root and the designated bridge for the particular segment.

Spanning Tree Templates   In order to modify the parameters of a particular STP process on the 1900 switch, one must make use of Spanning Tree templates. Cisco offers four templates in the 1900 switch that can each have a different set of properties. Once a template has been designed, one can add up to 10 VLANs to the template. Hence, when changing a VLAN's STP properties, one must first create a template and then add the VLAN to it.

The spantree-template global command enables the modification of the four STP templates as well as the capability to associate individual or groups of VLANs to the template. The following display illustrates the command syntax along with the available options:

```
sw1924_A(config)#spantree-template ?
  <1-4>  Bridge template identifier

sw1924_A(config)#spantree-template 1 ?
  forwarding-time     Set a Spanning Tree FORWARD Interval
  hello-time          Set a Spanning Tree HELLO Interval
  max-age             Set a Spanning Tree MAX AGE Interval
  priority            Set a Spanning Tree PRIORITY
  vlan                        Assign up to ten VLANs to a bridge
template
```

As shown in this example, after selecting the STP templates, one can then modify the parameters for the templates. Also, the last parameter, *vlan*, enables one to add VLANs or associate VLANs with the template.

To view the templates themselves, one can use the show spantree-template command from the command prompt. The following displays the output of the command:

```
sw1924_A#show spantree-template

                        Bridge Template 1
Bridge Priority                            : 32768 (8000 hex)
Max age when operating as root             : 20 second(s)
Hello time when operating as root          : 2 second(s)
Forward delay when operating as root       : 15 second(s)
VLANs assigned to option                              : 1-1005
—More—
                        Bridge Template 2
Bridge Priority                            : 32768 (8000 hex)
Max age when operating as root             : 20 second(s)
Hello time when operating as root          : 2 second(s)
Forward delay when operating as root       : 15 second(s)
VLANs assigned to option                              : None
—More—
                        Bridge Template 3
Bridge Priority                            : 32768 (8000 hex)
Max age when operating as root             : 20 second(s)
Hello time when operating as root          : 2 second(s)
Forward delay when operating as root       : 15 second(s)
VLANs assigned to option                              : None
—More—
                        Bridge Template 4
Bridge Priority                            : 32768 (8000 hex)
Max age when operating as root             : 20 second(s)
Hello time when operating as root          : 2 second(s)
Forward delay when operating as root       : 15 second(s)
VLANs assigned to option                              : None
```

Each of the four templates is displayed along with its respective configuration. Of note, only the first template is in use on this 1900, as indicated by the membership of VLANs 1 through 1005 noted in the display.

Chapter Summary

Within this chapter, the concept of VLANs and their implementation within the 1900 switch has been explored. When considering VLAN technology, the key element to remember is that a VLAN is simply a broadcast domain. With this in mind, other, more involved topics will become easier to grasp.

Future chapters dealing with the role of VLANs in IP and IPX networks will serve to enhance these concepts.

At this point, one should have a good grasp of the characteristics of VLANs and their general fit within an internetwork. The role of VLAN1 in a Cisco internetwork as it relates to VTP should also be understood. Also, the use of PVST and the role of Spanning Tree in general should also be clearly understood. Coupling this knowledge with a strong understanding of IP and IPX routing should position one well in the internetworking world.

From the Real World

As a designer of enterprise class networks, I have had the opportunity to leverage VLAN technology in a number of ways. VLANs are most often celebrated for their capability to reduce the size of the broadcast domain, and rightfully so. However, another benefit that is often overlooked and similarly underutilized is simply the capability to support multiple networks in one set of equipment.

Often, in large-scale internetworks with a number of isolated networks, administrators tend to leverage separate equipment. For example, it is not uncommon to see the hot side, or unprotected side, of a firewall connected to a stand-alone hub or switch. Further, many times specific-function networks are built alongside core-function, VLAN-capable networks to support specific applications. This generally represents a suboptimal use of the existing infrastructure. Beyond simply the capital cost in building parallel networks or using isolated devices lies the additional cost in management along with the less tangible increase in risk associated to a potential loss of fault tolerance. For example, most enterprise networks are laden with multiple levels of redundancy and governed by management tools that provide for maximum uptime. Given that these networks also support robust VLAN implementation, it seems odd that many choose not to leverage them for these other requirements.

The root of the problem in many cases stems from a lack of awareness on the part of the management teams. As most networks generally interconnect VLANs using high-speed switching, the concept of using VLANs that are not interconnected may seem foreign. As a design goal, I highly recommend building one robust network that serves all functions, irrespective of their interrelation, within an organization. In this way, the organization can take full advantage of their largest infrastructure investment and also benefit from the simplicity of a single network.

Peter Van Oene

Frequently Asked Questions (FAQ)

Question: Do I need a router for VLANs to work?

Answer: As a VLAN is simply a broadcast domain, it is not necessary for one to use a router to create VLANs. However, by the same token, without the services of a router or layer-three switch, users in one VLAN will not be able to communicate with users in another. Hence, in most situations, routing plays a significant role in VLAN-enabled networking.

Question: Can a port be a member of more than one VLAN?

Answer: Only trunk ports can participate in more than one VLAN. When a port is a member of more than one VLAN, some way of differentiating frames from each VLAN must exist. This differentiation is generally done through VLAN tagging, including methods like ISL and IEEE 802.1Q.

Question: If not all of my devices are made by Cisco, can I still use VLANs?

Answer: Port-based VLAN technology itself does not leverage any proprietary mechanisms in its simplest form. For that reason, simply connecting ports from one VLAN on one device to another device will enable complete VLAN interoperability between unlike devices. However, certain VLAN-oriented mechanisms like VTP and ISL are proprietary to Cisco and will not operate with devices from other manufacturers. For this reason, it is wise to investigate the protocol support of a set of devices so that one can design within them.

Case Study: Creating VLANs to Departmentalize Your LAN

The exercise will reinforce the concepts covered in this chapter. The required equipment is as follows:

- Three Catalyst 1900 switches
- Patch cords (Fiber SC-SC or Unshielded Twisted Pair [UTP], depending on the port configurations of the 1900s)

ABC Company has a small number of users spread out across four functional business units. Within the company, employees are members of Sales, Marketing, or Administration. The company would like to isolate the traffic from each of the business units completely, despite the fact that the desks in the office are mixed. The solution will involve the use of three Cisco 1900 switches.

The steps to take to solve this problem are as follows:

1. Cable the switches together so that one switch, the core switch, is connected to the two others via the Fast Ethernet interfaces.
2. Create a VTP domain called ABC.
3. Designate the core switch as a VTP server and the others as VTP clients.
4. Create three VLANs in addition to VLAN1.
5. Name the VLANs Sales, Market, and Admin.
6. Enable trunking on the each of the Fast Ethernet ports.
7. Set the core switch to the needed DISL mode.
8. Add at least one port on each switch to each VLAN.

Advanced steps would include the following:

1. Modify the bridge priority of the core switch to ensure it is the root bridge in VLAN1.
2. Associate the Sales VLAN with Spantree template 2.
3. Modify the bridge priority for the Sales VLAN so that one of the edge switches becomes the root bridge.

Questions

1. The collision domain is bound by which type of device(s)?

   a. Bridges
   b. Switches
   c. Nodes
   d. Repeaters

2. The broadcast domain is bound by which type of device(s)?

   a. Bridges
   b. Switches
   c. Routers
   d. Repeaters

3. A VLAN can be considered the same as which of the following?

   a. Broadcast domain
   b. Collision domain
   c. Local Area Network
   d. All of the above

4. A router is required to allow for communication between VLANs.

   a. True
   b. False

5. End nodes in a network require VLAN capabilities to connect to a VLAN.

   a. True
   b. False

6. VLANs operate in which layer of the OSI model?

   a. Layer one
   b. Layer two
   c. Layer three
   d. Layer four

7. VTP stands for what technology?

   a. VLAN Tunneling Protocol
   b. Virtual Trunking Protocol
   c. VLAN Trunking Protocol
   d. Virtual Tunneling Protocol

8. Which of the following are valid VTP modes?

   a. Server
   b. Client
   c. Host
   d. Transparent

9. VTP advertisements are sent out of which type of interface?

   a. Fast Ethernet
   b. Trunk
   c. Channel
   d. All of the above

10. VTP advertisements use which VLAN?

   a. VLAN0
   b. VLAN1
   c. All VLANs
   d. All VLANs configured for trunk mode

11. The VTP server with the lowest revision number is considered accurate.

   a. True
   b. False

12. Which of the following are VLAN tagging protocols?

   a. IEEE 802.1D
   b. IEEE 802.1Q
   c. IEEE 802.1P
   d. ISL

13. How many bytes does the ISL encapsulation add?

   a. 24
   b. 16
   c. 30
   d. 48

14. The standard that allows for priorities in the 802.1Q header is which of the following?

   a. IEEE 802.1R
   b. IEEE 802.1P
   c. IEEE 802.3Z
   d. IEEE 802.1A

15. Which acronym describes Cisco's capability to have one Spanning Tree per VLAN?

a. PSTN

b. PVST

c. PSTV

d. STPV

16. Which of the following are valid DISL modes?

a. Auto

b. Negotiate

c. Desirable

d. No-Negotiate

17. The correct syntax for viewing the trunk status on a Cisco 1900 is which of the following?

a. show trunk one

b. show FastEthernet 0/26

c. show trunk a

d. show trunking

18. Spanning Tree is enabled by default on the Cisco 1900 switch.

a. True

b. False

19. The correct syntax for removing Spanning Tree from VLAN2 is which of the following?

a. no spantree vlan 2

b. no spanning vlan 2

c. no spanning 2

d. no spantree 2

20. Cisco supports how many Spanning Tree templates in the 1900 switch?

a. Four

b. Eight

c. 10

d. 16

Answers

1. **a.** Bridges and **b.** Switches

   As the collision domain is a layer-one area, it can be segmented or bound by both bridges and switches at layer two.

2. **c.** Routers

   As the broadcast domain is a layer-two area, a router or layer-three switch at layer three can segment it.

3. **a.** Broadcast domain and **c.** Local Area Network

   Broadcast domains, LANs, and VLANs all represent essentially the same set of devices.

4. **a.** True

   A routing or layer-three functionality is always required to enable communication between VLANs. Future chapters dealing with layer-three network addressing and routing will serve to further illustrate this point.

5. **b.** False

   VLAN technology can occur completely transparent to the end node.

6. **b.** Layer two

   VLANs, as broadcast domains, occur at layer two.

7. **c.** VLAN Trunking Protocol

   VTP is a Cisco proprietary protocol that stands for VLAN Trunking Protocol.

8. a, b, d - Host is not a valid VTP Mode

9. **b.** Trunk

   VTP advertisements are transmitted out of trunked interfaces.

10. **b.** VLAN1

    VLAN1 is used for VTP advertisements, as always, throughout the network.

11. **b.** False

    The VTP server with the highest revision number is considered accurate.

12. **b.** IEEE 802.1Q and **d.** ISL

    Both ISL and IEEE 802.1Q are VLAN tagging protocols. ISL is Cisco proprietary and 802.1Q is an industry standard.

13. c. 30

The ISL header is 26 bytes long with four bytes added to the check-sum summing to 30 bytes in total.

14. b. IEEE 802.1P

The 16-bit 802.1Q header enables three bits for the priority as governed by IEEE 802.1P.

15. b. PVST

Per VLAN Spanning Tree (PVST) allows for this functionality.

16. a. Auto, **c.** Desirable, and **d.** No-Negotiate

Negotiate is not a valid DISL mode, while the rest are.

17. c. show trunk a

show trunk a represents the correct syntax for viewing the trunk status of a Fast Ethernet port on a Cisco 1900.

18. a. True

Spanning Tree is enabled for all VLANS on the Cisco 1900 by default.

19. d. no spantree 2

no spantree 2 represents the correct syntax for this functionality.

20. a. Four

Cisco provides four STP templates in the 1900 switch.

Interconnecting Networks with TCP/IP

Objectives

This chapter describes the TCP/IP architecture as well as the fundamental concepts underlying the TCP/IP protocol suite. The suite will be mapped to the OSI Reference Model and the protocols and functions that are performed at each layer will be thoroughly discussed. This chapter also presents a detailed discussion of IP addressing along with the use of subnet masks, network numbers, and host numbers. Lastly, this chapter will provide the reader with the knowledge and understanding to implement these concepts in a network environment.

On completion of this chapter, you will be able to do the following:

- Identify the *Internet Protocol* (IP) protocol stack, its protocol layer functions, and commonly used IP protocols.

- Identify IP address classes, IP addresses, IP subnet masks, IP network numbers, subnet numbers, and possible host numbers.

- Configure IP addresses and subnet masks on a router interface and optionally configure a host table.

- Interconnect the *Virtual Local Area Networks* (VLANs) with a Layer-three device such as a router on a stick.

Introduction to TCP/IP

The *Transmission Control Protocol / Internet Protocol* (TCP/IP) was first used in the mid-1970s when the government's Department of Defense Agency developed the *Department of Defense Advanced Research Projects Agency* (DARPA). DARPA was developed to create a packet-switched network to enable government agencies to share valuable data. Before DARPA and the use of TCP/IP, many government mainframes were unable to communicate with each other because they were using a different protocol or set of rules. Eventually, the government allowed researchers from universities access to their network. It was extended out to universities and the new network was called the *Advanced Research Projects Agency Network* (ARPANET). ARPANET transitioned into the Internet after the private sector was allowed access. Now the Internet is a conglomeration of computers and networks around the world with an estimated user base of 300 million by 2002.

IP as a Universal Protocol

The TCP/IP protocol suite consists of multiple protocols. The main two protocols in this suite and the protocols that run on the Internet are TCP and IP. Examples of other protocols in this suite are the *Address Resolution Protocol* (ARP), the *Internet Control Message Protocol* (ICMP), and the *User Datagram Protocol* (UDP). TCP/IP is the most widely used protocol in computer networks, allowing flexibility and scalability. Building a network based on the TCP/IP protocol suite will allow seamless integration with the Internet.

How the TCP/IP Protocol Suite Fits into the OSI Model

Figure 7-1 shows the TCP/IP protocol stack and how its layers map to the *Open Systems Interconnection* (OSI) Reference Model.

TCP/IP is the most important protocol in today's networks. Obtaining a solid understanding of the TCP/IP protocol suite and how it works will make it much easier to comprehend how other protocols function. It's also very important to understand not only the OSI Reference Model and how it works, but also how the TCP/IP protocol suite maps to it. The majority of network problems can be figured out by breaking down the problem into the different layers of the OSI and identifying where you may be losing the communication or where the source of the problem is occurring. Many tools, such as network analyzers, can assist in this process.

Figure 7-1
The TCP/IP protocol suite

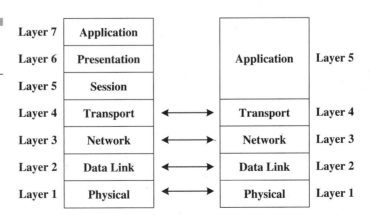

Layer 7	Application				
Layer 6	Presentation		Application	Layer 5
Layer 5	Session			
Layer 4	Transport	←→	Transport	Layer 4
Layer 3	Network	←→	Network	Layer 3
Layer 2	Data Link	←→	Data Link	Layer 2
Layer 1	Physical	←→	Physical	Layer 1

The application layer of the OSI Reference Model maps to many protocols in the TCP/IP protocol suite. Some of these protocols include *File Transfer Protocol* (FTP), *Trivial File Transfer Protocol* (TFTP), *Simple Network Management Protocol* (SNMP), *Simple Mail Transfer Protocol* (SMTP), *Domain Name System* (DNS), and Telnet. These protocols are also called network applications. They handle such tasks as file transfers, downloads, network management, e-mail, name resolution, and remote login. The application layer protocols in the TCP/IP suite incorporate the top three layers of the OSI Reference Model, application, session, and presentation, into their specific application. FTP, for example, will use functions of the top three layers during its process.

TCP and UDP are the two protocols that reside at the transport layer. The bottom four layers of the TCP/IP protocol stack map directly to their corresponding layers of the OSI Reference Model. Most TCP/IP-based applications map either to TCP or UDP. Both TCP and UDP use port numbers so that the transport layer knows which specific application it will interface with. These port numbers are found in either the TCP segment or the UDP datagram.

The TCP protocol is a connection-oriented protocol. Connection-oriented means that the protocol is acknowledged. So when a network application sends a request to another device using TCP, the device will send back an acknowledgement verifying that it received the data for every packet sent. This is also referred to as a *three-way handshake*. An example of a network application that uses TCP would be Telnet. Telnet would send a packet to the destination device with a source port of a number greater than 1023 and with a destination port of 23. When the destination device decapsulates the packet as it moves up the TCP/IP protocol stack, it will see that at layer 4 there is a destination port of 23. This tells the destination or receiving device that it is establishing a Telnet session because port 23 is designated to Telnet. The destination device would then send an acknowledgement back to the source and the negotiation for the remote login would start. TCP has a very large header and therefore has much more overhead than UDP. This causes TCP to be much slower and consumes more bandwidth than UDP.

UDP is a connectionless protocol. This means that for every byte sent across the wire, the receiving device does not need to respond. This causes UDP to be extremely fast and efficient. UDP relies on the protocols and the applications on the other layers to ensure that the datagram is delivered.

An example of a network application that uses UDP would be SNMP. SNMP uses UDP datagrams to request network devices to perform certain tasks. The network device does not to need to respond to every datagram sent, but to perform the task that was specified by the SNMP protocol. Such tasks could include pulling a router configuration, having the router pull a new router configuration from a TFTP server, or polling for the CPU usage of a router. All of these tasks and many more can be accomplished by using SNMP remotely.

The network layer is where the IP resides. The IP is responsible for determining the source and destination addresses and passing the TCP segment or UDP datagram information down the layer to be transmitted at the physical layer. IP has no retransmission capabilities, but it relies on upper layer protocols and network applications to handle the retransmissions. In addition, computers, router interfaces, and most network devices are usually assigned an IP address. An IP address consists of four bytes or octets and both the network and the host are determined by these four bytes with the use of a network or subnet mask. Furthermore, the network numbers are utilized by routing protocols during the routing process. A more in-depth discussion of network addresses and masks is discussed in detail later in this chapter.

The bottom two layers of the TCP/IP protocol, the physical layer and the data-link layer, are referenced in this chapter as the network interface layer. The data link layer is where the *Media Access Control* (MAC) address is found. Every network device and physical router interface has a MAC address. When an IP packet is transferred from one device to another, the source and destination MAC addresses change from one hop to the next. The source and destination IP address remain the same throughout this process.

During the course of communication, the data-link layer is responsible for retrieving the layer-three IP information and stripping off the IP header and mapping it to the type of network such as Ethernet or 802.2 Token Ring. Once the information transitions to the data-link layer, it is no longer considered a packet, but a frame.

The physical layer is where the frame is broken down into bits, or ones and zeros. The actual transmission of electrical signals or photons of light for fiber optic networks is done at this layer. 10BaseT, 10Base2, and RS-232 are examples of physical layer protocols. Connector pin-outs are also defined at the physical layer.

TCP Segment Format

This section describes the TCP segment format and each field in detail. Figure 7-3 illustrates the TCP segment format.

The TCP segment is broken down to give a better view of how this protocol functions. TCP uses segments to transmit data to the receiving station. The maximum size of the TCP segment is determined by the router interface that the segment is transitioning through to get to the receiving station. For example, if a PC on the Ethernet segment of a router sends a packet out the serial interface destined for another PC, the *Maximum Transmission Unit* (MTU) size defined on the serial interface determines the maximum TCP segment size.

Working down, each part of that TCP segment is described next. The number next to each name represents how many bits there are in that particular field inside the TCP segment.

The source port describes the connection to the specific upper layer protocol when a sending device sends the packet down the TCP/IP protocol

Figure 7-2
A single byte

1 Byte							
Bits 1	2	3	4	5	6	7	8

Figure 7-3

TCP segment format

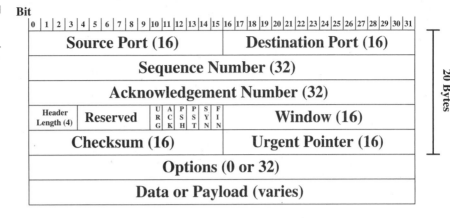

stack. The destination port is used to describe the upper layer protocol on which TCP will transfer its data up the protocol stack on a receiving station. The Sequence and Acknowledge numbers are responsible for establishing the reliability of the TCP communication. They are also located in the user's byte stream of this segment. HLEN stands for the header length and describes where the actual data begins. Six bits are marked as reserved and may be used in the future if such a need exists.

The Code Bits distinguish session management messages from the data. This is where the ACK or SYN bits are flagged. The window is the most complicated part in this puzzle and we will discuss this further later in the chapter. Let's refer to the window as the size of the receive buffers. The checksum is a *Cyclic Redundancy Check* (CRC). When a packet arrives at the destination, the receiving device calculates the CRC to determine if the packet arrived intact. If not, the receiving device will ask for the packet to be retransmitted. The Urgent Pointer is used to signify out-of-band data. Options are utilized by specific vendors to enhance their protocol services. The 0–32 after Options means that it can contain no bits up to 32 bits. The data portion of the frame describes the data handed down from the upper layer protocols. Remember that when the transport layer receives the data handed down from the session layer, it encapsulates that data with its own TCP information detailed above. Once this TCP segment gets handed down to the network layer or IP, it will encapsulate the TCP segment into an actual datagram or packet. This process of encapsulation works all the way down and it works in reverse, decapsulating when the receiving station receives the segment and moving it up the TCP/IP protocol stack.

Port Numbers and How TCP/IP Handles Multiple Applications Simultaneously

TCP/IP is what you might call a multi-tasking protocol. It can handle multiple applications at the same time, all by using port numbers. These will be either TCP or UDP port numbers. Remember that TCP is a connection-oriented protocol and when an application is mapped to TCP, it makes that application a connection-oriented application. The same applies to UDP but is connectionless. A network application such as TFTP uses UDP and is considered a connectionless application because it needs no response from the destination device. You may be connected to another router via Telnet from your source router, while your router is also sending the destination router *Routing Information Protocol* (RIP) updates, SMTP queries because of e-mail, and DNS inquires of the hostname of a router. This can all be done using the source router with a specific IP address, going to a destination router with a specific IP address. Even though the same IP addresses are being used for multiple processes, different TCP and UDP port numbers are utilized for these processes. This allows TCP/IP to use one address to talk to another device with one address but maintain many different network applications between these two devices simultaneously.

Well-Known Ports

Network traffic can be filtered via TCP port numbers. Therefore, extended access lists are utilized, specifying the TCP port number for the desired filter. Specific network applications can be allowed or restricted into your network by using extended access lists. Telnet, for example, would be allowed into your network by specifying an extended access list on the border router that would permit traffic destined to port 23 with a source port greater than 1023. The destination port of 23 is used because that is the TCP port that the Telnet application uses to connect to another device. A port greater than 1023 is used for the source port because these are considered local ports and are not in the range of well-known ports. Telnet has the capability to make numerous connections to the same device simultaneously. It will pick a different unused source port greater than 1023 for each session and will use the same destination port of 23. TCP port 23 is also known as a well-known port. Network applications such as Telnet that use the same port number each time it initiates a session use well-known ports. Some examples of these network applications and their ports are listed in Figure 7-4. Well-known ports can be either TCP or UDP ports and are dependent upon the network application as to which type of port it needs.

Figure 7-4
Well-known ports

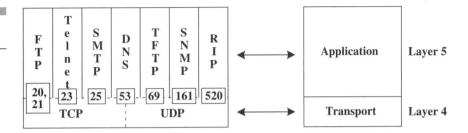

This figure shows how the different protocols use their assigned port numbers to map to either TCP or UDP. FTP uses both ports 20 and 21 because the workstation uses port 20 when connecting to the FTP server, and the FTP server uses port 21 to download the information back to the workstation. DNS uses port 53 in UDP and TCP. A workstation broadcasts for a DNS server using UDP port 53. The server then responds over TCP port 53. The figure also shows how the protocols or network applications map to the associated layer of the TCP/IP protocol stack.

NOTE: *Remember that layer five represents the application layer of the TCP/IP protocol stack, not the OSI model. When answering questions on the CCNA exam, be sure to understand which model the test is referring to, either the OSI model or the TCP/IP protocol stack. If the test uses the OSI model in the question, be sure to remember that the application layer is layer seven in the OSI model.*

NOTE: *Port numbers are standardized and described in detail in RFC 1700.*

TCP, a Connection-Oriented Protocol

The TCP protocol, as described earlier, is a connection-oriented protocol. It provides guaranteed delivery by using acknowledgements. When a sending station sends data to the receiving station, the receiving station sends back an acknowledgement for every data segment sent. TCP will also reassemble those data segments at the receiving station if they arrive out of order. If a segment is lost, the sending station automatically retransmits it. If TCP has to retransmit the data because of lost segments, it will reduce its transmission rate so that no more data segments get lost because of network congestion.

The Three-Way Handshake/Open Connection

The process that TCP uses to ensure guaranteed delivery of the packet is called the three-way handshake. Figure 7-5 illustrates an example of a three-way handshake.

The sending station starts off the communication process by sending a *Synchronous Sequence Numbers* (SYN) segment to the receiving station. This indicates that a new connection is requested and a sequence number is assigned to define which number will be used as the starting point for the messages that will be sent. The receiving station will receive the SYN segment and will send back a SYN *Acknowledgement* (ACK) packet, indicating that it received the SYN segment. The SYN ACK packet will also tell the sending station which sequence number it will use to start sending the data. The sending station will then send back an established packet containing an ACK, along with its first data segment. This communication process will continue with the sending station continuing to send data and the receiving station continuing to send back an ACK.

SYN/ACK DoS Attacks

Denial of Service (DoS) attacks have gained increased exposure lately. These attacks are one of the more popular schemes of hackers, and many Web servers and routers have been shut down because of this. A DoS attack consists of a hacker performing an action that would prevent an information system from performing its intended function. It usually consists of flooding a system so that it responds to the flooding and cannot respond to

Figure 7-5
The three-way
handshake

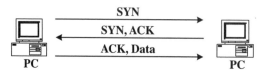

legitimate requests. An example of a DoS attack would be a SYN-flooding attack. This occurs when an attacker sends a flood of requests to the server and never completes the connection. These are called *half-open connections*. They tie up the server by allocating most of its resources to trying to respond to the flood of requests. The server can then no longer respond to legitimate requests and will often crash.

DoS attacks can be prevented in a variety of ways, the most popular being a firewall. A firewall will perform stateful inspections that will actually look at each frame to see whether the frame is established and if it is a response from an internal request. It can be set up so that if it doesn't meet those requirements, it will drop the frame.

Cisco also has a feature in its IOS firewall feature set called *Context-Based Access Control* (CBAC). CBAC intelligently inspects TCP and UDP packets based on application-layer protocol session information and can be used for intranets, extranets, and the Internet. CBAC can be configured to allow only specified TCP or UDP traffic if the connection is initiated from a specified network or interface. For example, if the firewall is set up to protect the internal network and CBAC is configured to filter on both TCP and UDP traffic, traffic originating from outside the network will only be allowed if it is a response from the internal network. CBAC inspects packet sequence numbers in TCP connections, and if they're not within an expected range, the router will drop the packet. The router will also issue an alert if it detects an unusually high amount of new connections.

If the router does not have the IOS firewall feature set, DoS attacks can still be filtered with the use of reflexive access lists. These lists filter IP traffic so that TCP or UDP session traffic is only permitted through the firewall if the session originated from within the internal network.

One reason that DoS attacks are becoming so prevalent is because hackers are using freeware applications on the Internet that will automatically initiate a DoS attack on whatever IP address is specified. These applications usually make it look like the source IP address of the hacker is from the internal network of the site that is being attacked. The packets sent to the station being attacked will have a spoofed source address, using an IP address from the internal network.

TCP Windows and ACKs

TCP uses windows to adjust the amount of traffic sent at one time. This is often called the *TCP sliding window*. This window enables multiple packets to be sent before waiting for an acknowledgment. The initial size of the

TCP window is established at the beginning of the TCP session and can vary during the data transfer based upon network congestion and other variables. This is also referred to as *flow control*. A TCP window size of zero equals "send no data." The receiving station specifies the TCP window size during the initial TCP three-way handshake. After the sending station sends a SYN, the receiving station responds with a SYN ACK packet and in that packet the window size will be indicated. For example, let's say the receiving station tells the sending station that the window size will be 10. The sending station needs to send a sequence of bytes of 20. It will put a window around the first 10 bytes and transmit them to the receiving station. Once the receiving station receives the data, it will respond back again that the window size is 10. It would also respond with an ACK=11, indicating that it received bytes 1 through 10 and expects 11 next. The sending station would then send the next bytes numbered 11 through 20.

Sequence Numbers

TCP uses sequence numbers to sequentially send and receive data. The sending station uses sequence numbers to tag bytes sent out to the receiving station. The receiving station uses them to organize the bytes in the same order as they were sent. A receiving station will process TCP packets in this manner because on multi-homed links, bytes sent to the receiving station may arrive out of order. This can occur because one link may be slower than the other link. TCP can get around this problem by organizing the bytes at the receiving end using the sequence numbers. The sequence numbers can start at any value and are incremented with every byte sent. The first sequence number identifies the first byte in the data stream and the length of the sequence numbers identifies the number of bytes sent.

UDP, a Connectionless Protocol

UDP is defined as a connectionless datagram protocol and resides at the transport layer of the OSI model, as described before. Connectionless means that the receiving station does not need to respond with an acknowledgement that it received the datagram. Therefore, UDP is also referred to as unreliable. UDP relies on the upper layer protocols to provide reliability. An example of a protocol that provides its own reliability at the upper layers is TFTP, which uses a checksum to provide this reliability. The checksum field

Figure 7-6
UDP datagram
format

Bit

| Bit | 0 | 1 | 2 | 3 | 4 | 5 | 6 | 7 | 8 | 9 |10 |11 |12 |13 |14 |15 |16 |17 |18 |19 |20 |21 |22 |23 |24 |25 |26 |27 |28 |29 |30 |31 | |

Source Port (16)	Destination Port (16)
Length (16)	Checksum (16)
Data or Payload (varies)	

8 Bytes

does a simple check of the contents of the segment. If the checksum does not match, then the file did not make it intact. With TFTP, the user will be notified and will have to retype the command again. Some other protocols that use UDP are TACAS+, DNS, SNMP, and BOOTP. All of these network applications rely on UDP for its fast and efficient delivery. These network applications also do not rely on an acknowledgement. UDP is covered in detail in RFC768. Figure 7-6 illustrates the UDP datagram format.

As discussed before, UDP is a lightweight and simple connectionless protocol. It requires little processing and therefore is ideal for certain network applications. Figure 7-6 breaks down the UDP segment to show how it differs from the TCP segment. UDP contains a source port and a destination port just as TCP does. This is then followed by a length field that specifies the length of the UDP segment. The 16-bit checksum field is next and, as described earlier, this determines if the segment made it to the destination intact. The Data field follows and this is where the actual data in the segment would be stored. It is important to remember that the UDP segment contains no sequence or acknowledgment fields.

Internet Layer

The Internet layer is the third layer of the TCP/IP conceptual model and maps to the network layer of the OSI model. Routing protocols are often considered layer-management protocols and they support the network layer. The IP protocol resides at the Internet layer of the TCP/IP model. IP is the main protocol used on the Internet today. IP is considered a routed protocol and is routed by other routing protocols. A routed protocol is a protocol that makes no actual routing decisions. Rather, it carries the data to the destination. Routing protocols, on the other hand, make routing decisions and determine the ideal path to the destination. Examples of routed protocols would be TCP/IP, IPX, or AppleTalk. Examples of routing protocols would include RIP, *Open Shortest Path First* (OSPF), *Enhanced Interior*

Gateway Routing Protocol (EIGRP), and *Border Gateway Protocol* (BGP). It is important to remember the difference between routed and routing protocols, as this is often a question on Cisco exams.

IP

IP resides at the Internet layer of the TCP/IP model. The Internet layer is also often referred to as the network layer. IP encapsulates the TCP segments or UDP datagrams and transfers the packet down the layers to be transmitted to the receiving device. IP is where the source and destination addresses are found and is the foundation of the addressing scheme used throughout the network. IP is defined as a packet delivery service. It relies on the upper layer protocols and network applications to provide retransmissions if needed. IP also has the capability to fragment packets if it is determined that they are too large for the network. This proves to be a costly process, as the sending device has to fragment the packets, and the receiving device must reassemble the fragmented packet before passing it up to the transport layer.

IP Datagram Format

This section describes the different fields and functions within the IP datagram. The IP datagram format is illustrated in Figure 7-7.

The IP datagram can be broken down into many pieces. This discussion will define those pieces so that a better understanding of the IP protocol can be achieved. The IP datagram starts with a version field. This contains ver-

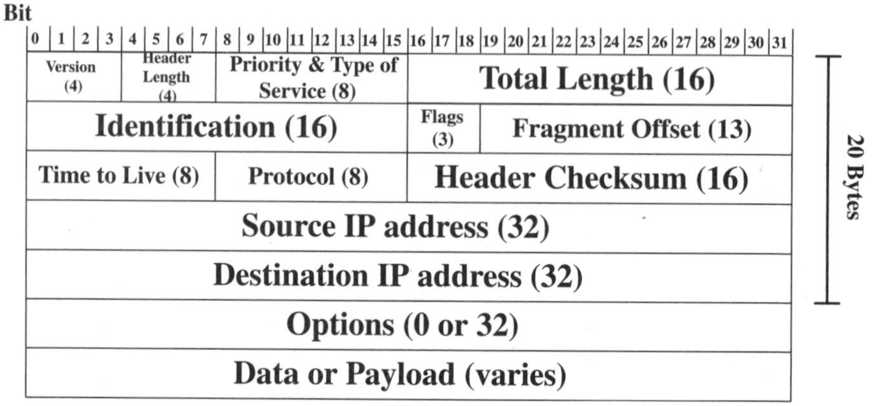

Figure 7-7
IP datagram format

sion 4, as we are currently using IPv4 of the IP protocol. Version 6 was developed to provide more addresses and more functionality as the amount of public IP addresses for version 4 were quickly depleting with the phenomenal growth of the Internet. However, IPv4 is still the main protocol being used and will likely continue that way for a while. This is because of *Network Address Translation* (NAT) and *Port Address Translation* (PAT), which use private IP addresses on the internal network and utilize one or a few public IP addresses to achieve connectivity to the Internet. The Internet only enables public IP addresses to be routed.

The next fields are the Header Length field, the Priority field, and the *Type-of-Service* (TOS) field. The TOS field enables the network application to specify the type of service the packet will receive from the network. Four TOS options are available and only one can be specified. The four TOS options are as follows:

- Low Delay
- Lowest Monetary Cost
- High Throughput
- High Reliability

The TOS field is not used in actual networking. Internetworking vendors never decided to implement this function.

The Total Length field consists of 16 bits and it specifies the total length of the entire IP packet. The maximum IP packet length is limited to 65,535 bytes. The Identification field also consists of 16 bits and is used to identify the individual packet. It can be used to identify duplicate packets on the network.

The Flags and Fragment Offset fields follow and this is the part of the IP that enables the packet to be fragmented if it is too large for the network. An example would be an Ethernet network where the MTU is 1500 bytes. This means that no frame can be transmitted onto the Ethernet where the data field is larger than 1500 or it will not be processed correctly. The MTU of a Token Ring network defaults to 4500 bytes. Therefore, if a device sends a frame onto a Token Ring network and the frame has to traverse an Ethernet network, the frame would have to be fragmented before it can enter the Ethernet segment. It would then be reassembled once it arrives at the destination. The receiving station will know which order to put the frames in because of the flag field that marks each fragmented frame.

The *Time-to-Live* (TTL) field is used as a countdown field. Every station that the packet passes through must decrement the number by one or by the number of seconds it holds the packet before transmitting it on to the next destination. When this number reaches zero, the packet is discarded.

An ICMP time exceeded message will be sent back informing the sending device that the packet was discarded. The reason the packet is dropped is to keep packets from continuously passing through devices looking for a device that no longer exists. This function is also used to avoid routing loops. A value is set to the TTL field before the packet is transmitted. A number such as 64 out of the possible 255 is usually specified.

The Protocol field specifies the individual protocol ID that will be used when passing the data up to the transport layer at the receiving station. The protocol ID specifies the actual upper layer protocol that is contained within the data. An example would be a protocol ID of six, which is mapped to TCP. UDP uses a protocol ID of 17. IP must know which port to use when decapsulating the data and sending it up to the transport layer.

The Header Checksum is the next field. This does a calculation to determine that the packet has not been changed since it was transmitted from the sender. If the header checksum does not calculate the same checksum as contained inside the packet, the packet will be discarded.

The next two fields are the Source and Destination Addresses. These are both 32-bit addresses and are defined as four octet addresses. An example of an IP address would be 172.16.15.254. The source and destination IP addresses remain the same inside the packet as it traverses the network to reach its destination. The source and destination MAC addresses, however, will change as the packet continues from one router to the next. The MAC address entries are stored in the data-link layer portion of the frame and are not included in this IP datagram. The IP addresses are used to determine the best path through the network. A further, detailed discussion of IP addresses will be discussed later in this chapter.

The last field is the Options field. This enables internetworking vendors to add specific code to the Options field, allowing the protocol more functionality. Data follows all of the fields and the size can vary.

Protocol Field

The Protocol field of the IP datagram serves an important function in the process of communication. Protocol numbers of protocol IDs are constant. These numbers are standardized and listed in RFC 1700. They are the method of mapping the IP to the appropriate transport layer protocol. IP will use the protocol ID when it needs to send the IP information up to the transport layer. IP will also need to know whether the network application it's communicating with is using UDP or TCP. This is defined by the protocol ID. UDP will always use a protocol ID of 17. For example, if an SNMP packet arrives at the receiving station, the packet would be decapsulated as it is brought up the protocol stack. Once it reaches the IP layer, it would have to associate the information to the UDP protocol ID of 17 so that it can make it up to the application layer where SNMP would read the information. By using UDP, SNMP knows that it does not have to send back an acknowledgement. Telnet, however, would use TCP. The packet would be sent to the receiving device and would decapsulate or strip off the headers as the packet moves up the OSI model. Once it reaches the IP layer, IP would know to associate the Telnet packet to TCP with a protocol ID of six so that it could ultimately reach the Telnet application at the application layer. By using TCP, Telnet knows that it has to send back an ACK, acknowledging that it received the packet. Extended access lists can also take advantage of the Protocol field to allow or disallow UDP or TCP segments to or from the network. Figure 7-8 illustrates the use of TCP and UDP protocol IDs and how they map to the IP layer.

ARP

ARP is used to associate IP addresses with MAC addresses. We'll use the following example to explain how the protocol works. A device on the network is assigned an IP address, a network mask identifying the network the device is on, and a MAC address, which will be the device's local address and will help determine which local segment or *Local Area Network* (LAN) the device resides on. The MAC address is statically configured and will never change. The IP address is determined by the network administrator in charge of the network topology. Network devices must know the 48-bit MAC address of the device it wants to communicate with. To determine that MAC address, the device must use ARP to map the destination device's IP address to its associated MAC address. ARP uses the IP address of the destination device to send a broadcast out to the LAN segment asking for the MAC address of the destination device. The destination device with the corresponding IP address sends back a reply directly to the sending device

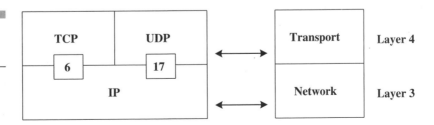

Figure 7-8
TCP and UDP
protocol Ids

Figure 7-9

An ARP example

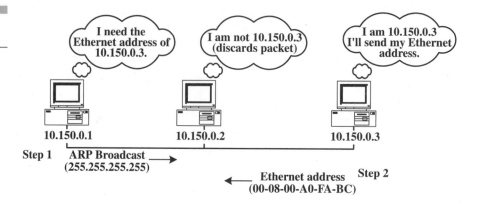

containing its MAC address. ARP then stores the IP-address-to-MAC-address association in an ARP cache. The next time the device needs to send data to the receiving device it will reference its ARP cache to determine if the IP address of the receiving device has an associated MAC address. If it does, it adds the MAC address into the destination MAC segment of the frame and will send off the packet. The process of referencing the ARP cache is faster and much more efficient than having to send out an ARP broadcast every time it needs to communicate with a device. Figure 7-9 illustrates an example of how ARP is used.

NOTE: *The default ARP cache timeout for a Cisco router is four hours. This value can be changed with the global configuration command* `arp timeout <value>`.

RARP

RARP works similar to ARP. Instead of broadcasting for a MAC address, a RARP request will broadcast for an IP address. Diskless nodes that do not know their IP addresses when they boot often use RARP. For RARP to work, it requires a RARP server on the local segment that will respond to RARP requests. The diskless workstation would send out a RARP request with its MAC address. The RARP server would then respond to the workstation with a RARP reply message, giving it its specified IP address. The workstation would now be able to send data because it can enter its source IP address into the packet so that the receiving station will know who to reply to. The reason the RARP server must be on the same local segment as the diskless workstation is because RARP broadcasts, like ARP broadcasts, do not travel past routers, thus limiting the broadcast to its own broadcast domain or network segment.

NOTE: *A Cisco communication server can be configured to act as a RARP server. This enables diskless booting between clients and servers that reside on different subnets. The command used to accomplish this is as follows:*

```
Router(config)#interface Ethernet0

Router(config-if)#ip address 172.16.5.1 255.255.0.0
Router(config-if)#ip rarp-server 172.16.5.1
```

The preceding commands enable interface Ethernet 0 to accept RARP requests. Support for RARP requests is configurable on a per-interface basis. This allows only the interfaces that need RARP assistance to be configured so that the router does not interfere with RARP requests on subnets that do not need assistance. A static ARP entry must also be entered for the diskless workstations to find the remote server. This static map entry will map the MAC address found in the RARP request to the IP address of the server. This way the router will receive the RARP request and be able to respond with the IP address of the remote server. RARP is documented in RFC 903.

ICMP

ICMP is the control and error message protocol for IP. It resides in an IP packet so it can be routed. Devices on the network can use ICMP messages to communicate to other devices about network congestion, unreachable destinations, redirects to better paths, TTL expirations, and many more. These are ICMP error messages. Destination unreachable messages include four basic types: network unreachable, host unreachable, port unreachable, and protocol unreachable. Network unreachable messages indicate that a failure has occurred in the routing or addressing of a packet. Host unreachable messages usually mean the wrong subnet mask is defined. Port unreachable messages imply that the TCP destination port is not available. Protocol unreachable messages usually indicate that the destination does not support the upper layer protocol specified in the packet.

Two kinds of ICMP messages are used: error messages and query messages. Query messages include echo requests and echo replies. When a router sends an ICMP destination unreachable message, it means that the router is unable to send the package to its final destination. The router then discards the original packet. A router would send an ICMP destination unreachable message because of the source specifying a non-existent network address or because a network link is down.

Two major applications use ICMP messages: *Packet Internet Groper* (ping) and trace route. Ping uses echo requests and echo replies. It is an extremely useful tool that can generate an ICMP echo-request message to test network reachability to another host. The receiving host will send back an ICMP echo-reply message to inform the host that originated the ping echo-request that it received the packet. Therefore, it has the capability to test network links to determine if certain paths are up and operational. It can also report if there is network congestion by reporting the time it took for the ICMP message to reach its destination. ICMP is documented in RFC 792.

NOTE: *To abort a ping session, type the escape sequence (by default, Ctrl-^ X, which is done by simultaneously pressing the Ctrl, Shift, and 6 keys, letting go, and then pressing the X key).*

Table 7-1 describes the characters that can be generated with the use of ping.

Table 7-1

Ping test characters

Char	Description
!	Each exclamation point indicates receipt of a reply.
.	Each period indicates the network server timed out while waiting for a reply.
U	Destination unreachable.
N	Network unreachable.
P	Protocol unreachable.
Q	Source quench.
M	Could not fragment.
?	Unknown packet type.

IP Addresses

An IP address is a 32-bit, layer-three software address. In TCP/IP, the address for a host is called the Internet address or best known as the IP address. All hosts on a TCP/IP network each have a unique IP address. IP addresses are specified and entered by the network administrator. This is a key process in network design as the addressing of hosts can have a key impact on the growth and expandability of the network. Routing decisions and path selection are based on IP addresses and how they are assigned. Hosts on the network will be able to communicate with each other because each host has a unique IP address. Throughout this discussion, we will describe why it's important to think about the network design in order to address future issues.

A 32-bit IP address is represented by a four-byte or octet number, which is in dotted-decimal notation format (see Figure 7-10). It contains a network number or prefix and a host or node number. The network number and network prefix are just two different names, both representing the network portion of the address. The same applies to the host number and node number. A host on a LAN must have the same network number as all the other hosts on that same LAN to communicate. However, that same host must have a unique host number to communicate. In this example, 172.16 is the network number and 3.1 is the host number.

For a host to communicate on the Internet, it must have a registered IP address. Registered IP addresses are most often obtained from the network's upstream *Internet Service Provider* (ISP). ISPs and larger networks can obtain their own class of addresses from the InterNIC. The InterNIC keeps a log of all IP addresses assigned and only assigns large groups of IP addresses if the requesting network warrants that many IP addresses.

Understanding IP addresses and how they are broken down is an extremely important aspect of networking to learn, as it plays an integral part of day-to-day work in the networking field. To those with little experience with IP addresses and how they function, it is my recommendation to read this chapter thoroughly and follow the examples. Once you've completed this, you may want to reread the section again until you have a solid understanding of the format of IP addresses.

Figure 7-10
The network number
and host number

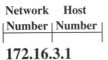

Network	Host
Number	Number

172.16.3.1

Classes of Addresses

IPv4 addresses are broken down into different classes. When the Internet was first developed and IP addresses first assigned, it was thought that there would be plenty of IP addresses to go around for a long time to come. They had reason to believe so, and why wouldn't they, with a possible 4,294,967,296 addresses available for hosts on the Internet? The problem wasn't necessarily the amount of IP addresses. It was how these addresses were initially distributed that started the depletion of IP addresses. The depletion of IP addresses is inevitable in retrospect to the dramatic growth of the Internet and the initial flaws with the process of distributing classes of IP addresses. The *Internet Engineering Task Force* (IETF) has developed a new version of IP called *IP next generation* (IPng) or *IP version 6* (IPv6). IPv6 is a 128-bit address, allowing for an almost infinite amount of addresses. IPv6 adds many features such as easier administration and tighter security and will scale extremely well as the Internet expands into the future.

IP addresses are broken down into four different classes: class A, class B, class C, and class D. Each class has a different amount of available networks and hosts. Class A allows for the largest amount of hosts and the fewest networks. Class A address spaces are meant for extremely large networks. Class B also provides a sizable amount of hosts and networks. Class B address spaces were initially intended for medium-sized networks. Class C allows for an extremely large amount of networks and the fewest hosts of the three classes. Class D is reserved for multicast and will be explained in detail further along in this discussion. Figure 7-11 illustrates how an IP address translates to a binary format.

To define which class an address is, we must first take a look at the first octet in the 32-bit address. The first octet always defines the address class. An octet defines the eight-bit number found in each one of the four segments of the address. That is why you will also see an octet referred to as a byte, because each part of the address has eight bits and eight bits equals a

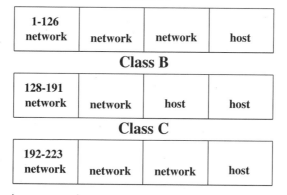

Figure 7-11
Decimal to binary example

| Decimal Address | 172. | 16. | 3. | 2 |

| Binary Address | 10101100. | 00010000. | 00000011. | 00000010 |

Octet/Byte
8 bits

Figure 7-12
Class address examples

Class A

| 1-126 network | network | network | host |

128 possible networks
16,777,216 possible hosts
per network

Class B

| 128-191 network | network | host | host |

16,384 possible networks
65,536 possible hosts per
network

Class C

| 192-223 network | network | network | host |

2,097,152 possible networks
256 possible hosts per
network

Octet/Byte

byte. Take another look at Figure 7-11. The first number in the address is an eight-bit number. The number can be broken down into binary format and you can see how the binary numbers equal the number in the example. Further discussion of binary-to-decimal translation and more examples will come later in the chapter.

Classes A, B, C, D, and E   In this section, each class of addresses will be detailed and broken down so that it can be fully understood. Figure 7-12 illustrates the class A, B, and C network ranges.

The class A address space was initially intended for extremely large networks, as mentioned earlier. Each class A address space can allow for a total of 16,777,216 hosts, and a total of 128 class A networks exists. Figure 7-12 shows that class A lists networks 1 through 126. This is because network 0.0.0.0 is used for the default network command and cannot be used as a valid network address. Also, network 127.0.0.0 is reserved for testing loop-back addresses and also cannot be used as a valid network address. There-fore, the useable networks for class A are 1 through 126. Many large corporations bought out the class A addresses when they were first being sold through the InterNIC. No, Microsoft doesn't have one. Neither does Cisco. They actually use class Bs. You may be asking, "How does a company use 16 million addresses in a network?" Well, truth be told, most corpora-tions don't need that many addresses and they now sell portions of their address space to ISPs and other corporations.

The first octet in the class A address is the network prefix and it always defines the network. The next three octets are the host number, which defines the host range for a class A address. This is why only 128 possible class A net-works are available and 16,777,216 possible hosts exist. The total combined combinations of addresses for the last three octets equal the possible amount of hosts on a class A network. The reason for the 128 possible networks instead of the 255 total possible combinations for the first octet is because the first bit in the first octet is always a zero and can never be a one for a class A address. Figure 7-13 illustrates the bit boundaries used in each class of address.

Figure 7-13
Bit boundaries
identifying the class
of the network
address

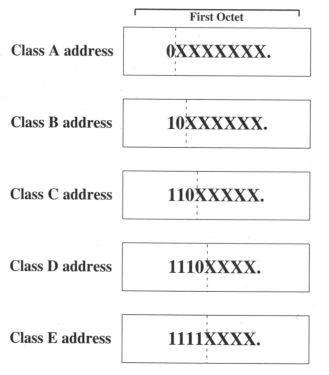

The first bit in the first octet will determine if the address is a class A. In binary format, the first bit in the first octet will always be a zero for the entire class A range. Routing used to be done on classful boundaries and the router would look at the first three bits of the address to determine which class the address fell under. If the first bit were a zero, the router would process it as a class A address. The reason that the first bit is always a zero for class A addresses is because if you put a zero in the first bit and then define all ones in the rest of the seven bits, the highest number that can be obtained will be 127. This is the high limit on the class A range.

The class B address range was initially intended for medium-sized networks. Each class B address range allows for a total of 65,534 ($2^{16} - 2$) hosts. A total of 16,384 (2^{14}) class B networks exists. Class B addresses range from 128 to 191. The reason for this range is because of the first two bits in the address. For a class B address, the two highest order bits determine that the address will be a class B. All class B addresses have the two highest order bits set to 1-0. The next 14 bits define the network number. Once the first two bits are defined as a 1-0 and if all the rest of the bit positions in the first octet are filled with ones, it would yield a 191 network number, the highest network number in a class B address range. If all zeros are filled in after the 1-0, it would yield a network number of 128. Refer to Figure 7-13 for a visual example. The network number for class B addresses is defined by the first two octets, and the host number is defined by the last two octets.

NOTE: *Highest order bits indicate the first bits of the first octet. For example, if a class B address is defined and it is stated that the two highest order bits will be 1-0, this will indicate that the first two bits in the first octet will be a one and a zero, as shown in Figure 7-13.*

The class C address is the most well-known address range because of the amount of networks available, the amount of Web sites on the Internet, and the many ISPs using class C addresses. A class C has the greatest amount of networks available of the classes with 2,097,152 (2^{21}). Each class C address range allows for 254 (2^8-2) addresses. Class C addresses range from 192 to 223. In the class C addresses, the three highest order bits are always set to 1-1-0. This indicates that the lowest range for a class C address will be 192. Looking at Figure 7-13, it can be seen that the 1-1-0 fills the bit positions 128, 64, 32. Since a zero occupies the bit with the 32 value, this bit will not be counted. Since the two highest order bits, 128 and 64, are marked with a one, this indicates that these bits will be counted and will equal 192, the lowest number in the allowable range for a class C address. If all ones are added to the rest of the first octet, it would equal 223, which is the highest allowable network number for a class C address. The network number for a class C address is defined by the first three octets. The last octet defines the host number.

The class D address range is reserved for multicast addresses. A multicast address is a class D range of addresses from 224.0.0.0 to 239.255.255.255. Many different routing protocols such as EIGRP and OSPF use multicast addresses to send routing updates. Many applications that send *Voice over IP* (VoIP) also use multicast addresses for IP multicasting. IP multicasting is the process of sending data to a selected group of hosts. These hosts are determined by a class D address. A class D address can be identified because the four highest order bits are 1-1-1-0. A class D address cannot be defined on a network host or router to allow communication with other devices.

The class E address range is reserved for experimental use. A class E address can be identified when the four highest order bits are set to 1-1-1-1.

Subnet Masks   This section covers subnet masks and how they are used to determine the network portion and the host portion of the IP address. IP addresses contain a network number and a host number, as described earlier. The mechanism for determining this is called a *subnet mask*. Figure 7-14 represents an example of a subnet mask.

In the IP address of 172.16.5.10, 172.16 is the network number and 5.10 is the host number. All hosts on that network segment have a network number of 172.16. Each host will have its own unique host number. A subnet mask is a 32-bit (four-octet) number like an IP address. A network that is routing an IP address will first look at the IP address and then the subnet mask to determine which network the IP address is destined for. Once the destination router receives the packet, it again looks at the IP address and

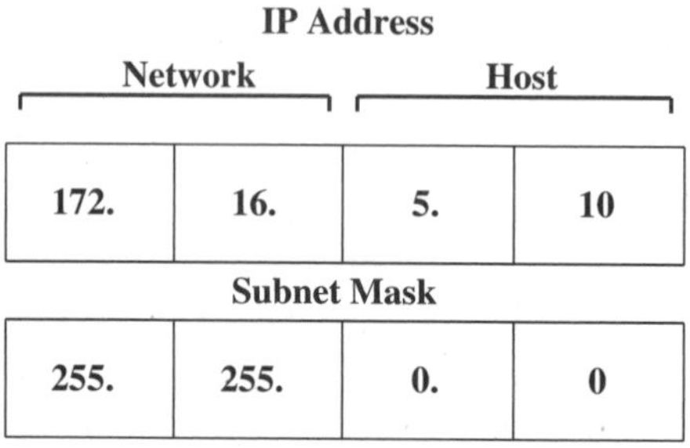

Figure 7-14
Subnet mask example

IP Address

Network		Host	
172.	16.	5.	10

Subnet Mask

255.	255.	0.	0

then the subnet mask to determine the actual host address. The destination router is only concerned with the host portion because the packet has already arrived at the specific network.

Default Subnet Masks for Classful Addresses   Default subnet masks determine the network number of the specific class of addresses. The class A, B, and C addresses have different sized network prefixes. In classful routing, the specific class of address is always routed on its network boundary. This means that a network device routing a class A address will process the first octet as the network number and the following three octets as the host number. This is because all IP addresses are sent with their corresponding subnet masks. Subnet masks for classful addresses in a classful routing environment will remain constant according to the specific class of the address. Figure 7-15 shows the default subnet masks used for each class of address.

Figure 7-15 shows examples of each address class along with their associated default subnet masks. It is shown that a class A address of 15.230.40.1 will have a subnet mask of 255.0.0.0. This is because the first octet with the value of 15 is the network number for that class A address. Each class of address has a subnet mask of 255 corresponding to its network number. Figure 7-15 also lists the default subnet masks for each class of address. It can be seen that the first three octets in the class C address of 198.168.67.2 represent the network number. This class C address will have a default subnet mask of 255.255.255.0. The 255 value is the highest value of an octet because every bit position is filled with a one. Bit positions along with binary numbers will be discussed in detail later in this chapter.

Subnetting

In the mid-1980s, the Internet started having problems because of the number of routes in the Internet routing tables. Subnetting was introduced in 1985 by RFC 950 to address these problems. Subnetting enables a single class A, B, or C network to be divided, or subnetted, into smaller networks. Instead of the classful, two-level hierarchy, subnetting allows a three-level hierarchy. Subnetting does this by splitting up the host number into two separate parts: the subnet number and the host number on that subnet. Subnetting also allows subnetworks to be created. Each subnetwork acts as an independent network. Subnetworks are generally created to better manage the design of the network and to reduce network traffic by splitting off a network into smaller subnetworks.

	Network		Host	
Class A Example	15.	230.	40.	1

Default Subnet Mask	255.	0.	0.	0

	Network		Host	
Class B Example	169.	228.	240.	5

Default Subnet Mask	255.	255.	0.	0

	Network			Host
Class C Example	198.	168.	67.	2

Default Subnet Mask	255.	255.	255.	0

Converting a Number from Decimal to Binary and Back   All decimal numbers that are used in IP addresses range from either 0 to 255. These numbers are determined by the values in the binary bit positions. In binary, the only available digits are one and zero. These digits represent how many times the number in the bit position will be used. Figure 7-16 shows how the decimal number 203 is broken down into binary format.

Notice in the figure that eight bit positions exist in a single octet. The rightmost bit position in the binary chart is always a one. The bit in the next position to the left is a two. These numbers, as shown by the example, go up exponentially until the final leftmost bit is reached, which is 128.

Figure 7-16
A binary to decimal
conversion

203 in Decimal format

203.

203 in Binary format

11001011.

Binary chart
+
Binary Number
=
Decimal Number

128	64	32	16	8	4	2	1
1	1	0	0	1	0	1	1
203							

In the figure, bit number 2 has a value of one, meaning that it will be used one time. Bit number 32 has a value of zero, meaning it will not be used. The bit positions that have a value of one are counted and, when added, equal the resulting factor of 203.

Decimal numbers can be broken down into binary by taking the decimal value and filling the bit positions starting with the largest possible number. For example, the decimal value of 197 is broken down accordingly in Figure 7-17.

Here it can be seen that the decimal value of 197 is greater than the highest binary number of 128. Thus, a one would be entered for the 128-bit position. The number 69 is now taken and can be filled in the next bit position of 64 (197 − 128 = 69). So the bit position of 64 now has a value of one. We are now left with a decimal value of five, as 69 − 64 = 5. The decimal value of five is not larger than the 32, 16, or eight binary bit positions. Thus, they each take a value of zero. The next bit position of four is less than our resulting value of five and takes a value of one (5 − 4 =1), as the remaining decimal value is at one. One is lower than the two bit position, so it

Figure 7-17
Another binary to
decimal conversion

Binary chart
+
Binary Number
=
Decimal Number

128	64	32	16	8	4	2	1
1	1	0	0	0	1	0	1
197							

takes a value of zero. The next bit position of one equals the remaining decimal value, so it takes a value of one. These binary numbers can now be converted back to decimal by simply adding the bit positions that have a value of one, thus $128 + 64 + 4 + 1 = 197$.

Determining the Number of Networks and Hosts   The equation to figure out the amount of hosts allowed on a subnet is $2^N - 2$. The first 2 symbolizes the possible numbers in a bit position. Those two possible numbers are one and zero, as described earlier. This number 2 is then increased to the power of N where N equals the amount of host bits. As shown in Figure 7-18, using an IP address of 172.16.5.1 with a subnet mask of 255.255.248.0, 11 bits are in the host portion. In this example, 2 is increased to the power of 11 because there are 11 host bits. This total is then decreased by 2, the last number in the equation, because two addresses cannot be used: the first address, which will be the network address, and the last address, which will be the broadcast address for that subnet.

The number of possible subnets is figured out similarly. Five bits are used for the subnet portion. The equation to figure out the amount of possible subnets is 2^N. The number 2 again symbolizes the possible numbers in a bit position. This number 2 is then increased to the power of N where N equals the amount of bits in the subnet portion. In the example, five bits are used in the subnet portion, so the equation for this example is 2^5, which equals 32. That's 32 possible subnets each with 2046 possible hosts.

Subnetting IP Addresses   Subnetting enables classful addresses to be further broken down to allow a more efficient use of IP addresses. Refer to Figure 7-18 to see an example of how a class B address can be subnetted.

In the earlier Figure 7-18, a class B address of 172.16.5.1 is subnetted. The 172.16 portion is the network number as defined by its default subnet mask. Further subnetting is now done with the host portion. A subnet mask of 255.255.255.0 has been randomly chosen. This new subnet mask now

Figure 7-18

A subnetted class B address

	Network		Subnet	Host
Class B Example	172.	16.	5.	1
Subnet Mask	255.	255.	255.	0

enables this class B address to take on the characteristics of a class C address with 254 possible hosts. The .5 portion is now the subnet number. The range for the 172.16.5.0 network with the 255.255.255.0 mask is a subnet range of 172.16.5.1 to 172.16.5.254. An IP address of 172.16.6.1 would be in a completely different subnet.

This example has a total of 256 possible subnets. This is because the 172.16 portion of the address will remain constant, as it is the network number. The subnet number can range from 0 to 255. The range for the subnet number is all of the possible numbers for the third octet, which is the subnet number. The subnet number uses all eight bits of the third octet; thus, the eight bits are entered into the 2^N equation to figure out the number of possible subnets ($2^8 = 256$). The range of the possible subnets is 172.16.0.0 to 172.16.255.0.

In Figure 7-19, the same class B address of 172.16.5.1 is used. Instead of subnetting with a class C subnet mask, a different subnet mask is used that will allow for more hosts per subnet.

In this example, a subnet mask of 255.255.248.0 is used. The first five bits in the third octet make up the subnet number. So to determine the amount of subnets possible, the first five bits are entered into the 2^N equation. Thus, 2^5 equals 32 possible subnets. The third octet of the subnet mask comes out to 248 because this is the sum of the first five bits in that third octet ($128 + 64 + 32 + 16 + 8 = 248$). These five bits in the subnet number along with the 16 bits in the first and second octet make up the *extended network prefix*.

The number of possible hosts per subnet is determined by a combination of the eight bits in the last octet and the remaining three bits in the third octet. In Figure 7-19, it can be seen that the combination of these last 11

Figure 7-19
A subnetted class
B example

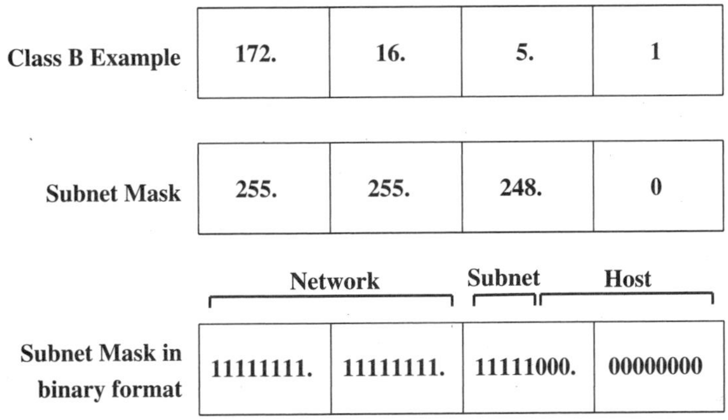

Class B Example	172.	16.	5.	1

Subnet Mask	255.	255.	248.	0

	Network		Subnet	Host
Subnet Mask in binary format	11111111.	11111111.	11111000.	00000000

Figure 7-20
The listed subnets

Subnet #1	172.16.0.0 -	172.16.7.255
Subnet #2	172.16.8.0 -	172.16.15.255
Subnet #3	172.16.16.0 -	172.16.23.255
Subnet #4	172.16.24.0 -	172.16.31.255
Subnet #5	172.16.32.0 -	172.16.39.255
	.....	
	.....	
	.....	
Subnet #30	172.16.232.0 - 172.16.239.255	
Subnet #31	172.16.240.0 - 172.16.247.255	
Subnet #32	172.16.248.0 - 172.16.255.255	

bits makes up the amount of possible hosts. This mask will enable 2046 (or $2^{11} - 2$) hosts per subnet. The range of addresses for the 172.16.5.1 address with the 255.255.248.0 subnet mask is defined in Figure 7-20.

Figure 7-20 shows how the first subnet range is from 172.16.0.0 to 172.16.7.255. The second subnet range is from 172.16.8.0 to 172.16.15.255. So 172.16.5.1 is an address in the first subnet. As shown in the figure, the subnet numbers increase by eight. This is because the subnet number is using the first five bytes in the third octet for the subnet number and eight is the lowest bit number in that subnet number. To determine the different ranges of subnets for different subnet masks, just find the lowest number bit in the subnet portion and that is the number that will be used to increment from zero. The first subnet, no matter which subnet mask is used, will always have a zero in the subnet portion. This is because all of the bits in the subnet number can be set to zero.

NOTE: *Subnet masks can be represented in three different formats:*

- Dotted-decimal notation (255.255.0.0)
- Bit count (/16)
- Hexadecimal (0XFFFFFF00)

If a subnet mask is represented as 255.255.255.0 in dotted-decimal notation, it would be /24 in bit count format. The reason for this is because 24 bits are used in the subnet mask, thus the /24. The subnet mask must be entered in dotted-decimal notation when configuring the IP address and subnet mask. However, you can choose to have the router represent the subnet mask in any of the three formats for the current session by entering the following command:

```
Router#term ip netmask-format {bitcount | decimal | hexadecimal}
```

The next command sets the format of the subnet mask for a specific line:

```
Router(config-line)#ip netmask-format {bitcount | decimal |
hexadecimal}
```

Network Addresses and Broadcast Addresses Using the same examples in Figure 7-20, one can see how the network address and the broadcast address is determined for each subnet. With a network address of 172.16.5.0 using a default class B subnet mask of 255.255.0.0, the range of addresses would be 172.16.0.0 to 172.16.255.255. The first address, 172.16.0.0, is the network address. This address is identified as the network address because when represented in binary, the host portion is all zeros (see Figure 7-21).

Figure 7-21
Class B network
address example

Class B Example	172.	16.	5.	1

Subnet Mask	255.	255.	0.	0

	Network		Host	
Subnet Mask in binary format	11111111.	11111111.	00000000.	00000000

Network Address	172.	16.	0.	0

Network Address in binary format	10101100.	00010000.	00000000.	00000000

This address is using a default class B subnet mask, which makes the last two octets the host number. The network address will have all zeros in the last two octets, identifying the host number as 0.0. Thus, the network address equals 172.16.0.0. This network address symbolizes the whole range of possible addresses. Network addresses are often entered into router configurations under a routing process. For example, let's say a router is running RIPv1 and the 172.16.0.0 network needs to be routed so that another router that is connected can reach this 172.16.0.0 network. This network address would be entered under the router rip statement. Network addresses are also used to reference the entire range of addresses. These network addresses cannot be used on router interfaces or other network devices.

Although the network address is the lowest possible number in the 172.16.0.0 to 172.16.255.255 range, the broadcast address is the highest possible number. This number is 172.16.255.255, as illustrated in Figure 7-22.

The broadcast address, when broken down into binary format, will have the host portion as all ones. The last two octets that identify the host portion have all ones, making the host number 255.255 and the broadcast address 172.16.255.255. The broadcast address does exactly as it sounds. A broadcast address is used when a network device needs to communicate with all hosts on that particular network (see Figure 7-23).

For example, if host A needs to request services from another host but doesn't know which host it needs, it could send out a broadcast. This broadcast would have the 172.16.255.255 address in its destination IP portion of the packet. The message would be sent to all of the hosts on the 172.16.0.0 network.

Now that we know what network and broadcast addresses do, we will subnet the network to create different network and broadcast address numbers. This may be difficult to grasp when first learning about subnetting, so it's recommended that the previous section be completely understood before proceeding with the next section.

Figure 7-22
Class B broadcast
address example

Broadcast Address	172.	16.	255.	255

Broadcast Address in binary format	10101100.	00010000.	11111111.	11111111

Figure 7-23

How a broadcast address is used

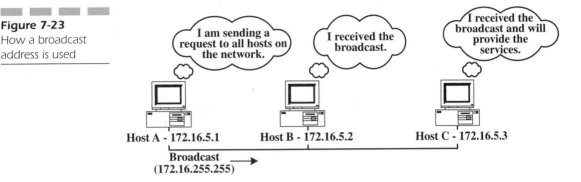

Host A - 172.16.5.1   Host B - 172.16.5.2   Host C - 172.16.5.3

Broadcast ⟶
(172.16.255.255)

The previous example of an address of 172.16.5.1 with a subnet mask of 255.255.248.0 will be used. As mentioned earlier, this address falls in the first subnet range of 172.16.0.0 to 172.16.7.255. For this subnetwork, 172.16.0.0 would be the network address. The address at the end of the subnet range, 172.16.7.255, would be the broadcast address for this subnetwork.

The 172.16.0.0 address is the network address of this first subnet because there is nothing but zeros in the 11-bit host portion. The five bits in the subnet number are also set to zero, as this is the first subnetwork. The broadcast address comes out to 172.16.7.255 because the 11 bits of the host number are all set to one. By specifying that this is the first subnetwork, we know that the five bits in the subnet number are set to zero. The rest of the bits in that octet, which are host bits, leave three bits. These three bits set to one give the third octet a value of seven, the last host number in the third octet subnet range. Specifying all ones in the last octet will give that octet a value of 255. In summary, we specify all ones in the last 11 host bits to get a value of 172.16.7.255, the broadcast address (see Figure 7-24).

Examples   Now that subnetting has been discussed, some more examples will be presented to better clarify the understanding of subnetting. Each different class of address will be subnetted using a random subnet mask. Each subnet mask will use different amounts of bits for the subnet number and will only use the bits in the next octet after the classful subnet mask.

Subnet Class A Address Space   As discussed earlier, a class A address uses a default subnet mask of 255.0.0.0. In this example, we will be using a class A address of 20.0.0.0 using a subnet mask of 255.192.0.0 (see Figure 7-25).

The subnet mask is broken down into binary. The second octet contains eight bits, the leftmost two being used for the subnet number. Those two bits are in bit positions with values of 128 and 64. These added together

Figure 7-24
How a subnet mask
determines the
broadcast address

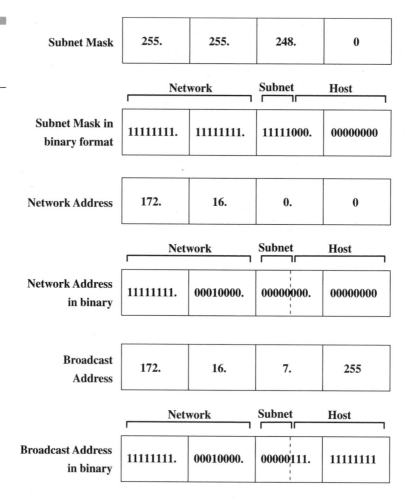

| Subnet Mask | 255. | 255. | 248. | 0 |

| | Network | | Subnet | Host |
| Subnet Mask in binary format | 11111111. | 11111111. | 11111000. | 00000000 |

| Network Address | 172. | 16. | 0. | 0 |

| | Network | | Subnet | Host |
| Network Address in binary | 11111111. | 00010000. | 00000000. | 00000000 |

| Broadcast Address | 172. | 16. | 7. | 255 |

| | Network | | Subnet | Host |
| Broadcast Address in binary | 11111111. | 00010000. | 00000111. | 11111111 |

equal 192, or the subnet number in the subnet mask. The last six bits in the second octet are used for the host number along with the 16 bits in the last two octets. This allows 22 bits to be used for the host portion of the address.

The 20.0.0.0 address uses the 255.192.0.0 subnet mask that is defined. This yields the first subnetwork to be 20.0.0.0 to 20.63.255.255. The reason for this range is because all zeros are entered into the subnet portion of the address, or the first two bits in the second octet, to define the first subnetwork. Since this is the first subnetwork, all the zeros in the subnet portion remain constant. All zeros are also entered into the host portion of the address to determine the first address. To determine the end of the range, all ones would be entered into the host portion, or the last 22 bits, to give the value of 20.63.255.255. The next subnetwork is 20.64.0.0 to 20.127.255.255 (see Figure 7-26).

Figure 7-25
A subnetted class
A address

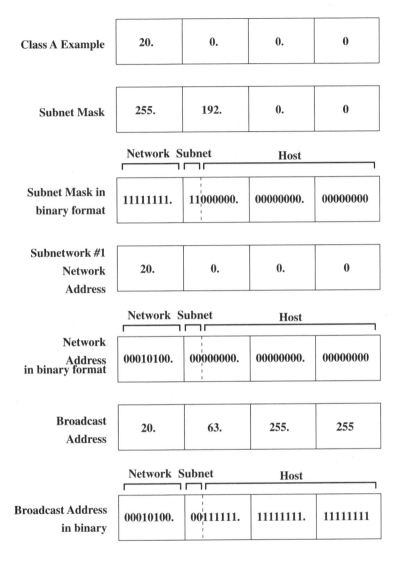

This next subnetwork is determined by changing the lowest value bit in the subnet number to one. In this case, the lowest bit in the subnet number is 64. Thus, the second subnetwork has a network address of 20.64.0.0. The range extends to 20.127.255.255 because all ones are entered into the 22-bit host portion, giving the last address or broadcast address for this value.

To determine the amount of possible networks, the 2^N equation is used. The N value in this scenario is 2 because two bits are available for the subnet portion. 2^2 equals 4, so there are four possible subnets.

Figure 7-26
A subnetted class A
address, the second
subnetwork

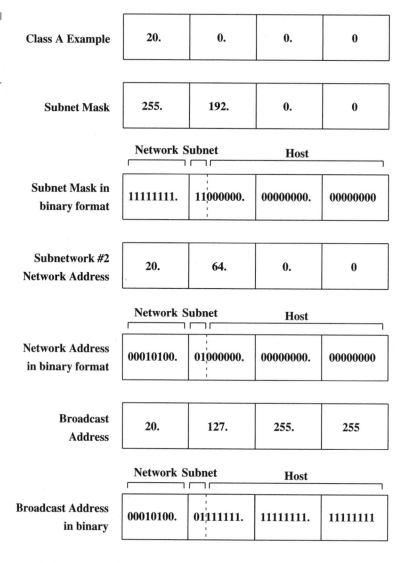

| | Network Subnet | | Host | |

| Class A Example | 20. | 0. | 0. | 0 |

| Subnet Mask | 255. | 192. | 0. | 0 |

| Subnet Mask in binary format | 11111111. | 11000000. | 00000000. | 00000000 |

| Subnetwork #2 Network Address | 20. | 64. | 0. | 0 |

| Network Address in binary format | 00010100. | 01000000. | 00000000. | 00000000 |

| Broadcast Address | 20. | 127. | 255. | 255 |

| Broadcast Address in binary | 00010100. | 01111111. | 11111111. | 11111111 |

The hosts are determined by using the $2^N - 2$ equation. In this scenario, 22 host bits exist, so the equation would look like $2^{22} - 2 = 4,194,302$. 4,194,302 is the amount of available hosts per subnet.

Subnet Class B Address Space In this example, a class B address of 172.32.4.120 will be subnetted with a subnet mask of 255.255.240.0. As described earlier, a class B address has a default subnet mask of 255.255.0.0. In this example, four bits in the third octet are used for the subnet number. Those first four leftmost bits in the third octet equal 240 (128 + 64 + 32 + 16 = 240), the value of the third octet in the subnet mask.

The first subnetwork will be 172.32.0.0 because all zeros are entered for the subnet portion. All zeros are also entered for the host portion to find the first address or the network address for the specific subnetwork. The range extends to 172.32.15.255. The reason for this value is because all ones are entered for the host portion. In this example, the last four bits in the third octet along with the eight bits in the last octet equal 12 bits that can be used for the host portion of the address.

The IP address of 172.32.4.120 falls within this first range of addresses or the first subnetwork. This address is broken down in Figure 7-27.

Figure 7-27
A subnetted Class B address

Class B Example	172.	32.	4.	120

Subnet Mask	255.	255.	240.	0

	Network	Subnet	Host
Subnet Mask in binary format	11111111. 11111111.	11110000.	00000000

Subnetwork #1 Network Address	172.	32.	0.	0

	Network	Subnet	Host
Network Address in binary format	10101100. 00100000.	00000000.	00000000

Broadcast Address	172.	32.	15.	255

	Network	Subnet	Host
Broadcast Address in binary	10101100. 00100000.	00001111.	11111111

The address falls within the first subnetwork because it has a subnet number of four, which is in the range of the first subnetwork, 0 to 15. This example has 16 possible networks. This again is determined by using the 2^N equation. The value of N in this scenario is four because four bits are available for the subnet number. Thus, 16 possible subnets are available (2^4).

To determine the amount of possible hosts, the $2^N - 2$ equation will be used again. Twelve bits are used for the host portion, so the equation would be $2^{12} - 2$, which equals 4094 possible hosts per subnet. It's important to remember that the $- 2$ in the equation states that the network address and the broadcast address cannot be used as addresses.

Subnet Class C Address Space   As class C addresses are the most prevalent in today's networks, two examples will be presented. In the first example, a class C address of 198.168.19.0 is used with a subnet mask of 255.255.255.128. Using a subnet mask of 255.255.255.128 enables us to basically split the host portion of a regular class C address. A class C address has a default subnet mask of 255.255.255.0. This mask allows for 254 host addresses ($2^8 - 2$). With the 255.255.255.128 subnet mask, the outcome equals 126 host addresses ($2^7 - 2$). Only one bit is being used in the subnet portion, the leftmost bit with the value of 128. This means that only two subnets are available, as there is only one bit to use in the equation to figure out the amount of networks, $2^1 = 2$. This type of subnet mask is used with a class C address when a network administrator wants to split a class C into two different networks.

In the second example, we will use the same class C address with a different mask of 255.255.255.252. To determine which bits add up to equal 252, we start with the leftmost bit in the last octet and add the bits up until they equal 252 ($128 + 64 + 32 + 16 + 8 + 4 = 252$). The leftmost six bits are being used for the subnet number. This means that only two bits are left over for the host portion. The number of subnets is determined by adding the six bits to the 2^N equation, $2^6 = 64$, while the number of hosts is determined by using the $2^N - 2$ equation. In this scenario, N = 2 because only two host bits are available; $2^2 - 2 = 2$. This means that only two hosts are available per subnet.

Many people may ask, "Why use a subnet mask that only allows for two hosts?" This subnet mask is in fact used quite often. It is most often used on point-to-point serial links using one address on one side of the connection and the other address on the other side. This subnet mask enables this to be done to 64 different connections.

Private Addresses   The IETF developed certain ranges of IP addresses that were to be used for internal networks wanting to use TCP/IP without connecting to the Internet. Private addresses are often referred to as non-routable addresses. This is false. Private addresses are no different than any other address and they could be routed through the Internet if all the filters aren't in place. All Internet routers and ISPs have access lists or other types of filters so that these addresses cannot be routed. These private addresses can be used on an internal network but will not work if a host tries to communicate with another host on the Internet. Each class of addresses has one address range that is defined as private. Figure 7-28 specifies the private ranges of addresses.

The class A address range that is private is the 10.0.0.0 network. This network has the default class A subnet mask of 255.0.0.0. The range of this network extends from 10.0.0.0 to 10.255.255.255. Many large organizations may decide to use this address range when going with internal addresses because of the scalability and the tremendous number of networks and hosts available. The 10.0.0.0 can be used with any subnet mask to give whatever number of networks or hosts a network administrator is looking for because any address starting with a 10.X.X.X cannot be routed through the Internet.

The class B address that is defined as private is the 172.16.0.0 network. This network is used with a subnet mask of 255.240.0.0. This subnet mask makes the range of private addresses from 172.16.0.0 to 172.32.255.255. This is the range that will be specified in access lists in the Internet and ISP routers. So any address in the range of 172.0.0.0 to 172.15.255.255 and 172.33.0.0 to 172.255.255.255 would be allowed through the Internet.

The class C address that is private is the 192.168.0.0 network. This network is used with a subnet mask of 255.255.0.0. This mask is actually a default subnet mask for a class B network. The address range with this mask is 192.168.0.0 to 192.168.255.255.

Classless Routing   The Internet used to route IP addresses based on classful boundaries. This was discussed earlier, how routers would look at the first three bits of the first octet in the address to determine if it was a class A, B, or C address. Well, the Internet has evolved and routing is no longer done on classful boundaries. Now it's referred to as *classless routing*.

Figure 7-28
Private address
ranges

Private Address Ranges

Class A range	10.0.0.0 - 10.255.255.255
Class B range	172.16.0.0 - 172.31.255.255
Class C range	192.168.0.0 - 192.168.255.255

Classless routing means that the router no longer looks at the first three bits of the address to determine its default subnet mask. IP addresses can now use any subnet mask. For example, a class C address of 199.204.56.0 can use a class A subnet mask of 255.0.0.0. Also, a class A address of 12.0.0.0 can use a subnet mask of 255.255.255.252. These are called *variable length subnet masks* (VLSM). The routing protocol used in the network must be able to support classless routing. RIPv1 and IGRP are two examples of routing protocols that do not support classless routing.

Router Concepts

This section discusses the different concepts defined on a router. Examples along with configurations of both physical and subinterfaces will be discussed as well as the encapsulation types for those interfaces.

Physical Interfaces

Physical interfaces are defined at the hardware level. This means that when looking at a router, each module or built-in interface is defined as an interface. Routers come in many shapes and sizes. Smaller scale routers, such as the 1600, are designed for smaller networks. They generally will have one Ethernet or Token Ring interface for the LAN and one serial or ISDN interface to connect to another router. The larger scale routers, such as the 7500, are modular. This means that modules can go into the router that have different interfaces such as ATM, Serial, Ethernet, Token Ring, or *Fiber Distributed Data Interface* (FDDI). These routers will often have many physical interfaces.

Subinterfaces

Subinterfaces are defined at the software level. This means that they do not physically exist and must be created with the Cisco IOS. Subinterfaces are often used on small routers that only have one physical serial interface but need to connect to multiple routers. The physical serial interface is split into subinterfaces and each subinterface is used to connect to a router. Subinterfaces also prove useful for reporting errors and bandwidth utilization on each link. Subinterfaces can also be used when running VLANs. They are used specifically to split up a trunk into multiple, logical subinterfaces.

To define a subinterface, the following commands would be typed:

```
Router#config t
Router(config)#interface serial 1
Router(config-if)#interface serial 1.1
```

The physical serial interface must first be defined before a subinterface can be created. This example creates a subinterface off serial 1. More subinterfaces can be created by typing in the desired subinterface under the interface configuration mode. Figure 7-29 shows multiple subinterfaces configured on a physical interface.

Encapsulation Types

Serial interfaces use different types of encapsulation to communicate with each other. Each serial interface must have the same encapsulation as the serial interface it wants to communicate with. The different types of encapsulation for serial interfaces are listed here:

- *Asynchronous Transfer Mode-Data Exchange Interface* (ATM-DXI)
- Frame Relay
- *High-level Data Link Control* (HDLC)
- *Link Access Procedure Balanced* (LAPB)
- *Point-to-Point Protocol* (PPP)

Figure 7-29
Subinterface example

Multiple sub-interfaces
configured on single
physical interface

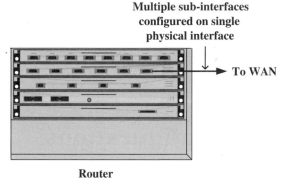

To WAN

Router

- *Synchronous Data Link Control* (SDLC)
- SDLC primary
- SDLC secondary
- *Switched Multimegabit Data Service* (SMDS)
- *Subnetwork Access Protocol* (SNAP)
- *Serial Tunnel* (STUN)
- X.25

The two most popular types of encapsulation are Frame Relay and HDLC. Frame Relay encapsulation is used on serial interfaces that connect to a Frame Relay network. Different types of Frame Relay encapsulations exist. These will be described in further detail later in the book.

HDLC is used on point-to-point serial interfaces. HDLC and PPP are two encapsulation types for point-to-point connections. HDLC is Cisco's default and is often the most preferred. Troubleshooting with HDLC is more advanced because it enables a network administrator to put the local *Channel Service Unit/Data Service Unit* (CSU/DSU) into loopback mode and do a *show interface serial X* (X represents the number of the serial interface that is being tested). If the interface and line protocol are in an "up" state, HDLC shows that the router and the CSU/DSU are working correctly. PPP does not allow for this test, as it will not show an up state for the line protocol. ATM-DXI and SMDS are both ATM-based layer-two encapsulation protocols.

LAPB is a data-link protocol linked to X.25 and provides reliable delivery. X.25 encapsulation is used in older X.25 networks. Two types of encapsulation are used for X.25: DTE and DCE. DTE encapsulation is the default when typing *encapsulation X.25*.

The following code example shows the use of the encapsulation command. The router's serial interface is configured to use a Frame Relay-type encapsulation for packets sent over the serial link.

```
Router(config)#interface serial 1
Router(config-if)#encapsulation frame-relay
```

Router Configurations

This section will discuss the basics on configuring the router. These are usually the first steps that need to be accomplished when setting up a network from scratch.

Setting up the IP Address of an Interface

IP addresses have been covered extensively throughout this chapter. Now we will assign an IP address to a router interface so that it can establish communication with other devices. An IP address will need to be assigned to each interface that will be used on the router. For example, the Ethernet interface would first have to have an IP address before being able to communicate with hosts on the internal network. In this example, the Ethernet interface is assigned an IP address:

```
Router#config t
Router(config)#interface ethernet 0
Router(config-if)#ip address 172.16.0.254 255.255.255.0
```

Here the IP address of 172.16.0.254 is assigned and will allow for 254 hosts on the network because of the 255.255.255.0 subnet mask. Hosts on this network will have their default gateway defined as this IP address.

Switches also have a default gateway. The IP address of the default gateway will be the Ethernet address of the router. This enables traffic that cannot be resolved locally to be sent to the router.

IP Host Names

Network devices often have names that identify the individual device. These names are called *host names*. The router can be configured to map IP addresses to host names. This allows for easier management of these network devices.

The Cisco IOS software maintains a host table that will store host-name-to-IP-address mappings. The router must know the IP address of the device to allow connectivity. When a router receives a request to connect to a particular host, it will look up the host in the host table to see if it has an IP address associated with it. If it does, it will use this IP address to connect to the host. Host-name-to-IP-address mappings can be assigned statically or dynamically.

Static Mappings   When IP-host-name-to-IP-address mappings are configured statically on the router, this allows the router to act as a DNS server. Network applications such as Telnet use host names to identify network devices. Telnet would reference the host table to determine the IP address that is associated with the host name and allow connectivity to the device. The most efficient way of handling host tables is to install a DNS server.

To define a static host-name-to-address mapping in the host cache, the ip host global configuration command is used. The following is an example of the ip host command. The router is configured to map the name server1 to the IP address of 172.16.0.2:

```
Router#config t
Router(config)#ip host server1 172.16.0.2
```

Multiple IP addresses can be mapped to a host name. This is done by typing the same line as was used to configure the first host name mapping, but using a different IP address.

A TCP port number can also be assigned to an ip host command. The specified TCP port number will be included when using the host name with an Exec connect or Telnet command. The default TCP port number is 23 for Telnet.

DNS   DNS can be installed on a server to have a central database where host-name-to-IP-address mappings are stored. The router can look up a DNS server with the command ip name-server. The router can use up to six DNS servers with this command. DNS is used widely throughout the Internet to translate names such as www.cisco.com to an IP address to allow connectivity. The following example describes the steps taken to configure a DNS server:

```
Router#config t
Router(config)#ip name-server 172.16.0.1
```

This example specifies a DNS server with an IP address of 172.16.0.1. The router will reference this DNS server anytime it receives a command or address it does not recognize in order to retrieve the IP address for the particular device.

DNS is enabled by default on a router. The router specifies a DNS server address of 255.255.255.255. This address is the local broadcast. So when a router cannot resolve a host name, it sends a local broadcast to find a DNS server. The command no ip domain-lookup is used to turn off this process. The router will no longer forward name system broadcast packets when this command is entered.

NOTE: *If a command is misspelled or typed incorrectly, the router will send a local broadcast trying to associate an IP address with the command. By typing the* no ip domain-lookup *command, the router will no longer try to translate misspelled commands.*

Working with the Hostname Table   The following example is the output from the show hosts command:

```
Router#show hosts
Default domain is not set
Name/address lookup uses domain service
Name servers are 255.255.255.255

Host            Flags          Age    Type    Address(es)
server1         (perm, OK)     0      IP      172.16.0.2
```

Table 7-2 describes the different line items in the previous code.

Routing from One VLAN to Another

VLANs are considered individual networks or broadcast domains. They are created on switches to segment network devices and the associated traffic to their own network. VLANs operate at layer two and need a layer-three device to communicate or route between VLANs. Routing between VLANs can be done in two different ways. *Route Switch Modules* (RSMs) can be placed in switches to enable communication between VLANs, or the switches can be connected to a router. Figure 7-30 illustrates a router connected to a core switch. This is often referred to as a "router on a stick."

The router can route packets received from one VLAN to another. For this to occur, the router must have a separate physical interface for each VLAN or have trunking enabled on a single physical interface. Each

Table 7-2 Descriptions of the show hosts field	**Term**	**Description**
	Host	Name of the learned host
	Flags	Describes how the host name was learned and specifies its current status
	Perm	Manually configured in the static host table
	Temp	Learned from DNS
	OK	Entry is current
	EX	Entry has aged out or expired
	Age	Last time the software referred to the entry, measured in hours
	Type	Protocol field
	Address(es)	IP addresses associated with the name of the host

Figure 7-30
A router on a stick

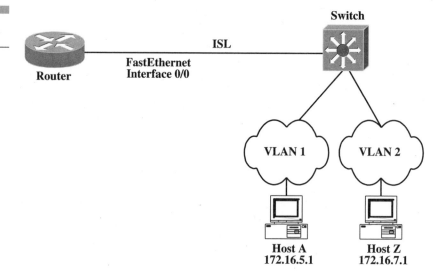

VLAN's network number must also be entered into the router so that the router knows how to route traffic to the VLAN.

ISL Configuration for VLANs   The *Inter Switch Link* (ISL) is a Cisco proprietary protocol that enables multiple VLANs to be interconnected and maintains VLAN information. ISL supports up to 1000 VLANs and operates in a point-to-point environment. ISL is most often configured on Fast Ethernet links in full- or half-duplex, allowing for wire speed performance.

ISL encapsulates the Ethernet frame with its own header that contains the VLAN IDs. The header consists of 26 bytes, 10 of which are used for the VLAN ID. Many different protocols can be routed over ISL. In this next example, IP will be configured to route over ISL. The following example shows the steps to configure VLAN 100 for ISL encapsulation:

```
Router#config t
Router(config)#interface FastEthernet 0/0.100
Router(config-if)#encapsulation isl 100
```

In this example, the interface FastEthernet 0/0.100 is configured to use ISL encapsulation. The 100 specified after `encapsulation isl` is the VLAN domain number. The ISL must also be configured on the switch port connected to the router.

Subinterfaces   Subinterfaces must be created from one physical interface to enable ISL trunking. The router's physical FastEthernet interface

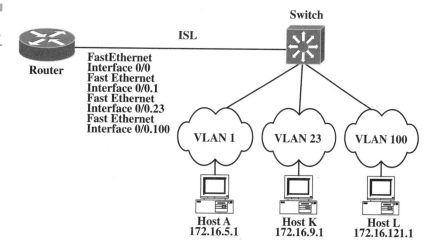

Figure 7-31
Subinterface example

is most commonly used. Each subinterface will be associated with a VLAN. A common naming standard for subinterfaces used for VLANs is shown in Figure 7-31.

In this example, each subinterface is attached to a VLAN. As shown in the figure, each subinterface is represented with the same number as the VLAN ID. This can be used to easily track which VLAN a subinterface is connected to when troubleshooting.

Routing between WANs

To route traffic across the WAN, the following must occur:

- The serial interface must be configured with a data-link serial protocol.

- An IP address must be assigned to the serial interface or each subinterface.

The data-link serial protocol is used for encapsulation at layer two. Cisco's default encapsulation for serial interfaces is HDLC. One can choose from a multitude of protocols when defining a data-link protocol for encapsulation of a serial interface. The protocol that you choose to assign will be determined by the type of traffic that is traversing the serial link and the functions that need to be provided. These protocols will be thoroughly discussed in Chapter 11, "Point-to-Point Serial Connections."

The IP address, along with a subnet mask, must be defined on the serial interface so that the router has a logical layer-three address. This IP address will be used when sending and receiving data, routing updates, and so on. A common subnet mask to use in point-to-point interfaces is 255.255.255.252. This subnet mask allows for two addresses. One of these addresses can be used on the serial interface of one of the routers and the other address can be assigned to the other end of the serial link.

IP Addresses   IP addresses have been covered extensively throughout this chapter. To enable the router to send and receive data, a protocol must be defined. The protocol in this example is IP. An IP address must be defined on each physical and logical interface to enable connectivity with another device using IP. The following example shows an IP address being assigned to a serial interface on a router:

```
Router#config t
Router(config)#interface Serial 1
Router(config-if)#ip address 172.16.5.1 255.255.255.252
```

Switches often have their IP addresses assigned globally. An IP address is assigned to a virtual interface on a switch, and assigning an IP address to the switch starts IP processing on the switch. The following example shows an IP address being assigned to a switch:

```
Switch#config t
Switch(config)#ip address 172.16.1.1 255.255.255.0
```

A switch also requires a default gateway. This is used to send traffic to that IP address when the switch cannot find the MAC address locally. The IP address of the default gateway is often defined as the IP address of the router's Ethernet interface. The following example shows the default gateway being configured on a switch:

```
Router#config t
Router(config)#ip default-gateway 172.16.1.254
```

Chapter Summary

The content of this chapter is often the most difficult to grasp for students. The learning process for more advanced routing protocols will progress much faster with a solid understanding of TCP/IP. If you found subnetting to be difficult and do not have a firm grasp on it, try doing the exercises below and then rereading the sections on subnetting. People often fully understand subnetting or do not at all. Once you have read this chapter and completed the exercises, the light should come on and you should be able to make up your own questions and answer them correctly.

The TCP/IP protocol suite was broken down and the associated protocols were defined in detail. Although this granular information may not be tested as thoroughly as IP subnetting, it is still important to understand, as it will help build your knowledge of protocols and their functions. The communication between protocols and how port numbers are used was also discussed. It is also very important to learn this interaction between the protocols and their associated port numbers, as this will make it easier to learn extended access lists.

If you are interested in pursuing more advanced and in-depth knowledge of TCP/IP, try looking up RFC 791, the TCP/IP standard. Although some people may fall asleep before ever reaching page five, it is an excellent way to learn all of the intricate details of TCP/IP.

From the Real World

Understanding IP addresses is a crucial part of being a qualified network engineer. With a clear understanding of the IP address format and subnetting, you will be better qualified to isolate and troubleshoot problems and eventually assume a design role in a networking company. IP addresses are at the foundation of learning in the networking field. Without a solid understanding of IP and many other protocols, applications and access lists will become much more difficult to learn.

Expect the CCNA exam to test your knowledge of TCP/IP, IP addressing, subnetting, and determining the amounts of networks and hosts, given a certain IP address and subnet mask. A tip to follow before starting the exam is to copy this table:

10000000 =	128
11000000 =	192
11100000 =	224
11110000 =	240
11111000 =	248
11111100 =	252
11111110 =	254
11111111 =	255
2^1 =	2
2^2 =	4
2^3 =	8
2^4 =	16
2^5 =	32
2^6 =	64
2^7 =	128
2^8 =	256
2^9 =	512
2^{10} =	1024
2^{11} =	2048
2^{12} =	4096

The first table will help you quickly identify the value of an octet when represented in binary format. It can also be used to find the value of a specific subnet mask. After finding out how many bits are used for subnetting, you will simply count down until finding the correct value. For example, if the test asked for 20 bits of subnet masking, you would know that the first 16 bits fill the first two octets, leaving four bits. You could then count down four numbers from the top of the chart at 128 to get the value of 240. This would give you the subnet mask of 255.255.240.

The second chart will help you quickly find the number of hosts or networks with a certain amount of bits used for that portion. For example, if eight bits are used for the network address, as in a default class A network, you would simply look for the 2^8 equation, therefore giving you the answer of 256 possible networks. The same can be applied when figuring out the amount of hosts, except for the fact that you must subtract the answer by two to get the final answer. This is because you cannot use the network address or broadcast address.

Let's say the test asked you to find the amount of hosts in a class B network subnetted with a 255.255.240.0 subnet mask. You would be able to quickly find the number of bits used for the host portion by referencing the first chart to see that 240 in the 255.255.240 mask leaves four bits for the host portion. These four bits would then be added to the last eight bits to equal 12 bits for the host portion. You would then look up this number 12 in the second chart to get the number 4096. Lastly, you would subtract two from 4096, giving you 4094 hosts ($4096 - 2 = 4094$).

As stated earlier, learning how IP is subnetted and differentiating among networks, subnetworks, and hosts is often the most difficult step for students taking the CCNA exam. My advice is to reread the sections you don't understand and continue to do the questions at the end of the chapter. After this is completed, try making your own questions and then reference this chapter to determine if you answered them correctly.

Michael Coker

Frequently Asked Questions (FAQ)

Question: What is the difference between a segment and a datagram?

Answer: A segment and a datagram both describe how the packet is encapsulated at layer four, as it moves up the protocol stack. A segment is defined at layer four and is used by TCP. A packet turns into a segment when moving up the protocol stack and using TCP. A datagram is used by UDP, also at layer four.

Question: What is the difference between a subnet mask of /24 and 255.255.255.0?

Answer: These both represent the same subnet mask. However, when configuring a router and entering the IP address and subnet mask, you must use the dotted-decimal notation.

Question: Why do some protocols use UDP while others use TCP?

Answer: When the developers create the protocols under IP, they develop them around either TCP or UDP. It is determined by whether the protocol will need to be connection-oriented such as Telnet or connectionless like SNMP.

Question: Is there another way of interconnecting switches without using ISL?

Answer: Yes, there is. ISL is a Cisco proprietary protocol that carries VLAN information from a switch. 802.1q is the IEEE standard that will provide this same function. 802.1q can also be used on Cisco routers and switches.

Question: What do the terms *all ones* or *all zeros* mean?

Answer: The term all zeros stands for the default network. This is used when creating a default route by specifying the 0.0.0.0 network out a specific interface. The all ones represents the broadcast address, which is 255.255.255.255. The reason for the name all ones and all zeros is because all zeros or all ones is entered in the bit positions to come up with the 0.0.0.0 and 255.255.255.255 addresses.

Case Study: Building a LAN with WAN connections

This lab will require three Cisco routers. One of these routers will need to have two serial interfaces. Here we'll demonstrate how to connect two Cisco routers to a core Cisco router. This is also known as a *hub and spoke design*. Connectivity will be established and then verified. This next section will take you step by step through the process. Figure 7-32 gives an example of the network that will be built during this exercise.

1. Connect your laptop or workstation to the console port of the router using the Cisco rolled cable. Set the terminal emulation program to 9600, 8, 1, and none. Connect to COM1. Power on the router and press enter on your machine. The router should come up at the router prompt.

2. Enter configuration mode and enter a hostname of `RouterA` for the router.

3. Enter interface configuration mode for Ethernet interface 0 and enter an IP address of `192.168.1.1` with a subnet mask of `255.255.255.0`. Enter the `no keepalive` statement for the interface.

4. Enter interface configuration mode for Serial interface 0 and enter an IP address of `192.168.5.2` with a subnet mask of `255.255.255.0`.

5. Enable RIP and add the networks `192.168.1.0` and `192.168.5.0`.

Figure 7-32
A hub and spoke network

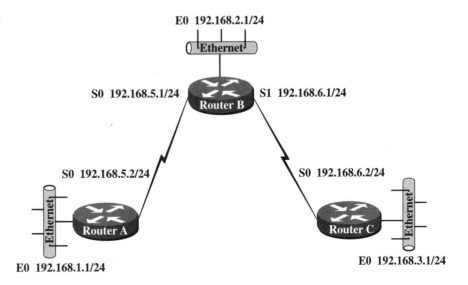

Configure Router B

1. Enter configuration mode and enter a hostname of `RouterB` for the router.

2. Enter interface configuration mode for Ethernet interface 0 and enter an IP address of `192.168.2.1` with a subnet mask of `255.255.255.0`. Enter the `no keepalive` statement for the interface.

3. Enter interface configuration mode for Serial interface 0 and enter an IP address of `192.168.5.1` with a subnet mask of `255.255.255.0`. Enter a clockrate of `38400` for the interface.

4. Enter interface configuration mode for Serial interface 1 and enter an IP address of `192.168.6.1` with a subnet mask of `255.255.255.0`. Enter a clockrate of `38400` for the interface.

5. Enable *RIP* and add the networks `192.168.2.0`, `192.168.5.0`, and `192.168.6.0`.

Configure Router C

1. Enter configuration mode and enter a hostname of `RouterC` for the router.

2. Enter interface configuration mode for Ethernet interface 0 and enter an IP address of `192.168.3.1` with a subnet mask of `255.255.255.0`. Enter the `no keepalive` statement for the interface.

3. Enter interface configuration mode for Serial interface 0 and enter an IP address of `192.168.6.2` with a subnet mask of `255.255.255.0`.

4. Enable RIP and add the networks `192.168.3.0` and `192.168.6.0`.

The configurations should look similar to Figures 7-33, 7-34, and 7-35 with the commands that should be entered in bold text.

The following configurations enable routers A, B, and C to communicate with each other. Routers A and C communicate via router B, the hub router. Use the ping command to verify the connectivity between routers.

```
RouterA#ping 192.168.3.1

Type escape sequence to abort.
Sending 5, 100-byte ICMP Echos to 192.168.3.1, timeout is 2
seconds:
!!!!!
Success rate is 100 percent (5/5), round-trip min/avg/max =
136/138/140 ms
```

Figure 7-33
RouterA
configuration

```
Current configuration:
!
version 12.0
no service udp-small-servers
no service tcp-small-servers
!
hostname RouterA
!
enable password cisco
!
interface Ethernet0
 ip address 192.168.1.1 255.255.255.0
 no keepalive
!
interface Serial0
 ip address 192.168.5.2 255.255.255.0
!
router rip
 network 192.168.1.0
 network 192.168.5.0
!
no ip classless
!
line con 0
line aux 0
line vty 0 4
 login
!
end
```

Figure 7-34
RouterB
configuration

```
Current configuration:
!
version 12.0
no service udp-small-servers
no service tcp-small-servers
!
hostname RouterB
!
enable password cisco
!
interface Ethernet0
 ip address 192.168.2.1 255.255.255.0
 no keepalive
!
interface Serial0
 ip address 192.168.5.1 255.255.255.0
 clockrate 38400
!
```

```
interface Serial1
 ip address 192.168.6.1 255.255.255.0
 clockrate 38400
!
router rip
 network 192.168.2.0
 network 192.168.5.0
 network 192.168.6.0
!
no ip classless
!
line con 0
line aux 0
line vty 0 4
 login
!
end
```

Figure 7-35
RouterC
configuration

```
RouterC

Current configuration:
!
version 12.0
no service udp-small-servers
no service tcp-small-servers
!
hostname RouterC
!
enable password cisco
!
interface Ethernet0
 ip address 192.168.3.1 255.255.255.0
 no keepalive
!
interface Serial0
 ip address 192.168.6.2 255.255.255.0
!
router rip
 network 192.168.3.0
 network 192.168.6.0
!
no ip classless
!
line con 0
line aux 0
line vty 0 4
 login
!
end
```

Questions

1. Which three protocols are part of the TCP/IP protocol suite?

   a. LAT
   b. SNA
   c. ICMP
   d. ARP
   e. IPX
   f. UDP

2. FTP falls under which layer of the OSI model?

   a. Physical layer
   b. Network layer
   c. Application layer

3. SNMP is a connection-oriented protocol.

   a. True
   b. False

4. When data reaches the transport layer, it is defined as a

   a. Datagram
   b. Frame
   c. Byte
   d. Segment
   e. Unit

5. Telnet uses port ___ to connect to a destination device.

   a. None
   b. One
   c. 23
   d. 25
   e. 1023

6. Telnet uses a source port of ___.

   a. None
   b. One
   c. 23
   d. 25
   e. Greater than 1023

7. During the TCP three-way handshake, what is the process that happens on the third step?

   a. An ACK is sent.

   b. An ACK with data is sent.

   c. A SYN is sent.

   d. No acknowledgment is sent at this step.

8. Which three protocols use UDP?

   a. SNA

   b. SNMP

   c. TCP

   d. BootP

   e. TFTP

   f. Telnet

9. UDP contains no sequence or acknowledgement fields.

   a. True

   b. False

10. The maximum IP packet length is limited to

   a. 1544 bytes

   b. 65,535 bytes

   c. 1028 bytes

   d. 64,500 bytes

   e. 4500 bytes

11. UDP uses a protocol ID of

   a. One

   b. Six

   c. 17

   d. 23

   e. 25

12. As a packet traverses the network, the source and destination IP address change at every router to indicate the next hop device.

   a. True

   b. False

13. Name the two kinds of ICMP messages.

    a. Time to Live expired

    b. Broadcast message

    c. Error message

    d. Query message

14. A default subnet mask for a class C network is

    a. 0.0.255.255

    b. 255.0.0.0

    c. 255.255.128.0

    d. 255.255.255.0

15. A class B network supports _____ networks or _____ hosts.

    a. 128; 16,777,216

    b. 2,097; 152,256

    c. 4,096; 128,000

    d. 16,384; 65,536

    e. 2,046; 256,000

16. An organization has a class C network of 195.160.10.0. There is a requirement for at least 12 different networks while supporting a minimum of 10 hosts per subnet. Which subnet mask do you use?

    a. 255.255.255.224

    b. 255.255.248.0

    c. 255.255.255.240

    d. 255.255.224.255

17. Identify the broadcast address for 198.168.110.5 255.255.248.0:

    a. 198.168.110.0

    b. 198.168.110.255

    c. 198.168.111.0

    d. 198.168.111.255

    e. 198.168.117.255

18. Translate the network address of 128.17.8.1 to binary format.

    a. 10000000.00010001.00001000.00000001

    b. 10000000.00001111.00000100.11111110

    c. 01111111.11101110.11110111.11111110

    d. 10000000.00001111.00001000.00001000

19. With the 16 subnetworks created by the subnet mask 255.255.240.0 what subnetwork does the IP address 172.16.17.1 fall into?

    a. First

    b. Second

    c. Fourth

    d. 16th

20. Identify the host range for 10.56.81.0/23.

    a. 10.56.81.0–10.56.82.255

    b. 10.56.81.0–10.56.83.0

    c. 10.56.78.0–10.56.84.255

    d. 10.56.80.0–10.56.81.255

Answers

1. **c.** ICMP, **d.** ARP, **f.** UDP

   ICMP, ARP, and UDP are all underlying protocols in the TCP/IP protocol suite.

2. **c.** Application layer

   FTP is an application layer protocol.

3. **b.** False

   SNMP uses UDP datagrams to request services from network devices. UDP is a connectionless datagram protocol, which makes SNMP connectionless as well.

4. **d.** Segment

   Data is considered a segment once it reaches the transport layer of the OSI Reference Model.

5. **c.** 23

   Port 23 is reserved for the use of Telnet.

6. **e.** Greater than 1023

   The Telnet application will use any source port greater than 1023 when initiating a session.

7. **b.** An ACK with data is sent.

   The third step of the three-way handshake consists of the sender sending an ACK along with the first amount of data.

8. **b.** SNMP, **d.** BootP, **e.** TFTP

   SNMP, BootP, and TFTP all use UDP and are considered connection-less network applications.

9. **a.** True

   UDP contains no sequence or acknowledgement fields. UDP relies on upper layer applications to provide reliability.

10. **b.** 65,535 bytes

    The maximum IP packet length is 65,535 bytes. If an IP packet is larger than the MTU of the router's interface, then the packet will be fragmented. The flags and fragment offset fields are used to reassemble the packet once it reaches the destination device.

11. c. 17

UDP uses a protocol ID of 17.

12. b. False

The source and destination IP address information will remain constant as the packet traverses the network. However, the source and destination MAC address fields will change as the packet traverses routers to reach its destination.

13. c. Error message and **d.** Query message

The two types of ICMP messages are error messages and query messages.

14. d. 255.255.255.0

A class C network address uses the first three octets to identify the network. Therefore, the default subnet mask will be 255.255.255.0.

15. d. 16,384; 65,536

A class B network will support 16,384 networks and 65,536 hosts. This can be determined by going back to the 2^N equation. The first two highest order bits in a class B network address are already used. This leaves 14 bits for the network portion of the address. Entering 14 into the 2^{14} equation equals 16,384 possible networks. The number of possible hosts is determined similarly by using the $2^N - 2$ equation. Sixteen possible bits are left over in the last two octets in a class B address. Entering 16 into the equation ($2^{16} - 2$) equals 65,534 possible hosts. The answer is 65,536 instead of 65,534 because the network address and broadcast addresses are still counted as possible addresses. It is important to notice if the CCNA exam asks for the possible amount of hosts or the possible amount of "usable" hosts. The network and broadcast addresses are not considered usable hosts.

16. c. 255.255.255.240

The subnet mask of 255.255.255.240 will yield 16 (2^4) possible subnets with 14 ($2^4 - 2$) usable hosts per subnet.

17. d. 198.168.111.255

The 198.168.110.5 address with a 255.255.248.0, or /21, subnet mask will yield a network address of 198.168.104.0 and a broadcast address of 198.168.111.255.

18. a. 10000000.00010001.00001000.00000001

Enter 128.17.8.1 into a binary chart with each octet representing 128, 64, 32, 16, 8, 4, 2, 1 and the outcome will be 10000000.00010001.00001000.00000001.

19. b. Second

The subnet mask of 255.255.240.0 has the four highest order bits in the third octet set to 1 (1111 | 0000). The first subnet would have all zeros in the subnet portion (0000 | 0000). The second subnet would have a one in the lowest value subnet bit of 16 (0001 | 0000). This allows the first subnet to be 172.16.0.0 to 172.16.15.255 and the second subnet to be 172.16.16.0 to 172.16.31.255. 172.16.17.1 falls within this second subnet range.

20. d. 10.56.80.0–10.56.81.255

10.56.80.0 to10.56.81.255 is the host range for the /23, or 255.255.254.0, subnet mask. The third octet of the subnet mask leaves one bit to be used for the host portion. After entering 81, the third octet address value, into a binary chart, it can be seen that the outcome is 0101000 | 1, leaving the last bit as a one. Changing the last bit to a zero will yield a subnet number of 80. This enables the network number to be 10.56.80.0 and the broadcast address to be 10.56.81.255.

IP Routing
Fundamentals

Objectives

This chapter provides an introduction to the fundamentals of IP routing. We will be looking at the basics and theory behind routing before progressing to routing concepts. These concepts include static and dynamic routing and the benefits associated with each routing type.

Dynamic routing protocols can also be broken into two main areas: distance vector and link state. We will explain the differences between these routing methods and explore the two main distance vector routing protocols, the *Routing Information Protocol* (RIP) and the *Interior Gateway Routing Protocol* (IGRP). Advanced knowledge of link state routing protocols is beyond the scope of this book.

Routing Overview

The growth of today's networks has seen the need for segmented networks. These segmented networks are split into hierarchical structures based around network layer addressing. The most common network layer addressing protocols are SPX/IPX and TCP/IP.

These segmented networks are interconnected using routers. This section is going to provide a brief overview of the basics of routing. Some technologies will be further explained later on in the chapter, so be sure to review this opening section again after reading the chapter.

The basic theory of routers is that they direct and forward packets received on an interface to another interface based upon the network layer addressing associated with the destination address within the packet. This is commonly referred to as *routing*. For the router to make this routing decision, it has to consult its internal routing table. This table can be created either manually or dynamically.

When a router is powered up in its default configuration, it is only aware of its directly connected interfaces.

In Figure 8-1, we can see that Router A has interfaces connected to networks 192.168.10.0 and 192.168.20.0. In its default state, the only networks

Figure 8-1
A basic Cisco router

192.168.10.0   192.168.20.0

Router A

that Router A can route between are 192.168.10.0 and 192.168.20.0. If Router A receives a packet from 192.168.10.1 destined for 192.168.20.1, it can route this because it knows how to. It simply moves the packet from one internal interface to another. This becomes slightly more complicated when more routers and networks are added.

Figure 8-2 now shows two routers, Router A and Router B. It also displays three networks, 192.168.10.0, 192.168.30.0, and a common one, 192.168. 192.168.20.0. From this figure we can ascertain that Router A has 10.0 and 192.168.20.0 directly connected and Router B has 192.168.20.0 and 192.168.30.0 directly connected.

Given this information, we can deduce that host 192.168.10.1 can communicate with host 192.168.20.1 through Router A and host 192.168.30.1 can communicate with host 192.168.20.1 through Router B. However, what happens if host 192.168.10.1 wants to communicate with host 192.168.30.1?

As you will probably have realized, this route will not occur and communication will fail. This is because Router A has no knowledge of the network 192.168.30.0 and vice versa: Router B has no knowledge of network 192.168.10.0. So what do you have to do to remedy this?

To facilitate this communication, you have to make Router A aware of the network 192.168.30.0 and Router B aware of the network 192.168.10.0. You may think it only necessary for Router A to see the network 192.168.30.0, but you also need a route back to the source in order for acknowledgements and replies to be received. This can be accomplished in two ways. You can either manually enter route information into each router, which is known as *static routing*, or you can configure a dynamic routing protocol on both routers to converge route information, which is known as *dynamic routing*.

So to facilitate communication between Router A and 192.168.30.1, you have to get Router A to store a route in its internal routing table that points to the network 192.168.30.0. At this point, it is immaterial how this route is added and this will be covered in depth later on in the chapter.

The basic information for a route in the routing table is the destination network along with the next hop address or interface and the administrative distance. This tells the router how to route packets destined for remote networks that it doesn't have a directly connected interface for.

Figure 8-2
Two Cisco routers

192.168.10.0   192.168.20.0   192.168.30.0

Router A   Router B

For example, on Router A there would be a route to 192.168.30.0 with the next hop interface being the interface connected to the 192.168.20.0 network. When a packet arrives destined for the 192.168.30.0 network, Router A looks up the destination in its internal routing table and forwards the packet out of the interface connected to the next router. Then Router B receives this packet and because 192.168.30.0 is connected to this router, it would know where to forward the packet based on the network layer address. The reverse of this would occur between Router B and the network 192.168.10.0.

Table 8-1 shows what the simplified routing tables would look like for Router A and Router B. Notice that the router to the remote network is shown on the same interface as the common network that is 192.168.20.0. This is self-explanatory, as shown earlier in Figure 8-2.

Each routing method and protocol is assigned an administrative distance. This is a numeric value between 0 and 255 and it relates to the trustworthiness of the route. The lower the value, the better the route, and the router will always use the route with the lowest administrative distance. The lowest administrative distance is 0 and this value is given to connected interfaces. The next value is 1 for static routes. The administrative distance for RIP is 120 and the administrative distance for IGRP is 100. So if RIP and IGRP routes both exist for the same network, the router would use the route provided by the IGRP process.

Table 8-1

Routing tables for
Router A and
Router B

Router A		
Network	**Type**	**Interface**
192.168.10.0	Connected	Ethernet 0
192.168.20.0	Connected	Ethernet 1
192.168.30.0	Static	Ethernet 1

Router B		
Network	**Type**	**Interface**
192.168.10.0	Static	Ethernet 0
192.168.20.0	Connected	Ethernet 0
192.168.30.0	Connected	Ethernet 1

This provides a simple overview to the routing process. We are now going to look at the two types of routing and the differences between them. Your understanding of routing will become more clear after reading the following sections that explain the process in more detail.

Static versus Dynamic Routing

As stated earlier, routers have two ways of obtaining routing information: through static and dynamic routing. Each of these methods has its advantages over the other. In the following section, we are going to look at each method and explain the fundamentals and benefits associated with each one.

Static Routes

Static routes are routes that have to be entered manually into the router. With static routes there is no interaction between routers and no automatic convergence of routing information after a network link change.

The major use of static routes is when you are designing a small- to medium-sized network with no or small plans for expansion. Static routes have to be entered manually; therefore, they also have to be administered manually. This means that when a network change or failure occurs, the routers must have their routing tables manually changed. Obviously, this becomes a problem when your internetwork grows or becomes susceptible to numerous failures. The administrative overhead can be a prohibitive burden to the implementation of static routes.

One advantage of static routes is that they carry no overhead as far as bandwidth goes. In dynamic routing protocols, an associated bandwidth issue exists for the routing protocols in order to maintain their relationships with adjoining routers. In large internetworks, the bandwidth requirement, especially for Distance Vector-based protocols, can be quite high and it increases with the complexity of the network.

The following is an example of how static routes are displayed on the output of a `show ip route` command:

```
Router#sh ip route
Codes: C - connected, S - static, I - IGRP, R - RIP, M - mobile, B
- BGP
        D - EIGRP, EX - EIGRP external, O - OSPF, IA - OSPF inter area
```

```
          N1 - OSPF NSSA external type 1, N2 - OSPF NSSA external type 2
          E1 - OSPF external type 1, E2 - OSPF external type 2, E - EGP
          i - IS-IS, L1 - IS-IS level-1, L2 - IS-IS level-2, * -
    candidate default
          U - per-user static route, o - ODR

Gateway of last resort is not set

S    20.0.0.0/8 is directly connected, BRI0
C    192.168.10.0/24 is directly connected, BRI0
S    192.168.0.0/24 is directly connected, BRI0
S    212.1.234.0/24 is directly connected, BRI0
Router#
```

You can see from this output that this router has a directly connected route to network 192.168.10.0. The C that precedes the route indicates this. We can also see the three static routes. These are 20.0.0.0, 192.168.0.0, and 212.1.234.0. All of these routes are preceded with an S, which indicates that they are static routes.

After each of the static routes we can see the next hop destination. For these three static routes, the next hop destination is the interface BRI0. This basically can be explained by saying that any packet destined for network 20.0.0.0, 192.168.0.0, or 212.1.234.0 will be sent out of interface BRI0.

Other uses of static routes include the gateway of last resort. We can see from the output listed earlier that the gateway of last resort has not been set for this router. This means that any packets received that have an unknown destination will be dropped. This may be a design requirement, but in most cases you would want all unknown traffic to be forwarded out on a specific interface. One example of this would be for an Internet connection.

In the following example, we have set a gateway of last resort with the `ip route 0.0.0.0 0.0.0.0 e0` command:

```
Router#sh ip route
Codes: C - connected, S - static, I - IGRP, R - RIP, M - mobile, B
- BGP
          D - EIGRP, EX - EIGRP external, O - OSPF, IA - OSPF inter area
          N1 - OSPF NSSA external type 1, N2 - OSPF NSSA external type 2
          E1 - OSPF external type 1, E2 - OSPF external type 2, E - EGP
          i - IS-IS, L1 - IS-IS level-1, L2 - IS-IS level-2, * -
    candidate default
          U - per-user static route, o - ODR

Gateway of last resort is 0.0.0.0 to network 0.0.0.0

S    20.0.0.0/8 is directly connected, BRI0
C    192.168.10.0/24 is directly connected, BRI0
S    192.168.0.0/24 is directly connected, BRI0
S    212.1.234.0/24 is directly connected, BRI0
S*   0.0.0.0/0 is directly connected, Ethernet0
Router#
```

Now you can see that the gateway of last resort is 0.0.0.0 to network 0.0.0.0. Basically, this means that any unknown traffic will be sent to network 0.0.0.0.

Also, a routing entry to 0.0.0.0 exists as a static route pointing to the Ethernet0 interface. So any unknown traffic will be sent out of the Ethernet0 interface. Note the asterisk next to the S for the static route. This identifies the route as the default route within the router. Static routes have an administrative distance of one.

IP Route Command   Static routes are entered into a router with the `ip route` command. This command manually assigns a route in the routing table with the type of S defined for static. As previously explained, these routes have an administrative distance of one.

The full syntax of the command is

```
Router(config)#ip route A.B.C.D E.F.G.H I.J.K.L/Interface X
```

where A.B.C.D is the destination network address, E.F.G.H is the destination network mask, I.J.K.L is the IP address of the next hop, or Interface is the interface name of the next hop. X represents the administrative distance (1 to 255).

For example,

```
Router(config)#ip route 10.0.0.0 255.0.0.0 Ethernet0
```

The previous command would add a static route to network 10.0.0.0 255.0.0.0. This route would direct any packets destined for this network to the interface Ethernet0 on the router.

```
Router(config)#ip route 10.0.0.0 255.0.0.0 192.168.10.1
```

The previous command would add a static route to network 10.0.0.0 255.0.0.0. This route would direct any packets destined for this network to the IP address 193.168.10.1.

One important point to note here is that the routing table must also have a routing entry for the next hop IP address. Therefore, an entry must exist for 192.168.10.0:

```
Router(config)#ip route 10.0.0.0 255.0.0.0 192.168.10.1 100
```

The previous command would add a static route to network 10.0.0.0 255.0.0.0. This route would direct any packets destined for this network to the IP address 193.168.10.1. Static routes usually have an administrative distance of one. A 100 is also listed after the next hop IP address. The command `no ip route` will remove the IP route from the routing table.

Special Case: Default Routes   When a router receives a packet, the destination IP address is checked against an entry in the router's internal routing table. If a match is made, the router is forwarded to the interface or address specified in the route, or else by default the packet is dropped. This may be suitable if your network has no external links to large networks such as the Internet. In fact, this obviously increases security, as only packets destined for the internal networks will be routed.

However, occasions will occur when a default route is required, such as for Internet connectivity. A default route is a destination that packets are sent to if a specific routing entry does not exist in the router's internal routing table. This can be achieved in two ways. You can either use the `ip default-network` command or you can apply a static route to the 0.0.0.0 network. To configure the default network using the ip default-network command, simply enter the following commands:

```
Router(config)#ip default network 192.168.10.0
```

These commands would send any packets not matched in the router's internal routing table to network 192.168.10.0. It is important to remember that a route to this network must exist in the router's internal routing table.

To apply the static route to network 0.0.0.0, you would perform the following steps. The router refers to the default route as the gateway of last resort. In the following output, which is the result of a `show ip route` command, we can see that the gateway of last resort has not been set:

```
Router#sh ip route
Codes: C - connected, S - static, I - IGRP, R - RIP, M - mobile, B
- BGP
        D - EIGRP, EX - EIGRP external, O - OSPF, IA - OSPF inter area
        N1 - OSPF NSSA external type 1, N2 - OSPF NSSA external type 2
        E1 - OSPF external type 1, E2 - OSPF external type 2, E - EGP
        i - IS-IS, L1 - IS-IS level-1, L2 - IS-IS level-2, * -
candidate default
        U - per-user static route, o - ODR

Gateway of last resort is not set

S    20.0.0.0/8 is directly connected, BRI0
C    192.168.10.0/24 is directly connected, BRI0
S    192.168.0.0/24 is directly connected, BRI0
S    212.1.234.0/24 is directly connected, BRI0
Router#
```

This indicates that any packets sent to the router destined for an external network would be dropped. The command to set the default route is `ip` `route 0.0.0.0 0.0.0.0 e0.` This would set the default route to be the Ethernet 0 Interface:

```
Router#sh ip route
Codes: C - connected, S - static, I - IGRP, R - RIP, M - mobile, B
- BGP
       D - EIGRP, EX - EIGRP external, O - OSPF, IA - OSPF inter area
       N1 - OSPF NSSA external type 1, N2 - OSPF NSSA external type 2
       E1 - OSPF external type 1, E2 - OSPF external type 2, E - EGP
       i - IS-IS, L1 - IS-IS level-1, L2 - IS-IS level-2, * -
candidate default
       U - per-user static route, o - ODR

Gateway of last resort is 0.0.0.0 to network 0.0.0.0

S    20.0.0.0/8 is directly connected, BRI0
C    192.168.10.0/24 is directly connected, BRI0
S    192.168.0.0/24 is directly connected, BRI0
S    212.1.234.0/24 is directly connected, BRI0
S*   0.0.0.0/0 is directly connected, Ethernet0
Router#
```

You can see by the first section that the gateway of last resort is now set to 0.0.0.0. A route entry for network 0.0.0.0 exists at the second section. This indicates that the route to network 0.0.0.0 is via the Ethernet 0 interface.

Default routes can be a useful tool to deploy, especially if you are providing Internet access to clients. A default route will not be required on every router and the removal of default routes can increase the security on the network, as only internal packets will be routed.

Dynamic Routing

As previously discussed, two main types of routing exist: static and dynamic. The last section looked at static routing and this section is concerned with dynamic routing.

The router's internal routing table must contain a route to every network in order for the internetwork to function. These routes can either be manually added or dynamically created based upon the topology of the internetwork.

A whole breed of protocols, called *routing protocols*, have been created and are used to dynamically build the routing tables of participating routers. These routing protocols include the following:

- *Routing Information Protocol* (RIP)
- *Interior Gateway Routing Protocol* (IGRP)
- *Open Shortest Path First* (OSPF)
- *Enhanced Interior Gateway Routing Protocol* (EIGRP)

The main function of these protocols is to ensure that every router that participates by running the dynamic protocol has a valid route to every network on the internetwork.

These protocols operate by advertising their directly connected interfaces to other routers on the network. This information is then computed in a way specific to the routing protocol, and the routing table is created. When a change in the internetwork occurs, such as the failure of a router interface, this information is propagated out to other routers and necessary changes to the routing table are made. The time it takes for the internetwork to make these changes is referred to as the *convergence time*. Obviously, the faster the convergence, the better, and this is something to keep in mind when designing internetworks that rely on dynamic routing protocols. The exact workings and differences between dynamic routing protocols will be explained in more detail in the next section.

Overview: Routing Protocols versus Routed Protocols

One important point to remember is the difference between routed and routing protocols. Routing protocols are protocols that are involved in the propagation of dynamic route information to participating routers. Routed protocols are the actual protocols that contain network layer addressing and are responsible for delivery of the datagrams. It is easy to misunderstand the differences between these two similar types of protocols. When you talk about TCP/IP, we know that it is a routable protocol. Therefore, IP is a routed protocol. IP does not involve itself in the routing decisions. These decisions are made by the routers that have gathered routing information via a routing protocol such as RIP or IGRP. NetBEUI, for example, doesn't contain any network layer addressing. Therefore, NetBEUI is not classified as a routed protocol. Examples of routing protocols are RIP, IGRP, EIGRP, and OSPF. Examples of routed protocols are IP and IPX.

Interior and Exterior Gateway Protocols

Dynamic routing protocols are classified as either interior or exterior gateway routing protocols. *Interior Gateway* (IGP) routing protocols are con-

Figure 8-3
Examples of IGP
and EGP

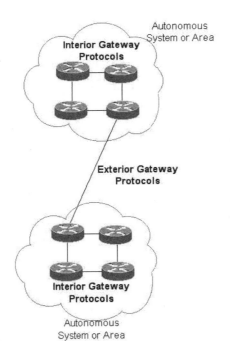

cerned with routing within networks that are under a common network administration. An example of this is IGRP. When you configure IGRP, you must enter an *Autonomous System* (AS) number. This AS number can be thought of as a routing domain, and IGRP routes will only be exchanged with other routers that are in the same AS. Therefore, IGRP is an interior gateway routing protocol that is concerned with routing within an AS.

In contrast, *Exterior Gateway* (EGP) routing protocols are used to exchange routing information between different ASs or networks that do not share a common administration. An example of an EGP would be the *Border Gateway Protocol* (BGP). This protocol is widely used on the Internet to pass routing information between differing routing systems, ASs, and areas. Figure 8-3 shows the placement of interior and exterior gateway routing protocols.

Dynamic Routing Protocols

Dynamic routing requires dynamic routing protocols in order for convergence to take place. Such routing protocols are responsible for route discovery, route removal, and route maintenance between all routers participating in dynamic routing. To further complicate matters, the dynamic routing protocols can also be broken up into two main types. These main types are distance vector and link state. Both of these protocols are dynamic in nature, but they both operate in differing ways. Because of this, it is important to select the correct protocol that matches the design criteria when designing the routing for a new network. Distance vector and link state routing are described in the next section.

Distance Vector

The differentiation between dynamic routing protocols is concerned with the way that the routing protocols learn about topology changes and the way this topology is recorded in the internal routing table of the router. Distance vector routing is based around an algorithm called the Bellman-Ford algorithm named after its creators. The basis of the distance vector routing is that all participating routers periodically pass copies of their routing table to other directly connected routers. These updates also communicate network topology changes as soon as they occur.

A router running a distance vector routing protocol receives route information from routers that are directly connected. By directly connected, we mean routers that are at the other end of a LAN or WAN interface on the router. These can be thought of as the routers' direct neighbors.

This route information will include the direct neighbor information of the routers that are classed as direct neighbors of the router that has received the routing information. In this way, the router learns about remote networks.

As you can see from Figure 8-4, Router A by default would not know about network 3. Router A would only know about networks 1 and 2. However, Router B does know about network 3. In fact, Router B knows about networks 2 and 3. So we can see that Router A learns about network 3 from a routing update sent by Router B.

This process occurs all over the network until each router knows about every route to every remote network. One important point is that in distance vector routing a single router can only see as far as its direct neigh-

Figure 8-4
Distance vector
routing information

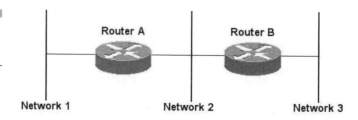

bors. It doesn't have a complete view of the network topology. It relies upon second-hand information.

Each router knows which networks are directly connected and it assigns a value of zero to these networks. This value is used as the metric for making routing decisions in distance vector routing. When a router receives a routing update from its direct neighbors, it automatically increments all of the route metric values by one. As this propagates throughout the network, the metric increases and this is called the *hop count*. The hop count is the number of routers that have to be passed to reach the destination network.

Distance vector routing uses the hop count as the metric of choice for routing decisions. If you have a remote network 172.18.16.0 and two routing entries in the routing table, one over interface Ethernet0 with a distance of five and one over Serial1 with a distance of three, the distance vector routing algorithm will choose the route with the lower hop count. In this case, the packets will be sent over the Serial1 interface.

This is a limitation of the distance vector algorithm due to the fact that no decision is made on bandwidth, but on distance alone. The route to 172.18.16.0 may have been available over five hops, but since all of these are at 10 Mbps, the serial route may have been transmitted over 64-Kbps lines. As the packets traverse the network, they stop at every router and get forwarded by that router depending on the best available (shortest) route in that router's routing table.

Network Discovery and Topology Changes   When a distance vector routing protocol is enabled on an interface, the router automatically discovers its direct neighbors based on a network or subnet broadcast. These broadcasts stay local to the network or subnet and all other routers running the same distance vector routing protocol will respond.

Distance vector routing protocols operate by sending their complete routing table to all direct neighbors. This identifies the state of the connected interfaces and it furnishes the direct neighbors with routing information for remote networks. The update includes the metric or hop count to the remote networks as well as the address of the first router on the path to each network. When a direct neighbor receives these updates, the neighboring router compares the update to its own routing table. If the newly received update contains any routes that are considered as better (defined as a lower metric or hop count), then the router updates its routing table with this information.

Problems and Limitations of Distance Vector Routing   The main problem with distance vector routing is the convergence time in large networks. This delay in convergence can cause routing loops. Several controls are built in to all distance vector-based routing protocols that protect against routing loops in the routing tables. These are as follows:

- Maximum hop count
- Split Horizon
- Hold down timers
- Triggered updates

Maximum Hop Count   One way that distance vector routing protocols prevent routing loops that can count to infinity is to impose a maximum hop count into the routing protocol. For example, RIP has a maximum hop count of 15. This means that the router considers any destination reachable in more than 15 hops unreachable. This can obviously have serious ramifications in very large networks that have more than 15 hops, which is a major reason why RIP isn't used in these installations.

This control also ensures that any routing loops do not propagate for longer than the maximum hop count. This control is similar to the *Time To Live* (TTL) field in the IP header that is covered in Chapter 9, "Access Lists and Traffic Management."

Split Horizon   The implementation of Split Horizon is a control to prevent routing loops. This works by ensuring that route information is never sent back over the interface that it was received on. If a route is identified from a routing update received from the direct neighbor on Ethernet0, it is unnecessary to send this routing information back to the router on Ethernet0. This control reduces routing loops and speeds up convergence.

Hold Down Timers   The implementation of hold down timers is a control to prevent routing loops. Routers have route timers that correspond to routes in the routing table. The routes in the routing table are valid for the duration of the route timer. When the route timer expires, the garbage collection timer is started and the routes metric is set to infinity. Until the garbage collection timer expires, the route cannot be removed from the routing table nor modified if another routing update for the route is received.

Triggered Updates   Triggered updates are routing updates that are sent or triggered by a metric or route change. By default, distance vector routing protocols advertise routing updates every 30 to 60 seconds. This can cause latency in convergence over a sizable network. Triggered updates speed up the convergence of routing information by immediately announcing the metric or route change as soon as it occurs. The two distance vector routing protocols that we are going to be looking at are RIP and IGRP.

Link State and Hybrid

We have just looked at the basics of distance vector routing. We are now going to look at the other category of routing protocols, link state. Link state dynamic routing protocols operate very differently compared to distance vector dynamic routing protocols. Unlike distance vector routing protocols, link state routing protocols know the complete topology of the whole network they operate in or the complete topology of the area they are members of, depending on the configuration. Link state protocols include the OSPF routing protocol and the *Intermediate System to Intermediate System* (IS-IS) routing protocol. Link state protocols are designed to improve on the limitations of distance vector routing protocols to provide more scalable solutions as networks grow. Link state routing algorithms maintain a complex database of topology information. This database includes full details about all distant routers and how they interconnect. This differs from distance vector protocols that only store remote network information against a simple metric.

One major feature of link state routing protocols is that they are classless. This enables discontiguous subnets and *Variable Length Subnet Masks* (VLSMs) to be used to improve router performance by reducing the number of advertised routes that are propagated into the network as routing updates or *Link State Packets* (LSPs).

Network Discovery and Topology Changes   Link state dynamic routing protocols operate by sending out LSPs. These packets are sent upon the introduction of a new router and also at frequent intervals or when a change occurs. The LSPs are sent as multicasts. All link state routers within the network or area receive these packets and they are used to create a common topology database that is held on every router within the network or area. The LSPs identify the direct neighboring routers as well as distant routers. The algorithm commonly known as the *Shortest Path First* (SPF) uses this information to work out the best route to these distant networks and maintains this information in the internal routing table. Once this information is in the routing table, the router uses this information to route packets.

Distance vector routing protocols send out regular routing table updates and this can also be forced as a triggered update if a network topology change occurs. Link state routing protocols work together and the first router that identifies a topology change would inform all the other routers participating in link state routing of the topology change. This is done by sending a multicast packet or a unicast packet to a designated router that is configured to inform all other participating routers of the update. All participating routers receive this information and again use the SPF algorithm to recalculate the route to the remote network.

Problems and Limitations of Link State Routing   Link state routing, although it appears to be extremely advantageous, still has inherent problems that must be considered. Link state protocols are more resource-hungry than distance vector routing protocols. Therefore, a router participating in link state routing requires more memory and more processing power in order to not burden its performance. More information is held about remote networks by link state protocols, and as the size of the network grows, so do the performance implications of the SPF algorithm in making routing decisions.

The initial link state operation of the addition of a new router can cause a situation known as *link state flooding*. This is when all participating routers send LSPs to each other advertising their existence and their connected networks. This floods the network with LSPs and reduces the overall network bandwidth for other network hosts. This initial flooding also takes a toll on the performance on the router while the CPU-intensive SPF algorithm is calculating.

Hybrid Dynamic Routing Protocols   Along with distance vector and link state dynamic routing protocols, there is also a third classification called *hybrid routing protocols*. A hybrid routing protocol is a dynamic routing protocol that performs both distance vector and link state functions. One such hybrid dynamic routing protocol is EIGRP, which is property of Cisco Systems, Inc. This has the advantage of utilizing the best features of both distance vector and link state protocols in one hybrid protocol.

Routing Information Protocol (RIP)

RIP is a distance vector-based dynamic routing protocol that uses the hop count as its metric. RIP is an IGP, so therefore it performs routing within a single AS. RIP has two main versions. RIP version 1 is a classfull routing protocol that strictly follows the classfull addressing scheme of IP. RIP version 2 (RIPv2) is the latest version of RIP and this is a classless routing protocol that enables more information to be included in the RIP packet header and supports VLSMs. RIP is also available for both IP routing and also IPX routing.

RIP is formally defined in RFC 1058 and 1723. RFC 1058 was defined in 1988 and describes the first implementation of RIP. RFC 1723 was defined in 1994 and this revision defines RIPv2 and the extended carrier features supported in the RIP packet header.

RIP operates by sending routing updates at regular intervals out of all the configured interfaces. The default time for this update is every 30 seconds. These routing updates contain the complete routing table minus any routes removed due to the Split Horizon rule. When a routing update is received from a direct neighbor, the route information is checked against the current routing table, and any better routes, ones with a lower metric or hop count, are updated in the routing table. RIP uses the hop count as the routing metric and the maximum allowable hop count using RIP is 15. The sixteenth hop is deemed unreachable.

On a Cisco router, simply adding the following command in global configuration mode enables RIP:

```
Router(config)#router rip
```

Networks are advertised and participate in RIP routing by entering the following command:

```
Router(config-router)network A.B.C.D
```

where A.B.C.D is the network address of the network to be advertised via RIP.

Other RIP configuration commands include the following:

```
Router configuration commands:
  address-family          Enter Address Family command mode
  auto-summary            Enable automatic network number
summarization
  default                 Set a command to its defaults
  default-information     Control distribution of default
information
  default-metric          Set metric of redistributed routes
  distance                Define an administrative distance
  distribute-list         Filter networks in routing updates
  exit                    Exit from routing protocol configuration
mode
  flash-update-threshold  Specify flash update threshold in second
  help                    Description of the interactive help system
  input-queue             Specify input queue depth
  maximum-paths           Forward packets over multiple paths
```

```
  neighbor                Specify a neighbor router
  network                 Enable routing on an IP network
  no                      Negate a command or set its defaults
  offset-list             Add or subtract offset from IGRP or RIP
metrics
  output-delay            Interpacket delay for RIP updates
  passive-interface       Suppress routing updates on an interface
  redistribute            Redistribute information from another
routing protocol
  timers                  Adjust routing timers
  validate-update-source  Perform sanity checks against source
address of routing updates
  version                 Set routing protocol version
```

Enabling RIP   RIP is enabled from global configuration mode on the router. From global configuration mode, enter the following command:

```
Router(config)#router rip
```

This enables RIP on the router and places you into router configuration mode. This is indicated by the `Router(config-router)#` prompt. This is all that is required to enable RIP on the selected router.

Configuring RIP   Once RIP has been enabled, you can assign an interface to be advertised via RIP. To do this, you enter the following command:

```
Router(config-router)#network A.B.C.D
```

This adds network A.B.C.D to the RIP routing process on the router. This identifies the network as a directly connected network. To add network 192.168.10.0 to the RIP routing process, you would enter:

```
Router(config-router)#network 192.168.10.0
```

For RIP, the network command does not include any information about the subnet mask. The default class of the IP address is always shown in the running configuration and is broadcast out in RIP updates. You cannot just advertise subnets with RIP. You have to advertise the whole network address.

Verifying RIP operation   A few commands can be used to verify the configuration of RIP on the router. These commands are as follows:

■ `show running-config`
■ `show ip protocol`

- show ip route
- debug ip rip

show running-config The show running-config command can be used to display the running configuration on the router. A breakdown of the specific routing commands will be displayed here and it is an excellent place to start to ensure that you have entered the correct networks into the RIP routing process.

The following code is a sample display from a router running RIP and it shows the entries under the router rip section:

```
!
router rip
 network 192.168.10.0
 network 192.168.20.0
 network 192.168.30.0
!.
```

We can see from the code that RIP has been enabled on the router and networks 192.168.10.0, 192.168.20.0, and 192.168.30.0 are directly connected and are participating in the RIP routing process.

If you are experiencing a routing problem where some networks are available and some are not, be sure to check the running-config to ascertain if the network has been added to the RIP routing process.

show ip protocol The show ip protocol command displays the IP routing protocol process parameters and statistics. Every IP routing protocol enabled on the router will be displayed along with its associated parameters and statistics.

```
Router#sh ip prot
Routing Protocol is "rip"
  Sending updates every 30 seconds, next due in 22 seconds
  Invalid after 180 seconds, hold down 180, flushed after 240
  Outgoing update filter list for all interfaces is
  Incoming update filter list for all interfaces is
  Redistributing: rip
  Default version control: send version 1, receive any version
    Interface      Send  Recv  Key-chain
    BRI0             1    1 2
    Ethernet0        1    1 2
  Routing for Networks:
    192.168.10.0
    192.168.20.0
    192.168.30.0
```

```
   Routing Information Sources:
     Gateway         Distance      Last Update
     192.168.40.1       120          0:00:18
     192.168.50.1       120          0:00:02
   Distance: (default is 120)

Router#
```

We can see from this output that the RIP updates are being sent every 30 seconds and the next one is due in 22 seconds. The invalid, hold down, and flush timers are also displayed. The outgoing and incoming update filters are concerned with distribute lists that are special access lists to control routing updates. We can see that no list is set either inbound or outbound. The router is identified as having Interface BRI0 and Ethernet0 participating in RIP routing and they are routing for networks 192.168.10.0, 192.168.20.0, and 192.168.30.0.

This command provides an excellent breakdown of the main parameters and statistics related to the routing protocol. You can check a number of settings from the output provided by this command.

show ip route   The show ip route command displays the router's internal routing table. This command in its native form will display routing information for all enabled IP routing protocols on the router.

```
Router#sh ip route
Codes: C - connected, S - static, I - IGRP, R - RIP, M - mobile, B
- BGP
       D - EIGRP, EX - EIGRP external, O - OSPF, IA - OSPF inter area
       E1 - OSPF external type 1, E2 - OSPF external type 2, E - EGP
       i - IS-IS, L1 - IS-IS level-1, L2 - IS-IS level-2, * -
candidate default

Gateway of last resort is not set

R    192.168.100.0 [120/5] via 194.35.35.13, 00:00:12, Ethernet0
                   [120/5] via 194.35.50.240, 00:00:12, Ethernet0
                   [120/5] via 129.3.1.241, 00:00:12, Ethernet0
     194.119.131.0 is variably subnetted, 2 subnets, 2 masks
R       194.119.131.0 255.255.255.0
           [120/5] via 194.35.35.13, 00:00:12, Ethernet0
           [120/5] via 194.35.50.240, 00:00:12, Ethernet0
           [120/5] via 129.3.1.241, 00:00:12, Ethernet0
D EX    194.119.131.65 255.255.255.255
           [170/307200] via 194.35.35.13, 20:06:44, Ethernet0
D    193.35.217.0 [90/307200] via 194.35.35.13, 20:06:44, Ethernet0
     212.159.2.0 is variably subnetted, 5 subnets, 2 masks
Router#
```

We can see from this output that this router has routes learned by RIP, EIGRP, and EIGRP External. These are indicated by the character that precedes the routing information. For RIP, the character is R.

This command also provides us with a breakdown of which networks have been identified via RIP and how to get to them. Here is an example of a route learned by RIP:

```
R       192.168.100.0 [120/5] via 194.35.35.13, 00:00:12, Ethernet0
```

This route is identified as a RIP route and it shows the destination network is 192.168.100.0. The default metric for RIP is 120 and the number of hops to the network is five. This is identified by the [120/5] output. We can see that the next hop address is 194.35.35.13 and is available out of Ethernet0. Therefore, any traffic destined for the 192.168.100.0 network will be forwarded out of interface Ethernet0 and will be addressed for 194.35.35.13.

This command can also be further restricted to an individual network or routing protocol. The following output shows the result of a show ip route rip command:

```
Router#sh ip route rip
R     192.168.100.0 [120/5] via 194.35.35.13, 00:00:13, Ethernet0
                    [120/5] via 194.35.50.240, 00:00:13, Ethernet0
                    [120/5] via 129.3.1.241, 00:00:13, Ethernet0
      194.119.131.0 is variably subnetted, 2 subnets, 2 masks
R        194.119.131.0 255.255.255.0
            [120/5] via 194.35.35.13, 00:00:13, Ethernet0
            [120/5] via 194.35.50.240, 00:00:13, Ethernet0
            [120/5] via 129.3.1.241, 00:00:13, Ethernet0
      212.159.2.0 is variably subnetted, 5 subnets, 2 masks
R        212.159.2.0 255.255.255.0
            [120/5] via 194.35.35.13, 00:00:13, Ethernet0
            [120/5] via 194.35.50.240, 00:00:13, Ethernet0
            [120/5] via 129.3.1.241, 00:00:13, Ethernet0
      212.159.1.0 is variably subnetted, 2 subnets, 2 masks
R        212.159.1.0 255.255.255.0
            [120/5] via 194.35.35.13, 00:00:13, Ethernet0
            [120/5] via 194.35.50.240, 00:00:13, Ethernet0
            [120/5] via 129.3.1.241, 00:00:13, Ethernet0
Router#
```

The show ip route rip command only displays the routing information that has been learned via RIP. This can also be run for any other supported routing protocol as well as static and directly connected routes.

debug ip rip The debug ip rip command displays routing information events for the RIP routing protocol. To show this in operation, we are going to examine two router listings that show a new network has been added to RIP and then has been removed. We are also going to change RouterA to RIP version 1 to show the problems it creates.

RouterA Listing

```
RouterA#conf t
Enter configuration commands, one per line.  End with CNTL/Z.
RouterA(config)#int s0
RouterA(config-if)#ip address 172.24.0.1 255.255.0.0 sec
RouterA(config-if)#exit
RouterA(config)#router rip
RouterA(config-router)#network 172.24.0.1
RouterA(config-router)#exit
RouterA(config)#router rip
RouterA(config-router)#version 1
RouterA(config-router)#exit
RouterA(config)#router rip
RouterA(config-router)#ver 2
RouterA(config-router)#no network 172.24.0.0
RouterA(config-router)#exit
RouterA(config)#int s0
RouterA(config-if)#no ip add 172.24.0.1 255.255.0.0 sec
RouterA(config-if)#^Z
RouterA#
```

RouterB Listing

```
RouterB#debug ip rip
RIP protocol debugging is on
RouterB#
07:23:22: RIP: sending v2 update to 224.0.0.9 via Ethernet0
(194.73.134.22)
07:23:22: RIP: build update entries
07:23:22:        0.0.0.0/0 metric 1, tag 0
07:23:25: RIP: received v2 update from 194.73.134.23 on Ethernet0
07:23:25:        172.19.0.0/16 via 0.0.0.0 in 1 hops
07:23:25:        172.20.0.0/16 via 0.0.0.0 in 1 hops
07:23:25: RIP: received v2 update from 172.18.0.11 on Ethernet0
07:23:25:        172.19.0.0/16 via 0.0.0.0 in 1 hops
07:23:25:        172.20.0.0/16 via 0.0.0.0 in 1 hops
07:23:50: RIP: sending v2 update to 224.0.0.9 via Ethernet0
(194.73.134.22)
07:23:50: RIP: build update entries
07:23:50:        0.0.0.0/0 metric 1, tag 0
07:23:55: RIP: received v2 update from 194.73.134.23 on Ethernet0
07:23:55:        172.19.0.0/16 via 0.0.0.0 in 1 hops
07:23:55:        172.20.0.0/16 via 0.0.0.0 in 1 hops
07:23:55: RIP: received v2 update from 172.18.0.11 on Ethernet0
07:23:55:        172.19.0.0/16 via 0.0.0.0 in 1 hops
07:23:55:        172.20.0.0/16 via 0.0.0.0 in 1 hops
07:24:19: RIP: sending v2 update to 224.0.0.9 via Ethernet0
(194.73.134.22)
07:24:19: RIP: build update entries
07:24:19:        0.0.0.0/0 metric 1, tag 0
07:24:21: RIP: received v2 update from 194.73.134.23 on Ethernet0
07:24:21:        172.19.0.0/16 via 0.0.0.0 in 1 hops
07:24:21:        172.20.0.0/16 via 0.0.0.0 in 1 hops
07:24:21: RIP: received v2 update from 172.18.0.11 on Ethernet0
```

```
07:24:21:          172.19.0.0/16 via 0.0.0.0 in 1 hops
07:24:21:          172.20.0.0/16 via 0.0.0.0 in 1 hops
07:24:39: RIP: received v2 update from 194.73.134.23 on Ethernet0
07:24:39:          172.24.0.0/16 via 0.0.0.0 in 1 hops
07:24:39: RIP: received v2 update from 172.18.0.11 on Ethernet0
07:24:39:          172.24.0.0/16 via 0.0.0.0 in 1 hops
07:24:41: RIP: sending v2 flash update to 224.0.0.9 via Ethernet0
(194.73.134.22)
07:24:41: RIP: build flash update entries - suppressing null update
07:24:46: RIP: sending v2 update to 224.0.0.9 via Ethernet0
(194.73.134.22)
07:24:46: RIP: build update entries
07:24:46:           0.0.0.0/0 metric 1, tag 0
07:24:51: RIP: received v2 update from 194.73.134.23 on Ethernet0
07:24:51:          172.19.0.0/16 via 0.0.0.0 in 1 hops
07:24:51:          172.20.0.0/16 via 0.0.0.0 in 1 hops
07:24:51:          172.24.0.0/16 via 0.0.0.0 in 1 hops
07:24:51: RIP: received v2 update from 172.18.0.11 on Ethernet0
07:24:51:          172.19.0.0/16 via 0.0.0.0 in 1 hops
07:24:51:          172.20.0.0/16 via 0.0.0.0 in 1 hops
07:24:51:          172.24.0.0/16 via 0.0.0.0 in 1 hops
07:25:15: RIP: sending v2 update to 224.0.0.9 via Ethernet0
(194.73.134.22)
07:25:15: RIP: build update entries
07:25:15:           0.0.0.0/0 metric 1, tag 0
07:25:16: RIP: ignored v1 packet from 194.73.134.23 (illegal
version)
07:25:16: RIP: ignored v1 packet from 172.18.0.11 (illegal version)
07:25:42: RIP: sending v2 update to 224.0.0.9 via Ethernet0
(194.73.134.22)
07:25:42: RIP: build update entries
07:25:42:           0.0.0.0/0 metric 1, tag 0
07:25:43: RIP: received v2 update from 194.73.134.23 on Ethernet0
07:25:43:          172.19.0.0/16 via 0.0.0.0 in 1 hops
07:25:43:          172.20.0.0/16 via 0.0.0.0 in 1 hops
07:25:43:          172.24.0.0/16 via 0.0.0.0 in 1 hops
07:25:43: RIP: received v2 update from 172.18.0.11 on Ethernet0
07:25:43:          172.19.0.0/16 via 0.0.0.0 in 1 hops
07:25:43:          172.20.0.0/16 via 0.0.0.0 in 1 hops
07:25:43:          172.24.0.0/16 via 0.0.0.0 in 1 hops
07:25:46: RIP: received v2 update from 194.73.134.23 on Ethernet0
07:25:46:          172.24.0.0/16 via 0.0.0.0 in 16 hops  (inaccessible)
07:25:46: RIP: received v2 update from 172.18.0.11 on Ethernet0
07:25:46:          172.24.0.0/16 via 0.0.0.0 in 16 hops  (inaccessible)
07:25:48: RIP: sending v2 flash update to 224.0.0.9 via Ethernet0
(194.73.134.22)
07:25:48: RIP: build flash update entries
07:25:48:           172.24.0.0/16 metric 16, tag 0
RouterB#
```

These listings show us adding the secondary ip address 172.24.0.1/16 to the Serial0 interface on RouterA. Next, we add this network to the RIP configuration so that it will be advertised using RIP. As soon as this is done, the next RIP routing update received by RouterB includes this network in the update.

Next, we change the RIP version on RouterA to be version 1. This area shows that this packet is considered illegal and is ignored. We then remove the route from the RIP configuration on RouterA, and RouterB receives the notification and marks it in the routing table as inaccessible. At this stage, the hold down timer would start.

The `debug ip rip` command is of paramount importance when debugging a RIP routing problem. A common RIP problem is the misconfiguration of the versions. This command identifies every RIP packet and provides output that can be used for diagnosing the problem.

Interior Gateway Routing Protocol (IGRP)

IGRP is a distance vector-based dynamic routing protocol that uses a combination of metrics. It is an IGP; therefore, it performs routing within a single AS. IGRP is formally defined in RFC 1074 and was designed in the mid-1980s by Cisco Systems to provide a more robust scalable intra-AS routing protocol to replace the de facto standard routing protocol, RIP. The problem with RIP was that its hop count was limited to 15 and this was the only metric used. No consideration was given to the bandwidth or reliability of a line for the computation of the best route to a given destination. The route was decided upon the lowest number of hops alone. IGRP is a propriety routing protocol designed and utilized by Cisco internetworking devices.

IGRP operates by sending routing updates at regular intervals out of all the configured interfaces. These routing updates contain the complete routing table minus any routes removed due to the Split Horizon rule. When a routing update is received from a direct neighbor, route information is checked against the current routing table and any better routes are updated in the routing table. IGRP uses a combination of factors to create the routing metric. These include the following:

- Internetwork delay
- Bandwidth
- Reliability
- Load
- *Maximum Transmission Unit* (MTU)

All of the above are factored into the routing decision. The network administrator can set weights for each of these values or you can accept the defaults. This inclusion of multiple values into the routing decision provides the router with a much more powerful means of establishing routing decisions. IGRP also has faster convergence than RIP. This is due to the IGRP implementation of flash updates. Flash updates are the IGRP equivalent of distance vector-triggered updates. A flash update is sent whenever a network topology change is noticed.

On a Cisco router, simply adding the following command in global configuration mode enables IGRP:

```
Router(config)#router igrp 101
```

The previous command would enable IGRP for the AS 101. You must specify the AS number when implementing IGRP.

Networks are advertised and participate in IGRP routing by entering the following command:

```
Router(config-router)network A.B.C.D
```

where A.B.C.D is the network address of the network to be advertised via IGRP.

Other IGRP configuration commands include the following:

```
Router configuration commands:
  default                Set a command to its defaults
  default-information    Control distribution of default
information
  default-metric         Set metric of redistributed routes
  distance               Define an administrative distance
  distribute-list        Filter networks in routing updates
  exit                   Exit from routing protocol configuration
mode
  help                   Description of the interactive help system
  maximum-paths          Forward packets over multiple paths
  metric                 Modify IGRP routing metrics and
parameters
  neighbor               Specify a neighbor router
  network                Enable routing on an IP network
  no                     Negate a command or set its defaults
  offset-list            Add or subtract offset from IGRP or RIP
metrics
  passive-interface      Suppress routing updates on an interface
  redistribute           Redistribute information from another
routing
                         protocol
  timers                 Adjust routing timers
  validate-update-source Perform sanity checks against source
address of
                         routing updates
  variance               Control load balancing variance
```

Enabling IGRP   IGRP is enabled from global configuration mode on the router. From this mode, enter the following command:

```
Router(config)#router igrp 1
```

This enables IGRP on the router and places you into router configuration mode. This is indicated by the `Router(config-router)#` prompt.

The 1 relates to the AS number. The valid AS numbers are between 1 and 65,535. An AS can be thought of as a grouping of routers and interfaces that share the same common information. This is similar to a domain in Microsoft Windows NT. If you have three routers all in AS 1, they would all share routing updates and information. However, if one of these is changed to AS 2, it would be separate from the others in relation to the routing updates and would not participate in AS 1 routing traffic.

Configuring IGRP   Once IGRP has been enabled, you can assign an interface to be advertised via IGRP. To do this, you enter the following command:

```
Router(config-router)#network A.B.C.D
```

This would add network A.B.C.D to the IGRP routing process on the router. This identifies the network as a directly connected network. To add network 192.168.10.0 to the IGRP routing process, you would enter

```
Router(config-router)#network 192.168.10.0
```

Verifying IGRP Operation   A few commands can be used to verify the configuration of IGRP on the router. These commands include the following:

- `show running-config`
- `show ip protocol`
- `show ip route`
- `debug ip igrp events`

show running-config   The `show running-config` command can be used to display the running configuration on the router. A breakdown of the routing-specific commands will be displayed here and it is an excellent place to start to ensure that you have entered the correct networks into the IGRP routing process.

The following is a sample display from a router running IGRP and it shows the entries under the router igrp 101 section:

```
!
router igrp 101
 network 192.168.10.0
 network 192.168.20.0
 network 192.168.30.0
!.
```

We can see from the code that IGRP has been enabled on the router and the networks 192.168.10.0, 192.168.20.0, and 192.168.30.0 are directly connected and are participating in the RIP routing process.

If you are experiencing a routing problem in which some networks are available and some are not, be sure to check the running-config to ascertain if the network has been added to the IGRP routing process.

show ip protocol The `show ip protocols` command displays all enabled routing protocols and the associated values relating to the routing protocol. This command is useful for displaying whether or not inbound or outbound distribution lists have been set. Distribution lists are a common cause of routing table abnormalities. The distribution lists filter the routing traffic that flows over the interface and are related to an access list.

```
Router#sh ip prot
Routing Protocol is "rip"
  Sending updates every 30 seconds, next due in 1 seconds
  Invalid after 180 seconds, hold down 180, flushed after 240
  Outgoing update filter list for all interfaces is
  Incoming update filter list for all interfaces is
  Redistributing: rip
  Default version control: send version 2, receive version 2
    Interface       Send  Recv  Triggered RIP  Key-chain
    Ethernet0        2     2
    Ethernet1        2     2
    Serial0          2     2
    Serial1          2     2
  Routing for Networks:
    172.18.0.0
    172.19.0.0
    172.20.0.0
    172.30.0.0
    194.73.134.0
  Routing Information Sources:
    Gateway         Distance     Last Update
    194.73.134.23       120       00:00:17
    194.73.134.22       120       11:43:51
    172.18.0.11         120       00:00:17
```

```
          Gateway        Distance      Last Update
          172.20.1.1          120      00:00:18
          172.19.1.1          120      00:00:18
        Distance: (default is 120)

    Routing Protocol is "ospf 1"
      Sending updates every 0 seconds
      Invalid after 0 seconds, hold down 0, flushed after 0
      Outgoing update filter list for all interfaces is
      Incoming update filter list for all interfaces is
      Redistributing: ospf 1
      Routing for Networks:
        172.18.0.0
        172.19.0.0
        172.20.0.0
      Routing Information Sources:
        Gateway        Distance      Last Update
      Distance: (default is 110)

    Routing Protocol is "bgp 1"
      Sending updates every 60 seconds, next due in 0 seconds
      Outgoing update filter list for all interfaces is
      Incoming update filter list for all interfaces is
      IGP synchronization is enabled
      Automatic route summarization is enabled
      Routing for Networks:
      Routing Information Sources:
        Gateway        Distance      Last Update
      Distance: external 20 internal 200 local 200

    Routing Protocol is "igrp 101"
      Sending updates every 90 seconds, next due in 60 seconds
      Invalid after 270 seconds, hold down 280, flushed after 630
      Outgoing update filter list for all interfaces is
      Incoming update filter list for all interfaces is
      Default networks flagged in outgoing updates
      Default networks accepted from incoming updates
      IGRP metric weight K1=1, K2=0, K3=1, K4=0, K5=0
      IGRP maximum hopcount 100
      IGRP maximum metric variance 1
      Redistributing: igrp 101
      Routing for Networks:
        172.18.0.0
        172.19.0.0
        172.30.0.0
        194.73.134.0
      Routing Information Sources:
        Gateway        Distance      Last Update
        Gateway        Distance      Last Update
        194.73.134.23       100      00:01:46
        172.19.1.1          100      00:00:13
      Distance: (default is 100)
    Router#
```

From this listing, we can see that RIP, OSPF, BGP, and IGRP are all enabled on this router. IGRP is advertising networks 172.18.0.0, 172.19.0.0, 172.30.0.0, and 194.73.134.0. We can also see that no distribution lists have been set for IGRP. This command is useful for getting a holistic view of the routing situation of a router.

show ip route The show ip route command displays the internal IP routing table for all enabled routing protocols. Static routes and connected routes are also displayed in this table.

```
Router#sh ip route
Codes: C - connected, S - static, I - IGRP, R - RIP, M - mobile, B
- BGP
        D - EIGRP, EX - EIGRP external, O - OSPF, IA - OSPF inter area
        N1 - OSPF NSSA external type 1, N2 - OSPF NSSA external type 2
        E1 - OSPF external type 1, E2 - OSPF external type 2, E - EGP
        i - IS-IS, L1 - IS-IS level-1, L2 - IS-IS level-2, ia - IS-
IS inter area
        * - candidate default, U - per-user static route, o - ODR
        P - periodic downloaded static route

Gateway of last resort is 172.19.1.2 to network 0.0.0.0

C    194.73.134.0/24 is directly connected, Ethernet0
C    172.19.0.0/16 is directly connected, Serial0
C    172.18.0.0/16 is directly connected, Ethernet0
C    172.20.0.0/16 is directly connected, Serial1
I    172.30.0.0/16 [100/1200] via 194.73.134.24, 00:00:29,
Ethernet0
R*   0.0.0.0/0 [120/1] via 172.19.1.2, 1d05h, Serial0
                [120/1] via 172.20.1.2, 1d05h, Serial1
C    212.0.0.0/8 is directly connected, Loopback0
Router#
```

The first part of this listing indicates all the codes that are used to identify the routing protocols in the actual routing table. You can see from the routing table that we have five connected networks that are over multiple interfaces. The connected interface is identified by a C. We also have one network that has been received via RIP. This is 0.0.0.0 or the default route. This default route is also identified by an asterisk next to the R. There is one static route to network 172.24.0.0. We can also see that 172.30.0.0 has been received over IGRP. Notice the values in the brackets after the route: [100/1200]. The first part (100) refers to the administrative distance of IGRP, and the second part (1200) refers to the metric of the route. This metric has been calculated by the IGRP algorithm.

This is a small routing table and it is not uncommon for routing tables to be a hundred or more lines long, depending on the size of the network. The show ip route command can be further divided by entering the exact route after the command or entering the routing protocol after the command. For example, Router#show ip route igrp would just display routes learned by IGRP. Router#show ip route 172.18.10.0 would just display protocol information about network 172.18.10.0

debug ip igrp events The debug ip igrp events command displays routing information events for the IGRP routing protocol. To show this in operation, we are going to examine two router listings that show that a new network has been added to IGRP and then been removed.

RouterA Listing

```
RouterA#conf t
Enter configuration commands, one per line.  End with CNTL/Z.
RouterA(config)#int s0
RouterA(config-if)#ip address 172.24.0.1 255.255.0.0 sec
RouterA(config-if)#

4w1d: RT: add 172.24.0.0/16 via 0.0.0.0, connected metric [0/0]
4w1d: is_up: 1 state: 4 sub state: 1 line: 0

RouterA(config-if)#exit
RouterA(config)#router igrp 101
RouterA(config-router)#network 172.24.0.0
RouterA(config-router)#exit
RouterA(config)#exit


RouterA#sh ip route
Codes: C - connected, S - static, I - IGRP, R - RIP, M - mobile, B
- BGP
        D - EIGRP, EX - EIGRP external, O - OSPF, IA - OSPF inter area
        N1 - OSPF NSSA external type 1, N2 - OSPF NSSA external type 2
        E1 - OSPF external type 1, E2 - OSPF external type 2, E - EGP
        i - IS-IS, L1 - IS-IS level-1, L2 - IS-IS level-2, ia - IS-
IS inter area
           * - candidate default, U - per-user static route, o - ODR
           P - periodic downloaded static route

Gateway of last resort is 194.73.134.1 to network 0.0.0.0

C    194.73.134.0/24 is directly connected, Ethernet0
C    172.19.0.0/16 is directly connected, Serial0
C    172.18.0.0/16 is directly connected, Ethernet0
C    172.20.0.0/16 is directly connected, Serial1
C    172.24.0.0/16 is directly connected, Serial0
C    172.30.0.0/16 is directly connected, Ethernet1
S*   0.0.0.0/0 [1/0] via 194.73.134.1


RouterA#conf t
Enter configuration commands, one per line.  End with CNTL/Z.
RouterA(config)#router igrp 101
RouterA(config-router)#no network 172.24.0.0
RouterA(config-router)#exit
RouterA(config)#int s0
RouterA(config-if)#no ip add 172.24.0.1 255.255.0.0 sec
RouterA(config-if)#

4w1d: RT: del 172.24.0.0 via 0.0.0.0, connected metric [0/0]
4w1d: RT: delete network route to 172.24.0.0
4w1d: is_up: 1 state: 4 sub state: 1 line: 0

RouterA(config-if)#^Z
```

```
RouterA#
4w1d: RT: add 172.24.0.0/16 via 172.19.1.1, igrp metric [100/10576]
4w1d: RT: delete route to 172.24.0.0 via 172.19.1.1, igrp metric
[100/10576]
4w1d: RT: no routes to 172.24.0.0, entering holddown

RouterA#sh ip route
Codes: C - connected, S - static, I - IGRP, R - RIP, M - mobile, B
- BGP
        D - EIGRP, EX - EIGRP external, O - OSPF, IA - OSPF inter area
        N1 - OSPF NSSA external type 1, N2 - OSPF NSSA external type 2
        E1 - OSPF external type 1, E2 - OSPF external type 2, E - EGP
        i - IS-IS, L1 - IS-IS level-1, L2 - IS-IS level-2, ia - IS-
IS inter area
        * - candidate default, U - per-user static route, o - ODR
        P - periodic downloaded static route

Gateway of last resort is 194.73.134.1 to network 0.0.0.0

C    194.73.134.0/24 is directly connected, Ethernet0
C    172.19.0.0/16 is directly connected, Serial0
C    172.18.0.0/16 is directly connected, Ethernet0
C    172.20.0.0/16 is directly connected, Serial1
I    172.24.0.0/16 is possibly down, routing via 172.19.1.1,
Serial0
C    172.30.0.0/16 is directly connected, Ethernet1
S*   0.0.0.0/0 [1/0] via 194.73.134.1

4w1d: RT: 172.24.0.0 came out of holddown
4w1d: RT: garbage collecting entry for 172.24.0.0

RouterA#sh ip route
Codes: C - connected, S - static, I - IGRP, R - RIP, M - mobile, B
- BGP
        D - EIGRP, EX - EIGRP external, O - OSPF, IA - OSPF inter area
        N1 - OSPF NSSA external type 1, N2 - OSPF NSSA external type 2
        E1 - OSPF external type 1, E2 - OSPF external type 2, E - EGP
        i - IS-IS, L1 - IS-IS level-1, L2 - IS-IS level-2, ia - IS-
IS inter area
        * - candidate default, U - per-user static route, o - ODR
        P - periodic downloaded static route

Gateway of last resort is 194.73.134.1 to network 0.0.0.0

C    194.73.134.0/24 is directly connected, Ethernet0
C    172.19.0.0/16 is directly connected, Serial0
C    172.18.0.0/16 is directly connected, Ethernet0
C    172.20.0.0/16 is directly connected, Serial1
C    172.30.0.0/16 is directly connected, Ethernet1
S*   0.0.0.0/0 [1/0] via 194.73.134.1

RouterA#no debug all
All possible debugging has been turned off
```

RouterB Listing

```
RouterB#debug ip igrp events
IGRP event debugging is on
RouterB#
```

```
4w1d: IGRP: sending update to 255.255.255.255 via Serial0
(172.19.1.1)
4w1d: IGRP: Update contains 0 interior, 3 system, and 0 exterior
routes.
4w1d: IGRP: Total routes in update: 3
4w1d: IGRP: sending update to 255.255.255.255 via Serial1
(172.20.1.1)
4w1d: IGRP: Update contains 0 interior, 3 system, and 0 exterior
routes.
4w1d: IGRP: Total routes in update: 3
4w1d: IGRP: received update from 194.73.134.24 on Ethernet0
4w1d: IGRP: Update contains 0 interior, 2 system, and 0 exterior
routes.
4w1d: IGRP: Total routes in update: 2
4w1d: IGRP: received update from invalid source 172.30.0.1 on
Ethernet0
4w1d: IGRP: received update from 172.19.1.2 on Serial0
4w1d: IGRP: Update contains 0 interior, 3 system, and 0 exterior
routes.
4w1d: IGRP: Total routes in update: 3
4w1d: IGRP: sending update to 255.255.255.255 via Serial0
(172.19.1.1)
4w1d: IGRP: Update contains 0 interior, 3 system, and 0 exterior
routes.
4w1d: IGRP: Total routes in update: 3
4w1d: IGRP: sending update to 255.255.255.255 via Serial1
(172.20.1.1)
4w1d: IGRP: Update contains 0 interior, 3 system, and 0 exterior
routes.
4w1d: IGRP: Total routes in update: 3
4w1d: IGRP: received update from 194.73.134.24 on Ethernet0
```

```
4w1d: RT: add 172.24.0.0/16 via 194.73.134.24, igrp metric
[100/8576]
```

```
4w1d: IGRP: Update contains 0 interior, 3 system, and 0 exterior
routes.
4w1d: IGRP: Total routes in update: 3
4w1d: IGRP: edition is now 4
4w1d: IGRP: sending update to 255.255.255.255 via Serial0
(172.19.1.1)
4w1d: IGRP: Update contains 0 interior, 4 system, and 0 exterior
routes.
4w1d: IGRP: Total routes in update: 4
4w1d: IGRP: sending update to 255.255.255.255 via Serial1
(172.20.1.1)
4w1d: IGRP: Update contains 0 interior, 4 system, and 0 exterior
routes.
4w1d: IGRP: Total routes in update: 4
4w1d: IGRP: received update from invalid source 172.30.0.1 on
Ethernet0
4w1d: IGRP: received update from 172.19.1.2 on Serial0
4w1d: IGRP: Update contains 0 interior, 3 system, and 0 exterior
routes.
4w1d: IGRP: Total routes in update: 3

RouterB#sh ip route
Codes: C - connected, S - static, I - IGRP, R - RIP, M - mobile, B
- BGP
```

```
            D - EIGRP, EX - EIGRP external, O - OSPF, IA - OSPF inter area
            N1 - OSPF NSSA external type 1, N2 - OSPF NSSA external type 2
            E1 - OSPF external type 1, E2 - OSPF external type 2, E - EGP
            i - IS-IS, L1 - IS-IS level-1, L2 - IS-IS level-2, ia - IS-
       IS inter area
            * - candidate default, U - per-user static route, o - ODR
            P - periodic downloaded static route

       Gateway of last resort is 172.19.1.2 to network 0.0.0.0

       C     194.73.134.0/24 is directly connected, Ethernet0
       C     172.19.0.0/16 is directly connected, Serial0
       C     172.18.0.0/16 is directly connected, Ethernet0
       C     172.20.0.0/16 is directly connected, Serial1
       I     172.24.0.0/16 [100/8576] via 194.73.134.24, 00:00:52,
       Ethernet0
       I     172.30.0.0/16 [100/1200] via 194.73.134.24, 00:00:52,
       Ethernet0
       R*    0.0.0.0/0 [120/1] via 172.19.1.2, 1d06h, Serial0
                       [120/1] via 172.20.1.2, 1d06h, Serial1
       C     212.0.0.0/8 is directly connected, Loopback0
       RouterB#

       4w1d: IGRP: sending update to 255.255.255.255 via Serial0
       (172.19.1.1)
       4w1d: IGRP: Update contains 0 interior, 4 system, and 0 exterior
       routes.
       4w1d: IGRP: Total routes in update: 4
       4w1d: IGRP: sending update to 255.255.255.255 via Serial1
       (172.20.1.1)
       4w1d: IGRP: Update contains 0 interior, 4 system, and 0 exterior
       routes.
       4w1d: IGRP: Total routes in update: 4
       4w1d: IGRP: received update from 194.73.134.24 on Ethernet0

       4w1d: RT: delete route to 172.24.0.0 via 194.73.134.24, igrp metric
       [100/8576]
       4w1d: RT: no routes to 172.24.0.0, entering holddown

       4w1d: IGRP: Update contains 0 interior, 3 system, and 0 exterior
       routes.
       4w1d: IGRP: Total routes in update: 3
       4w1d: IGRP: edition is now 5
       4w1d: IGRP: sending update to 255.255.255.255 via Serial0
       (172.19.1.1)
       4w1d: IGRP: Update contains 0 interior, 4 system, and 0 exterior
       routes.
       4w1d: IGRP: Total routes in update: 4
       4w1d: IGRP: sending update to 255.255.255.255 via Serial1
       (172.20.1.1)
       4w1d: IGRP: Update contains 0 interior, 4 system, and 0 exterior
       routes.
       4w1d: IGRP: Total routes in update: 4
       4w1d: IGRP: received update from invalid source 172.30.0.1 on
       Ethernet0
       4w1d: IGRP: received update from 172.19.1.2 on Serial0
       4w1d: IGRP: Update contains 0 interior, 3 system, and 0 exterior
       routes.
       4w1d: IGRP: Total routes in update: 3
       4w1d: IGRP: received update from 194.73.134.24 on Ethernet0
```

```
4w1d: IGRP: Update contains 0 interior, 3 system, and 0 exterior
routes.
4w1d: IGRP: Total routes in update: 3
4w1d: IGRP: received update from invalid source 172.30.0.1 on
Ethernet0
4w1d: IGRP: received update from 172.19.1.2 on Serial0
4w1d: IGRP: Update contains 0 interior, 4 system, and 0 exterior
routes.
4w1d: IGRP: Total routes in update: 4

RouterB#sh ip route
Codes: C - connected, S - static, I - IGRP, R - RIP, M - mobile, B
- BGP
       D - EIGRP, EX - EIGRP external, O - OSPF, IA - OSPF inter area
       N1 - OSPF NSSA external type 1, N2 - OSPF NSSA external type 2
       E1 - OSPF external type 1, E2 - OSPF external type 2, E - EGP
       i - IS-IS, L1 - IS-IS level-1, L2 - IS-IS level-2, ia - IS-
IS inter area
       * - candidate default, U - per-user static route, o - ODR
       P - periodic downloaded static route

Gateway of last resort is 172.19.1.2 to network 0.0.0.0

C     194.73.134.0/24 is directly connected, Ethernet0
C     172.19.0.0/16 is directly connected, Serial0
C     172.18.0.0/16 is directly connected, Ethernet0
C     172.20.0.0/16 is directly connected, Serial1
I     172.24.0.0/16 is possibly down, routing via 194.73.134.24,
Ethernet0
I     172.30.0.0/16 [100/1200] via 194.73.134.24, 00:00:11,
Ethernet0
R*    0.0.0.0/0 [120/1] via 172.19.1.2, 1d06h, Serial0
                [120/1] via 172.20.1.2, 1d06h, Serial1
C     212.0.0.0/8 is directly connected, Loopback0
RouterB#

4w1d: IGRP: received update from 194.73.134.24 on Ethernet0

4w1d: RT: 172.24.0.0 came out of holddown

4w1d: IGRP: Update contains 0 interior, 3 system, and 0 exterior
routes.
4w1d: IGRP: Total routes in update: 3
4w1d: IGRP: received update from invalid source 172.30.0.1 on
Ethernet0
4w1d: IGRP: received update from 172.19.1.2 on Serial0
4w1d: IGRP: Update contains 0 interior, 4 system, and 0 exterior
routes.
4w1d: IGRP: Total routes in update: 4
4w1d: IGRP: sending update to 255.255.255.255 via Serial0
(172.19.1.1)
4w1d: IGRP: Update contains 0 interior, 4 system, and 0 exterior
routes.
4w1d: IGRP: Total routes in update: 4
4w1d: IGRP: sending update to 255.255.255.255 via Serial1
(172.20.1.1)
4w1d: IGRP: Update contains 0 interior, 4 system, and 0 exterior
routes.
4w1d: IGRP: Total routes in update: 4
4w1d: IGRP: received update from 194.73.134.24 on Ethernet0
```

```
4w1d: IGRP: Update contains 0 interior, 3 system, and 0 exterior
routes.
4w1d: IGRP: Total routes in update: 3
4w1d: IGRP: received update from invalid source 172.30.0.1 on
Ethernet0
4w1d: IGRP: received update from 172.19.1.2 on Serial0
4w1d: IGRP: Update contains 0 interior, 4 system, and 0 exterior
routes.
4w1d: IGRP: Total routes in update: 4
```

```
4w1d: RT: garbage collecting entry for 172.24.0.0
```

```
RouterB#sh ip route
Codes: C - connected, S - static, I - IGRP, R - RIP, M - mobile, B
- BGP
       D - EIGRP, EX - EIGRP external, O - OSPF, IA - OSPF inter area
       N1 - OSPF NSSA external type 1, N2 - OSPF NSSA external type 2
       E1 - OSPF external type 1, E2 - OSPF external type 2, E - EGP
       i - IS-IS, L1 - IS-IS level-1, L2 - IS-IS level-2, ia - IS-
IS inter area
       * - candidate default, U - per-user static route, o - ODR
       P - periodic downloaded static route

Gateway of last resort is 172.19.1.2 to network 0.0.0.0

C    194.73.134.0/24 is directly connected, Ethernet0
C    172.19.0.0/16 is directly connected, Serial0
C    172.18.0.0/16 is directly connected, Ethernet0
C    172.20.0.0/16 is directly connected, Serial1
I    172.30.0.0/16 [100/1200] via 194.73.134.24, 00:01:20,
Ethernet0
R*   0.0.0.0/0 [120/1] via 172.19.1.2, 1d06h, Serial0
                [120/1] via 172.20.1.2, 1d06h, Serial1
C    212.0.0.0/8 is directly connected, Loopback0
RouterB#
Router2501#no debug all
All possible debugging has been turned off
```

In this listing, we add a new route to the IGRP routing process between two routers and track the events with the `debug ip igrp events` command. We start by adding a secondary IP address to Serial0 on RouterA. You can see this addition to the internal routing table on RouterA. We then add this new network to the IGRP routing process with the command `network 172.24.0.0`. We can see the periodic IGRP updates occurring on RouterB. Unlike RIP, the `debug ip igrp events` command does not show the individual route information in the debug output. Thus, we leave the process running for a few seconds and then enter a `show ip route` on RouterB. You can see that the network 172.24.0.0 is connected via 194.73.134.24, Ethernet0. This is also indicated as an IGRP route. This proves that RouterB has received the routing update from RouterA.

We then remove the route from the IGRP routing process on RouterA by entering the command `no network 172.24.0.0`. This forces RouterA to put the route into hold down. This propagates to RouterB and a `show ip` `route` on both routers indicates that this route is possibly down. Eventually, the route comes out of hold down on RouterA and the garbage collection removes the route. A `show ip route` command on both routers now shows that the route is absent from the routing table. This command provides a wealth of information for debugging IGRP problems. From the output though, you can see that this level of debugging in a large network can be very time-consuming and generate superfluous amounts of debug listings.

IP Classless

The *Internet Protocol* (IP) follows a classfull addressing scheme in which all unicast IP addresses are grouped into three main classifications: class A, class B, and class C. Each class of addresses specifies a range of IP addresses and has a default subnet mask that identifies the network and host portion of the IP address:

- *Class A—0.0.0.0 to 126.255.255.255* Class A addresses have a default subnet mask of 255.0.0.0 This provides for 255 networks and 16,777,214 hosts per network.

- *Class B—128.0.0.0 to 191.255.255.255* Class B addresses have a default subnet mask of 255.255.0.0 This provides for 65,536 networks and 65,534 hosts per network.

- *Class C—192.0.0.0 to 223.255.255.255* Class C addresses have a default subnet mask of 255.255.255.0 This provides for 16,777,216 networks and 254 hosts per network.

As you can see from these examples, the original classfull addressing scheme provides far too many hosts per network for class A and B addresses and too few hosts per network for class C addresses. The solution around this is to partition large networks internally into subnetworks or subnets. This enables you to create subnetworks (subnets) of the original network address.

Routing protocols are either classfull or classless in their design and operation. This doesn't correlate with the distance vector and link state grouping. However, most link state routing protocols are also classless. As always, there are exceptions to this rule.

Classfull dynamic routing protocols strictly adhere to the rules and restraints of the IP addressing scheme. Subnets and subnet masks are supported by classfull routing protocols, but they require that all subnet masks be the same for all IP addresses belonging to the same classfull network address. This point is key in understanding the difference between classfull and classless routing protocols. A network address of 172.18.1.0 and a subnet mask of 255.255.255.0 would provide a subnet for every change on the third octet. These would be 172.18.1.0, 172.18.2.0, 172.18.3.0, and so on. In this instance, a classfull dynamic routing protocol would insist that the subnet mask is the same for every subnet of 172.18.0.0. This would mean that the corporate-wide network address scheme would have to be based on the same subnet mask.

To use another subnet mask, you would have to use a different network address. For example, 172.19.1.0 is a different class B network and could have a subnet mask of 255.255.248.0.

The reason why classfull protocols only support one subnet mask is due to the fact that classfull dynamic routing protocols do not have the facility to include the subnet mask in the routing update. Because classfull routing protocols assume that the subnet mask is the same for all subnets of a network, they acquire the subnet mask from interfaces that they send and receive routing updates over.

Classless dynamic routing protocols have the capability to send the subnet mask along with the subnet information as part of the routing update. This enables VLSMs and route summarization to be used to conserve network resources. Table 8-2 outlines various routing protocols and specifies whether they are classfull or classless.

Chapter Summary

In this chapter, we have looked at the basics of IP routing and the associated technologies. We started by defining routing and providing an

Table 8-2	**Routing Protocol**	**Classfull or Classless**
Classfull and classless routing protocols	Routing Information Protocol (RIP)	Classfull
	Routing Information Protocol V2 (RIPv2)	Classless
	Interior Gateway Routing Protocol (IGRP)	Classfull
	Open Shortest Path First (OSPF)	Classless
	Border Gateway Protocol (BGP)	Classless
	Enhanced Interior Gateway Routing Protocol (EIGRP)	Classless

overview of the different types of routing. These included static and dynamic routing. We then explained the different types of dynamic routing protocols. RIP and IGRP were explained along with the Cisco IOS commands that are required to enable, configure, and monitor these two distance vector routing protocols. We finished by explaining the differences between classless and classfull routing protocols.

Frequently Asked Questions (FAQ)

Question: What is meant by a classfull routing protocol?

Answer: A classfull routing protocol is a routing protocol that strictly follows the classfull IP addressing scheme.

Question: Can multiple routing protocols be run over the same router at the same time?

Answer: Yes, multiple routing protocols can coexist, although they by default will not transfer or share routing information. You can redistribute routing information by using specific IOS commands.

Question: Are routing protocols enabled by default?

Answer: No, you have to manually enable every routing protocol. This also applies to static routes. The only routes that a router knows about by default are the directly connected interfaces.

Questions

1. Which of the following routing protocols considers the sixteenth hop unreachable?

    a. RIP

    b. IGRP

    c. EIGRP

    d. IS-IS

2. Which of the following routing protocols is a distance vector protocol and is proprietary to Cisco Systems?

    a. RIP

    b. OSPF

    c. IGRP

    d. BGP

3. Which command displays the internal IP routing table?

    a. `Router#show route`

    b. `Router(config)#show ip route`

    c. `Router#show ip route`

    d. `Router#show all routes ip`

4. Which command clears all dynamically learned IP routes from the internal routing table?

    a. `Router#clear ip route`

    b. `Router#clear ip route all`

    c. `Router(config)#clear ip route`

    d. `Router#clear ip route *`

5. What are the two main types of dynamic routing? Choose two.

    a. Link state

    b. Best path

    c. Distance vector

    d. Distance aware

6. Classfull routing protocols enable the subnet mask to be passed with the routing update.

    a. True

    b. False

7. You are using RIP as your routing protocol. You do not follow the classfull IP addressing scheme in your network. To continue using RIP, what should you do?

   a. Set the RIP version to version 2.
   b. Enable RIP VLSM support.
   c. Create a loopback interface.
   d. All of the above

8. After an IGRP hold down, what is performed to remove the route?

   a. Route recover
   b. Garbage collection
   c. Route removal
   d. Route clear

9. Which command displays all the configured routing protocols and their configurations on a router?

   a. `Router#show route`
   b. `Router(config)#show ip protocol`
   c. `Router#show ip protocol`
   d. `Router#show all protocols`

10. Which command would add network 172.18.0.0 to the RIP routing process?

   a. `network 172.18.0.0 RIP`
   b. `network 172.18.0.0`
   c. `network 172.0.0.0 0.255.255.255`
   d. `router network 172.18.0.0`

11. Which of the following routing protocols is classified as a hybrid?

   a. OSPF
   b. IGRP
   c. EIGRP
   d. IS-IS

12. Routing protocols are enabled by default.

   a. True
   b. False

13. Which command enables IGRP routing for AS 101?

   a. `Router(config)#router igrp`
   b. `Router(config-router)#router igrp 101`
   c. `Router#router igrp 101`
   d. `Router(config)#router igrp 101`

14. You have a large interconnected network. The network span from end to end is a possible 23 hops. Which routing protocol wouldn't you use?

   a. IGRP

   b. OSPF

   c. RIP

   d. EIGRP

15. You have a route in the routing table that is shown as 192.168.10.0 [120/1] via Ethernet 0. What does the first value in the brackets identify?

   a. The administrative distance

   b. The cost of the route

   c. The number of hops

   d. The metric

16. What is the administrative distance for a static route?

   a. 1

   b. 0

   c. 255

   d. 120

17. RIP is an _____ Gateway Routing Protocol.

   a. Exterior

   b. Anterior

   c. Posterior

   d. Interior

18. Which type of route has the best trustworthiness with regards to the administrative distance?

   a. Static

   b. RIP

   c. OSPF

   d. Connected

19. You have RIP and IGRP enabled on your router. You have a route to a network provided by both of these protocols. Which route will the router use?

   a. The route learned through RIP

   b. The route learned through IGRP

20. Which command is used to debug IP RIP routing activity?

    a. `debug ip rip`
    b. `debug routing rip`
    c. `show rip routing`
    d. `debug rip all`

Answers

1. a. RIP

RIP considers the sixteenth hop to be unreachable. This is a major design implication of using RIP in your internetwork.

2. c. IGRP

The *Interior Gateway Routing Protocol* (IGRP) is distance vector-based and also proprietary to Cisco Systems.

3. c. Router#show ip route

The Router#show ip route command displays the internal IP routing table. It is important to get the syntax correct for this command. It can only be entered from the privileged exec mode.

4. d. Router#clear ip route *

The command Routeraclear ip route * would clear all dynamically stored routes from the internal routing table. It is important to get the syntax correct for this command. It can only be entered from the privileged exec mode.

5. a. Link state and **c.** Distance vector

The two main types of dynamic routing protocols are link state and distance vector.

6. b. False

Classfull routing protocols do not enable the passing of the subnet mask with the network address within a routing update. Classless routing protocols, however, can perform this function. This is required for route summarization and the implementation of VLSMs.

7. a. Set the RIP version to version 2.

RIP version 1 is classfull. RIP version 2 is classless and supports route summarization and the implementation of VLSMs.

8. b. Garbage collection

After a hold down, garbage collection is performed to remove the route.

9. c. Router#show ip protocol

The Router#show ip protocol command will display all configured routing protocols on the router along with their specific configuration details.

10. **b.** `network 172.18.0.0`

    The command `network 172.18.0.0` would add this network to the RIP routing process on the router.

11. **c.** EIGRP

    The only hybrid routing protocol is the *Enhanced Interior Gateway Routing Protocol* (EIGRP). This is a Cisco proprietary protocol.

12. **b.** False

    Routing is not enabled by default.

13. **d.** `Router(config)#router igrp 101`

    The command `Router(config)#router igrp 101` would enable IGRP for AS 101 on the router.

14. **c.** RIP

    You wouldn't use RIP in this network due to RIP's maximum hop count of 15 with the sixteenth hop considered unreachable. This network spans 23 hops.

15. **a.** The administrative distance

    The first value identifies the administrative distance.

16. **a.** 1

    The administrative distance for a static route is 1.

17. **d.** Interior

    RIP is an *Interior Gateway Protocol* (IGP). There is no such thing as an Anterior or Posterior gateway routing protocol.

18. **d.** Connected

    Connected routes have an administrative distance of zero and are considered as the best route to a network. These will be used over any dynamically learned route.

19. **b.** The route learned through IGRP

    The administrative distance for IGRP is 100 and 120 for RIP. Therefore, the router would use the route learned through IGRP.

20. **a.** `debug ip rip`

    The command `debug ip rip` would debug all IP RIP routing activity.

Access Lists and Traffic Management

Objectives

This chapter provides an introduction to the fundamentals of access lists and traffic management. We will start with an overview of access lists and then move on to their use in today's internetworks.

Access lists are a powerful feature of Cisco IOS and, if used right, can improve the performance and security of your network. However, access lists can also be the root of many internetwork-related problems due to their misconfigurations, so a good understanding of their operation is required to succeed in the Cisco networking field.

We will be looking at the basics of access lists and their operations. This includes standard and extended access lists for both IP and IPX protocols.

Access List Overview

Access lists are rules that are created on the router to filter traffic that the router processes. These rules can be very specific in their operation, but generally they enable or disable access to areas of the network based on a selection of criteria such as the host address, destination address, or type of service. Access lists offer the network administrator a way to control and filter traffic on the internetwork for various reasons. Two main reasons include performance and security.

If you have a network design where specific users only access local resources, access lists can be used to ensure that the local users can only access these resources and no other. A block would be put on the external routers in the form of an access list to deny access from the local network to any other networks on the internetwork.

From a security point of view, access lists can be used to permit or deny specific resources to specific users based on the host address, destination address, or type of service. For example, it is possible to only allow FTP traffic to a particular host, or it is possible to only permit HTTP traffic inbound to the Web servers and not the e-mail servers.

Access lists are very powerful and serve many purposes on Cisco routers. They can provide the network designer with a set of tools for implementing a fine level of control over the network.

Access List Implementation

Cisco routers implement access lists based on either the inbound or outbound queue of an interface. This affects the order in which the packets are filtered against the access list. If you specify an outbound access list, any traffic entering the router will not be controlled against this list. Only the traffic leaving the router will be filtered against the access list.

Inbound versus Outbound Access Lists

Access lists can be applied to either an inbound or outbound interface. To grasp this, you have to think about this in relation to the router. An inbound access list is related to traffic entering the router, and an outbound access list is related to traffic leaving the router.

Another way to look at this is that inbound access lists occur before the packets are routed by the router, and outbound access lists occur after the packets have been routed by the router on the external or next hop interface (see Figure 9-1). So it makes more sense to filter inbound rather than outbound for the majority of cases. This saves *Central Processing Unit* (CPU) time by reducing the routing that the router's CPU has to perform.

It is obvious that the correct placement of the access list is important to ensure that it functions as it was designed. For example, you can create an access list to deny any traffic from the Internet apart from HTTP. You can see from Figure 9-2 that you would place this access list on the inbound interface to protect against any traffic coming into the private network.

Figure 9-1
Inbound and outbound access lists

Inbound Access List → **Outbound Access List** →

Figure 9-2
Sample Internet
access list scenario

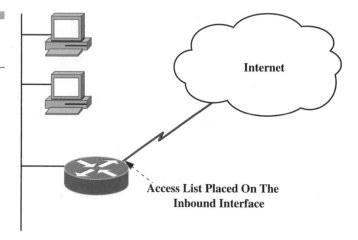

Access List Placed On The
Inbound Interface

Access List Commands

We are now going to look at the Cisco IOS commands that are required to configure access lists. We will also look at the four main types of access lists you will encounter and that you need to know for the ICND exam. These are

- IP standard access lists
- IP extended access lists
- IPX standard access lists
- IPX extended access lists

These four main types of access lists each have their own settings and configuration options that specify what they can and cannot achieve. When designing a network, it is important to have an overview of the functions of each type of access list to know what traffic they will permit and deny.

Entering the `access-list` command in global configuration mode followed by a number configures the access list. It is this number that informs the router as to the type of access list, and the router knows which options are available based on the type of access list. The access list configuration numbers are shown in Table 9-1.

As you can see from the table, these number ranges supply 100 of each type of access list. Access lists can, however, contain numerous permits and denies. So in theory you should never exhaust the 100 provided access lists of each type. IOS 11.2 introduced named access lists. With named access lists, you can give the access list a unique name. You also tell the access list whether it is a standard or extended list for which protocol. Descriptive

	Number Range	Type	Protocol
Table 9-1 Common access list configuration numbers	0–99	Standard	IP
	100–199	Extended	IP
	600–699	Standard	AppleTalk
	800–899	Standard	IPX
	900–999	Extended	IPX
	1000–1099	SAP filters	IPX SAP

comments can also be added to named access lists, so this eases the configuration and troubleshooting of complex access lists.

IP Access Lists

The most widely used access lists you will probably come across are IP access lists. IP access lists are designed to work with the TCP/IP protocol suite. IP access lists take two forms: standard IP access lists and extended IP access lists. Standard IP access lists work at the network layer of the OSI model and restrict access based on the source address only. Extended IP access lists work at the network and transport layers of the OSI model and can restrict access based on the network layer source address, destination address, or the transport layer *User Datagram Protocol* (UDP) and *Transmission Control Protocol* (TCP) port numbers. Common uses of IP access lists could be to restrict FTP access to a network, to deny access from one subnet to another subnet, and to permit only a specified host's Telnet access through the router.

The next section is going to look at IP standard and extended access lists and the associated commands required to configure these access lists on a Cisco router.

Standard IP Access Lists   IP access lists in the range 0 to 99 are classed as standard IP access lists. Standard IP access lists only filter traffic based on the source IP address. This IP address can be a specific host, complete

Figure 9-3
Standard IP access
lists

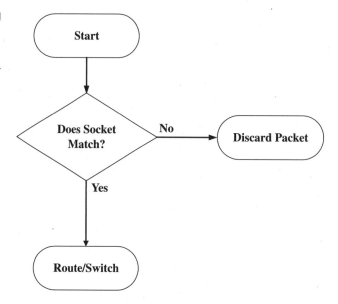

network, or specific hosts on a specific network. Figure 9-3 shows the standard IP access list process.

When the router receives a packet on an interface where a standard IP access list is set, the router checks the source IP address of the packet against the access list. If the access list matches a permit statement, then the packet is allowed through. If the packet doesn't match a permit statement, then the packet is discarded. Once through or permitted, the packet will then be routed to its destination by comparing the network address with the internal routing table on the router.

NOTE: *This brings to our attention an important topic that will be stressed the whole way through this chapter. At the end of every access list either standard or extended IP or IPX, there is always an implicit* deny all. *This means that if the packet doesn't match a permit statement, the implicit* deny all *will deny the packet.*

In light of this, it is important that you adopt the approach of permitting traffic that you require. Take the three following examples of access lists:

The following access list would permit traffic from the 192.168.10.0 network. Any other traffic would be denied by the implicit deny all *statement:*

```
Access-list 1 permit 192.168.10.0 0.0.0.255
```

The next access list would specifically deny traffic from the 192.168.10.0 network. The implicit deny all *statement would deny all other traffic as well, so no traffic whatsoever would pass through this access list:*

```
Access-list 2 deny 192.168.10.0 0.0.0.255
```

To remedy this, you would add a permit any, *as shown in the following code. This access list would deny all traffic from network 192.168.10.0 and permit any other traffic:*

```
Access-list 3 deny 192.168.10.0 0.0.0.255
Access-list 1 permit any
```

You can see from these examples the importance of specifying traffic to be permitted and allowing the deny all *to catch everything you do not want.*

Standard access lists are enabled from global configuration mode on the router. Global configuration mode is entered by typing

```
Router#configure terminal
Router(config)#
```

Note that the user prompt changes from Router# to Router(config)#. This identifies that you are in global configuration mode. Once in global configuration mode, the command that you enter in order to add any access list is simply access-list. We will now provide an example of a standard IP access list and then explain all of the components that make it up.

The following access list would permit only traffic from the 192.168.10.0 network. This is traffic with an IP address between 192.168.10.0 and 192.168.10.255. The first command is access-list. This tells the router that you are entering an access list. The 1 associates the access list with an IP standard access list. This is explained in Table 9-1 where it shows you the numbers associated with each protocol and the type of access list. We then enter the permit command. This indicates that this access list line permits traffic. The other option here is deny. Last comes the network address. The network address is 192.168.10.0 with what appears to be a subnet mask of 0.0.0.255 You will notice that the subnet mask appears to be reversed:

```
Router(config)#access-list 1 permit 192.168.10.0 0.0.0.255
```

Access lists use what are called `wildcard masks`. These are similar in operation to subnet masks, but they are used to tell the access list which part of the network address to ignore and which part to check against. The 0.0.0.255 tells the router to match the first three octets and ignore the fourth. At this stage, do not worry too much about this, as all will be explained in a coming section. Thus, this is the complete configuration of your first access list.

The full available syntax for an IP standard access list is

```
Router(config)#access-list access list number {permit _ deny}
source {source mask}
```

Here is a breakdown of the previous line:

- *Access list number*   This is the number of the access list. To specify an IP standard access list, you would use a number in the range of 0 to 99.
- *Permit/deny*   This indicates whether the access list is to permit or deny traffic.
- *Source*   This is the network address of the source to be filtered.
- *Source mask*   This is the wildcard mask that indicates which bits in the field are matched. Ones indicate that the bits are allowed to be different and zero indicates that the bits must match.

Other options that are available are the `any` and `host` commands. These commands can be used after the `permit` or `deny` statement to reference any host or a particular host. These two commands simplify things because they do not require a wildcard mask. The `any` command is the same as having a wildcard mask of 255.255.255.255 and the `host` command is the same as having a wildcard mask of 0.0.0.0.

Now we'll look at some examples of standard IP access lists. The following access list would deny the specific host 192.168.10.1 but allow everything else:

```
Router(config)#access-list 1 deny host 192.168.10.1
Router(config)#access-list 1 permit any
```

The following access list would deny any traffic from 192.168.0.0 to 192.168.255.255 but permit 192.167.0.0 to 192.167.255.255. Any other traffic outside of these ranges would also be denied by the implicit deny all:

```
Router(config)#access-list 2 deny 192.168.0.0 0.0.255.255
Router(config)#access-list 2 permit 192.167.0.0 0.0.255.255
```

The following access list would deny hosts 192.168.10.1 and 192.168.10.2 but permit all other traffic from the 192.168.10.0 network. As soon as the match is made, the access list stops. So even though the traffic is allowed by a permit lower down, the upper deny would drop the packet before it reaches the permit statement:

```
Router(config)#access-list 3 deny host 192.168.10.1
Router(config)#access-list 3 deny host 192.168.10.2
Router(config)#access-list 3 permit 192.168.10.0 0.0.0.255
```

Once you have created the standard IP access list, you have to apply it to an interface. To do this, you use the `ip access-group` command from interface configuration mode. Interface configuration mode is entered by typing the following commands:

```
Router#config t
Router(config)#interface ethernet0
Router(config-if)#
```

These commands put you into interface configuration mode for the Ethernet interface 0. Once in interface configuration mode, you enter the following command to apply the access list to the interface:

```
Router(config-if)#ip access-group 1 in
```

This command would apply IP access list 1 to the inbound queue on this interface. The command to set it to the outbound queue would be

```
Router(config-if)#ip access-group 1 out
```

As you can see, you just use `in` or `out` after the access list number to indicate the direction of the access list on the interface.

We have provided an overview and explanation of standard IP access lists and how to configure them. We are now going to move onto the extended IP access lists, which offer many more features.

Extended IP Access Lists   IP access lists in the range of 100 to 199 are classified as extended IP access lists. Extended IP access lists can filter traffic based on the source IP address, destination IP address, and transport layer TCP or UDP port information. Figure 9-4 shows the extended IP access list process.

When the router receives the packet on an interface where an extended IP access list is set, the router checks the source IP address of the packet

Figure 9-4
Extended IP access
lists

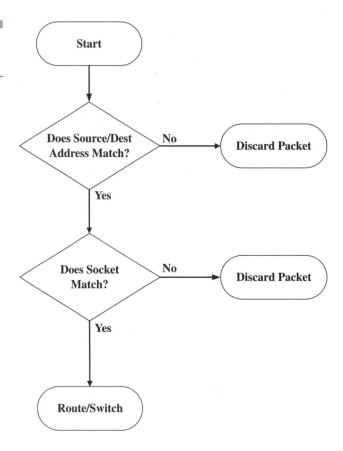

against the access list, then the destination IP address, and lastly the TCP or UDP port. If the access list matches a permit statement, then the packet is allowed through. If the packet doesn't match a permit statement, then the packet is discarded. Once through or permitted, the packet will then be routed to its destination by comparing the network address with the internal routing table on the router.

As with standard IP access lists, extended IP access lists have to be entered in global configuration mode. There is much more to extended IP access lists, so we are going to provide a breakdown of what every configuration option is before we explain any example access lists.

To start with, we know that IP extended access lists are in the range of 100 to 199, so the first start to the command syntax is

```
Router(config)#access-list 101
```

This identifies the access list as being an IP extended access list. As with the standard IP access list, the next part is to indicate whether this is a permit or deny access list:

```
Router(config)#access-list 101 permit
```

This is a permit statement for the access list. From now on, the syntax differs from the standard IP access lists. We now have to enter a protocol to permit or deny. In this case, we have to enter a protocol to permit. The choice of protocols is shown here:

```
Router(config)#access-list 101 perm ?
  <0-255>  An IP protocol number
  ahp      Authentication Header Protocol
  eigrp    Cisco's EIGRP routing protocol
  esp      Encapsulation Security Payload
  gre      Cisco's GRE tunneling
  icmp     Internet Control Message Protocol
  igmp     Internet Gateway Message Protocol
  igrp     Cisco's IGRP routing protocol
  ip       Any Internet Protocol
  ipinip   IP in IP tunneling
  nos      KA9Q NOS compatible IP over IP tunneling
  ospf     OSPF routing protocol
  pcp      Payload Compression Protocol
  pim      Protocol Independent Multicast
  tcp      Transmission Control Protocol
  udp      User Datagram Protocol
```

As you can see, many protocols can be chosen. For the ICND, we will concentrate only on IP, TCP, and UDP.

We have now chosen to permit traffic based on the TCP port information, as shown in the following code line. Remember that IP extended access lists can filter against the transport layer port. If you select TCP or UDP, this is an option. If you select IP or any other network-layer protocol, however, then you cannot filter by port, only by source and destination addresses.

```
Router(config)#access-list 101 permit tcp
```

Next comes the source address. As in the standard IP access lists, you can use a network address and a wildcard mask or the any and host commands:

```
Router(config)#access-list 101 permit tcp any
```

We have chosen to use the `any` command. This will permit any source address. After the source address is the destination address. The destination address uses the exact same syntax as the source address in that it can be a network address and a wildcard mask or the `any` and `host` commands.

The following command would permit TCP from any host to the specific host 192.168.10.1. The host 192.168.10.1 has been entered as the destination address:

```
Router(config)#access-list 101 permit tcp any host 192.168.10.1
```

Now because we have used a transport layer protocol, TCP, we can now specify an operator to match against it. The full list of operators is shown here:

```
Router(config)#access-list 101 perm tcp any host 192.168.10.1 ?
  ack          Match on the ACK bit
  eq           Match only packets on a given port number
  established  Match established connections
  fin          Match on the FIN bit
  gt           Match only packets with a greater port number
  log          Log matches against this entry
  log-input    Log matches against this entry, including input
interface
  lt           Match only packets with a lower port number
  neq          Match only packets not on a given port number
  precedence   Match packets with given precedence value
  psh          Match on the PSH bit
  range        Match only packets in the range of port numbers
  rst          Match on the RST bit
  syn          Match on the SYN bit
  time-range   Specify a time-range
  tos          Match packets with given TOS value
  urg          Match on the URG bit
  <cr>
```

Note that `<cr>` is also displayed in the previous code. This indicates that at this point you can complete the access list by pressing the carriage return and all further commands are optional. We will continue to add a command that matches HTTP traffic. The most common operator from the list above is `eq`, which stands for equal and it is to match a specific transport layer port:

```
Router(config)#access-list 101 permit tcp any host 192.168.10.1 eq
```

From here, we can see the full list of transport layer protocols that can be named. Here is the full list:

```
Router(config)#access-list 101 perm tcp any host 192.168.10.1 eq ?
  <0-65535>    Port number
```

```
bgp            Border Gateway Protocol (179)
chargen        Character generator (19)
cmd            Remote commands (rcmd, 514)
daytime        Daytime (13)
discard        Discard (9)
domain         Domain Name Service (53)
echo           Echo (7)
exec           Exec (rsh, 512)
finger         Finger (79)
ftp            File Transfer Protocol (21)
ftp-data       FTP data connections (used infrequently, 20)
gopher         Gopher (70)
hostname       NIC hostname server (101)
ident          Ident Protocol (113)
irc            Internet Relay Chat (194)
klogin         Kerberos login (543)
kshell         Kerberos shell (544)
login          Login (rlogin, 513)
lpd            Printer service (515)
nntp           Network News Transport Protocol (119)
pim-auto-rp    PIM Auto-RP (496)
pop2           Post Office Protocol v2 (109)
pop3           Post Office Protocol v3 (110)
smtp           Simple Mail Transport Protocol (25)
sunrpc         Sun Remote Procedure Call (111)
syslog         Syslog (514)
tacacs         TAC Access Control System (49)
talk           Talk (517)
telnet         Telnet (23)
time           Time (37)
uucp           Unix-to-Unix Copy Program (540)
whois          Nicname (43)
www            World Wide Web (HTTP, 80)
```

This list gives you the Cisco name and also the full name and TCP port. As well as using the name, you can also just use the port number from 1 to 65,535. We are now going to add HTTP to the configuration. This can be accomplished by adding either the HTTP word or the number 80 after the command. To keep it simple, we will add the number 80:

```
Router(config)#access-list 101 permit tcp any host 192.168.10.1 eq 80
```

At this point, most access lists would be complete. At this point, however, you can repeat the last step and add more TCP ports, such as 23 and 21, to permit Telnet and FTP as well as HTTP.

You can see from the earlier example that extended IP access lists are very powerful, and extreme care must be taken when designing and implementing them. We are now going to show a few examples of extended access lists and explain exactly what each access list is designed to achieve.

The following access list would permit HTTP, Telnet, and FTP traffic from network 192.168.10.0 to any destination:

```
Router(config)#access-list 101 permit tcp 192.168.10.0 0.0.0.255
any eq 80
Router(config)#access-list 101 permit tcp 192.168.10.0 0.0.0.255
any eq 23
Router(config)#access-list 101 permit tcp 192.168.10.0 0.0.0.255
any eq 21
Router(config)#access-list 101 permit tcp 192.168.10.0 0.0.0.255
any eq 20
```

The following access list would permit SMTP traffic from host 192.168.10.1 to host 212.1.1.2. This can be used in your network if you are using an SMTP relay. Only SMTP traffic from 192.168.10.1 would be allowed through the router. All other SMTP traffic would be blocked by the second line. The third line enables all other IP-based traffic through the router:

```
Router(config)#access-list 101 permit tcp host 192.168.10.1 host
212.1.1.2 eq 25
Router(config)#access-list 101 deny tcp any any eq 25
Router(config)#access-list 101 permit ip any any
```

Once you have created the extended IP access list, you have to apply it to an interface. To do this, you use the `ip access-group` command from interface configuration mode. Interface configuration mode is entered by typing the following commands:

```
Router#config t
Router(config)#interface ethernet0
Router(config-if)#
```

These commands put you into interface configuration mode for the Ethernet interface 0. Once in interface configuration mode, you enter the following command to apply the access list to the interface:

```
Router(config-if)#ip access-group 101 in
```

This command would apply IP access list 101 to the inbound queue on this interface. The command to set it to the outbound queue would be

```
Router(config-if)#ip access-group 101 out
```

As you can see, you just use in or out after the access list number to indicate the direction of the access list on the interface.

We have provided an overview and explanation of standard and extended IP access lists and how to configure these. Next, we are going to explain wildcard masks.

IP Wildcard Masks   As explained in the two previous sections, IP wildcard masks are similar to subnet masks. Wildcard masks are responsible for masking out the portion of a network address for use in an IP access list.

With IP wildcard masks, basically a mask bit of 0 instructs the router to check the corresponding bit in the network address. A mask bit of 1 instructs the router to ignore the corresponding bit in the network address. Table 9-2 shows this with an explanation.

So, given the examples above, you can see that if you use a wildcard mask of 0.0.0.255, you are checking every bit in the first three octets and ignoring every bit in the last octet. A network address of 192.168.10.0 and a wildcard mask of 0.0.0.255 would produce the following results:

```
192.168.10.1 would pass
192.168.10.233 would pass
192.169.10.1 would fail
192.168.1.1 would fail
```

So how can this be used in access lists? If you want to permit all hosts from 192.168.10.0 to 192.168.10.7 in a single command, you can use the network address of 192.168.10.0 and the wildcard mask of 0.0.0.7. This would check the first three octets and the first five bits of the third octet. The only hosts that would be allowed would be 192.168.10.0 to 192.168.

	Explanation	**128**	**64**	**32**	**16**	**8**	**4**	**2**	**1**	**Decimal**
Table 9-2	Check all bits in network address	0	0	0	0	0	0	0	0	0
IP wildcard masks	Ignore all bits in network address	1	1	1	1	1	1	1	1	255
	Ignore first two bits	1	1	0	0	0	0	0	0	192
	Ignore last four bits	0	0	0	0	1	1	1	1	15
	Check last three bits	1	1	1	1	1	0	0	0	248
	Check first two bits	0	0	1	1	1	1	1	1	63

10.7. If a host has the network address of 192.168.10.8, then the fourth octet would not match.

IPX Access Lists

As well as IP access lists, IPX access lists also exist. They function in virtually the same way as IP access lists, and similar to IP access lists, two types of IPX access lists are used: standard and extended. Standard IPX access lists enable the traffic to be filtered by the source and destination network (IPX) address. This differs from standard IP access lists as standard IP access lists can only filter traffic based on the source IP address. Extended IPX access lists filter traffic based on the source and destination network address as well as the source and destination sockets. The socket is the transport layer equivalent of an IP port. Remember that extended IP access lists can only filter traffic based on the port. With IPX extended access lists, you can filter traffic based on the source and destination sockets.

Standard IPX Access Lists   IPX access lists in the range of 800 to 899 are classified as standard IPX access lists. Standard IPX access lists filter traffic based on the source IPX address and destination IPX address. This IPX address can be a network address, a network and node address, or any network. Figure 9-5 shows the standard IPX access list process.

Figure 9-5
Standard IPX access lists

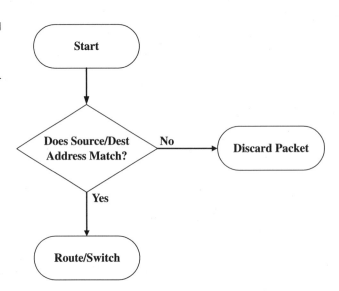

When the router receives the packet on an interface where a standard IPX access list is set, the router checks the source and destination IPX address of the packet against the access list. If the access list matches a permit statement, then the packet is allowed through. If the packet doesn't match a permit statement, then the packet is discarded. Once through or permitted, the packet is then routed to its destination by comparing the network address with the internal IPX routing table on the router.

Standard IPX access lists have to be entered into the router from global configuration mode. The following is an example of a standard IPX access list:

```
Router(config)#access-list 801 permit 100 -1
```

This IPX standard access list would permit any traffic from network 100 to any destination network.

NOTE: *In IPX access lists, –1 indicates any IPX network. The implicit* `deny all` *is also at the end of every IPX access list.*

As with IP standard access lists, the available options are permit or deny. As well as specifying the network address, you can also specify a host address. The following example expands the last to only enable a specific host access to a network:

```
Router(config)#access-list 801 deny 100.ac21.0002.2100 200
```

This access list denies the host 100.ac21.0002.2100 access to network 200.

Once you have created the standard IPX access list, you have to apply it to an interface. To do this, you use the `ipx access-group` command from interface configuration mode. Interface configuration mode is entered by typing the following commands:

```
Router#config t
Router(config)#interface ethernet0
Router(config-if)#
```

These commands put you into interface configuration mode for the Ethernet interface 0. Once in interface configuration mode, you enter the following command to apply the access list to the interface:

```
Router(config-if)#ipx access-group 801 in
```

This command would apply IPX access list 801 to the inbound queue on this interface. The command to set it to the outbound queue would be

```
Router(config-if)#ipx access-group 801 out
```

As you can see, you just use in or out after the access list number to indicate the direction of the access list on the interface.

We have provided an overview and explanation of standard IPX access lists and how to configure them. We are now going to move onto the extended IPX access lists. These offer even more features.

Extended IPX Access Lists   IPX access lists in the range of 900 to 999 are classified as extended IPX access lists. Extended IPX access lists can filter traffic based on the source IPX address/socket and destination IPX address/socket. Figure 9-6 shows the extended IPX access list process.

When the router receives the packet on an interface where an extended IPX access list is set, the router checks the source IPX address of the packet against the access list, then the destination IPX address, and lastly the sockets for both the source and destination. If the access list matches a permit statement, then the packet is allowed through. If the packet doesn't match a permit statement, then the packet is discarded. Once through or permitted, the packet is then routed to its destination by comparing the network address with the internal routing table on the router.

As with standard IPX access lists, extended IPX access lists have to be entered in global configuration mode. An extended IPX access list entails much more than what we have covered in this basic explanation, so we are going to provide a breakdown of what every configuration option is before we explain any example access lists.

To start with, we know that IPX extended access lists are in the range of 900 to 999, so the first start to the command syntax is

```
Router(config)#access-list 901
```

Next, you have to specify the permit or deny for the statement:

```
Router(config)#access-list 901 permit
```

This follows the same route as the standard IPX access lists. At this point, you specify the Novell protocol to filter. Here is a list of the available protocols:

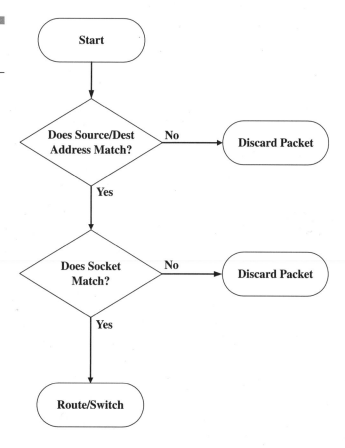

Figure 9-6
Extended IPX access
lists

```
Router(config)#access-list 901 permit ?
  <0-255>  Protocol type number (DECIMAL)
  any      Any IPX protocol type
  ncp      NetWare Core Protocol
  netbios  IPX NetBIOS
  rip      IPX Routing Information Protocol
  sap      Service Advertising Protocol
  spx      Sequenced Packet Exchange
```

For this example, we will filter the Novell SPX protocol, so we will enter this in the command syntax:

```
Router(config)#access-list 901 permit spx
```

The next step is to specify the source address and source socket. A difference in the IPX standard access lists is that you have to use the any command to specify any network. In this example, we will use the any command to specify any source:

```
Router(config)#access-list 901 permit spx any
```

The next component is the source socket. A list of the available sockets is displayed here:

```
Router(config)#access-list 901 permit spx any ?
  <0-FFFFFFFF>  Source Socket HEXADECIMAL
  all           All sockets
  cping         Cisco ipx ping
  diagnostic    Diagnostic packet
  eigrp         IPX Enhanced Interior Gateway Routing Protocol
  log           Log matches against this entry
  ncp           NetWare Core Protocol
  netbios       IPX NetBIOS
  nlsp          NetWare Link State Protocol
  nping         Standard IPX ping
  rip           IPX Routing Information Protocol
  sap           Service Advertising Protocol
  time-range    Specify a time-range
  trace         Trace Route packet
  <cr>
```

The <cr> indicates that all commands from this point onwards are optional and we could commit the access list now by pressing the carriage return. We are going to permit all source sockets so we use the `all` command:

```
Router(config)#access-list 901 permit spx any all
```

Next comes the destination network address and socket. We will use the network 100 and the socket RIP:

```
Router(config)#access-list 901 permit spx any all 100 rip
```

This is the completed IPX extended access list. This access list will permit all SPX traffic from any source address and all source sockets to network 100 on the socket that corresponds to IPX RIP.

Once you have created the extended IPX access list, you have to apply it to an interface. To do this, you use the `ipx access-group` command from interface configuration mode. Interface configuration mode is entered by typing the following commands:

```
Router#config t
Router(config)#interface ethernet0
Router(config-if)#
```

These commands put you into interface configuration mode for the Ethernet interface 0. Once in interface configuration mode, you enter the following command to apply the access list to the interface:

```
Router(config-if)#ipx access-group 901 in
```

This command would apply IPX access list 901 to the inbound queue on this interface. The command to set it to the outbound queue would be

```
Router(config-if)#ipx access-group 901 out
```

As you can see, you just use in or out after the access list number to indicate the direction of the access list on the interface.

Telnet VTY Access Restriction

You can restrict the Telnet VTY access to a router in two ways. The first is to filter out all inbound telnet traffic to the router. This is accomplished by an extended access list that blocks any source and any destination over port 23. Here's an example:

```
Router(config)#access-list 101 deny any any eq 23
```

This access list denies port 23 (Telnet) from any source to any destination. This has to be applied to an interface. The following command would apply this to the Ethernet 0 interface inbound:

```
Router(config-if)#ip access-group 101 in
```

Now no Telnet traffic will come inbound to the router through the Ethernet interface. This is well and good, but what happens if users require Telnet access through the router, and you want to disallow them access to the VTY lines on the router? This is where the second method comes into play. As well as assigning the access list to an interface, you can also assign it to the VTY lines on the router. This introduces another command, `access-class`. Using the same extended access list 101 from earlier, we can now apply this to the specific VTY lines on the router. The complete command syntax to do this is

```
Router(config)#line vty 0 4
Router(config-line)#access-class 101 in
```

The first line sets the line configuration mode from line 0 to line 4. These are all of the VTY lines available on the router. The second line, once in line configuration mode, sets the access list 101 inbound against the VTY lines.

This has the effect of blocking all Telnet access to the VTY ports but still allows Telnet traffic through the router. Another use of this would be to only allow specific users to access the VTY ports. This would be possible by permitting specific network addresses in the access list.

Named Access Lists

As well as access lists that are referred to by a number, you can also use named access lists. Named access lists make it easier to modify the access list as they facilitate the deletion of individual entries. With numbered access lists, you could only remove the entire list by using the no statement in front of the access list. You can also assign meaningful names to your access lists in order to help anyone looking at the configuration of the router. Named access lists are available for IP and IPX and support both standard and extended operations.

Named access lists are created from global configuration mode. We'll now demonstrate how to create a simple standard named access list. The first command to enter is the `ip access-list standard TestACL`. This creates a named access list called TestACL. The command tells the router that it is an IP standard access list. Notice that the router prompt changes from `Router(config)#` to `Router(config-std-nacl)#`. This indicates that we are in access list configuration mode. This is another new configuration mode and it is used specifically for named access lists.

```
Router(config)#ip access-list standard TestACL
Router(config-std-nacl)#
```

Next, we are going to add a few permit statements:

```
Router(config-std-nacl)#permit 192.168.10.0 0.0.0.255
Router(config-std-nacl)#permit 192.168.20.0 0.0.0.255
Router(config-std-nacl)#permit 192.168.30.0 0.0.0.255
```

Notice that these permit statements are entered directly from the prompt. You are already in access list configuration mode, so these commands are supported. The code enters three permit statements for networks 192.168.10.0, 192.168.20.0, and 192.168.30.0.

The full list of commands that are available from this configuration mode are as follows:

```
Router(config-std-nacl)#?
Standard Access List configuration commands:
  default  Set a command to its defaults
  deny     Specify packets to reject
  exit     Exit from access-list configuration mode
  no       Negate a command or set its defaults
  permit   Specify packets to forward
  remark   Access list entry comment
```

Typing Exit or pressing Ctrl-Z will take you back to exec mode. To apply the named access list to an interface, you use the ip access-group command from interface configuration mode. The following command would apply the named access list TestACL to the inbound queue on the interface:

```
Router(config-if)#ip access-group TestACL in
```

Breakout Box: Access List Tips and Tricks

We are now going to look at some tips and tricks on access lists. These will be very useful and time-saving when implementing access lists within your internetwork.

Applying Access Lists: Cut and Paste

Numbered access lists, once entered, cannot be modified. You have to remove the whole access list and retype it in. This is also true if you want to move a statement up or down in the access list. One way around this is by using the cut and paste functionality of your telnet/terminal client.

Once the access list is entered, simply highlight the entire access list from the output of a show running-configuration command. Then either cut or copy this information to the clipboard. Then go to global configuration mode and type no access-list 101 where 101 is the number of the access list you want to remove.

At this point, the access list is completely removed from the router. Now paste the access list into a text editor. Make the required changes and copy the new access list back into the clipboard. From global configuration mode you can now paste this information back to the router and the whole access list will be re-entered automatically with the changes intact. This is the reason why advanced access lists are better being named instead of numbered. With named access lists, you can remove and move around a single statement line without affecting the entire access list.

Access List Order

Access lists function from the top down and it is important to realize this. Once a match is made in the access list, either permit or deny, then the access list stops for that particular packet. No statements lower down will be checked. This has to be thought about when designing the access list as traffic permitted lower down may be denied higher up. This has the affect that the traffic is always denied by the higher statement.

As a design rule with access lists, always permit the majority of the traffic as high up the access list as possible. Each access list statement takes CPU time and increases latency, so it makes sense to have the rules that are matched the most towards the top of the list. The implicit `deny all` at the bottom of the access list is not visible but will always deny all traffic that doesn't match a previous access list permit or deny statement.

Monitoring and Verifying Access Lists

A few IOS commands can be used to monitor and verify the access lists configured on a Cisco router. These commands include

- `Show running-configuration`
- `Show ip interface`
- `Show ip access-list`
- `Show access-list`

Each of these tools is broken down and explained in the next sections. A detailed output will be given for each tool along with a supporting explanation.

Show running-configuration

Show running-configuration is one of the most useful commands for displaying information about access lists. From exec mode, simply type show run to display the output. Below we have provided sample output with the parts relative to access lists displayed:

```
!
access-list 1 permit 192.168.10.2
access-list 1 permit 192.168.10.3
access-list 1 permit 192.168.10.1
access-list 1 permit 192.168.10.4
access-list 1 deny    192.168.30.0 0.0.0.255
access-list 1 deny    192.168.50.0 0.0.0.255
access-list 101 permit tcp any 192.168.10.0 0.0.0.255 eq www
access-list 101 permit tcp any 192.168.10.0 0.0.0.255 eq ftp
access-list 101 permit tcp any 192.168.10.0 0.0.0.255 eq telnet
access-list 101 deny    udp any 192.168.0.0 0.0.255.255 eq domain
access-list 101 permit ip any any
access-list 801 permit 100.ac21.0002.2100 100
access-list 901 permit spx any all 100 rip
access-list 901 permit spx any ncp any
!
```

This output shows that access lists 1, 101, 801, and 901 are all configured on this router. You can also check each access list to ensure that it is doing exactly what it is supposed to be doing.

show ip interface

The show ip interface command displays detailed information about all interfaces on the router that are configured for IP. The useful part of information that is in relation to access lists is that it shows you which access lists are applied to the interface inbound and outbound:

```
Ethernet0 is up, line protocol is up
  Internet address is 194.73.134.242/24
  Broadcast address is 255.255.255.255
  Address determined by non-volatile memory
  MTU is 1500 bytes
  Helper address is not set
  Directed broadcast forwarding is disabled
  Outgoing access list is 1
  Inbound  access list is not set
  Proxy ARP is enabled
  Security level is default
  Split horizon is enabled
```

```
ICMP redirects are always sent
ICMP unreachables are always sent
ICMP mask replies are never sent
IP fast switching is enabled
IP fast switching on the same interface is disabled
IP Flow switching is disabled
IP Feature Fast switching turbo vector
IP multicast fast switching is enabled
IP multicast distributed fast switching is disabled
Router Discovery is disabled
IP output packet accounting is disabled
IP access violation accounting is disabled
TCP/IP header compression is disabled
RTP/IP header compression is disabled
Probe proxy name replies are disabled
Policy routing is disabled
Network address translation is disabled
WCCP Redirect outbound is disabled
WCCP Redirect exclude is disabled
BGP Policy Mapping is disabled
```

This code shows us that the outgoing access list is standard IP access list number 1 and that the inbound access list is not set. This information is useful for ascertaining if there is a problem communicating through the router. Sometimes engineers may apply the access list to the outbound queue on the router instead of the inbound queue. Looking at the results of this command makes it easy to see which access lists are applied where.

show ip access-list

The `show ip access-list` command displays details about the IP access lists configured on the router:

```
Router#sh ip access-lists
Standard IP access list 1
    permit 192.168.10.2
    permit 192.168.10.3
    permit 192.168.10.1
    permit 192.168.10.4
    deny    192.168.30.0, wildcard bits 0.0.0.255
    deny    192.168.50.0, wildcard bits 0.0.0.255
Extended IP access list 101
    permit tcp any 192.168.10.0 0.0.0.255 eq www
    permit tcp any 192.168.10.0 0.0.0.255 eq ftp
    permit tcp any 192.168.10.0 0.0.0.255 eq telnet
    deny udp any 192.168.0.0 0.0.255.255 eq domain
    permit ip any any
Router#
```

You can see from this output that IP access lists 1 and 101 are configured on this router. This command displays output similar to the output obtained from the show run command. Only IP access lists are shown here and any IPX or AppleTalk access lists will not show up.

show access-lists

The show access-list command displays information about all configured access lists on the router. This command displays information about every access list, regardless of protocol:

```
Router#sh access-lists
IPX standard access list 801
    permit 100.ac21.0002.2100 100
IPX extended access list 901
    permit spx any all 100 rip
    permit spx any ncp any
Standard IP access list 1
    permit 192.168.10.2
    permit 192.168.10.3
    permit 192.168.10.1
    permit 192.168.10.4
    deny   192.168.30.0, wildcard bits 0.0.0.255
    deny   192.168.50.0, wildcard bits 0.0.0.255
Extended IP access list 101
    permit tcp any 192.168.10.0 0.0.0.255 eq www
    permit tcp any 192.168.10.0 0.0.0.255 eq ftp
    permit tcp any 192.168.10.0 0.0.0.255 eq telnet
    deny udp any 192.168.0.0 0.0.255.255 eq domain
    permit ip any any
Router#
```

This command is similar in output as the show ip access-list command. The difference is that show access-list shows you the access list details for all types of access lists and not just IP access lists.

Chapter Summary

This chapter has looked at traffic management using access lists. We have covered access lists for the IP and IPX protocols. These access lists were further broken down to include standard and extended versions. We then looked at named access lists and provided some useful tips and tricks for access list usage. The last section looked at monitoring and verifying access lists.

Access lists are very useful tools to use in your internetwork. Careful design and planning has to be undertaken to ensure correct operation. Don't forget the implicit `deny all` at the end of every access list.

Frequently Asked Questions (FAQ)

Question: What is the difference between an IP standard and an IP extended access list?

Answer: IP standard access lists can only filter on the source address. IP extended access lists can filter on the source address, destination address, and transport layer port.

Question: What happens if you do not permit traffic in the access list. If it isn't caught by a deny statement, will it still get through?

Answer: No, at the end of every access list is an implicit `deny all`. This catches and denies all traffic that you have not specifically permitted.

Question: Do you have to apply an access list to an interface?

Answer: You do not have to apply any access lists to any interfaces, but they will not filter traffic on the interface if you don't.

Question: How many access lists can you have per interface?

Answer: You can only have one inbound and one outbound access list per interface.

Questions

1. What is the number range for standard IP access lists?

   a. 1–99
   b. 100–199
   c. 200–299
   d. 400–499

2. What mode do you have to be in to enter an access list?

   a. Global Configuration
   b. Interface Configuration
   c. Exec
   d. User

3. You have an access list numbered 834. What type is this?

   a. IP standard
   b. IPX extended
   c. IPX standard
   d. IPX SAP

4. Which command displays the content of an access list?

   a. `show all access list`
   b. `show access-list`
   c. `show interface access list`
   d. `write access-lists`

5. Which command will display information about IP access lists only?

   a. `router(config)#show access list`
   b. `router#show ip access list`
   c. `router#show ip access-list`
   d. `router(config)#show ip access-list`

6. What is the number range for an IPX extended access list?

   a. 1000–1099
   b. 100–199
   c. 800–899
   d. 900–999

7. Which protocol is the number range 600–699 related to?

   a. IPX
   b. IP
   c. Vines
   d. AppleTalk

8. With an outbound access list, is the access list applied before or after routing?

    a. Before

    b. After

9. The two main statements in an access list enable you to _____ or _____ traffic. Choose two.

    a. permit

    b. hold

    c. deny

    d. filter

10. What is the following access list designed to do: `access-list 800 deny 100 200`?

    a. Deny IP subnet 100 from subnet 200.

    b. Deny IPX traffic from network 100 to get to network 200.

    c. Deny SAP traffic communication between 100 and 200 networks.

    d. Deny type 200 packets from network 100.

11. What is the number range for IPX SAP access lists?

    a. 1000–1099

    b. 1–99

    c. 100–199

    d. 900–999

12. Which command refers to all networks in an IPX standard access list?

    a. any

    b. −1

    c. all

    d. 1

13. Which of the following access lists would disable all SMTP traffic?

    a. `access-list 101 deny tcp any any eq 80`

    b. `access-list 101 deny tcp any any eq 25`

    c. `access-list 101 deny tcp any any eq 21`

    d. `access-list 101 deny tcp any any eq 23`

14. What is the number range for IPX standard access lists?

    a. 1–99

    b. 100–199

    c. 800–899

    d. 900–999

15. With an inbound access list, is the access list processed before or after routing?

    a. Before

    b. After

16. How many access lists can be applied to an interface?

    a. One

    b. Two

    c. Four

    d. 255

17. What is at the end of every access list?

    a. `Deny all`

    b. `Permit all`

    c. `Deny host`

    d. `Permit host`

18. When applying an access list to an interface. You can specify the access list to be _____ or _____. Choose two.

    a. inbound

    b. recursive

    c. outbound

    d. static

19. Which of the following standard IP access lists are incorrect?

    a. `access-list 1 permit any`

    b. `access-list 101 permit 192.168.10.0 0.0.0.255`

    c. `access-list 54 permit 192.168.20.0 0.0.0.255`

    d. `access-list 99 permit host 12.2.3.4`

20. What is the number range for IP extended access lists?

    a. 1–99

    b. 100–199

    c. 200–299

    d. 400–499

Answers

1. **a.** 1–99

   The correct number range for standard IP access lists is 1–99.

2. **a.** Global configuration

   You have to be in global configuration mode to enter access list information.

3. **c.** IPX standard

   This access list will be an IPX standard as 834 falls in the 800–899 standard IPX access list range.

4. **b.** `show access-list`

   The correct command to display the contents of an access list is `show access-list`.

5. **c.** `router#show ip access-list`

   The correct command is `router#show ip access-list`. Note you have to be in exec mode, not global configuration mode. There is also a hyphen between access and list.

6. **d.** 900–999

   The correct range for IPX extended access lists is 900–999.

7. **d.** AppleTalk

   AppleTalk uses the access list range 600–699.

8. **b.** After

   Outbound access lists are applied after the traffic has been routed.

9. **a.** permit and **c.** deny

   The two main statements in an access list enable you to permit or deny traffic.

10. **b.** Deny IPX traffic from network 100 to get to network 200.

    The access list denies IPX traffic from network 100 to get to network 200.

11. **a.** 1000–1099

    IPX SAP access lists are the number range 1000–1099.

12. **b.** −1

    In an IPX standard access list −1 specifies any network.

13. b. `access-list 101 deny tcp any any eq 25`

SMTP uses TCP port 25. The correct access list therefore would be `access-list 101 deny tcp any any eq 25`.

14. c. 800–899

The correct range for IPX standard access lists is 800–899.

15. a. Before

Inbound access lists are applied before the traffic is routed.

16. b. Two

You can only apply two access lists per interface, one outbound and one inbound.

17. a. `Deny all`

An implicit `deny all` is at the end of every access list.

18. a. inbound and **c.** outbound

Access lists can be applied to interfaces either inbound or outbound.

19. b. `access-list 101 permit 192.168.10.0 0.0.0.255`

The following access list `access-list 101 permit 192.168.10.0 0.0.0.255` is numbered 101. Therefore, this is not classified as a standard IP access list, but an extended IP access list.

20. b. 100–199

The correct range for IP extended access lists is 100–199.

CHAPTER 10

Internetwork Packet Exchange (IPX)

Objectives

This chapter describes the *Internetwork Packet Exchange/Sequenced Packet Exchange* (IPX/SPX) protocol suite and the underlying protocols and functions that operate within IPX/SPX. The operation of IPX and the routing protocols that route IPX over a *Wide Area Network* (WAN) are explained. This chapter will also describe the steps to configure IPX on Cisco routers as well as implementing IPX access lists and SAP filters.

On completion of this chapter, you will be able to do the following:

- Describe basic IPX operations.
- Determine the required IPX network number and encapsulation type for a given interface.
- Enable the Novell IPX protocol.
- Configure and monitor IPX access lists and SAP traffic filters.

Introduction to IPX Protocols

IPX is a part of the IPX/SPX suite, a proprietary suite of protocols from Novell. The IPX/SPX suite is derived from the *Xerox Network Systems* (XNS) protocol suite. The IPX/SPX protocol suite is similar to the TCP/IP protocol suite in that many other protocols coexist and interact within the suite.

NetWare is a network operating system developed by Novell to enable seamless file and print services as well as database access and e-mail services to workstations using the Novell Client. NetWare uses IPX as its default protocol. Therefore, IPX has a large prevalence in today's LANs, as many of them run Novell NetWare servers. IPX/SPX is not as efficient as TCP/IP. With the ever-increasing use of the Internet and the efficient use in networks, TCP/IP is the de facto standard protocol for today's networks. Novell has realized this and has made TCP/IP the default protocol in NetWare 5.0.

IPX, SPX, SAP, NCP, and NetBIOS

IPX works at layer three of the OSI model. It was derived from XNS's *Internet Datagram Protocol* (IDP). IPX provides network layer addresses assigned to nodes. These addresses are represented as hexadecimal numbers and are 80 bits long. They consist of both the network number and the node number. IPX provides connectionless datagram delivery similar to UDP in the TCP/IP protocol suite. It does not require an acknowledgment from the end device. IPX uses sockets to communicate with the upper layer protocols, much like TCP/IP ports. Sockets enable IPX to handle multiple sessions on the same machine. The minimum IPX packet size is 30 bytes, and the maximum packet size is 65,535 bytes. Each IPX packet has a 30-byte packet header, as illustrated in Figure 10-1. The numbers in brackets are represented as bytes. The following section will describe each field in the IPX header.

The *Checksum* field contains a two-byte value used to verify packet integrity. The checksum was not used in NetWare systems until the release of NetWare 4.x, which enables the use of the checksum field, if desired. The reason that the checksum field is not required is because a *Cyclic Redundancy Check* (CRC) check is already done on the entire frame and data. The checksum field only verifies the IPX header. The checksum field cannot be used with the Novell Ethernet_802.3 frame type because the checksum field is used to indicate that the frame is a NetWare packet.

The *Packet Length* field contains a two-byte value defining the length of the entire packet. This includes the IPX header, which is 30 bytes.

The *Transport Control* is a one-byte field that indicates the number of routers (hops) a packet has traversed to reach its destination. This value starts at zero and can be as high as 15 in IPX Routing Information Protocol-enabled (RIP) networks. Each router that receives the packet will increment this value by one. After the packet has reached its sixteenth hop, the

Figure 10-1

An IPX header

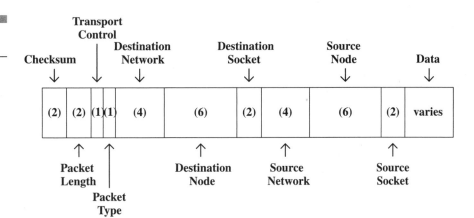

router will discard the packet. The use of the *NetWare Link Services Protocol* (NLSP) will enable the hop count to reach as high as 127 hops.

The *Packet Type* is a one-byte field indicating the type of service the packet will use. Table 10-1 lists the optional packet types.

The *Destination Network* field contains the four-byte network address of the destination node. This field is set to 0x00-00-00-00 if the packet is destined for the same network as the source node and will not be passed on by a router. However, a special case occurs when the workstation first initializes and sends out the *Service Advertisement Protocol* (SAP) *Get Nearest Server* (GNS) and RIP Get Local Target broadcast requests. The workstation sets its Source and Destination Network fields to zero (0x00-00-00-00) because it does not yet know which network it belongs to. The router will receive this request and will reply directly to the workstation, filling in the Source and Destination Network fields.

The *Destination Node* is a six-byte field that contains the node address of the destination node. A workstation can broadcast to all nodes on the local network by setting its Destination Node field to 0xFF-FF-FF-FF. This field will contain a value of 0x00-00-00-00 if the packet is destined for a NetWare 3.x or 4.x server. The destination server's actual hardware address will be in the Destination Address field of the Ethernet or Token Ring frame.

The *Destination Socket* is a two-byte field defining the socket address of the packet destination process. Sockets are used to route packets to different processes within a single node. Table 10-2 lists some processes with their corresponding socket numbers.

Table 10-1

Packet type
descriptions

Packet Type	Field Value (Hexadecimal)	Purpose
NLSP	0x00	NLSP packets
Routing information	0x01	RIP packets
Service advertising	0x04	SAP packets
Sequenced	0x05	SPX packets
NCP	0x11	NCP packets
Propagated	0x14	NetBIOS and other propagated packets

Table 10-2

Socket numbers
and their
associated
processes

Socket Number	Process
0x451	NCP
0x452	SAP
0x453	RIP
0x455	Novell NetBIOS
0x456	Novell Diagnostics
0x457	Serialization packet
0x9001	NLSP
0x9004	IPXWAN protocol

The *Source Network* contains a four-byte field that defines the source network address to which the source node is attached. The source node will set this field to 0 (0x00-00-00-00) if the source network is unknown. If the source node is a NetWare 3.x or 4.x server, it will set this field to the internal IPX address.

The *Source Node* is a six-byte field containing the address of the source node. This field cannot contain a broadcast address (0xFF-FF-FF-FF-FF-FF).

The *Source Socket* contains a two-byte field defining the socket number of the process from the source node transmitting the packet. Servers will reply from defined socket numbers, whereas workstations will use dynamically assigned socket numbers ranging from 0x4000 to 0x8000.

The *Data* field is of varying lengths and contains the data portion of the packet. This field is not included as part of the IPX header.

SPX

SPX, derived from the *Sequenced Packet Protocol* (SPP) of the XNS protocol, works at layer four of the OSI model and provides connection-oriented services to network applications that require a connection-oriented session. Novell's *Remote Console* (RCONSOLE), *Print Server* (PSERVER) and *Remote Printer* (RPRINTER) are all examples of programs that use SPX communications. SPX uses virtual circuits to establish sessions between nodes. Each virtual circuit is identified by a connection ID in the SPX header. An SPX header contains all the same fields as an IPX header, with an additional 12 bytes. These 12 bytes contain sequence and

Figure 10-2
An SPX header

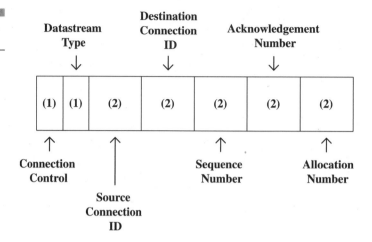

Table 10-3

Connection
Control field
values, names, and
descriptions

Value	Name	Description
0x04 (Introduced in SPX II)	Size	Negotiation size request/response
0x08 (Introduced in SPX II)	SPX2	SPX II type packet
0x10	End-of-Message	Indicates that the client requests to end the session
0x20	Attention	This field is not presently in use.
0x40	Acknowledgment Required	Data has been sent, and acknowledgment is required.
0x80	System Packet	Acknowledgement packet; this value is only used internally.

acknowledgement fields to support the connection-oriented services that SPX provides. The SPX header is 42 bytes long, as illustrated in Figure 10-2. The numbers in brackets are represented as bytes.

The *Connection Control* field contains a one-byte value that controls the bidirectional flow of data. Table 10-3 lists the possible values for this field.

The *Datastream Type* field contains a one-byte value that indicates the type of data stored in the packet. The value can be defined by the client or can contain one of the following values listed in Table 10-4.

Table 10-4

Datastream Type field values, names, and descriptions

Value	Name	Description
0xFC	Orderly release request	(Introduced in SPX II)
0xFD	Orderly release acknowledgement	(Introduced in SPX II)
0xFE	End-of-Connection	Indicates that the client requests to end the session
0xFF	End-of-Connection Acknowledgment	Transmitted after an End-of-Connection request is received

The *Source Connection ID* field contains a two-byte number defined by the source node. SPX may have multiple sessions running on a single machine, using the same socket numbers. To distinguish between each session, a virtual connection is identified with a number. The source node will use this number in the Source Connection ID field and the receiving station will use this same number in its Destination Connection ID field.

The *Destination Connection ID* field was described briefly in the last paragraph. It also contains a two-byte, connection ID number of the destination node. This field is set to 0xFFFF during the initial connection establishment. This is because the sending node does not yet know which number the destination node will use.

The *Sequence Number* field contains a two-byte value for the number of data packets sent by a single node. This value is incremented after receiving an acknowledgement for a data packet transmitted. This value does not increase after sending an acknowledgement packet.

The *Acknowledge Number* field contains a two-byte sequence number that is expected in the next SPX packet from the responding SPX node. This field is similar to the Acknowledgement number in TCP/IP. If the sequence number is incorrect, the receiving node assumes that an error occurred during transmission of the packet and will request a retransmission of the packet.

The *Allocation Number* field contains a two-byte value indicating the number of receive buffers at a workstation. The value starts at zero, which means that a value of four would equal five packet receive buffers. Each time the receiving station receives a packet, it increments this value. These buffers are then freed up each time a receiving device processes information.

NOTE: *Novell created an enhanced version of SPX called SPX II. SPX II was first implemented in NetWare 4.x. Enhancements include packet sizes up to the MTU of the network and more efficient windowing features. With the original SPX, packet size was limited to 576 bytes, including the 42-byte header. The original SPX also only allowed one packet to be sent at a time before receiving an acknowledgement. SPX II enables multiple packets to be sent before receiving an acknowledgement, thus greatly improving efficiency.*

SAP

SAP enables an end device to locate network services and servers to advertise their services and addresses to other servers and routers. SAP is a broadcast-type packet, and when a NetWare server is configured, it will send SAP broadcasts out every 60 seconds.

The three types of SAP packets are as follows:

- *Periodic updates* These are used by NetWare servers to advertise a list of their services and addresses on to the local network for other servers and routers to store. They are sent out every 60 seconds and can contain up to seven entries with a maximum packet size of 576 bytes. The servers and routers store the updates in their own *server information tables* (SITs). The SIT at each server or router stores a complete list of the available services on the network. The periodic updates are not sent across router boundaries. However, routers will build their own SAP table and will forward the complete SAP table to other routers. By default, this process happens every 60 seconds. However, the interval at which routers forward the SAP table is configurable. This process lets clients find remote services across the WAN. Each SAP update contains a hexadecimal number identifying the type of server that is broadcasting its services. Table 10-5 lists some examples of the different SAP updates.

- *Service queries* Clients do not receive SAP broadcasts. Instead, a client will send a service query SAP when it wants to know about services available on the network. Two types of service queries are available: General Service queries and Nearest Service queries. The most popular type of service query is the GNS request. It is used to find the nearest server, depending upon the type of service that is required. The service query packets define which type of server they are requesting. Figure 10-3 illustrates the service query packet format. The numbers in brackets are represented as bytes.

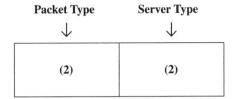

Figure 10-3
SAP service query
packet format

The service query packet follows the IPX header and defines both the
packet type and the server type that is requested. The *Packet Type* field
is a two-byte value defining whether the packet is a General Service
query with a value of 0x0001 or a Nearest Service query with a value of
0x0003. The *Service Type* field is a two-byte field defining the type of
service required in the request. Table 10-5 lists some of the possible
server types available, as defined by Novell.

■ *Service responses*   Service responses are used to reply to service
queries. Two types of service response packets exist: General Service
responses and Nearest Service responses. General Service responses
are used for service information broadcasts. Each General Service
response packet can contain information about a maximum of seven
servers. If the server needs to respond with additional servers available
for the request, an additional General Service response will have to be
sent. The Nearest Service response, also known as Get Nearest Server
response, contains information about only one server. The server listed
in the response will be the closest, in hops away, from the requester.
Figure 10-4 illustrates a Service Response packet. The numbers in
brackets are represented as bytes.

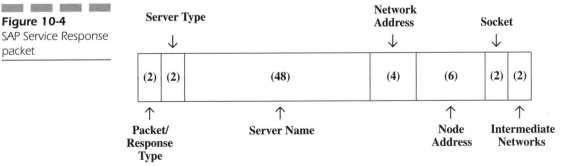

Figure 10-4
SAP Service Response
packet

Table 10-5

SAP Service Type
options

Type	Service
0X0001	User
0X0002	User group
0X0003	Print server queue
0X0004	File server
0X0005	Job server
0x0007	Print server
0x0009	Archive server
0x000A	Job server queue
0x002E	Dynamic SAP
0x0047	Advertising print server
0X004B	Btrieve VAP 5.0
0X004C	SQL VAP
0X007A	TES, NetWare for VMS
0x0098	Access server
0x009A	Named pipes server
0X009E	Portable NetWare, UNIX
0X0102	RCONSOLE
0x0111	Test server
0x0166	NetWare management (NMS)
0x026A	NetWare management (NMS console)
0x026B	Time synchronization (NetWare 4.x and later)
0x0278	Directory services (NetWare 4.x and later)

The *Packet / Response Type* is a two-byte field identifying the type of service response. The two possible values are 0x0002, for SAP General Service responses, or 0x0004, for Nearest Service responses.

The *Server Type* is a two-byte field identifying the type of service available. The list of possible server types is listed in Table 10-5.

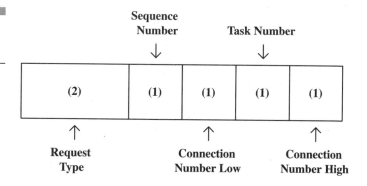

Figure 10-5
An NCP Request header

The *Server Name* is a 48-byte field containing the object name of the server. The server name must be unique per server type. For example, a file server (0x0004) can have the same name as a job server (0x0005). However, two file servers (0x0004) cannot use the same name. If a server's name is less than 48 bytes long, the field will be padded with zeros following the server name to maintain the 48-byte field length.

The *Network Address* is a four-byte field identifying the network address of the server.

The *Node Address* is a six-byte field identifying the node address of the server. This field will contain a value of 0x00-00-00-00-00-01 for NetWare 3.x and 4.x servers.

The *Socket* field contains a two-byte value identifying the socket number that the server will use to receive service requests for the server type.

NCP

The *NetWare Core Protocol* (NCP) is the protocol used for client and server communication. Clients send NCP requests to the server for file access and transfers, drive mappings, directory searches, print queue statuses, and more. NetWare servers reply to these requests with NCP replies. Once the server has processed and completed the request, the workstation will terminate the connection by sending a Destroy Service Connection request to the server.

An NCP header follows the frame and IPX/SPX header. An NCP Request header defines the service warranted by the sending workstation. The header is used in all communication from the client to the server and is six bytes long, followed by other NCP information defining the client's request. Figure 10-5 illustrates a NCP Request header. The numbers in brackets are represented as bytes.

The *Request Type* field contains a two-byte value indicating the type of request sent from the client to the server. Table 10-6 lists the possible request-type values.

Clients use the Create Service Connection and specify 1111 in the Request Type field to connect to a server. The client then sends a Destroy Service Connection and specifies 5555 in the Request Type field to detach from a server. Clients will specify 2222 in the Request Type field to request general services and will specify 7777 when using the Burst Mode protocol.

The *Sequence Number* field contains a one-byte value used to track the sequence of communication between the client and the server. The client will add a one to the last sequence number and place that value in this field.

The *Connection Number Low* field is a one-byte value containing the service connection number assigned to the client by the server upon login.

The *Task Number* field contains a one-byte value indicating which client task is making the request. The client will set this value to zero when all tasks have been executed.

The *Connection Number High* field is used in the 1000-user versions of NetWare. All other NetWare versions will have a value of 0x00 in this field.

The NCP Reply is used by the server to respond to NCP requests. The NCP Reply header follows the frame and IPX/SPX header. It also adds two additional fields to the NCP Request header. Figure 10-6 illustrates an NCP Reply header. The numbers in brackets are represented as bytes.

The *Reply Type* is a two-byte field containing the type of reply that the server is using to respond to the NCP Request. Table 10-7 lists the possible NCP Reply types.

The server will respond to most requests with a service reply, using 3333 as the value in the Reply Type field. If a workstation sends a NCP request and does not receive a response within a specified amount of time, it will send another NCP request. The server will receive the request and will respond with a Request Being Processed NCP reply by using 9999 in the

Table 10-6 NCP Request Types	**Value**	**Description**
	1111	Create Service Connection
	2222	Service Request
	5555	Destroy Service Connection
	7777	Burst Mode Transfer

Figure 10-6
An NCP Reply header

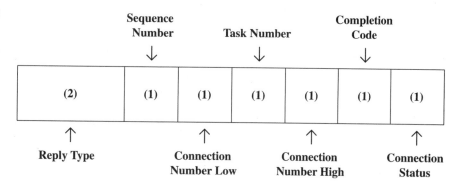

Table 10-7

The NCP Reply Types

Value	Description
3333	Service Reply
7777	Burst Mode Connection
9999	Request Being Processed

Reply Type field. The Burst Mode Connection with the 7777 value is used when using Burst Mode to transfer files.

The *Completion Code* is a one-byte field added for the NCP Reply header. The Completion Code is used to indicate that the request was processed correctly. If an error occurs on the server while processing the request, it will use a number in this field to indicate that an error occurred during the process. If the server completes the request successfully, it will use a zero in this field.

The *Connection Status Flags* field is a one-byte value indicating the connection status between the client and the server. The server will mark the fourth bit in this byte as one when the Down command is issued at the server.

NCP also uses a term called *function codes*. These function codes work in conjunction with the NCP Reply and Request headers to specify specific functions that the client is requesting, such as opening a file. Some functions apply to a range of functions and require subfunction codes.

NetBIOS

Network Basic Input/Output System (NetBIOS) is a non-routable protocol that can be used over IPX to obtain information about the named nodes on the network. NetBIOS is a broadcast-type protocol that uses type-20 broadcast packets to flood the network. Routers do not forward broadcasts, so to propagate the type-20 broadcasts to external networks, the router's IPX interfaces, either Ethernet or Token Ring and Serial, must be configured to enable the type-20 broadcasts to be forwarded.

NetBIOS uses a type-20 (0x14) IPX packet with a socket number of 0x455 to identify itself as a NetBIOS packet. The Destination Node field in the IPX header is set to 0xFF-FF-FF-FF-FF-FF. Figure 10-7 shows how routers must be configured to forward IPX NetBIOS packets.

Routing IPX with RIP, NLSP, and EIGRP

RIP is a distance vector routing protocol derived from XNS and uses IPX to route over the WAN. RIP exchanges IPX routing information to neighboring IPX routers. As soon as new routing information is learned, an IPX RIP router will immediately broadcast its entire routing table to its neighboring routers. Those routers will then broadcast their routing tables to their neighboring routers until all the IPX RIP routers in the WAN have been updated with the new routing information. The time that it takes to complete this entire process is called the *convergence time*. IPX RIP will also send periodic routing updates every 60 seconds to its neighboring routers.

Figure 10-7
An IPX NetBIOS example

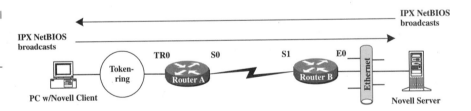

Configuration - Router A	Configuration - Router B
hostname RouterA	hostname RouterB
!	!
ipx routing 00e0.00a4.1579	ipx routing 00e0.00a4.ee1c
!	!
interface TokenRing0	interface Ethernet0
ipx network 100	ipx network 150
ring-speed 16	ipx type-20-propogation
ipx type-20-propogation	!
!	interface Serial1
interface Serial0	bandwidth 128
bandwidth 128	ipx network 200
ipx network 200	ipx type-20-propogation
ipx type-20-propogation	

This happens even if no new changes take place in the network. These broadcasts can often cause excessive overhead traffic in the network, leading to oversubscribed circuits and latency delays for other types of traffic trying to traverse the network.

IPX RIP uses two metrics during its routing decision process. These metrics are ticks (delay) and hop count (the number of routers a packet traverses to get to its destination). One tick is equal to 1/18 of a second. The router will first look at the tick count of the route to determine which path to take. The route with the lowest tick count, or delay, will be chosen as the best path to the destination. If two routes exist with the same tick count, the router will choose the route with the lowest hop count to the destination. The hop count is determined by counting the number of routers that the packet will traverse to reach the destination router. The maximum hop count used by IPX RIP is 15. This means that the packet will be discarded after it has reached its sixteenth hop. The hop count is incremented and counted in the Transport Control field of the IPX header. The reason for the maximum hop count used by RIP is to alleviate routing loops in the network. Figure 10-8 illustrates an example.

In this example, San Jose needs to send data to New York. San Jose has a 56K connection to Chicago and a T1 connection to Dallas. New York has T1 connections to both Miami and Chicago. IPX RIP will first look at the tick information to decide which path it will take to reach New York. Even though there are less hops (two) from San Jose to New York via the Chicago router, the 56K connection is much less desirable than a T1 connection. The cumulative ticks from the source to the destination calculate the tick count. This cumulative tick count is passed via IPX RIP updates. So assuming that the 56K link is being saturated with a large amount of traffic, the tick count for the path over the 56K link to New York will be higher than the tick

Figure 10-8

RIP example

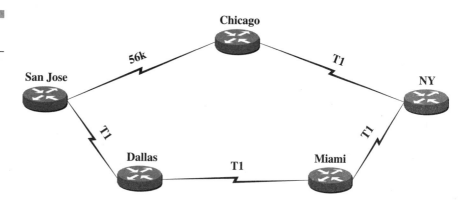

count for the path through Dallas and Miami. Therefore, IPX RIP will find that the tick count is smaller via the route to Dallas and Miami to get to New York, and this is the best route that will be chosen by the San Jose router. If it is decided to upgrade the 56K connection to a T1, then the San Jose router would choose the path to New York via the Chicago router because of a lower tick value.

However, circumstances may occur where the route through the 56K link will be chosen. This may occur if little to no traffic is traversing the link. This will cause the delay time to be low and the router will maintain a low tick count across this link. This would ultimately result in the San Jose router sending packets across the 56K link to Chicago to get to New York. To alleviate this problem, the tick count can be inflated so that the San Jose router will never choose the route through the 56K link over the route through Dallas and Miami.

This example also shows the configuration of the San Jose router. The tick count can be manually adjusted by using the following command in interface configuration mode:

```
Router(config-if)#ipx delay tick
```

The `tick` portion of the command will be replaced with a number to define the tick count. By default, all LAN interfaces have a RIP delay of one and all WAN interfaces have a delay of six. The higher the tick count, the less desirable the link becomes.

EIGRP

The *Enhanced Interior Gateway Routing Protocol* (EIGRP) is a hybrid routing protocol, using some of the advantages of a link-state routing protocol and a distance vector routing protocol. EIGRP is a more efficient protocol with a faster convergence time over IPX RIP. The only drawback is that EIGRP can only be used on the WAN links. This means that IPX RIP will be used on the LAN and either static routes will have to be entered for the NetWare servers to access routers across the WAN or redistribution must be done at the router. By default, EIGRP redistributes IPX RIP internal routes into EIGRP external routes and EIGRP routes into IPX RIP. Figure 10-9 shows a basic IPX EIGRP configuration.

Going through the configurations, the relevant commands will be discussed. The first command is `ipx routing`. This command starts the IPX routing process and will take the Media Access Control (MAC) address of the router for the node address unless a node address is specifically defined. This command is entered in global configuration mode.

```
Router(config)#ipx routing [node]
```

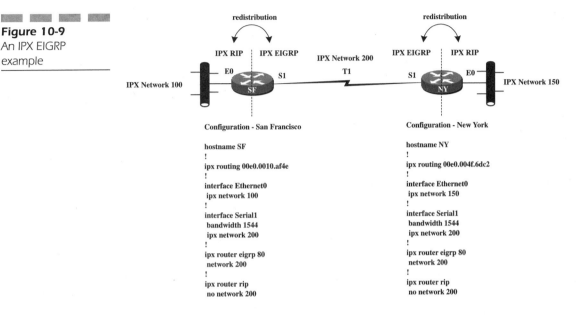

Figure 10-9
An IPX EIGRP
example

> redistribution
>
> **IPX RIP** | **IPX EIGRP**
>
> E0
> S1
>
> **SF**
>
> **IPX Network 100**
>
> **IPX Network 200**
> T1
>
> redistribution
>
> **IPX EIGRP** | **IPX RIP**
>
> S1
> E0
>
> **NY**
>
> **IPX Network 150**

Configuration - San Francisco

```
hostname SF
!
ipx routing 00e0.0010.af4e
!
interface Ethernet0
 ipx network 100
!
interface Serial1
 bandwidth 1544
 ipx network 200
!
ipx router eigrp 80
 network 200
!
ipx router rip
 no network 200
```

Configuration - New York

```
hostname NY
!
ipx routing 00e0.004f.6dc2
!
interface Ethernet0
 ipx network 150
!
interface Serial1
 bandwidth 1544
 ipx network 200
!
ipx router eigrp 80
 network 200
!
ipx router rip
 no network 200
```

This command enables IPX RIP and SAP services on the router. The node part of the command is optional; a four-digit hexadecimal number can be entered (xxxx.xxxx.xxxx). If a node is not specified, the router will use the MAC address of the first Ethernet, Token Ring, or *Fiber Distributed Data Interface* (FDDI) interface card.

The ipx network commands are entered on each interface defining the IPX network number for that specific interface. Notice that both routers share the same IPX network number on their respective serial interfaces. This is because the link between both routers is considered to be a single network, similar to operation in a TCP/IP environment.

The network portion of this command is the IPX network number used on the interface. The ipx router eigrp command is used to enable the Enhanced IGRP protocol on the router. This command is entered in global configuration mode:

```
Router(config)#interface Ethernet0
Router(config-if)#ipx network network
```

The autonomous-system-number argument is the EIGRP autonomous system (AS) number. This number can range from one to 65,535. The EIGRP AS number must be the same for each network. In this example, the number 80 is used.

The network statement after the ipx router eigrp command is used to list all the networks that EIGRP will be routing for. In this example, network 200 is used because it is the IPX network running on the WAN interfaces in which EIGRP is routing.

```
Router(config)#ipx router eigrp autonomous-system-number
Router(config-router)#network network
```

The last command discussed in the configuration is the `ipx router rip` command. This command is also entered in global configuration mode:

```
Router(config)#ipx router rip
Router(config-router)#no network network
```

The `ipx router rip` command is used to enable IPX RIP, which is enabled by default once the *ipx routing* command is entered.

The `no network` command is used to deny IPX RIP from routing this network. Because IPX RIP is enabled by default, it will route all IPX networks listed on the interfaces. In this scenario, the no network command is used so that IPX RIP does not route for IPX network 200 and rather leaves the routing to EIGRP. IPX RIP will route for the internal IPX network 100 on the San Francisco router and the internal IPX network 150 on the New York router, even though these networks aren't explicitly defined under the ipx router rip process. It is important to remember to deny all IPX networks that EIGRP will be routing under the ipx router rip process.

EIGRP uses hello packets to establish neighbor relationships with its directly connected routers. Hello packets also enable the router to dynamically learn about new routers on directly connected networks. They are also used to identify when a neighbor becomes unreachable. Hello packets are sent to all neighbor routers every five seconds by default (or 60 seconds by default for low-speed NBMA links). If a router does not receive hello packets for a specified interval, known as the *hold down timer*, it believes that the neighbor has become unreachable. The hold down timer is three times the hello packet interval, or 15 seconds. Hello packets do not have a priority higher than any other packet. This means that if a circuit becomes oversubscribed and packets are being dropped, the hello packets could be discarded, causing the router to lose its neighbor relationships and basically dropping from the network.

Hello packets also cause an increase in WAN bandwidth utilization because of the rate at which they are sent. Increasing the interval in which hello packets are sent can alleviate these problems. The hold down timer will also have to be increased to compensate for the delay in hello packets. The recommended setting for the hold down timer is three times the hello interval. The following example shows the configuration steps necessary to increase the hello interval and hold down timer:

```
Router(config)#ipx hello-interval eigrp autonomous-system-number
seconds
Router(config)#ipx hold-time eigrp autonomous-system-number seconds
```

The `autonomous-system-number` argument is the EIGRP AS number used for the network. The `seconds` statement in the `ipx hello-interval` command is the interval between hello packets in seconds. The default hello-interval is five seconds for T1 links and higher.

The `seconds` statement in the `ipx hold-time eigrp` is the hold time in seconds. The hold time is advertised in hello packets and indicates to neighbors the length of time they should consider the sender valid. The default hold time is 15 seconds for T1 links and higher, which is three times the hello interval.

Some additional enhancements that EIGRP has over IPX RIP include the following features:

- The support of incremental SAP updates is the first enhancement. NetWare servers send out SAP updates every 60 seconds regardless of whether any changes have occurred. EIGRP can be configured to send out SAP updates only when changes have occurred and will send only the changed SAP information instead of the entire SAP table. The command used to configure EIGRP so that it supports this feature is as follows:

```
Router(config)#interface Serial1
Router(config-if)#ipx sap-incremental eigrp autonomous-system-
number [rsup-only]
```

This command enables SAP updates to be sent out of Serial Interface 1 incrementally only when changes occur, instead of periodically every 60 seconds. The command is entered in interface configuration mode and the interface specified should be the interface that the router is sending the SAP updates out to. The `autonomous-system-number` argument is the EIGRP AS number used for the network. The `[rsup-only]` is a option that enables the router to use IPX RIP for the routing updates and will only use EIGRP to transport incremental SAP updates.

- EIGRP IPX networks support up to 224 hops, instead of the limited 15 hops of IPX RIP.
- EIGRP IPX determines the best path to a destination by performing a calculation including the bandwidth and delay of a link. This is a much more optimal solution for determining the best path than IPX RIP's ticks and hop count.

The *NetWare Link-Services Protocol* (NLSP) is a link-state routing protocol from Novell designed to overcome some of the limitations of IPX RIP and SAP. NLSP is based upon the OSI *Intermediate System to Intermediate System* (IS-IS) and is similar to other link-state protocols such as OSPF for IP. The main difference between NLSP and other link-state protocols is that NLSP does not support the use of areas. Using NLSP is similar to having all routers in an OSPF network in area 0.

NLSP provides many benefits over the use of RIP and SAP. NLSP allows for better efficiency, improved routing, and greater scalability. As with other link-state protocols, every router in an NLSP network maintains an identical copy of the link-state database containing the entire topology of the network. Routers in an NLSP network send routing updates only when there is a topology change in the network. This is in contrast to routers in a RIP environment that send routing updates every 60 seconds. In addition, routers will send service-information updates only when services change, not every 60 seconds as SAP does. NLSP also provides improved routing by guaranteeing delivery using a reliable delivery protocol. NLSP can also scale up to 127 hops compared to RIP, which supports only 15 hops.

Adjacencies, similar to neighbor relationships in EIGRP, are established between routers with the use of hello packets. These adjacencies contain information regarding the link to the neighboring routers as well as the attributes of the neighboring routers. Each router will then build an adjacency database that will store the adjacency information. Adjacency establishment can be accomplished over a WAN or LAN. Establishing adjacencies over a WAN requires that the routers first exchange identities. This is done with the use of IPXWAN. IPXWAN is a connection start-up protocol that enables a router that is running IPX routing to connect via a serial link. IPXWAN must be configured on the serial interfaces that will be using NLSP. Once this is accomplished, the routers will then send hello packets to establish their adjacency databases. Once the adjacency database is built, the routers will send *link-state packets* (LSPs) to each other to establish their link-state database. LSPs are flooded to all other NLSP devices on the network to inform them of a topology change. Each router then updates its respective link-state database. LSPs are flooded through the network to all NLSP devices every time a link state changes. LSPs are refreshed every two hours.

Besides the adjacency database and the link-state database, NLSP also uses a forwarding database. The forwarding database is simply a computation calculated from the adjacency and link-state databases using Dijkstra's *Shortest Path First* (SPF) algorithm. NLSP also uses a *designated router* (DR). This DR is a router that is elected to represent a network.

SAP Updates

This section describes how SAP updates work in an IPX network. NetWare servers send SAP updates to all other servers on the network to inform them of the services they offer. Once a server receives a SAP update from another

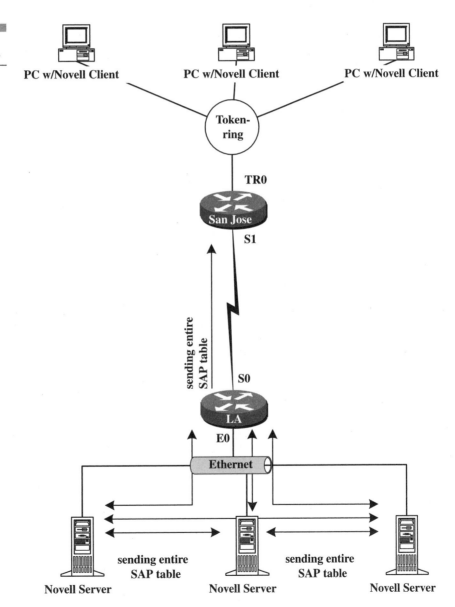

Figure 10-10
SAP update example

server, it updates its own SAP table and sends out that new information in the next SAP update. The local router also receives these SAP updates. The router does not forward broadcasts, so it builds its own SAP table and sends its SAP table to all its neighbor routers. These neighbor routers will now update their SAP tables. This process enables a remote client to learn about NetWare services on a remote network. Figure 10-10 outlines this process.

As shown in the figure, the NetWare servers send SAP updates carrying information about all the services they have learned from other servers as well as their own services. The arrows represent the NetWare servers sending their SAP updates to the other NetWare servers as well as the router. The Los Angeles router then sends its entire SAP table to the San Jose router. The San Jose router then updates its own SAP table and the clients attached to its Token Ring segment will be able to learn about the NetWare services in L.A. via the San Jose router.

Where IPX Protocols Fit into the OSI Model

Figure 10-11 shows how IPX/SPX and its underlying protocols map to the OSI model. A description follows on how the protocols map to their associated OSI layers.

The IPX/SPX protocol suite, much like the TCP/IP protocol suite, has many underlying protocols that interact and work with each other to enable communication in an IPX/SPX environment. The MAC protocols, along with IPX, handle the addressing of the nodes, allowing packets to be delivered to the correct destinations. RIP, SAP, and NLSP all provide routing capabilities, storing routing information about the network and handling the

Figure 10-11

IPX/SPX mapped to the OSI model

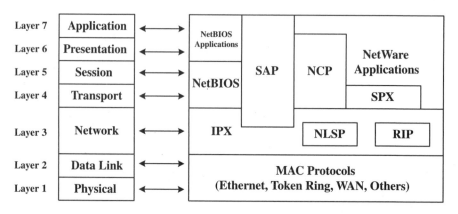

delivery process to the individual nodes. NCP is an upper layer protocol that handles the client-to-server interaction and works with the individual processes between nodes. NCP also provides session control and packet-level error checking between NetWare workstations and the routers. SPX is a connection-oriented transport layer protocol providing a guaranteed delivery of packets.

NetWare Addresses

NetWare uses a layer-three, IPX address that is assigned to nodes on the network. Each address is represented as a hexadecimal address. This means that each digit in the address can be a value from zero to nine or A to F. The hexadecimal address is represented in the format *network.node*. The network number of the address is four bytes long (32 bits) and identifies a physical network. Each IPX network is assigned a globally unique network number. The network number is represented as eight hexadecimal numbers, such as C0.A8.33.00. IPX network numbers are often represented as fewer numbers than eight because the leading zeros are not shown in the address. For example, a network number of 00.00.00.12 could be shown simply as 12. The network administrator assigns the IPX network number to routers and servers. The clients will learn the network number dynamically upon startup of the workstation.

The node number of the IPX address consists of a six-byte (48-bit) number. It is represented as 12 hexadecimal numbers, such as 00.00.62.65. A3.7F. The node number is taken from the device's MAC address. This allows IPX to know the MAC address of the end station it needs to communicate with when it already knows the device's IPX address. This eliminates the need to use ARP to find the MAC address. IPX requires that each node number be unique per the IPX network. This means that a node on network 10 can have a node number of 00.00.10.AF.AA.11, and a node on network 11 can have the same node number of 00.00.10.AF.AA.11. Each address is considered unique because they have different network numbers.

IPX also uses a socket number. The socket number is a two-byte hexadecimal number that is appended after the node number to create a "complete" 12-byte IPX address. The socket number identifies the server process or the ultimate destination of an IPX packet. IPX uses different processes, and each process has a unique socket number. A process that needs to communicate on the network will request that a socket number be assigned to the IPX packet. Once the IPX packet is received, it will pass it directly to the process. Table 10-8 lists some processes with their corresponding socket numbers.

Table 10-8

IPX socket numbers

Socket Number	Process
0x451	NCP
0x452	SAP
0x453	RIP
0x455	Novell NetBIOS
0x456	Novell Diagnostics
0x457	Serialization packet
0x9001	NLSP
0x9004	IPXWAN protocol

Socket numbers are dynamically used by the process and are not configured on the router. Therefore, an IPX address that is configured on a router or server will be a 10-byte (80-bit) address. The IPX address changes to the 12-byte (96-bit) length when sockets are used.

NOTE: *During the CCNA exam, if a question comes up about the format or length of an IPX address, read to see if they are asking for the socket number as well. If not, then remember the network.node format along with its 10-byte (80-bit) length.*

Basic NetWare Operation

The following section discusses some of the basic operations in a NetWare environment. The use of GNS as well as the interaction between RIP and SAP is thoroughly discussed.

GNS

Get Nearest Server (GNS) is a SAP service query to find the closest server. Clients use GNS requests when they are first booted to find a server to login to. The client will send a GNS request and all local NetWare servers will respond with a GNS reply. The client will then choose the closest server or the first to respond to the request. Once the client is logged in to the server, it can start using resources from additional servers. If no local servers are available to log in to, the router will reference its Server Information Table (SIT), also known as a SAP table, and reply with a GNS reply specifying the IPX address of the closest remote server. Figure 10-12 steps through this process.

In the figure, Workstation C gets booted and sends out a GNS request broadcast to all nodes on the Token Ring segment. No servers on the local segment are available to respond to the GNS request. Therefore, the router will respond with a GNS reply telling Workstation C about Novell Server A in L.A., including the IPX address of the server.

RIP

This section discusses the operation of IPX RIP in an IPX environment. Continuing on with the previous discussion, Workstation C now knows about Novell Server A and has the associated IPX address. However, Workstation C does not have a route to Novell Server A. Therefore, a RIP broadcast will be sent from Workstation C asking for the route to network 150, in which Novell Server A resides. The San Jose router can process this request and send a RIP response packet indicating that it knows a route to IPX network 150. The San Jose router knows of this route because it exchanges *Routing Information Tables* (RITs) with the L.A. router. Workstation C can now send packets to Novell Server A to log in and use server resources. Figure 10-13 illustrates this process.

NOTE: *IPX RIP can be configured to send out RIP updates less frequently, creating less overhead and utilizing a smaller percentage of bandwidth. The command to initiate this feature is listed here:*

```
Router(config)#interface Serial0

Router(config-if)#ipx update interval rip 120
```

This command enables IPX RIP updates to be sent out of Serial Interface 0 every 120 seconds.

SAP

A previous example earlier in this chapter discussed the use of SAP updates in an IPX network. This section will instead focus on how the SAP

Figure 10-12
A GNS request
example

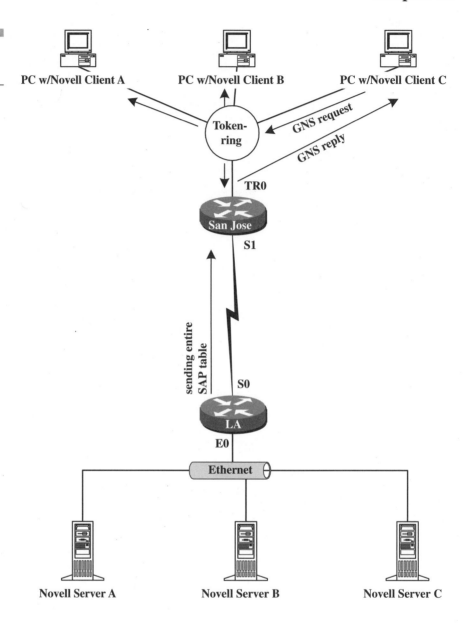

query and response is used in an IPX environment. Figure 10-14 shows an example of how a SAP query and response is used.

In this scenario, the L.A. router has already built up its routing tables from the SAP updates of the NetWare servers. Workstation A needs to be able to print a document. Therefore, it will send out a SAP query with a packet type of 0x0001, indicating that this query is a General Service query.

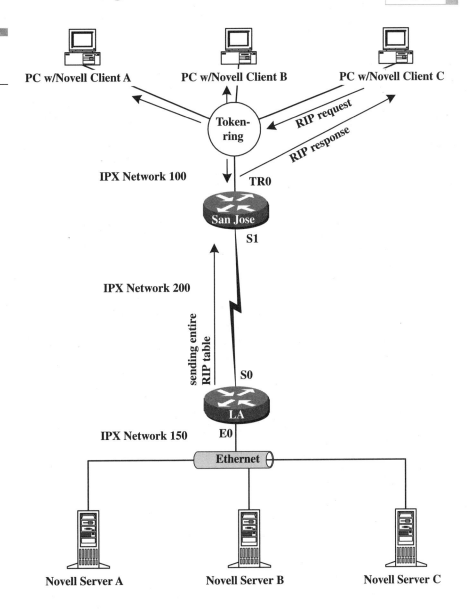

Figure 10-13
An IPX RIP update example

PC w/Novell Client A

PC w/Novell Client B

PC w/Novell Client C

Token-ring

RIP request

RIP response

IPX Network 100

TR0

San Jose

S1

IPX Network 200

sending entire RIP table

S0

LA

IPX Network 150

E0

Ethernet

Novell Server A

Novell Server B

Novell Server C

It will also add 0x0007 in the server type field, indicating that it is requesting print services. This SAP query is broadcast to the local network. The local router, L.A., responds to the SAP query with a SAP response packet. The SAP response packet will include the IPX address of the Novell Server "Printsrv." Workstation A now has the IPX address of the server with the requested services and will send packets directly to the server.

Figure 10-14
A SAP query and
response example

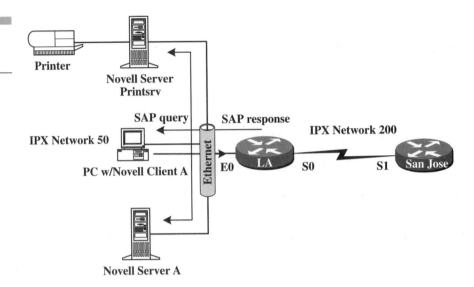

It is important to remember that SAPs are used prevalently in NetWare 3.x networks. With the release of NetWare 4.x, Novell servers went to a directory services structure where a client references a *Novell Directory Services* (NDS) server to locate services. SAP requests are still required, in the form of GNS requests, to locate an NDS server during boot up.

NOTE: *SAP updates are sent periodically, every 60 seconds, just as RIP updates are. A problem occurs when a remote router receives a SAP update containing new services but has yet to receive a RIP update that defines the path to this new service. The following command configures the router to send SAP updates immediately after RIP updates, allowing remote networks to always have a path to new network services:*

```
Router(config)#interface Serial1
Router(config-if)#ipx update sap-after-rip
```

This command enables SAP periodic updates to be synchronized with IPX RIP updates and be sent out of Serial Interface 1.

Encapsulations of IPX

IPX can run on Ethernet, Token Ring, and FDDI. Novell supports four different encapsulation types for use over these layer-two protocols. Novell uses these encapsulation settings to package upper layer protocol information and data into a frame. Each of these encapsulation types uses a different MAC frame. If a workstation is configured for one of these encapsulation settings and uses a certain MAC frame, it will not be able to communicate with other workstations on the same LAN that are using a different type of MAC frame, without first going through a router.

NetWare supports the following four encapsulation types:

- *802.2*   Referred to as SAP encapsulation by Cisco, this encapsulation type includes an *Institute of Electrical and Electronics Engineers* (IEEE) 802.3 Length field followed by a IEEE 802.2 (LLC) header.

- *802.3*   Referred to as Novell-Ether encapsulation by Cisco, this is also called 802.3 raw or Novell Ethernet_802.3. 802.3 is the initial encapsulation scheme used by Novell and is also the default encapsulation on a Cisco Ethernet interface.

- *Ethernet II*   Referred to as ARPA encapsulation by Cisco, Ethernet II consists of an Ethernet II frame including Source and Destination Address fields followed by an EtherType field.

- *SNAP*   Referred to as SNAP encapsulation by Cisco, this encapsulation type is also referred to as Ethernet_SNAP. SNAP extends the 802.2 (LLC) header to include a type code similar to the type code in Ethernet II.

Table 10-9 lists the encapsulation types supported for Ethernet, Token Ring, and FDDI.

Figure 10-15 illustrates the different IPX encapsulation types.

Table 10-9	**Interface Type**	**Encapsulation Type**	**IPX Frame Type**
The encapsulation types supported on different interface types	Ethernet	Novell-Ether (default) ARPA SAP SNAP	Ethernet_802.3 Ethernet_II Ethernet_802.2 Ethernet_Snap
	Token Ring	SAP (default)	Token-Ring Token-Ring_Snap
	FDDI	SNAP (default) SAP Novell_FDDI	FDDI_Snap FDDI_802.2 FDDI_Raw

Figure 10-15

IPX encapsulation types

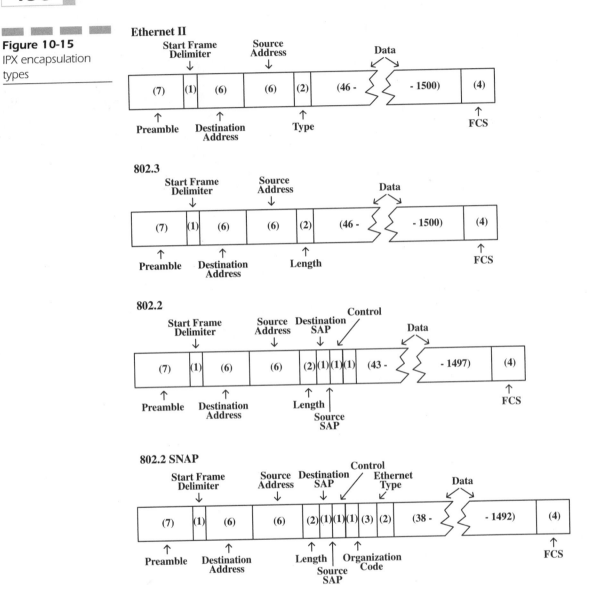

Configuring IPX on Cisco Routers

This next section will demonstrate the steps necessary to configure IPX on a Cisco router. Secondary addresses as well as subinterfaces will be discussed.

IPX Routing

The first step for enabling IPX on a Cisco router is to enter the command `ipx routing`. This begins the IPX routing process and allows IPX networks to be entered on the interfaces. This command also enables IPX RIP and SAP services on all interfaces with an IPX address. The command is entered in global configuration mode:

```
Router(config)#ipx routing
```

As described in an earlier section, a *node* can be specified and is an optional command. In this example, the router will use the MAC address of its Ethernet 0 card.

IPX Addresses on Interfaces

The next step to take is to enter the networks for the interfaces that will be using IPX. In this example, Ethernet Interface 0 and Serial Interface 1 on Router A will be configured.

```
RouterA(config)#interface Ethernet0
RouterA(config-if)#ipx network 100
RouterA(config)#interface Serial1
RouterA(config-if)#ipx network 200
```

In this example, Ethernet 0 is configured to use an IPX network number of 100. Serial 1 is configured to use an IPX network number of 200. These steps are all that is required for basic IPX routing. Figure 10-16 illustrates the preceding configuration.

Multiple Networks and Encapsulation Types on One Interface
IPX enables multiple networks to be configured on a single interface. It is also possible to define different types of encapsulation settings on a single interface. The following example configures a secondary network address on an Ethernet interface:

```
Router(config)#interface Ethernet0
Router(config-if)#ipx network 150 secondary
```

The `secondary` option sets ipx network 150 as a secondary network on Ethernet 0. Multiple networks can be configured by duplicating the steps above and entering a different ipx network number. This next example will define primary and multiple secondary networks with different encapsulation settings:

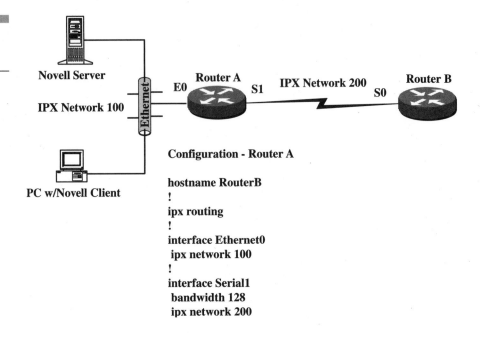

Figure 10-16
An IPX routing
example

Novell Server

IPX Network 100

PC w/Novell Client

Router A   E0   S1   **IPX Network 200**   S0   **Router B**

Configuration - Router A

```
hostname RouterB
!
ipx routing
!
interface Ethernet0
 ipx network 100
!
interface Serial1
 bandwidth 128
 ipx network 200
```

```
Router(config)#interface Ethernet0
Router(config-if)#ipx network 100 encapsulation novell-ether
Router(config-if)#ipx network 120 encapsulation arpa secondary
Router(config-if)#ipx network 150 encapsulation sap secondary
```

Three different encapsulation settings are used on this single Ethernet interface. Figure 10-17 shows how the different encapsulation settings may look on the workstations and servers, and also shows the configuration for the router.

The IPX networks are listed next to each workstation and server. Each encapsulation type has its own network, both on the router, the workstations, and the servers.

In this scenario, Workstation C can communicate only with Novell Server B. This is because they are both using the same type of encapsulation. If Workstation C needs to use Printsrv, it would have to first go through the router. Since the router is configured to support the Ethernet 802.3/Novell-Ether encapsulation, it will route the packet to Printsrv. If the router is not configured for Novell-Ether, it would not be able to forward the packet, and Workstation C would only be able to communicate with Novell Server B. This principle applies to all workstations and servers.

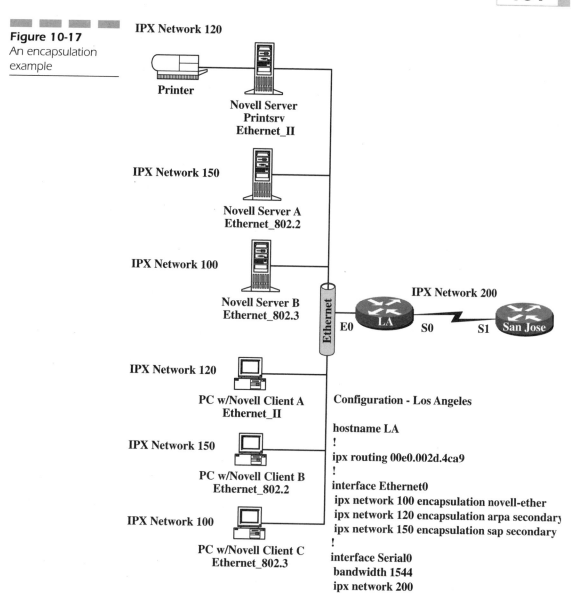

Figure 10-17
An encapsulation example

IPX Network 120

Printer

Novell Server
Printsrv
Ethernet_II

IPX Network 150

Novell Server A
Ethernet_802.2

IPX Network 100

Novell Server B
Ethernet_802.3

Ethernet

E0   LA   S0

IPX Network 200

S1   San Jose

IPX Network 120

PC w/Novell Client A
Ethernet_II

IPX Network 150

PC w/Novell Client B
Ethernet_802.2

IPX Network 100

PC w/Novell Client C
Ethernet_802.3

Configuration - Los Angeles

hostname LA
!
ipx routing 00e0.002d.4ca9
!
interface Ethernet0
 ipx network 100 encapsulation novell-ether
 ipx network 120 encapsulation arpa secondary
 ipx network 150 encapsulation sap secondary
!
interface Serial0
 bandwidth 1544
 ipx network 200

Verifying and Monitoring IPX Routing

This section describes the show commands that can be used to verify the operation of IPX routing. Show commands are used to troubleshoot problems in an IPX environment. They provide detailed output on how the communication is taking place and how much traffic is traversing the network. The following section describes some of the possible `show` commands that can be used in an IPX environment.

Show Commands

The `show ipx traffic` command displays valuable information about the type of routing protocol used and how much traffic is traversing the network. SAP requests and replies are also counted as well as GNS requests to the servers. This command also displays the number of broadcasts sent and received on the router. Figure 10-18 shows a sample output of the `show ipx traffic` command.

Table 10-10 describes the fields in the `show ipx traffic` display.

The `show ipx interface` command gives valuable output on the current state of the interfaces. This command lists all the interfaces configured on the router. The IPX address of each interface is listed as well as the encapsulation type. This command also displays the type of filters set on the interface and the delays for the routing protocols. See Figure 10-19 for the output of the `show ipx interface` command.

Table 10-11 describes the fields displayed in the `show ipx interface` output.

Debug Commands

Debug commands are used on the router to perform more extensive IPX troubleshooting. The following debug command is beneficial when troubleshooting IPX:

```
debug ipx sap
```

The following shows the syntax of the `debug ipx sap` command:

```
debug ipx sap [activity | events]
```

The `debug ipx sap` command provides the option of entering either the `activity` or `events` command. The `activity` command provides more detailed output of SAP packets, including displays of services in SAP packets.

Figure 10-18
Output of the show
ipx traffic
command

```
Router#sh ipx traffic
System Traffic for 0.0000.0000.0001 System-Name: RouterA
Rcvd:   1051062605 total, 129218869 format errors, 0 checksum
errors, 640 bad hop count, 536080 packets pitched, 115351932
local destination, 0 multicast

Bcast:  109377883 received, 127013421 sent
Sent:   301516796 generated, 938931977 forwarded
        7405 encapsulation failed, 29115 no route
SAP:    670319 Total SAP requests, 11433902 Total SAP replies,
2581
  servers
        624020 SAP general requests, 28235 ignored, 11433714
replies
        40702 SAP Get Nearest Server requests, 75 replies
        5597 SAP Nearest Name requests, 113 replies
        0 SAP General Name requests, 0 replies
        39125817 SAP advertisements received, 98797581 sent
        1301203 SAP flash updates sent, 0 SAP format errors
RIP:    43566472 RIP requests, 27 ignored, 13131183 RIP replies,
722
  routes
        3084742 RIP advertisements received, 3902642 sent
        252562 RIP flash updates sent, 0 RIP format errors
Echo:   Rcvd 4 requests, 0 replies
        Sent 5 requests, 8 replies
        428 unknown: 0 no socket, 0 filtered, 0 no helper
        0 SAPs throttled, freed NDB len 0
Watchdog:
        0 packets received, 0 replies spoofed
Queue lengths:
        IPX input: 0, SAP 0, RIP 0, GNS 0
        SAP throttling length: 0/(no limit), 0 nets pending lost
route
  reply Delayed process creation: 0
EIGRP:  Total received 25535904, sent 25255112
        Updates received 658015, sent 769232
        Queries received 852599, sent 569527
        Replies received 612276, sent 855657
        SAPs received 29316, sent 2063658
Trace:  Rcvd 0 requests, 0 replies
        Sent 0 requests, 0 replies
```

The events command limits the amount of detailed output for SAP packets to those that contain interesting events. Figure 10-20 shows some sample debug ipx sap output.

Table 10-12 describes the fields in the debug ipx sap output.

The type 0x4 field in the SAP output describes the type of service that the server sending the packet provides. Refer to Table 10-5 for a list of the possible values. Table 10-13 lists the options for the IPX socket number.

	Field	Description
Table 10-10	Rcvd:	The description of the packets the router has received.
The `show ipx traffic` command fields	total	The total number of packets the router has received.
	format errors	The number of bad packets discarded (for example, packets with a corrupted header).
	checksum errors	The number of packets containing a checksum error. This number should always be zero because IPX does not use a checksum.
	bad hop count	The number of packets discarded because its hop count exceeded 16 (that is, the packets timed out).
	packets pitched	The number of times the router received its own broadcast packet.
	local destination	The number of packets sent to the local broadcast address or specifically to the router.
	multicast	The number of packets received that were addressed to multiple destinations.
	Bcast:	The description of the broadcast packets the router has received and sent.
	received	The number of broadcast packets received.
	sent	The number of broadcast packets sent. It includes broadcast packets the router is either forwarding or has generated.
	Sent:	The description of those packets that the router generated and then sent, and also those the router has received and then routed to other destinations.
	generated	The number of packets the router transmitted that it generated itself.
	forwarded	The number of packets the router transmitted that it forwarded from other sources.
	encapsulation failed	The number of packets the router was unable to encapsulate.
	no route	The number of times the router could not locate a route to the destination in the routing table.
	SAP:	The description of the SAP packets the router has sent and received.
	SAP requests	The number of SAP requests the router has received.
	SAP replies	The number of SAP replies the router has sent in response to SAP requests.

Table 10-10	Field	Description
Continued	SAP advertisements received	The number of SAP advertisements the router has received from another router.
	sent	The number of SAP advertisements the router has generated and then sent.
	SAP flash updates sent	The number of SAP advertisements the router has generated and then sent as a result of a change in its routing table.
	SAP poison sent	The number of times the router has generated an update indicating that a service is no longer reachable.
	SAP format errors	The number of SAP advertisements that were incorrectly formatted.
	RIP:	The description of the RIP packets the router has sent and received.
	RIP format errors	The number of RIP packets that were incorrectly formatted.
	freed NDB length	The number of *Network Descriptor Blocks* (NDBs) that have been removed from the network but still need to be removed from the router's routing table.
	Watchdog:	The description of the watchdog packets the router has handled.
	packets received	The number of watchdog packets the router has received from IPX servers on the local network.
	replies spoofed	The number of times the router has responded to a watchdog packet on behalf of the remote client.
	Echo:	The description of the ping replies and requests the router has sent and received.
	Rcvd 55 requests, 0 replies	The number of ping requests and replies received by the 0 router.
	Sent 0 requests, 55 replies	The number of ping requests and replies sent by the router.
	unknown	The number of incomprehensible ping packets received by the router.
	SAPs throttled	The number of ping packets discarded because they exceeded the buffer capacity.
	Queue lengths	The description of outgoing packets currently in buffers that are waiting to be processed.
	IPX input	The number of incoming packets waiting to be processed.

continued

	Field	Description
Table 10-10 Continued	SAP	The number of outgoing SAP packets waiting to be processed.
	RIP	The number of outgoing RIP packets waiting to be processed.
	GNS	The number of outgoing GNS packets waiting to be processed.
	Total length for SAP throttling purposes	The maximum number of outgoing SAP packets allowed in the buffer. Any packets received beyond this number are discarded.
	EIGRP:	The description of the Enhanced IGRP packets the router has sent and received.
	Updates	The number of Enhanced IGRP updates the router has sent and received.
	Queries	The number of Enhanced IGRP queries the router has sent and received.
	Replies	The number of Enhanced IGRP replies the router has sent and received.
	SAPs	The number of SAP packets the router has sent to and received from Enhanced IGRP neighbors.
	unknown counter	The number of packets the router was unable to forward, perhaps because of a misconfigured helper address or because no route was available.
	NLSP:	The description of the NLSP packets the router has sent and received.
	Level-1 Hellos	The number of LAN hello packets the router has sent and received.
	PTP Hello	The number of point-to-point packets the router has sent and received.
	Level-1 LSPs	The number of LSPs the router has sent and received.
	Level-1 CSNPs	The number of complete sequence number PDU (CSNP) packets the router has sent and received.
	Level-1 PSNPs	The number of partial sequence number PDU (PSNP) packets the router has sent and received.
	Level-1 DR Elections	The number of times the router has calculated its designated router election priority.
	Level-1 SPF Calculations	The number of times the router has performed the SPF calculation.
	Level-1 Partial Route Calculations	The number of times the router has recalculated routes without running SPF.

Figure 10-19

Output of the show
ipx interface
command

```
Router#sh ipx interface
TokenRing0/0 is up, line protocol is up
  IPX address is AD531800.0008.fffb.0400, SAP [up]
  Delay of this IPX network, in ticks is 1 throughput 0 link delay
0
  IPXWAN processing not enabled on this interface.
  IPX SAP update interval is 60 seconds
  IPX type 20 propagation packet forwarding is disabled
  Incoming access list is not set
  Outgoing access list is not set
  IPX helper access list is not set
  SAP GNS processing enabled, delay 0 ms, output filter list is
not set
  SAP Input filter list is not set
  SAP Output filter list is not set
  SAP Router filter list is not set
  Input filter list is not set
  Output filter list is not set
  Router filter list is not set
  Netbios Input host access list is not set
  Netbios Input bytes access list is not set
  Netbios Output host access list is not set
  Netbios Output bytes access list is not set
  Updates each 60 seconds aging multiples RIP: 3 SAP: 3
  SAP interpacket delay is 55 ms, maximum size is 480 bytes
  RIP interpacket delay is 55 ms, maximum size is 432 bytes
  RIP response delay is not set
  IPX accounting is disabled
  IPX fast switching is configured (enabled)
  RIP packets received 2130117, RIP packets sent 1789063
  SAP packets received 680965, SAP packets sent 18217613
Ethernet1/0 is up, line protocol is up
  IPX address is AD531000.aa00.0400.6304, NOVELL-ETHER [up]
  Delay of this IPX network, in ticks is 1 throughput 0 link delay
0
  IPXWAN processing not enabled on this interface.
  IPX SAP update interval is 60 seconds
  IPX type 20 propagation packet forwarding is enabled
  Incoming access list is not set
  Outgoing access list is not set
  IPX helper access list is not set
  SAP GNS processing enabled, delay 0 ms, output filter list is
not set
  SAP Input filter list is not set
  SAP Output filter list is not set
  SAP Router filter list is not set
  Input filter list is not set
  Output filter list is not set
  Router filter list is not set
  Netbios Input host access list is not set
  Netbios Input bytes access list is not set
  Netbios Output host access list is not set
  Netbios Output bytes access list is not set
  Updates each 60 seconds aging multiples RIP: 3 SAP: 3
  SAP interpacket delay is 50 ms, maximum size is 480 bytes
  RIP interpacket delay is 55 ms, maximum size is 432 bytes
```

```
    RIP response delay is not set
    IPX accounting is disabled
    IPX fast switching is configured (enabled)
    RIP packets received 42921400, RIP packets sent 12520477
    SAP packets received 15552172, SAP packets sent 18484980
Serial2/0.13 is up, line protocol is up
    IPX address is 8DC340FE.0060.3e31.f520 [up]
    Delay of this IPX network, in ticks is 6 throughput 0 link delay
0
    IPXWAN processing not enabled on this interface.
    IPX SAP update interval is 60 seconds
    IPX type 20 propagation packet forwarding is disabled
    Incoming access list is not set
    Outgoing access list is not set
    IPX helper access list is not set
    SAP GNS processing enabled, delay 0 ms, output filter list is
not set
    SAP Input filter list is not set
    SAP Output filter list is not set
    SAP Router filter list is not set
```

Additional debug commands that can be used for IPX troubleshooting include the following:

- Debug ipx routing This command displays information on IPX routing packets that the router sends and receives.
- Debug ipx packet This command displays information about packets received, transmitted, and forwarded.
- Debug ipx ipxwan This command displays debug information relating to interfaces that are configured to use IPXWAN.

The problem that is occurring on the network will ultimately decide which IPX debug command should be used.

IPX Ping

IPX ping is a troubleshooting tool used in IPX environments. It enables the router to send IPX echo packets to IPX nodes or interfaces and to receive a response to indicate network connectivity between the two devices. To use IPX ping, the protocol ipx must be specified after entering the ping command using extended ping.

	Field	Description
Table 10-11 The `show ipx interface` command fields	Ethernet1 is . . . , line protocol is . . .	The type of interface and whether it is currently active and inserted into the network (up) or inactive and not inserted (down).
	IPX address is . . .	The network and node address of the local router interface, followed by the type of encapsulation configured on the interface and the interface's status. Refer to the `ipx network` command for a list of possible values.
	NOVELL-ETHER	The type of encapsulation being used on the interface, if any.
	[up] line-up	Indicates whether IPX routing is enabled or disabled on the interface. "line-up" indicates that IPX routing has been enabled with the `ipx routing` command. "line-down" indicates that it is not enabled. The word in square brackets provides more details about the status of IPX routing when it is in the process of being enabled or disabled.
	RIPPQ:	The number of packets in the RIP queue.
	SAPPQ:	The number of packets in the SAP queue.
	Secondary address is . . .	The address of a secondary network configured on this interface, if any, followed by the type of encapsulation configured on the interface and the interface's status. Refer to the `ipx routing` command for a list of possible values. This line is displayed only if you have configured a secondary address with the `ipx routing` command.
	Delay of this IPX network, in ticks . . .	The value of the ticks field (configured with the `ipx delay` command).
	throughput	The throughput of the interface (configured with the `ipx spx-idle-time` interface configuration command).
	link delay	The link delay of the interface (configured with the `ipx link-delay` interface configuration command).
	IPXWAN processing . . .	Indicates whether IPXWAN processing has been enabled on this interface with the `ipx ipxwan` command.
	IPX SAP update interval	Indicates the frequency of outgoing SAP updates (configured with the `ipx sap-interval` command).

Table 10-11

Continued

Field	Description
IPX type 20 propagation packet forwarding . . .	Indicates whether the forwarding of IPX type-20 propagation packets (used by NetBIOS) is enabled or disabled on this interface, as configured with the `ipx type-20-propagation` command.
Outgoing access list	Indicates whether an access list has been enabled with the `ipx access-group` command.
IPX Helper access list	The number of the broadcast helper list applied to the interface with the `ipx helper-list` command.
SAP Input filter list	The number of the input SAP filter applied to the interface with the `ipx input-sap-filter` command.
SAP Output filter list	The number of the output SAP filter applied to the interface with the `ipx output-sap-filter` command.
SAP Router filter list	The number of the router SAP filter applied to the interface with the `ipx router-sap-filter` command.
SAP GNS output filter	The number of the GNS response filter applied to the interface with the `ipx output-gns-filter` command.
Input filter	The number of the input filter applied to the interface with the `ipx input-network-filter` command.
Output filter	The number of the output filter applied to the interface with the `ipx output-network-filter` command.
Router filter	The number of the router entry filter applied to the interface with the `ipx router-filter` command.
Netbios Input host access list	The name of the IPX NetBIOS input host filter applied to the interface with the `ipx netbios input-access-filter host` command.
Netbios Input bytes access list	The name of the IPX NetBIOS input bytes filter applied to the interface with the `ipx netbios input-access-filter bytes` command.
Netbios Output host access list	The name of the IPX NetBIOS output host filter applied to the interface with the `ipx netbios input-access-filter host` command.
Netbios Output bytes access list	The name of the IPX NetBIOS output bytes filter applied to the interface with the `ipx netbios input-access-filter bytes` command.

Field	Description
Update time	How often the router sends RIP updates, as configured with the `ipx update-time` command.
Watchdog spoofing . . .	Indicates whether watchdog spoofing is enabled of disabled for this interface, as configured with the `ipx watchdog-spoof` command. This information is displayed only on serial interfaces.
IPX accounting	Indicates whether IPX accounting has been enabled with the `ipx accounting` command.
IPX Fast switching, IPX Autonomous switching	Indicates whether IPX fast switching is enabled (default) or disabled for this interface, as configured with `ipx route-cache` command. (If IPX autonomous switching is enabled, it is configured with the `ipx route-cache cbus` command.)
IPX SSE switching	Indicates whether IPX SSE switching is enabled for this interface, as configured with the `ipx route-cache sse` command.
IPX NLSP is running on primary network E001	Indicates that NLSP is running and the number of the primary IPX network on which it is running.
RIP compatibility mode	The state of RIP compatibility (configured by the `ipx nlsp rip` interface configuration command).
SAP compatibility mode	The state of SAP compatibility (configured by the `ipx nlsp sap` interface configuration command).
Level 1 Hello interval	The interval between the transmission of hello packets for nondesignated routers (configured by the `ipx nlsp hello-interval` interface configuration command).
Level 1 Designated Router Hello interval	The interval between the transmission of hello packets for designated routers (configured by the `ipx nlsp hello-interval` interface configuration command).
Level 1 CSNP interval	The CSNP interval (as configured by the `ipx nlsp csnp-interval` interface configuration command).
LSP retransmit interval	The LSP retransmisison interval (as configured by the `ipx nlsp restransmit-interval` interface configuration command).
Level 1 adjacency count	The number of Level 1 adjacencies in the adjacency database.
Level 1 circuit ID	The system ID and pseudo-node number of the designated router. In this example, 0000.0C02. 8CF9 is the system ID, and 02 is the pseudo-node number.

Figure 10-20

Output of the debug
`ipx sap` command

```
NovellSAP: at 00004EAB
I  SAP Response type 0x2 len 160 src:100.0000.0e40.0ab1
dest:100.ffff.ffff.ffff(452)
  Type 0x4, "FLSRV1", 200.0010.0200.0004 (451), 2 hops
  Type 0x4, "FLSRV1", 200.0010.0200.0008 (451), 2 hops
NovellSAP: sending update to 200
NovellSAP: at 001609BB:
 0 SAP Update type 0x2 len 96 ssoc:0x452 dest:100.ffff.ffff.ffff
(452)
Novell: type 0x4, "NOVLSRV2", 50.0000.0000.0001 (451), 2 hops
```

Table 10-12

The debug ipx
sap command
fields

Field	Description
I	The indication as to whether the router received the SAP packet as input (I) or is sending an update as output (O).
SAP Response type 0x2	The packet type. The format is 0xn and the possible values for n include 1: General query 2: General response 3: Get Nearest Server request 4: Get Nearest Server response
len 160	Length of this packet (in bytes).
src: 100.000.0c00.070d	Indicates the source address of the packet.
dest: 100.ffff.ffff.ffff	Indicates the IPX network number and broadcast address of the destination IPX network that the message is intended for.
(452)	The IPX socket number of the process sending the packet at the source address. This number is always 452, which is the socket number for the SAP process.

Table 10-13

IPX socket options

Field	Description
ssoc:0x452	Indicates the IPX socket number of the process sending the packet at the source address. Possible values include 451: Network Core Protocol 452: Service Advertising Protocol 453: Routing Information Protocol 455: NetBIOS 456: Diagnostics 4000 to 6000: Ephemeral sockets used for interaction with file servers and other network communications

The following display is a sample output of the extended IPX `ping` command:

```
Router# ping
Protocol [ip]: ipx
Target IPX address: 100.0000.04e1.ad39
Repeat count [5]:
Datagram size [100]:
Timeout in seconds [2]:
Verbose [n]:
Novell Standard Echo [n]:
Type escape sequence to abort. Sending 5 100-byte IPX echoes to
100.0000.04e1.ad39, timeout is 2 seconds.
!!!!!
Success rate is 100 percent (5/5)
```

Table 10-14 describes the IPX ping test characters.

IPX Routing Tables

The `show ipx route` command displays information regarding the router's Routing Information Table (RIT). This table is updated with routing updates from neighboring routers. These routing updates can come from any IPX routing protocol. The `Codes` section under the `show ipx route` display defines how the route was learned. Figure 10-21 shows a sample output of the `show ipx route` command:

Table 10-15 describes the fields in the `show ipx route` output display.

Table 10-14	**Character**	**Meaning**
Character descriptions from IPX ping	!	Each exclamation point indicates the receipt of a reply from the target address.
	.	Each period indicates the network server timed out while waiting for a reply from the target address.
	U	A destination unreachable error PDU was received.
	C	A congestion-experienced packet was received.
	I	A user interrupted the test.
	?	Unknown packet type.
	&	Packet lifetime exceeded.

Figure 10-21
Output of the
show ipx route
command

```
Router#sh ipx route
Codes: C - Connected primary network,    c - Connected secondary
network
       S - Static, F - Floating static, L - Local (internal), W -
IPXWAN
       R - RIP, E - EIGRP, N - NLSP, X - External, A - Aggregate
       s - seconds, u - uses, U - Per-user static

722 Total IPX routes. Up to 2 parallel paths and 16 hops allowed.

No default route known.

C    5AC3108C (NOVELL-ETHER),   Fa9/1/1
C    5AC350FE (FRAME-RELAY),    Se1/0.15
C    5AC353FE (FRAME-RELAY),    Se1/0.28
C    5AC358FF (FRAME-RELAY),    Se1/2.22
C    5AC369FF (FRAME-RELAY),    Se1/1.24
C    5AC397FD (FRAME-RELAY),    Se1/3.19
C    5AC398FE (FRAME-RELAY),    Se1/2.32
C    5AC399FE (FRAME-RELAY),    Se1/3.33
C    5AC39AFE (FRAME-RELAY),    Se1/3.15
C    5AC39BFE (FRAME-RELAY),    Se1/3.3
C    5AC39CFE (FRAME-RELAY),    Se1/3.18
C    5AC39DFE (FRAME-RELAY),    Se1/3.12
C    5AC39EFE (FRAME-RELAY),    Se1/3.13
C    5AC39FFE (FRAME-RELAY),    Se1/3.11
```

IPX Server Table

The show ipx servers command is listed in Figure 10-22. This command displays all of the servers that the router is aware of and has listed in its Server Information Table (SIT). This table is updated from SAP updates from other servers and neighboring routers.

The show ipx servers command displays all the servers in the SIT. Other important information such as through which interface the server exists as well as the IPX address of the server is contained in this display. Table 10-16 lists the descriptions of the show ipx servers fields.

If a particular server or multiple servers exist on the network and are not being displayed in the show ipx servers display, it may indicate that the SAP updates propagating the network are having problems.

Table 10-15

The `show ipx route` command fields

Field	Description
Codes	Codes defining how the route was learned.
L	Internal network number.
C	Directly connected primary network.
c	Directly connected secondary network
R	Route learned from a RIP update.
E	Route learned from an EIGRP update.
S	Statically defined route via the `ipx route` command.
Total IPX routes	The number of routes in the IPX routing table.
No parallel paths allowed	The maximum number of parallel paths that the router has been configured for with the `ipx maximum-paths` command.
Novell routing algorithm variant in use	Indicates whether the router is using the IPX-compliant routing algorithms (default).
Net 1	The network to which the route goes.
[3/2]	Delay/Metric. Delay is the number of IBM clock ticks (each tick is 1/18 seconds) reported to the destination network. Metric is the number of hops reported to the same network. Delay is used as the primary routing metric, and the metric (hop count) is used as a tie breaker.
via *network.node*	The address of a router that is the next hop to the remote network.
age	The amount of time in hours, minutes, and seconds that has elapsed since information about this network was last received.
uses	The number of times this network has been looked up in the route table. This field is incremented when a packet is process-switched, even if the packet is eventually filtered and not sent. As such, this field represents a fair estimate of the number of times a route gets used.
Ethernet0	Interface that packets to the remote network are sent through.
(NOVELL-ETHER) (HDLC) (SAP) (SNAP)	Encapsulation (frame) type. This is shown only for directly connected networks.
is directly connected	Indicates that the network is directly connected to the router.

Figure 10-22
Output of the show
ipx servers
command

```
Router#show ipx servers
Codes: S - Static, P - Periodic, E - EIGRP, N - NLSP, H -
Holddown, + = detail
U - Per-user static
2581 Total IPX Servers

Table ordering is based on routing and server info

    Type Name        Net      Address      Port     Route  Hops  Itf
P     4  CD1      C4268297.0000.0000.0001:0451     2/01    1    Et1/0
P     4  CD2      C4268406.0000.0000.0001:0451     2/01    1    Et1/0
P     4  CD3      C4268683.0000.0000.0001:0451     2/01    1    Et1/0
P+    4  FILESRV1 C4268801.0000.0000.0001:0451     2/01    1    Et1/0
P     4  FILESRV2 D5990A01.0000.0000.0001:0451     2/01    1
Et8/0/0
P     4  FILESRV3 D5990A02.0000.0000.0001:0451     2/01    2
Et8/0/0
P     4  FILESRV4 D5990A0D.0000.0000.0001:0451     2/01    1
Et8/0/0
P     4  FILESRV5 D5990A15.0000.0000.0001:0451     2/01    1
Et8/0/0
P     4  FILESRV6 AC31280B.0000.0000.0001:0451     2/01    1    Et1/0
P     4  FILESRV7 AC31207B.0000.0000.0001:0451     2/01    1    Et1/0
P     4  GW01     AC312034.0000.0000.0001:0451     2/01    1    Et1/0
P     4  GW02     AC31208D.0000.0000.0001:0451     2/01    1    Et1/0
P     4  GW03     AC312080.0000.0000.0001:0451     2/01    1    Et1/0
P     4  PROXY1   AC312306.0000.0000.0001:0451     2/01    1    Et1/0
P     4  PROXY2   AC312401.0000.0000.0001:0451     2/01    1    Et1/0
P+    4  PROXY3   AC312308.0000.0000.0001:0451     2/01    1    To0/0
```

IPX Access Lists

IPX access lists are used to filter out unwanted networks and control broadcasts across the network. IPX access lists are similar to other access lists in that they are always processed in order. This means that each entry is checked in order, and if there is no entry for the network or service, the packet is not permitted.

IPX uses standard and extended access lists. Standard access lists are used to permit or deny specific networks or hosts. Extended access lists are more granular and enable the filtering of specific nodes and services.

A standard IPX access list uses an access list number between 800 and 899. Any access list using a number in that range is considered to be a standard access list. The access lists are entered in global configuration mode and are assigned to an interface with the ipx access-group command. This command filters all outgoing packets to the interface in which it is assigned. Only one ipx access group can be assigned per interface. The following describes the syntax for a standard IPX access list:

Table 10-16

The `show ipx servers` command fields

Field	Description
Code	Codes defining how the route was learned.
S	Statically defined route via the `ipx route` command.
P	Route learned via a SAP update.
E	Route learned via EIGRP.
N	Route learned via NLSP.
H	Indicates that the entry is in hold down mode and is not reachable.
+	Indicates that multiple paths to the server exist.
Type	Indicates how the route was learned.
Name	The name of the server.
Net	The network on which server is stored.
Address	The network address of server.
Port	The source socket number.
Route	Ticks/hops (from the routing table).
Hops	Hops (from the SAP protocol).
Itf	The interface in which the server can be reached.

```
Router(config)#access-list access-list-number {deny | permit}
source-network[.source-node [source-node-mask]] [destination-
network[.destination-node [destination-node-mask]]]
```

To remove a specific access list, the `no` form of the preceding command must be used exactly as it was entered.

Table 10-17 describes each field and option of the standard IPX access list syntax.

Figure 10-23 shows how an access list can be configured to block a network from being advertised to an additional router.

The figure shows three routers in an IPX network. San Jose exchanges routing updates to Dallas, and Dallas exchanges routing updates with Miami. Assuming that Miami or San Jose will never need to communicate with each other, the Dallas router will be configured to deny the propagation of their networks.

Table 10-17

The IPX access list
fields and options

Field	Description
access-list-number	The number of the access list, which is a decimal number from 800 to 899.
deny	Denies access if the conditions are matched.
permit	Permits access if the conditions are matched.
source-network	The number of the network the packet is being sent from. This is an eight-digit hexadecimal number that uniquely identifies a network cable segment. It can be a number in the range of one to FFFFFFFE. A network number of zero matches the local network. A network number of -1 matches all networks. You do not need to specify leading zeroes in the network number. For example, for the network number 000000AA, you can enter AA.
source-node	(Optional) The node on source-network that the packet is being sent from. This is a 48-bit value represented by a dotted triplet of four-digit hexadecimal numbers (xxxx.xxxx.xxxx).
source-node-mask	(Optional) The mask to be applied to source-node. This is a 48-bit value represented as a dotted triplet of four-digit hexadecimal numbers (xxxx.xxxx.xxxx). Place ones in the bit positions you want to mask.
destination-network	(Optional) The number of the network to which the packet is being sent. This is an eight-digit hexadecimal number that uniquely identifies a network cable segment. It can be a number in the range one to FFFFFFFE. A network number of zero matches the local network. A network number of -1 matches all networks. You do not need to specify leading zeroes in the network number. For example, for the network number 000000AA, you can enter AA.
destination-node	(Optional) The node on destination-network to which the packet is being sent. This is a 48-bit value represented by a dotted triplet of four-digit hexadecimal numbers (xxxx.xxxx.xxxx).
destination-node-mask	(Optional) The mask to be applied to destination-node. This is a 48-bit value represented as a dotted triplet of four-digit hexadecimal numbers (xxxx.xxxx.xxxx). Place ones in the bit positions you want to mask.

Figure 10-23
IPX access list
example

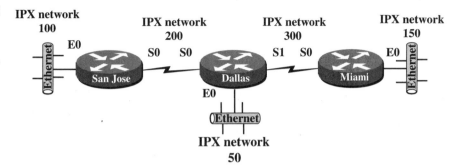

The following commands are entered in global configuration mode:

```
Dallas(config)#access-list 800 permit  200
Dallas(config)#access-list 801 permit  300
```

These commands create access list 800 and 801. Access list 800 is permitting IPX network 200, and access list 801 is permitting IPX network 300.

The following commands are entered in a specific configuration mode and apply the access lists to specific interfaces:

```
Dallas(config)#interface Serial0
Dallas(config-if)#ipx access-group 800
Dallas(config-if)#interface Serial1
Dallas(config-if)#ipx access-group 801
```

The IPX access group 800 is applied to Serial0, out to San Jose. IPX access group 801 is applied to Serial1, out to Miami. This enables the specific IPX networks to be permitted and advertised out of their specified interfaces. All other IPX networks will be implicitly denied. The IPX networks 100 and 200 will be advertised from San Jose to Dallas. Dallas receives the information about these networks in IPX RIP updates. The same applies to Miami. Miami will advertise the IPX networks 300 and 150 to Dallas in IPX RIP updates. Dallas builds its own RIP table and when sending it out serial interface 0 towards San Jose, it will first reference the access list. Since only IPX network 200 is permitted to be advertised out of serial interface 0, all the other networks will be excluded from the RIP update. This allows San Jose to only know about IPX network 200 externally.

The same scenario applies to IPX RIP updates to Miami. Dallas knows about the IPX networks on all three routers. However, when it sends the IPX RIP update out serial interface 1 towards Miami, it will first reference the access list and find that only IPX network 300 is permitted to be advertised. Therefore, the only external IPX networks that Miami will know about will be IPX network 300.

Extended access lists enable the router to filter on source or destination nodes as well as source and destination sockets. This allows specific services to be filtered, such as specific SAP services. A number range of 900 to 999 identifies extended access lists. Any access lists that fall into this range are considered to be extended access lists. The following describes the syntax for an extended access list:

```
Router(config)#access-list access-list-number {deny | permit}
protocol [source-network][[[.source-node] source-node-mask] |
[.source-node source-network-mask.source-node-mask]] [source-
socket] [destination.network][[[.destination-node] destination-
node-mask] | [.destination-node destination-network-
mask.destination-nodemask]] [destination-socket]
```

To remove a specific extended access list, the no form of the preceding command must be used exactly as it was entered. Table 10-18 describes each field and option of the extended IPX access list syntax.

Table 10-19 lists some of the possible IPX protocol numbers used for access lists.

Table 10-20 lists some of the possible socket numbers used for access lists.

Controlling Overhead on IPX Networks

In an IPX RIP environment, each server on the network sends out SAP updates. The router receives these SAP updates and builds its own SAP table to advertise to its neighbor routers. This causes massive overhead on the network because all of the available services on each server are being broadcast across the network to remote routers. In most situations, Novell clients at remote sites will need only a few select services from the servers. Therefore, the additional SAP services that are being broadcast across the WAN are not being utilized and are creating overhead on the WAN.

This situation can be rectified in a few ways. This first step is to increase the interval in which the SAP updates are advertised. By default, these updates are sent every 60 seconds. Increasing the interval will lower the amount of broadcasts traversing the network, thus saving overhead. This is especially important over slower links where the SAP updates consume a

Table 10-18	Field	Description
The extended IPX access list	access-list-number	The number of the access list, which is a decimal number from 900 to 999.
	deny	Denies access if the conditions are matched.
	permit	Permits access if the conditions are matched.
	protocol	The number of an IPX protocol type in decimal. This is sometimes referred to as the packet type.
	source-network	(Optional) The number of the network that the packet is being sent from. This is an eight-digit hexadecimal number that uniquely identifies a network cable segment. It can be a number in the range one to FFFFFFFE. A network number of zero matches the local network. A network number of −1 matches all networks. You do not need to specify leading zeroes in the network number; for example, for the network number 000000AA, you can enter AA.
	source-node	(Optional) The node on source-network that the packet is being sent from. This is a 48-bit value represented by a dotted triplet of four-digit hexadecimal numbers (xxxx.xxxx.xxxx).
	source-network-mask	(Optional) The mask to be applied to source-network. This is an eight-digit hexadecimal mask. Place ones in the bit positions you want to mask. The mask must immediately be followed by a period, which must in turn immediately be followed by source-node-mask.
	source-node-mask	(Optional) The mask to be applied to source-node. This is a 48-bit value represented as a dotted triplet of four-digit hexadecimal numbers (xxxx.xxxx.xxxx). Place ones in the bit positions you want to mask.
	source-socket	The socket number that the packet is being sent from in hexadecimal.
	destination-network	(Optional) The number of the network that the packet is being sent to. This is an eight-digit hexadecimal number that uniquely identifies a network cable segment. It can be a number in the range one to FFFFFFFE. A network number of zero matches the local network. A network number of −1 matches all networks. You do not need to specify leading zeroes in the network number. For example, for the network number 000000AA, you can enter AA.
	destination-node	(Optional) The node on destination-network that the packet is being sent to. This is a 48-bit value represented by a dotted triplet of four-digit hexadecimal numbers (xxxx.xxxx.xxxx).

Table 10-18

Continued

Field	Description
destination-network-mask	(Optional) The mask to be applied to destination-network. This is an eight-digit hexadecimal mask. Place ones in the bit positions you want to mask. The mask must immediately be followed by a period, which must in turn immediately be followed by destination-node-mask.
destination-node-mask	(Optional) The mask to be applied to destination-node. This is a 48-bit value represented as a dotted triplet of four-digit hexadecimal numbers (xxxx.xxxx.xxxx). Place ones in the bit positions you want to mask.
destination-socket	(Optional) The socket number that the packet is being sent to in hexadecimal.

Table 10-19

IPX protocol numbers

IPX Protocol Number (Decimal)	Protocol (Packet Type)
− 1	Wildcard that matches any packet type in 900 lists.
0	Could be any protocol. Refer to the socket number to determine the packet type.
1	RIP
4	SAP
5	SPX
17	NCP
20	IPX NetBIOS

larger percentage of the bandwidth. The following command is entered in interface configuration mode and enables the router to send SAP updates out Serial Interface 1 at an interval of every five minutes:

```
Router(config)#interface Serial1
Router(config-if)#ipx sap-interval 5
```

The 5 in the `ipx sap-interval` command specifies the number of minutes in between each SAP update. This number can be changed to reflect a different time interval. Network links should be monitored and analyzed to

| **Table 10-20**

IPX socket numbers	**IPX Socket Number (Hexadecimal)**	**Socket**
	0	All sockets, wild card used to match all sockets
	451	NCP process
	452	SAP process
	453	RIP process
	455	Novell NetBIOS process
	456	Novell diagnostic packet
	457	Novell serialization socket
	4000–7FFF	Dynamic sockets used by workstations for interaction with file servers and other network servers
	8000–FFFF	Sockets as assigned by Novell, Inc.

determine the correct interval in which this should be set. Setting this interval too high could result in a loss of services for the clients.

If multiple servers on the LAN provide multiple services, the SAP table at the router will grow too large to be sent in one SAP update packet. Therefore, the router will break up the SAP update into multiple packets and send them simultaneously to the neighbor routers, informing them of their entire SAP table. This can cause overhead by having multiple broadcasts sent at one time and can cause problems in X.25 and slow-speed Frame Relay links. Cisco offers a solution by adjusting the interpacket delay, which adjusts the time in which the individual packets of a multiple-packet SAP update are sent. This can be done on an individual interface by entering the following command in interface configuration mode:

```
Router(config)#interface Serial1
Router(config-if)#ipx output-sap-delay 55
```

By default, Cisco routers set the delay to five milliseconds (ms), after IOS release 11.0. Novell recommends a delay of 55 ms. This configuration example sets the interpacket delay to 55 ms. The 55 in the command `ipx output-sap-delay` represents ms. This setting can be adjusted to a number other than 55 ms, but it is not recommended. This setting can also be implemented globally on every interface by using the following command:

```
Router(config)#ipx default-output-sap-delay 55
```

This configuration sets the interpacket delay for all interfaces in which SAP updates are sent out to 55 ms.

The commands in this section describe different ways to reduce overhead on IPX networks. It is important to implement these solutions in IPX environments to keep down broadcast traffic on the WAN.

The next step to take to reduce overhead on an IPX network is to restrict unwanted SAP services from propagating the network. The next section will describe in detail the steps to take to configure the router to implement these SAP filters.

SAP Filters

As described earlier, SAP services are sent by all Novell servers and are gathered by the router to build its SAP table. The router then sends its entire SAP table in an SAP update to its neighbor routers. Included in these SAP updates are all of the services that the router knows about on its LAN. Remote clients often have no use for most of these services across the WAN. SAP filters allow the router to only advertise the specific SAP services required by remote users.

Figure 10-24 shows a situation in which a Novell print server and a Novell file server exist in Orlando. The Orlando router has a connection to the New York router. The New York clients need to be able to get to the file server and any other services that exist on the Orlando LAN, except for print services. Therefore, a SAP filter is placed on the Orlando router that permits everything except for print servers to be advertised out the serial interface.

The configuration to implement this SAP filter is as follows and is entered in global configuration mode:

```
Router(config)#access-list 1000 deny -1 47
Router(config)#access-list 1000 permit -1
```

This command defines an access-list 1000 that denies print services from being announced.

The following command is entered in interface configuration mode:

```
Orlando(config)#interface Serial0
Orlando(config-if)#ipx output-sap-filter 1000
```

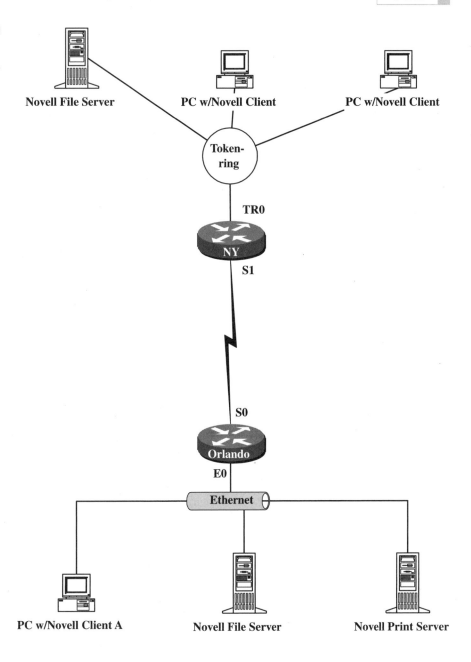

Figure 10-24
SAP filter example

This command applies the access list to Serial Interface 0 of the Orlando router in order to restrict the print services from being advertised to New York. The same solution can also be accomplished by only allowing file servers and denying all other IPX servers from advertising services out to New York.

The following command is entered in global configuration mode:

```
Orlando(config)#access-list 1000 permit -1 4
```

This command allows only the file server's services to be advertised out to New York.

SAP filters enable the router to restrict the amount of SAP traffic that is sent over the WAN. The access list number range of 1000 to 1099 identifies SAP filters. It is important to design the IPX network in such a way that most relevant services are obtained locally by the client. The services needed remotely should be allowed and all other services advertised by the servers should be restricted via SAP filters on the router.

This section showed examples of SAP filters applied outbound. Inbound SAP filters can also be applied by entering the command ipx inbound-sap-filter. This command can filter incoming SAP updates and allow only specific services through the router. Inbound access lists are often less desirable than outbound access lists because the entire SAP updates are still being sent across the WAN before the selected services are denied.

Chapter Summary

During the course of this chapter, we have broken down the IPX/SPX protocol suite and examined its components. Each component plays a key role in the communication process between the servers, routers, and workstations. IPX addressing, along with the encapsulation settings for the protocol, was also discussed. The implications of RIP and SAP in a large network environment were discussed, along with other design alternatives to support such a network. Lastly, the configuration of IPX and troubleshooting IPX was covered.

From the Real World

IPX is the second most popular routed protocol behind IP. With the introduction of NetWare 5.0 using native TCP/IP, IPX will eventually be phased out. However, it still plays a major role in many large-scale networks today because of the use of NetWare 3.x and 4.x servers. It's important to understand IPX and its capabilities so that you can diagnose problems as they occur and assist with the design of IPX in your environment. It's important to understand IPX, its associated protocols, and how it uses them for the communication process between the servers, routers, and workstations. With this understanding, you will be able to use the knowledge towards more extensive troubleshooting techniques, such as using a network analyzer.

Michael Coker

Case Study: Building an IPX LAN

This lab will require three Cisco routers. One of these routers will be used as a hub router, as in a hub and spoke configuration, and will need to have two serial interfaces. The lab will demonstrate how to route IPX over a WAN. Connectivity will be established and then verified. This next section will take you step by step through the process. Figure 10-25 illustrates a diagram of the network that will be built.

Configure Router A

1. Connect your laptop or workstation to the console port of the router using the Cisco rolled cable. Set the terminal emulation program to 9600, 8, 1, and none. Connect to COM1. Power on the router and press enter on your machine. The router should come up at the router prompt.

2. Enter configuration mode and enter a hostname of `RouterA` for the router.

3. Enter the `ipx routing` command and specify `aaaa.aaaa.aaaa` as the node address for the router.

4. Enter an `ipx network` of `100` on the Ethernet interface.

5. Enter an `ipx network` of `200` on the serial interface.

Configure Router B

1. Follow Step 1 under Router A's configuration steps to connect to the router.

Figure 10-25
An IPX network diagram

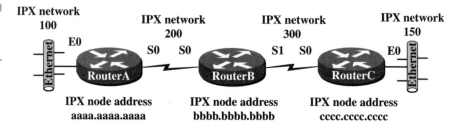

2. Enter configuration mode and enter a hostname of `RouterA` for the router.

3. Enter the `ipx routing` command and specify `bbbb.bbbb.bbbb` as the node address for the router.

4. Enter an `ipx network` of `200` on Serial Interface 0.

5. Enter an `ipx network` of `300` on Serial Interface 1.

Configure Router C

1. Follow Step 1 under Router A's configuration steps to connect to the router.

2. Enter configuration mode and enter a hostname of `RouterA` for the router.

3. Enter the `ipx routing` command and specify `aaaa.aaaa.aaaa` as the node address for the router.

4. Enter an `ipx network` of `150` on the Ethernet interface.

5. Enter an `ipx network` of `300` on the Serial interface.

The following configurations (see Figures 10-26, 10-27, 10-28, and 10-28) allow all of the routers to communicate with each other. It's important to remember that the `ipx router rip` command does not have to be used because IPX RIP will route all IPX networks listed on the interface by entering the command `ipx routing`. Use the IPX `ping` command along with the other `show` commands explained in this chapter to verify the IPX connectivity.

Figure 10-26
Output of the IPX
`ping` command

```
Router# ping
Protocol [ip]: ipx
Target IPX address: 100.aaaa.aaaa.aaaa
Repeat count [5]:
Datagram size [100]:
Timeout in seconds [2]:
Verbose [n]:
Novell Standard Echo [n]:
Type escape sequence to abort. Sending 5 100-byte IPX echoes to
100.0000.04e1.ad39, timeout is 2 seconds.
!!!!!
Success rate is 100 percent (5/5)
```

Figure 10-27
RouterA
configuration

```
RouterA

Current configuration:
!
version 12.0
no service udp-small-servers
no service tcp-small-servers
!
hostname RouterA
!
enable password cisco
!
!
ipx routing aaaa.aaaa.aaaa
!
interface Ethernet0
 no ip address
 no keepalive
 ipx network 100
!
interface Serial0
 no ip address
 encapsulation ppp
 ipx network 200
 no fair-queue
!
!
line con 0
line aux 0
line vty 0 4
 login
!
end
```

Figure 10-28
RouterB
configuration

```
RouterB

Current configuration:
!
version 12.0
no service udp-small-servers
no service tcp-small-servers
!
hostname RouterB
!
enable password cisco
!
!
ipx routing bbbb.bbbb.bbbb
!
```

```
interface Ethernet0
interface Ethernet0
 no ip address
 no keepalive
!
interface Serial0
 no ip address
 encapsulation ppp
 ipx network 200
 no fair-queue
!
interface Serial1
 no ip address
 encapsulation ppp
 ipx network 300
 no fair-queue
!
line con 0
line aux 0
line vty 0 4
 login
!
end
```

Figure 10-29
RouterC
configuration

```
RouterC

Current configuration:
!
version 12.0
no service udp-small-servers
no service tcp-small-servers
!
hostname RouterC
!
enable password cisco
!
!
ipx routing cccc.cccc.cccc
!
interface Ethernet0
 no ip address
 no keepalive
 ipx network 150
!
interface Serial0
 no ip address
 encapsulation ppp
 ipx network 300
```

```
 no fair-queue
!
!
line con 0
line aux 0
line vty 0 4
 login
!
end
```

Questions

1. Identify the valid IPX address.

   a. ABC.0000134589AB

   b. 0000AHAB.000000AE1414

   c. 00000010.00001414404040

   d. FFFFFFFF.000000009090

2. How many bytes is an IPX header?

   a. One

   b. 30

   c. 33

   d. 50

3. Which fields in the IPX header cannot contain a broadcast address?

   a. Source Node

   b. Destination Node

   c. Source Network

   d. Destination Network

4. Name the four types of encapsulation supported by Novell.

   a. 802.1

   b. 802.2

   c. 802.3

   d. 802.3 SNAP

   e. 802.5

   f. 802.10

   g. SNAP

   h. Ethernet

   i. Ethernet II

   j. Token Ring

5. Which type of encapsulation can be used on a Token Ring interface?

   a. 802.2 SAP

   b. 802.3 SNAP

   c. 802.10

   d. 802.3

6. _____ are used by servers to identify a process.

   a. SAP updates

   b. RIP requests

   c. Addresses

   d. Sockets

7. Which two encapsulation types are correctly matched with their Cisco names?

   a. SNAP, SNAP

   b. 802.2, Novell-Ether

   c. 802.3, SAP

   d. Ethernet II, ARPA

8. Which command is used to start the IPX RIP and SAP services on a router?

   a. `ipx router`

   b. `ipx routing`

   c. `ipx network`

   d. `ipx address`

9. If you are using a FDDI interface, which type of encapsulation setting would you use?

   a. ARPA

   b. SNAP

   c. 802.5

   d. Ethernet II

10. Novell uses this protocol for client-to-server communication:

   a. RIP

   b. SAP

   c. NCP

   d. ARP

11. An access list in the range of 1000 to 1099 identifies which type of access list?

   a. RIP

   b. Standard

   c. Extended

   d. SAP

12. Name the three types of SAP packets.

    a. Service query

    b. Network query

    c. Network response

    d. Incremental update

    e. Periodic update

    f. Service response

13. The following protocol provides enhanced convergence and efficiency over IPX RIP.

    a. OSPF

    b. IPX WAN

    c. IPX RIP 2

    d. IPX EIGRP

14. _____ is a SAP query to find the nearest server.

    a. GNC

    b. GNS

    c. SAP

    d. RIP

15. IPX RIP discards a packet after it has reached the _____ hop.

    a. tenth

    b. fifteenth

    c. sixteenth

    d. hundredth

16. SAP updates are sent out every _____ seconds by default.

    a. 10

    b. 30

    c. 60

    d. 120

17. 802.3 is referred to by Cisco as

    a. Novell-Ether

    b. Novell-SAP

    c. SAP

    d. ARPA

    e. SNAP

18. IPX EIGRP sends hello packets every ___ seconds. The hold down timer is set by default to ____ seconds.

    a. five, 10

    b. 10, 20

    c. five, 15

    d. 10, 30

19. The difference between the Ethernet II and 802.3 frames is that Ethernet II uses a Type field and 802.3 uses a Length field.

    a. True

    b. False

20. `Access-list 1011 permit -1 4` performs which function?

    a. It enables only print services to be advertised.

    b. It enables only file services to be advertised.

    c. It enables only RIP updates to be advertised.

    d. It enables only EIGRP hello packets to be sent.

Answers

1. **a.** ABC.0000134589AB

   An IPX address consists of a four-byte network number (eight hexadecimal numbers) and a six-byte node number (12 hexadecimal numbers). ABC.0000134589AB is the correct answer because it has the correct amount of hexadecimal numbers in the host number and the network number can be represented as less than eight hexadecimal numbers because the preceding zeros are transparent. It is also important to remember that a hexadecimal number can be in the range of zero to nine and A to F. Any number out of this range would not be a valid number.

2. **b.** 30

   The IPX header is 30 bytes long.

3. **a.** Source Node, **c.** Source Network, **d.** Destination Network

   It is important to remember that the only field in an IPX header that can contain a broadcast address is the destination node.

4. **b.** 802.2, **c.** 802.3, **g.** SNAP, **i.** Ethernet II

   As discussed in this chapter, the four types of encapsulation supported by Novell are 802.2, 802.3, SNAP, and Ethernet II.

5. **a.** 802.2 SAP

   Token Ring uses an encapsulation setting of 802.2 SAP.

6. **d.** Sockets

   Sockets are used by servers to identify the process that is to be run, such as a RIP or SAP process.

7. **a.** SNAP, SNAP, **d.** Ethernet II, ARPA

   The Novell encapsulation types mapped to their Cisco names, are as follows:

   802.2—SAP

   802.3—Novell-Ether

   Ethernet II—ARPA

   SNAP—SNAP

8. b. `ipx routing`

The `ipx routing` command is used to start the IPX RIP and SAP services on a router. The IPX networks would then have to be defined on the interfaces that are to use IPX.

9. b. SNAP

FDDI can use SAP, SNAP, and Novell_FDDI. SNAP is the default encapsulation type for FDDI interfaces.

10. c. NCP

NCP works at the upper layers of the OSI model and is used for client-to-server communication.

11. d. SAP

SAP access lists fall in the range of 1000 to 1099.

12. a. Service query, **e.** Periodic update, **f.** Service response

13. d. IPX EIGRP

IPX EIGRP provides many enhancements over IPX RIP including enhanced convergence and efficiency. OSPF is not used for IPX and IPX WAN is used in conjunction with NLSP.

14. b. GNS

GNS is a type of SAP query used to find the nearest server. A workstation sends a GNS request to find the nearest server to log in and get file access.

15. c. sixteenth

IPX RIP has a hop limit of 15. However, the sixteenth hop or router will discard the packet.

16. c. 60

SAP updates are sent out every 60 seconds by default. This interval can be changed with the use of the `ipx sap-interval` command followed by the number in minutes for how often you want the router to send the SAP updates.

17. a. Novell-Ether

The 802.3 encapsulation type is referred to as Novell-Ether by Cisco. This will be the name to use when defining this type of encapsulation on a Cisco router.

18. **c.** five, 15

    IPX EIGRP sends out hello packets every five seconds and the hold down timer defaults to 15 seconds. This can be adjusted with the use of the `ipx hello-interval eigrp` command followed by the EIGRP AS number and the number in seconds in which to send the hello packets. The hold down timer is adjusted with the use of the `ipx hold-time eigrp` command followed by the EIGRP AS number and the number in seconds in which the hold down timer is to be set.

19. **a.** True

    Ethernet II does in fact use a Type field, whereas 802.3 uses a length field.

20. **b.** It enables only file services to be advertised.

    This access list defines that only file services can be advertised. The − 1 represents all networks and the 4 represents the SAP file service.

11

Point-to-Point Serial Connections

Objectives

In today's world, exchanging information is a fact of life. In order for computers to exchange information, they need to be connected by networks. Over the last 10 years, the computing industry has seen a tremendous increase in the number of networking products in *Local Area Networks* (LANs) and *Wide Area Networks* (WANs). In this chapter, we will cover how to configure *High-Level Data Link Control* (HDLC) and *Point-to-Point Protocol* (PPP) and their various attributes on a WAN link.

The objectives covered in this chapter are as follows:

- Understand HDLC and PPP encapsulations
- Configure HDLC and PPP configurations
- Verify and debug HDLC and PPP configurations

WAN Overview

A WAN connection is very different than a LAN. Frequently, it is this misunderstanding between WANs and LANs that leads to poorly designed applications. We will now look at how a WAN is different than a LAN and some of the issues involved with setting up a WAN connection.

LAN versus WAN

LANs provide high-speed data communications between hosts in a relatively small geographic area. LANs typically are confined to a single building or even a floor within a large building. WANs provide data communication over relatively slow links (as compared to their LAN counterparts) to large geographic areas.

The costs associated with building the necessary infrastructure to support a global network can be enormous. Therefore, WAN services are generally leased from service providers. Think of these service providers as your telephone company. The telephone companies own the infrastructure; you are just paying for the right to use their infrastructure.

WAN Services

Numerous WAN services are provided by telecommunication companies (T1, T3, ISDN, xDSL, POTS, Frame Relay, and X.25). These can all be broken down into three different types of WAN connections:

- *Dedicated connections*   T1, T3, xDSL
- *Circuit-switched*   Analog (POTS) and ISDN
- *Packet-switched*   X.25 and Frame Relay

Dedicated Connections Dedicated connections, often called leased lines, provide a point-to-point link between two sites. Figure 11-1 shows an example of a point-to-point connection.

The sites, as shown in Figure 11-1, can be as close as across the street or hundreds of miles away. The data path provided by the telcos in a dedicated connection is a reserved line for the customer. This means that no one else uses the data path but you. These types of connections enable a business to maximize its control over the WAN connection. They are ideal for high-traffic connections with speeds up to T3/E3. Unfortunately, this speed and control does have a downside: they are expensive. These types of lines tend to be cost-effective when you have long connect times and the distances are relatively short.

A dedicated leased line typically requires the use of a router's synchronous serial port. Cisco supports the following synchronous serial standards:

- EIA/TIA-232
- EIA/TIA-449
- V.35
- X.21
- EIA-530
- HSSI

Figure 11-1
A dedicated serial connection

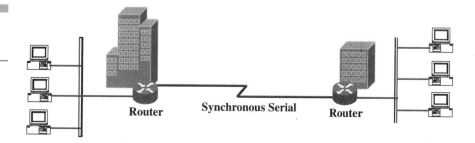

Router   Synchronous Serial   Router

NOTE: *The HSSI interface is typically available only on high-end routers.*

Synchronous communication works by using a precise clock to transmit data. Because data is sent and received using a fixed known frequency, data can be transmitted without gaps between characters. On the other hand, asynchronous transmissions usually encapsulate individual characters in control bits (called start and stop bits) that designate the beginning and end of each character. This adding of start and stop bits increases overhead, thus decreasing efficiency.

In order to connect your Cisco router to a synchronous line, you must have a *Channel Service Unit / Digital Service Unit* (CSU/DSU). The function of a CSU/DSU is to convert a signal from the data terminal equipment device (such as a router) to a signal the data circuit-terminating switch in a carrier network can understand. Figure 11-2 shows an example of the placement of a CSU/DSU in a dedicated WAN connection.

The CSU physically terminates the line while providing amplification and responding to remote loop-back operations. The loop-back operations are used by the telcos to verify connectivity to the customer site. In addition, it is responsible for providing electrical protection from either side of the CSU. The DSU is responsible for converting WAN signals into a format suitable for your router. Other responsibilities include timing recovery, signaling, and synchronous sampling.

Figure 11-2

The relationship of a CSU/DSU, router, and WAN connection

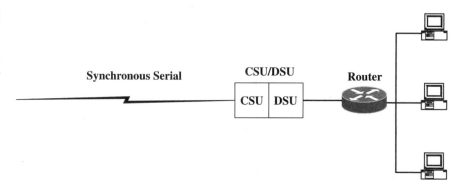

Circuit-Switched Connections Circuit-switched connections are a WAN switching method. This means that a dedicated circuit is created through a carrier network during call setup and destroyed during call teardown. The most commonly used form of this type of communication is your telephone. Call setup happens when you pick up the phone and call a friend, while call teardown is what happens when you hang up. In order to use a circuit-switched connection, we need to know the termination point ahead of time (the phone number of your friend). Figure 11-3 shows an example of a circuit-switched connection.

However, unlike the dedicated serial connection, the destination of the circuit can be set up and torn down as quickly as we can dial our phone .

Packet-Switched Networks Packet-switched networks are not so much a WAN connection type as they are a WAN service. There is no end-to-end physical connection. Instead they must use virtual circuits through a *Public Data Network* (PDN) to communicate with remote sites. These PDNs typically use the first three layers of the OSI model to move your data on its own internal network. Your router has no idea how many different networks it takes to get through the public network. It thinks the next hop is the remote router. If you were to run a traceroute from one site to the next, it would appear as if you were connected directly to the remote site, just like with a dedicated serial connection. Some additional configuration is required by your Cisco router to use a packet-switched network, but this effort can be minimized using certain techniques. Packet-switched networks dynamically enable the sharing of the network medium, as shown in Figure 11-4.

Packet-switched networks use statistical multiplexing techniques to control network access. This paradigm enables a more efficient use of bandwidth, allowing telcos to provide WAN connections at a lower cost to the end

Figure 11-3
A circuit-switched network

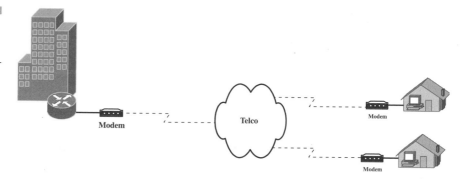

Figure 11-4
A packet-switched
network

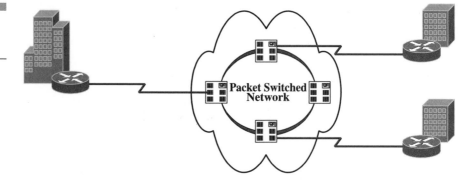

user. Unfortunately, these types of networks offer less control to the administrator than a point-to-point connection. If a business needs to cover large geographic ranges and needs long connect times, this type of connection tends to be the most cost-effective.

Working with Service Providers

When working with service providers, it is important to understand the nomenclature used when describing the different components used to make a WAN connection. This vocabulary is extremely important when provisioning and troubleshooting WAN connections. Without it, you and your service provider representative may be talking about different components and time is wasted trying to establish where a problem may lie.

You must understand five basic concepts in order to interface with your WAN service provider:

- *Customer premise equipment* (CPE)
- Demarcation
- Local loop
- Central office
- Toll network

In Figure 11-5, we can see a visual representation of the concepts used to connect to a WAN service provider.

The CPE is considered to be the devices that are physically located at the customer's site. This includes the router and any devices leased to the customer by the service provider.

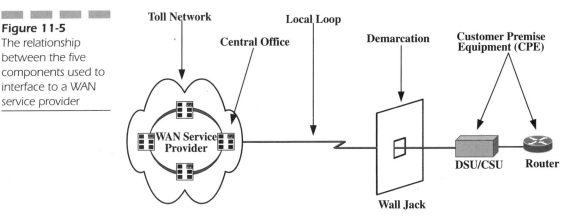

Figure 11-5
The relationship between the five components used to interface to a WAN service provider

The demarcation is generally considered to be the jack that you plug your CSU/DSU into. Its purpose is to indicate the separation of the WAN service provider's responsibility and the customer's responsibility. For example, if the problem exists on the WAN service provider's side of the jack, then it is the WAN service provider's problem. However, when a problem occurs, it can take both a WAN service provider representative and a representative from the local site to troubleshoot where the problem is occurring.

The local loop is used to describe the line that connects your building to the central office. When dealing with 56K-modem technologies, it is the quality of this last leg that frequently limits your ability to get 56K-modem service.

The *Central Office* (CO) switch is the nearest point of presence for the WAN provider's service. The toll network is the compilation of switches and facilities inside the WAN provider's cloud, as shown in Figure 11-5.

Serial Connections

In order to connect to any WAN service provider (point-to-point or packet-switched), we must be able to connect the cable to the interface on a Cisco router. Many different types of cables exist. Today's serial interfaces are generally the high-density DB-60 pin connector that can support the following signaling standards:

- EIA/TIA-232
- EIA/TIA-449

- V.35
- X.21
- EIA-530

As a general rule of thumb for serial cables, the shorter the cable, the higher its maximum speed transfer. Table 11-1 indicates the maximum recommended distances and speed for each signaling standard.

When you order a Cisco router with a serial interface, you must also order the type of cable you want with it. It is important to remember to specify the correct cable or you could end up with the proverbial square peg for a round hole.

In order for two devices to communicate over a synchronous serial interface, one end must be the *Data Circuit-Terminating Equipment* (DCE), while the other end must be the *Data Terminal Equipment* (DTE). In all cases, the DCE end always provides the clocking on the WAN link. In almost all of the cases, either side of the WAN link can be configured as a DTE or a DCE, but generally the Telco provides clocking on the WAN link.

WAN Encapsulation

In order for data to cross a WAN circuit, the data must be encapsulated in frames. The type of encapsulation used is dependent upon the type of WAN technology you have subscribed. In order to communicate across a WAN

Table 11-1

Maximum recommended distances

Rate (bps)	EIA/TIA-232 Max. Length (feet)	EIA/TIA-449, V.35, X.21 and EIA-530 Max. Length (feet)
2400	200	4100
4800	100	2050
9600	50	1025
19200	25	513
38400	12	256
56000	8.6	102
1544000	—	50

link, both sides of the WAN connection must use the same type of encapsulation in order to communicate.

HDLC

HDLC is an *Internal Organization for Standardization* (ISO) standard data-link protocol that encapsulates data on synchronous serial data links. Unfortunately, the ISO standard HDLC was never really adopted because of its limited capability to indicate which network protocol it is carrying. In order to make HDLC useful, many vendors, including Cisco, have developed their own proprietary HDLC with an additional control field so that they can carry more than a single network protocol, as shown in Figure 11-6.

Because of this difference in functionality, HDLC can usually only be used when the same vendor's routers are being used on both sides of a WAN link. If we are connecting a Cisco router to a non-Cisco router over a WAN link, we should use PPP encapsulation.

PPP

PPP is another method for transporting frames over a point-to-point link. It is a bit-oriented protocol that can run over synchronous or asynchronous links. PPP uses a variant of HDLC as the foundation for encapsulation. This encapsulation provides for the multiplexing of multiple network-layer protocols simultaneously over the same link. The PPP encapsulation

Figure 11-6
Comparison of ISO HDLC and Cisco HDLC

Flag	Address	Control	Data	FCS	Flag

ISO HDLC

Flag	Address	Control	Proprietary	Data	FCS	Flag

CISCO HDLC

protocol, while based upon ISO HDLC, is not Cisco's proprietary HDLC protocol. For more information about PPP, go to www.netcerts.com/RFCs/1548.txt.

SLIP

In the early 1980s, 3COM implemented a packet-framing protocol that defined a sequence of characters in a framed IP packet on a serial line (SLIP). In 1984, Rick Adams implemented SLIP in version 4.2 Berkeley Unix and Sun Microsystems. Its ease of configuration and reliability made it a *de facto* standard for serial lines. Unfortunately, SLIP had many problems that made it difficult to use in a medium or large environment.

One of SLIP's biggest drawbacks was the lack of a field to indicate the type of protocol. By not giving SLIP the capability to distinguish between network layer protocols, it could only transport a single network layer protocol. As Novell NetWare took off in the late '80s and early '90s, users needed access to their NetWare servers running IPX/SPX as well as TCP/IP. Aside from this deficiency, it had other problems as well.

Few SLIP implementations had the capability to dynamically assign an IP address when using dialup. This means the user had to configure an IP address on his local machine before he could establish a dialup session.

SLIP's shortcomings also made it a difficult protocol for end users. Although SLIP had many imperfections, it provided a low-cost way to access the Internet. For more information about SLIP, go to www.netcerts.com/RFCs/rfc1055.txt.

X.25/LAPB

In the early days of remote access data communication, the transmission protocols were not as sophisticated as they are today. In addition, the transmission circuits were unreliable and prone to errors compared to today's robust transmission facilities. Consequently, a significant amount of overhead occurred in data transmissions. X.25, first adopted by the ITU-T in 1976, is a suite of protocols used to connect end user devices to network devices. *Link Access Procedure for the D-Channel* (LAPB), a data-link layer protocol, manages the flow of data between the DTE and DCE devices.

Frame Relay

Frame Relay is a switched data-link layer protocol that can handle multiple virtual circuits. It is generally considered the next generation of X.25. One of the interesting aspects of Frame Relay is that it only specifies the connection between the customer router and the Frame Relay switch and not the WAN network. This enables service providers to build Frame Relay clouds with differing technologies. These differences in implementation play an important role in the overall performance, cost, and reliability of the network. For example, a Frame Relay frame sent from the local router could be converted to an ATM cell and sent through the Frame Relay cloud until it reaches its destination, at which point it is converted back to a Frame Relay frame and sent to the remote router device.

ATM

Asynchronous Transfer Mode (ATM) is an ITU-T standard for carrying multiple services such as voice, video, and data using a small fixed-sized cell (53 bytes). By using a predetermined, fixed-length cell, the processing of a packet can occur within the hardware, thus reducing latency. ATM combines the guaranteed bandwidth of circuit-switching with the flexibility and efficiency of packet-switching networks.

NOTE: *ATM, SLIP, and X.25 will not be covered any further in the rest of this chapter.*

Configuring HDLC

Synchronous serial lines use HDLC encapsulation by default, so it is not necessary to configure a serial port to use HDLC during a new installation.

However, if your interface is configured with another encapsulation protocol, such as PPP, it may be necessary to change back to HDLC encapsulation. In order to execute the command that tells the interface to use HDLC encapsulation, we must already be in interface configuration mode (indicated by the router prompt). Use the following command to configure HDLC encapsulation on an interface:

```
Router(config-if)#encapsulation hdlc
```

Configuring PPP

PPP consists of three major components:

- The encapsulation method (HDLC)
- The *Link Control Protocol* (LCP)
- The *Network Control Protocol* (NCP)

PPP uses a variant of HDLC as the foundation for encapsulation. This encapsulation provides for the multiplexing of multiple network-layer protocols simultaneously over the same link. The PPP encapsulation protocol, while based upon ISO HDLC, is not Cisco's proprietary HDLC protocol. As shown in Figure 11-7, PPP encapsulation is made up of six distinct fields.

LCP gives PPP its versatility, allowing for the negotiation of packet formats, packet sizes, and authentication. It also gives PPP the capability to determine when the line is failing or functioning properly.

The NCP is actually a suite of protocols. Each subprotocol is designed to handle the configuration intricacies required by its respective network layer protocol.

Figure 11-7
PPP frame format

Flag	Address	Control	Protocol	Data	FCS	Flag

Link Control Protocol (LCP)

Before any network layer protocols can be routed, like TCP/IP and IPX/SPX, LCP must open a connection and negotiate the configuration. Three components within LCP will be discussed:

- Authentication
- Compression
- Multilink PPP

NOTE: *PPP Callback is an option within the LCP suite of protocols. However, it will not be discussed in this book. For more information about PPP callback, refer to McGraw-Hill's* Building Cisco Remote Access Networks *by Adam Quiggle.*

PPP Authentication   PPP authentication is the very first protocol to be negotiated within the LCP suite of protocols after a client has connected. Two authentication protocols are commonly used: the *Password Authentication Protocol* (PAP) and the *Challenge Handshake Authentication Protocol* (CHAP).

NOTE: *Although authentication is not necessary to connect using PPP, it is definitely an integral part of any security strategy.*

Password Authentication Protocol (PAP)   PAP is the simplest authentication protocol. Once the link has been established, authentication will take place (if configured). During this period, the username and password pair is repeatedly sent to the Cisco router until the authentication is accepted or rejected.

When the username and password is sent using PAP, no encryption scheme will hide the username or password, as shown in Figure 11-8.

Because the username and password are sent unencrypted, it is subject to a playback attack. A playback attack is when an intruder "listens" to the

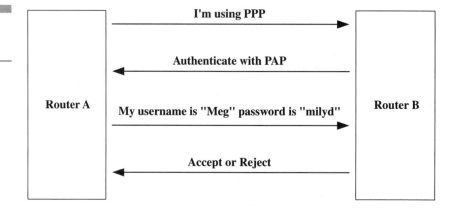

Figure 11-8
PAP authentication
process

line during the authentication process, intercepts, and records the authentication process. An intruder would then be able to use that recorded authentication process to gain access to your system. Although this is not an easy process, it can be done.

In order to configure your Cisco router to use PAP encapsulation, you must be in interface configuration mode on the interface on which you want to configure PAP authentication. The format of the command is

```
Router(config-if)#ppp authentication pap
```

Challenge Handshake Protocol (CHAP) To improve security, we can use a more secure authentication method called CHAP. During a CHAP authentication, the Cisco router sends a challenge to the connecting host, as shown in Figure 11-9.

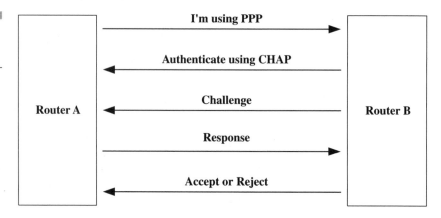

Figure 11-9
CHAP authentication
process

The challenge is in the form of a random number. This number, called an *encryption key*, is generated by the Cisco router and must be unique and unpredictable. The host will then encrypt the username and password using a one-way hash function, typically using MD5. This newly encrypted message sent by the host is called the *response*.

When the Cisco Router receives the response, it decrypts the username and password using the key sent for that connection and compares it against the valid usernames and passwords in its database. These security features in CHAP make it more secure than PAP. Because the random number sent in the challenge is unique and unpredictable, CHAP protects against playback. In addition, the host uses the encryption key to encrypt the username and password; neither the password nor the username is sent over the wire in clear text form.

Lastly, CHAP provides additional protection by repeatedly challenging the host every two minutes. These repeated challenges limit your exposure to any single attack.

Configuration of your Cisco router is almost identical to that of PAP. The format of the command is

```
Router(config-if)#ppp authentication chap
```

For more information about PAP and CHAP, go to `www.netcerts.com/RFCs/rfc1334.txt` (PPP Authentication Protocols).

Creating User Accounts   Now that we have a basic understanding of PAP and CHAP authentication, we now need to know how to create a user account so that we have something to compare authentication requests against.

Cisco routers have the capability to create a local user account database. Creating a username on the local Cisco router to authenticate to another router is a two-step process. First, we must configure the hostname of the router. We can do that by using the following command:

```
Router(config)#hostname router-name

router-name     WORD     The name of the user (such as RouterA)
```

The second step is to create a password and username on the remote router. To create a username and password for a Cisco router, use the following command:

```
Router(config)#username user-account-name encryption-type password
```

user-account-name	**WORD**	*The name of the user (such as RouterA)*
encryption-type	**0, 7**	*(Optional) The level of encryption used to encrypt the password for the user. This keeps the password from being displayed as clear text in the configuration file.*
password	**WORD**	*The password*

In Figures 11-10 and 11-11, we can see how the hostname, username, and password must be used in combination in order for a Cisco router to authenticate another Cisco router.

Notice that the password used in both examples is identical. This is critical for the successful authentication of a PPP synchronous link.

Two different encryption types are available when creating a user account on a local Cisco router. It is important to understand the distinction between the two different levels and how to make passwords unreadable in the configuration file. The first encryption type is 0, which specifies that the password that is about to be entered is unencrypted. This enables a plain

Figure 11-10
Configuration file for RouterA to authenticate RouterB

```
!
hostname RouterA
!
username RouterB password 0 jaguar
!
interface Serial0
 ip address 192.168.1.3 255.255.255.0
 encapsulation ppp
 ppp authentication chap
!
```

Figure 11-11
Configuration file for RouterB to authenticate RouterA

```
!
hostname RouterB
!
username RouterA password 0 jaguar
!
interface Serial1
 ip address 192.168.1.2 255.255.255.0
 encapsulation ppp
 ppp authentication chap
!
```

text password to be entered during user account creation. The second encryption type is 7 and specifies that a Cisco router has already encrypted the password that is about to be entered. Although it may not be apparent why this is important, it should become clear in just a moment.

If a user account is created using the encryption type 0, we may not necessarily want everyone who has access to the configuration file to know this password. In order to encrypt user passwords in a configuration file, the `service password-encryption` must be turned on. This is easily accomplished using the following command:

```
Router(config)#service password-encryption
```

Once password-encryption has been enabled, all passwords in the configuration file are encrypted. If a user's password has been encrypted, disabling password-encryption does not decrypt the user's password; it still remains encrypted.

Figure 11-12 shows us that service password-encryption is disabled and we can view the password for user Suzy.

In Figure 11-13, we can see that after password-encryption has been enabled that we can no longer see the password for Suzy's user account.

Now if we wanted to copy Suzy's user account from RouterA to Router B, we can use the encryption type 7 to create the user's account and password without actually knowing the value of the password, as shown in Figure 11-14.

NOTE: *How the service-password encryption command works is not on the CCNA exam.*

Figure 11-12
User account's password before password-encryption is enabled

```
RouterA#show running-config
Building configuration . . .

Current configuration:
!
version 11.3
service timestamps debug uptime
service timestamps log uptime
no service password-encryption
service udp-small-servers
service tcp-small-servers
```

```
!
hostname RouterA
!
username suzy password 0 suzy
!
```

Figure 11-13
User account's password before password-encryption is disabled

```
RouterA#show running-config
Building configuration . . .

Current configuration:
!
version 11.3
service timestamps debug uptime
service timestamps log uptime
service password-encryption
service udp-small-servers
service tcp-small-servers
!
hostname RouterA
!
username suzy password 7 1404071115
!
```

Figure 11-14
Creating a user account with encryption type 7

```
RouterB(config)#username suzy password 7 1404071115
```

PPP Compression   Compression can be a useful facility for slow links. It has the capability to speed up the transfer rates, thus giving the appearance of having more bandwidth. Because compression is a negotiated option within LCP, both the client and the access server must support compression or it will be disabled. Two different kinds of compression on a Cisco Router will be discussed: Predictor and Stacker.

NOTE: *Other forms of compression can be configured for a PPP connection, but we are only going to cover Predictor and Stacker.*

The capability to compress a file is directly related to the type of file that needs to be compressed. Standard text files are readily compressible, but GIFs, JPEGs, and any other multimedia file are not. These types of files (GIFs and JPEGs) have already undergone a compression algorithm to minimize their storage requirements.

Unfortunately, when trying to compress a file that has already undergone some kind of compression, the end result is not always beneficial. This is because a compressed file that undergoes compression again can frequently end up being larger than before it was compressed. In addition, the CPU of a Cisco router is taxed during the compressing and uncompressing of this data. Therefore, you should make sure that there would be some benefits by turning on compression.

Predictor Originally developed by Novell, the compression algorithm Predictor works by trying to predict the next sequence of characters in a data stream by using a guess table with predefined values based on a hash of the previous characters.

One of the advantages of Predictor compression is that it takes into account whether the data has already been compressed or not. Predictor can do this because it will add a flag bit for every byte of data. This flag bit is used to indicate whether the data for this packet has been compressed or not. This alerts the decompressor to the status of the frame (compressed or uncompressed). For more information about the Predictor compression algorithm, go to www.netcerts.com/RFCs/rfc1978.txt (PPP Predictor Compression Protocol).

Stacker Stacker, developed by STAC Electronics, is based upon the Lempel-Ziv compression algorithm. Stacker looks at the data stream and replaces a continuous stream of characters withuses this information to reconstruct the data stream.

```
Router(config-if)#compress compression-type compression-option
```

compression-type	stac	Use STAC compression
	predictor	Use Predictor compression

Although each compression method seeks to do a similar task, they have different repercussions on the Cisco router when implemented. For example, Predictor tends to be more memory-intensive, while Stacker tends to be more CPU-intensive. When planning your WAN, you should keep this in mind so that you can order appropriately configured equipment.

PPP Multilink   PPP Multilink gives a router the capability to split and recombine packets over multiple interfaces. Multilink is an LCP option that is negotiated during call connection. During LCP negotiation, a client can indicate that it can combine multiple physical links into a bundle. This bundle can then appear to operate as a single WAN link, as shown in Figure 11-15.

The Multilink protocol addresses several problems related to load balancing across multiple WAN links, including the following:

- Multi-vendor interoperability
- Packet fragmentation
- Packet sequence and load balancing

During LCP negotiation, a client can indicate its ability to use Multilink by sending the *Maximum Received Reconstructed Unit* (MRRU). Similar to all of the other LCP options, both sides must support Multilink in order for a successful negotiation of Multilink PPP. To configure Multilink PPP, use the following command:

```
Router(config-if)#ppp multilink
```

Network Control Protocol (NCP)

NCP is a collection of independently defined protocols that are responsible for negotiating a network layer's attributes during PPP setup. The use of NCP layer protocols is generally used when one side of the WAN connection is missing information for the successful operation of a particular protocol. For example, if a user were to dial into a Cisco router, the user's machine

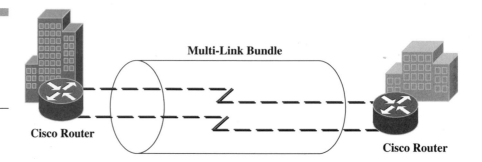

Figure 11-15
Multilink PPP
bundling two lines
into one single
logical WAN
connection

would generally have no idea of which IP address to use and must therefore obtain one from the Cisco router through NCP/IPCP negotiations. However, when using PPP over a dedicated connection, the network administrator assigns all network layer attributes and thus the capabilities of NCP are not important. For more information about NCP and dialup connections, refer to *Building Cisco Remote Access Networks*.

Monitoring and Verifying WAN Connections

Monitoring and troubleshooting PPP connections is easy with the tools that Cisco has provided in their IOS. These commands enable various attributes to be viewed, as we will see in this section.

Show Interface

The `show interface` command is one of the most basic commands that can be used to verify the status of a serial link and to identify its encapsulation method. In Figure 11-16, we can see that interface serial 0 is up (the physical layer) and the line protocol is up (the data-link layer).

This means that whatever the encapsulation is, it is operational. In addition, we can see that the encapsulation is PPP. Using all of this information, we can see that our PPP WAN link is up and operational.

Debug PPP Authentication

Using the `debug ppp authentication` command, we can see the outcome of two routers attempting to negotiate a PPP connection. In Figure 11-17, we can see two routers going through the authentication process.

From this example, we can see that once RouterB and RouterA successfully negotiate a connection, the line protocol comes up. If authentication is not successful, the two routers continually attempt to authenticate until the username/password combination is correct or the lines are physically disconnected, as shown in Figure 11-18.

Notice that every two seconds the routers are attempting to authenticate.

Figure 11-16
Output from the
show interface
serial 0
command on a PPP
WAN link

```
RouterA#show interface serial 0
Serial0 is up, line protocol is up
  Hardware is HD64570
  Internet address is 192.168.1.3/24
  MTU 1500 bytes, BW 1544 Kbit, DLY 20000 usec,
    reliability 255/255 , txload 1/255 , rxload 1/255
  Encapsulation PPP, loopback not set, keepalive set (10 sec)
  LCP Open
  Open: IPCP, CDPCP
  Last input 00:00:01, output 00:00:02, output hang never
  Last clearing of "show interface" counters never
  Queueing strategy: fifo
  Output queue 0/40 , 0 drops; input queue 0/75 , 0 drops
  5 minute input rate 0 bits/sec, 0 packets/sec
  5 minute output rate 0 bits/sec, 0 packets/sec
    4724 packets input, 223881 bytes, 0 no buffer
    Received 30 broadcasts, 0 runts, 0 giants, 0 throttles
    0 input errors, 0 CRC, 0 frame, 0 overrun, 0 ignored, 0
abort
    4810 packets output, 224300 bytes, 0 underruns
    0 output errors, 0 collisions, 170 interface resets
    0 output buffer failures, 0 output buffers swapped out
    291 carrier transitions
    DCD=up  DSR=up  DTR=up  RTS=up  CTS=up
```

Figure 11-17
Output from
debug ppp
authentication
during PPP
authentication

```
RouterB#debug ppp authentication
03:36:44: %LINK-3-UPDOWN: Interface Serial1, changed state to up
03:36:45: Se1 PPP: Treating connection as a dedicated line
03:36:45: Se1 PPP: Phase is AUTHENTICATING, by both
03:36:45: Se1 CHAP: O CHALLENGE id 94 len 28 from "RouterB"
03:36:45: Se1 CHAP: I CHALLENGE id 90 len 28 from "RouterA"
03:36:45: Se1 CHAP: O RESPONSE id 90 len 28 from "RouterB"
03:36:45: Se1 CHAP: I RESPONSE id 94 len 28 from "RouterA"
03:36:45: Se1 CHAP: O SUCCESS id 94 len 4
03:36:45: Se1 CHAP: I SUCCESS id 90 len 4
03:36:46: %LINEPROTO-5-UPDOWN: Line protocol on Interface
Serial1, changed state to up
```

NOTE: *HDLC does not have any facilities for authentication and therefore we do not need the capability to debug authentication when HDLC is our encapsulation.*

Figure 11-18
Output from
`debug ppp`
`authentication`
with incorrectly
configured
usernames and
passwords

```
03:40:37: Se1 PPP: Phase is AUTHENTICATING, by both
03:40:37: Se1 CHAP: O CHALLENGE id 118 len 28 from "RouterB"
03:40:37: Se1 CHAP: I CHALLENGE id 114 len 28 from "RouterA"
03:40:37: Se1 CHAP: O RESPONSE id 114 len 28 from "RouterB"
03:40:37: Se1 CHAP: I RESPONSE id 118 len 28 from "RouterA"
03:40:37: Se1 CHAP: O FAILURE id 118 len 25 msg is "MD/DES
compare failed"
03:40:39: Se1 PPP: Phase is AUTHENTICATING, by both
03:40:39: Se1 CHAP: O CHALLENGE id 119 len 28 from "RouterB"
03:40:39: Se1 CHAP: I CHALLENGE id 115 len 28 from "RouterA"
03:40:39: Se1 CHAP: O RESPONSE id 115 len 28 from "RouterB"
03:40:39: Se1 CHAP: I RESPONSE id 119 len 28 from "RouterA"
03:40:39: Se1 CHAP: O FAILURE id 119 len 25 msg is "MD/DES
compare failed"
03:40:41: Se1 PPP: Phase is AUTHENTICATING, by both
03:40:41: Se1 CHAP: O CHALLENGE id 120 len 28 from "RouterB"
03:40:41: Se1 CHAP: I CHALLENGE id 116 len 28 from "RouterA"
03:40:41: Se1 CHAP: O RESPONSE id 116 len 28 from "RouterB"
03:40:41: Se1 CHAP: I RESPONSE id 120 len 28 from "RouterA"
03:40:41: Se1 CHAP: O FAILURE id 120 len 25 msg is "MD/DES
compare failed"
```

Chapter Summary

In this chapter, we have discussed the various WAN connections employed today. In addition, we have learned about the various encapsulation methods (HDLC and PPP) used over synchronous WAN links and how to debug PPP connections. In the next chapter, we will learn how to configure ISDN *Basic Rate Interface* (BRI) connections.

From the Real World

Most likely, you are reading this book in the pursuit of the CCNA certification. Although the feeling of passing an exam to achieve the certification you are interested in is great, don't forget that just memorizing a series of commands does not make you an expert. It is the ability to quickly recall the appropriate command and apply it to the right interface. Nothing is more embarrassing than trying to apply an IP address while in global configuration mode. So how does one develop this ability? Practice, practice, practice.

You can gain experience in several ways; the first most obvious is to build a home lab. The 2500 series router is the quintessential router used for those pursuing a Cisco certification. However, less expensive alternatives exist, such as the Cisco 3100 or 3200 series routers. Just because they are older doesn't mean you can't get the experience you need. They can easily run IOS 11.0.22 (assuming you have enough Flash and RAM).

Another method for getting practice on a Cisco router is to rent time on the many router labs that are available on the Internet. Many of the router labs offer simple scenarios, or you can design simple scenarios yourself.

Remember that you are not just pursuing a certification through rote memorization, but trying to understand the structure of the Cisco IOS so that it becomes second nature. As you practice, think about the attributes that need to be set and where they need to be set. For example, an IP address needs to be set on an interface configuration mode, while the hostname needs to be set in global configuration mode. You will find that this understanding of the Cisco IOS will help you more than you can imagine when trying to find a command that you aren't totally familiar with.

Adam Quiggle

Frequently Asked Questions (FAQ)

Question: What is the difference between a synchronous connection and an asynchronous connection?

Answer: Synchronous communication uses a precise clock to define data communication transmissions. It embeds the signal inside the communications. It is used with Frame Relay, X.25, T1, and T3 connections. Asynchronous connections do not have a precise clock to define when data can be transferred, but it uses start bits and stop bits to identify when data is being sent (such as dialup).

Question: My WAN connection is plugged directly into my router. Where is my CSU/DSU?

Answer: Many Cisco routers have built-in CSU/DSUs to minimize the number of problems that can happen at a remote site.

Question: I need to move my router to a different room. Should I move the demarcation?

Answer: No, the WAN service provider will move the demarcation to a location of your choosing (you will probably be charged for moving your demarcation).

Question: I have a non-Cisco router in which I am trying to bring up an HDLC connection. Why won't the protocol come up?

Answer: Many vendors' implementations of HDLC are proprietary and they won't work together. Use PPP to establish a WAN connection with a non-Cisco router.

Question: I have configured multilink PPP on my router, but I can't get both lines to come up.

Answer: You must configure multilink PPP on both ends, not just one end, in order for PPP multilink to work.

Question: Should I configure compression on my WAN links?

Answer: If you are experiencing congestion on your WAN links, then congestion may be an option. However, you will want to evaluate the type of data that is being sent and make sure that it will be susceptible to compression. Otherwise, you will be wasting CPU cycles trying to compress already compressed data.

Case Study: Connecting to an Internet Service Provider

The objective here is to configure two routers to use PPP encapsulation over a WAN link. Quiggle Inc. wants to use PPP encapsulation between two of their sites with Cisco routers. Figure 11-19 shows us the scenario.

The equipment required is as follows:

- Two Cisco routers with at least one serial interface (Cisco 25xx)
- A back-to-back cable

Here is the required information:

- Central office information

  - DCE device
  - Serial 0 IP address: 192.168.100.1
  - Ethernet IP address: 192.168.1.1
  - Use EIGRP for the routing protocol.

- Remote site information:

  - Serial 0 IP address: 192.168.100.2
  - Ethernet IP Address: 192.168.2.1
  - Use EIGRP for routing protocol

Figure 11-19

Configuring two routers using PPP encapsulation over a dedicated connection

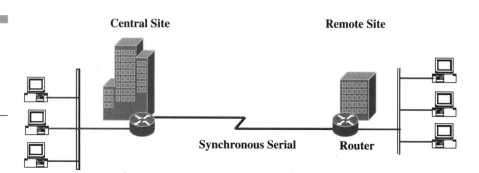

Central Site   Remote Site

Synchronous Serial   Router

To solve this problem, we need to break it down into two tasks:

1. Configure the central site

   a. Configure the Ethernet interface.

   b. Configure the serial interface.

   c. Set up EIGRP routing.

2. Configure the remote site.

   a. Configure the Ethernet interface.

   b. Configure the serial interface.

   c. Set up EIGRP routing.

Task 1: Configure Central Site

1. Enter enable mode on the router.

   ```
   Router>ena
   ```

2. Enter global configuration mode.

   ```
   Router#config t
   ```

3. Name the router.

   ```
   Router(config)#hostname CentralSite
   ```

4. Configure the Ethernet interface.

   ```
   CentralSite(config)#interface ethernet0
   ```

5. Specify the IP address for the Ethernet interface.

   ```
   CentralSite(config-if)#ip address 192.168.1.1 255.255.255.0
   ```

6. Configure the Serial0 interface.

   ```
   CentralSite(config)#interface serial0
   ```

7. Describe the interface for future reference.

   ```
   CentralSite(config-if)#description Interface to the Remote site
   ```

8. Define PPP encapsulation for the interface.

   ```
   CentralSite(config-if)#encapsulation ppp
   ```

9. Specify the CHAP authentication.

   ```
   CentralSite(config-if)#ppp authentication chap
   ```

10. Specify the IP address for the serial 0 interface.

    ```
    CentralSite(config-if)#ip address 192.168.100.1 255.255.255.0
    ```

11. Specify the clock rate to set the clock on the synchronous line (this is not needed if you are using a real WAN service provider).

```
CentralSite(config-if)#clock rate 640000
```

12. Configure the username and password so that the router may authenticate the remote site.

```
CentralSite(config)#username RemoteSite password cisco
```

13. Configure the EIGRP routing protocol (autonomous system [AS] #109).

```
CentralSite(config)#router eigrp 109
```

14. Advertise the LAN network within the AS.

```
CentralSite(config-router)#network 192.168.1.0
```

15. Advertise the WAN network within the AS.

```
CentralSite(config-router)#network 192.168.100.0
```

Task 2: Configure Remote Site A

1. Enter enable mode on the router.

```
Router>ena
```

2. Enter global configuration mode.

```
Router#config t
```

3. Name the router.

```
Router(config)#hostname RemoteSite
```

4. Configure the Ethernet interface.

```
RemoteSite(config)#interface ethernet0
```

5. Specify the IP address for the Ethernet interface.

```
RemoteSite(config-if)#ip address 192.168.2.1 255.255.255.0
```

6. Configure the Serial0 interface.

```
RemoteSite(config)#interface serial0
```

7. Describe the interface for future reference.

```
RemoteSite(config-if)#description Interface to the Central site
```

8. Define the PPP encapsulation for the interface.

```
RemoteSite(config-if)#encapsulation ppp
```

9. Specify the CHAP authentication.

```
RemoteSite(config-if)#ppp authentication chap
```

10. Specify the IP address for the serial 0 interface and set up the user accounts.

```
RemoteSite(config-if)#ip address 192.168.100.2 255.255.255.0
```

11. Configure the username and password so that the router can authenticate the remote site.

```
RemoteSite(config)#username CentralSite password cisco
```

12. Configure the EIGRP routing protocol (AS #109).

```
RemoteSite(config)#router eigrp 109
```

13. Advertise the LAN network within the AS.

```
RemoteSite(config-router)#network 192.168.1.0
```

14. Advertise the WAN network within the AS.

```
RemoteSite(config-router)#network 192.168.100.0
```

The configuration files are shown in Figures 11-20 and 11-21.

Figure 11-20
Configuration file for the central site router

```
!
hostname CentralSite
!
username RemoteSite password 0 cisco
!
interface Ethernet0
 ip address 192.168.1.1 255.255.255.0
!
interface Serial0
 description Interface to the Remote site
 ip address 192.168.100.1 255.255.255.0
 encapsulation ppp
 no ip mroute-cache
 ppp authentication chap
!
router eigrp 109
 network 192.168.1.0
 network 192.168.100.0
!
ip classless
!
!
line con 0
line aux 0
line vty 0 4
 login
!
```

Figure 11-21
Configuration file for
the remote site router

```
!
hostname RemoteSite
!
username CentralSite password 0 cisco
ip subnet-zero
!
interface Ethernet0
 ip address 192.168.2.1 255.255.255.0
 no ip directed-broadcast
!
interface Serial1
 description Interface to the Central site
 ip address 192.168.100.2 255.255.255.0
 no ip directed-broadcast
 encapsulation ppp
 clockrate 64000
 ppp authentication chap
!
router eigrp 109
 network 192.168.1.0
 network 192.168.100.0
 !
ip classless
 !
 !
line con 0
line aux 0
line vty 0 4
 !
```

████ ████ # Questions

1. Typically, a LAN connection is slower than a WAN connection.

    a. True

    b. False

2. Dedicated circuits typically use which type of communication?

    a. Frame Relay

    b. X.25

    c. ISDN

    d. Synchronous connection

    e. Asynchronous connection

3. What is the purpose of a CSU/DSU?

    a. To convert the ISDN switch signals to a connection a router can interpret

    b. To enhance the security of a Web site

    c. None, it is an old piece of equipment not required anymore.

    d. To transform the signal from a telco to a synchronous connection that a router can understand

4. Which of the following are circuit-switched technologies?

    a. Frame Relay

    b. ISDN

    c. X.25

    d. Analog telephone

5. Which type of WAN encapsulation can be used on a dedicated connection on a Cisco router?

    a. SLIP

    b. PPP

    c. HDLC

    d. Frame Relay

6. Which encapsulation protocol is PPP based on?

    a. LAPB

    b. LAPD

    c. HDLC

    d. PAP

7. Which command correctly encapsulates PPP on a serial line?

   a. `Router(config)#ppp encapsulation`

   b. `Router(config)#encapsulation ppp`

   c. `Router(config-if)#ppp encapsulation`

   d. `Router(config-if)#encapsulation ppp`

8. Which authentication protocol sends the password in clear text over the dialup link? Select all that apply.

   a. PAP

   b. CHAP

   c. MS-CHAP

   d. BAP

9. What is the purpose of Multilink?

   a. To carry multiple protocols over the same dialup link

   b. To aggregate multiple lines to give additional bandwidth to a single site

   c. To link multiple sites together using various routing protocols

10. What is the correct command to debug PPP authentication requests?

    a. `Router#debug ppp`

    b. `Router#debug ppp authentication requests`

    c. `Router#debug ppp authentication`

    d. `Router#debug ppp requests`

11. Frame Relay is which type of network?

    a. Dedicated connection

    b. Circuit-switched network

    c. Packet-switched network

    d. Broadcast network

12. Frame Relay uses which data-link layer protocol?

    a. LAPB

    b. LAPD

    c. PPP

    d. SDLC

    e. HDLC

13. X.25 uses which data-link layer protocol?

    a. LAPB

    b. LAPD

    c. PPP

    d. SDLC

    e. HDLC

14. Which command correctly configures a user account on a Cisco router?

    a. `Router(config)#hostname sam`

    b. `Router(config)#username sam password cisco`

    c. `Router(config)#username sam cisco`

    d. `Router(config)#hostname sam password cisco`

15. Which of the following are compression techniques that can be used with PPP encapsulation?

    a. Zipper

    b. Stacker

    c. Predictor

    d. Compactor

    e. Crusher

16. Which command can we use to verify the encapsulation of interface serial 0?

    a. `Show interface serial 0`

    b. `Show encapsulation serial 0`

    c. `Show interface encapsulation`

    d. `Show PPP interfaces`

17. Which compression protocol is more memory-intensive?

    a. Stacker

    b. Predictor

    c. Zipper

18. CHAP Authentication _____.

    a. sends the password in clear text

    b. can be subject to playback attacks

    c. sends an encrypted password

    d. can be used with HDLC encapsulation

19. Which is a valid protocol that makes up the PPP protocol?

    a. LCP

    b. Modem

    c. ATM

    d. ISDN

20. SLIP is _____.

    a. the *de facto* dialup standard

    b. capable of encapsulating multiple network protocols

    c. an older dialup protocol that has been replaced by PPP

Answers

1. **b.** False

   Local Area Networks are generally much faster than a Wide Area Network. Ethernet runs at 10mb/sec compared to a T1 at 1.544mb/sec. There are WAN connections that run faster than 10mb/sec, but within they are run out of the ICND exam scope.

2. **d.** Synchronous connection

   WAN circuits like a T1 (dedicated circuit) use synchronous communication. Synchronous communications uses a precise clock for sending data. Asynchronous connections are used with modems.

3. **d.** To transform the signal from a telco to a synchronous connection that a router can understand

   The function of a CSU/DSU is to convert a signal from the data terminal equipment device (such as a router) to a signal the data circuit-terminating switch in a carrier network can understand.

4. **b.** ISDN and **d.** Analog telephone

   ISDN and the *Plain Old Telephone Service* (POTS) are a circuit-switched technology while Frame Relay and X.25 are packet switched network technologies. Circuit-switched technology forms a physical point-to-point path during call setup. This type of behavior is associated with the telephone system.

5. **b.** PPP and **c.** HDLC

   PPP and HDLC encapsulations can be used on a dedicated connection. SLIP is an older dialup encapsulation and Frame Relay is a packet-switched technology.

6. **c.** HDLC

   PPP is based upon HDLC. LAPB is used for X.25 and LAPD is used for ISDN. PAP is an authentication protocol.

7. **d.** `Router(config-if)#encapsulation ppp`

   The format of the command is `encapsulation ppp` and it must be executed on the interface, which is indicated by the keyword `-if` in the router prompt.

8. **a.** PAP

   PAP is the most basic authentication protocol and sends the password in clear text over the dialup link. CHAP and MS-CHAP do not send the password in clear text.

9. b. To aggregate multiple lines to give additional bandwidth to a single site.

Multilink PPP is used to aggregate the bandwidth between multiple WAN links and give the appearance of a single WAN link to the router. This minimizes the problems associated with routing over two links.

10. c. `Router#debug ppp authentication`

The command `debug ppp authentication` displays a subnet of information provided by `debug ppp negotiation`. The keywords pap and chap are not valid within the `debug ppp authentication` command.

11. c. Packet-switched network

A Frame Relay network is considered a packet-switching network.

12. b. LAPD

Frame Relay uses *Link Access Protocol-D* (LAPD) as its data link layer protocol. LAPD is a subnet of the Integrated Services Digital Network specification.

13. a. LAPB

X.25 uses *Link Access Procedure Balanced* (LAPB) as its data link layer protocol.

14. b. `Router(config)#username sam password cisco`

When creating a user account you must be in global configuration mode. In addition, the format of the command is `username xxx password yyy`.

15. b. Stacker and **c.** Predictor

Predictor and Stacker are the only two compression methods listed that can be used with PPP.

16. a. `Show interface serial 0`

The `show interface` can be used to see the encapsulation type used on an interface.

17. b. Predictor

STAC compression protocol utilizes the Lempel-Ziv encoding method. It is more memory intensive but less CPU intensive.

18. c. sends an encrypted password

CHAP and MS-CHAP do not send the password in clear text.

19. a. LCP

PPP is made up of two different protocols, *Link Control Protocol* (LCP) and *Network Control Protocol* (NCP).

20. c. an older dialup protocol that has been replaced by PPP

SLIP is an older dialup protocol that has been replaced by PPP.

Integrated Services Digital Network (ISDN)

Objectives

In this chapter, we are going to discuss the *Integrated Services Digital Network's* (ISDN) *Basic Rate Interface* (BRI). Although ISDN still utilizes the same infrastructure that the *Plain Old Telephone System* (POTS) uses, the way it delivers that service is unique. In addition, because of its flexibility and its speed, it has many different uses, as we will see in this chapter.

- Overview of ISDN BRI
- Understand ISDN components
- Configure ISDN BRI with *Dial on Demand Routing* (DDR)
- Monitor and troubleshoot ISDN and DDR

ISDN Overview

Over the last 40 years, communication networks have been evolving. The first discussions revolving around ISDN started in 1968. It was envisioned that this new technology would integrate access to a broad range of services, including voice, networking, packet switching, and cable television.

Although ISDN is fundamentally different than analog communications, it has been designed to enable end-to-end compatibility for analog communications (that is, standard telephone). ISDN has several advantages over analog communications:

- Extremely fast call setup
- Less expensive than leased lines
- Faster transmission speeds than analog lines

Analog versus ISDN

Although both analog and ISDN connections have the same objective, which is to use circuit switched networks to create dynamic paths from one site to another, they use fundamentally different technologies to achieve that goal. If we look at Figure 12-1, we can see that both technologies pro-

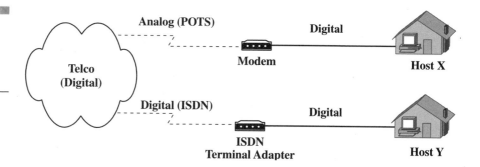

Figure 12-1
The difference
between analog
and ISDN
communications

vide us with access to the telco cloud, but the signal used to get to the telco cloud is different.

In this figure, the modem serving Host X must convert the digital signal to analog before sending to the Telco, where it is then converted back to digital by the Telco. Host Y's transmission starts as a digital transmission and never gets converted to an analog signal, therefore it is a more efficient transmission medium.

B Channel versus D Channel

ISDN and analog lines are similar in that they enable you to set up and tear down connections on demand using the public telephone infrastructure. However, ISDN provides increased bandwidth over a typical dialup connection. Its increased bandwidth is the result of sending data in a completely digital form instead of trying to represent the digital data in an analog medium.

Two different varieties of ISDN are provided by the telcos: BRI and *Primary Rate Interface* (PRI). The primary difference between the types is the number of channels. ISDN has two different types of channels: bearer channels (B channels) and data channels (D channel). The B channels carry all of the voice/data communications at 64 Kbps (some older ISDN switches only enable 56 Kbps of throughput on the B channel), while the D channels are responsible for signaling call setup and teardown. The speed of the D channel is dependent upon the type of ISDN you are using. The D channel for a BRI is 16 Kbps, while the D channel for a PRI is 64 Kbps.

Figure 12-2
The difference
between analog and
ISDN call setup and
call teardown

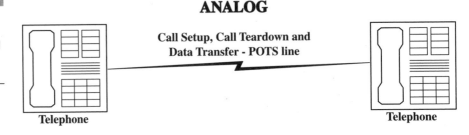

ANALOG

Call Setup, Call Teardown and
Data Transfer - POTS line

Telephone   Telephone

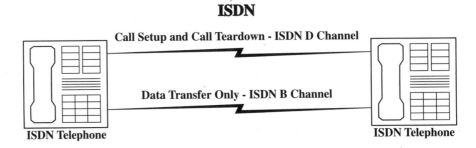

ISDN

Call Setup and Call Teardown - ISDN D Channel

Data Transfer Only - ISDN B Channel

ISDN Telephone   ISDN Telephone

Unlike asynchronous connections, ISDN call setup and teardown is handled out of band, as shown in Figure 12-2.

These different channels (B and D) are not actually physical channels, but logical channels using a single physical circuit. This is accomplished by using *Time Division Multiplexing* (TDM).

ISDN Reference Points

The devices used in ISDN include terminal equipment (TE1 and TE2), *terminal adapters* (TAs), network-termination equipment (NT1 and NT2), and exchange-termination equipment (telco switch). ISDN terminals have two different designations: *Terminal Equipment type 1* (TE1) and *Terminal Equipment type 2* (TE2). In addition, the equipment that makes up an ISDN network is also composed of several logically defined reference points. The following reference points provide connectivity:

- *R* connects TE2 equipment (standard phone) and a TA.
- *S* connects TE1 equipment (ISDN phones and TAs) to the NT2 device.

- *T* connects NT2 equipment to the NT1 device.
- *U* connects NT1 equipment to the telco's ISDN switch.

NOTE: *Reference points identify the signaling characteristics used between two devices.*

TE2 equipment predates the ISDN standards and thus must connect to the ISDN network through a TA. TE1 equipment adheres to the ISDN user-network interface and can connect directly to the S-type reference point that supports B and D channels. In Figure 12-3, we can see that a TA has two interfaces: an R interface and an S interface.

The next point when connecting to an ISDN network is the *Network Termination 2* (NT2). NT2 equipment performs functions similar to the first three layers of the OSI Reference Model. The type of equipment used here can include PABXs, *Local Area Networks* (LANs), terminal controllers, concentrators, and multiplexers. NT1 equipment only performs functions equivalent to the first layer of the OSI model. It enables the ISDN user network to interface with the telco ISDN switch.

So why are all these reference points important? In the U.S., the telco is only allowed to provide up to the NT1 interface, as opposed to Europe where

Figure 12-3
ISDN reference points

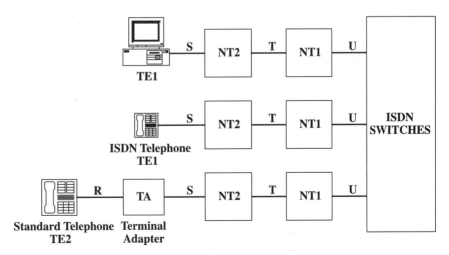

the telcos typically provide up to the NT2 interface. Although this distinction may seem meaningless, it does provide a different level of functionality.

For example, today's standard analog phones work without a separate power source. This is because your local telephone company provides power through the telephone connection. Due to the specification of ISDN, power cannot be provided at the NT1 interface, but it can be provided at the NT2 interface. The end result? In the United States, all ISDN equipment must have an external power source because we have standardized the telcos providing up to the NT1 interface. However, in many European countries where ISDN is commonly the only type of connection in the home, the telco provides power to your ISDN equipment. Although this may seem trivial, consider the fact that in the United States during a blackout your ISDN equipment will not work without an external power source. Our European neighbors, however, can continue to use their ISDN equipment even during a blackout (assuming the telephone company hasn't lost power). Figure 12-4 shows how all of these reference points come together.

The S/T reference point is a passive bus network with four wires. This architecture enables multiple devices to connect to the reference point,

Figure 12-4

The relationship of ISDN reference points and physical equipment

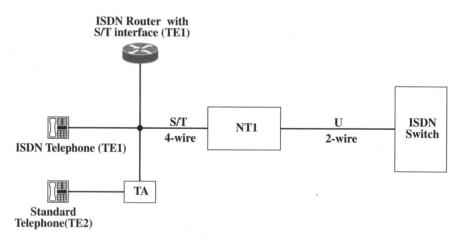

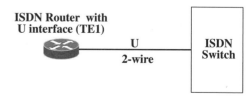

similar to connecting multiple telephones to a standard POTS line. The U reference point can only have a single device attached to it.

Most Cisco ISDN routers offered in the U.S. have an NT1 interface and can connect to the U reference point. This removes the need for an NT1 device. The protocol ANSI T1.601 has been defined to specify the signaling characteristics across the U interface in the United States.

NOTE: *You will want to memorize the ISDN reference points for the CCNA exam.*

ISDN BRI

A typical ISDN BRI service provides two B channels and one D channel, commonly referred to as 2B+D. However, many different flavors of ISDN BRI including 1B+D and 0B+D. Each B channel operates at 64 Kbps or 56 Kbps, while the D channel operates at 16 Kbps. The B channels can be used independently or joined together to form a single 128-Kbps connection. Remember that the D channel is typically used for call setup and teardown, but it can also can be used for data transmission using X.25. Some banks purchase 0B+D for *Automated Teller Machine* (ATM) connections.

If we consider that a single B channel can carry 64 Kbps of information and the D channel can carry 16 Kbps of information, we can see that the total throughput for an ISDN BRI is 144 Kbps, not including framing. However, because we can only use 128 Kbps for data, remember that the D channel is typically only used for call signaling.

ISDN PRI (T1/E1)

The ISDN PRI service offered in North America and Japan provides 23 B channels and a single D channel. The B channels are identical to the B channels used in BRI 64 Kbps. The D channel, however, operates at 64 Kbps, unlike the 16 Kbps provided in an ISDN BRI. Thus, a single ISDN PRI line yields a total of 1.536 Mbps of total throughput.

NOTE: *A channelized T1 uses eight bits for framing, thus providing the well-known value of 1.544 Mbps. For more information about framing, refer to McGraw-Hill's* Building Cisco Remote Access Networks *by Adam Quiggle.*

The ISDN PRI service in Europe (E1) is a bit different in that, instead of offering 23 B channels and a single D channel, they offer 30 B channels and a single D channel for a total of 1.984 Mbps. Remember that for both the T1 and E1 generally only the B channels are used for data and the D channel is reserved for call signaling.

NOTE: *A channelized E1 uses 64 bits for framing, thus providing the well-known value of 2.048 Mbps. For more information about framing, refer to* Building Cisco Remote Access Networks.

ISDN Protocols

The *International Telecommunication Union* (ITU-T) has organized the ISDN protocols into three different types of protocols: Q, E, and I.

The Q Series The Q series of protocols defined by the ITU-T specifies the switching and signaling protocols used between devices. Examples include the following:

- *Q.921* An ISDN user-network interface data-link layer for general aspects
- *Q.931* An ISDN user-network interface network layer specification for basic call control

The I Series The I series of protocols is used to define concepts and interfaces associated with ISDN:

- *I.430* A basic user-network interface for a physical layer specification
- *I.431* A primary rate user-network interface for a physical layer specification

The E Series Lastly, the E series of protocols is used to define telephone network standards:

- *E.164* A numbering plan for the ISDN era
- *E.172* Call routing in the ISDN era

It is important to note that some protocols have been defined in multiple categories, such as the following:

- Q.921 is also I.441, an ISDN user-network interface data-link layer specification.
- Q.931 is also I.451, an ISDN user-network interface network layer specification.

For a more complete list of ISDN protocols, go to `www.cisco.com/warp/public/84/6.html`.

To better understand how these protocols come together, Figure 12-5 shows us how each channel's protocols relate to the OSI model.

This is an important diagram to understand so that you can better understand the context of all the protocols and how they relate to each other.

Figure 12-5

ISDN protocols and the OSI model

	B-Channel	D-Channel
Network Layer	**TCP/IP** or **IPX/SPX** or **AppleTalk**	**Q.931**
Data Link Layer	**HDLC** or **PPP**	**Q.921**
Physical Layer	**I.430 BRI** or **I.431 PRI**	

NOTE: *Make sure that you memorize the purpose of the different series'*
ISDN protocols and their purposes.

Configuring ISDN BRI

The main focus of this section is to configure the physical layer attributes of ISDN BRI. We will also discuss the configuration of setting up a call. Two components need to be configured to make an ISDN BRI line support incoming and outgoing calls:

- The switch type
- The service provider identifiers

Switch Type

We must configure the switch type on an ISDN BRI interface. The selection of the switch type is dependent upon the version of IOS you are running. Prior to IOS 11.3, the switch type selection was limited to the global configuration, but with IOS 11.3 and later, the switch type selection can be configured two ways: globally and on the interface. By configuring the switch type on the interface, we can support multiple switch types (assuming we have multiple BRI interfaces).

The format of the command used to configure the switch type of an ISDN BRI interface is identical, but the options to configure an ISDN BRI line are slightly different, as shown here:

```
Router(config)#isdn switch-type telco-switch-type

telco-switch-type    basic-1tr6     1TR6 switch type for Germany
                     basic-5ess     AT&T 5ESS switch type for the U.S.
                     basic-dms100   Northern DMS-100 switch type
                     basic-net3     NET3 switch type for U.K. and
                                    Europe
                     basic-ni       National ISDN switch type
                     basic-qsig     QSIG switch type
                     basic-ts013    TS013 switch type for Australia
                     ntt            NTT switch type for Japan
                     vn3            VN3 and VN4 switch types for France
```

Service Profiler Identifier (SPID)

A *Service Profile Identifier* (SPID) is typically a 13-digit numeric number that enables service providers to associate the terminal with a terminal service profile. This allows the service provider to assign service characteristics to your equipment (such as call forwarding, caller ID, call waiting, and so on).

Not all switch types require a SPID. Currently, only DMS-100 and NI1 require SPIDs. Similar to a DLCI for Frame Relay, it is only locally significant. Configuration of the SPID is performed on the ISDN BRI interface. To configure an ISDN BRI SPID, use the following command:

```
Router (config-if)#isdn B-channel-number spid-number phone-number
```

B-channel-number	spid1	The specific SPID for the first B-channel
	spid2	The specific SPID for the second B-channel
spid-number	xxxxxxxxxxxxx	The specific SPID for the second B-channel
phone-number	xxxxxxx	phone number associated with the SPID.

Overview of Dial on Demand Routing (DDR)

DDR is a useful feature when using ISDN as your connectivity solution. Unlike dedicated connections that typically charge a flat rate per month, circuit switched connections charges can be based upon a number of different attributes including the following:

- Time connected
- Long-distance charges
- Tariffs

Although some aspects of these charges may be different depending upon the proximity of the two sites, your state's tariffs, and other various attributes, one thing is for certain: the less time you stay connected, the less expensive your ISDN charges.

In recognition of the costs associated with ISDN, technologies have been developed to minimize your connection times. Although these technologies can be used with analog connections as well as ISDN connections, we will focus on ISDN because of its quick call setup times and capability to aggregate the bandwidth of both B channels when needed.

The basic concept of DDR is to enable a router to set up a connection with a remote site when there is "interesting traffic" destined for that remote network. The type of service that we need to access is what is usually known as interesting traffic. For example, if we need to retrieve mail from our mail server, we can classify *Simple Mail Transfer Protocol* (SMTP) packets as interesting traffic and have the ISDN line call the central site when SMTP packets need to go to the remote site. We can also classify certain traffic as "uninteresting" and not allow it to bring up an ISDN line. An example of this could be when a Windows 95/98/NT/2000 computer boots up. It tries to contact the WINS server to tell the server its IP address. We probably don't want to bring up the ISDN line every time we reboot a computer.

Configuring Dial on Demand Routing (DDR)

Cisco has provided us with many options to configure an ISDN line for DDR. We can use DDR for basic connectivity or we can use it to backup our WAN connection. When configuring ISDN for DDR, three main components must be determined, as outlined in Table 12-1.

Dialer-list

As previously mentioned, the `dialer-list` command specifies which traffic should bring the line up. This is important because of the need to keep uninteresting traffic from bringing the line up while still allowing the line to come up when we need it to, as shown in Figure 12-6.

Table 12-1	**Topic**	**Function**
DDR commands and their function	dialer-list	Determines what is interesting traffic
	dialer-group	Determines which interface we should use
	dialer-map	Determines where the traffic is going

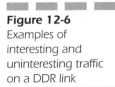

Figure 12-6

Examples of interesting and uninteresting traffic on a DDR link

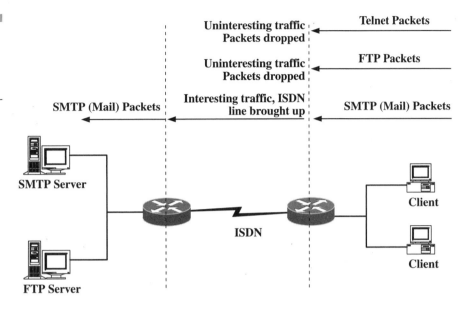

CENTRAL SITE

REMOTE SITE

When defining a dialer-list, we can use the simple form and allow or deny an entire protocol, or we can use access lists for a more refined control over which traffic we want to block or pass. To specify which protocols are interesting and/or uninteresting, use the following command:

```
Router(config)#dialer-list list-number protocol protocol-type
permission
```

list-number	1-10	Specify which dialer-group this list applies to
protocol-type	appletalk	AppleTalk
	ip	IP
	ipx	Novell IPX
permission	deny	Deny specified protocol (simple form).
	list	Add access list to dialer list.
	permit	Permit specified protocol (simple form).

NOTE: *The previous protocol type is only a partial list.*

Access control lists enable an administrator to be more selective about which protocols can bring the line up. Before you start using access lists to specify which protocols can pass or will be blocked, you must understand the environment you are working in. Otherwise, you could inadvertently block protocols that are required for the operation of the remote office.

You can specify protocol selections when using access lists to define interesting traffic with the following command:

```
Router(config)#access-list list-number permission protocol-option
```

list-number	1-99	The IP standard access list
	100-199	The IP extended access list
	200-299	The protocol type-code access list
	300-399	The DECnet access list
	600-699	The AppleTalk access list
	700-799	The 48-bit MAC address access list
	800-899	The IPX standard access list
	900-999	The IPX extended access list
	1000-1099	The IPX SAP access list
	1100-1199	The extended 48-bit MAC address access list
	1200-1299	The IPX summary address access list
permission	deny	Reject packets.
	list	Allow packets.
protocol-option	attribute that is specific to the protocol selected in the access list.

NOTE: *You can only use one access list to define interesting traffic.*

You need to be careful about what is defined as interesting traffic and what types of traffic are allowed to flow. Once the line comes up any traffic is allowed to flow across the line. This can potentially cause problems. Take the situation in which we only allow SMTP (e-mail) traffic to bring our line up. It is possible for SMTP traffic to legitimately bring the line up, and once up, another host could establish a Telnet session with an outside host. Because the timeout timers only reset when they see interesting traffic, the expiration of a timer will drop the line even though there is an active Telnet session. In this scenario, it is important that we block potentially problematic protocols using access control lists instead of allowing the definition of interesting traffic to keep from establishing a connection. Although this particular situation is not likely to occur, it does represent the type of problem that could occur using DDR. For a complete list of options on access lists, go to `www.cisco.com/univercd/cc/td/doc/product/software/ ios120/12 cgcr/secur_c/scprt3/scacls.htm`.

Dialer-group

Now that we've specified what is interesting traffic, we must indicate which interfaces use a particular dialer-list. The `dialer-group` command is used to associate a dialer-list to an interface, as shown in Figure 12-7.

A packet that is designated as interesting has special capabilities, such as the capability to force the router to set up a call to a remote router so that the packet can be sent to a remote router. Because the `dialer-group` command associates an interface with a dialer-list, it specifies when the router should drop the packet or enable a specific interface to bring the line up.

Because we are associating a command that is executed at the global configuration mode (`dialer-list`) with an interface, we need to execute this command on the interface we want associated with this traffic. The format of the `dialer-group` command is as follows:

```
Router(config-if)#dialer-group dialer-list-number

dialer-list-number    1-10      Dialer-group number assigned in a
                                dialer-list statement.
```

Figure 12-7

A dialer-group associating a dialer-list with an interface

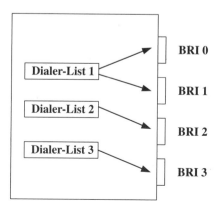

CISCO ROUTER

Dialer-List 1 → BRI 0, BRI 1
Dialer-List 2 → BRI 2
Dialer-List 3 → BRI 3

Dialer-map

At this point, we have defined interesting traffic and the interface responsible for handling those packets. We now need to specify a destination for those packets. Figure 12-8 shows us how the `dialer-map` command can make decisions on which number to call based upon the destination IP address.

To assign a phone number to a next-hop address, use the following command:

```
Router(config-if)#dialer map protocol next-hop-address name host
broadcast dial-string
```

protocol	**ip**	IP
next-hop-address	*a.b.c.d*	Protocol-specific address
host	**WORD**	Name of the remote system (used for authentication purposes)
dial-string	*xxxxxxx*	The phone number to dial to reach this IP address.

NOTE: *Any references to Legacy DDR are in reference to the dialer-map statements.*

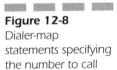

Figure 12-8
Dialer-map
statements specifying
the number to call

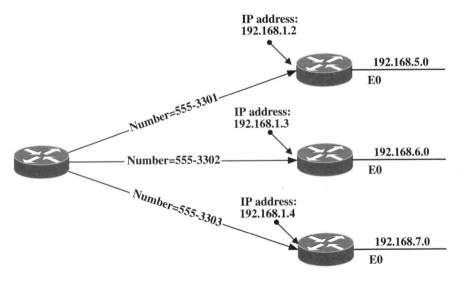

A `dialer map` command allows us to manually map a layer-two address to a network address. Think of the `dialer map` command as a manual form of the *Address Resolution Protocol* (ARP).

DDR Summary

We have seen the three main components of configuring DDR and should have an understanding of how they operate. Figure 12-9 gives us an overview of how these commands come together to establish a link with a remote site.

Even though the router has set the call up for us, it does not mean that it knows how to route packets.

Default Route

Just like any other interface, the router still needs to know when to send traffic to an interface. This means that we must have an entry in the route table so that the router knows where to direct packets. The use of a static route to direct traffic is a common practice in a DDR environment. This keeps us from having to send routing updates over our expensive ISDN line.

Setting a static route is particularly useful if the remote office's only network connection is through the dialup link. This is also called a *stub network*, as shown in Figure 12-10.

To configure a static route, we can use the following command:

```
Router(config)#ip route 0.0.0.0 0.0.0.0 gateway

gateway       a.b.c.d       IP address of the next hop
```

Optional Configuration Issues with DDR

Looking back at the previous sections, we discussed the commands used to bring an ISDN line up on demand. However, that is only half the battle. We must now focus on authentication, when to bring the line down, and

Figure 12-9
A flowchart of DDR
establishing a
connection

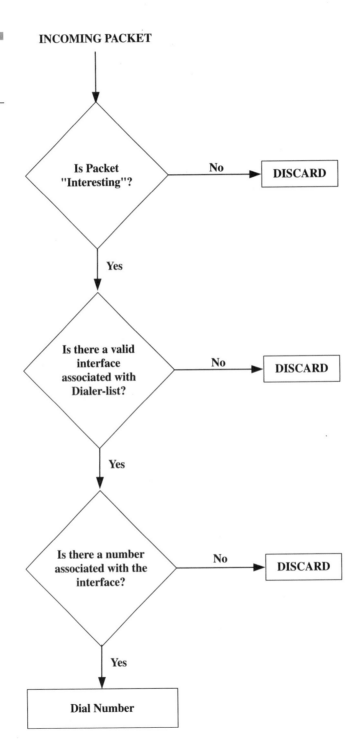

Figure 12-9
A flowchart of DDR
establishing a
connection

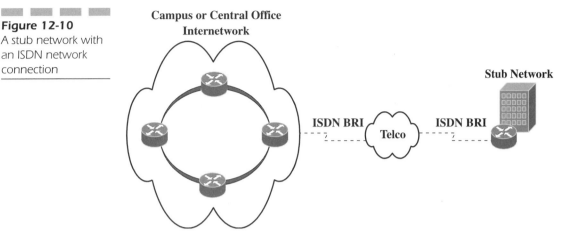

Figure 12-10
A stub network with
an ISDN network
connection

when to bring the second B channel up to support additional bandwidth requirements.

Authentication

The encapsulation protocol we are using dictates the type of authentication we can use. This is important depending upon the level of security required. If we are using the *High-Level Data Link Control* (HDLC) as our encapsulation protocol, then there is no authentication. However, if we are using PPP, we can choose whether or not we want to authenticate. If we do want to authenticate, then we will need to use the following command on an interface:

```
Router(config-if)#ppp authentication authentication-protocol

authentication-protocol    chap    Challenge handshake authentication
                                   protocol
                           pap     The password authentication
                                   protocol
```

Dialer idle-timeout

Once a call has been established between routers, a method needs to be established to terminate the connection between the two routers. Otherwise, the connection charges could cost as much or more than a dedicated connection.

In order to establish a DDR connection with a remote router, we need to define interesting traffic. Using access lists, we can refine our selection so that only certain traffic can activate the line. However, once a connection has been established, a packet can be routed even if it doesn't qualify as interesting. One of the problems with allowing uninteresting traffic to cross the dialup line is that we don't want it to keep the line up. Therefore, the `dialer idle-timeout` command only resets its counters anytime interesting traffic is passed, as shown in Figure 12-11.

In Figure 12-11, assuming all traffic is allowed to flow (no access lists restrict the routing of a packet) and that SMTP and the *Hypertext Transfer Protocol* (HTTP) have been defined as interesting traffic, Telnet, *Routing Information Protocol* (RIP), SMTP, and HTTP packets will flow between both sites once a connection has been established. However, only when SMTP and HTTP packets are sent across the ISDN line is the timer reset. In order for this to be the case, we would have to use the more complex form of DDR that utilizes access lists to define interesting traffic and not the simpler form that enables all IP packets to flow, as in Figure 12-12.

The default value for the dialer idle-timeout command is 120 seconds. This means that when 120 seconds pass and the Cisco router has not

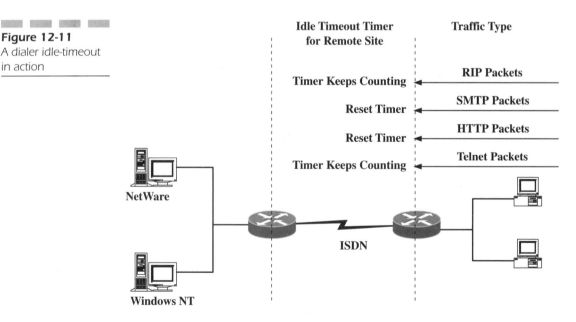

Figure 12-11
A dialer idle-timeout in action

Figure 12-12
Defining Interesting
Traffic

```
Router(config)#dialer-list1 protocol ip list 101
Router(config)#access-list 101 permit tcp any any eq www
Router(config)#access-list 101 permit tcp any any eq smtp
```

passed any SMTP or HTTP packets (based on Figure 12-9), then the ISDN link will be brought down, as shown in the following code. `time` represents *x*, which is the time in seconds:

```
Router(config-if)#dialer idle-timeout time
```

time   *x*   **time in seconds**

It is important to note that both the calling router and the called router use timers. This is important when trying to troubleshoot why this timer may not be functioning as expected. In addition, even though we only set the value once, the idle-timeout exists for each B-channel.

Multilink PPP

Multilink PPP enables the aggregation of multiple channels to form a single logical channel. This is done by fragmenting them in a round-robin fashion out both channels, as shown in Figure 12-13.

Figure 12-13
PPP using the
multilink protocol

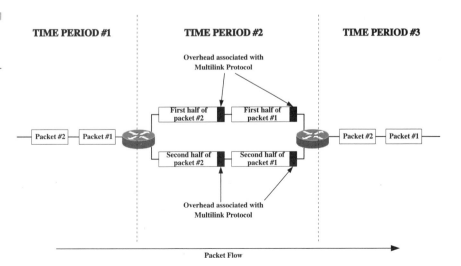

NOTE: *Although PPP is a layer-two protocol and should use the term frame, RFC 1990 uses the term packet to describe the individual fragments for the multilink protocol.*

In time period #1 in Figure 12-13, we can see packet #1 and packet #2 directed to the router with respect to time. When multilink is enabled with multiple logical channels, the router will fragment the packet into as many pieces as there are channels, in this case two. The router will add a header, which contains a sequence number for reassembly at the other end, and then send each fragmented packet simultaneously over each channel. Once the two fragmented packets have reached the receiving router, the router will reassemble the packet for delivery. You should also be aware that there is a minimal size packet, in which case a Cisco router will not fragment the packet.

To enable Multilink PPP, the following command needs to be applied to an interface:

```
Router (config-if)#ppp multilink
```

For more information about Multilink PPP, go to

```
www.netcerts.com/RFCs/rfc1990.txt
```

Dialer load-threshold

When establishing a connection with DDR, we only use one of the two B channels to establish that connection. However, if the load becomes great enough, we can activate the second B channel and aggregate the bandwidth between the two channels.

To specify the load when the dialer will establish another call to the destination, use the following command:

```
Router (config)#dialer load-threshold load direction

load          0-255        Percentage based upon 255 (128=50%)


direction     outbound     Outbound traffic only
              inbound      Inbound traffic only
              either       Either direction
```

NOTE: *Counting starts at zero, so between zero and 255 are actually 256 possibilities.*

The value for the variable `load` defines a percentage based upon 255. If we wanted the second line to become active instantly, we would use the value one. However, if we want the line to become active at 50 percent load, we will need to multiply our percentage by the number 255 (.5 * 256 = 128).

Lastly, in order to use the `dialer load-threshold` command to dial into the same site twice, Multilink PPP must be configured on both the remote and local routers.

Monitoring and Verifying ISDN Connections

We have seen how to configure DDR to access a remote site. We will now look at the various commands used to verify the installation of ISDN and debug a DDR connection.

Show Commands

One of the simplest commands we can use to verify that an interface is set up correctly is through the use of the `show interface` command. When performing this command on a BRI interface, you will see three different interfaces. They are categorized in Table 12-2.

Table 12-2

Logical BRI interfaces and what they represent

Interface	Command Used to View Status	Description
BRI0	`show interface bri0`	D channel
BRI0:1	`show interface bri0 1`	First B channel
BRI0:2	`show interface bri0 2`	Second B channel

In Figure 12-14, we can see that the `show interface` command has been used to view the interfaces. Note that the output has been edited to show only the relevant information.

NOTE: *The output "BW 64 Kbit" from Figure 12-14 does not indicate the bandwidth available on the line to transport data. Instead, it is used by sophisticated routing protocols such as IGRP, EIGRP, and OSPF so that they may consider the line speed of a WAN link when calculating the best route. This enables a network engineer to use the bandwidth command on an interface to artificially tweak the paths an OSPF network will use.*

Also notice that both B channels are down, BRI0:1 and BRI0:2. For more information about the DDR activity, we can use the `show dialer interface` command. This command gives us information about both timers, how many calls have been placed, and how long those calls lasted. This command is useful to make sure there haven't been any problems.

Debug Commands

The single most important `show` command for verifying the installation of an ISDN line is the `show isdn status` command. The output of this command depends upon the type of interfaces that are installed in the Cisco router. In Figure 12-15, we can see the `show isdn status` command being used on a Cisco router with a BRI interface.

In Figure 12-15, we can quickly determine where any problems might be taking place because of the organization of the command. If we look at ISDN BRI1/0 , we can see that layer one is active, meaning that we have physical connectivity. In the layer-two section, we can see that a *Terminal Endpoint Identifier* (TEI) has been assigned and that the value for the *Service Access Point Identifier* (SAPI) is zero. Lastly, currently no active layer-three calls exist.

We can use a handful of commands to debug any dialer problems. One of the most useful is the `debug dialer` command, shown in Figure 12-16.

This command shows us when any activity brings the line up. In addition, it shows us the the traffic that brought the line up, its source, and its destination.

Two main commands are used to debug an ISDN connection. Each command is used to debug the transactions happening at that particular layer of the OSI model. The command `debug isdn q921`, shown in Figure 12-17, is used to verify that your TEI and SAPI values are being properly assigned.

Figure 12-14

Edited output
from the show
interface
command

```
Router#show interfaces
BRI0 is up, line protocol is up (spoofing)
  Hardware is BRI with U interface and POTS
  Internet address is 192.168.150.2/24
  MTU 1500 bytes, BW 1000 Kbit, DLY 20000 usec,
  reliability 255/255, txload 1/255, rxload 1/255
  Encapsulation HDLC, loopback not set
  Last input 00:00:07, output 00:00:07, output hang never
  Last clearing of "show interface" counters never
  Input queue: 0/75/0 (size/max/drops); Total output drops: 0
  Queueing strategy: weighted fair
  Output queue: 0/1000/64/0 (size/max total/threshold/drops)
  Conversations 0/1/256 (active/max active/max total)
  Reserved Conversations 0/0 (allocated/max allocated)
  5 minute input rate 0 bits/sec, 0 packets/sec
  5 minute output rate 0 bits/sec, 0 packets/sec
  44 packets input, 196 bytes, 0 no buffer
  Received 2 broadcasts, 0 runts, 0 giants, 0 throttles
  0 input errors, 0 CRC, 0 frame, 0 overrun, 0 ignored, 0 abort
  45 packets output, 220 bytes, 0 underruns
  0 output errors, 0 collisions, 1 interface resets
  0 output buffer failures, 0 output buffers swapped out
  1 carrier transitions
BRI0:1 is down, line protocol is down
  Hardware is BRI with U interface and POTS
  MTU 1500 bytes, BW 64 Kbit, DLY 20000 usec,
  reliability 255/255, txload 1/255, rxload 1/255
  Encapsulation HDLC, loopback not set, keepalive set (10 sec)
  Last input never, output never, output hang never
  Last clearing of "show interface" counters never
  Input queue: 0/75/0 (size/max/drops); Total output drops: 0
  Queueing strategy: weighted fair
  Output queue: 0/1000/64/0 (size/max total/threshold/drops)
  Conversations 0/0/256 (active/max active/max total)
  Reserved Conversations 0/0 (allocated/max allocated)
  5 minute input rate 0 bits/sec, 0 packets/sec
  5 minute output rate 0 bits/sec, 0 packets/sec
  0 packets input, 0 bytes, 0 no buffer
  Received 0 broadcasts, 0 runts, 0 giants, 0 throttles
  0 input errors, 0 CRC, 0 frame, 0 overrun, 0 ignored, 0 abort
  0 packets output, 0 bytes, 0 underruns
  0 output errors, 0 collisions, 0 interface resets
  0 output buffer failures, 0 output buffers swapped out
  0 carrier transitions
BRI0:2 is down, line protocol is down
  Hardware is BRI with U interface and POTS
  MTU 1500 bytes, BW 64 Kbit, DLY 20000 usec,
  reliability 255/255, txload 1/255, rxload 1/255
  Encapsulation HDLC, loopback not set, keepalive set (10 sec)
  Last input never, output never, output hang never
  Last clearing of "show interface" counters never
  Input queue: 0/75/0 (size/max/drops); Total output drops: 0
  Queueing strategy: weighted fair
  Output queue: 0/1000/64/0 (size/max total/threshold/drops)
  Conversations 0/0/256 (active/max active/max total)
  Reserved Conversations 0/0 (allocated/max allocated)
```

```
5 minute input rate 0 bits/sec, 0 packets/sec
5 minute output rate 0 bits/sec, 0 packets/sec
0 packets input, 0 bytes, 0 no buffer
Received 0 broadcasts, 0 runts, 0 giants, 0 throttles
0 input errors, 0 CRC, 0 frame, 0 overrun, 0 ignored, 0 abort
0 packets output, 0 bytes, 0 underruns
0 output errors, 0 collisions, 0 interface resets
0 output buffer failures, 0 output buffers swapped out
0 carrier transitions
```

Figure 12-15

Output from show
ISDN status
command on a
Cisco router with
BRI interfaces

```
Router#show isdn status
Global ISDN Switchtype = basic-dms100
ISDN BRI1/0 interface
  dsl 8, interface ISDN Switchtype = basic-dms100
  Layer 1 Status:
  ACTIVE
  Layer 2 Status:
  TEI = 64, Ces = 1, SAPI = 0, State = MULTIPLE_FRAME_ESTABLISHED
  TEI = 65, Ces = 2, SAPI = 0, State = MULTIPLE_FRAME_ESTABLISHED
  Spid Status:
  TEI 64, ces = 1, state = 5(init)
  spid1 configured, no LDN, spid1 sent, spid1 valid
  Endpoint ID Info: epsf = 0, usid = 1, tid = 1
  TEI 65, ces = 2, state = 5(init)
  spid2 configured, no LDN, spid2 sent, spid2 valid
  Endpoint ID Info: epsf = 0, usid = 2, tid = 2
  Layer 3 Status:
  0 Active Layer 3 Call(s)
  Activated dsl 8 CCBs = 0
```

Figure 12-16

Output from the
debug dialer
command

```
Router#debug dialer
Dial on demand events debugging is on
00:55:46: BRIO: Dialing cause ip (s=192.168.150.2, d=192.168.1.1)
00:55:46: BRIO: Attempting to dial 384000
00:55:47: %LINK-3-UPDOWN: Interface BRI0:1, changed state to up
00:55:47: dialer Protocol up for BR0:1
00:55:48: %LINEPROTO-5-UPDOWN: Line protocol on Interface BRI0:1,
changed state to up
```

Notice that every 10 seconds there is an exchange of Q921 information. This enables the Cisco router to determine the status of the Layer-two connections. Remember that Q.921 is only locally significant. It only deter-

Figure 12-17
Output from debug
isdn q921

```
Router#debug isdn q921
ISDN Q921 packets debugging is on
Router#
00:01:37: ISDN BR1/0: TX -> RRp sapi = 0 tei = 64 nr = 0
00:01:37: ISDN BR1/0: RX <- RRf sapi = 0 tei = 64 nr = 0
00:01:47: ISDN BR1/0: TX -> RRp sapi = 0 tei = 64 nr = 0
00:01:47: ISDN BR1/0: RX <- RRf sapi = 0 tei = 64 nr = 0
00:01:57: ISDN BR1/0: TX -> RRp sapi = 0 tei = 64 nr = 0
00:01:57: ISDN BR1/0: RX <- RRf sapi = 0 tei = 64 nr = 0
00:02:07: ISDN BR1/0: TX -> RRp sapi = 0 tei = 64 nr = 0
00:02:07: ISDN BR1/0: RX <- RRf sapi = 0 tei = 64 nr = 0
```

Figure 12-18
Output from debug
isdn q931 during
call setup

```
Router#debug isdn q931
ISDN Q931 packets debugging is on
Router#
04:19:54: ISDN Se0:23: RX <- SETUP pd = 8 callref = 0x1624
04:19:54: Bearer Capability i = 0x8090A2
04:19:54: Channel ID i = 0xE980830D
04:19:54: Calling Party Number i = '!', 0x83, '9193033304'
04:19:54: Called Party Number i = 0xA1, '9198390637'
04:19:54: ISDN Se0:23: TX -> CALL_PROC pd = 8 callref = 0x9624
04:19:54: Channel ID i = 0xE980830D
04:19:54: ISDN Se0:23: TX -> ALERTING pd = 8 callref = 0x9624
04:19:54: ISDN Se0:23: TX -> CONNECT pd = 8 callref = 0x9624
04:19:54: ISDN Se0:23: RX <- CONNECT_ACK pd = 8 callref = 0x1624
```

mines what is going on between your Cisco router and the Telco's ISDN
switch.

Q931 is the protocol responsible for end-to-end communication with
another remote device. In Figure 12-18, we can see the use of Q931 during
call setup.

In this output, we can see the series of Q.931 commands being issued to
set the call up, while in Example 12-5 we can see the other half of this connection in which the call is released.

For the CCNA exam, it is important to remember that debug isdn
q921 is for troubleshooting connections between your Cisco router and the
Telco switch, while debug isdn q931 is used to resolve end-to-end connections (one Cisco router to another Cisco router).

Chapter Summary

In this chapter, we have discussed the basics of ISDN and how to configure an ISDN BRI line. In addition, we have covered how to configure simple legacy DDR environments using ISDN. DDR can be a very useful feature when designed correctly. We must watch out for pitfalls, however, like making sure that only interesting traffic brings the DDR line up.

From the Real World

Sometimes when starting out in this particular area, it is difficult to find other people you can converse with about the internetworking technologies in any meaningful manner. So where is a internetworking newbie to go in order to talk about a common interest?

In addition to this book, a network professional can explore many different avenues for additional peer support. This support can come in a variety of forms and take on several different variations. If you are interested in pursuing a Cisco certification, listservs from www.groupstudy.com can provide an additional viewpoint on the technologies covered within this book. This is a great place to either listen to other people's questions and answers (known as *lurking*), ask your own questions, or impart the wisdom you've found after reading this book to others. Although the last method may not seem worthwhile, remember that by explaining a topic to someone else, you gain a greater understanding of the topic. This not only allows you to solidify the knowledge you know, but maybe you can gain a friend that can help you understand a difficult topic in the future.

Adam Quiggle

Frequently Asked Questions (FAQ)

Question: Why does my router establish a connection to the remote router even though I am not using any applications that need to access the remote network?

Answer: You need to be more specific about what qualifies as interesting traffic by using access lists in your `dialer-list` command. It is very possible that your computer is performing a service that you are not aware of, such as updating a WINS server.

Question: Why can't my second B channel connect successfully with the remote router even though I have configured my local router to use Multilink PPP?

Answer: Multilink PPP needs to be enabled on the remote link as well as the local link.

Question: How can I get both B channels to come up immediately after the router dials a remote site?

Answer: Set the dialer load-threshold to one.

Question: Every time I reload my router I get a different TEI. Is this a problem?

Answer: No, this is not a problem. Some service providers dynamically assign a TEI when your router boots up.

Case Study: Remote Office Connectivity with ISDN

The objective here is to configure a simple DDR environment. The equipment required is as follows:

- Two computers with Windows 95 and an Ethernet *Network Interface Card* (NIC)
- Two Cisco routers with a single ISDN BRI interface
- Two ISDN BRI lines

Dwyer Inc. is setting up a remote office with ISDN BRI so the remote location can communicate with the headquarters using SMTP and the Web. To minimize operational impact on their newly implemented ISDN PRI solution, they will use a dedicated ISDN BRI router. Configure their two ISDN BRI routers to support a remote site (see Figure 12-19).

The Central Office information is as follows:

- Switch type: dms-100
- Central Office SPID1: 3840000001, Phone number: 384000
- Central Office SPID2: 3840000002, Phone number: 384000
- Ethernet interface IP address: 192.168.1.1/24
- ISDN BRI0 IP address: 192.168.100.1/24
- Central Office network IP subnet: 192.168.200.0/24
- Use static routing at the remote site to get to the central site.

Figure 12-19
Configuring ISDN BRI lines for DDR

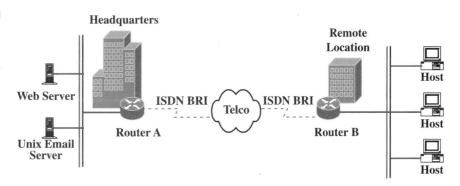

The required information for the Remote Office is as follows:

- Switch type: dms-100
- Remote Office SPID1:   3840200001, Phone #: 384020
- Remote Office SPID2:   3840200002, Phone #: 384020
- Ethernet interface IP address: 192.168.10.1/24
- ISDN BRI0 IP address: 192.168.100.2/24
- Use static routing at the remote site to get to the central site.

Lastly, use CHAP authentication.
To solve this problem, we need to break it down into two tasks:

- Configure the headquarters
  - Configure the ISDN interface.
  - Configure the Ethernet interface.
  - Define the usernames and passwords of remote sites.
  - Define interesting traffic.
  - Configure static route.

- Configure the remote site
  - Configure the Ethernet interface.
  - Configure the ISDN interface.
  - Define the usernames and passwords of remote sites.
  - Define the interesting traffic.
  - Configure the static route.

Task 1: Configure the Central Site

Configure the headquarters:

1. Enter enable mode on the router.

   ```
   Router>ena
   ```

2. Enter global configuration mode.

   ```
   Router#config t
   ```

3. Describe the name of the router (for authentication purposes).

   ```
   Router(config)#hostname HeadQuarters
   ```

4. Select the ISDN switch type and configure ISDN BRI Interface.

   ```
   HeadQuarters(config)#isdn switch-type basic-dms100
   ```

5. Select the BRI interface for configuration.

   ```
   HeadQuarters(config)#interface bri0
   ```

6. Describe the interface for future reference.

   ```
   HeadQuarters(config-if)#description ISDN interface to remote site
   ```

7. Define SPID #1.

   ```
   Remote(config-if)#isdn spid1 3840000001
   ```

8. Define SPID #2.

   ```
   Remote(config-if)#isdn spid2 3840000002
   ```

9. Define PPP encapsulation on the ISDN BRI line.

   ```
   HeadQuarters(config-if)#encapsulation ppp
   ```

10. Use CHAP authentication.

    ```
    HeadQuarters(config-if)#ppp authentication chap
    ```

11. Assign the IP address to the BRI interface.

    ```
    HeadQuarters(config-if)#ip address 192.168.100.1 255.255.255.0
    ```

12. Assign the number to dial in order to reach the next hop at the remote site.

    ```
    HeadQuarters(config-if)#dialer map ip 192.168.100.2 name remote
    3840200
    ```

13. Assign the dialer-list (the interesting traffic definition) to this interface.

    ```
    HeadQuarters(config-if)#dialer-group 1
    ```

14. Select the Ethernet interface for configuration.

    ```
    HeadQuarters(config-if)#interface e0
    ```

15. Describe the interface for future reference.

    ```
    HeadQuarters(config-if)#description Ethernet interface for HeadQ
    ```

16. Assign the IP address to the Ethernet interface.

    ```
    HeadQuarters(config-if)#ip address 192.168.1.1 255.255.255.0
    ```

17. Stop configuring the Ethernet interface and configure the usernames and passwords of the central site.

    ```
    HeadQuarters(config-if)#exit
    ```

18. Enter the username and password for the remote site router to connect to the central site.

    ```
    HeadQuarters(config)#username remote password cisco
    ```

19. Define interesting traffic using access lists.

```
HeadQuarters(config)#dialer-list 1 list 101
```

20. Define Telnet traffic as interesting.

```
HeadQuarters(config)#access-list 101 permit tcp any any eq www
```

21. Define SMTP traffic as interesting. Also configure the route to the remote site and the routing protocols to redistribute the static routes.

```
HeadQuarters(config)#access-list 101 permit tcp any any eq smtp
```

22. Set a gateway of last resort (remember this is just a stub network).

```
HeadQuarters(config)#ip route 192.168.10.0 255.255.255.0
192.168.100.2
```

Task 2: Configure the Remote Site

1. Enter enable mode on the router.

```
Router>ena
```

2. Enter global configuration mode.

```
Router#config t
```

3. Describe the name of the router (for authentication purposes).

```
Router(config)#hostname Remote
```

4. Select the ISDN switch type and configure the ISDN BRI interface.

```
Remote(config)#isdn switch-type basic-dms100
```

5. Select the BRI interface for configuration.

```
Remote(config)#interface bri0
```

6. Describe the interface for future reference.

```
Remote(config-if)#description ISDN interface to central site
```

7. Define SPID #1.

```
Remote(config-if)#isdn spid1 3840200001
```

8. Define SPID #2.

```
Remote(config-if)#isdn spid2 3840200002
```

9. Define the PPP encapsulation on the ISDN BRI line.

```
Remote(config-if)#encapsulation ppp
```

10. Use CHAP authentication.

```
Remote(config-if)#ppp authentication chap
```

11. Assign the IP address to the BRI interface.

    ```
    Remote(config-if)#ip address 192.168.100.2 255.255.255.0
    ```

12. Assign the number to dial in order to reach the next hop.

    ```
    Remote(config-if)#dialer map ip 192.168.100.1 name HeadQuarters
    3840000
    ```

13. Assign the dialer-list (the interesting traffic definition) to this interface.

    ```
    Remote(config-if)#dialer-group 1
    ```

14. Select the Ethernet interface for configuration.

    ```
    Remote(config-if)#interface e0
    ```

15. Describe the interface for future reference.

    ```
    Remote(config-if)#description Ethernet interface for remote site
    ```

16. Assign the IP address to the Ethernet interface.

    ```
    Remote(config-if)#ip address 192.168.10.1 255.255.255.0
    ```

17. Stop configuring the Ethernet interface.

    ```
    Remote(config-if)#exit
    ```

18. Enter username and password for the central site router to connect to the remote site.

    ```
    Remote(config)#username HeadQuarters password cisco
    ```

19. Define interesting traffic using access lists.

    ```
    Remote(config)#dialer-list 1 list 101
    ```

20. Define Telnet traffic as interesting.

    ```
    Remote(config)#access-list 101 permit tcp any any eq telnet
    ```

21. Define SMTP traffic as interesting and set up the static route to the central site.

    ```
    Remote(config)#access-list 101 permit tcp any any eq smtp
    ```

22. Set a gateway of last resort (remember this is just a stub network).

    ```
    Remote(config)#ip route 0.0.0.0 0.0.0.0 192.168.100.1
    ```

Case Study Summary

This case study shows how to configure two Cisco routers to support dial on demand environments using ISDN BRI to call an ISDN BRI connection. Figures 12-20 and 12-21 are example configuration files for each router.

Figure 12-20

Configuration file for the headquarters Cisco router

```
!
hostname HeadQuarters
!
username remote password 0 cisco
ip subnet-zero
!
isdn switch-type basic-dms100
!
interface Ethernet0
 description Ethernet interface for HeadQ
 ip address 192.168.1.1 255.255.255.0
 no ip directed-broadcast
!
interface BRI0
 description ISDN interface to remote site
 ip address 192.168.100.1 255.255.255.0
 no ip directed-broadcast
 encapsulation ppp
 dialer map ip 192.168.100.2 name remote 3840200
 dialer-group 1
 isdn switch-type basic-dms100
 isdn spid1 38400000001 3840000
 isdn spid2 38400000002 3840000
 ppp authentication chap
 hold-queue 75 in
!
ip classless
ip route 192.168.10.0 255.255.255.0 192.168.100.2
!
access-list 101 permit tcp any any eq telnet
access-list 101 permit tcp any any eq smtp
dialer-list 1 protocol ip list 101
!
line con 0
 transport input none
line aux 0
line vty 0 4
!
```

Figure 12-21

Configuration file for the remote site Cisco router

```
!
hostname Remote
!
username HeadQuarters password 0 cisco
!
ip subnet-zero
!
isdn switch-type basic-dms100
!
interface Ethernet0
 description Ethernet interface for remote site
```

```
ip address 192.168.10.1 255.255.255.0
no ip directed-broadcast
!
interface BRI0
 description ISDN interface to central site
 ip address 192.168.100.2 255.255.255.0
 no ip directed-broadcast
 encapsulation ppp
 dialer map ip 192.168.100.1 name HeadQuarters 3840000
 dialer-group 1
 isdn switch-type basic-dms100
 isdn spid1 38402000001 3840200
 isdn spid2 38402000002 3840200
 ppp authentication chap
 hold-queue 75 in
!
ip classless
ip route 0.0.0.0 0.0.0.0 192.168.100.1
!
access-list 101 permit tcp any any eq telnet
access-list 101 permit tcp any any eq smtp
dialer-list 1 protocol ip list 101
!
line con 0
 transport input none
 stopbits 1
line vty 0 4
!
```

Questions

1. Which attributes does ISDN have over standard analog communications?

   a. Faster setup

   b. Faster connection speeds

   c. Longer connection times

2. How many ISDN B channels are in an ISDN BRI?

   a. 2

   b. 23

   c. 24

   d. 30

3. What is the bandwidth of an ISDN BRI D channel?

   a. 16 Kbps

   b. 56 Kbps

   c. 64 Kbps

   d. 128 Kbps

4. What is the purpose of multiplexing?

   a. To be a movie house that can show multiple movies at the same time

   b. To combine multiple physical media, allowing for the aggregation of bandwidth

   c. To create the appearance of multiple physical channels by dividing some aspect of the channel (time, frequency, and so on)

   d. To use multiple routers for route redundancy

5. The total available bandwidth (B channels and D channels combined) on a ISDN BRI is

   a. 128 Kbps

   b. 144 Kbps

   c. 192 Kbps

   d. 64 Kbps

6. The Q series of protocols defines _____.

   a. switching and signaling

   b. concepts and interfaces

   c. telephone network standards

   d. quantization protocols

7. The E series of protocols defines _____.

  a. switching and signaling

  b. concepts and interfaces

  c. telephone network standards

  d. quantization protocols

8. The I series of protocols defines _____.

  a. switching and signaling

  b. concepts and interfaces

  c. telephone network standards

  d. quantization protocols

9. The protocol Q.931 acts at which layer of the OSI model?

  a. Physical

  b. Data-link

  c. Network

  d. Transport

10. What is the purpose of DDR?

  a. Data-link Downstream Routing enables the routing of packets over a WAN connection.

  b. Dial on Demand Routing enables a circuit-switched connection to be brought up on demand.

  c. Datagram Dialing Routing encapsulates packets in a PPP packet for use with multiple ISPs.

  d. Distant Dialing Router tells remote routers to connect to us for a data exchange.

11. What are some of the factors that make DDR attractive? Select all that apply.

  a. It does not need a permanent connection with the central site.

  b. It has fast connection times.

  c. It has LAN speed connections.

12. What is the definition of *interesting traffic*?

  a. Data that is destined for a remote network

  b. Data that contains e-mail

  c. Data that we want to send to a remote site

  d. Data that carries JPEGs and GIFs

13. What is the correct command to associate a dialer-list (which defines interesting traffic) with the interface we want to send the data out of?

    a. `Router(config-if)#dialer-group 1`
    b. `Router(config-if)#dialer-group ip 1`
    c. `Router(config)#dialer-group 1 interface BRI0`
    d. `Router(config)#dialer-group 1`

14. Which command is required in order to specify telnet traffic as interesting?

    a. `Router(config-if)#dialer-list 1 protocol ip permit`
    b. `Router(config)#dialer-list 1 protocol ip permit`
    c. `Router(config-if)#dialer-list 1 protocol ip list 101`
    d. `Router(config)#dialer-list 1 protocol ip list 101`
    e. `Router(config)#dialer-list 1 protocol ip list 10`

15. Which command enables an ISDN line to be brought up, assuming it is considered interesting traffic?

    a. `RouterA(config-if)#dialer map 555-3304 name RouterB broadcast ip 172.16.1.1`
    b. `RouterA(config-if)#dialer map ip 172.16.1.1 name RouterB broadcast 555-3304`
    c. `RouterA(config)#dialer map ip 172.16.1.1 name RouterB broadcast 555-3304`
    d. `RouterA(config)#dialer map ip 555-3304 name RouterB broadcast 172.16.1.1`

16. What is the purpose of the `dialer idle-timeout` command?

    a. It specifies the length of time that must pass without any interesting packets before a line can be brought down.
    b. It specifies the length of time that must pass with no packets being passed before a line can be brought down.
    c. It specifies the length of time that must pass while other traffic is waiting to establish communications with a remote site before a line can be brought down.

17. What is the default value for the idle-timeout timer?

    a. 5
    b. 10
    c. 20
    d. 120

18. Which authentication protocols can we use with HDLC as our encapsulation method?

   a. PAP only

   b. CHAP only

   c. PAP and CHAP

   d. None

19. What authentication protocols can we use with PPP as our encapsulation method?

   a. PAP only

   b. CHAP only

   c. PAP and CHAP

   d. None

20. Which command tells the second B channel to initiate a connection when the load is 50 percent?

   a. `RouterA(config-if)#dialer load-threshold 50`

   b. `RouterA(config-if)#dialer load-threshold 128`

   c. `RouterA(config)#dialer load-threshold 50`

   d. `RouterA(config)#dialer load-threshold 128`

Answers

1. **a.** Faster setup and **b.** Faster connection speeds

   When using ISDN you can setup a call very quickly (compared to two modems). In addition, the connection speed of an ISDN connection is very fast compared to an analog POTS line.

2. **a.** Two

   There are two B-channels and one D-channel in an ISDN BRI T1.

3. **a.** 16 Kbps

   The D-channel on an ISDN BRI line is 16kps.

4. **c.** To create the appearance of multiple physical channels by dividing some aspect of the channel (time frequency and so on)

   Multiplexing gives the perception that there are multiple physical lines, but there really is only one physical wire. There are many methods for creating these logical channels, one example is *Time Division Multiplexing* (TDM). TDM works by logically dividing the channel up into time slices.

5. **c.**

   ISDN BRI B-channels

   (16 bits per frame/channel × 2 chanels) × 4000 samples per second = 128,000bps

   ISDN BRI D-channels

   (4 bits per frame) × 4000 samples per second = 16,000bps

   ISDN BRI Overall Bit Rate:
   128.000bps + 16,000 = 144,000bps

6. **a.** switching and signaling

   The Q-series of protocols defined by the ITU-T specifies the switching and signaling protocols used between devices.

7. **c.** telephone network standards

   The E-Series of protocols defined by the ITU-T defines telephone network standards (phone number schemes).

8. **b.** concepts and interfaces

   The I-Series of protocols defined by the ITU-T defines concepts and interfaces associated with ISDN.

9. c. Network

Q.931 identifies the path across the Telco network (e.g. multiple switches) and thus operates at the network layer.

10. b. Dial on Demand Routing enables a circuit-switched connection to be brought up on demand.

The basic concept of DDR is to allow a router to setup a connection with a remote site using a circuit-switched network (ISDN or POTS) when there is "interesting traffic" destined for that remote network.

11. a. It does not need a permanent connection with the central site.

DDR is used to make a connection to a site on-demand, thus there is no need for a permanent connection with the central site. The amount of time required to establish a connection is directly dependent upon the technology used (e.g., ISDN or POTS) and both of those technologies are slow in comparison to LAN technologies (e.g., Ethernet or Token-Ring).

12. c. Data that we want to send to a remote site

The type of service that we need to access characterizes "interesting traffic". For example, if we need to retrieve mail from our mail server, we can classify SMTP packets as "interesting traffic" and have the ISDN line call the central site when there are SMTP packets that need to go to the remote site.

13. a. `Router (config-if)#dialer-group 1`

The `dialer-group` command is used to associate a dialer-list to an interface. It must be applied to an interface and you must indicate which dialer-list you want to associate with the interface.

14. d. `Router (config)#dialer-list 1 protocol ip list 101`

The `dialer-list` command is used to identify interesting traffic. Because we are defining a specific type of packet (telnet) we must use an extended access list (i.e., between 100–199) to identify interesting traffic.

15. b. `RouterA(config-if)#dialer map ip 172.16.1.0. name RouterB broadcast 555-3304`

This command must be applied to an interface. The format of the command is

```
dialer map protocol next-hop-address name host broadcast dial-string
```

16. a. It specifies the length of time that must pass without any interesting packets before a line can be brought down.

The dialer idle-timeout command allows us to disconnect a circuit-switched connection after a predefined period of time. The default for this command is 120 seconds.

17. d. 120

The default value for the idle-timeout timer is 120 seconds.

18. d. None

HDLC does not support authentication.

19. c. PAP and CHAP

PPP support both PAP and CHAP authentication.

20. b. `RouterA(config-if)#dialer load-threshold 128`

This command must be executed from within interface configuration mode. It also uses a relative value between 0 and 255 to indicate the percentage of utilization that must occur before the second B channel will become active.

Frame Relay

Objectives

This chapter describes the use of Frame Relay, a high performance *Wide Area Network* (WAN) protocol. Frame Relay terminology and the use of congestion control used in Frame Relay are discussed in detail. The configuration and operation of Frame Relay is also covered as well as the relevant commands to troubleshoot problems in a Frame Relay network.

Upon completion of this chapter, you will be able to do the following:

- Determine how Frame Relay operates
- Configure Frame Relay
- Configure Frame Relay subinterfaces
- Verify Frame Relay operation

Frame Relay Overview

Frame Relay consists of sending information over a *public data network* (PDN) or a WAN while dividing the information into frames. Frame Relay is a *Consultative Committee on International Telephone and Telegraphy* (CCITT) and an *American National Standards Institute* (ANSI) standard. *Personal Computers* (PCs), servers, and other end user devices began requiring a need to connect to a high-speed network with low network delays and efficient bandwidth allocated to accommodate bursts in network traffic. Thus, Frame Relay was developed to provide such a high-performance, cost-effective solution often replacing older and slower packet-switching networks such as X.25. Frame Relay was originally designed for use across *Integrated Services Digital Network* (ISDN) interfaces.

Frame Relay is a purely layer-two protocol and thus provides high throughput and reliability by relying on upper layer protocols such as *Transmission Control Protocol/Internet Protocol* (TCP/IP) to handle retransmissions and other high-level services. Frame Relay can support multiple upper layer protocols. *Permanent Virtual Circuits* (PVCs) and *Switched Virtual Circuits* (SVCs) are used to establish connections between devices. They will be discussed in detail later in the chapter.

Frame Relay is a packet-switching network. Packet-switching networks enable end devices to dynamically share the network and available bandwidth. Frame Relay networks use statistical multiplexing techniques that multiplex many logical data conversations, or virtual circuits, over one physical link. This allows for a more efficient use of bandwidth along with greater flexibility. Other examples of packet-switching networks are X.25, Token Ring, and Ethernet.

Frame Relay is used between the *customer premise equipment* (CPE) and the carrier's Frame Relay switch. This does not affect how traffic gets routed after it leaves the carrier's Frame Relay switch. The CPE defines the customer's equipment on the edge of their network that is used to communicate with the Frame Relay switch. This usually consists of the customer's router. The Frame Relay switch is a high-end switch owned and used by the public carrier, such as AT&T or MCI WorldCom, to receive incoming frames and forward outgoing frames based on destination. It is possible for large enterprise networks to own their own Frame Relay switch, in which case the particular Frame Relay network would be private. A Frame Relay switch is considered a *Data Communication Equipment* (DCE) device. These DCE devices communicate with the customer's router, a *Data Terminal Equipment* (DTE) device.

Frame Relay uses a variable length framing structure. This enables the frame to consist of a few or more than a thousand characters depending upon the user data. Frame Relay can then accommodate multiple *Local Area Network* (LAN) protocols with varying frame sizes. This also equates to varying traffic delays based upon frame size.

The router encapsulates the upper layer protocol data and encapsulates it into a frame. The frame is then forwarded on to the Frame Relay switch. Figure 13-1 is an example of a Frame Relay network.

NOTE: *Frame Relay is implemented up to T1 (1.544 Mbps) speeds. At the time of this writing, one carrier supports up to T3 (45 Mbps) speeds.*

How Frame Relay Saves Money

Frame Relay is an extremely cost-effective solution for high-speed networks with low network delays. Frame Relay can provide this lower cost of ownership for many reasons:

- It can support multiple protocols such as TCP/IP, *Systems Network Architecture* (SNA), *Network Basic Input / Output System* (NetBIOS), and voice. This enables any combination of these protocols to be run

Figure 13-1
Frame Relay network
example

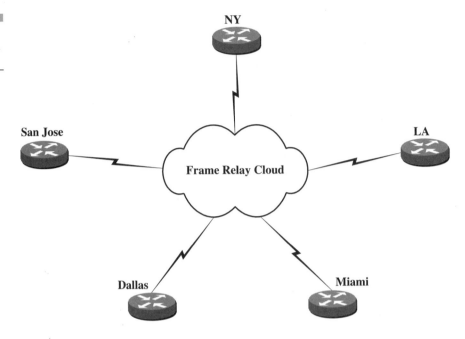

over one physical circuit, instead of having multiple leased lines to
support the different protocols coming into a single site.

- Costs are saved by not having to purchase more equipment, such as
  higher end routers and more *Channel Service Unit / Data Service Units*
  (CSU/DSUs), to support multiple point-to-point circuits. Frame Relay
  solves this by utilizing one physical circuit and using PVCs to establish
  multiple virtual circuits.

- Multiple users can simultaneously use a single access circuit and
  Frame Relay port. It also efficiently uses bandwidth and accommodates
  to bursty traffic, thanks in part to the statistical multiplexing
  capability that Frame Relay provides.

Virtual Circuits within the Cloud

Frame Relay is often represented in network diagrams as a cloud. The cloud
represents the carrier's network infrastructure. Inside this network infrastructure lies the high-end Frame Relay switches, core routers, and

switches that the carriers use to route all the packets that traverse their network. The Frame Relay service defines the interconnection process between the customer's router and the carrier's Frame Relay switch at the edge of their network. All internal devices that the frame traverses inside the carrier's network are not defined as Frame Relay.

A router using Frame Relay will have one physical access circuit to the *frame cloud*, or carrier network, and will have multiple virtual circuits within the frame cloud. These virtual circuits are used to connect LANs across a WAN. A virtual circuit is a logical connection created between two *data terminal equipment* (DTE) devices (routers) across a Frame Relay *packet-switched network* (PSN). Virtual circuits provide a bidirectional, private communications path from one DTE device to another and are uniquely identified by a *data-link connection identifier* (DLCI). A number of virtual circuits can be multiplexed into a single physical circuit for transmission across the network. This capability can often reduce the equipment and network complexity required connecting multiple DTE devices. A virtual circuit can pass through any number of intermediate DCE devices (switches) located within the Frame Relay PSN. Frame Relay virtual circuits fall into two categories: SVCs and PVCs. They will be discussed in detail later in this chapter.

Virtual circuits enable enhanced flexibility with the capability to add or delete more virtual circuits as needed. Figure 13-2 shows three routers connecting to a frame cloud. We will discuss how virtual circuits are used in this example.

All three of these routers have a single physical access circuit connecting to the carrier network. In this example, each of these physical access circuits has a bandwidth of a T-1 (1.544 Mbps). Dallas needs to communicate with both L.A. and N.Y. A virtual circuit will be created between Dallas and L.A. and then between Dallas and N.Y. These virtual circuits are assigned a *Committed Information Rate* (CIR). The CIR specifies the bandwidth of the virtual circuit. Each of these virtual circuits will utilize a bandwidth of 384K for this example. Figure 13-3 illustrates how virtual circuits are used.

The virtual circuits have been assigned and a subinterface has been used for each virtual circuit. This enables enhanced troubleshooting and monitoring capabilities. N.Y. can now communicate with Dallas and L.A. by traversing the Dallas router. One of the main reasons that Frame Relay is used is because of the cost. The low cost allows network administrators to add redundancy in their network. In this example, an additional virtual circuit is added between L.A. and N.Y. This way if one of the virtual circuits goes down, the traffic can traverse the alternate path. Frame Relay is a

Figure 13-2
Physical circuits

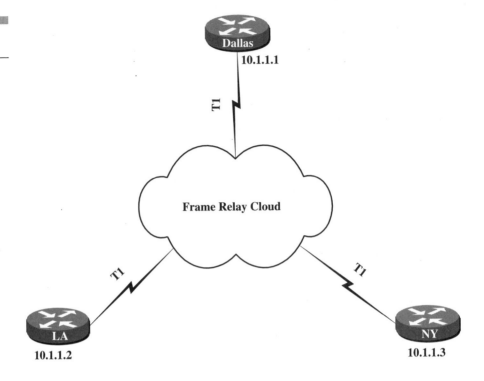

cost-effective solution for redundancy. Figure 13-4 illustrates an example of redundancy in a Frame Relay network.

Frame Relay in the OSI Model

Frame Relay is purely a layer-two protocol. Unlike X.25, Frame Relay does no layer-three processing. It does not handle any upper layer tasks and therefore depends on those upper layer protocols at the end points to handle those tasks. Some of these tasks include retransmission and error recovery. For example, Frame Relay will use TCP at layer four to recover from the loss of a frame by requesting a retransmit from the source if the sequence numbers are incorrect.

Problems can occur with the upper layer protocols providing these services, such as retransmission. Some of these problems include having to retransmit all unacknowledged frames when a single frame is lost. This process utilizes additional bandwidth by having to retransmit the frames

Figure 13-3
Virtual circuits

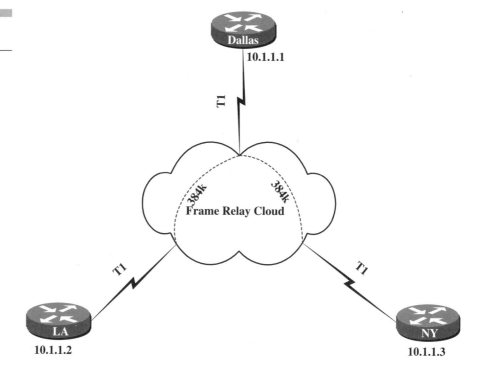

again. This also causes an increase in memory usage in the routers or other devices that are handling the retransmission. This retransmission also causes larger network delays from the fact that the receiving host has to wait for the frames to be retransmitted before it can accept any other frames.

Frame Relay goes through only three processes when transmitting a frame. The first step it takes is to verify if the frame is valid. The Frame Relay switch receives the frame and uses the *Frame Check Sequence* (FCS) field in the frame to determine if any errors occurred during transmission. The most common error for a frame is noise on the line. Frame Relay requires clean lines, which is why Frame Relay has become so adopted, since networks have moved to digital and fiber optic lines. These types of lines do not accumulate errors like the networks of old.

The second step in the process is to look up the DLCI. The Frame Relay switch will try to reference the DLCI with the destination link. If this DLCI does not exist, the Frame Relay switch will discard the frame. The last step

Figure 13-4
Redundant virtual
circuits

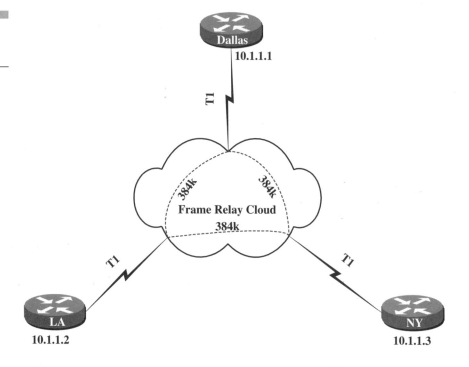

in this process is for the Frame Relay switch to forward the frame out the specified port to the destination. A frame may be discarded for two reasons:

- *Congestion in the network* The network can become oversubscribed; that is, too much data is attempting to traverse the network than the network can handle. If this happens, frames may be discarded.

- *Errors detected in the frame* These are also referred to as *bit errors*. The FCS field is checked to verify if any errors occurred during transmission. If so, the frame is discarded.

Frame Relay Terminology

This section will discuss the different terminology that is found in Frame Relay. The standard frame is shown in Figure 13-5. This frame is the source of many Frame Relay terms.

The standard Frame Relay frame consists of 48 bytes plus the data portion of the packet. The data portion is a variable amount of bytes depend-

Figure 13-5
Frame Relay frame

ing on how much upper layer data is encapsulated. The first eight bits are the Flags field. This field delimits the beginning and end of the frame. This field is always the same and is represented as either the binary number 01111110 or the hexadecimal number 7E.

The next 16 bits contain the Frame Relay header. Figure 13-6 illustrates the Frame Relay header portion of the Frame Relay frame.

The Frame Relay header contains the following information:

- Data Link Connection Identifier *(DLCI)* The 10-bit DLCI address is defined in this portion of the frame. The DLCI is split across the two bytes, with six bits in the first byte and four bits in the second byte. It is not contiguous across the frame. The use of the DLCI is discussed in detail later in this section.

- Call Reference *(C/R)* The C/R bit is currently not defined.

- Extended Address *(EA)* The EA determines the last DLCI octet. If the value is one, then that current byte is determined to be the last DLCI octet. The EA enables DLCIs to be longer. The eighth bit of each byte in the address field indicates the EA.

- *Congestion control* The congestion control consists of the last three bits in the address field. These three bits represent the *Forward Explicit Congestion Notification* (FECN), *Backward Explicit Congestion Notification* (BECN), and *Discard Eligible* (DE) bits used to provide congestion control in a Frame Relay network environment. These three bits are discussed thoroughly later in this section.

Following the 16-bit header is the data field, as shown in Figure 13-5. The size of the data portion in the frame varies, depending on the amount

Figure 13-6
Frame Relay header

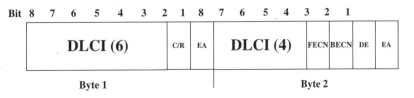

of upper layer data encapsulated in the frame. This value generally consists of no more than 4096 bytes of user data.

The last field is the *Frame Check Sequence* (FCS). The source device uses FCS to compute a value. This value is then in turn verified by the destination device to ensure that the frame was delivered error-free. This process ensures integrity during the transmission of the frame.

PVC

PVCs are statically defined and are permanently established. The customer would send a request for service to their Frame Relay service provider. The service provider would then configure a PVC between two specified locations via a network management station. The bandwidth of this link, the CIR, is defined by the customer. The PVC is a fixed path and represents a point-to-point circuit. PVCs are popular because of their low cost and efficiency. They can be used to create alternate routes and provide redundancy.

SVC

SVCs are created dynamically on a per-call basis. This means that when a connection needs to be made to a remote host, a SVC will be dynamically created. SVCs use the SVC signaling protocol (Q.933) to establish these circuits. This SVC signaling provides call setups and call disconnects. Think of SVCs as a telephone call. Just as you would dial the number of the person you want to talk to, a user specifies the address of the remote device that it wants to communicate with. This process is transparent to the user. The network creates these connections on an as-needed basis.

To create the SVC, the user would first request to be connected to the destination device. Starting an application that needs to connect to a remote server may do this. Once the user sends this request, the network receives it and communicates with the destination device to determine if it should create the connection. The destination device then decides whether to accept or to deny the request. If the destination device accepts, the network will build the SVC between the two end points. Once the end points no longer need the connection and have stopped communicating, one of them will notify the network to remove the SVC.

NOTE: *Frame Relay SVCs have been supported in Cisco IOS™ 11.2 or later.*

CIR

The CIR is defined on each PVC and specifies the bandwidth for each PVC, represented in bits per second. A router has a physical access circuit to the Frame Relay provider and multiple PVCs can be configured off this circuit. The PVCs will have variable amounts of traffic at any certain time depending upon the amount of data the network applications are sending. Frame Relay can accommodate bursty traffic and each PVC is able to burst above its configured CIR if the utilization of the physical circuit is low.

The CIR also allows a customer to have a guaranteed throughput for the circuit. If the customer has important data that cannot afford to be discarded, they would subscribe to a high CIR. A CIR of zero is also available, but it puts all data at risk as the frames are marked as DE, which is discussed in detail later in this chapter.

Subscribing to a higher CIR results in a significant cost increase. Therefore, a baseline should be configured to determine the average amount of data sent across the PVC in a specified amount of time. Once the average amount of data per second is determined, the customer can determine the appropriate CIR for the PVC. A customer can oversubscribe the physical access circuit by having a higher CIR total across all PVCs configured on the physical access circuit than the actual bandwidth of the physical access circuit. This can be done because all of the PVCs would rarely be fully allocated. Each of the PVCs would still be able to burst above their CIR. Figure 13-7 shows how CIRs are used in a Frame Relay network.

This figure shows that each router has a PVC connection to its neighbor routers. Each of these PVCs has a CIR of 384K. This 384K bandwidth is the guaranteed throughput for the circuit. The Frame Relay service provider allows bursty traffic that may exceed the 384K CIR. In this scenario, there is no oversubscription of the physical access circuits because the total CIR of the two PVCs per router is a total of 768K, which is less than the 1.544 Mbps (T1) of the physical access circuit.

Figure 13-7
CIR example

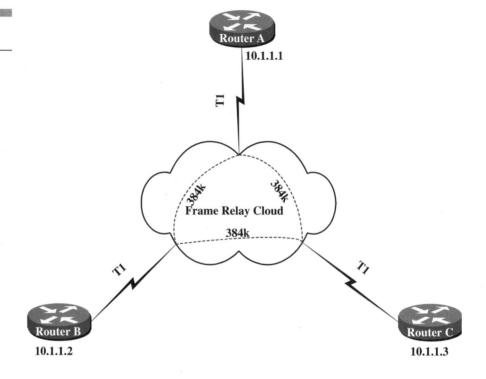

It's important to subscribe to the right CIR. Depending on the traffic rates and the utilization of the circuit, the CIR may need to be adjusted after the circuit is installed.

DLCI

Frame Relay is a layer-two WAN protocol. It does no layer-three processing, so therefore it has no layer-three address. Frame Relay defines layer-two addresses called DLCIs, which represent the layer-two addresses for this WAN protocol similar to how a MAC address represents a layer-two address for LAN protocols. A DLCI identifies a virtual circuit and represents a particular destination with local significance. The Frame Relay switch will forward the frame out the port in which the DLCI for the destination is specified.

Value	Usage
0	Used for call control signaling
1–15	Reserved
16–1007	Available for assignment of Frame Relay PVCs
1008–1018	Reserved
1019–1022	Used for Multicast group
1023	Used for *Local Management Interface* (LMI) specification

Table 13-1

DLCI values

The DLCI is a 10-bit number contained in the Frame Relay header. With 10 bits, a DLCI can be assigned 1024 possible numbers. Some of these numbers are reserved, as shown in Table 13-1.

Locally Significant

DLCI numbers are *locally significant*, which means they identify the connection between the local router and the Frame Relay switch that it is connected to. The DLCI is identified specifically on the port configured on the Frame Relay switch that connects to the LAN. Any number that is locally available on the Frame Relay switch can be used for the DLCI number. This also means that numerous LANs can contain the same DLCI number as long as they are not connected to the same Frame Relay switch.

Local Loop

The local loop is identified as the connection between the *Customer Premise Equipment* (CPE) and the *Central Office* (CO). This is often the physical access circuit from the customer router to the Frame Relay switch (see Figure 13-8).

In this example, the New York site has a T1 physical access circuit to the Frame Relay provider. The router also has multiple virtual circuits connecting to the other remote sites. In this example the T1 circuit would be

Figure 13-8
Local loop example

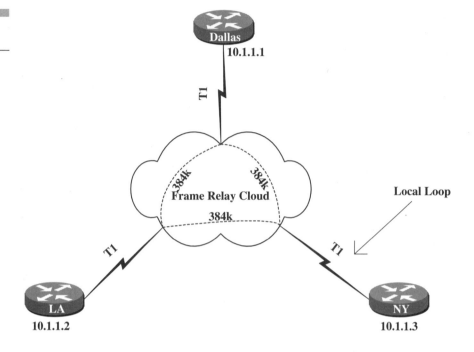

defined as the local loop. The local loop is often one of the first things to test when troubleshooting a circuit. A call would be made to the Frame Relay provider asking them to test the local loop between their equipment and the CSU/DSU at the customer site.

LMI

In 1990, the "Gang of Four" got together to create standards for Frame Relay. This gang consisted of Cisco, Stratacom, Northern Telecom, and Digital. They later formed the Frame Relay Forum in 1991 and helped create standards such as the *Local Management Interface* (LMI), which extends the capabilities of Frame Relay.

LMI provides a connection status mechanism that reports information on the connection between the router and the Frame Relay switch. LMI consists of management frames that the router sends when enabled for LMI to the Frame Relay switch. The router can send keep-alive messages to report that the router is up and will in turn get keep-alive responses from the Frame Relay switch. The router can also determine the PVC status of the port by sending a status request. The network will respond with a full report on the PVCs.

LMI extends the capabilities of Frame Relay in many ways. Some of these features include

- The use of Inverse ARP, which enables the router to dynamically learn the protocol addresses on the other end of each DLCI-defined PVC.

- The capability to provide simple flow control. This flow control feature includes the use of the FECN, BECN, and DE bits to help throttle the traffic sent onto the network and to alleviate congestion on the network. These terms are described later in this chapter.

- The capability to send multicast frames. Multicasting enables the router to send a frame destined to multiple recipients. This is used often for routing updates.

- The capability to learn the PVC status from the Frame Relay switch by sending queries or status requests. The router could also simply request keep-alives. This process enables LMI-enabled networks to learn if a PVC goes down.

The following bullets describe a Frame Relay frame that conforms to the LMI specification as illustrated in Figure 13-9.

- *Flag*   This delimits the beginning and end of the frame.

- *LMI DLCI*   This identifies the frame as being an LMI frame instead of a basic Frame Relay frame. The LMI-specific DLCI value is 1023, as defined in the LMI consortium specification.

Figure 13-9
The LMI frame format

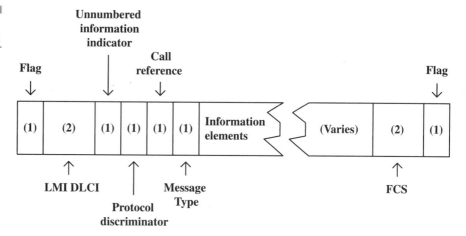

- *Unnumbered Information Indicator*   This sets the poll/final bit to zero.

- *Protocol Discriminator*   This field always contains a value indicating that the frame is an LMI frame.

- *Call Reference*   This field consists of all zeros. The field is currently not defined.

- *Message Type*   This field labels the frame as either a status-inquiry message or a status message. The status-inquiry message enables the router to determine the status of the network. Status messages are used to respond to status-inquiry messages. PVC status messages and keep-alives are examples of status messages.

- *Information Elements*   This field contains a variable number of individual *information elements* (IEs). IEs consist of the following fields:

    - *IE Identifier*   This uniquely identifies the IE.

    - *IE Length*   This indicates the length of the IE.

    - *Data*   The data portion consists of at least one byte of encapsulated upper-layer data.

- Frame Check Sequence *(FCS)*   The FCS field provides the same function as it does in a regular Frame Relay frame, which ensures the integrity of each frame.

NOTE: *Stratacom later merged with Cisco, and Compaq Computers acquired Digital Equipment Corporation.*

FECN

Congestion can occur on the network when too much data tries to traverse a link. With the use of LMI, Frame Relay can provide enhanced capabilities such as congestion notification. Before such a standard arrived, Frame Relay relied on the upper layer protocols such as TCP to provide windowing, or flow control. Now with this enhanced capability, Frame Relay does not have to rely solely on TCP, thus saving many processing cycles at the end points because the flow control is also processed at layer two on the network. Frame Relay has two bits in its header that define two aspects of congestion notification. The first is FECN, which is defined in one bit in the Frame Relay header. The bit can be set to either a one or a zero. Figure 13-10 shows how FECN operates.

San Jose is sending data to Miami and is connected via Frame Relay to its service provider locally. The frame will then travel across the U.S., traversing two additional Frame Relay switches before reaching the destination switch in Miami. Miami's Frame Relay switch D then passes the frame to the Miami router. In this scenario, a saturated circuit is set up between Frame Relay switch B and C. Therefore, when the frame reaches switch B, it sees that the link is congested and switches the FECN bit in the frame from zero to one. By doing this, switch B has notified switches C and D of the congestion on the link. The destination router will also be informed that FECNs have occurred during the transmission.

BECN

Using the same example, let's say that congestion is still occurring between Frame Relay switch B and C, and Miami is now responding, or sending data, to San Jose. Switch B will see that the link between itself and switch C is still saturated. It will then switch the *Backward Explicit Congestion Notification* (BECN) bit from a "0" to a "1" going in the "backwards" direction towards San Jose. The San Jose router will receive the frames with the

Figure 13-10
FECN operation

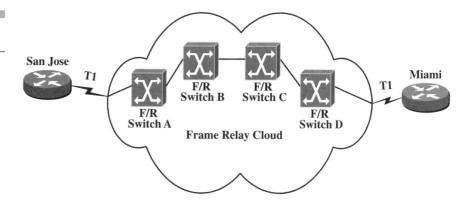

BECN bit flagged and will know to throttle down the amount of frames it is sending out to Miami.

DE

A DE bit resides in every Frame Relay frame header. The frames become eligible for discard every time the DE bit is set to one and the frames that have their DE bit set to zero are not eligible for discard. The DE bit is an important part of the congestion control process of Frame Relay because it provides a method of predetermining which frames may be discarded. To truly understand how the DE bit and congestion control process works, we will discuss the process of provisioning the circuit.

An office in N.Y. needs to establish a circuit with the headquarters in San Francisco. The company will order physical access circuits for the routers at N.Y. and San Francisco. Each router will have a T1 connection to the public Frame Relay network or carrier network. The company will then order a PVC between the two routers with a 384K CIR. The carrier will provision the virtual circuit and define the CIR of 384K. This will be the company's guaranteed throughput on this circuit. The carrier will also set the *committed burst* (Bc). This is the maximum number of bits of user data that the carrier's network will commit to transfer during a specified amount of time, or *Tc*. All frames that exceed the Bc are marked with the DE bit set to one by the Frame Relay switch. The router can also set the DE bit, but only if the customer implements *Quality of Service* (QoS) on the router. Tc is the committed rate measurement interval and is equal to Bc/CIR. Tc is most often referred to as the time interval and is usually set to one second. The last parameter that is set is called the *Be*, or excess burst. The Be is the maximum number of bits in excess of the Bc that the network will attempt to transfer over the Tc (the time interval) under normal conditions. All frames in excess of the Be are discarded. Figure 13-11 illustrates this process.

Understandably, this process can appear complicated. Most network engineers understand the congestion process as being "whatever frames exceed the CIR get marked as DE" and "If the network experiences congestion, the frames marked DE are discarded."

Although this is a true explanation, it only touches the surface of how the congestion process works within Frame Relay. The easiest way to understand how the components of Frame Relay work (that is, Bc, Be, Tc, and CIR) is to break down the process. Think of the Bc and Be as buffers for the

Figure 13-11
The DE process

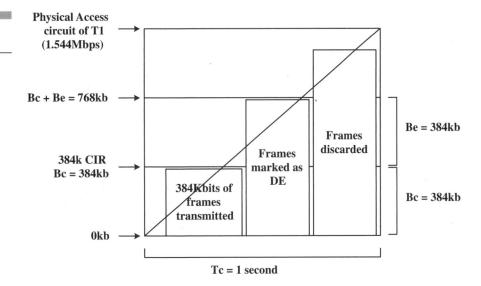

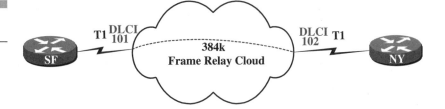

Figure 13-12
The DE process

frames. Figure 13-12 show the steps that the frames make during the congestion process.

San Francisco is performing large FTP file transfers to N.Y. The frames are sent out of the San Francisco router to the local Frame Relay switch. As the frame comes into the switch, they are put in the Bc buffer. The Bc is set to 384K. Once that buffer is exceeded (384K+), the frames are marked as DE and are sent to the Be buffer. Once the Be buffer is full, the rest of the frames are discarded until the Tc expires, in which time the buffers are cleared and the process starts over again. It's important to remember that this whole process takes place in a very short period of time, which is the Tc, as it is usually set to one second. This process is known as the *leaky bucket algorithm*.

NOTE: *An important concept to remember is that Frame Relay does not provide any error notification of frames that were discarded. Frame Relay relies on upper layer protocols such as TCP for the retransmission of discarded frames.*

Frame Relay Address Mapping

As discussed earlier, Frame Relay uses layer-two addresses called DLCIs. DLCIs have local significance and are mapped to destination network layer addresses, such as an IP address. DLCIs can be mapped to IP addresses in two ways. The first way is done dynamically using Inverse ARP in conjunction with LMI to find the next-hop IP address for a specific PVC. This is done by the router sending Inverse ARP requests out each DLCI to find the IP address on the other side of the PVC. The other way to map DLCIs to IP address is via static frame maps. These static frame maps take each local DLCI and map it to the next-hop IP address on that PVC. Frame maps provide the same function as Inverse ARP, but it is done manually. Frame maps are generally used on much smaller networks or in a test lab where one central router connects to many stub networks. The addition and deletion of frame maps in an enterprise environment would prove tiresome.

Frame Relay Signaling

The Gang of Four developed the LMI protocol because no current standards at the time supported these extended capabilities of Frame Relay. Later, standards committees such as the *International Telecommunication Union* (ITU-T) Standardization Sector, formerly the CCITT, and the *American National Standards Institute* (ANSI) developed their own standards. Table 13-2 outlines the three different versions of the LMI specification. Cisco supports all three of these LMI protocols.

The implementation of LMI enables only one-way status requests. This limits status requests from the router to the network, or the *User-to-Network Interface* (UNI). LMI will not work in a *Network-to-Network Interface* (NNI) because of its one-way communication.

Table 13-2	Protocol	Specification
LMI specifications	LMI	Frame Relay Forum *Implementation Agreement* (IA); FRF.1 is superseded by FRF.1.1
	Annex A	ITU Q.933, referenced in FRF.1.1
	Annex D	ANSI T1.617

ANSI recognized the importance of this and included it in its standard, Annex D of T1.617. Annex D enables NNI to provide a bidirectional mechanism for PVC signaling. This bidirectional mechanism is symmetric in that it allows both the router and the Frame Relay switch to issue both queries and responses. Annex D also enables networks to send queries and responses to each other, thus extending the capability of Frame Relay.

Annex A defines a standard for SVC signaling and is not supported by as many vendors as Annex D and LMI. Annex D is supported by most vendors and LMI is the most supported management protocol. Annex A uses DLCI 0 in its protocol, as does Annex D, whereas LMI uses DLCI 1023. Although LMI is the first protocol to be created to provide these extended functions, all the protocols can generically be defined as LMI.

Cisco routers will attempt to autosense which LMI type the Frame Relay switch is using. The router does this by sending full status requests to the Frame Relay switch. The Frame Relay switch will then respond with one or more LMI types. The router will then automatically configure the LMI type with the last LMI type received from the Frame Relay switch. The LMI type can also be configured manually.

The router, or DTE device, will send LMI status requests to the Frame Relay switch every 10 seconds. These status requests are sent over DLCI 1023 if configured for `cisco` LMI or will be sent over DLCI 0 if configured for `ansi` or `q933i` type signaling. The Frame Relay switch responds with a status response or keep-alive. Every sixth status request from the router or DTE device is sent as a full status request. The Frame Relay switch will respond with all of the DLCIs configured on the port of the Frame Relay switch.

The router updates the status of its PVCs when it receives LMI information from the Frame Relay switch. It updates its PVCs on one of the following three states:

- *Active state* This is when the router's connection to the Frame Relay switch is up and active. The router can exchange information with the Frame Relay switch.

- *Inactive state* This is when the router's connection to the Frame Relay switch is up and active, but the router at the end of the PVC is not communicating with its local Frame Relay switch.

- *Deleted state* The router is not receiving any LMI from the Frame Relay switch. This could be a circuit problem or a problem with the network.

Frame Relay Inverse ARP

One of the features that LMI provides is the use of Inverse ARP. Inverse ARP enables the router to dynamically find the next-hop IP address for a PVC. The first step in this process is accomplished with the Frame Relay switch sending the router all of the DLCI numbers that are configured for the physical circuit between the router and the Frame Relay switch. The router then sends Inverse ARP requests out each DLCI to determine the IP address of the router on the other end of the PVC. The router can then build a table of DLCI-to-IP-address mappings called a Frame Relay map table. The use of Inverse ARP saves the manual task of configuring multiple Frame Relay mappings. Inverse ARP is enabled by default on Cisco routers when LMI is configured. Figure 13-13 illustrates an example of how Inverse ARP operates.

Figure 13-13
Inverse ARP

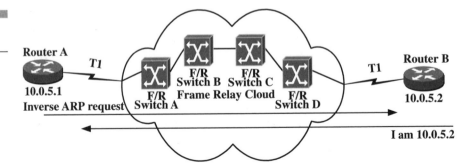

Configuring Frame Relay

Frame Relay is an efficient and cost-effective way to connect network devices over a WAN. The following section describes the steps to take to configure Frame Relay in a network.

Interface Settings

The following example shows the steps to take to configure an IP address for the interface:

1. Go into specific configuration mode on the router:

```
Router#config t
Router(config)#interface serial 1
```

2. Enter an IP address for the interface:

```
Router(config-if)#ip address 172.16.5.1 255.255.255.0
```

Encapsulation

This section discusses configuring different encapsulation types on Frame Relay interfaces. The following configuration examples continue from the preceding section.

Specify the encapsulation type for the interface. The options are either cisco or ietf. In this example, we will use the cisco encapsulation setting. The encapsulation setting must be the same on each router connected. The ietf encapsulation type would be used if you were connecting to a non-Cisco router. The default encapsulation setting is cisco:

```
Router#config t
Router(config-if)#encapsulation frame-relay cisco
```

LMI Type

This section discusses the steps to configure LMI on Frame Relay interfaces. The following configuration examples continue from the preceding section:

1. Specify the LMI type that will be used on this interface. The LMI options are `ansi`, `cisco`, and `q933i`. We will use Cisco in this example, which is the default LMI type. After IOS release 11.2, the LMI type is autosensed and no configuration is necessary for LMI. If you are using an IOS release prior to 11.2 that does not support the LMI autosense feature, you must ask your carrier or Frame Relay provider for the LMI type to use.

```
Router(config-if)#frame-relay lmi-type cisco
```

2. Configure the bandwidth for the serial link. The bandwidth statement is used to determine metrics in many routing protocols. The router will default each link to a T1 that does not have the bandwidth statement specified and it will not appear in the configuration. The following example configures the serial link with a bandwidth of 128K. This is the bandwidth of the physical access circuit:

```
Router(config-if)#bandwidth 128
```

3. Inverse ARP is enabled on the router by default. If it is disabled, it can be reenabled by entering the following command. The protocol options are `ip`, `ipx`, `appletalk`, `decnet`, `vines`, and `xns`. The DLCI on the local interface in which you want to exchange Inverse ARP messages is defined after the protocol.

```
Router(config)#frame-relay inverse-arp ip 102
```

The following example shows the results of the router configuration:

```
interface serial 1
 ip address 172.16.5.1 255.255.255.0
 encapsulation frame-relay
 bandwidth 128
 frame-relay lmi-type cisco
```

Static Mappings

If Inverse ARP is not supported by the router, or if you want to control the broadcast traffic, the router must be configured with Frame Relay static mappings. These static mappings are defined manually and with them you can build the IP-address-to-DLCI table.

The following is an example showing how to configure a Frame Relay static map:

Figure 13-14
DLCI example

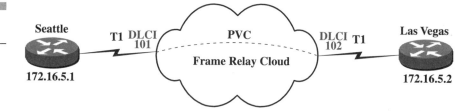

```
Router(config)#interface serial 1
Router(config-if)#frame-relay map ip 172.16.5.2 101 broadcast
```

Figure 13-14 illustrates an example of how DLCIs are used in a Frame Relay network.

This figure statically maps the Seattle router's DLCI to the IP address of its destination, the Las Vegas router. This statement tells the router that to reach the IP address of 172.16.5.2, the Las Vegas router, it must use DLCI 101. Once both routers are configured with their `frame-relay map` statements, communication can start occurring. The broadcast argument at the end of the command enables the router to send broadcast routing updates to the Las Vegas router through the PVC. The actual syntax for the `frame-relay map` command is as follows:

```
Router(config-if)#frame-relay map protocol protocol-address dlci
[broadcast] [ietf | cisco | payload-compress packet-by-packet]
```

Table 13-3 explains the uses of each option.

NOTE: *The* `payload-compress` `packet-by-packet` *option in the* `frame-relay` `map` *statement can be extremely processor-intensive. It should be verified that the router has enough memory and processor power to support compression. Compression is usually reserved for use over slow links on routers that can support the compression.*

Cisco uses the STAC method of packet-by-packet compression. If the router contains a data compression *Advanced Interface Module* (AIM), it will perform hardware compression. Otherwise, compression is performed in the software installed on the router's main processor.

	frame-relay map	Description
Table 13-3	protocol	Defines the protocol in use (ip, ipx, appletalk, decnet, vines, or xns).
`frame-relay` `map` Descriptions	protocol address	Defines the network layer address of the destination router interface.
	dlci	Defines the local DLCI used to connect to the remote router's protocol address.
	broadcast (optional)	Enables the use of broadcasts and multicasts over the virtual circuit. Routing protocols can broadcast routing updates over the virtual circuit when this statement is added.
	ietf | cisco	Enables the encapsulation of either cisco (default) or ietf (standard).
	payload-compress packet-by-packet (optional)	The packet-by-packet compression of the payload using the Stacker (STAC) method.

Verifying Frame Relay

Once you have configured the routers for Frame Relay, you can verify that the connections are active and operational by using the available show commands. If a problem occurs with a circuit or connection, the correct show commands can often help determine where the problem is occurring. Also, debug commands can be used to assist in more extensive troubleshooting of the Frame Relay connections. The following section discusses the different show and debug commands and explains their usage.

Show Commands

One of the most basic and resourceful commands is the show interface command. This command displays a lot of relevant information regarding the Frame Relay network. The following example shows the output of the show interface command:

```
Router#show interface s0/0
Serial0/0 is up, line protocol is up
  Hardware is PowerQUICC Serial
  Internet address is 172.16.1.4/24
  MTU 1500 bytes, BW 1544 Kbit, DLY 20000 usec,
```

```
        reliability 255/255, txload 1/255, rxload 1/255
     Encapsulation FRAME-RELAY, loopback not set
     Keepalive set (10 sec)
     LMI enq sent  2726, LMI stat recvd 2709, LMI upd recvd 0, DTE LMI up
     LMI enq recvd 0, LMI stat sent  0, LMI upd sent  0
     LMI DLCI 1023  LMI type is CISCO  frame relay DTE
     Broadcast queue 0/64, broadcasts sent/dropped 1091/0, interface
  broadcasts 544
     Last input 00:00:05, output 00:00:07, output hang never
     Last clearing of "show interface" counters 07:41:01
     Queueing strategy: fifo
     Output queue 0/40, 0 drops; input queue 0/75, 0 drops
     5 minute input rate 0 bits/sec, 0 packets/sec
     5 minute output rate 0 bits/sec, 0 packets/sec
        3871 packets input, 152211 bytes, 0 no buffer
        Received 0 broadcasts, 0 runts, 0 giants, 0 throttles
        0 input errors, 0 CRC, 0 frame, 0 overrun, 0 ignored, 0 abort
        3870 packets output, 103120 bytes, 0 underruns
        0 output errors, 0 collisions, 16 interface resets
        0 output buffer failures, 0 output buffers swapped out
        12 carrier transitions
        DCD=up  DSR=up  DTR=up  RTS=up  CTS=up
```

The previous lines show the Frame Relay information that is output when doing a show interface command. The first item, Encapsulation FRAME-RELAY, shows that the encapsulation setting is set to frame-relay for this serial interface. The next item LMI DLCI 1023 shows that the DLCI used by LMI is 1023. This is the DLCI used for Cisco LMI. The following statement LMI type is Cisco shows that the LMI type is specified as Cisco LMI. The last item frame relay DTE shows that the serial interface is acting as a DTE device.

Another useful command to display information regarding Frame Relay is the show frame-relay lmi. This command displays LMI traffic statistics. The following example shows the output of the show frame-relay lmi command:

```
Router#show frame-relay lmi

LMI Statistics for interface Serial0/0 (Frame Relay DTE) LMI TYPE
= CISCO
    Invalid Unnumbered info 0          Invalid Prot Disc 0
    Invalid dummy Call Ref 0           Invalid Msg Type 0
    Invalid Status Message 0           Invalid Lock Shift 0
    Invalid Information ID 0           Invalid Report IE Len 0
    Invalid Report Request 0           Invalid Keep IE Len 0
    Num Status Enq. Sent 2730          Num Status msgs Rcvd 2713
    Num Update Status Rcvd 0           Num Status Timeouts 17
```

The output of the show frame-relay lmi command shows the number of status messages sent and received from the router to the Frame Relay switch.

The command show frame-relay pvc is one of the most informative show commands that can be used to troubleshoot and monitor Frame Relay connections. The following is an example of the show frame-relay pvc command:

```
Router#show frame-relay pvc

PVC Statistics for interface Serial0/0 (Frame Relay DTE)

                Active      Inactive      Deleted      Static
   Local          2            0             0           0
   Switched       0            0             0           0
   Unused         0            0             0           0

DLCI = 201, DLCI USAGE = LOCAL, PVC STATUS = ACTIVE, INTERFACE =
Serial0/0

   input pkts 1150          output pkts 569        in bytes 108520
   out bytes 34140          dropped pkts 0         in FECN pkts 0
   in BECN pkts 0           out FECN pkts 0        out BECN pkts 0
   in DE pkts 0             out DE pkts 0
   out bcast pkts 549       out bcast bytes 32060
   pvc create time 07:32:33, last time pvc status changed 07:28:03

DLCI = 301, DLCI USAGE = LOCAL, PVC STATUS = ACTIVE, INTERFACE =
Serial0/0

   input pkts 16            output pkts 563        in bytes 1594
   out bytes 33586          dropped pkts 0         in FECN pkts 0
   in BECN pkts 0           out FECN pkts 0        out BECN pkts 0
   in DE pkts 0             out DE pkts 0
   out bcast pkts 548       out bcast bytes 32026
   pvc create time 07:32:35, last time pvc status changed 07:32:25
```

This command shows a lot of information about the Frame Relay circuit. The PVC status listed for each DLCI can be active, inactive, or deleted. The PVC status is active when the PVC has been created and the Frame Relay link between the two routers is up.

The PVC will be in an inactive state if the router is not using the correct DLCI assigned to the PVC. For example, if you have a PVC on serial interface 1/1 with a DLCI of 110 and you accidentally entered the DLCI number as 101, the router would show that PVC status as inactive. If the router shows an inactive status for a PVC, you may want to contact the Frame Relay provider to ensure that you are using the correct DLCI. Another troubleshooting tip is to ensure that you don't have the DLCIs reversed from your local router to the remote router.

The last option of the PVC status is deleted. The PVC status will show up as deleted if the Frame Relay provider has yet to provision the PVC. It will also show up as deleted if the Frame Relay provider does not support the DLCI that is entered.

If you are having problems getting an active PVC status, you may want to also check that the encapsulation settings are correct. The router must have the same encapsulation type as the Frame Relay switch. Verify this with your Frame Relay provider.

This output also shows the amount of FECN and BECN packets received and sent out of the interface. It is important to monitor these fields when troubleshooting. If the FECN and BECN packets are increasing, it could be a sign that the bandwidth of the circuit is too low. Raising the CIR of the physical access circuit could help reduce the number of packets being discarded.

NOTE: *The* `show frame-relay pvc` *command will show the status of all the DLCIs configured on the interfaces. You can also use the command* `show frame-relay pvc <number>` *and enter a specific PVC that you want to check the status on. This will show the status of only that specific PVC.*

An additional command that can be used to verify Frame Relay connectivity is the `show frame-relay map` command. This command will display all the map entries configured on the router. The following is an example of the `show frame-relay map` command:

```
R4#show frame-relay map
Serial0/0 (up): ip 172.16.1.3 dlci 301(0x12D,0x48D0), dynamic,
              broadcast,, status defined, active
Serial0/0 (up): ip 172.16.1.1 dlci 201(0xC9,0x3090), dynamic,
              broadcast,, status defined, active
```

This command shows that the serial link is up and that the IP addresses of the remote routers interface mapped to the local DLCI numbers. The `0x12D` value is the hexadecimal conversion of the DLCI number `301`. The `0x48D0` value is how it would appear on the wire. This is because of the way the bits are spread out in the Frame Relay frame. The `active` value defines the status of the PVC, as described earlier. The command `clear frame-relay-inarp` is used to delete the dynamically created Frame Relay maps that are created with Inverse ARP.

Debug Commands

A more extensive method of troubleshooting a Frame Relay connection is to use the associated debug commands. One of the most useful debug Frame Relay commands is `debug frame-relay lmi`. This command lets you troubleshoot the Frame Relay circuit by monitoring the LMI passed between the router and the Frame Relay switch. The following is an example of output from the `debug frame-relay lmi` command:

```
Router#debug frame-relay lmi
Frame Relay LMI debugging is on
Displaying all Frame Relay LMI data
Router#
1w3d:Serial 1 (out):   StEnq, myswq 140, yourseen 139, DTE up
1w3d:datagramstart    =       0XE008EC,       datagramsize    =
13
1w3d:FR  encap  =  0xFCF10309
1w3d:00 75 01 01 01 03 02 8C 8B
1w3d:
1w3d:Serial 1 (in):   Status, myseq 140
1w3d:RT IE 1, length 1, type 1
1w3d:KA IE 3, length 2, yourseq 140, myseq 140
1w3d:Serial 0 (out): StEnq, myseq 141, yourseen 140, DTE up
1w3d:datagramstart = 0xE008EC, datagramsize = 13
1w3d:FR encap = 0xFCF10309
1w3d:00 75 01 01 01 03 02 8D 8C
1w3d:
1w3d:Serial 1 (in):   Status,  myseq 142
1w3d:RT IE 1, length 1, type 0
1w3d:KA IE 3, length 2, yourseq 142, myseq 142
1w3d:PVC IE 0x7 , length 0x6 , dlci 100, status 0x2 , bw 0
```

This output reflects whether the Frame Relay switch is sending and receiving LMI packets properly. The (out) is an LMI status message sent by the router. The (in) is a message sent by the Frame Relay switch. The type 0 is a full LMI status message. The type 1 is an LMI exchange. The dlci 100 defines the dlci, and the status 0x2 shows that DLCI 100 is active. Different status values can be defined for the DLCI during the debug. These possible values are listed below:

- *0x0* Inactive/Added indicates that the Frame Relay switch has the DLCI programmed, but the router cannot use the PVC. The reasons for this include mismatched DLCIs or the other end of the PVC is down.

- *0x2* Active/Added indicates that the Frame Relay switch has the DLCI programmed and the PVC is up and operational.

- *0x4* Deleted indicates that the Frame Relay switch does not have the DLCI currently programmed for the router. This often occurs once the Frame Relay switch deletes the PVC after the customer requests to remove it. The router will show the PVC status as deleted. The router must be rebooted before the PVC will be deleted.

Depending upon which protocols and services you are running across the Frame Relay network, some other `debug frame-relay` commands may be useful. Figure 13-15 lists the other options for debugging `frame-relay` information.

Figure 13-15

Debug options for frame relay

```
Router#debug frame-relay ?
  dlsw         Frame Relay dlsw
  end-to-end   Frame-relay end-to-end VC information
  events       Important Frame Relay packet events
  foresight    Frame Relay router ForeSight support
  fragment     Frame Relay fragment
  hpr          Frame Relay APPN HPR
  ip           Frame Relay Internet Protocol
  llc2         Frame Relay llc2
  lmi          LMI packet exchanges with service provider
  packet       Frame Relay packets
  ppp          PPP over Frame Relay
  rsrb         Frame Relay rsrb
  verbose      Frame Relay
```

Designing Frame Relay

Many issues must be considered when designing a Frame Relay network. This section describes three different Frame Relay designs. Each of these designs has its own advantages and disadvantages. To determine the ideal design for a network, the advantages and disadvantages, such as redundancy and cost, must be weighed.

Full-Mesh

A full-mesh network is exactly as it sounds. It consists of each router having a dedicated virtual circuit to every other router in the network. This design allows for full redundancy because if a link goes down, the router can traverse a multitude of other links to reach its destination. Figure 13-16 illustrates an example of a full-mesh design.

Each router has a virtual circuit to every other router. This design has both advantages and disadvantages. They are listed in Table 13-4.

Figure 13-16
Full-mesh design

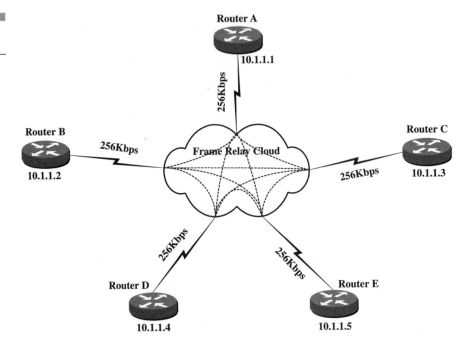

Table 13-4

A full-mesh design's
advantages and
disadvantages

Advantages	Disadvantages
It provides a full redundant network.	A large number of virtual circuits must be set up between all the routers, increasing the complexity of the router configurations and resulting in a significant cost to the customer.
If a link goes down, the routing protocol chooses the next best path to the destination.	The routing tables become huge and can cause problems with the amount of broad cast traffic passed over the links.
This topology facilitates support of all network protocols.	

Star

The star topology, often referred to as a *hub and spoke configuration*, is
the most popular Frame Relay network topology. In a hub and spoke configuration, the remote sites would all have connections back to the core

site. The hub site generally provides the main applications and services that the remote sites need. Figure 13-17 shows a typical star, or hub-and-spoke, design.

This design also has its advantages and disadvantages, which are listed in Table 13-5.

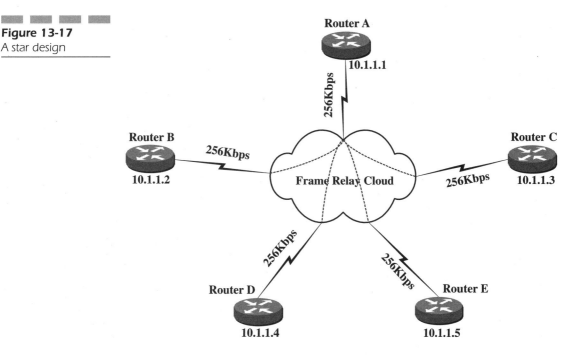

Figure 13-17

A star design

Table 13-5	Advantages	Disadvantages
A star design's advantages and disadvantages	It is the least expensive design because it requires the least amount of circuits.	The hub site is a single point of failure in this design. If the hub router or its physical circuit goes down, the remote sites are unable to access the hub to get their required services to operate.
	All network services and applications can be run from the hub, with the remote sites connecting to get the services they need. This also equates to simplified management.	All the remote sites traverse a single physical link, creating a bottleneck in the network. This does not provide scalability.

Partial Mesh

A partial mesh design combines some of the features of both the mesh topology and the star topology. For a non-meshed router to communicate with another non-meshed router, it must traverse through a collection point router. In Figure 13-18, if Router B needs to communicate with Router C, it could not do so directly because it does not have a direct connection. It

Figure 13-18
A partial mesh topology

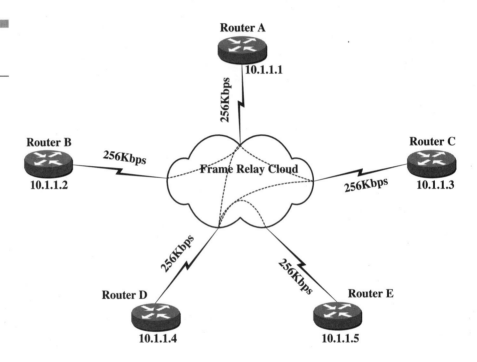

Table 13-6	Advantages	Disadvantages
A partial mesh design's advantages and disadvantages	The partial mesh topology provides somewhat of a hybrid network. It provides more redundancy than the star topology.	This design does not provide as much redundancy as the full mesh topology.
	This has fewer costs than the mesh topology because not as many virtual circuits are required.	Circuit costs are higher in this design than the star topology.

would pass the traffic to Router A, which would then route the traffic to Router C.

The advantages and disadvantages of this design are listed in Table 13-6.

A partial mesh network is often referred to as a *hybrid design*. The advantages of both the mesh topology and the star topology can be brought together to create a hybrid hierarchical design. We will discuss this more advanced design in the Subinterfaces section.

Frame Relay as a NBMA Network

Frame Relay is by default a nonbroadcast multi-access network. This means that although all sites can reach each other, many routers will not be able to retransmit routing broadcast updates out the interface in which it was learned. The reason for this is because Frame Relay uses Split Horizon to reduce routing loops in the network. Split Horizon defines that a router cannot retransmit routes it has learned from the same interface. The next section shows an example of a NBMA network using Split Horizon.

How Frame Relay Complicates the Routing Update Process

A NBMA network inherently causes problems for most routing protocols, mainly because of the use of Split Horizon. Figure 13-19 shows an example of some of the problems that can occur.

In this NBMA network, Router A has one physical interface with multiple PVCs to the spoke routers B, C, and D. Each spoke router also has one physical interface with one PVC back to the hub site, Router A. Router A can send routing updates to all of the other routers. Likewise, Routers B, C, and D can send routing updates to Router A. However, when Router B, C, or D sends routing updates to Router A, Router A will not be able to retransmit those routing updates back out to the other spoke routers in the network. For example, if Router B sends a routing update to Router A, the hub site, Router A will not be able to retransmit that routing update back out to Routers C and D. Therefore, the spoke routers will not learn about routing updates from other spoke routers. The reason Router A cannot retransmit routing updates is because of the Split Horizon rule, which states that a

Figure 13-19

Split Horizon example

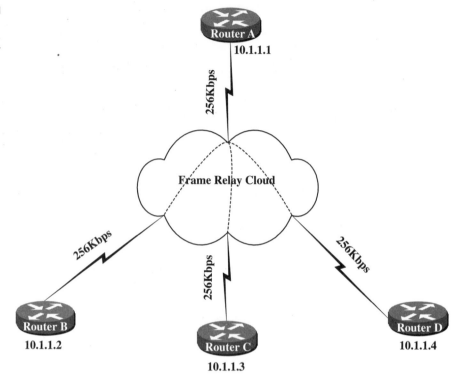

broadcast cannot be retransmitted out the same interface from which it was learned. Remember that Router A only has one physical interface in which it uses multiple PVCs to connect to the other routers.

Split Horizon can be disabled to overcome some of these limitations and is disabled by default in IP-only networks. However, Split Horizon should not be disabled in this type of environment for two main reasons. Some protocols, such as AppleTalk, will not allow Split Horizon to be turned off. Therefore, routing updates will not be able to reach the other routers. To disable Split Horizon and still accommodate these types of routing protocols, the network must be fully meshed. The drawback of a fully meshed network is the significant cost in circuits.

The second reason that the network design should be carefully thought out before disabling Split Horizon is because of the chance of routing loops in the network. Split Horizon reduces routing loops by not allowing a routing update received on an interface to be retransmitted out that same interface.

NOTE: *To disable Split Horizon, enter the following command in the router using specific configuration mode:*

```
Router(config-if)#no ip split-horizon
```

Subinterfaces

Many of Frame Relay's problems can be overcome by one solution, and that is to create subinterfaces. By creating subinterfaces, it moves the network away from being a NBMA network and creates multiple point-to-point leased lines between routers. The routers still use virtual circuits to connect to each other, but each connection will have its own defined subinterface. Each subnetwork will also have its own network number. Therefore, routing protocols can send routing updates out of a subinterface and they can be rebroadcast out other subinterfaces without violating the rule of Split Horizon (see Figure 13-20).

Figure 13-20
Subinterface example

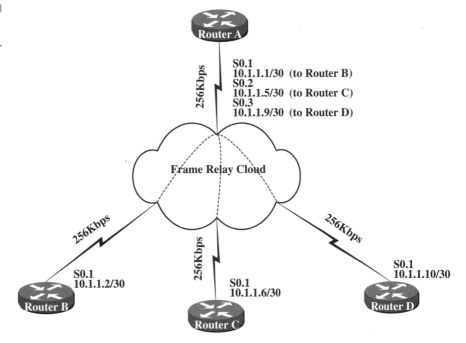

In this figure, Router A has one physical interface with multiple subinterfaces. The subinterfaces are used as logical connections to the spoke routers. Each subinterface has an associated PVC that maps to a spoke router. The spoke routers B, C, and D all have a single subinterface associated to a PVC mapped to Router A.

Router B sends a routing update to Router A. Router A is now able to receive that routing update and retransmit it out the other subinterfaces. The Split Horizon rule is still in effect in this example and does not allow Router A to retransmit the routing update back to Router B. All of the spoke routers can now send routing updates to the hub router, Router A, and expect the routing update to be propagated throughout the network.

Notice that in this example a separate network is used for each PVC. The network addresses use a 255.255.255.252, or /30 subnet mask, which enables two usable addresses. One of the addresses will be used on a subinterface on the hub router, and the second address will be used on the subinterface at the spoke router. A single class C address can be broken down with the 255.255.255.252 subnet mask and will enable 64 different subnetworks to be used on the subinterfaces for the network.

The command `frame-relay interface-dlci` must be used when configuring subinterfaces. The reason for this is because LMI does not know about subinterfaces. Therefore, to link the LMI-derived PVC to a subinterface, this command must be used. Figure 13-21 shows how the command is used in the configuration of Router A.

Using subinterfaces in a Frame Relay network is one of the most efficient designs. Large-scale Frame Relay networks often use subinterfaces in a hybrid hierarchical design using both the partial mesh topology along with the full mesh topology (see Figure 13-22).

An enterprise network will often consist of multiple partial mesh configurations. These configurations are actually dual hub and spoke configurations but are considered partial mesh because more than one hub site exists. The hub site of each hub and spoke configuration will have a high-speed connection, either via Frame Relay or ATM, back to the core backbone of the network. Each spoke site will have two connections back to the hub routers for redundancy. One of the hub routers will often be the backup router, and the PVCs to the spoke sites will have a much lower CIR than the PVCs originating from the main hub router. It is useful to exchange full routing tables between the hub sites and the core backbone, while configuring the spoke sites to only advertise their own network to the hub site. This helps limit the amount of broadcast traffic across the low-speed links to the spoke sites.

Figure 13-21

Subinterface example with the `frame-relay interface-dlci` command

Configuration

```
interface Serial0
no ip address
encapsulation frame-relay
!
interface Serial0.1 point-to-point
ip address 10.1.1.1 255.255.255.0
bandwidth 64
frame-relay interface-dlci 101
!
interface Serial0.2 point-to-point
ip address 10.1.1.5 255.255.255.0
bandwidth 64
frame-relay interface-dlci 102
!
interface Serial0.3 point-to-point
ip address 10.1.1.9 255.255.255.0
bandwidth 64
frame-relay interface-dlci 103
```

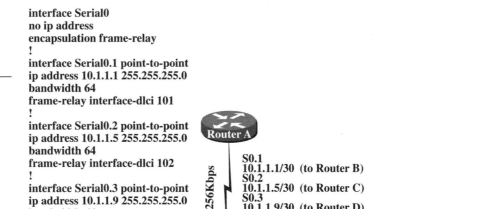
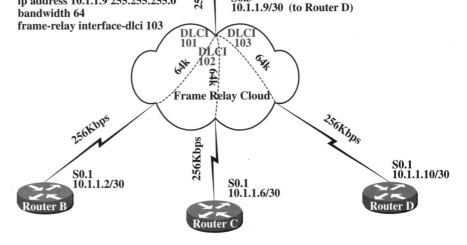

The core network represents the backbone, the hub sites represent the distribution layer, and the spoke sites represent the access layer. This design is the most redundant while still remaining cost-effective. The hybrid hierarchical design also provides scalability in the internetwork by allowing additional sites and networks to be added without disrupting the backbone.

Multipoint Subinterfaces   Cisco routers also support the use of multipoint subinterfaces that divide the physical interface into separate virtual multipoint subinterfaces. Multipoint subinterfaces use a single network

Figure 13-22
A hybrid hierarchical
design

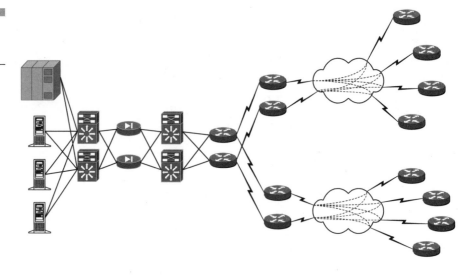

layer address. Configuring the network with multipoint subinterfaces makes the network an NBMA network and is subject to the rules of Split Horizon (see Figure 13-23). Multipoint subinterfaces are not often used because of this reason.

This example uses the same example from the discussion on subinterfaces, except it is utilizing multipoint subinterfaces instead of point-to-point subinterfaces. Router A now only has one subinterface, but the subinterface is defined as multipoint, which allows it to map logical connections to the other spoke routers. All devices on the multipoint subinterface belong to the same network number. The spoke routers all have a single subinterface pointing back to the hub site. The hub site, Router A, is the only router that can utilize the multipoint subinterface because it has the multiple connections.

Chapter Summary

During this chapter, we have taken a comprehensive look at Frame Relay. The contents in this chapter present enough material to give the

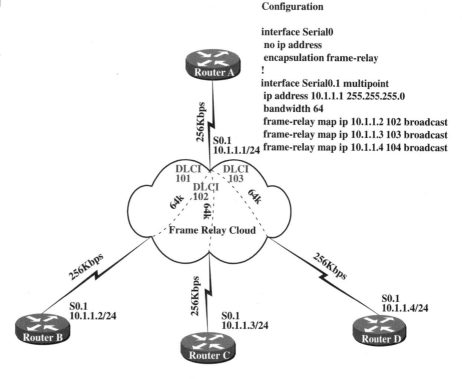

Figure 13-23
Multipoint
subinterface example

Configuration

interface Serial0
 no ip address
 encapsulation frame-relay
 !
interface Serial0.1 multipoint
 ip address 10.1.1.1 255.255.255.0
 bandwidth 64
 frame-relay map ip 10.1.1.2 102 broadcast
 frame-relay map ip 10.1.1.3 103 broadcast
 frame-relay map ip 10.1.1.4 104 broadcast

reader a solid understanding of Frame Relay and its components. The individual frame is broken down and each piece is thoroughly discussed, describing its function and purpose. The reader will be able to obtain the knowledge to effectively design and configure the pieces in a Frame Relay environment.

This chapter also presents the different design scenarios that can be applied in real-world environments, along with the advantages and disadvantages that encompass each design. Features such as subinterfaces and Frame Relay map commands are explained along with examples of their use.

Lastly, configuration examples of the different types of networks are given throughout this chapter. The configurations are mapped to design scenarios to give the reader a feel for how the configurations would look in real-life examples. Tips for troubleshooting and debugging Frame Relay information are also covered.

From the Real World

Frame Relay is one of the most popular WAN technologies used today. If you are in this industry or have future plans for pursuing a career in this industry, chances are you will experience it. If you have a desire to work in the service provider field, knowledge of Frame Relay is necessary. It's important to understand the underlying technologies of Frame Relay so that other WAN technologies such as ATM can be better understood.

As you gain more experience using Frame Relay, you will find that many different designs exist, and that different companies will use those designs in different ways. Depending on the Frame Relay service provider, the configurations of those designs may vary. The contents of this chapter will give you the knowledge to implement these designs and understand their configurations.

Michael Coker

Frequently Asked Questions (FAQ)

Question: What RFCs cover Frame Relay?

Answer: 1596 and 1604 cover the definitions of managed objects for Frame Relay services. 1586 covers guidelines for running OSPF over Frame Relay networks. 1294 and 1490 are concerned with multiprotocol interconnections over Frame Relay. 1315 deals with the Management Information Base for Frame Relay DTEs. 1483 covers multiprotocol encapsulation over ATM adaptive layer five.

Question: What is the highest speed that Frame Relay can operate at?

Answer: The highest speed used to be T1 (1.544 Mbps). Currently, Frame Relay providers offer Frame Relay services with speeds up to T3 (45 Mbps).

Question: What is the maximum frame size for Frame Relay?

Answer: 4096 bytes is generally the largest frame allowed, because the FCS can only detect errors in frames less than 4096 bytes.

Question: I heard Frame Relay is similar to ATM. Is this true?

Answer: Frame Relay and ATM have many similarities. They are both layer-two protocols that utilize packet-switching technologies. Frame Relay and ATM also use similar algorithms for flow control.

Question: How is Frame Relay better than X.25?

Answer: Frame Relay provides many enhanced services over X.25. For starters, X.25 doesn't have the capability to provide high-speed connections as Frame Relay can. Although many say X.25 is limited to 64-Kbps connections, real-life implementations have gotten up to 256 Kbps. This is still significantly lower than the possible T3 speeds (45 Mbps) that some Frame Relay carriers provide. X.25 also uses addresses called *logical channels* that reside at layer three of the OSI model. X.25, being a layer-three protocol, provides acknowledgments and functions at layer three. This equates to much more processing at the X.25 switch with higher transit delays. Frame Relay is a purely layer-two protocol with DLCIs. Functioning as a layer-two protocol, Frame Relay does not have the overhead of X.25 and can provide lower transit delays and faster processing at the Frame Relay switch.

Case Study: Building a Frame Relay Network

This lab will require three Cisco routers. One of these routers will be used as a Frame Relay switch and will need to have two serial interfaces. The lab will demonstrate how to connect two Cisco routers via a Frame Relay switch. Connectivity will be established and then verified. The following section will take you step-by-step through the process. Figure 13-24 illustrates an example of the design of the network that is to be built.

Configure Router A

1. Connect your laptop or workstation to the console port of the router using the Cisco rolled cable. Set the terminal emulation program to 9600, 8, 1, and none. Then connect to COM1. Power on the router and press enter on your machine. The router should come up at the router prompt.
2. Enter configuration mode and enter a hostname of RouterA for the router.
3. Enter the specific configuration mode for serial interface 0 and enter an IP address of 10.0.0.1 with a subnet mask of 255.255.255.0.
4. Encapsulate the interface for frame-relay.
5. Enter an LMI type of cisco.
6. Enable rip and add the network 10.0.0.0

Configure Router B

Follow the steps above to configure Router B. However, use a hostname of RouterB and an IP address of 10.0.0.2 255.255.255.0.

Figure 13-24
Frame Relay practical exercise

DLCI 101   DLCI 102

RouterA   Frameswitch   RouterB

Configure the Frame Relay Switch

1. Enter configuration mode and enter a hostname of Frameswitch for the router.
2. Enter specific configuration mode for serial interface 0.
3. Enter a clock rate of 38400 for the connection to Router A.
4. Enter the interface type to reflect dce for the serial interface.
5. Enter the LMI as cisco.
6. Enter the frame-relay route command and map DLCI 101 out serial interface 1, mapping to DLCI 102 at Router B.
7. Enter specific configuration mode for serial interface 1.
8. Enter the frame-relay switching command to enable the router to act as a Frame Relay switch.
9. Enter a clock rate of 38400 for the connection to Router B.
10. Enter the interface type to reflect dce for the serial interface.
11. Enter the LMI as cisco.
12. Enter the frame-relay route command and map DLCI 102 out serial interface 0, mapping to DLCI 101 at Router A.

The configurations should look similar to the following (see Figures 13-25, 13-26 and 13-27).

Figure 13-25
RouterA
Configuration

```
RouterA

Current configuration:
!
version 12.0
no service udp-small-servers
no service tcp-small-servers
!
hostname RouterA
!
enable password cisco
!
interface Serial0
  ip address 10.0.0.1 255.255.255.0
  encapsulation frame-relay
```

```
 frame-relay lmi-type cisco
!
router rip
 network 10.0.0.0
!
no ip classless
!
line con 0
line aux 0
line vty 0 4
 login
!
end
```

Figure 13-26
RouterB
configuration

```
Current configuration:
!
version 12.0
no service udp-small-servers
no service tcp-small-servers
!
hostname RouterB
!
enable password cisco
!
interface Serial0
 ip address 10.0.0.2 255.255.255.0
 encapsulation frame-relay
 frame-relay lmi-type cisco
!
router rip
 network 10.0.0.0
!
no ip classless
!
line con 0
line aux 0
line vty 0 4
 login
!
end
```

Figure 13-27
Frameswitch
configuration

```
Current configuration:
!
version 12.0
no service udp-small-servers
```

```
no service tcp-small-servers
!
hostname Frameswitch
!
enable password cisco
!
frame-relay switching
!
interface serial0
 no ip address
 encapsulation frame-relay
 clockrate 38400
 frame-relay lmi-type cisco
 frame-relay intf-type dce
 frame-relay route 101 interface Serial1 102
!
interface serial1
 no ip address
 encapsulation frame-relay
 clockrate 38400
 frame-relay lmi-type cisco
 frame-relay intf-type dce
 frame-relay route 102 interface Serial0 101
!
no ip classless
!
line con 0
line con aux 0
line vty 0 4
 login
!
end
```

The following configurations enable Router A to communicate with Router B via the Frame Relay switch. Use the ping command, along with the other commands explained in this chapter, to verify the connectivity and Frame Relay status:

```
RouterA#ping 10.0.0.2

Type escape sequence to abort.
Sending 5, 100-byte ICMP Echos to 10.0.0.2, timeout is 2 seconds:
!!!!!
Success rate is 100 percent (5/5), round-trip min/avg/max =
136/138/140 ms
```

Questions

1. Frame Relay was developed to replace this type of network:

   a. ATM

   b. X.25

   c. SMDS

   d. ISDN

2. Frame Relay is a layer-___ protocol.

   a. one

   b. two

   c. three

   d. four

3. Choose the two reasons that a frame may get discarded in Frame Relay.

   a. Misconfigured circuit

   b. Errors detected in frame

   c. Incorrect DLCI

   d. Congestion in network

4. Frame Relay uses a layer-two address called a

   a. Logical channel number

   b. Data Link Connection Identifier

   c. Frame address

   d. Circuit identifier

5. How many bytes does the Frame Relay header consist of?

   a. One

   b. Two

   c. Four

   d. Eight

6. How many possible DLCI's are available in a Frame Relay?

   a. 512

   b. 1000

   c. 1024

   d. 2056

7. DLCI addresses are globally significant.

   a. True

   b. False

8. What is the connection between the customer router and the Frame Relay switch called?

   a. Local loop

   b. Local circuit

   c. PVC

   d. Virtual circuit

9. _____ provides a connection status mechanism that reports information on the connection between the router and the Frame Relay switch.

   a. DLCI

   b. PVC monitoring

   c. Circuit management

   d. LMI

10. What is used to dynamically find the protocol addresses at the end of each DLCI-defined PVC?

   a. Circuit management

   b. Inverse ARP

   c. RARP

   d. ARP

11. When Frame Relay passes information to a remote router, how does it alert the router if it experiences congestion?

   a. FECN

   b. BECN

   c. DE

   d. LMI

12. When the CIR is exceeded during the transfer of traffic, which bit may get set in the Frame Relay header?

   a. FECN

   b. BECN

   c. DE

   d. LMI

13. Name the three types of Frame Relay signaling.

   a. Annex A

   b. Annex B

   c. Annex C

   d. Annex D

   e. LMI

14. Annex A uses which DLCI number?

    a. 0

    b. 1

    c. 1023

    d. 1024

15. Inverse ARP is disabled by default on Cisco routers when LMI is configured.

    a. True

    b. False

16. During configuration of a Cisco router, choose the two options for Frame Relay encapsulation.

    a. cisco

    b. lmi

    c. annex a

    d. ietf

17. During configuration of a Cisco router, choose the three options for LMI.

    a. cisco

    b. lmi

    c. annex a

    d. ietf

    e. q933i

    f. ansi

18. Type the command to create a Frame Relay map using the local DLCI of 100 and the remote address of 10.10.10.2 enabled for broadcasts.

19. Which commands will show the LMI type for interface Serial 0?

    a. Show frame relay lmi

    b. Show frame relay serial 0

    c. Show interface serial 0

    d. Show frame-relay lmi

    e. Show frame relay pvc

20. Which commands will show the status of a PVC?

    a. Show frame relay pvc

    b. Show interface serial 0

    c. Show frame-relay map

    d. Show frame-relay lmi

    e. Show frame-relay pvc

Answers

1. b. X.25

Frame Relay was developed to replace slower X.25 networks and provide a high-speed, cost-effective solution.

2. b. two

Frame Relay is purely a layer-two protocol and does not perform any layer-three functionality.

3. b. Errors detected in frame, **d.** Congestion in network

Frames can get discarded in a Frame Relay network when congestion occurs and frames are marked as DE. Frames can also be discarded when errors are detected in a frame.

4. b. Data Link Connection Identifier

The layer-two address used by Frame Relay is a 10-bit address called a *Data Link Connection Identifier* (DLCI).

5. b. Two

The Frame Relay header consists of two bytes where the 10-bit DLCI address resides along with the FECN, BECN and DE bits.

6. c. 1024

1024 total possible DLCIs exist. However, DLCIs 16 through 1007 are used for general deployment in Frame Relay networks.

7. b. False

DLCIs are considered locally significant because they specify the address of the connection between the customer router and the port on the local Frame Relay switch.

8. a. Local loop

The local loop is the circuit between the customer router and the service provider's Frame Relay switch. The customer can have the service provider test the local loop if problems occur with the Frame Relay circuit.

9. d. LMI

The `Local Management Interface` (LMI) provides information about the circuit between the router and the Frame Relay switch. Sta-

tus requests are sent by the DTE device and status responses or keep-
alives are sent back to the DTE device from the Frame Relay switch
(DCE device).

10. b. Inverse ARP

Inverse ARP is used to request the DLCI information for PVCs from
the Frame Relay switch.

11. a. FECN

The FECN bit is set to one in the frame if congestion occurs during its
transition to the destination device.

12. c. DE

The `Discard Eligible` (DE) bit is set to one in the frame if the
frame is being transmitted at a time when the CIR of the PVC is
being exceeded.

13. a. Annex A, **d.** Annex D, **e.** LMI

These are the three types of Frame Relay signaling.

14. a. 0

Annex A uses DLCI number 0 to communicate connection management information between the Frame Relay switch to the DTE device
(router). Annex D also uses DLCI 0 and LMI uses DLCI 1023 for this
same operation.

15. a. True

This statement is true. LMI defines the DLCIs defined on each PVC
and the Frame Relay reports this information to the DTE device
(router). Once this is accomplished, the router then sends Inverse
ARP requests out each DLCI to determine the IP address of the
router on the other end of the PVC.

16. a. `cisco` and **d.** `ietf`

The only two encapsulation options for a Frame Relay interface are
Cisco and IETF.

17. a. `cisco`, **e.** `q933i`, and **f.** `ansi`

These are the three options for LMI during the configuration of a
Cisco router. The *cisco* option represents standard LMI, whereas
q933I represents Annex A and *ansi* represents Annex D.

18. `frame-relay map ip 10.10.10.2 100 broadcast`

19. c. `Show interface serial 0,` **and d.** `Show frame-relay lmi`
These two options will display the LMI type for a serial interface.

20. c. `Show frame-relay map,` **e.** `Show frame-relay pvc`
These two options will display the PVC status.

APPENDIX A

OSI Model

The OSI Model is used to describe how information from one application on one computer can move to an application on another computer. Developed by the *International Organization for Standardization* (ISO) in 1984, it is the primary architectural model for internetworking communications. The OSI Model has seven layers:

- Physical layer
- Data link layer
- Network layer
- Transport layer
- Session layer
- Presentation layer
- Application layer

We will now take a look at their purposes within the OSI Model and give an example of a technology that correlates to that particular layer.

Layer 1: The Physical Layer

The definition of the physical layer is that it is Layer 1 of the OSI Reference Model. The physical layer defines the electrical, mechanical, procedural, and functional specifications for activating, maintaining, and deactivating the physical link between end systems. It is comprised of three components. These components, in some instances, are the same in *Local Area Network* (LAN) and *Wide Area Network* (WAN) environments. They are cables or wires, connectors, and encoding.

Cables and Wires

The majority of the cable in place today falls into three types: *Unshielded Twisted Pair* (UTP), coaxial, and fiber optic. The majority of modern internal cable plant wiring is UTP. However, coaxial cable is still used today for specific LAN applications as well as for some high-speed WAN applications. Finally, the high-speed cable of choice is fiber. Fiber is used as the backbone for all high-speed LAN and WAN connections today.

Unshielded Twisted Pair (UTP)   UTP has many uses. It is used for voice communication, key card readers, alarm systems, and data communications. The first distinction in the type of UTP that can be used is the rating of the cable. UTP cable is rated for *either* or *plenum* use. If an area is a plenum or air return space, plenum rated cable must be used. Otherwise, standard cable is acceptable for use.

NOTE: *Plenum-rated cable is approximately twice the cost of standard UTP cable.*

The next distinction, and probably most important, is the category designator. The category, often abbreviated as CAT, levels officially run from Category 1 to Category 5:

- *CAT 1*   Here cable performance is intended for basic communications and power-limited circuit cable. No performance criteria exist for cable at this level.

- *CAT 2*   Low performance UTP. Typical applications are voice and low-speed data. This is not specified in the *Electronic Industries Association / Telecommunications Industry Association* (EIA/TIA) 568A for data use.

- *CAT 3*   This is data cable that complies with the transmission requirements in the EIA/TIA 568A. It has a maximum transmission speed of 16Mbps. In current installations, this is the grade most often used for voice cabling.

- *CAT 4*   An infrequently used category. It has a maximum transmission speed of 20Mbps.

- *CAT 5*   The most commonly used UTP category. Its maximum transmission speed is 100Mbps.

Coaxial cable   The coaxial cable used in networks is a relative of the coax cable used in many households for cable TV reception. Just like UTP, there can be both PVC and plenum-rated varieties for each variation. Many variations of this cable exist, but only three are used for data communications. The impedance or resistance of the cable is the item that differentiates the specific cables. RG58, RG59, and RG62 have approximately the same diameter, but each cable has a different amount of impedance. Table A-1 summarizes the coax categories, as follows:

- *RG58*   Also called ThinNet. Rated for 10MHz transmissions over a distance of 185 meters.
- *RG8*   Also called ThickNet. Rated for 10MHz transmissions over a distance of 500 meters.
- *RG62*   Used for IBM controller cabling.
- *RG59*   Not used for data transmissions. Used primarily for video transmissions and household cable TV.

Fiber optic cable   Fiber optic cable is the cable of choice for high-speed, long-distance communications. Simply put, a light source such as a low-powered laser is used to generate the optical or light signals down this type of cable. These cables are constructed out of small, thin strands of glass that look like fibers. The distance limitation of fiber is often measured in kilometers. Fiber optic cable, like UTP and coax, is rated either for PVC or plenum use. Two different types of fiber optic cable exist:

- *Multimode Fiber (MMF)*   Multimode fiber enables light to travel over one of many possible paths. Light, for example, could bounce under various angles in the core of the multimode cable. Because of the larger diameter of the core, it is much easier to get the light within it, allowing for less expensive electronics and connectors. The maximum distance for MMF is two km.

Table A-1	**Type of Coaxial Cable**	**Impedance**	**Cable Diameter**	**Usage**
Coaxial Cable Variations	RG8	50 Ohm	10mm	10Base5, Thick Ethernet
	RG58	50 Ohm	5mm	10 Base2, Thin Ethernet
	RG59	75 Ohm	6mm	Video
	RG62	93 Ohm	6mm	IBM 3270, Arcnet

- *Single Mode Fiber (SMF)* This offers the light only one route to travel through. SMF has a much smaller core than MMF (eight micron for SMF versus 50 or 62.5 micron for MMF). The smaller core enables much longer distances than MMF. Telephone companies interconnect their network equipment with SMF. The typical distance is between five and 1,000 miles. Simply put, if you want more distance, use a stronger laser.

NOTE: *SMF equipment is much more expensive than the equipment for MMF.*

Physical Terminations and Connectors

Without connectors and terminations, cables would have to be "hard-wired" to the end device. This would make quick disconnects and reconnects impossible. Connectors usually vary depending on the media type.

UTP Four basic modular jack styles are used in UTP. Figure A-1 shows the eight-position and eight-position keyed modular jacks. These jacks are commonly and incorrectly referred to as RJ45 and keyed RJ45 respectively.

The six-position modular jack is commonly referred to as RJ11. Using these terms can sometimes lead to confusion since the RJ designations actually refer to specific wiring configurations called *Universal Service Ordering Codes* (USOC).

Figure A-1
UTP jacks

8-position

8-position keyed

6-position

6-position modified

The designation RJ means "registered jack." Each of these three basic jack styles can be wired for different RJ configurations. For example, the six-position jack can be wired as an RJ11C (one-pair), RJ14C (two-pair), or RJ25C (three-pair) configuration. An eight-position jack can be wired for configurations such as RJ61C (four-pair) and RJ48C. The keyed eight-position jack can be wired for RJ45S, RJ46S, and RJ47S.

The fourth modular jack style is a modified version of the six-position jack (modified modular jack or MMJ). It was designed by *Digital Equipment Corporation*® (DEC) along with the *modified modular plug* (MMP) to eliminate the possibility of connecting DEC data equipment to voice lines and vice versa.

Cable Termination Practices for UTP   Two primary wiring standards exist. One set of standards is set by the EIA/TIA; the other is set by the USOC. The various pinouts are detailed in Figure A-2.

Two wiring schemes have been adopted by the EIA/TIA 568-A standard. They are nearly identical, except that pairs two and three are reversed. T568A is the preferred scheme because it is compatible with one or two-pair USOC systems. Either configuration can be used for *Integrated Services Digital Network* (ISDN) and high-speed data applications.

USOC wiring is available for one-, two-, three-, or four-pair systems. Pair 1 occupies the center conductors; pair 2 occupies the next two contacts out, and so on. One advantage to this scheme is that a six-position plug configured with one or two pairs can be inserted into an eight-position jack and maintain pair continuity.

Ethernet uses either of the EIA/TIA standards in an eight-position jack. However, only two pairs are used. On the other hand, Token Ring wiring uses

Figure A-2
EIA/TIA and USOC
jack pinouts

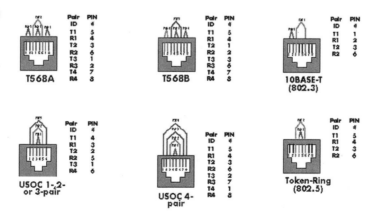

either an eight-position or six-position jack. The eight-position format is compatible with T568A, T568B, and USOC wiring schemes. The six-position format is compatible with one- or two-pair USOC wiring.

Coaxial connectors Coaxial cables use two different connectors. One type is used specifically for ThickNet. All other types of coax use the same type of connector.

All ThinNet and other coax cables, except RG8 (ThickNet), use the *Bayonet Neil-Concelman* (BNC) connector, shown in Figure A-3. The acronym BNC has also been purported to mean British Naval Connector and Bayonet Nut Connector, but those references are incorrect.

NOTE: *If the connector is not firmly connected to the cable, the connection will have intermittent connection issues. This is not acceptable for DS3 WAN circuits.*

ThickNet (RG8) uses an *Attachment Unit Interface* (AUI) connector to connect devices to the cable. The AUI connector itself is a standard male DB-15M with studs instead of mounting screws; the female is a DB-15F with a slide-clip that attempts to lock onto the studs. Table A-2 lists the pinouts for an AUI connector as well as an RJ45-pinned connector.

Fiber optic connectors Five popular types of fiber connectors exist. They can be used for both MMF and SMF. The most common types of connectors, ST, SC, and MIC, are pictured in Figure A-4. The less common connector types are ESCON and MT-RJ. The following is a brief description of each of the connectors:

Figure A-3
BNC connector for
coaxial cable

Table A-2

AUI and RJ45
Pinouts

AUI Pin No.	Ethernet V2.0	IEEE 802.3	RJ45 (EIA/TIA568A) Pin #
1	Shield	Control in Shield	
2	Collision Presence +	Control in A	
3	Transmit +	Data out A	1
4	Reserved	Data in Shield	
5	Receive +	Data in A	3
6	Power Return	Voltage Common	
7	Reserved	Control out A	
8	Reserved	Control out Shield	
9	Collision Presence −	Control in B	
10	Transmit −	Data out B	2
11	Reserved	Data out Shield	
12	Receive −	Data in B	6
13	Power	Voltage	
14	Reserved	Voltage Shield	
15	Reserved	Control out B	
Connector Shield ───────────────────			Protective Ground

Figure A-4
Common types of
fiber connectors

A) ST Connector   B) SC Connector

C) MIC Connector

- *ST* A commonly used connector in the earlier days of fiber installations.
- *SC* The most commonly used connector type today. Almost every connector on Cisco equipment uses an SC connector.
- *MIC/FSD* The *Medium Interface Connector/Fiber Shroud Duplex* (MIC/FSD) connector is used for fiber-based Fiber Distributed Data

Interfaces (FDDI) connections. It is polarized so that TX/RX are always correct.

- *ESCON* This is used to connect to IBM equipment as well as channel interface processors.

- *MT-RJ* A new fiber connector that is able to fit into a standard 110 patch panel. It almost doubles the port capacity of an SC module.

Physical Encoding Methods

An encoding method is the method that a device uses to put data on the media. Although the media and connectors for LANs and WANs are similar, the encoding variations for LANs and WANs are different.

LAN encoding Four basic LAN encoding schemes exist. The first encoding scheme is the foundation for all the other encoding schemes. Thus, it is important that you understand the basic encoding scheme that everything is based on, the *Non-Return To Zero-Level* (NRZ-L). Figure A-5 shows how the various encoding methods reduce the binary numbers to electrical or optical signals.

The common encoding methods are as follows:

- *Non-Return to Zero-Level (NRZ-L)* This is the basic type of encoding upon which all others are based. A *one* is positive voltage; a *zero* is no voltage. The problem with this is that timing information cannot be retrieved from a string of zeros. Thus, other encoding methods have been developed to overcome this problem.

- *Non-Return to Zero Inverted (NRZI)* Used in 100Base-Fx fiber networks, NRZI uses a change in signal to represent a one.

Figure A-5
Common encoding methods

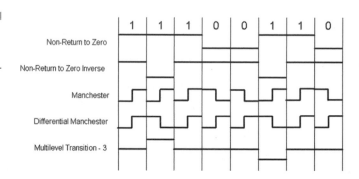

- *Manchester* Used in Ethernet, this encoding is based on the signal transition in the middle of the bit. An upward transition is a one. A downward transition represents a zero.

- *Differential Manchester* Used in Token Ring networks, this always has a transition in the middle. However, the encoding is based on the transition at the bit boundaries. A transition indicates a zero. No transition indicates a one.

- *MLT-3* Used in Fast Ethernet Networks. Instead of two voltage levels (voltage and no voltage), MLT-3 uses three layers: positive voltage, no voltage, and negative voltage. Changing the voltage represents a one. For instance, a series of ones would be represented as $0,1,0,-1,0,1,0.-1$.

WAN connectors Remember that the same types of media are used in WANs as LANs. However, the connectors used in WANs differ depending upon their use. Too many WAN connectors exist for us to cover every type, but the most common WAN connectors terminate T1 and E1 lines. Table A-3 displays the pinouts of T1 and E1 Lines.

NOTE: *The use of the terms tip and ring are typically not used today. Their usage is historical in perspective when testing was done with a tone tester. This test would allow a different tone to be present depending on which tip or ring was tested.*

Table A-3

The Pinouts of T1 and E1 Lines

Eight Position Jack Pinouts	T1/EI
1	Receive (tip)
2	Receive (ring)
3	Not used
4	Transmit (tip)
5	Transmit (ring)
6	Not used
7	Not used
8	Not used

WAN encoding   Before the topic of WAN encoding can be addressed, the concept of the digital hierarchy must be familiar to the reader. The digital hierarchy is a classification of circuit speeds. In North America, it is called the North American Digital Hierarchy. In Europe and the majority of the world, it is called the CCITT Digital Hierarchy. Both begin at the DS0 level with a single 64Kbps circuit. Then differences appear in the two systems.

In the North American Digital Hierarchy, this DS0 circuit is multiplied 24 times into a DS1 circuit with a speed of 1.544Mbps. This DS1 is then multiplied 28 times into a DS3 circuit with a speed of over 44Mbps.

The CCITT Digital Hierarchy combines 30 DS0s into an E1 circuit with a speed of 2.048Mbps. Next, 16 E1 circuits are combined to form an E3 circuit with a speed of over 34Mbps.

The WAN media type used depends on the circuit speed. T1 and E1 circuits generally use UTP. DS3 and E3 circuits use coax. However, all speeds above DS3/E3 require the use of fiber optic cables. The terms *North American Synchronous Optical Network* (SONET) and *International Synchronous Digital Network* (SDH) identify the circuits in this range. Table A-4 denotes the various circuit names and speeds.

The variations in WAN encoding first occur at the DS1 level. When a DS1 line is ordered, it is necessary to specify the framing and line coding. These settings must match the Channel Service Unit/Data Service Unit (CSU/DSU) and the other end of the circuit.

NOTE: *One of the most difficult issues to troubleshoot is the incorrect encoding of a circuit. More that once, I have seen a service provider finally determine that the cause of a line fault is improper encoding at one end of the circuit.*

Table A-4

Various Circuit
Names and Speeds

Optical Circuit	Speed
OC-1	51.8Mbps
OC-3	155.5Mbps
OC-12	622.1Mbps
OC-48	2488.3Mbps

The two frame types available for DS1s are *D4/Super Frame* (SF) and *Extended Super Frame* (ESF). The two frame types for E1s are CRC4 and no CRC4.

The available line codings for DS1s are *Alternate Mark Inversion* (AMI) and *Bipolar Eight-Zero Substitution* (B8ZS). The only available line codings for E1s are AMI and *High-Density Bipolar 3* (HDB3).

Conclusion

The physical layer may be seen as the most trivial or least important of the seven layers. After all, no fancy things like routing or switching happen at this layer. No addresses are used at the physical layer. However, many of the issues faced in the networking world are solved at the physical layer. A UTP cable might run too close to a fluorescent light or an OC-3 fiber patch cord might get accidentally crushed. When troubleshooting network problems, one of the most effective methods is to follow the OSI Model and troubleshoot by layers. Thus, you would start at the physical layer and move up once you have determined each layer is operating correctly.

Layer 2: The Data Link Layer

Layer 2 of the OSI Reference Model is the data link layer. Figure A-6 shows the placement of the network layer in the OSI Reference Model.

The data link layer is responsible for describing the specifications for topology and communication between local systems. Many examples of data link layer technology exist:

- Ethernet
- Fast Ethernet
- Token Ring
- Frame Relay
- HDLC
- Point-to-Point Protocol (PPP)
- Serial Line Interface Protocol (SLIP)

Figure A-6
The data link layer in
the OSI Reference
Model

7	Application Layer
6	Presentation Layer
5	Session Layer
4	Transport Layer
3	Network Layer
2	**Data Link Layer**
1	Physical Layer

Figure A-7
An example of data
link layer
conversations

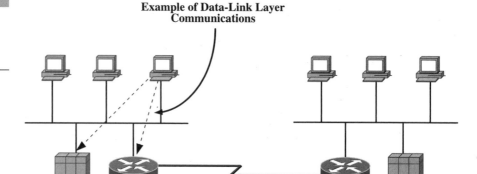

**Example of Data-Link Layer
Communications**

All of these services describe how conversations take place between two devices on the same media. Remember that the data link layer implementation used is independent of the physical layer. For example, Ethernet can use UTP or coaxial cable. It does not matter which physical layer media it uses; the rules that govern the technology are the same. This is the beauty of the OSI Model: any layer can be replaced without concerns about the lower or upper layers.

Communication at the data link layer is between two hosts on the same network. Those two hosts can be a desktop computer communicating with a local file server or a local host sending data to a router that is destined for a remote host (see Figure A-7).

Data Link Layer Example

The following section focuses on Ethernet, one of the most commonly used data link layer standards. If we look at the frame format of an Ethernet frame, we can get a better understanding of each component's purpose. In Figure A-8, we see a standard IEEE 802.3 Ethernet frame format. If we look at each component, we can easily see its purpose.

Preamble The preamble is an alternating pattern of ones and zeros. It tells the other stations on the media that a frame is coming. The IEEE 802.3 preamble ends with two consecutive ones, which serves to synchronize the frame reception of all stations on the LAN.

Data link layer addressing (Destination and source address) The capability to distinguish one host from another is critical when multiple hosts have access to the same media. Compare that to point-to-point connections in which the capability to distinguish the end point is irrelevant because there is only one other node on the network that can hear the data.

The address used by end hosts to identify each other is called the *Media Access Control* (MAC) address. It is often referred to as the physical address, burned-in address, or hardware address. The MAC address of each Ethernet *Network Interface Card* (NIC) is by definition unique. It is a 48-bit address built into the NIC that uniquely identifies the station. It is generally represented in one of three formats:

- 00-60-94-EB-41-9F
- 00:60:94:EB:41:9F
- 0060.94EB.419F

If we look closely at the MAC address, we will see that it can be broken down into two distinct components: the vendor's address and a unique host

Figure A-8
Ethernet frame format

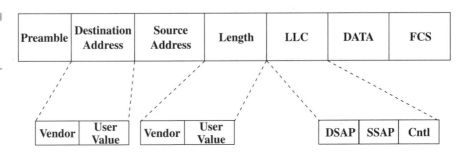

identifier. The first three octets (24 bits) identify the vendor. Using the example listed above, we can look up 00-60-94 at `http://standards.ieee.org/regauth/oui/oui.txt`.

We can see that this NIC was manufactured by IBM. This can be useful when attempting to locate a device on the network that is malfunctioning.

Length   The Length field indicates the number of bytes contained in the Data field. Although all of the other fields are of a predetermined length (the Destination and Source addresses are six bytes) the Data field can be up to 1,500 bytes. If the data in the frame is insufficient to fill the frame to a minimum 64-byte size, the frame is padded to ensure at least a 64-byte frame.

Logical Link Control (LLC)   The IEEE 802.2 *Logical Link Control* (LLC) header is used to specify which upper layer protocol is contained in the data. Without the capability to distinguish which upper layer protocol a packet belongs to, it is impossible to carry multiple network layer protocols over a data link layer implementation. For example, because Novell's 802.3 RAW frame format does not have a method to distinguish between network layer protocols, it could only carry a single network layer protocol. This is one of the reasons why Novell's 802.3 frame format is generally not employed.

Another example of a data link layer technology not using a type field is SLIP. Even though it enjoyed some success in the late '80s and early '90s as a dialup protocol, its incapability to distinguish between different network layer protocols has allowed PPP to become the standard dialup protocol.

The following fields all play a part in LLC identification:

- *DSAP*   The *Destination Service Access Point* (DSAP) is a one-byte field that acts like a pointer in the receiving station. It tells the receiving NIC which buffer to put this information in. This function is critical when users are running multiple network layer protocols.

- *SSAP*   The *Source Service Access Point* (SSAP) is identical to the DSAP, except that it indicates the source of the sending application.

- *Control*   This one-byte field is used to indicate the type of LLC frame of this data frame. Three different types of LLC frames exist:

  - *LLC1*   An unacknowledged connectionless service. It uses unsequenced information to set up communication between two network stations. This type of LLC is generally used with Novell's *Internetwork Packet Exchange* (IPX), TCP/IP, and Vines IP.

- *LLC2*   A connection-oriented service between two network stations. This type of service is generally used in SNA and NetBIOS sessions.
- *LLC3*   A connectionless but acknowledged-oriented service between two different stations. This type of service can be used by SDLC.

Data   The Data field in an IEEE 802.3 frame can be between 43 and 1,497 bytes. However, depending upon the type of frame being used, this size can vary. For example, an Ethernet II frame can hold between 46 and 1,497 bytes of data, while a frame using Novell's RAW 802.3 frame format can hold between 46 and 1,500 bytes of data.

Frame Check Sequence (FCS)   The last four bytes of a IEEE 802.3 frame are used to verify that the frame is not corrupt. By using a complex polynomial, the NIC can detect errors in the frame. If errors are detected, then the frame is discarded and it never reaches the memory buffers.

Now that we understand the frame format of an IEEE 802.3 frame, we need to discuss how those frames get on the wire.

Carrier Sense Media Access with Collision Detection (CSMA/CD)
Ethernet is one of the most common network topologies. The basic rule behind Ethernet communication is called *Carrier Sense Multiple Access with Collision Detection* (CSMA/CD). If we break down each phrase, we can interpret its meaning:

- *Carrier Sense*   All Ethernet stations are required to listen to the network to see if any other devices are sending data. This serves two purposes: one, it keeps the station from sending data when someone else is sending data and, two, it enables the station to be ready when another station wants to send it data.
- *Multiple Access*   This means more than two stations can be connected to the same network at the same time and that all stations can transmit data whenever the network is free. In order for data to be transmitted, the station must wait until the Ethernet channel is idle. Once the channel is idle, the station can transmit a frame, but it must listen to see if there is a collision.
- *Collision Detection*   If there is a collision, then both stations must immediately back off and use a backoff algorithm to randomly determine how long they should wait before trying to transmit again. It

is important that a random number be generated for this timer, because if some standard number were used, then both stations would wait the same length of time and then attempt to transmit again, thus causing another collision.

NOTE: *A collision is the simultaneous transmitting of a frame by two different stations. A station can detect a collision within the first 64 bytes of the transmission.*

Conclusion

Many different types of data link layer technologies exist, and Ethernet is one of those technologies. Although a data link layer technology can theoretically use any physical layer implementation, generally the actual implementation of a data link layer technology goes hand in hand with the physical layer implementation. For example, PPP is generally used over dialup networks or WAN networks, while Ethernet and Token Ring are used in LAN environments. This means that you probably won't see very many implementations of PPP using CAT 5 cable for its wiring infrastructure. Likewise, you probably won't see Token Ring being deployed from a corporate office to a telecommuter's home using the Telco's wiring infrastructure.

Layer 3: Network Layer

Layer 3 of the OSI Reference Model is the network layer. Figure A-9 shows the placement of the network layer in the OSI Reference Model.

This layer is responsible for providing routing for the network. Routing, in a generic sense, is simply finding a path to a destination. In the context of the network layer, routing means finding a path to a destination that is a member of a different Layer 2 network than the source. Physical networks can be connected together with bridges to form larger Layer 2 networks. Unfortunately, Layer 2 networks cannot scale to an infinite size. As these networks grow, more bandwidth is used to transmit broadcast packets that flood the entire Layer 2 network. These broadcast packets are used to find the destination host.

Figure A-9
The network layer
and the OSI
Reference Model

7	Application Layer
6	Presentation Layer
5	Session Layer
4	Transport Layer
3	**Network Layer**
2	Data Link Layer
1	Physical Layer

Routing enables Layer 2 networks to be broken into smaller segments, enabling the network to grow to support more hosts. Figure A-10 shows the concept of routing.

The data link control layer passes packets up to the network layer. These packets have headers to define the source and destination addresses and other network layer parameters of the data in the packet. The network layer only uses the data in the network layer packet header for information to perform its functions. This maintains the modularity of the network layer. Therefore, there is no dependency on the information from the data link control layer headers and the transport layer headers.

Network layer communication is not guaranteed. This means that there is no mechanism to determine if the destination node received the network layer packets. Guaranteed delivery is maintained at other layers in the OSI Reference Model. The most obvious reason for not implementing guaranteed delivery at the network layer is because this layer has no concept of end-to-end delivery. It would be more appropriate for upper layer protocols that implement more connection-oriented services to make sure that the data reaches its destination. The network layer routes data on a packet-by-packet basis.

Only one network layer process exists for each network node. Several data link control layer processes may be found below the network layer, depending on the number of physical interfaces in the node, and several transport layer processes may be found above the network layer, depending

Figure A-10
Routing between
Layer 2 networks

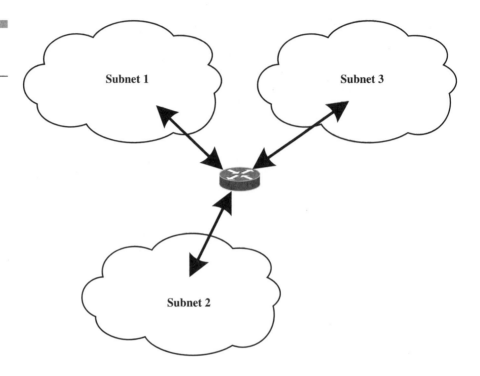

on the number of connection-oriented streams terminating at the node. Several network layer protocols may be running on a node, but each of these protocols corresponds to a separate logical internetwork and they do not intercommunicate.

A special node called a *gateway* connects logical networks formed by network layer addressing schemes. Gateways have a special sublayer in the upper portion of the network layer called the *Internet sublayer*. This sublayer handles the intercommunication between subnets. When a packet arrives from one subnet that is destined for another, the packet will be passed from the network layer to the Internet sublayer. The Internet sublayer in turn determines the destination subnet and forwards the packet back down to the lower portion of the network layer to the destination subnet. This is the basic idea behind routing. Figure A-11 illustrates the concept of a network node.

Each network layer process at each node is a peer process. These peer processes work together to implement distributed algorithms. These distributed algorithms are the routing algorithms corresponding to various routing protocols. These protocols provide a means to automatically discover and transmit routing information between gateways.

Figure A-11
Network node model

3	**Internet Sublayer**

	Network Layer
2	Data Link Layer
1	Physical Layer

The Internet Protocol (IP)

The most familiar protocol that operates at the network layer is the *Internet Protocol* (IP). IP is by far the most widely deployed network layer protocol due to the success of the Internet. This protocol is the foundation of the Internet in terms of addressing and packet routing. The Internet employs multiple protocols in the other OSI Reference Model layers, but it only uses IP in the network layer.

Another example of a network protocol is Novell's *Internet Packet Exchange* (IPX). Novell has since refined NetWare to use IP as the native network layer protocol instead of IPX.

IP Node Operation

If an IP host wants to communicate with another IP host, the transmitting IP source must determine if the destination IP address is in the same subnet or not. If the destination is in the same subnet, the host must send an *Address Resolution Protocol* (ARP) request packet to obtain the MAC address of the destination, assuming the destination MAC address isn't already in its ARP table. If the destination is not in the same subnet as the source, the source must send the packet to the MAC address of the gateway for that subnet. Most IP hosts have one IP address to send their packets to if they are destined for any subnet other than their own. This is called the *default gateway* or *default router address*. The user configures the default gateway address.

Once the default gateway (router) gets the packet and sees that the packet is destined for its own MAC address and at the same time destined for another IP host, the router knows that it must forward the packet to another interface to move the packet closer to its destination.

The mechanism for determining if the destination IP host is in the same subnet is as follows. The subnet mask is bitwise ANDed with both the source IP address and the destination IP address. The logic table for the AND operation is shown in Table A-5.

The result of these two functions is exclusively ORed (XORed). If this final result is not zero, then the destination IP address is in another subnet. The logic table for the XOR operation is shown in Table A-6.

Here is an example of determining if the destination address is in the same subnet as the host:

Source IP address:

$(100.1.43.1)_{\text{dotted-decimal}}$ $(01100100.00000001.00101011.00000001)_{\text{binary}}$

Subnet mask:

$(255.255.255.0)_{\text{dotted-decimal}}$ $(11111111.11111111.11111111.00000000)_{\text{binary}}$

Destination IP address:

$(100.1.44.2)_{\text{dotted-decimal}}$ $(01100100.00000001.00101100.00000010)_{\text{binary}}$

Table A-5

Logic table for
AND operations

	1	0
1	1	0
0	0	0

Table A-6

Logic table for OR
operations

	1	0
1	0	1
0	1	0

Source IP address ANDed with subnet mask:

01100100.00000001.00101011.00000001

<u>11111111.11111111.11111111.00000000</u>

01100100.00000001.00101011.00000000

Destination IP address ANDed with subnet mask:

01100100.00000001.00101100.00000010

<u>11111111.11111111.11111111.00000000</u>

01100100.00000001.00101100.00000000

The two results XORed:

01100100.00000001.00101011.00000000

<u>01100100.00000001.00101100.00000000</u>

00000000.00000000.00000111.00000000

The result of the XOR function is not zero. Therefore, the destination IP address is in another subnet than the source and the packet must be sent to the default gateway to be routed to the destination subnet.

When the router gets a packet to be forwarded to another subnet, the router must manipulate the MAC and IP header fields to ensure that the packet is forwarded toward its destination.

Three things must happen when the router forwards the packet at the network layer:

- The interface to forward the packet to must be determined.
- The destination MAC address must be updated with the MAC address of the next-hop router or destination host.
- The *Time to Live* (TTL) field must be decremented in the IP header.

The interface that the packet is forwarded out of is determined by looking through the route table that the router maintains. This route table associates a route to a destination with a physical interface.

The destination MAC address must be updated with the MAC address of the destination IP host if the host is directly connected to the router. If the destination host is not directly connected to one of the ports of the router, the router must forward the packet to the next router to move the packet toward the destination IP host. In either case, if the router doesn't know the

MAC address of the next hop toward the destination, it must ARP for the MAC address.

The TTL field is then decremented. This field provides a mechanism for the packet to be removed from the network if it gets caught in a loop. Without such a mechanism, the packet may be forwarded for as long as the routing loop is active. The packet is removed by a router if its TTL field is zero.

Internetwork Packet Exchange (IPX) Operation

Another example of a Layer 3 protocol is the IPX protocol. The IPX protocol was developed by Novell NetWare. Novell NetWare is a *Network Operating System* (NOS) that provides network file and print services. IPX is quickly being replaced by IP since NetWare now provides native IP support, but there remains a large installed base of IPX networks in campus networks.

Unlike IP, IPX has no concept of multiple subnets per the Layer 2 network. Instead, IPX has only one address per physical network called a *network number*. The full network layer address for a network device is made of two parts: the 32-bit network number and the node's 48-bit MAC address.

Some argue that the combination of Layer 2 and Layer 3 addresses to form a Layer 3 address undermines the modularity of the OSI Reference Model. This is due to the fact that IPX (Layer 3) network numbers depend on the Layer 2 addressing scheme. This argument is purely academic since the MAC address scheme is so prevalent. The real limitation to IPX is its inability to logically subnet hosts on the same physical network.

Layer 4: Transport Layer

Layer 4 of the OSI Reference Model is the transport layer. Figure A-12 shows the placement of the network layer in the OSI Reference Model.

The transport layer is responsible for data transfer issues such as reliability of the connection, establishing error detections, recovery, and flow control. In addition, this layer is responsible for delivering packets from the network layer to the upper layers of the OSI Model.

If we think of the network layer as responsible for delivering packets from one host to another, the transport layer is responsible for identifying the conversations between two hosts. For example, Figure A-13 shows an

Figure A-12
The transport layer
and the OSI
Reference Model

7	Application Layer
6	Presentation Layer
5	Session Layer
4	**Transport Layer**
3	Network Layer
2	Data Link Layer
1	Physical Layer

Figure A-13
The transport layer
differentiating
between
conversations

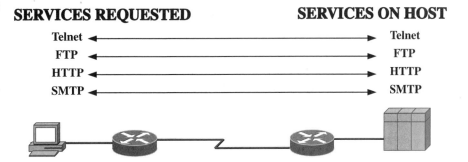

SERVICES REQUESTED   SERVICES ON HOST

Telnet ⟷ Telnet
FTP ⟷ FTP
HTTP ⟷ HTTP
SMTP ⟷ SMTP

example of how the transport layer keeps the conversations between the different applications separate.

Two different variants of transport layer protocols are used. The first provides a reliable, connection-oriented service, while the second method is a best-effort delivery. The difference between these two protocols dictates the paradigm in which they operate. When using TCP/IP, the two different protocols are TCP and UDP. Inside an IP packet is a protocol number that enables the host to identify whether the packet contains a TCP message or a UDP message. The TCP protocol value is 6 and for UDP it is 17. Many other (~130) protocols types exist, but these two are commonly used to transport user messages from one host to another.

Transport Layer Protocol Examples

In this section, we'll examine some examples of transport layer protocols.

Transmission Control Protocol (TCP)   The TCP described in RFC 793 provides applications with a reliable connection-oriented service. Three basic instruments are used to make TCP a connection-oriented service:

■ Sequence numbers

■ Acknowledgments

■ Windowing

In order for data to be handed down to the network layer, the data must be broken down into messages. These messages are then given a sequence number by TCP before being handed off to the network layer. The purpose of the sequence number is so that in case the packets arrive out of order the remote host can reassemble the data using the sequence numbers. This only guarantees that the data is reassembled correctly.

In addition to sequence numbers, acknowledgements are used by the remote host to tell the local host that the data was received, guaranteeing the delivery of data. If, for whatever reason, a packet gets dropped along the way, the remote host can see that it is missing a message and request it again, as shown in Figure A-14.

Although windowing enables TCP to regulate the flow of packets between two hosts, this minimizes the chances of packets being dropped because the buffers are full in the remote host.

Figure A-14
Using acknowledgements for guaranteed delivery

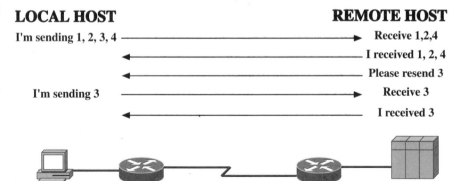

LOCAL HOST

REMOTE HOST

I'm sending 1, 2, 3, 4 ⟶ Receive 1,2,4

⟵ I received 1, 2, 4

⟵ Please resend 3

I'm sending 3 ⟶ Receive 3

⟵ I received 3

In order for a TCP connection to be established, a three-step handshake is exchanged between the local host and the remote host. This three-way handshake starts with the local host initiating a conversation by sending a *Synchronize Sequence Numbers* (SYN) packet to the remote host, as shown in Figure A-15.

The remote host acknowledges the SYN and sends an SYN acknowledgement back to the local host. The local host responds by sending an acknowledgement and then starts sending data. The purpose of this handshake is to synchronize the sequence numbers that identify the proper order used to reconstruct the messages throughout the conversation.

User Datagram Protocol (UDP)   The UDP, as described in RFC 768, provides applications with a connectionless best-effort delivery service. Because there is no time wasted setting up a connection, applications that utilize UDP are very fast. Applications that send short bursts of data can take advantage of UDP's speed, but if the messages get delivered out of order or a message gets dropped, then the entire message fails.

Well-Known Ports   We've seen how we can guarantee the delivery of a packet through the use of TCP and how we can improve throughput by using a connectionless delivery service, but how are discrete conversations between two hosts handled? Both TCP and UDP utilize a mechanism called a port (also known as a socket). By utilizing a source port and a destination port, two hosts can distinguish between multiple conversations.

In order to provide services to unknown callers, a host will use a well-known port number. Well-known port numbers are assigned by the *Internet Assigned Numbers Authority* (IANA). By adhering to the well-known port numbers published by the IANA, we can make sure that various services do not utilize the same port. Both TCP and UDP use port numbers and when

Figure A-15
Three-way
handshake to initiate
a connection

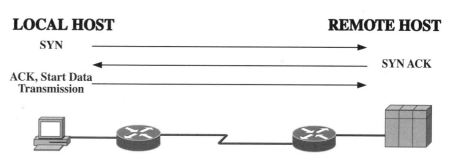

LOCAL HOST   **REMOTE HOST**

SYN

SYN ACK

ACK, Start Data
Transmission

Table A-7

Well-Known Port
Numbers

Port Number	Service
20	FTP (Data)
21	FTP (Control)
23	Telnet
25	SMTP
42	Host Name Server
53	Domain Name Service
80	HTTP

a service can utilize both TCP and UDP, the port number is identical. Table A-7 shows us a sampling of the well-known port numbers.

Until recently, the assigned port range was from 0 to 255. However, the range has been expanded from 0 to 1,023.

Conclusion

The transport layer protocol helps end devices distinguish between simultaneous conversations between the same two hosts. The protocol that is used, connection-oriented or connectionless, is dependent upon the needs of the upper layer application. Some applications want the speed of UDP and will implement their own form of reliability-checking in an effort to speed up the transmission of the data. Although this obviously adds a lot of overhead to the programmer's job, it can be worth it, depending upon the applications requirements.

Layer 5: Session Layer

Layer 5 of the OSI Reference Model is the session layer. Figure A-16 shows the placement of the session layer in the OSI Reference Model.

The session layer is responsible for providing such functions as directory service and access rights. The session layer has a defined role in the OSI Reference Model, but its functions are not as critical as the lower layers to all networks. For example, a network without the physical layer, the data

Figure A-16
The session layer and
the OSI Reference
Model

7	Application Layer
6	Presentation Layer
5	**Session Layer**
4	Transport Layer
3	Network Layer
2	Data Link Layer
1	Physical Layer

link layer, network layer, or the transport layer would be lacking basic functionality that would make the network useful. Until recently, the session layer has been ignored or at least not seen as absolutely necessary in data networks. Session layer functionality has been seen as a host responsibility, not a network function. As networks become larger and more secure, functions such as directory services and access rights become more necessary.

Access rights functionality deals with a user's access to various network resources such as computer access and authentication, file access, and printer access. Devices providing the service such as file and print servers have typically implemented access rights. There has been a shift in responsibility for these functions in recent years. Authentication can now be distributed using authentication services such as Kerberos. File and print service access control is moving to network directory services such as Novell's *Network Directory Service* (NDS) or Microsoft's *Active Directory Services* (ADS). These services control what resources a host may access.

Directory services are services that find resources on the network. Typically, a user would have to have prior knowledge of a service to gain access to the service. Some services have the capability of broadcasting their presence, but that methodology does not scale well in a large network with many hosts and many services. True directory services act as a redirection point for hosts to be given addressing information to find a particular resource. Novell's NDS or Microsoft's ADS can act as directory services as well as define a user's access rights, as mentioned above.

The session layer has no hard and fast rules for interfacing with the presentation layer since the presentation layer is optional in many cases. The session layer services are typically accessed via TCP or UDP port numbers, therefore defining the interface to the transport layer.

Layer 6: Presentation Layer

Layer 6 of the OSI Reference Model is the presentation layer. Figure A-17 shows the placement of the network layer in the OSI Reference Model.

The presentation layer is responsible for providing data encryption, data compression, and code conversion. The functions in this layer have not been considered a function of the network and have been handled by various applications. In recent years, data encryption, compression, and code conversion have moved into the mainstream of the network protocol functionality.

Data encryption is moving to the forefront of networking since networks are carrying more sensitive data. Encryption can be handled in a number of ways. The easiest and most secure method for encrypting data is to encrypt all the data on a particular link. This requires a device on both ends of a path to encrypt and decrypt the payload of each packet that passes over the link. This requires that sensitive data always pass over a path installed with an encryption device. This does not scale well for a large network. The more scalable method for encryption is for the applications at both ends of

Figure A-17
The presentation layer and the OSI Reference Model

7	Application Layer
6	**Presentation Layer**
5	Session Layer
4	Transport Layer
3	Network Layer
2	Data Link Layer
1	Physical Layer

a session to set up a means for encrypting the data. This method of encryption requires that a device have more processing power to handle the application and the data encryption in real time.

Data compression conserves bandwidth over a link. Like data encryption, data compression can be done on both ends of a path through a network. This requires an external device to compress the network data. This method does not scale well in large networks where there can be many paths through a network. A more scalable method for data compression is to allow the application at both ends of a session to compress the data. The tradeoff in this method is more processing power is required on the host to support the application and real-time compression/decompression.

Code conversion involves converting a set of data or a data stream from one format to another. Data formats can be for character sets, video formats, graphics formats, and presentation formats. Examples of character set formats are ASCII and EBCDIC, video formats are MPEG and MJPEG, graphics formats are GIF, TIFF, JPEG, and bitmap, and presentation formats are HTML, XML, and SHTML.

No hard and fast rules define the interface between the presentation layer and the session layer since the session layer may be optional for a particular network. The presentation layer communicates to the application layer by addressing the application with an appropriate transport layer (session) address such as a TCP port number.

Layer 7: Application Layer

The final layer, Layer 7, of the OSI Model is the application layer. This section will define the application layer and examine in moderate detail what takes place at Layer 7.

The application layer consists of an application that requires the use of a network to perform its task. Communication between applications takes place at Layer 7. As with the previous layers, Layer 7 exchanges messages with Layer 7 only. Restated, an application communicates with only a peer application. Figure A-18 depicts this layer-to-layer communication.

An example application could be something as simple as a *chat* program. The application connects to its peer application and sends characters that are entered on the keyboard. It also displays characters received from the peer application. The applications communicating at Layer 7 use the lower layers and the services they provide to send and receive application-specific information.

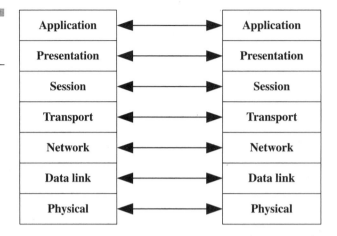

Figure A-18
Layer 7 application
communication

Furthermore, it is common for applications to further define the contents of the data that is being exchanged. Even with the simple chat program, a protocol is defined: "Each message received from a peer application contains a single character." This creates a challenge for troubleshooting network-related problems.

Although only a handful of protocols are used at the lower layers, the protocols are usually well specified. As you can see, anyone can define a new protocol for his or her specific application. This makes it difficult for vendors that develop network analyzers to provide the capability of troubleshooting application, or Layer 7, problems.

As you can see, this layer can be any application that requires network communication. The application communicates with its peer application at Layer 7, and an application may arbitrarily define a protocol that specifies application-to-application communication.

Conclusion

It is important to remember that the OSI Model is only for reference. Not all protocols and technologies have a direct correlation to one of the seven layers. Frequently, a protocol may straddle different layers, such as ARP, which is used when a computer knows the IP address it needs to communicate with (network layer) but it doesn't know its MAC address (data link layer). ARP enables a computer to map an IP address to a MAC address. So is ARP a data link layer-protocol or a network-layer protocol? Technically, it straddles both layers, so it doesn't really fit the OSI Model, but without it IP communication on a LAN couldn't happen.

INDEX

10Base-F, 49
10Base-FX cabling, 26
10Base-T, 47
10Base-T cabling, 26
10Base-TX cabling, 26
10Base2, 46
10Base2 cabling, 26
10Base5, 46
10Base5 cabling, 26
100Base-FX, 50
100Base-T4, 53
100Base-TX, 50
1000Base-SX/LX cabling, 27
1900 series switches, POST, 87–88
    front panel LEDs, 88
2513 series routers, 68
2900XL switches, POST, 88
802.1Q VLAN tagging, 269

A

abbreviating commands, 112
Access layer, networks, 6–7
access lists, 396
    adding to interfaces, 403
    configuring, 398
    cut-and-paste editing, 417
    extended IP, 403–404, 407–408
        destination addresses, 406
        source addresses, 406
    extended Telnet, 415
    implicit deny all, 400
    inbound, 397
    IP, 399
    IPX, 410–411, 476–478, 480
        destination addresses, 414
        extended, 412
        source addresses, 413
        source sockets, 414
        standard, 410
    monitoring, 418
    named, 416
    outbound, 397
    permission order, 418
    standard IP, 399–401
        wildcard masks, 402–403
    verifying, 418
access-class command, 415
access-list command, 398
access-list deny command, 401, 484
access-list list-number permission protocol-option
        command, 552
access-list permit command, 401, 484
accounts, user, 515–516
ACK packets (SYN Acknowledgement), TCP,
        292–294
Acknowledge Number field, SPX headers, 435
acknowledge numbers, TCP, 289
active state, Frame Relay LMI, 604
adaptive switching, 23
addresses
    broadcast, 194
    Frame Relay, DLCI mappings, 602
    helper, 167
    IP, 299, 303
        classless, 384
        subnet masks, 17
        VLAN1, 262
    IPX, 430
        interfaces, 459
    logical, 16
    MAC, 287, 299
    multicast, 195
    NetWare, 451
    network layer, 17
adjacencies, EIGRP, 448
adjacency databases, NLSP, 448
administrative distances, routers, 352
advertisements
    CDP, VLAN1, 262
    VTP, 260
    VTP, VALN1, 262
age values, MAC addresses, 188
algorithms
    Spanning Tree, 203
    SPF, 363

Allocation Number field, SPX headers, 435

Application layer, OSI model, 12

ARP (Address Resolution Protocol), 285, 299
  broadcasts, 299

ARPANET (Advanced Research Projects Agency
      Network), 284

ASs (Autonomous Systems), interior gateway
      routing, 359

ATM (Asynchronous Transfer Mode), 511

AUI (Attachment Unit Interface) cables, 47

AUI connectors, 54

authentication
  CHAP, encryption keys, 515
  ISDN DDR, 557
  WANs
    CHAP, 514
    PPP, 513

bridging, transparent, 183

broadband networks, 45

broadcast addresses, 194
  subnet masks, 316

broadcast domains, 195, 248
  LANs, 250
  LANs, performance issues, 249
  multiple, 251
  VLANs, 251

broadcast frames, 193

broadcast storms, 196

broadcasts
  ARP, 299
  RARP, 300

bytes, 288

B

B channel, ISDN, 541, 545

bandwidth command, 606

baseband networks, 45

basic management setup, routers, 106–107

Bc (committed burst), Frame Relay, 600

Be (excess burst), Frame Relay, 600

BECN (Backward Explicit Congestion
      Notification), Frame Relay, 599

BGP (Border Gateway Protocol), 359

binary number conversion, IP addresses, 310

bits, 288

blades, 123

blocking state, switches, 208

boot command, 164

boot loops, 93

boot process, IOS, 86

boot system flash command, 168

BPDUs (Bridge Protocol Data Units), 203
  configuration, 203
  topology change, 203, 209–210

branch offices, networks, 3–5

BRI ISDN (*See* ISDN BRI)

bridges
  designated ports, 208
  differences from switches, 184
  root bridges, 205
  root ports, 206

C

cabling
  console ports, 71
  crossover cables, 59
  crosstalk, 58
  Ethernet, 26, 57
  fiber connections, 60
  networks, Ethernet, 46–49
  performance categories, 58
  RJ-45 connectors, 54
  roll over cables, 71

cache table, CDP, 141

CAM (Content Address Memory) table,
      switches, 186

capability codes, CDP, 142

Catalyst 1900 series switches
  commands, 96–97, 101–102, 105
  configuration file, 231–232
  configure terminal command, 103
  configuring, 210, 215–216
    CDP, 213
    console passwords, 214
    duplex, 214, 220
    duplex mismatches, 221
    enable passwords, 218
    hostnames, 216
    IOS CLI, 212
    IP addresses, 213
    menu-driven CLI, 211
    permanent MAC addresses, 228

port security, 230
ports, 214–215
remote management, 217
restricted MAC addresses, 229
spanning trees, 214
switching modes, 213
user interfaces, 210
VSM, 212
enable command, 96
hostname command, 104
ip address command, 105
late collisions, 221
maintenance, 222
MAT (MAC Address Table), 227
NVRAM, 233
show ip command, 102
show running configuration command, 98
show version command, 97
catalyst switches, 30
POST, 87–88
errors, 89
front panel LEDs, 88
CBAC (Context-Based Access Control), 293
CDP advertisements, VLAN1, 262
CDP (Cisco Discovery Protocol), 140, 213
cache table, 141
capability codes, 142
Catalyst 1900 series switches, 213
interfaces, viewing, 143
remote connections, 142
remote devices, network addresses, 143
viewing, traffic, 143
CHAP (Challenge Handshake Authentication
Protocol), 513
authentication, 514
encryption keys, 515
Checksum field, IPX headers, 431
CIR (Committed Information Rate), 587
Frame Relay, 593
Frame Relay VCs, 587
circuit-switched connections, WANs, 505
circular routes, 160
Cisco
Catalyst 1900 series switches, 210
catalyst switches, 30
fixed port routers, 68
IOS (Internetwork Operating System), 84, 85
modular routers, 69
routers, 31

configuring, 90–93
serial ports, 61
Class A address space, subnets, 317
Class B address space, subnets, 320–321
Class C address space, subnets, 322
classes, IP addresses, 304–307
classless addresses, IP, 384
classless routing, IP addresses, 323–324
clear frame-relay inarp command, 611
CLI (command line interface), 210
Catalyst 1900 series switches, 211
routers, 70
access options, 71
client mode, VLANs, 259
clouds, Frame Relay, 586
code bits, TCP, 289
collision domains, 247
segmentation, 183
collision rates, LANs, 248
Command Completion Help, routers, 112
command history, 113
Command-List Help, routers, 111
commands
ipx sap-interval, 482
abbreviations, 112
access-class, 415
access-list, 398
access-list deny, 401, 484
access-list list-number permission protocol-
option, 552
access-list permit, 401, 484
bandwidth, 606
boot, 164
boot system flash, 168
Catalyst 1900 series switches, 96–97,
101–102, 105
clear frame-relay inarp, 611
compress compression type, 519
config register, 163
configure terminal, 401
copy flash tftp, 168
copy nvram tftp, 232
copy running-config startup-config, 118, 166
copy running-config tftp, 167
copy startup-config running-config, 119
copy tftp, 232
copy tftp flash, 167
debug dialer, 562
debug frame-relay lmi, 612

debug ip igrp events, 377–382
debug ip rip, 369–371
debug ipx sap, 462
    output fields, 472
debug isdn q921, 562
debug ppp authentication, 521
delete nvram, 233
description, 123
dialer idle-timeout, 558
dialer load-threshold, 560
dialer-group, 553
dialer-list, 551
dialer-map, 554
disable, 95
enable, 94
enable password, 121, 219
enable secret, 121
encapsulation frame-relay, 326
encapsulation frame-relay cisco, 605
encapsulation hdlc, 512
encapsulation isl, 330
encapsulation x.25, 326
exec timeout, 122
exit, 96
extended ping, IPX, 473
frame relay map ip, 606
frame-relay interface-dlci , 620
frame-relay inverse-arp, 606
frame-relay lmi-type, 606
hostname, 119
hostname router-name, 515
IGRP configuriation, 373
interface Ethernet, 459
interface serial, 325, 459, 605
ip access-group, 403
ip access-list standard TestACL, 416
ip address, 123, 327
ip default-gateway, 332
ip default-network, 356
ip host, 146, 328
ip name-server, 328
ip netmask-format, 315
ip rarp-server, 301
ip route, 354–355, 555
ipx access-group, 411, 414, 476
ipx delay tick, 444
ipx hello-interval eigrp autonomous-system-
    number seconds, 447

ipx output-sap-delay, 483
ipx output sap-filter, 486
ipx router eigrp, 445
ipx router eigrp autonomous-system-number, 446
ipx router rip, 446
ipx routing, 444, 459
ipx sap-incremental eigrp autonomous-system-
    number, 447
ipx update interval rip, 453
ipx update sap-after-rip, 456
isdn B-channel-number spid-number, 549
isdn switch type, 548
line vty, 120, 415
logging synchronous, 122
login, 119
network a.b.c.d., 365
network troubleshooting, 144
no ip domain-lookup, 328
no network, 446
no shutdown, 123
password, 120
payload-compress packet-by-packet, 607
permit, 416
ping, 153
ping apple, 153
port secure, 231
ppp authentication, 557
ppp authentication chap, 515
ppp authentication pap, 514
ppp multilink, 520, 560
RIP configuration, 365
router igrp, 373
router rip, 365–366
service password encryption, 121, 517
show vtp, 262
show access-list, 421
show cdp, 141
show cdp entry, 143
show cdp interface, 143
show cdp neighbor, 141
show cdp neighbor detail, 142
show cdp traffic, 143
show frame-relay lmi, 609
show frame-relay map, 611
show frame-relay pvc, 610
show history, 113
show hosts, 329
show interface, 521, 561, 608

show interface-serial, 326
show interfaces, 124–125, 223
show ip access-list, 420
show ip interface, 419
show ip protocol, 367, 375
show ip route, 353, 368, 377
show ip route rip, 369
show ipx interface, 462
    output fields, 469–471
show ipx route, 473
    output fields, 475
show ipx servers, 474, 477
show ipx traffic, 462
    output fields, 464–466
show isdn status, 562
show mac-address-table, 227
show running-config, 118, 165, 222–224, 367,
    374, 419
show sessions, 148
show spantree, 271
show spantree-template, 273
show startup config, 116, 165
show trunk, 270
show version, 115, 162, 227
show vlan, 263
show vlan-membership, 264
shutdown, 123
spantree, 271
spantree-template, 272
term ip netmask-format, 315
traceroute, 159
tracert, 161
trunk, 268
username user-account-name encryption-type
    password, 515
vlan name, 263
vlan-membership static, 264
vtp pruning enable, 261
vtp-domain, 258
Completion Code field, NCP headers, 441
compression
    PPP, 518–519
    Predictor, 519
    Stacker, 519
config register command, 163
configuration BPDUs, 203
configuration files
    1900 series switches, 231–232

encrypting user names, 517
routers, 162
configuration mode, 95
configure terminal command, 401
    Catalyst 1900 switches, 103
configuring
    access lists, 398
        extended IP, 403–408
        standard IP, 399–403
    Catalyst 1900 series switches, 210, 215–216
        CDP, 213
        configuration file, 231–232
        console passwords, 214
        duplex, 214, 220
        duplex mismatches, 221
        enable passwords, 218
        hostnames, 216
        IOSCLI, 212
        IP addresses, 213
        MAT, 227
        menu-driven CLI, 211
        NVRAM, 233
        permanent MAC addresses, 228
        port security, 230
        ports, 214–215
        remote management, 217
        restricted MAC addresses, 229
        spanning trees, 214
        switching modes, 213
        user interfaces, 210
        VSM, 212
    catalyst switches, 87–88
        front panel LEDs, 88
    DNS, servers, 328
    encapsulation, PPP Multilink, 520
    Frame Relay, 605
        encapsulation, 605
        interfaces, 605
        LMI, 605–606
        static mappings, 606–607
    HDLC encapsulation, 512
    IGRP, 374
    IPX access lists, 410–411
    IPX extended access lists, 412
    ISDN BRI, 548
        SPIDs, 549
    ISDN, DDR, 549–553
    PPP encapsulation, 512, 516, 519

RIP, 366
routers, 90–93, 119, 326
    basic management setup, 106–107
    initial setup, 105–106
    interface setup, 108
    IPX routing, 459
    protocols setup, 108
    troubleshooting, 124
subinterfaces, 330
switches
    default gateways, 332
    IP addresses, 332
    VLANs, 256
        client mode, 259
        ISL, 330
        server mode, 258
        spanning trees, 271
        transparent mode, 259
        trunks, 265–269
        VTP domains, 258
    VTs, 120
congestion control, 16
Connection Control field, SPX headers, 434
Connection Number High field, NCP headers, 440
Connection Number Low field, NCP
        headers, 440
Connection Status Flags field, NCP headers, 441
connection-oriented protocols, 286
connectionless protocols, 286
connections
    circuit-switched, 505
    Frame Relay, verifying, 608
    IPX, troubleshooting, 468
    ISDN, verifying, 561
    networks, routers, 18
    packet switched, 505
    remote hosts
        checking via Ping, 151
        viewing, 144
    serial, WANs, 507
    WANs, 521, 524
connectors
    AUI, 54
    MIC, 53
    MTRJ, 52, 55
    RJ-45, 54
    SC, 55
    ST, 53–55

console passwords, Catalyst 1900 series
        switches, 214
console ports, routers, 71
consoling into IOS, 85
convergence, 210
    IPX, 442
copy flash tftp command, 168, 232
copy running-config startup-config command,
        118, 166
copy running-config tftp command, 167
copy startup-config running-config command, 119
copy tftp command, 232
copy tftp flash command, 167
copying, IOS to TFTP server, 173
Core layer, networks, 6, 9
cost efficiency of VLANs, 254
cost of ownership, Frame Relay, 585
CPE (customer premise equipment), 506
    Frame Relay, 585
CRC (Cyclic Redundancy Check), 190
    TCP, 289
crossover cables, 57–59
crosstalk, 58
CSU/DSUs (Channel Service Unit/Data Service
        Unit), 326, 504
cut and paste access list editing, 417
cut-through switching, 22, 190

D

D channel ISDN, 541, 545
DARPA (Defense Advanced Research Projects
        Agency), 284
Data field
    Frame Relay, 591
    IPX headers, 433
Data link layer (*See also* network interface
        layer), 287
    OSI model, 19
datagrams
    extended Ping, 156
    IP, 296–298
Datastream Type field, SPX headers, 434
DCE (Data Circuit-Terminating Equipment), 508
DCE (Data Communication Equipment), 67
    Frame Relay, 585

DDR (Dail-on-Demand Routing), ISDN, 549–550, 552–553
  authentication, 557
  default routes, 555
  dialer idle timeouts, 557–558
  dialer load threshold, 560
  Multilink PPP, 559–560
  stub networks, 555
DE bit (Discard Eligible), Frame Relay, 600
debug commands, IPX, 468
debug dialer command, 562
debug frame-relay lmi command, 612
debug ip igrp events command, 377–378, 380–382
debug ip rip command, 369–371
debug ipx sap command, 462
  output fields, 472
debug isdn q921 command, 562
debug ppp authentication command, 521
decimal number conversion, IP addresses, 310
dedicated connections, WANs, 503
default gateways, switches, 332
default routes, 356
  ISDN DDR, 555
defaults, subnet masks, 309
delete nvram command, 233
deleted state, Frame Relay LMI, 604
demarcation, WANs, 507
description command, 123
designated ports, 208
destination addresses
  extended IP access lists, 406
  extended IPX access lists, 414
  IP datagrams, 298
  MAC frames, 20
Destination Connection ID field, SPX headers, 435
Destination Network field, IPX headers, 432
Destination Node field, IPX headers, 432
destination ports, TCP, 289
Destination Socket field, IPX headers, 432
destination unreachable messages, ICMP, 301
dialer idle timeouts, ISDN DDR, 557–558
dialer idle-timeout command, 558
dialer load threshold, ISDN DDR, 560
dialer load-threshold command, 560
dialer-group command, 553
dialer-list command, 551
dialer-map command, 554

disable command, 95
DISL (Dynamic Inter-Switch Link), 268
distance vector protocols, 360
Distribution layer, networks, 6–8
DLCIs (data-link connection identifiers), Frame Relay, 587–589, 594
  IP address mapping, 602
  local significance, 595
  troubleshooting, 612
DMACs (destination MAC addresses), switches, 189
DNS (Domain Name System), 286
DNS
  configuring servers, 328
  host name resolution, 146
domain lookup, 146
domains, 246
  broadcast, 195, 248
  collision, 247
  VTP, pruning, 261
  VTP, revision numbers, 260
DoS (Denial of Service) attacks, 292–293
DRs (Designated Routers), NLSP, 448
DTE (Data Terminal Equipment), 67, 508
  Frame Relay, 585
duplex
  1900 series switches, 220–221
  Catalyst 1900 series switches, 214
  Ethernet, 55
dynamic routing, 351, 357–360
  hold down timers, 362
  hop counts, 361
  hop counts, 361
  maximum hop counts, 362
  neighbor discovery, 361
  Split Horizon, 362
  triggered updates, 362

E

E series protocols, ISDN, 547
echo-reply messages, ICMP, 302
echo-request messages, ICMP, 302
editing, access lists, 417
EGP (Exterior Gateway Protocol), 359
EIA/TIA-232-E standard, 62

EIA/TIA-449 standard, 62
EIGRP (Enhanced Interior Gateway Routing
    Protocol), 444
  adjacencies, 448
  hello packets, 446
  hold down timer, 446
  neighbors, identifying, 446
EMI (electromagnetic interference), 58
enable command, 94
  Catalyst 1900 switches, 96
enable password command, 121, 219
enable passwords, 1900 series switches, 218
enable secret command, 121
encapsulation, 13
  Frame Relay, configuring, 605
  HDLC, 512
  IPX, 456
    multiple settings, 459
  PPP, 512, 516, 519
  PPP Multilink, 520
  serial interfaces, 325
    HDLC, 326
  WANs, 508
    ATM, 511
    Frame Relay, 511
    HDLC, 509
    LAPB, 510
    PPP, 509
    SLIP, 510
    X.25, 510
encapsulation frame-relay cisco command, 605
encapsulation frame-relay command, 326
encapsulation hdlc command, 512
encapsulation isl command, 330
encapsulation x.25 command, 326
encryption keys, CHAP authentication, 515
error checking, 16
error messages
  Catalyst POST, 89
  ICMP, 301
Ethernet, 45
  cabling, 26, 46–49, 57
    crossover cables, 59
  catalyst switches, 30
  Fast Ethernet, 26
  flow control, 27
  full duplex, 55
  half duplex, 55

hubs, 27, 30
  MAC frames, 20
    FCS field, 21
    Length fields, 20
  routers, 31
  switches, 22
    MAC table, 23
exec timeout command, 122
exit command, 96
extended access lists, IPX, 480–481
extended IP access lists, 403–404, 407–408
  applying to interfaces, 414
  destination addresses, 406
  source addresses, 406
extended IPX access lists, 412
  destination addresses, 414
  source addresses, 413
  source sockets, 414
extended Ping, 155
  parameters, 155
  source address variable, 157
extended ping command, IPX, 473
extended Telnet access lists, 415
extended traceroute, 159

F

FAQs
  access lists, 423
  cabling, 75
  Frame Relay, 625
  IP routing, 387
  ISDN, 568
  network concepts, 34
  router configuration, 128, 170
  router connections, 525
  TCP/IP, 336
  VLANs, 276
Fast Ethernet, 26
FastHubs, 30
FCS (Frame Check Sequence) field
  Frame Relay, 592
  MAC frames, 21
FECN (Forward Explicit Congestion Notification),
    Frame Relay, 598

fiber connections, 60
fields
  debug ipx sap command, 472
  Frame Relay
    data, 591
    FCS, 592
    Flags, 591
  IPX headers, 431
  show ipx interface command, 469–471
  show ipx route command, 475
  show ipx traffic output, 464–466
files, configuration, 232
filtering
  frames, 193
  SPX, 412
  Telnet traffic, 415
  SAP, 484
firewalls, 293
fixed port routers, 68
Flags field
  Frame Relay, 591
  IP datagrams, 297
flash memory, routers, 163
flash updates, IGRP, 373
flooding, link state, 364
flow control, 27
  TCP, 294
forwarding state, switches, 209
forwarding tables, inaccurate entries, 201
Fragment Offset field, IP datagrams, 297
fragment-free switching, 23, 191
Frame Relay, 511, 584
  Bc (committed burst), 600
  Be (excess burst), 600
  BECN (Backward Explicit Congestion
    Notification), 599
  CIR, 593
  configuring, 605
    encapsulation, 605
    interfaces, 605
    LMI, 605–606
    static mappings, 606–607
    verifying, 608
  cost of ownership, 585
  CPE (customer premise equipment), 585
  data field, 591
  DCE (Data Communication Equipment), 585
  DE (Discard Eligibility) bit, 600

DLCIs (data-link connection identifiers), 587,
    589, 594
  IP address mapping, 602
  local significance, 595
DTE (Data Terminal Equipment), 585
FCS (Frame Check Sequence) field, 589, 592
FECN (Forward Explicit Congestion
    Notification), 598
Flags field, 591
frame clouds, 586
full-mesh networks, 613
headers, 591
Inverse ARP, 604
LMI (Local Management Interface), 596–597
  status requests, 603
local loop, 595
NNI (Network-to-Network Interface), 602
OSI model, 588
partial-mesh networks, 616
PVCs (Permanent Virtual Circuits), 584, 592
  checking status, 610
routing updates, 617
  troubleshooting, 618
signaling, 602–603
Split Horizon, 617–618
star networks, 614
subinterfaces, troubleshooting, 619–621
SVCs (Switched Virtual Circuits), 584, 592
troubleshooting, 611
  DLCIs, 612
UNI (User Network Interface), 602
VCs (Virtual Circuits), 587
frame-relay interface-dlci command, 620
frame-relay inverse-arp command, 606
frame-relay lmi-type command, 606
frame-relay map ip command, 606
frames, 19
  broadcast, 193
  filtering, 193
  Frame Relay, FCS field, 589
  MAC, Ethernet, 20
  multicast, 193–195
  multiple copies, 198
  SAP (Service Access Point), 21
  SNAP (Subnetwork Access Protocol), 21
front panel LEDs, Catalyst switches, 88
FTP (File Transfer Protocol), 286
full duplex, Ethernet, 55

full-mesh Frame Relay, 613
function codes, NCP, 441

G

gateway of last resort, static routing, 354
gateways, switches, default, 332
general service queries, SAP, 454
gigabit Ethernet, 27
global configuration mode, 216
GNS (Get Nearest Server), 452
    requests, NetWare, 452

H

half duplex, 55
HDLC (High level Data Link Control), 20, 326,
    509, 512
header vhecksum, IP datagrams, 298
Header Length fields, IP datagrams, 297
headers, 13
    Frame Relay, 591
    IPX, 431–432
    NCP, 439
    SPX, 434–435
Hello packets, EIGRP, 446
help options, routers, 111
helper addresses, routers, 167
hierarchical model, networks, 6
HLENs (header lengths), TCP, 289
hold down timers
    EIGRP, 446
    dynamic routing, 362
home offices, networks, 3–5
hop counts, 361
    IPX, 443
host names, 327
host unreachable messages, ICMP, 301
hostname command
    Catalyst 1900 switches, 104
    routers, 119
hostname router-name command, 515
hostname tables, 329
hostnames, 1900 series switches, 216

hosts
    IP addresses, 303
    IP pinging, 154
    subnets, determining number, 312
HSSI (High-Speed Serial Interface), 64
hubs, 26
    Cisco, 30
    Ethernet, 27
hybrid routing protocols, 364

I

I series protocols, ISDN, 546
ICMP (Internet Control Message Protocol), 150,
    285, 301
    error messages, 301
    packets, 150
    query messages, 302
IEEE (Institute of Electrical and Electronic
    Engineers), 802.3 standard, 25
IGP (Interior Gateway Protocol), 358
IGRP (Interior Gateway Routing Protocol),
    16, 372
    adding routes, 383
    configuration commands, 373
    configuring, 374
    flash updates, 373
    routing metrics, 372
    routing updates, 372
    verifying configuration, 374
implicit deny all
    access lists, 400
    IPXaccess lists, 411
in-band access, routers, 70
inactive state, Frame Relay LMI, 604
inbound access lists, 397
initial Configuration dialog, routers, 105–106
    basic management setup, 106–107
    interface setup, 108
    protocols setup, 108
interesting traffic, ISDN, 552
interface configuration mode, 123, 216
interface Ethernet command, 459
interface serial command, 325, 459, 605
interface setup, routers, 108

interfaces
  access lists, 403
  CDP, viewing for devices, 143
  extended IP access lists, 414
  Frame Relay, configuring, 605
  IP addresses, 327
  IPX addresses, 459
    multiple networks, 459
  ISDN BRI, switch type, 548
  ISDN, verifying, 561
Internet layer, TCP/IP model, 295
InterNIC, registering IP addresses, 303
interpacket delay, IPX, 483
inverse ARP, Frame Relay, 604
IOS (Internetwork Operating System), 84–85
  boot process, 86
  command history, 113
  commands, Catalyst 1900 switches, 96–97,
      101–102, 105
  configuration files, 109–110
  configuration mode, 95
  image files, routers, 164
  privileged exec mode, 94
  routers, copying to TFTP server, 173
  user exec mode, 93–94
IOSCLI, Catalyst 1900 series switches, 212
IP (Internet Protocol), 287, 296
  access lists, 399
  addresses, 299, 303
    Catalyst 1900 series switches, 213
    classes, 304–307
    classless routing, 323–324
    decimal to binary number
      confversions, 310
    DNS servers, 328
    Frame Relay, DLCI mappings, 602
    interfaces, 459
    private, 323
    registering, 303
    router interfaces, 327
    serial interfaces, 332
    subnet masks, 17, 308–309, 313–314
    subnets, 312–314
    switches, 332
    VLAN1, 262
  classless addresses, 384
  datagrams, 296–298

  Destination Addresses, 298
  host names, 327
  NAT (Network Address Translation), 297
  PAT (Port Address Translation), 297
  source addresses, 298
  wildcard masks, 409
ip access-group command, 403
ip access-list standard TestACL command, 416
ip address command, 123, 327
  Catalyst 1900 switches, 105
ip default-gateway command, 332
ip default-network command, 356
ip host command, 146, 328
iP hosts, pinging, 154
ip name-server command, 328
ip netmask-format command, 315
Ip rarp-server command, 301
ip route command, 354–355, 555
IPX
  access lists, 410–411, 476–478, 480
    destination addresses, 414
    extended, 412
    source addresses, 413
    source sockets, 414
    standard, 410
  addresses, 430
  convergence, 442
  debug commands, 468
  encapsulation, 456
    multiple settings, 459
  extended access lists, 481
  extended ping command, 473
  headers, 431–432
  hop count, 443
  interfaces, multiple networks, 459
  interpacket delay, 483
  network numbers, 451
  node numbers, 451
  overhead control, 480
  packets, 431
  RIP, 442–443, 453
  router configuration, 459
  routing, 442
    tables, 473
    monitoring, 461–462
  SAP
    queries, 454

responses, 454
viewing, 474
socket numbers, 451–452
sockets, 431
tick count, 443
troubleshooting, connections, 468
ipx access-group command, 411, 414, 476
ipx delay tick command, 444
ipx hello-interval eigrp autonomous-system-number seconds command, 447
ipx output-sap-delay command, 483
ipx output-sap-filter command, 486
ipx router eigrp autonomous-system-number command, 446
ipx router eigrp command, 445
ipx router rip command, 446
ipx routing command, 444, 459
ipx sap-incremental eigrp autonomous-system-number command, 447
ipx sap-interval command, 482
ipx update interval rip command, 453
ipx update sap-after-rip command, 456
IPX/SPX (Internetwork Packet Exchange/Sequenced Packet Exchange), 430
OSI model relationship, 450
IPXWAN, 448
IS-IS (Intermediate System to Intermediate System), 363
ISDN (Integrated Services Digital Network), 65, 540
DDR (Dial on Demand Routing), 549–550, 552–553
authentication, 557
default routes, 555
dialer idle timeouts, 557–558
dialer load threshold, 560
Multilink PPP, 559–560
stub networks, 555
debugging, 562
E series protocols, 547
I series protocols, 546
interesting traffic, 552
interfaces, verifying, 561
NT1 (network-terminating device type, 1), 65
NT2 (network-terminating device type, 2), 65
NT1/NT2, 543
Q series protocols, 546

reference points, 65, 542–544
TAs (Terminal Adapters), 65
U interface, 66
uninteresting traffic, 550
isdn B-channel-number spid-number command, 549
ISDN BRI (Basic Rate Interface), 541, 545
configuring, 548
interfaces, switch types, 548
SPIDs (Service Profile Identifiers), 549
ISDN PRI (Primary Rate Interface), 541, 545
isdn switch type command, 548
ISL (Inter Switch Link), 330
configuring VLANs, 330
VLAN tagging, 267
ISPs (Internet Service Providers), registering IP addresses, 303

J–L

LANs
broadcast domains, 248–250
broadcast domains, performance issues, 249
collision domains, 247
collision rates, 248
domains, 246
Ethernet, 45
VLANs, 250
LAPB (Link Access Procedure Balanced), 326, 510
late collisions, Catalyst 1900 series switches, 221
layer-two switches (*See also* switches), 185
layer-two switching, 183
LCP (Link Control Protocol), 512
PPP authentication, 513
learning state, switches, 209
leased lines, WANs, 503
LEDs, catalyst switches, 88
length fields, MAC frames, 20
line vty command, 120, 415
link state flooding, 364
link state protocols, 363
link state routing, 364
listening state, switches, 208
LLC (Logical Link Control) sublayer, 19
SAP (Service Access Point) frames, 21

SNAP (Subnetwork Access Protocol) frames, 21
LMI (Local Management Interface), Frame Relay, 596–597
   configuring, 605–606
   states, 604
   status requests, 603
load balancing, 520
local loop, 507
   Frame Relay, 595
local significance, Frame Relay DLCIs, 595
logging synchronous command, 122
logical addresses, 16
login command, 119
loops, 196
   multiple, 201
LSPs (Link State Packets), 363
   NLSP, 448

M

MAC addresses (Media Access Control), 287, 299
   age values, 188
   permanent, 228
   restricted, 229
   switches, 185
MAC frames
   destination addresses, 20
   Ethernet, 20
   FCS fields Frame Check Sequence, 21
   length fields, 20
   source addresses, 20
MAC sublayer, 19
MAC tables
   switches, 186
   Ethernet switches, 23
main offices, networks, 3–4
maintenance, Catalyst 1900 series switches, 222
managing networks, 140
mapping
   host names to IP addresses, 327
   switch ports to VLANs, 253
MAT (MAC Address Table), 1900 series switches, 227
maximum hop counts, dynamic routing, 362

metrics, IGRP routing, 372
MIC connectors, 53
MicroHubs, 30
mismatched duplex, 221
MMF (multi-mode fiber) cabling, 49
modular routers, 69
monitoring
   access lists, 418
   IPX routing, 461–462
   WAN connections, 521, 524
MTRJ connectors, 52, 55
MTU (Maximum Transmission Unit), 288
multicast addresses, 195
multicast frames, 193–195
mMultilink PPP, ISDN DDR, 559–560
multiple broadcast domains, 251
multiple frame copies, 198
multiple loops, 201
multiple network IPX interfaces, 459
multiple Telnet sessions, 147

N

name resolution
   DNS, 146
   remote hosts, 146
named access lists, 416
naming VLANs, 263
NAT, (Network Address Translation), IP, 297
NCP (NetWare Core Protocol), 439, 512, 520
   function codes, 441
   headers, 439
NDS (Novell Directory Services), servers, 456
neighbor discovery, dynamic routing, 361
neighbors, EIGRP, identifying, 446
NetBIOS (Network Basic Input/Output System), 441
NetWare
   addresses, 451
   GNS requests, 452
   IPX/SPX, 430
   network numbers, 451
   node numbers, 451
network a.b.c.d command, 365
Network Address field, SAP packets, 439

network addresses
  remote devices, 143
  subnet masks, 316
network interface layer, OSI model, 287
Network layer, OSI model, 16, 287
  addresses, 17
network loads, 162
network management, 140
network masks, 299
network numbers
  IPX, 451
  NetWare, 451
network unreachable messages, ICMP, 301
networks
  100Base-FX, 50
  100Base-T4, 53
  100Base-TX, 50
  10Base-F, 49
  10Base-T, 47
  10Base2, 46
  10Base5, 46
  access layer, 6–7
  access lists
    configuring, 398
    IP, 399
  application layer, 12
  AUI connectors, 54
  baseband, 45
  branch offices, 3–5
  broadband, 45
  cabling
    crossover cables, 59
    Ethernet, 49
    fiber connections, 60
    performance categories, 58
  connections, routers, 18
  core layer, 6, 9
  data link layer, 19
  default routes, 356
  distribution layer, 6–8
  dynamic routing, 357–358
  dynamic routing protocols, 359–384
    hold down timers, 362
    hop counts, 361
    maximum hop counts, 362
    neighbor discovery, 361
    Split Horizon, 362
    triggered updates, 362

encapsulation, 13
Ethernet
  cabling, 26, 46–47, 57
  flow control, 27
  hubs, 27, 30
  MAC frames, 20
  routers, 31
  switches, 30
Frame Relay, 584
  topologies, 613–617
headers, 13
home offices, 3–5
main offices, 3–4
MTRJ connectors, 55
network layer, 16
  addresses, 17
OSI model, 10
physical layer, 25
presentation layer, 12
remote users, 4–5
RJ-45 connectors, 54
routing, 350–351
routing
  loops, 361
  static, 353–355
SC connectors, 55
session layer, 12
ST connectors, 55
static routing, ip route command, 355
transit areas, 9
transport layer, 14
troubleshooting commands, 144
VLANs, security, 254
NLSP (NetWare Link Services Protocol), 432, 448
  adjacency databases, 448
  DRs (Designated Routers), 448
  LSPs (Link State Packets), 448
NNI (Network-to-Network Interface), Frame
      Relay, 602
no ip domain-lookup command, 328
no network command, 446
no shutdown command, 123
node Address field, SAP packets, 439
node numbers
  IPX, 451
  NetWare, 451
Novell (See also NetWare), 430
  access lists, protocol filtering, 412

NT1 (network-terminating device, type 1), 65
NT2 (network-terminating device, type 2), 65
NT1/NT2 (network-termination equipment),
    ISDN, 542–543
NVRAM (Non-Volatile RAM), 233

O

options bit, TCP, 289
Options field, IP datagrams, 298
OSI model (Open Systems Interconnect), 10, 285
    application layer, 12
    data link layer, 19
    encapsulation, 13
    Frame Relay, 588
    IPX/SPX relationship, 450
    network interface layer, 287
    network layer, 16, 287
        addresses, 17
    physical layer, 25
    presentation layer, 12
    session layer, 12
    TCP/IP relationship, 285–286
    transport layer, 14, 286
out-of-band access, routers, 70
outbound access lists, 397
overhead control, IPX, 480

P

packet switched connections, 505
packet switching, Frame Relay, 584
Packet Type field
    IPX headers, 432
    SAP packets, 437
Packet/Response Type field, SAP packets, 438
packets
    EIGRP, hello, 446
    ICMP, 150
    IPX, 431
    routing, 352
    runts, 192
    SAP, 436–437
PAP (Password Authentication Protocol), 513

parameters, extended Ping, 155
partial-mesh Frame Relay, 616
password command, 120
passwords, routers, recovering, 171
PAT (Port Address Translation), IP, 297
payload-compress packet-by-packet command, 607
PDNs (Public Data Networks), 505
PDUs (Protocol Data Units), 13
performance categories, cabling, 58
performance
    LANs, broadcast domains, 249
    LANs, collision rates, 248
    VLANs, 254
periodic updates, SAP packets, 436
permanent MAC addresses, 1900 series
    switches, 228
permissions, access lists, 418
permit command, 416
physical interfaces, routers, 324
Physical layer (*See also* network interface
    layer), 287
    OSI model, 25
ping, 150–151
    extended form, 155
    IPhosts, 154
    timeouts, 152
    user form, 153
    Windows systems options, 157
ping apple command, 153
ping command, 153
PING (Packet Internet Groper), 302
playback attacks, 513
port secure command, 231
port unreachable messages, ICMP, 301
ports
    Catalyst 1900 series switches, 214–215, 230
    console, 71
    designated, 208
    root, 206
    switches, VLAN assignments, 264
    VLAN membership discovery, 253
    VLANs, verifying memberships, 264
POST (Power On Self Test), 87–88
    2900XL switches, 88
    Catalyst switches, 87–88
        errors, 89
        front panel LEDs, 88
    routers, 162

PPP (Point-to-Point Protocol), 20, 509
  authentication, 513
  compression, 518–519
  encapsulation, 512, 516, 519
ppp authentication chap command, 515
ppp authentication command, 557
ppp authentication pap command, 514
ppp multilink command, 520, 560
predictor compression, 519
Presentation layer, OSI model, 12
priority field, IP datagrams, 297
private IP addresses, 323
privileged exec mode, 94
protocol field, IPdatagrams, 298
protocol unreachable messages, ICMP, 301
protocols
  ARP, 285, 299
  BGP, 359
  CDP, 140, 213
  CHAP, 513
  connection-oriented, 286
  connectionless, 286
  DISL, 268
  distance vector, 360
  EGP, 359
  EIGRP, 444
  extended Ping, 155
  FTP, 286
  HDLC, 20, 509
  hybrid routing, 364
  ICMP, 150, 285, 301
  IGP, 358
  IGRP, 16, 372
  IP, 287, 296
  IPX/SPX, 430
  IPXWAN, 448
  IS-IS, 363
  ISL, 330
  LAPB, 326, 510
  LCP, 512
  link state, 363
  NCP, 439, 520
  NLSP, 432, 448
  PAP, 513
  PPP, 20, 509
  RARP, 300
  RIP, 16, 290, 364
  routed, 295

  routing, 295, 358
  SAP, 432
  setup, routers, 108
  SLIP, 510
  SMTP, 286
  SNMP, 286–287
  SPX, 433
  TCP, 15
  TCP/IP, 284
  Telnet, 144–145
  TFTP, 286
  UDP, 16, 285–286, 294
  VLAN flexibility, 255
  VTP, 257
pruning, VTP domains, 261
PVCs (Permanent Virtual Circuits), 584
  Frame Relay, 592, 610

Q–R

Q series protocols, ISDN, 546
queries, SAP, IPX, 454
query messages, ICMP, 302
RARP (Reverse ARP), 300
  broadcasts, 300
  requests, 300
recovering router passwords, 171
reference points, ISDN, 65, 542–544
reflexive access lists, 293
registering IP addresses, 303
remote connections, CDP, 142
remote devices, network addresses, 143
remote hosts
  connections, checking via ping, 151
  name resolution, 146
  viewing connections, Telnet, 144
remote management, 1900 series switches, 217
remote users, networks, 4–5
repeat counts, extended ping, 155
repeaters, 26
Reply Typefield, NCP headers, 440
Request Type field, NCP headers, 440
requests
  GNS, NetWare, 452
  RARP, 300

responses, SAP, IPX, 454
restricted MAC addresses, 1900 series
    switches, 229
revision numbers, VTP domains, 260
RIP (Routing Information Protocol), 16, 290, 364
    configuration commands, 365
    configuring, 366
    IPX routing, 442–443
    updates, IPX, 453
    verifying configuration, 366
RJ-45 connectors, 48, 54
roll over cables, 71
ROM, routers, 164
root bridges, 204–205
    designated ports, 208
root ports, 206
routed protocols, 16, 295
router igrp command, 373
router on a stick, 329
router rip command, 365–366
routers, 31
    2513 series, 68
    blades, 123
    CLI (command-line interface), 70
        access options, 71
    Command Completion Help, 112
    Command-List Help, 111
    configuration files, 109–110
    configuration files, 162
    configuration mode, 95
    configuring, 90–93, 119, 326
        IPX routing, 459
    console ports, 71
    copying IOS to TFTP server, 173
    description command, 123
    enable password command, 121
    enable secret command, 121
    exec timeout command, 122
    fixed port, 68
    flash memory, 163
    helper addresses, 167
    hostname command, 119
    in-band access, 70
    Initial Configuration dialog, 105–106
        basic management setup, 106–107
        interface setup, 108
        protocols setup, 108
    Interface Config mode, 123

interfaces, IP addresses, 327
IOS image files, 164
ip address command, 123
IP routing parameters, 367
line vty command, 120
logging synchronous command, 122
login command, 119
modular, 69
network connections, 18
no shutdown command, 123
out-of-band access, 70
password command, 120
passwords, recovering, 171
physical interfaces, 324
POST (Power On Self Test), 162
PPP compression, 518–519
privileged exec mode, 94
ROM, 164
routing process, 350–352
routing tables, viewing, 368
running configuration, 165
serial interfaces, 325
    IPaddresses, 332
service password encryption command, 121
show interfaces command, 124–125
show running-config command, 118
show startup config command, 116
show version command, 115
shutdown command, 123
startup configuration, 165
startup sequence, 162
sticks, 123
subinterfaces, 324
    configuring, 330
troubleshooting, 124
user accounts, 515–516
user exec mode, 93–94
viewing configuration, 367
RIP routing events, 369
viewing, RIP routing events, 371
routing, 350–351
    administrative distances, 352
    defaults, 356
    dynamic, 357–360
        hop counts, 361
        hop counts, 361
        neighbor discovery, 361
    IGRP, adding routes, 383

IPX, 442–443
  configuring, 459
  monitoring, 461
  monitoring, 462
link state, 364
metrics, IGRP, 372
static, 353–355
  gateway of last resort, 354
routing loops, 361
routing protocols, 16, 295, 358
routing tables
  IPX, 473
  viewing, IP parameters, 368
routing updates
  Frame Relay, 617–618
  IGRP, 372
RS-232C standard, 62
RS-449 standard, 62
RSMs (Route Switch Modules), 329
running configuration, routers, 165
runts, 192

S

SAP frames (Service Access Point), 20–21
SAP (Service Advertisement Protocol), 432
  filters, 484
  General Service queries, 454
  packets, 436–437
  queries, IPX, 454
  responses, IPX, 454
  SITs (server information tables), 436
  updates, 449–450
    intervals, 480
SC connectors, 55
security, VLANs, 254
segmentation, collision domains, 183
segments, TCP, 288
sequence Number field
  NCP headers, 440
  SPX headers, 435
sequence numbers, TCP, 289, 294
serial connections, 507
serial interfaces, encapsulation, 325
  HDLC, 326

IP addresses, 332
  routers, 325
serial ports, 61
server mode, VLANs, 258
Server Name field, SAP packets, 439
Server Type field, SAP packets, 438
servers
  DNS, configuring, 328
  NDS, 456
service password encryption command, 121, 517
service providers, 506
service queries, SAP packets, 436
service responses, SAP packets, 437
Service Type field, SAP packets, 437
Session layer, OSI model, 12
show access-list command, 421
show cdp command, 141
show cdp entry command, 143
show cdp interface command, 143
show cdp neighbor command, 141
show cdp neighbor detail command, 142
show cdp traffic command, 143
show frame-relay lmi command, 609
show frame-relay map command, 611
show frame-relay pvc command, 610
show history command, 113
show hosts command, 329
show interface command, 521, 561, 608
show interface-serial command, 326
show interfaces command, 124–125, 223
show ip access-list command, 420
show ip command, Catalyst 1900 switches, 102
show ip interface command, 419
show ip protocol command, 367, 375
show ip route command, 353, 368, 377
show ip route rip command, 369
show ipx interface command, 462
  output fields, 469–471
show ipx route command, 473
  output fields, 475
show ipx servers command, 474, 477
show ipx traffic command, 462
  output fields, 464–466
show isdn status command, 562
show mac-address-table command, 227
show running configuration command, Catalyst
    1900 switches, 98

show running-config command, 118, 165, 222–224, 367, 374, 419

show sessions command, 148

show span command, 271

show spantree-template command, 273

show startup-config command, 116, 165

show trunk command, 270

show version command, 115, 162, 227

   Catalyst 1900 switches, 97

show vlan command, 263

show vlan-membership command, 264

show vtp command, 262

shutdown command, 123

signaling, Frame Relay, 602–603

SITs (server information tables)

   SAP updates, 436

   IPX, viewing, 474

sliding window, TCP, 293

SLIP (Serial Line Internet Protocol), 510

SMACs (Source MAC addresses), 189

SMTP (Simple Mail Transfer Protocol), 286

SNAP frames (Subnetwork Access Protocol), 21

SNMP (Simple Network Management Protocol), 286–287

Socket field, SAP packets, 439

socket numbers, IPX, 451–452

sockets, IPX, 431

SOHOs (Small Office/Home Offices), 5

source address variable, extended Ping, 157

source addresses

   extended IP access lists, 406

   extended IPX access lists, 413

   IP datagrams, 298

   MAC frames, 20

Source Connection ID field, SPX headers, 435

Source Network field, IPX headers, 433

Source Node field, IPX headers, 433

source ports, TCP, 288

Source Socket field, IPX headers, 433

source sockets

   extended IPX access lists, 414

   extended IPX access lists, 414

spanning trees, 203

   BPDUs, 203

   Catalyst 1900 series switches, 214

   root bridges, 204–205

   templates, 272

   VLANs, 271

spantree command, 271

spantree-template command, 272

SPF algorithm (Shortest Path First), 363

SPIDs (Service Profile Identifiers), ISDN BRI, 549

split horizon

   dynamic routing, 362

   Frame Relay, 617–618

SPX (Sequenced Packet eXchange), 433

   filtering, 412

   headers, 434–435

ST connectors, 53–55

stacker compression, 519

standard access lists, IPX, 476

standard IP access lists, 399–401

   wildcard masks, 402–403

standard IPX access lists, 410

star topology, Frame Relay, 614

startup configuration, routers, 165

startup sequence, routers, 162

states, Frame Relay LMI, 604

static mapping

   IP host name to address, 327

   Frame Relay, configuring, 606–607

static routing, 351–355

   gateway of last resort, 354

   ip route command, 355

status requests, LMI, Frame Relay, 603

sticks, 123

store and forward switching, 22, 190

stub ISDN DDR, 555

subinterfaces, 330

   Frame Relay, troubleshooting, 619–621

   routers, 324

subnet masks, 385

   broadcast addresses, 316

   IP addresses, 17, 308–309, 313–314

   network addresses, 316

subnets, 309, 317

   class A address space, 317

   class B address space, 320–321

   class C address space, 322

   hosts, determining number, 312

   IP addresses, 312–314

suspending Telnet sessions, 147

SVCs (Switched Virtual Circuits), 584

   Frame Relay, 592

switch types, ISDN BRI interface, 548
switches
    2900XL, POST, 88
    blocking state, 208
    broadcast storms, 196
    CAM table, 186
    Catalyst 1900 series, 210
        commands, 96–97, 101–102, 105
    catalyst series, 30
    catalyst, front panel LEDs, 88
    catalyst, POST, 87–88
    catalyst, POST errors, 89
    default gateways, 332
    differences from bridges, 184
    DMACs (destination MAC addresses), 189
    Ethernet, 22
        MACtables, 23
    forwarding state, 209
    forwarding tables, inaccurate entries, 201
    frames
        filtering, 193
        multiple copies, 198
    IP addresses, 332
    learning state, 209
    listening state, 208
    MAC addresses, 185
        age values, 188
    multiple loops, 201
    ports, VLAN assignments, 264
    ports, VLAN membership discovery, 253
    SMACs (Source MAC addresses), 189
    spanning trees, 203
        BPDUs, 203
        templates, 272
    VLANs, 252
        configuring spanning trees, 271
        naming, 263
        trunks, 265–269
    vtp-domain command, 258
switching modes, Catalyst 1900 series
        switches, 213
switching
    adaptive, 23
    cut-through, 22, 190
    fragment-free, 23, 191
    store and forward, 22, 190
synchronization, VLANs, 260

SYNs (Synchronous Sequence Numbers),
        TCP, 292

T

tagging VLANs, 267
    ISL, 267
TAs (terminal adapters), ISDN, 65, 542
Task Number field, NCP headers, 440
TCP, 15
    ACK packets (SYN Acknowledgement),
        292–294
    acknowledge numbers, 289
    code bits, 289
    CRC (Cyclic Redundancy Check), 289
    destination ports, 289
    flow control, 294
    header lengths, 289
    options bit, 289
    segments, 288
    Sequence numbers, 289, 294
    sliding window, 293
    source ports, 288
    SYNs (Synchronous Sequence Numbers), 292
    three-way handshake, 292
    urgent pointers, 289
    well-known ports, 290–291
TCP/IP (Transmission Control Protocol/Internet
        Protocol), 284
    IP addresses, 303
    OSI model relationship, 285–286
    multiple applications, 290
TE1/TE2 (terminal equipment), ISDN, 542
telecommuting, 5
Telnet, 145, 286
    filtering traffic, 415
    multiple sessions, 147
    remote host connections, 144
    suspending sessions, 147
    switch administration, 105
telnetting into IOS, 85
templates, spanning trees, 272
term ip netmask-format command, 315
TFTP servers, copying router running
        configuration, 167

TFTP (Trivial File Transfer Protocol), 286
Thick Ethernet, 46
thicknet, 46
  cabling, 26
thin Ethernet, 46
thinnet, 46
  cabling, 26
three-way handshake, 286
  TCP, 292
tick count, IPX RIP, 443
timeouts
  extended Ping, 156
  ping, 152
timers, EIGRP, 446
topologies, Frame Relay, 613–616
Topology Change BPDUs, 203, 209–210
TOS field (Type of Service), IPdatagrams, 297
Total Length field, TCP datagrams, 297
traceroute, 158, 302
  circular routes, 160
  extended form, 159
tracert command, 161
traffic filtering, Telnet, 415
traffic routing, WANs, 331
traffic viewing, 143
transit areas, networks, 9
transparent bridging, 183
transparent mode, VLANs, 259
transparent switching, MAC addresses, 185
Transport Control field, IPX headers, 431
Transport layer, OSI model, 14, 286
triggered updates, dynamic routing, 362
troubleshooting, 124
  access lists, 418
  Frame Relay, 611
    DLCIs, 612
    routing updates, 617–618
    subinterfaces, 619–621
  IPX, connections, 468
  ISDN, 562
  WAN connections, 521, 524
trunk command, 268
trunks
  verifying, 270
  VLANs, 265–267
    802.1 Q method, 269
    ISL method, 268

TTL field (Time-to-Live), IP datagrams, 297
twisted pair cabling, 26

U

U interface, ISDN, 66
UDP (User Datagram Protocol), 16, 285–286, 294
UNI (User Network Interface), Frame Relay, 602
uninteresting traffic, ISDN, 550
updates
  Frame Relay, routing, 617–618
  RIP, IPX, 453
  SAP, 449–450
    intervals, 480
urgent pointers, TCP, 289
user accounts, 515–516
user exec mode, 94
  routers, 93
user form, ping, 153
user interfaces, Catalyst 1900 series switches, 210
username user-account-name encryption-type
    password command, 515
UTP (Unshielded Twisted Pair), 48

V

V.11 standard, 62
V.24 interface, 63
V.35 interface, 63
vampire taps, 47
VCs (Virtual Circuits), Frame Relay, 587
verifying
  access lists, 418
  Frame Relay connections, 608
  Frame Relay, PVCs, 610
  RIP configuration, 366
  VLAN memberships, 264
  VLAN trunks, 270
version field, IP datagrams, 296
viewing
  CDP interfaces, 143
  CDP traffic, 143
  IPX SITs, 474

remote host connections, Telnet, 144
vlan name command, 263
vlan-membership static command, 264
VLAN1
  CDP advertisements, 262
  IP addresses, 262
  VTP advertisements, 262
VLANs (Virtual Local Area Networks), 246,
    250, 329
  broadcast domains, 251
  client mode, 259
  configuring, 256
    ISL, 330
    VTP domains, 258
  cost efficiency, 254
  naming, 263
  network security, 254
  performance, 254
  port membership discovery, 253
  protocol flexibility, 255
  server mode, 258
  show vtp command, 262
  spanning trees, 271
    templates, 272
  switch ports, 264
  switches, 252
  synchronization, 260
  tagging, 267
    ISL, 267
  transparent mode, 259
  trunks, 265–267
    802.1Q method, 269
    ISL method, 268
    verifying, 270
  verifying port memberships, 264
  VLAN1, 262
  VTP (VLAN Trunking Protocol), 257, 260
  vtp pruning enable command, 261
VLSMs (variable length subnet masks), 324, 363
VSM (Virtual Switch Manager), 212
  Catalyst 1900 series switches, 212
VTP domains
  pruning, 261
  revision numbers, 260
  VLANs, 258
vtp-domain command, 258
VTP (VLAN Trunking Protocol), 257
  advertisements, 260–262

vtppruning enable command, 261
VTs (Virtual Terminals), 120
  configuring, 120
VTYs, Telnet traffic filtering, 415

W

WANs
  CHAP authentication, 514
  circuit-switched connections, 505
  connections, monitoring, 521, 524
  connections, troubleshooting, 521, 524
  dedicated connections, 503
  demarcation, 507
  differences from LANs, 502
  encapsulation, 508
    ATM, 511
    Frame Relay, 511
    HDLC, 509
    LAPB, 510
    PPP, 509
    SLIP, 510
    X.25, 510
  Frame Relay, 584
  IPX/SPX, 430
  leased lines, 503
  local loop, 507
  packet switched connections, 505
  PAP authentication, 513
  serial connections, 507
  serial ports, 61
  service providers, 506
  traffic routing, 331
well-known ports, TCP, 290–291
wildcard masks, 409
  standard IP access lists, 402–403
Windows systems
  Ping options, 157
  tracert command, 161

X

X.21, 63
X.25, 510

ABOUT THE CD-ROM ▬ ▬ ▬ ▬ ▬ ▬

FastTrakExpress™

FastTrak Express provides interactive certification exams to help you prepare for certification. With the enclosed CD, you can test your knowledge of the topics covered in this book with over 200 multiple choice questions.

To Install FastTrak Express:

1. Insert the CD-ROM in your CD-ROM drive.
2. From your computer, choose Run. Select the CD-ROM drive and Run the file called "setupfte.exe." This will launch the Installation Wizard.
3. When the Setup is finished, you may immediately begin using FastTrak Express.
4. To begin using FastTrak Express, enter your license key number: 603142443951

FastTrak Express offers two testing options: the Adaptive exam and the Standard exam.

The Adaptive Exam

The Adaptive exam style does not simulate all of the exam environments that are found on certification exams. You cannot choose specific subcategories for the adaptive exam and once a question has been answered you cannot go back to a previous question.

You have a time limit in which to complete the adaptive exam. This time varies from subject to subject, although it is usually 15 to 25 questions in 30 minutes. When the time limit has been reached, your exam automatically ends.

To take the Adaptive Exam:

1. Click the Adaptive Exam button from the Main window. The Adaptive Exam window will appear.
2. Click the circle or square to the left of the correct answer.

NOTE: *There may be more than one correct answer. The text in the bottom left corner of the window instructs you to Choose the Best Answer (if there is only one answer) or Mark All Correct Answers (if there is more than one correct answer.*

3. Click the Next button to continue.
4. To quit the test at any time, click the Finish button. After about 30 minutes, the exam exits to review mode.

After you have completed the Adaptive exam, FastTrak Express displays your score and the passing score required for the test.

- Click Details to display a chapter-by-chapter review of your exam results.
- Click on Report to get a full analysis of your score.

To review the Adaptive exam After you have taken an Adaptive exam, you can review the questions, your answers, and the correct answers. You may only review your questions immediately after an Adaptive exam. To review your questions:

1. Click the Correct Answer button.
2. To see your answer, click the Your Answer button.

The Standard Exam

After you have learned about your subject using the Adaptive sessions, you can take a Standard exam. This mode simulates the environment that might be found on an actual certification exam.

You cannot choose subcategories for a Standard exam. You have a time limit (this time varies from subject to subject, although it is usually 75 minutes) to complete the Standard exam. When this time limit has been reached, your exam automatically ends.

To take the Standard exam:

1. Click the Standard Exam button from the Main window. The Standard Exam window will appear.
2. Click the circle or square to the left of the correct answer.

NOTE: *There may be more than one correct answer. The text in the bottom left corner of the window instructs you to Choose the Best Answer (if there is only one answer) or Mark All Correct Answers (if there is more than one correct answer).*

3. If you are unsure of the answer and wish to mark the question so you can return to it later, check the Mark box in the upper left hand corner.
4. To review which questions you have marked, which you have answered, and which you have not answered, click the Review button.
5. Click the Next button to continue.
6. To quit the test at any time, click the Finish button. After about 75 minutes, the exam exits to review mode.

After you have completed the Standard exam, FastTrak Express displays your score and the passing score required for the test.

- Click Details to display a chapter-by-chapter review of your exam results.
- Click on Report to get a full analysis of your score.

To review a Standard Exam   After you have taken a Standard exam, you can review the questions, your answers, and the correct answers.

You may only review your questions immediately after a Standard exam.

To review your questions:

1. Click the Correct Answer button.
2. To see your answer, click the Your Answer button.

Changing Exams   FastTrakExpress provides several practice exams to test your knowledge. To change exams:

1. Select the exam for the test you want to run from the Select Exam window.

If you experience technical difficulties please call (888) 992-3131. Outside the U.S. call (281) 972-3131. Or, you may e-mail brucem@bfq.com. For more information, visit the BeachFrontQuizzer site at www.bfq.com.

SOFTWARE AND INFORMATION LICENSE

The software and information on this diskette (collectively referred to as the "Product") are the property of The McGraw-Hill Companies, Inc. ("McGraw-Hill") and are protected by both United States copyright law and international copyright treaty provision. You must treat this Product just like a book, except that you may copy it into a computer to be used and you may make archival copies of the Products for the sole purpose of backing up our software and protecting your investment from loss.

By saying "just like a book," McGraw-Hill means, for example, that the Product may be used by any number of people and may be freely moved from one computer location to another, so long as there is no possibility of the Product (or any part of the Product) being used at one location or on one computer while it is being used at another. Just as a book cannot be read by two different people in two different places at the same time, neither can the Product be used by two different people in two different places at the same time (unless, of course, McGraw-Hill's rights are being violated).

McGraw-Hill reserves the right to alter or modify the contents of the Product at any time.

This agreement is effective until terminated. The Agreement will terminate automatically without notice if you fail to comply with any provisions of this Agreement. In the event of termination by reason of your breach, you will destroy or erase all copies of the Product installed on any computer system or made for backup purposes and shall expunge the Product from your data storage facilities.

LIMITED WARRANTY

McGraw-Hill warrants the physical diskette(s) enclosed herein to be free of defects in materials and workmanship for a period of sixty days from the purchase date. If McGraw-Hill receives written notification within the warranty period of defects in materials or workmanship, and such notification is determined by McGraw-Hill to be correct, McGraw-Hill will replace the defective diskette(s). Send request to:

Customer Service
McGraw-Hill
Gahanna Industrial Park
860 Taylor Station Road
Blacklick, OH 43004-9615

The entire and exclusive liability and remedy for breach of this Limited Warranty shall be limited to replacement of defective diskette(s) and shall not include or extend any claim for or right to cover any other damages, including but not limited to, loss of profit, data, or use of the software, or special, incidental, or consequential damages or other similar claims, even if McGraw-Hill has been specifically advised as to the possibility of such damages. In no event will McGraw-Hill's liability for any damages to you or any other person ever exceed the lower of suggested list price or actual price paid for the license to use the Product, regardless of any form of the claim.

THE McGRAW-HILL COMPANIES, INC. SPECIFICALLY DISCLAIMS ALL OTHER WARRANTIES, EXPRESS OR IMPLIED, INCLUDING BUT NOT LIMITED TO, ANY IMPLIED WARRANTY OF MER-CHANTABILITY OR FITNESS FOR A PARTICULAR PURPOSE. Specifically, McGraw-Hill makes no representation or warranty that the Product is fit for any particular purpose and any implied warranty of merchantability is limited to the sixty day duration of the Limited Warranty covering the physical diskette(s) only (and not the software or information) and is otherwise expressly and specifically disclaimed.

This Limited Warranty gives you specific legal rights; you may have others which may vary from state to state. Some states do not allow the exclusion of incidental or consequential damages, or the limitation on how long an implied warranty lasts, so some of the above may not apply to you.

This Agreement constitutes the entire agreement between the parties relating to use of the Product. The terms of any purchase order shall have no effect on the terms of this Agreement. Failure of McGraw-Hill to insist at any time on strict compliance with this Agreement shall not constitute a waiver of any rights under this Agreement. This Agreement shall be construed and governed in accordance with the laws of New York. If any provision of this Agreement is held to be contrary to law, that provision will be enforced to the maximum extent permissible and the remaining provisions will remain in force and effect.